THE PATH TO FREEDOM

Vimuttimagga

The Path to Freedom

Vimuttimagga

Volume 2

by

Upatissa Thera

Translated from the Chinese by

Bhikkhu Nyanatusita

BPE

BPS PARIYATTI EDITIONS

BPS Pariyatti Editions
an imprint of
Pariyatti Publishing
www.pariyatti.org

Published with the consent of the original publisher.
First BPS Pariyatti Edition, 2024

ISBN: 978-1-68172-718-9 (paperback)
ISBN: 978-1-68172-719-6 (hardback)
ISBN: 978-1-68172-802-5 (PDF)
ISBN: 978-1-68172-803-2 (ePub)
ISBN: 978-1-68172-804-9 (Mobi)
Library of Congress Control Number: 2024953089

Contents

Volume 01

Abbreviations xix
Translator's Preface xxi
Translator's Introduction xxvii
Chapter 1 Introduction (*Nidāna*) ... 3
Chapter 2 Exposition of Virtue (*Sīlaniddesa*) ... 15
Chapter 3 Asceticism ... 53
Chapter 4 Exposition of Concentration (*Samādhiniddesa*) ... 81
Chapter 5 The Search for a Good Friend ... 99
Chapter 6 Exposition of Temperaments (*Caritaniddesa*) ... 107
Chapter 7 Exposition of the Meditation Subjects (*Kammaṭṭhānaniddesa*) 121
Chapter 8 The Way to Practise [the Meditation Subjects] ... 135

Volume 02

Abbreviations xix
Chapter 9 Five Direct Knowledges ... 397
Chapter 10 Exposition of Wisdom (*Paññāniddesa*) ... 425
Chapter 11 The Five Skills ... 437
Chapter 12 Exposition of the Truths (*Saccaniddesa*) ... 547
Appendices I-V 639
Bibliography 777
Index 795

Detailed Content

Volume 01

Abbreviations xix
Translator's Preface xxi
Translator's Introduction xxvii

1. The Vimuttimagga xxvii

1. General description ... xxvii
2. A Theravāda work ... xxviii
3. Structure ... xxix
4. Title ... xxxi
5. Author ... xxxi
6. Relation to the *Visuddhimagga* and Paṭisambhidāmagga ... xxxii
7. Reasons for the composition of the *Vimuttimagga* ... xxxvi
8. Modern relevance ... xxxviii

2. Overview of the chapters of the Vimuttimagga xxxviii

3. Tibetan translations of the Vimuttimagga xl

4. Uncertainties xlii

1. School affiliation ... xlii
2. Language ... xlvii
3. Country of origin ... li
4. Alterations ... lii
5. Date of composition ... lxx
6. Disappearance ... lxxv
7. Subcommentary ... lxxvi
8. Sources ... lxxvi
9. Influences ... lxxxii

5. Passages attributed to "some" that can be found in the Vimuttimagga xcvi

6. Quotations from the Peṭakopadesa in the Vimuttimagga cviii

7. The modern fabrication of a Pali text of the Vimuttimagga cxiv

8. How the Vimuttimagga came to China cxvii

9. Biography of the translator Saṅghapāla cxxii

10. Saṅghapāla or Saṅghabhara? cxxxii

11. How and why the Chinese translation was made cxxxiv

12. Quotations from the Vimuttimagga in other works in the Chinese Tripiṭaka cxxxvi

13. Headings and subheadings in the Chinese text cxli

14. Editions and manuscripts of the Chinese text cxlii

15. Translating the Chinese text cxliii

Chapter 1: Introduction (*Nidāna*)

1. Preface 3
2. Explanation of the preface 4
3. Purpose of teaching the path to freedom 5
4. Aggregates of virtue, concentration, wisdom 7
5. Three kinds of purity 11
6. Three kinds of goodness 12
7. Three kinds of pleasure 13
8. Middle way 13

Chapter 2: Exposition of Virtue (*Sīlaniddesa*)

1. Introduction 15
2. Definition of virtue 15
3. Characteristic of virtue 19
4. Function, manifestation and footing of virtue 20
5. Benefits of virtue 20
6. Meaning of virtue 21
7. Origin of virtue 24
8. Stages in virtue 24
9. Obstacles and causes of virtue 24
10. Kinds of virtue 25
11. Two kinds of virtue: 1 25
12. Two kinds of virtue: 2 26
13. Two kinds of virtue: 3 27
14. Two kinds of virtue: 4 27
15. Two kinds of virtue: 5 27
16. Two kinds of virtue: 6 28
17. Two kinds of virtue: 7 28
18. Two kinds of virtue: 8 29
19. Two kinds of virtue: 9 29
20. Two kinds of virtue: 10 30
21. Three kinds of virtue: 1 30
22. Three kinds of virtue: 2 31
23. Three kinds of virtue: 3 31
24. Three kinds of virtue: 4 32
25. Three kinds of virtue: 5 32
26. Three kinds of virtue: 6 33
27. Three kinds of virtue: 7 33
28. Three kinds of virtue: 8 34
29. Four kinds of virtue: 1 34
30. Four kinds of virtue: 2 35
31. Four kinds of virtue: 3 35
32. Four kinds of virtue: 4 36
33. Four kinds of virtue: 5 37
34. Virtue of the Pātimokkha restraint 37
35. Conduct 38
36. Seeing danger in tiny faults 41
37. Trains himself in the training rules 41
38. Virtue of the purity of livelihood & wrong livelihood 42
39. Virtue of the restraint of the sense-faculties 44
40. Virtue connected with the requisites 45
41. Four reflections 46
42. Three reflections 46
43. Virtue connected with the use of requisites 47
44. Miscellaneous topics 48
45. Purity of virtue and its characteristic 49
46. Causes of virtue 51

Chapter 3: Asceticism

1. Introduction 53
2. Thirteen kinds of asceticism 54
3. Rag-robe-wearer 57
4. Three-robes-wearer 58
5. Alms-food-gatherer 59
6. Uninterrupted-alms-round-goer 60
7. One-sitting-eater 61
8. Food-limiter 62
9. Later-food-denier 63
10. Wilderness-dweller 64
11. Tree-root-dweller 66
12. Open-air-dweller 67
13. Charnel-ground-dweller 67
14. User-of-any-dwelling 69

15. Sitter 69
16. Expediencies 70
17. Eight and three kinds of asceticism 74
18. Miscellaneous topics 75

Chapter 4: Exposition of Concentration (*Samādhiniddesa*)

1. Introduction....81
2. Definition of concentration....81
3. Characteristics, essential function, manifestation and footing of concentration....82
4. Undertaking of concentration....83
5. Differences between jhāna, liberation, concentration and attainment....84
6. Causes of concentration....84
7. Benefits of concentration 85
8. Obstacles to concentration....87
9. Aids and requisites of concentration 87
10. Kinds of concentration: two kinds ..88
11. Three kinds of concentration....89
12. Four kinds of concentration 91
13. Five kinds of concentration 96

Chapter 5: The Search for a Good Friend

1. Introduction....99
2. Qualities of the good friend....99
3. How to search for a good friend ...102

Chapter 6: Exposition of Temperaments (*Caritaniddesa*)

1. Introduction....107
2. Fourteen kinds of temperament....107
3. Fourteen persons by way of temperament 108
4. Seven Persons 109
5. Quick and slow practice 111
6. Three persons 112
7. Seven ways of knowing temperament 113
8. Object 113
9. Afflictions 114
10. Gait 114
11. Wearing robes....115
12. Eating....116
13. Work....116
14. Lying down....117
15. Which practice is suitable for which temperament? 117
16. Miscellaneous topics 119

Chapter 7: Exposition of the Meditation Subjects (*Kammaṭṭhānaniddesa*)

1. Introduction....121
2. Thirty-eight meditation subjects...121
3. Nine ways of knowing the differences....122
4. Jhāna 122
5. Transcending....124
6. Extending 124
7. Condition....125
8. Object 125
9. Specialness 128
10. Plane....129
11. Grasping....130
12. Person 130

Chapter 8: The Way to Practise [the Meditation Subjects]

Earth Totality *135*

1. Introduction....135
2. Definition, practice, characteristic, function, footing, benefits, and meaning....135

3. Kinds of earth to be used 137
4. Making a disc 140
5. Method of practice: mental preparation 140
6. Physical preparation 145
7. Three ways of grasping the sign 145
8. Looking evenly 146
9. Skills 147
10. Abandoning of distraction 148
11. The sign 149
12. Threshold jhāna and jhāna 152
13. Extending of the totality 155
14. Skill in absorption concentration 156

First Jhāna 161

15. Factors of the first jhāna 161
16. Seclusion from sense-pleasures .. 161
17. Seclusion from unwholesome states 163
18. Thinking and exploring 167
19. The difference between thinking and exploring 168
20. Seclusion 170
21. Rapture and pleasure 170
22. Five factors of the first jhāna 174
23. Factors, characteristics, benefits, etc. 175
24. Five hindrances 176
25. Five jhāna factors 179
26. Three kinds of goodness 182
27. Ten characteristics 182
28. Twenty-five benefits 184
29. Benefit of rebirth as a Brahmā 187

Second Jhāna 190

30. Disadvantage of the first jhāna and the benefit of the second jhāna 190
31. Factors of the second jhāna 193
32. Benefit of rebirth as a radiant deity 199

Third Jhāna 199

33. Disadvantage of the second jhāna 199
34. Factors of the third jhāna 200
35. Benefit of rebirth as a deity of refulgent lustre 209

Fourth Jhāna 209

36. Disadvantage of the third jhāna ... 209
37. Factors of the fourth jhāna 210
38. Benefit of rebirth as a deity of great fruit 215

Base of Boundless Space 217

39. Disadvantage of the fourth jhāna 217
40. Attaining the base of boundless space 218
41. Definition of the base of boundless space 219

Base of Boundless Consciousness 223

42. Disadvantage of the base of boundless space 223
43. Attaining the base of boundless consciousness 224
44. Definition of the base of boundless consciousness 225

Base of Nothingness 226

45. Disadvantage of the base of boundless consciousness 226
46. Attaining the base of nothingness 227

47. Definition of the base of nothingness 228

Base of Neither-perception-nor-non-perception *229*

48. Disadvantage of the base of nothingness....229
49. Attaining the base of neither-perception-nor-non-perception....230
50. Definition of the base of neither-perception-nor-non-perception 231
51. Miscellaneous topics 233

Other Totalities *236*

52. Water totality 236
53. Fire totality 238
54. Wind totality....240
55. Blue totality 241
56. Yellow totality 243
57. Red totality....244
58. White totality 245
59. Light totality 246
60. Space totality 247
61. Consciousness totality....248
62. Miscellaneous topics 249

Ten Perceptions of the Foul *252*

63. Perception of the bloated 252
64. Procedure 253
65. Perception of the livid....259
66. Perception of the festering....259
67. Perception of the cut up 259
68. Perception of the gnawed....260
69. Perception of the scattered....261
70. Perception of the slain and scattered 261
71. Perception of the blood-smeared...262
72. Perception of the maggot-infested 262
73. Perception of the skeleton....263
74. Miscellaneous topics 263

Ten Recollections *267*

Recollection of the Buddha *267*

75. Introduction....267
76. Procedure 268
77. Four ways of practice....275
78. Jātakas....275
79. Pulling himself out 277
80. Distinctive states....278
81. Compassion for the world 282
82. Conclusion....283
83. Miscellaneous topics 284

Recollection of the Dhamma *285*

84. Introduction....285
85. Procedure 286
86. Conclusion....288

Recollection of the Saṅgha *288*

87. Introduction....288
88. Procedure 289
89. Conclusion....291

Recollection of Virtue *292*

90. Introduction....292
91. Procedure 292
92. Conclusion....293

Recollection of Generosity *294*

93. Introduction....294
94. Procedure....294
95. Conclusion....295

Recollection of Deities *295*

96. Introduction....295
97. Procedure....296
98. Conclusion....296
99. Miscellaneous topics....296

Mindfulness of Breathing *297*

100. Introduction....297
101. Procedure....298
102. Explanation....299
103. The sign....302
104. Four ways of practice....305
105. The sixteen training grounds....308
106. Miscellaneous topics....319

Recollection of Death *320*

107. Introduction....320
108. Procedure....321
109. Eight ways of practice....323
110. Being followed by an executioner....323
111. There being no means....323
112. Comparison....324
113. Being shared with many....324
114. Fragility....325
115. Limitedness of the duration....326
116. Signlessness....327
117. Momentariness....327
118. Conclusion....328
119. Miscellaneous topics....328

Mindfulness of the Body *328*

120. Introduction....328
121. Procedure....329
122. Thirteen ways of practice....332
123. Seed....333
124. Location....333
125. Condition....333
126. Oozing....334
127. Gradual physical formation....335
128. Kinds of worms....336
129. Support....339
130. Mass....340
131. Repulsiveness....340
132. Dirtiness....340
133. [Breeding] ground....341
134. Ingratitude....341
135. Finiteness....342
136. Conclusion....342

Recollection of Stillness *342*

137. Introduction....342
138. Procedure....343
139. Conclusion....345
140. Miscellaneous topics....345

Four Immeasurables *346*

Loving-kindness *346*

141. Introduction....346
142. Procedure....347
143. Disadvantages of anger and resentment....347
144. Developing loving-kindness....349
145. Skilful means for removing anger....352
146. Pervading the directions....356
147. Roots, manifestation, success, failure, and object....357

148. Ten perfections 359
149. The four resolves 361

Compassion *362*

150. Introduction 362
151. Procedure 363
152. Success and failure 364
153. Miscellaneous topics 364

Appreciative gladness *364*

154. Introduction 364
155. Procedure 365
156. Success and failure 365

Equanimity *366*

157. Introduction 366
158. Procedure 366
159. Success and failure 367
160. Miscellaneous topics 368

Defining of the Four Elements *374*

161. Introduction 374
162. Grasping the elements in brief ... 375
163. Grasping the elements in detail .. 376
164. Ten ways of defining the elements 377
165. Word meaning 378
166. Function 382
167. Clusters 383
168. Powder 384
169. Inseparability 385
170. Conditions 385
171. Characteristics 387
172. Similarity and dissimilarity 388
173. Unity and difference 388
174. Element puppet 389
175. Conclusion 390

Perception of Repulsiveness of Food *391*

176. Introduction 391
177. Five ways of practice 392
178. Searching 392
179. Breaking up and using 393
180. Location 393
181. Oozing 394
182. Assemblage 394
183. Conclusion 394

Base of nothingness and base of neither-perception-nor-non-perception *395*

Chapter Conclusion *395*

Volume 02

Abbreviations xix

Chapter 9: Five Direct Knowledges

1. Introduction....397
2. Three kinds of supernormal power 397
3. Seven kinds of supernormal power 398
4. Supernormal power due to the pervasive force of knowledge....399
5. Supernormal power due to the pervasive force of concentration 399
6. Supernormal power of the noble ones 400
7. Supernormal power born of result of kamma....401
8. Supernormal power of the meritorious 401
9. Supernormal power sprung from magic knowledge....402
10. Supernormal power due to [right] application....402
11. Procedure of developing supernormal power 402
12. Supernormal power of resolve....407
13. Supernormal power of miraculous transformation 410
14. Supernormal power of [producing a] mind-made [body] 411
15. Miscellaneous topics 412
16. Divine ear 413
17. Knowledge of others' minds....415
18. Recollection of past lives 416
19. Divine eye....420
20. Miscellaneous topics 423

Chapter 10: Exposition of Wisdom (*Paññāniddesa*)

1. Introduction....425
2. Definition, characteristic, function, manifestation, and footing of wisdom....425
3. Benefits of wisdom....426
4. Meaning of wisdom 427
5. Qualities needed for obtaining wisdom....427
6. Kinds of wisdom....428
7. Two kinds of wisdom....428
8. Three kinds of wisdom 429
9. Four kinds of wisdom 431

Chapter 11: The Five Skills

1. Introduction....437

Skill in the Aggregates *437*

2. What is skill in the aggregates 437

Aggregate of Matter *437*

3. What is the aggregate of matter?...437
4. Four great primaries....438
5. Dependent matter....438
6. Sense bases....439
7. Other kinds of dependent matter...442
8. Difference between the four great primaries and dependent matter 443
9. Five ways of knowing matter 443
10. Producing....443
11. Clusters....444
12. Birth 451

13. Diversity 452
14. Two kinds of matter 453
15. Three kinds of matter....454
16. Four kinds of matter....455
17. Unity 456

Aggregate of Feeling *458*

18. What is the aggregate of feeling? 458

Aggregate of Perception *460*

19. What is the aggregate of perception? 460

Aggregate of Formations *462*

20. What is the aggregate of formations? 462
21. Meaning and similes 462

Aggregate of Consciousness *469*

22. What is the aggregate of consciousness? 469
23. Three ways of knowing consciousness 470
24. Bases and objects 470
25. Objects 471
26. States....473
27. Four ways of knowing the five aggregates 475
28. Word meaning....475
29. Characteristic 475
30. Analysis....476
31. Inclusion 477

Skill in the Sense Bases *479*

32. What is the skill in the sense bases?....479
33. Five ways of knowing the sense bases 482
34. Word meaning 482
35. Sense object 483
36. Condition....483
37. Occurrence of the process of mind 487
38. Simile of the mango 490
39. Inclusion....493

Skill in the Elements *494*

40. What is skill in the elements?....494
41. Inclusion....495

Skill in Dependent Arising *498*

42. What is skill in dependent arising? 498
43. Explanation of the twelve factors....499
44. Simile of the seed 500
45. Simile of the sun and the simile of the two bundles of reeds 502
46. Simile of the seed and sprout....504
47. In a single mind-moment 506
48. Questions on kamma, afflictions, results, etc. 510
49. Seven ways of knowing dependent arising....513
50. Three links 513
51. Existence-link....514
52. Kamma, kamma-sign, destination, and destination-sign....515
53. Four collections....518
54. Twenty modes 518
55. Wheel 520
56. Way....521
57. Analysis....521
58. Inclusion....523

Skill in the Noble Truths 525
59. What is skill in the noble truths? 525
60. Truth of suffering 525
61. Kinds of suffering........................526
62. Truth of the origination of suffering 528
63. Truth of the cessation of suffering 529
64. Truth of the path leading to the cessation of suffering 529
65. Why four noble truths are taught 532
66. Eleven ways of knowing the four noble truths 532
67. Word meaning..............................532
68. Characteristics..............................534
69. Sequence 535
70. Collection 536
71. Simile 537
72. Analysis...538
73. Enumeration 539
74. Oneness..540
75. Diversity 541
76. Successive explanation 542
77. Inclusion.......................................545

Chapter 12: Exposition of the Truths (*Saccaniddesa*)

1. Introduction....................................547
2. Procedure of defining the four noble truths................................547
3. Defining the truth of suffering.....548
4. Defining the truth of origination...550
5. Defining the truth of cessation.....552
6. Defining the truth of the path leading to the cessation of suffering 552
7. Comprehension of the five aggregates by way of the three characteristics 552
8. Grasping the Sign...........................556
9. Grasping the aggregates in three ways 556
10. Grasping of the sign of mind.......558
11. Knowledge of rise and fall 559
12. Obtaining the higher knowledge...561
13. Four states....................................563
14. Knowledge of delimitation of formations 568
15. Knowledge of the contemplation of dissolution 568
16. Three ways of seeing dissolution...569
17. Clusters 569
18. Pairs...570
19. Analysis..570
20. Knowledge of what is appearing as fearful 578
21. Knowledge of desire for release ...579
22. Knowledge of conformity 581
23. Knowledge of change of lineage...582
24. Knowledge of the path 584
25. Comprehension of the truths in a single moment 584
26. Three fetters 590
27. Stream-enterer.............................592
28. Once-returner...............................595
29. Non-returner 595
30. Arahant 596
31. Three kinds of stream-enterer and the non-returner 597
32. Five kinds of non-returner 599
33. No further existence for the arahant 600
34. Gradual realization of the fruit.....601
35. Flaw one..602
36. Flaw two..602
37. Flaw three......................................603
38. Flaw four..604
39. Flaw five..604
40. Flaw six 605
41. Flaw seven 605
42. Objection 605

Miscellaneous topics *606*

43. Insight.......606
44. Thinking.......607
45. Rapture.......608
46. Feelings.......609
47. Noble planes.......609
48. Three supramundane faculties.......610
49. Three liberations.......611
50. One hundred and thirty-four afflictions.......616
51. Three roots of unwholesomeness.......616
52. Three searches.......617
53. Four contaminations.......617
54. Four ties.......617
55. Four torrents and four yokes.......618
56. Four clingings.......619
57. Four kinds of going the wrong way.......619
58. Five kinds of selfishness.......619
59. Five hindrances.......620
60. Six roots of dispute.......620
61. Seven latent tendencies.......621
62. Eight worldly states.......621
63. Nine conceits.......622
64. Ten grounds for afflictions.......622
65. Ten grounds for anger.......622
66. Ten courses of unwholesome kamma.......623
67. Ten fetters.......623
68. Ten kinds of wrongness.......624
69. Twelve distortions.......624
70. Twelve arisings of the unwholesome mind.......625
71. Two attainments not shared with the worldling.......626
72. Attainment of fruition.......626
73. Attainment of the cessation of perception and feeling.......631

Conclusion *637*

Appendix I

Translation of the Vimuktimārgadhutaguṇanirdeśa *639*

1. Introduction.......639
2. Thirteen kinds of asceticism.......639
3. Rag-robe-wearer.......640
4. Three-robes-wearer.......641
5. Alms-food-gatherer.......641
6. Uninterrupted-alms-round-goer.......642
7. One-sitting-eater.......643
8. Food-limiter.......643
9. Later-food-denier.......644
10. Wilderness-dweller.......645
11. Tree-root-dweller.......645
12. Open-air-dweller.......646
13. Charnel-ground-dweller.......646
14. User-of-any-dwelling.......647
15. Sitter.......648
16. Expediencies.......648
17. Eight and three ascetic qualities.......650
18. Miscellaneous topics.......651

Appendix II

Quotations from the Vimuttimagga in the Saṃskṛtāsaṃskṛtaviniścaya *654*

2 § 2. Definition of virtue.......654
4 § 13. Five kinds of concentration.......655
10 § 1. Introduction.......656
10 § 2. Definition, characteristic, function, manifestation, and footing of wisdom.......656
10 § 3. Benefits of wisdom.......657
10 § 4. Meaning of wisdom.......657
10 § 5. Qualities needed for obtaining wisdom.......657
10 § 6–7. Two kinds of wisdom.......658
10 § 8. Three kinds of wisdom.......658
10 § 9. Four kinds of wisdom.......659
11 § 1. Introduction.......661
11 § 2–4. Skill in the aggregates.......662
11 § 5. Dependent matter.......662

11 § 7. Kinds of dependent matter (end) ... 662
11 § 9. Five ways of knowing matter ... 662
11 § 10. Producing ... 662
11 § 11. Clusters ... 663
11 § 12. Birth ... 663
11 § 13. Diversity ... 664
11 § 14. Two kinds of matter ... 664
11 § 15. Three kinds of matter ... 665
11 § 16. Four kinds of matter ... 665
11 § 17. Unity ... 666
11 § 18. What is the aggregate of feeling? ... 666
11 § 19. What is the aggregate of perception? ... 667
11 § 20. What is the aggregate of formations? ... 668
11 § 22. What is the aggregate of consciousness? ... 668
11 § 27. Four ways of knowing the five aggregates ... 668
11 § 28. Word meaning ... 668
11 § 29. Characteristic ... 668
11 § 30. Analysis ... 669
11 § 31. Inclusion ... 669
11 § 32. Skill in the sense bases ... 670
11 § 39. Skill in the sense bases (end) 671
11 § 40. Skill in the elements ... 671
11 § 41. Differences between the aggregates, sense bases and element methods ... 671
11 § 42. Skill in dependent arising ... 672
11 § 43. Explanation of the twelve factors ... 673
11 § 44. Simile of the seed ... 673
11 § 45. Simile of the sun and the two bundles of reeds ... 674
11 § 46. Simile of the seed and sprout ... 674
11 § 47. In a single mind moment ... 675
11 § 48. Questions on kamma, defilements, results, etc. ... 676
11 § 49. Seven ways of knowing dependent arising ... 677
11 § 50. Three links ... 677
11 § 51. Existence link ... 677
11 § 52. Kamma, kamma-sign, destination, and destination-sign ... 677
11 § 53. Four collections ... 678
11 § 54. Twenty modes ... 678
11 § 55. Wheel ... 679
11 § 56. Way ... 679
11 § 57. Analysis ... 679
11 § 58. Inclusion ... 680
11 § 59. Skill in the noble truths ... 681
11 § 60. Truth of suffering ... 681
11 § 61. Kinds of suffering ... 682
11 § 62. Truth of the origination of suffering ... 683
11 § 63. Truth of the cessation of suffering ... 683
11 § 64. Truth of the path leading to the cessation of suffering ... 683
11 § 65. Why four noble truths are taught ... 684
11 § 66. Eleven ways of knowing the four noble truths ... 684
11 § 67. Word meaning ... 685
11 § 68. Characteristic ... 685
11 § 69. Sequence ... 685
11 § 70. Collection ... 686
11 § 71. Simile ... 686
11 § 72. Analysis ... 686
11 § 73. Enumeration ... 687
11 § 74. Oneness ... 688
11 § 75. Diversity ... 688
11 § 76. Successive explanation ... 688
11 § 77. Inclusion ... 691
12 § 23. Knowledge of change of lineage ... 691
12 § 24. Knowledge of the path ... 692
12 § 25. Comprehension of the truths in a single moment ... 692
12 § 26. Three fetters ... 693
12 § 27. Stream-enterer ... 694
12 § 28. Once-returner ... 694
12 § 29. Non-returner ... 695
12 § 30. Arahant ... 695

12 § 31. Three kinds of stream-enterer and the non-returner 696
12 § 32. Five kinds of non-returner ...696
12 § 33. No further existence for the arahant...697
12 § 47. Noble planes 697
12 § 48. Three supramundane faculties 698
12 § 49. Three liberations...................698
12 § 50. Hundred thirty-four defilements 698
12 § 51. Three roots of unwholesomeness......................699
12 § 52. Three searches.......................699
12 § 53. Four contaminations 699
12 § 54. Four ties.................................699
12 § 55. Four torrents..........................699
12 § 56. Four clingings 700
12 § 57. Four kinds of going the wrong way 700
12 § 58. Five kinds of selfishness.......700
12 § 59. Five hindrances 700
12 § 60. Six roots of dispute..............700
12 § 61. Seven latent tendencies.......700
12 § 62. Eight worldly states.............701
12 § 63. Nine conceits 701
12 § 64. Ten grounds for afflictions..701
12 § 65. Ten grounds for anger..........701
12 § 66. Ten unwholesome actions...702
12 § 67. Ten fetters.............................702
12 § 68. Ten kinds of wrongness 702
12 § 69. Twelve distortions 703
12 § 70. Twelve arisings of the unwholesome mind 703
12 § 71. Attainments not shared with the worldling 704
12 § 72. Attainment of fruition 704
12 § 73. Attainment of the cessation of perception and feeling.............705

Appendix III

The Pali Commentaries and their Sources 708

1. The origins of the Pali commentaries (*aṭṭhakathā*).................................708
2. *Sīhaḷaṭṭhakathā* 726
3. *Porāṇā*...732
4. *Aṭṭhakathā* in other Theravāda traditions....................................734
5. The sources of the *Visuddhimagga* and other commentaries of Buddhaghosa...............................735
6. Translation of the *Sīhaḷaṭṭhakathā* ...739
7. Structural changes.........................742
8. Differences in commentaries as pointed out in the *Sāratthamañjūsā*......................... 747
9. *Dīpavaṃsa* and *Mahāvaṃsa* 750
10. Different attributions of ideas 753
11. Reasons for Buddhaghosa's commentary project..................755

Appendix IV

The Reasons for the Split between the Mahāvihāra and Abhayagirivihāra 759

Appendix V

Attabhāvavatthu and Ātmavastu 766

1. *Attabhāvavatthu*................................766
2. Translations of Pali passages.........768
3. *Ātmavastu*..771

Bibliography 777

Vimuttimagga Bibliography 777

General Bibliography 779

Index 795

Abbreviations

A	Aṅguttara Nikāya
Abhidh-s	*Abhidhammatthasaṅgaha*
Abhi-av	*Abhidhammāvatāra*
Ap	Apadāna
As	*Atthasālinī* (= *Dhammasaṅgaṇi-aṭṭhakathā*)
Bej:	Comparative Beijing edition of *Saṃskṛtāsaṃskṛtaviniścaya.*
Chin:	Chinese text of the *Vimuttimagga*, Taishō edition
CJKV-E	*CJKV-English Dictionary*, edited by Charles Muller
Cp	Cariyāpiṭaka
CPD	*Critical Pali Dictionary*
CS	Chaṭṭha Saṅgāyana edition of the Tipiṭaka, as digitized by the Vipassana Research Institute
Cv	*Cūḷavaṃsa*
D	Dīgha Nikāya
DDB	*Digital Dictionary of Buddhism*, edited by Charles Muller
Der:	Dergé edition of *Saṃskṛtāsaṃskṛtaviniścaya*
Dg	Dergé edition
Dhp	Dhammapada
Dhp-a	*Dhammapada-aṭṭhakathā*
Dhs	Dhammasaṅgaṇi
DPPN	*Dictionary of Pali Proper Names*
EKS	Ehara, Kheminda, and Soma
GRETIL	Göttingen Register of Electronic Texts in Indian Languages (at http://gretil.sub.uni-goettingen.de)
It	Itivuttaka
J-a	*Jātaka-aṭṭhakathā*
LC	Lance Cousins
Nidd I	Mahā Niddesa
Nett	*Nettipakaraṇa*
Paṭis	Paṭisambhidāmagga
Paṭis-a	*Paṭisambhidā-aṭṭhakathā* (= *Saddhammappakāsinī*)
Pe	Old Peking edition of *Saṃskṛtāsaṃskṛtaviniścaya*
Peṭ	*Peṭakopadesa*
PED	*Pali English Dictionary*, Rhys-Davids and Stede
PTS	Pali Text Society
PoF	*The Path of Freedom*
PoP	*The Path of Purification: Visuddhimagga*, Bhikkhu Ñāṇamoli
PtF	*The Path to Freedom*
M-a	*Papañcasūdanī* (= *Majjhimanikāya-aṭṭhakathā*)

M	Majjhima Nikāya
Mhv	*Mahāvaṃsa*
Mil	*Milindapañhā* (V. Trenckner's ed.)
Mvy	*Mahāvyutpatti*
MW	*A Sanskrit English Dictionary*, Monier Williams
Rūpār	*Rūpārūpavibhāga*
Lal	*Lalitavistara*
S	Saṃyutta Nikāya
Saddh	*Saddhammopāyana*
Sav	*Saṃskṛtāsaṃskṛtaviniścaya*
Skt	Sanskrit
Sn	Suttanipāta (Harvard Oriental Series)
Sn-a	Suttanipāta-aṭṭhakathā (= Paramatthajotikā)
Snar:	Snar Thang or Narthang edition of *Saṃskṛtāsaṃskṛtaviniścaya*
Sp	*Samantapāsādikā* (= *Vinaya-aṭṭhakathā*)
Spk	*Sāratthappakāsinī* (= *Saṃyuttanikāya-aṭṭhakathā*)
Sv	*Sumaṅgalavilāsinī* (= *Dīghanikāya-aṭṭhakathā*)
Ud	Udāna
Ud-a	*Udāna-aṭṭhakathā*
Th	Theragāthā
Thī	Therīgāthā
THL	Tibetan and Himalaya Library (www.thlib.org)
Vibh	Vibhaṅga
Vibh-a	*Vibhaṅga-aṭṭhakathā* (= *Sammohavinodanī*)
Vim	*Vimuttimagga*
Vin	Vinaya
Vism	*Visuddhimagga*
Vism-mhṭ	*Paramatthamañjūsā* (= *Visuddhimagga-mahāṭikā*)

Chapter 9

Five Direct Knowledges

1. Introduction

Now, the meditator, who has thus mastered concentration and is dwelling in the fourth jhāna, can give rise to the five direct knowledges (*abhiññā*), namely: (1) the direct knowledge of supernormal power (*iddhividha, iddhi*); (2) the direct knowledge of the divine ear (*dibbasota*); (3) the direct knowledge of the knowledge of others' minds (*paracittavijānana*); (4) the direct knowledge of [the recollection of] former lives (*pubbenivāsānussati*); and (5) the direct knowledge of the divine eye (*dibbacakkhu*).

"Supernormal power" means miraculous transformation (*vikubbana, pāṭihāriya*).

"Divine ear" means surpassing the human ear.[1]

"Knowledge of others' minds" means cognising others' minds.[2]

"[Recollection of] former lives" means the recollection of previous births.[3]

"Divine eye" means surpassing the vision of the human eye.[4] **[441b]**

2. Three kinds of supernormal power

Q. How many kinds of supernormal power[5] are there? Who practises supernormal power? How should one give rise to supernormal power?

A. There are three kinds of supernormal power, namely, the supernormal power of resolve (*adhiṭṭhānā-iddhi*), the supernormal power of miraculous

1. D I 79: ... *So dibbāya sotadhātuyā visuddhāya atikkantamānusikāya ubho sadde suṇāti dibbe ca mānuse ca ye dūre santike ca.*

2. D I 79: ... *So parasattānaṃ parapuggalānaṃ cetasā ceto paricca pajānāti,* ... The text has 他心智 which corresponds to *paracittavijānana* "knowing/knowledge of others' minds" as found in Mil 359, etc., and Abhidh-s 359: *Iddhividhaṃ dibbasotaṃ, paracittavijānanā; / Pubbenivāsānussati, dibbacakkhūti pañcadhā.* Cf. Abhidh-av-pṭ II 18: *parehi vā katakusalassa anussaraṇakāle paracittavijānanakāle.*

3. D I 80: ... *So anekavihitaṃ pubbenivāsaṃ anussarati, seyyathidaṃ ekam-pi jātiṃ dvepi jātiyo...*

4. D I 82: *So dibbena cakkhunā visuddhena atikkantamānusakena satte passati cavamāne upapajjamāne ...*

5. 變 usually means *vikubbana*, or *pāṭihāriya*, as at 441a28—where 身通 corresponds to *iddhividha*—but from here onwards it corresponds to *iddhi* in the Pali parallels. Apparently Saṅghapāla could not find suitable characters for *iddhividha*. At 441c14 he uses 變辯 for *iddhividha*.

transformation (*vikubbanā-iddhi*), and the supernormal power of [producing a] mind-made [body] (*manomayā-iddhi*).

Q. What is "the supernormal power of resolve"?
A. The meditator, being one, he becomes many; and being many, he becomes one. ... Through the body, he extends influence as far as the world of Brahmā—this is called "the supernormal power of resolve".[6]

Q. What is "the supernormal power of miraculous transformation"?
A. The meditator discards his natural physical appearance and manifests the physical appearance of a boy or a dragon (*nāga*) or Brahmā, etc.—this is called "the supernormal power of miraculous transformation".[7]

Q. What is "the supernormal power of [producing a] mind-made [body]"?
A. The meditator, according to his wish, conjures from this body another body created [complete] with all limbs and complete in faculties—this is called "the supernormal power of [producing a] mind-made [body]".[8]

3. Seven kinds of supernormal power

Furthermore, there are seven kinds of supernormal power, namely, (1) supernormal due to the pervasive force of knowledge (*ñāṇa-vipphārā-iddhi*), (2) supernormal power due to the pervasive force of concentration (*samādhi-vipphārā-iddhi*), (3) supernormal power of the noble ones (*ariyiddhi*), (4) supernormal power born of result of kamma (*kamma-vipākajā-iddhi*), (5) supernormal power of the meritorious (*puññavato-iddhi*), (6) supernormal power sprung from magic knowledge (*vijjāmayā-iddhi*), and (7) supernormal power due to [right] application (*sammāpayoga-paccayā ijjhanaṭṭhena iddhi*).[9]

---

6. This passage is abridged in the Chinese text. Otherwise, Upatissa quotes an abbreviated repetition (*peyyāla*). Cf. Paṭis II 207–10: *Katamā adhiṭṭhānā iddhi? Idha bhikkhu anekavihitaṃ iddhividhaṃ paccanubhoti: eko pi hutvā bahudhā hoti, bahudhā pi hutvā eko hoti ... yāva brahmalokā pi kāyena vasaṃ vatteti ...*

7. Paṭis II 210: *Katamā vikubbanā iddhi? ... So pakativaṇṇaṃ vijahitvā kumārakavaṇṇaṃ vā dasseti, nāgavaṇṇaṃ vā dasseti, supaṇṇavaṇṇaṃ vā dasseti, yakkhavaṇṇaṃ vā dasseti, indavaṇṇaṃ vā dasseti, devavaṇṇaṃ vā dasseti, Brahmavaṇṇaṃ vā dasseti.*

8. Paṭis II 210–11: *Katamā manomayā iddhi? Idha bhikkhu imamhā kāyā aññaṃ kāyaṃ abhinimmināti rūpiṃ manomayaṃ sabbaṅgapaccaṅgaṃ ahīnindriyaṃ ....* Vism-mhṭ II 11: *Abhiññāñāṇassa hi yathā manomayo kāyo nipphajjati, tathā pavatti manomayiddhi.*

9. Paṭis II 173: *Katamāni dasa iddhibalāni? Adhiṭṭhānā iddhi, vikubbanā iddhi, manomayā iddhi, ñāṇavipphārā iddhi, samādhivipphārā iddhi, ariyā iddhi, kammavipākajā iddhi, puññavato iddhi, vijjāmayā iddhi, tattha tattha sammā payogappaccayā ijjhanaṭṭhena iddhi, imāni dasa iddhibalāni.*

The text omits 辯, "pervasive force", after the first two powers. However, in the explanation below, from 441b11 onward, it is included.

4. Supernormal power due to the pervasive force of knowledge

Q. What is "supernormal power due to the pervasive force of knowledge"?

A. Through the contemplation of impermanence, one succeeds in abandoning the perception of permanence—this is supernormal power due to the pervasive force of knowledge. [...][10] Through the path of arahantship, one succeeds in abandoning all afflictions—this is supernormal power due to pervasive force of knowledge, as [possessed by] Venerable Bakkula, Venerable Saṅkicca, and Venerable Bhūtapāla.[11]

This is called "supernormal power due to the pervasive force of knowledge".

5. Supernormal power due to the pervasive force of concentration

Q. What is "supernormal power due to the pervasive force of concentration"?

A. Through the first jhāna, one succeeds in abandoning the hindrances—this is supernormal power due to the pervasive force of concentration. [...] Through the attainment of the base of neither-perception-nor-non-perception, one succeeds in abandoning the perception of the base of nothingness—this is supernormal power due to the pervasive force of concentration, as [possessed by] the Venerable Sāriputta, Venerable Sañjīva, Venerable Koṇḍañña, the female lay follower Uttarā, and the female lay follower Sāmāvatī.

This is called "supernormal power due to the pervasive force of concentration".[12]

---

10. There is a long sequence missing here and also in the 2nd and 7th noble power since the abbreviated repetitions (*peyyāla*) in the Paṭisambhidāmagga are quoted. The full sequences are given at Paṭis I 45 & 100–01, and are included in the long sequence in Ch. 2 § 2, 400c08ff; see fn. 223.

11. Paṭis 211: *Katamā ñāṇavipphārā iddhi? Aniccānupassanāya niccasaññā niccasaññāya pahānaṭṭho ijjhatī ti ñāṇavipphārā iddhi, dukkhānupassanāya sukhasaññāya, anattānupassanāya attasaññāya ... paṭinissaggānupassanāya ādānassa pahānaṭṭho ijjhatī ti ñāṇavipphārā iddhi. Āyasmato bakkulassa ñāṇavipphārā iddhi, āyasmato saṅkiccassa ñāṇavipphārā iddhi, āyasmato bhūtapālassa ñāṇavipphārā iddhi.*

12. Cf. Paṭis 211–12: *Katamā samādhivipphārā iddhi? Paṭhamajjhānena nīvaraṇānaṃ pahānaṭṭho ijjhatī ti samādhivipphārā iddhi, ... nevasaññānāsaññāyatanasamāpattiyā ākiñcaññāyatanasaññā pahānaṭṭho ijjhatī ti samādhivipphārā iddhi. Āyasmato sāriputtassa samādhivipphārā iddhi, āyasmato sañjīvassa samādhivipphāra iddhi, āyasmato khāṇukoṇḍaññassa samādhivipphārā iddhi; uttarāya upāsikāya samādhivipphārā iddhi, sāmāvatiyā upāsikāya samādhivipphārā iddhi.* A I 26: *Etad-aggaṃ bhikkhave mama sāvikānaṃ upāsikānaṃ (paṭhamaṃ) jhāyīnaṃ yadidaṃ uttarā nandamātā.*

6. Supernormal power of the noble ones

Q. What is "supernormal power of the noble ones"?
A. "If a bhikkhu wishes "I should dwell perceiving the non-repulsive in the repulsive", he dwells perceiving the non-repulsive [in that].

If a bhikkhu wishes "I should dwell perceiving the repulsive in the non-repulsive", he dwells perceiving the repulsive [in that].

If a bhikkhu wishes "I should dwell perceiving the non-repulsive in the non-repulsive and in the repulsive", he dwells perceiving the non-repulsive [in that].

If a bhikkhu wishes "I should dwell perceiving the repulsive in the repulsive and in the non-repulsive", he dwells perceiving the repulsive [in that].

If a bhikkhu wishes "I should avoid both the non-repulsive and the repulsive and dwell equanimous, mindfully and clearly knowing", he dwells equanimous therein, mindfully and clearly knowing".[13]

Q. How does he "dwell perceiving the non-repulsive in the repulsive"?
A. He pervades an unattractive object with loving-kindness or regards it as elements.[14]

Q. How does he "dwell perceiving the repulsive in the non-repulsive"?
A. He pervades an attractive object with the [perception of the] foul or regards it as impermanent.[15]

---

13. Paṭis II 212–13: *Katamā ariyā iddhi? Idha bhikkhu sace ākaṅkhati paṭikūle appaṭikūlasaññī vihareyyan-ti, appaṭikūlasaññī tattha viharati. ... Kathaṃ paṭikūle appaṭikūlasaññī viharati? Aniṭṭhasmiṃ vatthusmiṃ mettāya vā pharati, dhātuto vā upasaṃharati. Evaṃ paṭikūle appaṭikūlasaññī viharati. Kathaṃ appaṭikūle paṭikūlasaññī viharati? Iṭṭhasmiṃ vatthusmiṃ asubhāya vā pharati, aniccato vā upasaṃharati. Evaṃ ... Kathaṃ paṭikūle ca appaṭikūle ca appaṭikūlasaññī viharati? Aniṭṭhasmiñca iṭṭhasmiñca vatthusmiṃ mettāya vā pharati, dhātuto vā upasaṃharati. ... Kathaṃ appaṭikūle ca paṭikūle ca paṭikūlasaññī viharati? Iṭṭhasmiñca aniṭṭhasmiñca vatthusmiṃ asubhāya vā pharati, aniccato vā upasaṃharati. ... Kathaṃ paṭikūle ca appaṭikūle ca tadubhayaṃ abhinivajjetvā upekkhako viharati sato sampajāno? Idha bhikkhu cakkhunā rūpaṃ disvā ... manasā dhammaṃ viññāya neva sumano hoti na dummano, upekkhako viharati sato sampajāno. ... Ayaṃ ariyā iddhi.* M III 301: *Kathañcānanda, ariyo hoti bhāvitindriyo? Idhānanda, bhikkhuno cakkhunā rūpaṃ disvā uppajjati manāpaṃ, uppajjati amanāpaṃ, uppajjati manāpāmanāpaṃ. So sace ākaṅkhati paṭikūle appaṭikūlasaññī vihareyyan-ti, ... upekkhako tattha viharati sato sampajāno. ...* Cf. D III 112, S V 119, A III 169.

14. The last *ariya-iddhi* in the list and the question and answer about the first *ariya-iddhi* are omitted in the Taishō text itself, and are given as variant readings in footnotes.

15. D-a III 895: *Paṭikūlasaññī tattha viharatī ti appaṭikūle satte asubhasaññaṃ pharati, saṅkhāre aniccasaññaṃ upasaṃharati.*

Q. How does he "dwell perceiving the non-repulsive in the repulsive and in the non-repulsive"?
A. He pervades non-attractive and attractive objects with loving-kindness or regards them as elements.

Q. How does he "dwell perceiving the repulsive in the non-repulsive and in the repulsive"?
A. He pervades attractive and non-attractive objects with the [perception of the] foul or regards them as impermanent. **[441c]**

Q. How does he "avoid both the non-repulsive and the repulsive and dwell equanimous, mindful, and aware"?
A. Here a bhikkhu, seeing a form with the eye is neither glad nor sad, but dwells equanimous, mindful, and clearly knowing. And so for the other sense doors.

This is called "supernormal power of the noble ones".

7. Supernormal power born of result of kamma

Q. What is "supernormal power born of result of kamma"?
A. All deities, all birds, some men, and some born in the bad destinations (*duggati*), perform the supernormal power of flying in the sky.[16]

This is called "supernormal power born of result of kamma".

8. Supernormal power of the meritorious

Q. What is "supernormal power of the meritorious"?
A. [The supernormal power of a] Wheel-turning King, [the supernormal power of] the eminent householder Jotika, the eminent householder Jaṭila, and the eminent householder Ghosita. It is also said: "The five persons of great merit have it".[17]

---

16. Paṭis II 213: *Katamā kammavipākajā iddhi? Sabbesaṃ pakkhīnaṃ, sabbesaṃ devānaṃ, ekaccānaṃ manussānaṃ, ekaccānaṃ vinipātikānaṃ. Ayaṃ kammavipākajā iddhi.*

17. Meṇḍaka is missing. In Paṭis-a 685, Meṇḍaka is one of five persons in a separate list of persons with great merit. Instead of 居士 "householder" *gahapatī*, as used earlier, 長者 is used here, which possibly corresponds to *seṭṭhi*, since Jotika and the others, besides being called *gahapati*, are also called *seṭṭhi* in Paṭis-a 677–84. A *seṭṭhi* is a "chief merchant", "head of a guild", or "eminent/wealthy man". 長者 lit. "one who is superior", can correspond to *mahā-dhanin; āyuṣmat, dhanin, mahā-śāla,* or *śreṣṭhi.*

Paṭis II 213: *Katamā puññavato iddhi? Rājā cakkavatti vehāsaṃ gacchati saddhiṃ caturaṅginiyā senāya antamaso assabandhagopake purise upādāya; jotikassa gahapatissa puññavato iddhi, jaṭilassa gahapatissa puññavato iddhi, meṇḍakassa gahapatissa puññavato iddhi, ghositassa gahapatissa puññavato iddhi, pañcannaṃ mahāpuññānaṃ puññavato iddhi.*

This is called "supernormal power of the meritorious".

9. Supernormal power sprung from magic knowledge

Q. What is "supernormal power sprung from magic knowledge"?
A. [The supernormal power of a] sorcerer who [by] reciting charms can fly through the sky and manifest elephants, horses, chariots, infantry, or various arrays of troops.

This is called "supernormal power sprung from magic knowledge".[18]

10. Supernormal power due to [right] application

Q. What is "supernormal power due to [right] application"?
A. Through renunciation, one succeeds in abandoning sensual desire; [...]; through the path of arahantship, one succeeds in abandoning all afflictions.[19] It is like a potter, etc., completing his work. Thus, because of giving rise to right application, one succeeds in all one's goals.

This is called "supernormal power due to [right] application".

11. Procedure of developing supernormal power

Q. Who develops supernormal power?
A. One who practises the fourth jhāna with mastery on the [nine] totalities with the space totality as the ninth, or on the [five] totalities with the space totality as the fifth,[20] is one who develops supernormal power.

Paṭis-a 685: *Pañcannaṃ mahāpuññānaṃ puññavato iddhi ti ettha puññiddhi pañcannaṃ mahāpuññānaṃ daṭṭhabbā ti attho. pañca mahāpuññā nāma meṇḍakaseṭṭhi, tassa bhariyā candapadumā, putto dhanañcayaseṭṭhi, suṇisā sumanadevī, doso puṇṇo nāmā ti ime pañca janā paccekasambuddhe katādhikārā.*

18. Paṭis II 213: *Katamā vijjāmayā iddhi? Vijjādharā vijjaṃ parijapetvā vehāsaṃ gacchanti: ākāse antalikkhe hatthim pi dassenti, assam pi dassenti, ratham pi dassenti, pattim pi dassenti, vividham pi senābyūhaṃ dassenti.*

19. Upatissa quotes the abbreviated sequence from the Paṭisambhidāmagga; see fn. 223. Cf. Paṭis II 213–14: *Kathaṃ tattha tattha sammāpayogapaccayā ijjhanaṭṭhena iddhi? Nekkhammena kāmacchandassa pahānaṭṭho ijjhatī ti ... Arahattamaggena sabbakilesānaṃ pahānaṭṭho ijjhatī ti tattha tattha sammāpayogapaccayā ijjhanaṭṭhena iddhi.*

20. Lit. "... with the space totality as the ninth, or with the space totality as the fifth, ...". In the explanations of the divine ear and recollection of past lives, it is said that one "attains the fourth jhāna with mastery on the eight totalities and the two totalities" as a prerequisite. These 8 probably refer to the 4 element totalities and 4 colour totalities, which are mentioned together as the "eight totalities" in commentarial Pali works, while the other two totalities, i.e. light and space, are also mentioned as a separate pair (Nett 89, As 400). So, what could be intended here is that he attains the 4th jhāna

It is also said: "One who practises the fourth [jhāna] of the material sphere with distinction, is one who develops supernormal power".

It is also said: "One who practises the fourth [jhāna] a second time with mastery [after emerging from the immaterial attainments], is one who develops supernormal power".

Q. How should one give rise to supernormal power?

A. "Here a bhikkhu develops the basis of supernormal power which is endowed with the activities of endeavour and the concentration due to motivation, ... concentration due to energy, ... concentration due to mind, ... concentration due to examination".[21]

"Motivation" (*chanda*) is the wish for performing supernormal power.

"Concentration" is undistractedness of the mind.[22]

The meditator desires and wishes for supernormal power and the bases of supernormal power. He develops concentration and resolves upon the four kinds of energy: [He arouses energy] for the non-arising of evil unwholesome states that have not yet arisen; for the abandoning of the evil unwholesome states that have already arisen; for the arising of wholesome states that have not yet arisen; for the fullness, non-losing, increase, development, and fulfilment of the wholesome states that have already arisen. This is called "the activities of endeavour" (*padhāna-saṅkhārā*).[23]

---

through the nine totalities, i.e. the eight totalities including the space totality, or the five totalities, i.e. the four element (or colour) totalities and the space totality. Given that space is also an element, it could be that the four element totalities are intended. In the divine eye section, the same phrase is given with the light totality.

LC: "The point is that one either practises the nine totalities ending with the space totality or the five elements ending with the space element. When one attains to the fourth jhāna (in these), one develops supernormal power. Alternatively, when one attains to the fourth jhāna of form with distinction (e.g. by breathing mindfulness), one develops supernormal power".

21. D I 213: *Idha bho bhikkhu chandasamādhippadhānasaṅkhārasamannāgataṃ iddhipādaṃ bhāveti. Vīriyasamādhippadhānasaṅkhārasamannāgataṃ iddhipādaṃ bhāveti. Cittasamādhippadhānasaṅkhārasamannāgataṃ iddhipādaṃ bhāveti. Vīmaṃsāsamādh ippadhānasaṅkhārasamannāgataṃ iddhipādaṃ bhāveti. Ime kho, bho, tena bhagavatā jānatā passatā arahatā sammāsambuddhena cattāro iddhipādā paññattā iddhipahutāya iddhivisavitāya iddhivikubbanatāya.* Cf. Vism XII.50–54/p.385.

22. Vibh 216: *Yo chando chandikatā kattukamyatā kusalo dhammacchando, ayaṃ vuccati chando. ... Yā cittassa ṭhiti saṇṭhiti avaṭṭhiti avisāhāro avikkhepo avisāhaṭamānasatā samatho samādhindriyaṃ samādhibalaṃ sammāsamādhi, ayaṃ vuccati samādhi.*

23. Vibh 216: *Chandaṃ ce bhikkhu adhipatiṃ karitvā labhati samādhiṃ, labhati cittassekaggataṃ, ayaṃ vuccati chandasamādhi. So anuppannānaṃ pāpakānaṃ akusalānaṃ dhammānaṃ anuppādāya chandaṃ janeti ... padahati, uppannānaṃ pāpakānaṃ akusalānaṃ dhammānaṃ pahānāya ... padahati, anuppannānaṃ kusalānaṃ dhammānaṃ uppādāya*

"Endowed" (*samannāgata*)[24] means that one is endowed with just these three states (*dhamma*) for fulfilling the six factors of the term "endowed".[25]

"Basis of supernormal power" (*iddhipāda*): [that which] creates the path for the obtaining of supernormal power, just that state is the basis of supernormal power.[26]

Furthermore, it is endowed with the activities of endeavour and the concentration due to motivation—this is called the "basis of supernormal power".

"For the obtaining of supernormal power" is the principal meaning.

"Develops" (*bhāveti*) means: "practises these states and practises them much".[27]

This is called "the development of the basis of supernormal power endowed with the activities of endeavour and the concentration due to motivation".

If the practice (*payoga*) of the meditator who is thus developing [these states] falls back or stagnates, [then] by arousing energy he accomplishes the basis of power that is endowed with activities of endeavour and concentration due to energy.[28] **[442a]**

If, while practicing, there is sluggishness, falling back, or fright, when the mind is sluggish, he attends to the sign of exertion; when the mind falls back, he attends to the sign of concentration; when the mind is frightened, he attends to the sign of equanimity.[29] Thus, he accomplishes the basis of

---

... padahati, uppannānaṃ kusalānaṃ dhammānaṃ ṭhitiyā asammosāya bhiyyobhāvāya vepullāya bhāvanāya pāripūriyā ... padahati. Ime vuccanti padhānasaṅkhārā. Iti ayañ-ca chandasamādhi, ime ca padhānasaṅkhārā. Tadekajjhaṃ abhisaññahitvā abhisaṅkhipitvā chandasamādhipadhānasaṅkhāro tveva saṅkhaṃ gacchati.

24. Vibh 216: *Iti iminā ca chandena, iminā ca samādhinā, iminā ca padhānasaṅkhārena upeto hoti samupeto upāgato samupāgato upapanno sampanno samannāgato. Tena vuccati chandasamādhipadhānasaṅkhārasamannāgato ti.*

25. The three qualities would refer to *chanda, samādhi, padhānasaṅkhāra;* and the six factors to *upeta, samupeta, upāgata, samupāgata, upapanna, sampanna,* of the Vibh passage given the previous footnote.

26. Cf. Paṭis II 205: *Iddhiyā ime cattāro pādā iddhilābhāya iddhipaṭilābhāya iddhivikubbanatāya iddhivisavitāya iddhivasībhāvāya iddhivesārajjāya saṃvattantī ti.*

27. Vibh 216: *Iddhī ti: yā tesaṃ dhammānaṃ iddhi samiddhi ... upasampadā. ... Iddhipādaṃ bhāvetī ti: te dhamme āsevati bhāveti bahulīkaroti.*

28. Cf. the "roots of success" passage in Paṭis II 206 (§ 8).

29. Cf. A I 256: *Adhicittamanuyuttena ... bhikkhunā tīṇi nimittāni kālena kālaṃ manasi kātabbāni kālena kālaṃ samādhinimittaṃ manasi kātabbaṃ, kālena kālaṃ paggahanimittaṃ manasi kātabbaṃ, kālena kālaṃ upekkhānimittaṃ manasi kātabbaṃ. Sace, bhikkhave, adhicittamanuyutto bhikkhu ekantaṃ samādhinimittaṃ yeva manasi kareyya, ṭhānaṃ taṃ cittaṃ kosajjāya saṃvatteyya. Sace ... paggahanimittaṃ yeva manasi kareyya, ṭhānaṃ taṃ*

supernormal power that is endowed with concentration due to mind (*citta-samādhi*), and the activities of endeavour.

If the mind is without defilement (*kilesa*), he easily discriminates the beneficial and the harmful. He practises, [thinking]: "It is the time to develop this state", or "It is not the time to develop this state". Thus, he accomplishes the basis of supernormal power that is endowed with concentration due to examination (*vīmaṃsā-samādhi*), and the activities of endeavour.

The meditator develops the four bases of supernormal power. When he has achieved mastery of mind [in these], he makes his mind correspond to his body, and his body correspond to his mind. The meditator settles his mind in his body, and in his body, he settles his mind; by means of his body, he transforms his mind, and by means of his mind, he transforms his body; by means of his body, he resolves on his mind, and with his mind, he resolves on his body. He dwells imbuing the body with the perception of pleasure and the perception of lightness.[30]

The body of the meditator who is practising thus becomes exceedingly soft, light, and malleable, just as a ball of iron heated in a fire can be fashioned into any shape one wishes. Thus, through developing the mind, his body becomes light and, owing to the lightness, he enters upon the fourth jhāna. Mindfully emerging from it, he adverts to space[31] and resolves with

---

cittaṃ uddhaccāya saṃvatteyya. Sace ... upekkhānimittaṃ yeva manasi kareyya, ṭhānaṃ taṃ cittaṃ na sammā samādhiyeyya āsavānaṃ khayāya.

30. Cf. the parallel in the "supernormal power of transformation section" below, which is translated differently. Cf. Paṭis I 111: *So imesu catūsu iddhipādesu cittaṃ paribhāvetvā paridametvā muduṃ karitvā kammaniyaṃ kāyam-pi citte samodahati, cittam-pi kāye samodahati, kāyavasena cittaṃ pariṇāmeti, cittavasena kāyaṃ pariṇāmeti, kāyavasena cittaṃ adhiṭṭhāti, cittavasena kāyaṃ adhiṭṭhāti; kāyavasena cittaṃ pariṇāmetvā cittavasena kāyaṃ pariṇāmetvā kāyavasena cittaṃ adhiṭṭhahitvā cittavasena kāyaṃ adhiṭṭhahitvā sukhasaññañ-ca lahusaññañ-ca kāye okkamitvā viharati. So tathābhāvitena cittena parisuddhena pariyodātena iddhividhañāṇāya cittaṃ abhinīharati abhininnāmeti.*

31. 能分別虛空, or "he is able to analyse/discriminate/investigate space". 分別 corresponds to *paricchindati vibhajjati*, as well as *vīmaṃsati*, but here 能分別, in accordance with Paṭis II 208, it would correspond to *āvajjana*; cf. DDB s.v. 能分別. According to Vism XII.131–132/p.404 one adverts to the wind totality and according to Vism XII.87—90/p.394, the space-totality is used as basis for the *iddhi* of going through walls, etc.

Cf. Vism XII.98/p.396ff.: *Pakkhī sakuṇo ti pakkhehi yuttasakuṇo. Evaṃ kātukāmena pana pathavīkasiṇaṃ samāpajjitvā vuṭṭhāya sace nisinno gantumicchati, pallaṅkappamāṇaṃ ṭhānaṃ paricchinditvā parikammaṃ katvā vuttanayeneva adhiṭṭhātabbaṃ. ... sace padasā gantukāmo hoti maggappamāṇan-ti evaṃ yathānurūpaṃ ṭhānaṃ paricchinditvā vuttanayeneva pathavī hotū ti adhiṭṭhātabbaṃ, saha adhiṭṭhānena pathavī yeva hoti. Tatrāyaṃ pāḷi (Paṭis II 208): Ākāsepi pallaṅkena kamati, seyyathā pi pakkhī sakuṇoti. Pakatiyā pathavīkasiṇasamāpattiyā lābhī hoti, ākāsaṃ āvajjati. Āvajjitvā ñāṇena adhiṭṭhāti, pathavī*

knowledge upon it thus: "This body will rise up into space". By resolving with knowledge, he rises up into the sky like a fibre of silk blown by the wind.[32]

Therefore, the beginner meditator should not go far away hastily. Why? Because seeing where he has gone to could give rise to fear. If fear arises, he falls away from jhāna. Therefore, the beginner meditator should not go far away hastily, but should go gradually. At first [he should rise up] one foot, then after observing [where he is, he should rise up] higher little by little. Then again, depending on the indications (*nimitta*), he applies energy [and rises up] one fathom (1.8 m). Through this method of [rising] gradually, he can rise up as [far as] he wishes.

Q. If a meditator who is in the sky falls away from jhāna, would he fall to the ground from the sky?

A. This is not the case. If he has risen up and has gone far away from his former sitting place, and would fall away [from jhāna], then he returns to his former sitting place. He sees himself sitting in his former sitting place

---

hotū ti. Pathavī hoti. So ākāse antalikkhe caṅkamatipi tiṭṭhatipi nisīdatipi seyyam-pi kappeti. ....

32. This is likely to be a Chinese adaptation of the original text's "tuft of cotton wool", *tūlapicu*. Cf. S V 283: *Yasmiṃ, ānanda, samaye tathāgato kāyam-pi citte samodahati, cittam-pi kāye samodahati, sukhasaññañ-ca lahusaññañ-ca kāye okkamitvā viharati; tasmiṃ, ānanda, samaye tathāgatassa kāyo lahutaro ceva hoti mudutaro ca kammaniyataro ca pabhassarataro ca. Seyyathāpi, ānanda, ayoguḷo divasaṃ santatto lahutaro ceva hoti mudutaro ca kammaniyataro ca pabhassarataro ca; evam-eva ... pabhassarataro ca. Yasmiṃ, ānanda, samaye ... tathāgatassa kāyo appakasireneva pathaviyā vehāsaṃ abbhuggacchati, so anekavihitaṃ iddhividhaṃ paccanubhoti- eko pi hutvā ... yāva brahmalokāpi kāyena vasaṃ vatteti. Seyyathāpi, ānanda, tūlapicu vā kappāsapicu vā lahuko vātūpādāno appakasireneva pathaviyā vehāsaṃ abbhuggacchati; evam-eva ...*

Vism XII.131–132/p.404, Paṭis-a III 662: *Sukhasaññañ-ca lahusaññañ-ca okkamitvā ti pādakajjhānārammaṇena iddhicittena sahajātaṃ sukhasaññañ-ca lahusaññañ-ca okkamitvā pavisitvā phusitvā pāpuṇitvā. Sukhasaññā ca nāma upekkhāsampayuttasaññā. Upekkhā hi santaṃ sukhan-ti vuttā, sā yeva saññā nīvaraṇehi ceva vitakkādipaccanīkehi ca vimuttattā lahusaññā ti pi veditabbā. Taṃ okkantassa panassa karajakāyo pi tūlapicu viya sallahuko hoti. So evaṃ vātakkhittatūlapicunā viya sallahukena dissamānena kāyena brahmalokaṃ gacchati. Evaṃ gacchanto ca sace icchati, pathavīkasiṇavasena ākāse maggaṃ nimminitvā padasā gacchati. ... Sace icchati, vāyokasiṇavasena vātaṃ adhiṭṭhahitvā tūlapicu viya vāyunā gacchati. Api ca gantukāmatāva ettha pamāṇaṃ. Sati hi gantukāmatāya evaṃkatacittādhiṭṭhāno adhiṭṭhānavegakkhitto va so jiyāvegakkhitto saro viya dissamāno gacchati.* Cf. Th-a I 222: *Tattha lahuko vata me kāyo ti nīvaraṇādivikkhambhanena cuddasavidhena cittaparidamanena caturiddhipādakabhāvanāya suṭṭhu ciṇṇavasībhāvena ca me rūpakāyo sallahuko vata, yena dandhaṃ mahābhūtapaccayam-pi nāma imaṃ karajakāyaṃ cittavasena pariṇāmemīti adhippāyo. ... Tenāha tūlam-iva eritaṃ mālutena, pilavatīva me kayo ti. Tassattho yadāhaṃ brahmalokaṃ aññaṃ vā iddhiyā gantukāmo homi, tadā mālutena vāyunā eritaṃ cittaṃ tūlapicu viya ākāsaṃ laṅghanto yeva me kāyo hotī ti.*

[and thinks]: "This is the person with supernormal power. This is his state of dwelling".[33]

Thus, the meditator goes gradually with observation until he resolves with mastery.

12. Supernormal power of resolve

He wields the various kinds of miraculous transformation: Being one, he becomes many; being many, he becomes one. He appears or disappears.[34] He goes unimpeded through a wall, through a rampart, through a mountain, just as if [going] through space. He dives into the earth or emerges from it, as if in water. He walks on water as on earth. He goes through the sky like a bird flying. He strokes the sun and the moon, such is his great supernormal power, such is his great might. His body rises as far as the Brahmā world.[35]

"Being one, he becomes many": He, being one, makes himself many, a hundred or a thousand, or a 10,000 and so on through miraculous transformation. [**442b**] He enters upon the fourth jhāna, emerges mindfully from it, and immediately after[36] resolves through knowledge: "May I be many", like Cullapanthaka, the arahant.

"Being many, he becomes one": Desiring to change from many to one, he resolves through knowledge: "May I change from many to one!", like venerable Cullapanthaka, the arahant.[37]

---

33. 止法, "state of calm" (*samatha-dhamma*) or "dwelling state" (*vāsa-dhamma*)? Elsewhere, at 455b29ff., 止法 corresponds to *dhammatā*.

34. Read 或現或不現 as at 442b04.

35. D I 77, Paṭis I 111: *So anekavihitaṃ iddhividhaṃ paccanubhoti. Eko pi hutvā bahudhā hoti, bahudhā pi hutvā eko hoti; āvibhāvaṃ tirobhāvaṃ; tirokuṭṭaṃ tiropākāraṃ tiropabbataṃ asajjamāno gacchati, seyyathā pi ākāse; pathaviyā pi ummujjanimujjaṃ karoti, seyyathā pi udake; udake pi abhijjamāne gacchati, seyyathā pi pathaviyaṃ; ākāse pi pallaṅkena kamati seyyathā pi pakkhī sakuṇo ime pi candimasūriye evaṃ mahiddhike evaṃ mahānubhāve pāṇinā parāmasati parimajjati; yāva brahmalokā pi kāyena vasaṃ vatteti.*

36. 次第 = *anupubba, paṭipāṭiyā, kama, samanantara*, etc. Cf. Vism XII.57: *Ñāṇena adhiṭṭhahanto ti svāyam-ete iddhiyā bhūmipādapadabhūte dhamme sampādetvā abhiññāpādakaṃ jhānaṃ samāpajjitvā vuṭṭhāya sace sataṃ icchati sataṃ homi sataṃ homī ti parikammaṃ katvā puna abhiññāpādakaṃ jhānaṃ samāpajjitvā vuṭṭhāya adhiṭṭhāti, adhiṭṭhānacittena saheva sataṃ hoti. Sahassādīsu pi eseva nayo. Sace evaṃ na ijjhati puna parikammaṃ katvā dutiyam-pi samāpajjitvā vuṭṭhāya adhiṭṭhātabbaṃ.*

37. Cf. Vism XII.59. Paṭis I 207: ... *Yathāyasmā cullapanthako eko pi hutvā bahudhā hoti, evam-evaṃ so iddhimā cetovasippatto eko pi hutvā bahudhā hoti. Bahudhā pi hutvā eko hotī ti. Pakatiyā bahulo ekaṃ āvajjati; āvajjitvā ñāṇena adhiṭṭhāti eko homī ti, eko hoti.* .... Cf. A I 24: *Etad aggaṃ bhikkhave mama sāvakānaṃ bhikkhūnaṃ manomayaṃ kāyaṃ abhinimminantānaṃ yadidaṃ cullapanthako.* (Cf. Mp I 216).

"He appears or disappears": What is the meaning of "appears"? It means, "revealed".

What is the meaning of, "Disappears"? It means, "Not revealed". The meditator reveals what is not revealed.[38]

"He goes unimpeded through a wall, through a rampart, through a mountain, just as if [going] through space": The meditator, through developing the space totality, enters upon the fourth jhāna. Emerging mindfully from it, he adverts to a wall, a rampart, or a mountain. Having adverted, he resolves through knowledge: "Let this be space". There being space, the meditator, in space goes through the wall, goes through the rampart, and goes through the mountain. He goes unimpeded, just as through space.

"He dives into the earth or emerges from it as if in water": The meditator, through developing the water totality, enters upon the fourth jhāna. Emerging mindfully from it, he adverts to earth, demarcates [an area of earth], and resolves through knowledge: "Let this be water!" [There being water,] the meditator can dive into the earth or emerge from it like in normal water.[39]

---

38. There is no mention of a method of development of this power, as found in Vism XII.69–70/p.390 & XII.81/p.392 and Paṭis-a 347. It could be lost, or else Upatissa follows Paṭis closely, which also does not mention it.

Paṭis I 207–8: *Āvibhavan ti. Kenaci anāvaṭaṃ hoti appaṭicchannaṃ vivaṭaṃ pākaṭaṃ. Tirobhāvan ti. Kenaci āvaṭaṃ hoti paṭicchannaṃ pihitaṃ paṭikujjitaṃ. Tirokuḍḍaṃ tiropākāraṃ tiropabbataṃ asajjamāno gacchati, seyyathā pi ākāse ti. Pakatiyā ākāsakasiṇasamāpattiyā lābhī hoti, tirokuḍḍaṃ tiropākāraṃ tiropabbataṃ āvajjati; āvajjitvā ñāṇena adhiṭṭhāti ākāso hotū ti, ākāso hoti. .... Paṭhaviyā pi ummujjanimujjaṃ karoti, seyyathā pi udake ti. Pakatiyā āpokasiṇa-samāpattiyā lābhī hoti, paṭhaviṃ āvajjati; āvajjitvā ñāṇena adhiṭṭhāti udakaṃ hotū ti udakaṃ hoti. So pathaviyā ummujjanimujjaṃ karoti.*

The text is garbled: The power of going through walls comes before the power of appearing, which is followed again by the same sentence on going through walls, etc. For clarity, the translation has been amended here in accordance with similar instructions earlier in this section and at Vism XII.87. According to the Vism, after emerging from the fourth jhāna, one resolves "Let this which is dark become light" or "Let this which is hidden be revealed", etc. The Vism gives no particular totality attainment for developing these powers, but the dispelling of darkness (*andhakāravidhamana*) is listed as one of the benefits of the white and the light totality in both the Vim (423c) and the Vism (V.35/p.176), while Vism V.37 (but not Vim) lists "revealing what is hidden" (*paṭicchannānaṃ vivaṭakaraṇaṃ*) as a benefit of the space totality, and Vism V.3 lists "making darkness" (*andhakārakaraṇa*) as one of the benefits of the blue totality.

39. Vism XII.92: *Pathaviyā pi ummujjanimujjan-ti ettha ummujjanti uṭṭhānaṃ vuccati. Nimujjanti saṃsīdanaṃ. Ummujjañ-ca nimujjañ-ca ummujjanimujjaṃ. Evaṃ kātukāmena āpokasiṇaṃ samāpajjitvā uṭṭhāya ettake ṭhāne pathavī udakaṃ hotū ti paricchinditvā parikammaṃ katvā vuttanayeneva adhiṭṭhātabbaṃ. Saha adhiṭṭhānena yathā paricchinne ṭhāne pathavī udakam-eva hoti. So tattha ummujjanimujjaṃ karoti. Tatrāyaṃ pāḷi: Pakatiyā āpokasiṇasamāpattiyā lābhī hoti. ...*

"He can walk on water": unimpeded, just as if he is going on earth. The meditator practises the earth totality and enters upon the fourth jhāna. Emerging mindfully from it, he adverts to water, demarcates [an area of water], and resolves through knowledge: "Let this be earth!" There being earth, the meditator is able to go on water unimpeded, just as if he is going on normal earth.[40]

"He goes through the sky like a flying bird": Herein there are three kinds of going: going by foot, going by wind, and going by mind.

Herein, [to go by foot] the meditator attains the attainment of the earth totality, resolves through knowledge upon a path in space, and goes by foot [on it].

[To go by wind] he attains the attainment of the wind totality, resolves upon wind, and goes by wind like a fibre of silk.

To go by mind, he imbues his body and mind with the perception of pleasure and the perception of lightness. Through imbuing, the body becomes light, and he goes by mind [through the sky] like a flying bird. Thus, he goes by mind.[41]

"He strokes the sun and the moon, such is his great power, such is his great might": The meditator, having supernormal power, achieves mastery of his mind. Through developing his mind, he attains the fourth jhāna and, emerging mindfully from it, he strokes the sun and the moon by resolving through knowledge: "Let this be within hand's reach!", and, being within hand's reach, the meditator, whether sitting or lying down, strokes them with his hand.[42]

"His body rises as far as the Brahmā world": When the meditator who has supernormal power and has achieved mastery of his mind desires to go as far as the Brahmā world,[43] **[442c]** then with such [development of the] the four bases of supernormal power, and with such development of mind, he resolves the far as near, or the near as far. He resolves much as little, or little as much.

---

40. Paṭis I 208: *Udake pi abhijjamāne gacchati, seyyathā pi paṭhaviyan ti. Pakatiyā paṭhavīkasiṇa-samāpattiyā lābhī hoti, udakaṃ āvajjati; āvajjitvā ñāṇena adhiṭṭhāti paṭhavī hotū ti paṭhavī hoti.*

41. A fuller description of this method is at 442a10; cf. 442c09. Cf. Paṭis II 208: *Ākāse pi pallaṅkena kamati, seyyathā pi pakkhī sakuṇo ti pakatiyā pathavīkasiṇasamāpattiyā lābhī hoti. Ākāsaṃ āvajjati. Āvajjitvā ñāṇena adhiṭṭhāti pathavī hotū ti. Pathavī hoti. So ākāse antalikkhe caṅkamati pi tiṭṭhati pi nisīdati pi...*

42. Paṭis I 208–9: *Ime pi candimasuriye evam-mahiddhike evam-mahānubhāve pāṇinā parāmasati parimajjatī ti. Idha so iddhimā cetovasippatto nisinnako vā nipannako vā candimasuriye āvajjati; āvajjitvā ñāṇena adhiṭṭhāti hatthapāse hotū ti, hatthapāse hoti, ...*

43. Paṭis II 209: *Sace so iddhimā cetovasippatto dissamānena kāyena brahmalokaṃ gantukāmo hoti, kāyavasena cittaṃ pariṇāmeti, kāyavasena cittaṃ adhiṭṭhāti. Kāyavasena cittaṃ pariṇāmetvā, kāyavasena cittaṃ adhiṭṭhahitvā, sukhasaññañ-ca lahusaññañ-ca okkamitvā dissamānena kāyena brahmalokaṃ gacchati.*

By means of the divine eye, he sees Brahmā's form. By means of the divine ear, he hears the sound of Brahmā. By means of the knowledge of others' minds, he knows Brahmā's mind.[44]

The meditator, having three formations, goes to Brahmā's world through two formations.[45]

This is the teaching of the supernormal power of resolve in full.

The supernormal power of resolve is finished.

13. Supernormal power of miraculous transformation

Now, the meditator who wishes to give rise to the supernormal power of miraculous transformation, having developed the four bases of supernormal power and having achieved mastery of his mind [in them], settles his mind in his body, and in his body he settles his mind; by means of his body he transforms his mind, and by means of his mind he transforms his body; by means of his body he resolves on his mind, and with his mind he resolves on his body.[46] He dwells imbuing the body with the perception of pleasure and the perception of lightness. The body of the meditator who is practising thus becomes exceedingly soft, exceedingly light, and malleable, just as a ball of iron heated in a fire can be fashioned into any shape one wishes.

The meditator, who has practised thus and whose mind is exceedingly soft and malleable, imbues his body with his mind. The meditator, if he wishes to discard his physical appearance and manifest the physical appearance of a boy, enters upon the fourth jhāna and, emerging mindfully from it, gradually adverts to the physical appearance of a boy. Having adverted, he resolves through knowledge: "Let me have the physical appearance of a boy!" Attending thus he accomplishes the physical appearance of a boy.[47] In the

---

44. Paṭis I 209: *Yāva brahmalokā pi kāyena vasaṃ vattetī ti. Sace so iddhimā cetovasippatto brahmalokaṃ gantukāmo hoti, dūre pi santike adhiṭṭhāti santike hotū ti santike hoti, Santike pi dūre adhiṭṭhāti dūre hotū ti. Dūre hoti. Bahukam-pi thokaṃ adhiṭṭhāti thokaṃ hotū ti. Thokaṃ hoti. Thokam-pi bahukaṃ adhiṭṭhāti bahukaṃ hotū ti. Bahukaṃ hoti. Dibbena cakkhunā tassa brahmuno rūpaṃ passati. Dibbāya sotadhātuyā tassa brahmuno saddaṃ suṇāti. Cetopariyañāṇena tassa brahmuno cittaṃ pajānāti.... Yaññad-eva hi so iddhimā karoti, tan tad eva hi so nimmito karotī ti.*

45. This probably refers to not being able to wield bodily power (i.e. the bodily formation, *kāyasaṅkhāra*) in the Brahmāloka, but only verbal and mental power (i.e. *vacī-* and *citta-saṅkhāra*). Cf. Vism XII.136.

46. This passage is corrupt in places; see the parallel above at 442a07–10.

47. According to Paṭis-a and Vism, first he should emerge and attend to his appearance as a boy, then he should again attain the fourth jhāna and after emerging from it he should resolve "Let me be a boy!" The same procedure is found in the next section, on supernormal power of mind.

same way in transforming into the physical appearance of a dragon (*nāga*), a harpy (*supaṇṇa*), a yakkha, an asura, or into the appearance of Inda[48] or Brahmā, the ocean, a mountain, a forest, a lion, a tiger, a leopard, an elephant, a horse, infantry, and an array of troops. He resolves through knowledge thus: "Let me be an array of troops!" Attending thus he accomplishes the physical appearance of an array of troops.[49]

Q. What is the difference between the supernormal power of resolve and the supernormal power of miraculous transformation?
A. Through the supernormal power of resolve, one resolves without discarding one's material appearance. Through the supernormal power of miraculous transformation, one discards one's physical appearance. This is the difference.

The supernormal power of miraculous transformation is finished.

14. Supernormal power of [producing a] mind-made [body]

Now, the meditator who wishes to give rise to the supernormal power of [producing a] mind-made [body], and has thus developed the four bases of supernormal power, and has achieved mastery of his mind, enters upon the fourth jhāna. Emerging mindfully from it, he attends to the interior of his body [thinking]: "It is just like an empty pot". The meditator attending thus [thinks]: "In this empty body I will perform miraculous transformation

---

Paṭis-a III 665: *Tattha soti heṭṭhā vuttavidhānena mudukammaññakatacitto so iddhimā bhikkhu. Sace vikubbaniddhiṃ kātukāmo hoti, attano pakativaṇṇaṃ pakatisaṇṭhānaṃ vijahitvā kumārakavaṇṇaṃ vā dasseti. Kathaṃ? Pathavīkasiṇāramma ṇābhiññāpādakacatutthajjhānato vuṭṭhāya evarūpo kumārako homi ti nimminitabbaṃ kumārakavaṇṇaṃ āvajjitvā kataparikammāvasāne puna samāpajjitvā vuṭṭhāya evarūpo nāma kumārako homī ti abhiññāñāṇena adhiṭṭhāti, saha adhiṭṭhānena kumārako hotī ti.* Vism XII.138/p.406: *Vikubbanaṃ tāva karontena, so pakativaṇṇaṃ vijahitvā kumārakavaṇṇaṃ ... dīpivaṇṇaṃ vā dasseti, hatthim-pi dasseti, assam-pi dasseti, ratham-pi dasseti, pattim-pi dasseti, vividham-pi senābyūhaṃ dassetī ti* (Paṭis II 209) *kumārakavaṇṇādīsu yaṃ yaṃ ākaṅkhati, taṃ taṃ adhiṭṭhātabbaṃ. Adhiṭṭhahantena ca pathavīkasiṇādīsu aññatarārammaṇato abhiññāpādakajjhānato vuṭṭhāya attano kumārakavaṇṇo āvajjitabbo. Āvajjitvā parikammāvasāne puna samāpajjitvā vuṭṭhāya evarūpo nāma kumārako homī ti adhiṭṭhātabbaṃ. Saha adhiṭṭhānacittena kumārako hoti devadatto viya.*

48. A *nāga* is a serpent-king or dragon. A *supaṇṇa* is a mythical bird or a harpy. A *yakkha* is an (evil) spirit. An *asura* is a fallen deity or Titan. EKS rendered "Sakka-Inda" but the text has 帝釋 = "King Sakka," i.e. Inda; see DDB s.v. 帝釋. Cf. *sakko devānaṃ indo*: "sakka the lord of deities," M I 252, S I 220, 230.

49. Paṭis I 210: *Katamā vikubbanā iddhi? Sikkhissa bhagavato abhibhū nāma sāvako brahmaloke ṭhito sahassīlokadhātuṃ sarena viññāpeti. So dissamānena pi kāyena dhammaṃ deseti, ... vividhaṃ pi senābyūhaṃ dasseti.*

as I wish" and adverts accordingly. Having adverted, he resolves through knowledge thus: "Like that [body], let there be [a mind-created body]!" Thus, attending, he gives rise to a representation [of that body]. He practises much the miraculous transformation through this method. When he has performed the miraculous transformation, he goes.

If the meditator wishes to go to the world of Brahmā with a body created [by transformation], before approaching the Brahmā world, he transforms his body in accordance with the physical appearance of a Brahmā. [The body] which he created according to his wish is complete with all limbs, lacking no faculty.[50] **[443a]**

If the one who possesses supernormal power walks back and forth, that created person also walks back and forth. If the one who possesses supernormal power sits, or lies down, or issues smoke and flames, or asks questions, or answers, that created person also sits or lies down, issues smoke and flames, or asks questions, or answers. Whatever the one who possesses supernormal power and who has performed the miraculous transformation does, that created person also does.

Supernormal power of [producing a] mind-made [body] is finished.

15. Miscellaneous topics

Q. What are the miscellaneous topics?

A. Forms created by [the supernormal power of] miraculous transformation disappear when the [previously] determined time is reached. If the determined time has not yet been reached, but should he wish to speak during this period, he resolves that they shall disappear. If he has not determined a time, they momentarily disappear.

50. Paṭis I 210–11: *Katamā manomayā iddhi? Idha bhikkhu imamhā kāyā aññaṃ kāyaṃ abhinimmināti rūpiṃ manomayaṃ sabbaṅgapaccaṅgaṃ ahīnindriyaṃ. ...* Vism XII.139: *Manomayaṃ kātukāmo pana pādakajjhānato vuṭṭhāya kāyaṃ tāva āvajjitvā vuttanayeneva susiro hotūti adhiṭṭhāti, susiro hoti. Athassa abbhantare aññaṃ kāyaṃ āvajjitvā parikammaṃ katvā vuttanayeneva adhiṭṭhāti, tassa abbhantare añño kāyo hotūti. So taṃ muñjamhā īsikaṃ viya kosiyā asiṃ viya karaṇḍāya ahiṃ viya ca abbāhati. ...* Paṭis-a III 666: *... imamhā kāyā aññaṃ kāyaṃ abhinimminātī ti ādīsu iddhimā bhikkhu manomayiddhiṃ kātukāmo ākāsakasiṇārammaṇapādakajjhānato vuṭṭhāya attano rūpakāyaṃ tāva āvajjitvā vuttanayeneva susiro hotū ti adhiṭṭhāti, susiro hoti. Atha tassa abbhantare pathavīkasiṇavasena aññaṃ kāyaṃ āvajjitvā parikammaṃ katvā vuttanayeneva adhiṭṭhāti, tassa abbhantare añño kāyo hoti. ... Ettha ca yathā īsikādayo muñjādīhi sadisā honti, evamidaṃ manomayaṃ rūpaṃ iddhimatā sabbākārehi sadisam-eva hotī ti dassanatthaṃ imā upamā vuttāti. Manomayena kāyena iddhiyā upasaṅkamī ti ettha abhiññāmanena katakāyo manomayakāyo nāma. Aññataraṃ manomayaṃ kāyaṃ upapajjatī ti ettha jhānamanena nibbittitakāyo tena manena katattā manomayakāyo nāma. Idha pana abhiññāmanena uppāditakāyo tena manena katattā manomayakāyo nāma.*

The created person has no life faculty. That which has been created, [such as] food, is an object (*ārammaṇa*). Knowledge of supernormal power[51] occurs with regard to nine kinds of object, namely, limited object, exalted object, object that is not to be spoken of (*navattabba*), past object, future object, present object, internal object, external object, and internal-external object.[52]

The miscellaneous topics are finished.

16. Divine ear

Q. Who .gives rise to the divine ear? How does one give rise to it?

A. One who has achieved mastery in the fourth jhāna with the eight totalities and the two totalities[53] gives rise to the divine ear element from his natural ear.

It is also said: "Why is the material sphere [the basis for this knowledge]? When he has achieved mastery in the fourth jhāna it can be given rise to".

It is also said: "It can also be given rise to in [all] the four jhānas".[54]

Q. How does one give rise to it?

A. The beginner meditator, who has developed the four bases of supernormal power and has achieved mastery [in them], enters upon the fourth jhāna. Emerging mindfully from it, he immediately subsequently [adverts to sounds] by means of the natural ear element: If hearing a distant sound, he attends to the sign of the sound; if hearing a nearby sound, he attends to the sign of the sound. If hearing a gross sound, he attends to the sign of the sound; if hearing a subtle sound, he attends to the sign of the sound. If hearing a sound from

---

51. 於化人無壽命根所化飲食事變種智成九事. 所化飲食事 literally means " that has been created food object". Since there is no mention of food (*āhāra*) earlier in this chapter, and nothing corresponding to this can be found in the Pali, this likely is a corruption. Perhaps the original text had "That which has been created is an object". Cf. Nidd-a I 16: ... *yathārucitaṃ ārammaṇaṃ nimminitvā nimminitvā ramantī ti nimmānaratīnaṃ devānaṃ.* ...

52. Cf. Vism XIII.106/p.430, Paṭis-a 382: *Tattha iddhividhañāṇaṃ parittamahaggata-atītānāgatapaccuppanna-ajjhattabahiddhārammaṇavasena sattasu ārammaṇesu pavattati.* ...

53. Probably these are the four element totalities and four colour totalities, which are mentioned together as the "eight totalities" in non-canonical Pali works, while the other two are mentioned together separately (Nett 89, As 400). This is also found at the start of the recollection of past lives section.

54. This same passage is also found at the start of the recollection of previous lives section below at 443c05–07. In both places the text has "four jhānas", 四禪, not "fourth jhāna" 第四禪. This statement would suggest that one can also produce it on the first jhāna, etc. Below, at 443c06, the text has "obtains arising/production", 得起, instead of "also arises/is produced", 亦起.

the eastern direction, he attends to the sign of the sound, and likewise for all the directions.

The meditator, through developing purity of mind and purity of the ear element, extends the mind's range. Through the purified divine ear element, the meditator hears what is beyond the reach of the human ear.

He hears both sounds, namely, divine sounds and human sounds, those that are distant as well as near.[55] Herein, the former teachers said: "The beginner meditator first hears the sounds of the beings inside his own body,[56] then he hears the sounds of the beings outside his body, and then he hears the sounds of the beings residing in his dwelling place. Thus, he gradually attends and extends [the range]".

It is also said: "The beginner meditator cannot at first hear the sounds of beings inside his own body. Why? He cannot hear subtle sounds with the natural ear because they are not within its range".

The beginner meditator hears the sounds of distant conches, drums, and so on—the sounds that depend on the natural ear. For the divine ear knowledge, he should attend to the signs of these sounds as this gives rise to the divine ear knowledge. Subtle sounds or coarse sounds, [**443b**] distant sounds or nearby sounds should be grasped with just the divine ear.

Herein, the beginner meditator should not attend to [agreeable sounds and to] frightening sounds. Why? It is said that he will have sensual desire towards agreeable sounds, and that he becomes frightened of fearful sounds.

Knowledge of the divine ear occurs with regard to three kinds of object, namely, limited object, present object, and external object.[57]

If one loses the natural ear, one will also lose the divine ear element

Herein, disciples who achieve mastery hear the sounds of a thousand world-systems; Paccekabuddhas hear more than that; the Tathāgatas' hearing is unlimited.[58]

The divine ear is finished.

---

55. D I 79: *Seyyathā pi mahā-rāja puriso addhāna-magga-paṭipanno so suṇeyya bheri-saddam pi ... Tassa evam assa: bheri-saddo iti pi, "... Evam eva ... evaṃ samāhite citte parisuddhe .... dibbāya sota-dhātuyā cittaṃ abhinīharati abhininnāmeti. So dibbāya sota-dhātuyā visuddhāya atikkanta-mānusikāya ubho sadde suṇāti, dibbe ca mānuse ca, ye dūre santike ca.*

56. Cf. Vism XIII.3 *sadehakanissitā pāṇakasaddā.*

57. Vism XIII.109 adds internal object and As 426 internal-external object as well.

58. See in relation to the *pubbenivāsānussati* Sv II 407: *Sāvakā kappasatasahassaṃ anussaranti. Dve aggasāvakā asaṅkhyeyyañceva kappasatasahassañ-ca. Paccekabuddhā dve asaṅkhyeyyāni kappasatasahassañ-ca. Buddhānaṃ pana ettakan-ti paricchedo natthi, yāvatakaṃ ākaṅkhanti, tāvatakaṃ anussaranti.* Cf. Paṭis–a I 364.

The same passage is found at 444b20–22 in relation to the *dibbacakkhu.*

17. Knowledge of others' minds

Q. Who can give rise to the knowledge of others' minds? How does one give rise to it?
A. One who has achieved mastery in the fourth jhāna with the light totality obtains the divine eye and gives rise to the knowledge of others' minds.

Q. How does one give rise to it?
A. The beginner meditator, who has thus developed the four bases of supernormal power, and has achieved mastery of his mind, which is pure and immovable, enters upon [the fourth jhāna by way of] the light totality. Emerging mindfully from the fourth jhāna, he, at first, pervades his own body with light.

He sees the colour of his own mind (*cittamano*)[59] through the divine eye. He knows "Dependent upon this colour, mind consciousness (*manoviññāṇa*) arises". He sees the changes of colour through the changes in his own mind (*citta*):[60] "This colour has arisen from the faculty of joy; this colour has arisen from the faculty of distress; this colour has arisen from the faculty of equanimity".

If there is the arising of mind (*citta*) accompanied by the faculty of joy, the colour of the mind (*mano*) is like the colour of curd. If there is the arising of mind accompanied by the faculty of distress, it is like the colour purple. If there is the arising of mind accompanied by the faculty of equanimity, it is like the colour of honey. If there is the arising of mind accompanied by sensual desire, it is like the colour yellow. If there is the arising of mind accompanied by ill will, it is like the colour black. If there is the arising of mind accompanied by delusion, it is like a murky (*āvila*) colour. If there is the arising of mind accompanied by faith, it is like a pure (*suddha*) colour. Thus, the meditator investigates the changes within himself through the changes in colour.

---

59. Whereas the *Visuddhimagga* says that the meditator sees the colour of the blood of the physical heart, *hadaya*, the *Vimuttimagga*, or at least the Chinese translation of it, stresses that he sees the colour of the mind or mind-consciousness.

Vism XIII.9/p.409: *Tasmā tena bhikkhunā ālokaṃ vaḍḍhetvā dibbena cakkhunā parassa hadayarūpaṃ nissāya vattamānassa lohitassa vaṇṇaṃ passitvā cittaṃ pariyesitabbaṃ. Yadā hi somanassacittaṃ vattati, tadā rattaṃ nigrodhapakkasadisaṃ hoti. Yadā domanassacittaṃ vattati, tadā kāḷakaṃ jambupakkasadisaṃ. Yadā upekkhācittaṃ vattati, tadā pasannatilatelasadisaṃ. Tasmā tena idaṃ rūpaṃ somanassindriyasamuṭṭhānaṃ, idaṃ domanassindriyasamuṭṭhānaṃ, idaṃ upekkhindriyasamuṭṭhānan-ti parassa hadayalohita-vaṇṇaṃ passitvā cittaṃ pariyesantena cetopariyañāṇaṃ thāmagataṃ kātabbaṃ.*

60. When contemplating the minds at others at 443b21–22 "and he sees the changes in his mind through the changes in colours" is added. Perhaps the original had this here too.

Then he pervades the bodies of others with light. With the divine eye, he analyses[61] the colour of others' minds. He analyses the changes of colours by means of the changes in their minds, and analyses the changes in their minds by means of the changes in colours. Having analysed thus he gives rise to the knowledge of others' minds. When he has given rise to the knowledge of others' minds, he abandons analysing the changes of colour and only takes the mind as the object.

If the [other's] mind is with lust, the meditator, with his mind thus developed, purified, and cleansed, knows "the mind is with lust". If the mind is without lust, he knows "the mind is without lust". If the mind is with hate, he knows "the mind is with hate". If the mind is without hate, he knows "the mind is without hate".[62] Thus, he knows all [states of mind].

The knowledge of others' minds occurs with regard to eight objects, namely, limited object, exalted object, path object, immeasurable object, past object, future object, present object, and external object.[63]

The knowledge of the minds of those who are without contaminations (*anāsavā*) is not within the range of the worldling. The minds of the beings of the immaterial sphere are within the range only of the Buddhas. [**443c**]

Herein, disciples who achieve mastery know the minds [of beings] of a thousand world-systems; Paccekabuddhas know more than that; and the Tathāgatas' [knowledge] is unlimited.[64]

Knowledge of others' minds is finished.

18. Recollection of past lives

Q. Who gives rise to the knowledge of the recollection of past lives? How many kinds of knowledge of the recollection of past lives are there? How does one give rise to it?

[Q. Who gives rise to the knowledge of the recollection of past lives?]

---

61. 分別 can correspond to *vibhaṅga, paricchindana, pariccheda, abhisamaya*, etc. The Vism (XIII.9) has *pariyesana*, "seeking out, investigating".

62. Cf. A I 255; D I 79–80; S V 265: *Evaṃ bhāvitesu kho bhikkhu catusu iddhipādesu evaṃ bahulīkatesu parasattānaṃ parapuggalānaṃ cetasā ceto paricca pajānāti. Sarāgam vā cittaṃ sarāgam cittan ti ... vimuttaṃ vā cittaṃ vimuttaṃ cittan ti pajānāti.* Paṭis I 112: *So imesu catūsu iddhipādesu cittaṃ paribhāvetvā paridametvā, muduṃ karitvā kammaniyaṃ evaṃ pajānāti idaṃ rūpaṃ somanassindriyasamuṭṭhitaṃ, idaṃ rūpaṃ domanassindriyasamuṭṭhitaṃ, idaṃ rūpaṃ upekkhindriyasamuṭṭhitanti. So tathābhāvitena cittena parisuddhena pariyodātena cetopariyañāṇāya cittaṃ abhinīharati abhininnāmeti. So parasattānaṃ parapuggalānaṃ cetasā ceto paricca pajānāti sarāgaṃ vā cittaṃ sarāgaṃ cittan-ti pajānāti ...*

63. Vism XIII.110: *Cetopariyañāṇaṃ paritta-mahaggata-appamāṇa-magga-atītānāgata-paccuppanna-bahiddhārammaṇa-vasena aṭṭhasu ārammaṇesu pavatti.*

64. See fn. 1601.

A. One who achieves mastery in the fourth jhāna with the eight totalities and the two totalities gives rise to the knowledge of the recollection of past lives.

Q. It is also said: "Why is the material sphere the basis [for this knowledge]?

A. When he has achieved mastery in the fourth jhāna, then it is given rise to". It is also said: "In [all] the four jhānas it arises".[65]

Q. How many kinds of knowledge of the recollection of past lives are there?

A. There are three kinds of recollection of past lives: produced by maintenance, produced naturally,[66] and produced through practice.

"Produced by maintenance": In four ways, there is knowledge of the recollection of past lives: one grasps the sign well, sees the counterpart-sign, cleans the faculties, and encompasses (*saṅgahati*?) [previous] births. These four ways born of much maintenance [produce] the recollection of past lives. At most, one recalls seven past lives.

"Produced naturally": deities, dragons (*nāga*), and harpies (*supaṇṇa*) remember their past lives naturally. At most, they recall fourteen past lives.

"Produced through practice" is [recollection developed through] the practice of the four bases of supernormal power.

Q. How does one give rise to the knowledge of the recollection of past lives?

A. The beginner meditator, who has thus developed the four bases of supernormal power, and through confidence has achieved mastery [over his mind], which is pure and immovable,[67] recollects the actions (*kamma*) through body, speech, or mind that he has done during the day [beginning] from [the action of] sitting down. Likewise, the actions done during the night. Likewise, he gradually recollects all actions that he has done during [the past] one day, during two days until one month. Likewise, he gradually recollects all the actions that he had done during two months, one year, two years, three years, a hundred years until [he recollects] the preceding birth.[68]

---

65. This passage is also in the divine ear section at 443a15.

66. Read 性所成 "naturally produced" or "produced naturally" (*pakatisamuṭṭhāna, pakatija*?), instead of 生所成, "birth produced" or "accomplished by birth", *jātisamuṭṭhāna*. The characters 性 and 生 are very similar.

67. In the sections on the knowledge of others' minds and the divine eye this same passage occurs in slightly different words. The words "through confidence", 以信, are not found there and probably are out of place here.

68. 初生. At 439c19, 448b02, 449a19 this corresponds to *purejāta (-paccaya)*, "pre-arising (condition)". Here it could correspond to *paṭhamābhinibbatti*, "first arising"; cf. Ud-a 43; Vibh-a 95: *Tattha tattha bhave paṭhamābhinibbattilakkhaṇā jāti* ... However, the way the Vim text continues indicates that the meditator has already recollected previous births, which supports *purejāta*.

Then [he contemplates] the mind and mental properties of long past existences and rebirths, and the mind and mental properties of the present birth: "Dependent on the preceding mind and mental properties, one obtains birth". Through the mind and the succession of births, he contemplates the causes (*nidāna*) [of birth]. He recollects that the stream of consciousness (*viññāṇasota*) is not cut off with regard to both birth in this world and birth in the other world.[69]

The meditator, with his mind thus developed, purified, and cleansed, [recollects] manifold past lives: one birth, two births, three births, four births, and so forth.[70] If the beginner meditator who has recollected everything in this birth is not able to recollect other births, he should not give up making effort. Again and again, he should properly enter upon and emerge from jhāna, until he achieves mastery. It is like the teaching about the well-polished mirror.[71] Having achieved mastery, when he is recollecting [this birth] as before, there will be recollection of the other [births]. If his mind goes beyond [this] one birth, then he succeeds in recollecting [his past births]. [**444a**] Having seen the means, he becomes very glad.

---

69. 憶識流轉兩俱不斷，於此世生，於彼世生. Cf. D III 105: ... *tathārūpaṃ cetosamādhiṃ phusati, yathāsamāhite citte imam-eva kāyaṃ uddhaṃ pādatalā adho kesamatthakā tacapariyantaṃ pūraṃ nānappakārassa asucino paccavekkhati: atthi imasmiṃ kāye kesā lomā ... lasikā muttanti. Atikkamma ca purisassa chavimaṃsalohitaṃ aṭṭhiṃ paccavekkhati. Purisassa ca viññāṇasotaṃ pajānāti, ubhayato abbocchinnaṃ idha loke patiṭṭhitañ-ca paraloke patiṭṭhitañ-ca. Ayaṃ tatiyā dassanasamāpatti.* Sv III 888: *Viññāṇasotan-ti viññāṇam-eva. Ubhayato abbocchinnan-ti dvīhipi bhāgehi acchinnaṃ. Idha loke patiṭṭhitañcā ti chandarāgavasena imasmiñca loke patiṭṭhitaṃ. ... Kammaṃ vā kammato upagacchantaṃ idha loke patiṭṭhitaṃ nāma.*

70. Paṭis I 113: *So tathābhāvitena cittena parisuddhena pariyodātena pubbenivāsānussatiñāṇāya cittaṃ abhinīharati abhininnāmeti. So anekavihitaṃ pubbenivāsaṃ anussarati, seyyathidaṃ ekam-pi jātiṃ dvepi jātiyo tisso pi jātiyo catasso pi jātiyo pañcapi jātiyo ...*

71. Cf. Vism XVIII.16: *Yathā hi cakkhumato purisassa aparisuddhe ādāse mukhanimittaṃ olokentassa nimittaṃ na paññāyati, so nimittaṃ na paññāyatī ti na ādāsaṃ chaḍḍeti, atha kho naṃ punappunaṃ parimajjati. Tassa parisuddhe ādāse nimittaṃ sayam-eva pākaṭaṃ hoti.* Vism-mhṭ II 355: ... *ādāsassa aparisuddhakālo viya rūpapariggahassa avikkhālitakālo, tadā mukhanimittassa apaññāyanaṃ viya rūpapariggahassa avisuddhatāya arūpadhammānaṃ anupaṭṭhānaṃ, ādāsassa punappunaṃ parimajjanaṃ viya rūpapariggahassa punappunaṃ visodhanaṃ, suparimajjite ādāse subyattaṃ mukhanimittassa paññāyanaṃ viya suvikkhālite nijjaṭe rūpapariggahe arūpadhammānaṃ suṭṭhu upaṭṭhānanti.* D I 80; M I 19–20: *Seyyathāpi, udāyi, itthi vā puriso vā daharo yuvā maṇḍakajātiko ādāse vā parisuddhe pariyadāte acche vā udakapatte sakaṃ mukhanimittaṃ paccavekkhamāno sakaṇikaṃ vā sakanikan ti jāneyya, akaṇikaṃ vā akaṇikan ti jāneyya, evam eva kho, ūdāyi, akkhātā mayā sāvakānaṃ paṭipadā, yathā paṭipannā me sāvakā parasattānaṃ parapuggalānaṃ cetasā ceto paricca pajānanti, sarāgaṃ vā cittaṃ: sarāgaṃ cittan ti pajānāti ...*

He should not recollect animal births, immaterial births, and births [as a being] without perception (*asaññasatta*) because there is no perception [in those births].

The Venerable Sobhita is foremost in this [recollection].[72]

The knowledge of the recollection of past lives occurs with regard to seven objects: limited, exalted, not to be spoken of, past, internal, an external, and internal-external.[73]

When one has already attained paths and fruits in the past, the country or the village [where one attained them] should be recollected.

To have perception of the past is knowledge of the recollection of past lives. To recollect the continuity of aggregates through knowledge is knowledge of the recollection of past lives.

Sectarians (*titthiya*) recollect forty aeons; they cannot recollect more than that because of their weakness.[74] Noble disciples (*ariyasāvaka*) recollect 10,000 aeons; great disciples (*mahāsāvaka*) [recollect] more than that; Paccekabuddhas (*paccekabuddha*) [recollect] more than that; and Tathāgatas [recollect] more than that.[75]

Rightly Enlightened Ones (*sammāsambuddhā*) recollect their own and others' previous lives, kamma, places, and everything. The others recollect only their own previous lives and a few of others' previous lives.

---

72. A I 25: *Etad aggaṃ mama sāvakānaṃ bhikkhūnaṃ pubbenivāsaṃ annussarantānaṃ yadidaṃ Sobhito.*

73. Cf. Vism XIII.120/p.433: *Pubbenivāsañāṇaṃ paritta-mahaggata-appamāṇa-magga-atīta-ajjhattabahiddhā na vattabbārammaṇavasena aṭṭhasu ārammaṇesu pavattati.*

74. 身無力故, lit. "because of bodily/body weakness", but this must be a corruption since this recollection cannot refer to the body, 身, because it is based on concentration (D I 13) and wisdom (Vism XIII.16). The Vism parallel has *dubbalapaññattā*. Perhaps Saṅghapāla's manuscript read *dubbalattā*, which Saṅghapāla misunderstood as *dubbala* + *attā*. 身 can mean *attā*, "(one-)self", as in 身性, *attabhāva*.

Vism XIII.16/p.411: *Tattha titthiyā cattālīsaṃ yeva kappe anussaranti, na tato paraṃ. Kasmā, dubbalapaññattā. Tesañ-hi nāmarūpaparicchedavirahitattā dubbalā paññā hoti. Pakatisāvakā kappasatam-pi kappasahassam-pi anussarantiyeva, balavapaññattā. Asītimahāsāvakā satasahassakappe anussaranti. Dve aggasāvakā ekaṃ asaṅkhyeyyaṃ satasahassañ-ca. Paccekabuddhā dve asaṅkhyeyyāni satasahassañ-ca. Ettako hi etesaṃ abhinīhāro. Buddhānaṃ pana paricchedo nāma natthi.* Cf. D I 13: *... ekacco samaṇo ... tathārūpaṃ cetosamādhiṃ phusati, yathāsamāhite citte anekavihitaṃ pubbenivāsaṃ anussarati. Seyyathidaṃ ... anekānipi jātisatasahassāni amutrāsiṃ evaṃnāmo ...* Sv II 407: *Sāvakā kappasatasahassaṃ anussaranti. Dve aggasāvakā asaṅkhyeyyañceva kappasatasahassañ-ca. Paccekabuddhā dve asaṅkhyeyyāni kappasatasahassañ-ca. Buddhānaṃ pana ettakan-ti paricchedo natthi, yāvatakaṃ ākaṅkhanti, tāvatakaṃ anussaranti.* Cf. Paṭis–a I 364.

75. In the preceding and following parallel passages at the end of the other direct knowledges, the Tathāgatas' knowledge is said to be unlimited. The Pali parallels also state this; see preceding note.

Rightly Enlightened Ones recollect everything as they wish; the others recollect only sequentially. Rightly Enlightened Ones, whether entering upon concentration or not entering upon concentration, are always able to recollect; the others can recollect only through entering upon concentration.

The recollection of past lives is finished.

19. Divine eye

Q. Who gives rise to the divine eye? How many kinds of divine eye are there? How does one give rise to the divine eye?

A. One who achieves mastery in the fourth jhāna through the [nine] totalities, with the light totality as the ninth, or through the [five] totalities with the light totality as the fifth,[76] gives rise to the divine eye element from his natural eye.

Q. How many kinds of divine eye are there?

A. There are two kinds of divine eye: born of result of kamma (*kammavipākaja*) and sprung from development (*bhāvānāmaya*).

Herein, the treasure trove divine eye is "born of [kamma] result". Thereby one can see whether a treasure trove is with gems or without gems.[77]

"Sprung from development": [produced by the] development of the four bases of supernormal power.[78]

Q. How does one give rise to the divine eye?

A. The beginner meditator, having developed the four bases of supernormal power through achieving mastery of his mind, which is pure and immovable, enters upon the fourth jhāna on the light totality. He attends to perception of light and resolves upon the perception of day thus: "This day is like night; this night is like day". With a mind that is unimpeded and open, he develops

---

76. See note 491 above (under "Procedure of developing supernormal power").

77. Supposedly, 典藏 is a corruption or synonym of 寶藏, *nidhi*, which is used later in the same sentence (444a17). Cf. 典藏寶 "treasure store", at T 0309: 1030b23, etc. 或有珠或無珠, "with gems or without gems (*maṇi*)" is due to a misunderstanding of *sassāmikam-pi assāmikampi*, "with owner or without owner"; see D II 176, M III 175: *Puna caparaṃ, ānanda, rañño mahāsudassanassa gahapatiratanaṃ pāturahosi. Tassa kammavipākajaṃ dibbacakkhu pāturahosi yena nidhiṃ passati sassāmikam-pi assāmikampi.*

78. Cf. Sv II 56: *Duvidhañ-hi dibbacakkhuṃ kammamayaṃ bhāvanāmayanti. Tatridaṃ kammamayan-ti āha na bhāvanāmayanti. Bhāvanāmayaṃ pana bodhimūle uppajjissati.* Cf. Sv II 453: *Kammavipākajan-ti na bhāvanāmayaṃ, kammavipākavasena pana devatānaṃ cakkhusadisam-eva maṃsacakkhu ahosi.* Mil 122: *Yaṃ pana sutte vuttaṃ maṃsacakkhusmiṃ naṭṭhe ahetusmiṃ avatthusmiṃ natthi dibbacakkhussa uppādo ti. Taṃ bhāvanāmayaṃ cakkhuṃ sandhāya vuttaṃ.*

a mind accompanied by brilliance.[79] The meditator who develops a mind accompanied by brilliance and unobstructed by darkness, surpasses the sun in brilliance.

The meditator, with a mind thus developed, pervades [himself] internally with light and attends to forms. When through knowledge he [just] pervades [himself] with light, it is not the divine eye. When through knowledge he sees illuminated forms internally, it is the divine eye.[80]

The meditator with the divine eye, which is purified, which surpasses the human eye, sees beings passing away and rearising, inferior and superior, fair and ugly, born in good destinations and born in bad destinations, faring according to their kamma.[81] [**444b**]

Now, if he is to give rise to the divine eye, the lesser afflictions should be abandoned, namely, doubt, inattention, sloth and torpor, fear, exhilaration, grossness, overly exerted effort, overly lax effort, longing, perceptions of diversity, and excessive reflection on forms.[82] If any one of these lesser

---

79. Cf. D III 223: *Idh' avuso bhikkhu ālokasaññaṃ manasikaroti, divāsaññaṃ adhiṭṭhāti yathā divā tathā rattiṃ, yathā rattiṃ tathā divā, iti vivaṭena cetasā apariyonaddhena sappabhāsaṃ cittaṃ bhāveti.*

80. Perhaps: "[When] through knowledge he sees [with] light forms inside". 以智令滿光明彼非天眼, 以智見内光明色此謂天眼. This could stress the difference between the development of perception of light, *ālokasaññā,* which is for repelling sleepiness, and the proper development of light for the seeing of forms. For "seeing forms internally", see D II 109: *Ajjhattaṃ rūpasaññī eko bahiddhā rūpāni passati parittāni suvaṇṇadubbaṇṇāni. Tāni abhibhuyya jānāmi passāmī ti evaṃsaññī hoti. Idaṃ paṭhamaṃ abhibhāyatanaṃ.* Sv II 561: *Ajjhattaṃ rūpasaññī ti ādīsu pana ajjhattarūpe parikammavasena ajjhattaṃ rūpasaññī nāma hoti. Ajjhattañ-hi nīlaparikammaṃ karonto kese vā pitte vā akkhitārakāya vā karoti.* M III 156: *... obhāsañceva sañjānāmi dassanañ-ca rūpānaṃ. So kho pana me obhāso nacirasseva antaradhāyati dassanañ-ca rūpānaṃ.*

81. It 100; A IV 178: *Iti dibbena cakkhunā visuddhena atikkantamānusakena satte passāmi cavamāne upapajjamāne, hīne paṇīte suvaṇṇe dubbaṇṇe sugate duggate yathākammūpage satte pajānāmi.* Cf. D III 111–12.

82. Cf. M III 158ff: *So kho ahaṃ, anuruddhā, vicikicchā cittassa upakkileso ti iti viditvā vicikicchaṃ cittassa upakkilesaṃ pajahiṃ, amanasikāro ... thīnamiddhaṃ ... chambhitattaṃ ... ubbillaṃ ... duṭṭhullaṃ ... accāraddhavīriyaṃ ... atilīnavīriyaṃ ... abhijappā ... nānattasaññā ... atinijjhāyitattaṃ rūpānaṃcittassa upakkileso ti iti viditvā atinijjhāyitattaṃ rūpānaṃ cittassa upakkilesaṃ pajahiṃ.*

Instead of *chambhitatta,* "consternation", the Chinese text has *māna,* "conceit", 慢. However, the characters used for conceit and fright, 慢 and 畏, are somewhat similar and must have been confused during transmission. Below, at 444b12, there is a reference back to "fear", 畏怖 ("... should neither delight in forms nor fear forms, as in the faults taught above".). *Ubbilla,* "exhilaration" or "elation", is rendered as "wrong rapture", 邪喜. The characters 惡口 literally mean "bad speech", but correspond to *duṭṭhulla,* "grossness" or "inertia" due to a misinterpretation of

afflictions manifests during the arousing of the divine eye, his concentration falls away. If concentration falls away, light and vision of objects also disappears.[83] Therefore, these lesser afflictions should be abandoned well.

If he has abandoned these afflictions, but does not achieve mastery in concentration, the divine eye is limited due to non-mastery. The meditator perceives limited light with a limited divine eye and the vision of forms is limited. Therefore, the Fortunate One said: "At the time when my concentration is limited, at that time my eye is limited; and with a limited eye I perceive limited light and I see limited forms. At the time when my concentration is immeasurable, at that time my divine eye is immeasurable; and with this immeasurable divine eye, I perceive immeasurable light and I see immeasurable forms".[84]

Now, the beginner meditator should neither delight in forms nor fear forms, as was taught in the [lesser affliction] faults above.

[The knowledge of] the divine eye occurs with regard to five objects, namely, limited object, present object, internal object, external object, and an internal-external-object.[85]

Four kinds of knowledge are produced by means of the divine eye: knowledge of the future, knowledge of the ownership of kamma, knowledge of the faring according to kamma, and knowledge of the result of kamma.[86]

---

duṭṭhulla as *duṭṭhullavācā*, "lewd speech". *Abhijappā*, "talk" or "prayer", and "longing", is 多語, "much talk".

83. Cf. M III 160: ... *atinijjhāyitattādhikaraṇañ-ca pana me rūpānaṃ samādhi cavi. Samādhimhi cute obhāso antaradhāyati dassanañ-ca rūpānaṃ.*

84. M III 161: *Yasmiṃ kho samaye paritto samādhi hoti, parittam me tamhi samaye cakkhu hoti; so 'haṃ parittena cakkhunā parittañ c' eva obhāsaṃ sañjānāmi parittāni ca rūpāni passāmi. Yasmiṃ pana samaye apparitto me samādhi hoti, appamāṇaṃ me tamhi samaye cakkhu hoti; so 'haṃ appamāṇena cakkhunā appamāṇañ c' eva obhāsaṃ sañjānāmi appamāṇāni ca rūpāni passāmi kevalam pi rattiṃ kevalam pi divasaṃ kevalaṃ pi rattindivan ti.*

85. Cf. Vism XIII.124/p.434: *Dibbacakkhuñāṇaṃ paritta-paccuppanna-ajjhatta-bahiddhārammaṇa-vasena catūsu ārammanesu pavattati.* The fifth, *ajjhattabahiddha-ārammaṇa*, is not in Vism. Cf. As 426: *Dibbacakkhucatutthaṃ attano kucchigatādirūpadassanakāle ajjhattārammaṇaṃ, avasesarūpadassanakāle bahiddhā-rammaṇaṃ, ubhayavasena ajjhattabahiddhārammaṇaṃ.*

LC: "It is perhaps incorrect to say that *ajjhattabahiddhārammaṇa* is excluded by Buddhaghosa in Vism. Possibly the comment at Vism XIII.129/p.435 is meant to apply to the three preceding knowledges. In any case, it is included at As 426f.; Vibh-a 375, but not at Abhidh-av 1153, Nidd-a II 381f.; Paṭis-a I 383."

86. *Anāgataṃsa-ñāṇa, kammassakata-ñāṇa, yathākammūpaga-ñāṇa, kammavipāka-ñāṇa.* The Vism (XIII.80/p.424, XIII.103/p.429) mentions only the first and the third as being based on the divine eye. According to Vism XIX.17, Paṭis-a III 576, Abhidh-av II 320 the *kammavipāka-ñāṇa* is a knowledge that is exclusive to Buddhas, not shared by disciples: *Iti imesaṃ dvādasannaṃ kammānaṃ kammantarañceva vipākantarañ-*

Herein, through knowledge of the future, he knows: "In the future [these] forms will arise".[87]

Through knowledge of the ownership of kamma, he sees the kamma that another person has done: "Through this kamma this person will go to that destination".

Through knowledge of the faring according to kamma, he sees the rebirth-destination of [another] person and knows: "Through this kamma, this person's former rebirth was here".

Through knowledge of the result of kamma, he knows: "He arrived at this time. He arrived at this destination. He arrived through this affliction (*kilesa*). He arrived through this means. This kamma will mature; this kamma will not mature. This kamma will be experienced much; this kamma will be experienced little".[88]

Herein, disciples who achieve mastery see a thousand world-systems; Paccekabuddhas see more than that; and the Tathāgatas' vision is limitless.[89]

The divine eye is finished.

20. Miscellaneous topics

Herein, these are the miscellaneous topics:

If one develops one kind of concentration for the purpose of seeing forms with the divine eye, one only sees forms and does not hear sounds. If one develops one kind of concentration for the purpose of hearing sounds with the divine ear, one only hears sounds and does not see forms. If one develops both concentrations for the purpose of seeing [forms] and hearing [sounds],

---

ca buddhānaṃ kammavipākañāṇasseva yāthāvasarasato pākaṭaṃ hoti, asādhāraṇaṃ sāvakehi.* (* Abhidh-av adds *buddhāveṇikañhetaṃ*.)

87. Vibh-a 373: *Anāgataṃsañāṇacatutthaṃ anāgate kāmadhātuyā nibbattijānanakāle parittārammaṇaṃ, rūpārūpabhavesu nibbattijānanakāle mahaggatārammaṇaṃ, ...* As 426: *Anāgataṃsañāṇacatutthaṃ attano anāgatakkhandhānussaraṇakāle ajjhattārammaṇaṃ, ...*

88. Cf. Peṭ 35: ... *kammantaraṃ tathāgato evaṃ pajānāti: iminā sattena evaṃ dhātukena evarūpaṃ kammaṃ kataṃ, taṃ atītamaddhānaṃ iminā hetunā tassa evarūpo vipāko vipaccati etarahi vipaccissati vā anāgatamaddhānanti. Evaṃ paccuppannamaddhānaṃ ... Taṇhāya ca diṭṭhiyā ca iminā hetunā na tassa vipāko diṭṭhe yeva dhamme nibbattissati, upapajje vā ti aparamhi vā pariyāye evaṃ pajānāti ayaṃ puggalo evarūpaṃ kammaṃ karissati anāgatamaddhānaṃ, iminā hetunā tassa evarūpo vipāko nibbattissati, iminā hetunā yāni cattāri kammaṭṭhānāni idaṃ kammaṭṭhānaṃ paccuppannasukhaṃ āyatiṃ ca sukhavipākaṃ ... iti ayaṃ atītānāgatapaccuppannānaṃ kammasamādānānaṃ hetuso ṭhānaso vipākavemattataṃ pajānāti uccāvacā hīnapaṇītatā, idaṃ vuccati kammavipākañāṇaṃ pañcamaṃ tathāgatabalaṃ.*

89. The same passage is found at 443c01–02 in relation to the knowledge of others' minds.

one sees [forms] and hears [sounds]. If one develops concentration for the purpose of seeing [forms], hearing [sounds] and knowing others' minds, one sees [forms], hears [sounds], and knows others' minds. If one develops concentration for the purpose of seeing [forms] in one direction, one does not see [forms in] the other directions, does not hear [sounds], and does not know others' minds. If one develops [all three kinds of] much concentration [in all directions], one sees [forms], hears [sounds], and knows others' minds in all directions. [**444c**]

The five direct knowledges are: (1) mundane direct knowledge subject to contaminations, connected to the material sphere and shared with the worldling;[90] (2) the wholesome direct knowledge of the trainee and of the worldling; and (3) the indeterminate direct knowledge of the arahant.

The five kinds of direct knowledge are not produced in the immaterial sphere.

[The miscellaneous topics are finished.]

[The ninth chapter of] the Path to Freedom, the Exposition of the [Five] Direct Knowledges, is finished.

90. Paṭis II 191: *Puthunānāabhiññāsu ñāṇaṃ pavattatī ti puthupaññā. Puthujjanasādhāraṇe dhamme atikkamma paramatthe nibbāne ñāṇaṃ pavattatī ti puthupaññā.* Sv III 931: ... *puthunānāariyamaggesu sāmaññaphalesu abhiññāsu puthujjanasādhāraṇe dhamme samatikkamma paramatthe nibbāne ñāṇaṃ pavattatī ti puthupaññā.* Paṭis-a I 249: ... *sā āsavuppattihetuto oghaniyato ... saṃkilesikato puthujjanasādhāraṇato ...*

Chapter 10

Exposition of Wisdom (*Paññāniddesa*)

1. Introduction

Q. What is "wisdom" (*paññā*)? What is its characteristic? What is its essential function? What is its manifestation? What is its footing? What are its benefits? What is the meaning of wisdom? How many qualities [are needed] for obtaining wisdom? How many kinds of wisdom are there?

2. Definition, characteristic, function, manifestation, and footing of wisdom

Q. What is "wisdom"?

A. The mind that sees the object as it is—this is called "wisdom".[1]

Furthermore, the attending to what is beneficial and harmful, and to the sublime, is called "wisdom".[2]

A. is taught in the Abhidhamma: "What is wisdom? This wisdom is understanding, investigation of the Dhamma, discerning, contemplation, insight, cleverness, clarity, analysis, consideration, examination, comprehensiveness,

---

1. Cf. S III 13: *Samādhim bhikkhave bhāvetha, samāhito bhikkhave bhikkhu yathābhūtam pajānāti.* S II 31–2: *... pītūpanisā passaddhi, passaddhūpanisaṃ sukhaṃ, sukhūpaniso samādhi, samādhūpanisaṃ yathābhūtañāṇadassanaṃ, ...*

2. "Sublime" or 莊嚴 corresponds to *alaṅkara, sobhana,* etc. The Tibetan instead has "practising much (*bahulīkaraṇa*) the cause-aspect of the mind (*rgyu rnam pa* , = *cittanimitta?*) ...".

Cf. S V 151: *Sa kho so ... paṇḍito byatto kusalo bhikkhu lābhī ceva hoti diṭṭheva dhamme sukhavihārānaṃ, lābhī hoti satisampajaññassa. Taṃ kissa hetu? Tathā hi so ... paṇḍito byatto kusalo bhikkhu sakassa cittassa nimittaṃ uggaṇhātī ti.* M I 118: *... yaṃ nimittaṃ āgamma yaṃ nimittaṃ manasikaroto uppajjanti pāpakā akusalā vitakkā chandūpasaṃhitāpi dosūpasaṃhitāpi mohūpasaṃhitāpi, tena ... bhikkhunā tamhā nimittā aññaṃ nimittaṃ manasi kātabbaṃ kusalūpasaṃhitaṃ.* Cf. Th 85: *cittanimittassa kovido.* Cf. Nidd-a I 156, As 123: *Yathā pana cheko bhisakko āturānaṃ sappāyāsappāyāni bhojanādīni jānāti, evaṃ paññā uppajjamānā kusalākusale sevitabbāsevitabbe hīnappaṇīta-kaṇhasukka-sappaṭibhāga-appaṭibhāge dhamme pajānāti. Vuttam-pi cetaṃ dhammasenāpatinā: Pajānāti pajānātī ti kho, āvuso, tasmā paññavā ti vuccati. Kiñca pajānāti? Idaṃ dukkhan-ti pajānātī ti vitthāretabbaṃ. Evamassā pajānanalakkhaṇatā veditabbā.* Ud-a 222: *So satiyā kusalānaṃ dhammānaṃ gatiyo samanvesamāno paññāya sattānaṃ hitāhitaṃ yathābhūtaṃ jānitvā, samādhinā tattha ekaggacitto hutvā, vīriyena satte ahitā nisedhetvā hite niyojeti.* Cp-a 267: *sattānaṃ hitāhitavicāraṇavasena dānasīlādisaṃvidahanavasena ca paññāpāramī.* Cp-a 321: *sattānaṃ hitāhitavinicchayakaraṇavasena tisso paññāpāramiyo.*

intelligence, reasoning, clear knowing; the goad of wisdom, faculty of wisdom, power of wisdom, sword of wisdom, palace of wisdom, light of wisdom, brilliance of wisdom, lamp of wisdom, gem of wisdom; the non-delusion, investigation of the Dhamma, right view—this is called "wisdom".[3]

Penetration of reality is its characteristic. Investigation is its essential function. Non-delusion is its manifestation. The four noble truths are its footing.

Furthermore, elucidating is its characteristic; the entering into the True Dhamma (*saddhamma*) is its essential function; the dispelling of the darkness of ignorance is its manifestation; the four discriminations (*paṭisambhidā*) are its footing.[4]

3. Benefits of wisdom

Q. What are its benefits?

A. The benefits of wisdom are incalculable (*appamāṇa*). They will be made known in brief by these verses:

> Through wisdom one purifies all virtue,
> Entering jhāna is the second wisdom,
> Through wisdom one develops the paths,
> Through wisdom one sees their fruits.
>
> Wisdom is the superior goodness,
> The eye of wisdom is unsurpassed,
> The decline of wisdom is impurity,

---

3. Cf. Dhs 11, § 16: *Yā tasmiṃ samaye paññā pajānanā vicayo pavicayo dhammavicayo sallakkhaṇā upalakkhaṇā paccupalakkhaṇā paṇḍiccaṃ kosallaṃ nepuññaṃ vebhavyā cintā upaparikkhā bhūrī medhā pariṇāyikā vipassanā sampajaññaṃ patodo paññā paññindriyaṃ paññābalaṃ paññāsatthaṃ paññāpāsādo paññā-āloko paññā-obhāso paññāpajjoto paññāratanaṃ amoho dhammavicayo sammādiṭṭhi—idaṃ tasmiṃ samaye paññindriyaṃ hoti.* Cf. Dhs 191, Vibh 250, Paṭis I 119, Nidd I 44, 77, Nett 76, Pug 125, Kv 595, Sv 759.

The Pali has 30 synonyms. The Chinese has 24 synonyms, several of which are not found in the Pali, probably due to difficulty in translation. The introductory sentence in the Tibetan (Sav 244b–45a) says that there are thirty synonyms (*rnam grangs*), and if *sems nye bar yongs su rtogs pa* is taken as two words corresponding to *cintā upaparikkhā* "consideration, examination", then thirty are listed. Several of these are also different than the ones in the Pali. Instead of *paññāratana*, "gem of wisdom", the Tibetan has *shes rab de kho na nyid* "reality of wisdom", *paññā-tathatā/prajñā-tattva*. Taishō reads 慧實 = "reality/thusness of wisdom" but has 慧寶 = *paññāratana* as a variant reading.

4. Mil 39: ... *kiṃlakkhaṇā paññā ti? ... api ca obhāsanalakkhaṇā paññā ti. ... Paññā, mahārāja, uppajjamānā avijjandhakāraṃ vidhameti, vijjobhāsaṃ janeti, ñāṇālokaṃ vidaṃseti, ariyasaccāni pākaṭāni karoti. Tato yogāvacaro aniccan-ti vā dukkhan-ti vā anattā ti vā sammappaññāya passatī ti.*

Growth in wisdom is unsurpassed.
Wisdom crushes the arguments of outsiders,
And is not sullied by worldly states.[5]

Those endowed with wisdom, the most excellent,
Expound in good words,
About this world and the other, and freedom.
When hearing about suffering, happiness,
And the goal, they apply energy.

Those endowed with wisdom,
Fully seeing this whole Dhamma
The teachings of dependent arising,
When instructed about name-and-matter
They are drawn to the teaching of the four truths

Those who have wisdom as their pasture (*gocara*),
Through wisdom abandon the evils
Of craving, hatred, and ignorance,
Through wisdom they abandon saṃsāra,
They abandon what others cannot abandon.

4. Meaning of wisdom

Q. What is the meaning of wisdom?
A. It means understanding (*pajānana*) and it means abandoning (*pahāna*).[6]

5. Qualities needed for obtaining wisdom

Q. How many qualities (*dhammā* or *guṇā*) [are needed] for obtaining wisdom? **[445a]**
A. Eleven qualities, namely, (1) examining the meaning of discourses; (2) many good deeds;[7] (3) a clean dwelling place;[8] (4) calm and insight; (5)

---

5. At 444c20 in accordance with the Tibetan *'jig rten chos kyis,* "by worldly states", the Chinese text should be amended to 世法, instead of 世至.

6. 能除為義. Tibetan: "Also, the abandoning of all faults—this is wisdom". Cf. Paṭis I 87 (§ 415): *Taṃ ñātaṭṭhena ñāṇaṃ, pajānanaṭṭhena paññā. Tena vuccati: abhiññā paññā ñātaṭṭhe ñāṇaṃ, pariññā paññā tīraṇaṭṭhe ñāṇaṃ, pahāne paññā pariccāgaṭṭhe ñāṇaṃ, ...*

7. 多善事. Sav 245b has *yang dag pa mang du gtam pa nyid* = "much discussion", *sambahula kathā/sākacchā*? Or *paripucchakatā* of Paṭis II 1 (see fn. 1644). Cf. M I 294: *Pañcahi kho ... aṅgehi anuggahitā sammādiṭṭhi ... paññāvimuttiphalānisaṃsā ca. Idhāvuso, sammādiṭṭhi sīlānuggahitā ca hoti, sutānuggahitā ca hoti, sākacchānuggahitā ca hoti, samathānuggahitā ca hoti, vipassanānuggahitā ca hoti.*

8. 清淨居, also used for "pure abode" (*suddhāvāsa*). Sav has *btegs gnas su gnas pa*

[reflecting on] the four noble truths;[9] (6) cleansing of the physical basis;[10] (7) the mind dwelling regularly in jhāna; (8) a mind without hindrances; (10) avoidance of unwise persons and (10) association with wise persons; and (11) intentness upon that [wisdom] (*tadadhimuttatā*).[11]

6. Kinds of wisdom

Q. How many kinds of wisdom are there?
A. Two kinds, three kinds, and four kinds.

7. Two kinds of wisdom

Q. What are the two kinds of wisdom?
A. Mundane wisdom and supramundane wisdom.

Herein, the wisdom associated with the noble paths and fruits is supramundane wisdom. Other wisdom is mundane wisdom.[12]

Mundane wisdom is subject to contaminations, is subject to fetters, ties, torrents, yokes, hindrances, to holding on to, clinging, and affliction.

---

nyid, "dwelling in a supportive abode".

9. Sav omits *samatha-vipassanā* and has "reflection on the Truths", *bden pa la rtog pa.*

10. In the Pali commentaries *vatthuvisadakiriyā*, "cleansing of the physical basis", is explained as cleaning the body and the surroundings as a preliminary for meditation practice. See Vibh-a 276: *Vatthuvisadakiriyā ti ajjhattikabāhirānaṃ vatthūnaṃ visadabhāvakaraṇaṃ. Yadā hissa kesanakhalomāni dīghāni honti, sarīraṃ vā ussannadosañceva sedamalamakkhitañ-ca, tadā ajjhattikaṃ vatthu avisadaṃ hoti aparisuddhaṃ. ...*

11. Cf. Vism IV 54, Vibh-a 276: *satta dhammā dhammavicayasambojjhaṅgassa uppādāya saṃvattanti: paripucchakatā, vatthuvisadakiriyā, indriyasamattapaṭipādanā, duppaññapuggalaparivajjanā, paññavantapuggalasevanā, gambhīrañāṇacariyapaccavekkhaṇā, tadadhimuttatā ti.* Paṭis II 1: *Assaddhe puggale parivajjayato, saddhe puggale sevato bhajato payirupāsato, pasādanīye suttante paccavekkhato imehi tīhākārehi saddhindriyaṃ visujjhati. Kusīte puggale parivajjayato, āraddhavīriye puggale sevato bhajato payirupāsato, sammappadhāne paccavekkhato imehi tīhākārehi vīriyindriyaṃ visujjhati. Muṭṭhassatī puggale parivajjayato, upaṭṭhitassatī puggale sevato bhajato payirupāsato, satipaṭṭhāne paccavekkhato imehi tīhākārehi satindriyaṃ visujjhati. Asamāhite puggale parivajjayato, samāhite puggale sevato bhajato payirupāsato, jhānavimokkhe paccavekkhato imehi tīhākārehi samādhindriyaṃ visujjhati. Duppaññe puggale parivajjayato, paññavante puggale sevato bhajato payirupāsato, gambhīrañāṇacariyaṃ paccavekkhato imehi tīhākārehi paññindriyaṃ visujjhati.*

12. Cf. Ps I 196: *Sā cāyaṃ sammādiṭṭhi duvidhā hoti lokiyā lokuttarāti. Tattha kammassakatāñāṇaṃ saccānulomikañāṇañ-ca lokiyā sammādiṭṭhi, saṅkhepato vā sabbāpi sāsavā paññā. Ariyamaggaphalasampayuttā paññā lokuttarā sammādiṭṭhi.*

Supramundane wisdom is not subject to contaminations, is not subject to fetters, ties, torrents, yokes, hindrances, holding on to, clinging, and affliction.[13]

8. Three kinds of wisdom

The three kinds of wisdom are: wisdom sprung from thought, wisdom sprung from learning, and wisdom sprung from development.

Herein, when one obtains knowledge of the ownership of kamma[14] or knowledge in conformity with the truths or [knowledge] in the sphere of crafts or the field of sciences, without having heard it from another—this is called "wisdom sprung from thought".

When one acquires wisdom in these areas (*vatthu*), having heard it from another—this is called "wisdom sprung from learning".

All wisdom developed by one who has entered upon [concentration]—this is called "wisdom sprung from development".[15]

---

13. Vibh 322: *Tīsu bhūmīsu kusalābyākate paññā lokiyā paññā, catūsu maggesu catūsu phalesu paññā lokuttarā paññā. ... Tīsu bhūmīsu kusalābyākate paññā sāsavā paññā, catūsu maggesu catūsu phalesu paññā anāsavā paññā. ... āsavavippayuttā sāsavā paññā, catūsu maggesu catūsu phalesu paññā āsavavippayuttā anāsavā paññā. ... saṃyojaniyā ... asaṃyojaniyā ... saṃyojanavippayuttā saṃyojaniyā ... saṃyojanavippayuttā asaṃyojaniyā ... ganthaniyā ... aganthaniyā ... ganthavippayuttā ... oghaniyā ... anoghaniyā ... oghavippayuttā .... yoganiyā ... ayoganiyā ... yogavippayuttā ... nīvaraṇiyā ... anīvaraṇiyā ... nīvaraṇavippayuttā ... parāmaṭṭhā ... aparāmaṭṭhā ... parāmāsavippayuttā ... Tīsu bhūmīsu vipāke paññā upādinnā paññā, tīsu bhūmīsu kusale tīsu bhūmīsu kiriyābyākate ... anupādinnā paññā. ... upādāniyā ... anupādāniyā ... upādānavippayuttā ... saṃkilesikā ... asaṃkilesikā ... kilesavippayuttā ....* Cf. Dhs 125 § 584: *Lokiyaṃ sāsavaṃ saṃyojaniyaṃ ganthaniyaṃ oghaniyaṃ, yoganiyaṃ, nīvaraṇiyaṃ parāmaṭṭhaṃ upādāniyaṃ saṅkilesikaṃ.*

14. According to the Pali tradition, *kammassakata* means "ownership of kamma", however, the Tibetan *rang gi las las*, and Chinese 自作業 mean "kamma done by oneself". The Pali tradition interprets *kammassakatā* as *kamma* + *saka* [= Skt: *svaka*] + *tā* = "one's-own-state/owner-ship" while the Tibetan and Chinese traditions interpret it as *karma* + *svakṛta*: "kamma + done by oneself". Cf. Vibh-a 411: *Kammassakataṃ vā ti idaṃ kammaṃ sattānaṃ sakaṃ, idaṃ no sakan-ti evaṃ jānanañāṇaṃ.* A III 185: *kammassakatā tasmiṃ puggale adhiṭṭhātabbā kammassako ayamāyasmā kammadāyādo kammayoni kammabandhu kammappaṭisaraṇo, yaṃ kammaṃ karissati kalyāṇaṃ vā pāpakaṃ vā tassa dāyādo bhavissatī ti.*

15. Cf. D III 219: *Cintā-mayā paññā, suta-mayā paññā, bhāvanā-mayā paññā.* Vibh 324: *... Yogavihitesu vā kammāyatanesu yogavihitesu vā sippāyatanesu yogavihitesu vā vijjāṭṭhānesu kammassakataṃ vā saccānulomikaṃ vā rūpaṃ aniccan-ti vā vedanā... saññā... saṅkhārā... viññāṇaṃ aniccan-ti vā, yaṃ evarūpiṃ anulomikaṃ khantiṃ diṭṭhiṃ ruciṃ mudiṃ pekkhaṃ dhammanijjhānakkhantiṃ parato assutvā paṭilabhati—ayaṃ vuccati cintāmayā paññā. ... Yogavihitesu vā ... aniccan-ti vā, yaṃ evarūpiṃ anulomikaṃ khantiṃ diṭṭhiṃ dhammanijjhānakkhanti... parato sutvā paṭilabhati—ayaṃ vuccati sutamayā paññā.*

Furthermore, there are three kinds of wisdom: skill in increasing, skill in declining, and skill in means.

Herein, when one is attending to these [states], unwholesome states decline and wholesome states increase. The wisdom therein—this is called "skill in increasing".

Furthermore, when one is attending to these [states], unwholesome states increase, and wholesome states decrease. The wisdom therein—this is called "skill in decreasing".

The wisdom of all the means therein—this is called "skill in means".[16]

Furthermore, there are three kinds of wisdom, namely, wisdom leading to accumulation, wisdom leading to disaccumulation, wisdom leading neither to accumulation nor to disaccumulation.

Wisdom with regard to the wholesome in the three planes (*tebhūmika*) is called "wisdom leading to accumulation".

The wisdom with regard to the four paths is called "wisdom leading to disaccumulation".

The wisdom with regard to the result in the four planes and with regard to the functional-indeterminate[17] in the three planes—this is "wisdom leading neither to accumulation nor to disaccumulation".[18]

Sabbā pi samāpannassa paññā bhāvanāmayā paññā. Cf. Vism XIV.16/Vibh 324–25. Cf. Moh 267: *Bhāvanāmayā panettha samathavipassanāvasena pavattā catubhūmakapaññā. Niddese panassa kiñcāpi samāpannassa paññā ti evaṃ mahaggatalokuttarapaññāva vuttā, tathā pi taṃ ukkaṭṭhavasena vuttaṃ. Kāmāvacarānaṃ pana pubbabhāgabhāvanānaṃ, anussati-upacārabhāvanānañ-ca bhāvanāmaye saṅgahoti daṭṭhabbaṃ. Purimattike panetāsaṃ cintāmaye saṅgahitattā bhāvanāmaye asaṅgaho, tatthā pi bhāvanābalanipphannānam-eva saṅgaho daṭṭhabbo.*

16. D III 220 *Tīṇi kosallāni: Āyakosallaṃ, apāyakosallaṃ, upāyakosallaṃ.* Vibh 325: *Ime dhamme manasikaroto anuppannā ceva akusalā dhammā na uppajjanti, uppannā ca akusalā dhammā pahīyanti. Ime vā panime dhamme manasikaroto anuppannā ceva kusalā dhammā uppajjanti, uppannā ca kusalā dhammā bhiyyobhāvāya ... saṃvattantī-ti. Yā tattha paññā ... idaṃ vuccati āyakosallaṃ. ... Ime dhamme manasikaroto anuppannā ceva kusalā dhammā na uppajjanti, uppannā ca kusalā dhammā nirujjhanti. Ime vā panime dhamme manasikaroto anuppannā ceva akusalā dhammā uppajjanti, uppannā ca akusalā dhammā bhiyyobhāvāya vepullāya saṃvattantī-ti. Yā tattha paññā ... idaṃ vuccati apāyakosallaṃ. Sabbā pi tatrupāyā paññā upāyakosallaṃ.* Sv-ṭ III 281: *Sabbāpīti āyakosallapakkhikāpi apāyakosallapakkhikāpi. Tatrupāyā ti tatra tatra karaṇīye upāyabhūtā.* Cf. Vism XIV.16–18/pp.439–440, Vibh-a 414.

17. 事有記 = "functional-determinate". The Tibetan (Sav 246a) has *bya ba lung du ma bstan pa*, which corresponds to *kiriyāvyākata*, "functional-indeterminate". Saṅghapāla misunderstood the *sandhi* in *kiriyāvyākate* as *kiriyā-vyākate* instead of *kiriyā-avyākate*; see also fn. 1875 & 2049.

18. Cf. Vibh 326: *Tīsu bhūmīsu kusale paññā ācayagāminī paññā. Catūsu maggesu paññā apacayagāminī paññā. Catūsu bhūmīsu vipāke tīsu bhūmīsu kiriyābyākate paññā nevācayagāmināpacayagāminī paññā.* Cf. M III 288: *Tassa asārattassa asaṃyuttassa*

9. Four kinds of wisdom

The four kinds of wisdom are: knowledge of the ownership of kamma, knowledge in conformity with the truths, knowledge of one who possesses the paths, and knowledge of one who possesses the fruits.

Herein, right view endowed with ten grounds[19]—this is called "knowledge of the ownership of kamma".

When one sees the aggregates as impermanent, suffering, and without self, such acceptance in conformity (*anulomika-khanti*) is called "knowledge in conformity with the truths".

The wisdom with regard to the four paths is called "knowledge of one who possesses the paths".

The wisdom with regard to the four fruits is called "knowledge of one who possesses the fruits".[20]

Furthermore, there are four kinds of wisdom, namely, wisdom with regard to the sensuous sphere, wisdom with regard to the material sphere, wisdom with regard to the immaterial sphere, and wisdom with regard to the unincluded.

---

asammūḷhassa ādīnavānupassino viharato āyatiṃ pañcupādānakkhandhā apacayaṃ gacchanti. ... Evamassāyaṃ ariyo aṭṭhaṅgiko maggo bhāvanāpāripūriṃ gacchati. Cf. A V 242: *Sammādiṭṭhi ... sammāvimutti—ayaṃ vuccati ... apacayagāmī dhammo ti.* Cf. Dhs 238: *Catūsu bhūmīsu vipāko, tīsu bhūmīsu kiriyābyākataṃ, rūpañ-ca, nibbānañca—ime dhammā nevācayagāmināpacayagāmino.* Dhs 184: *Kusalākusalānaṃ dhammānaṃ vipākā kāmāvacarā, rūpāvacarā, arūpāvacarā, apariyāpannā; vedanākkhandho... pe... viññāṇakkhandho; ye ca dhammā kiriyā neva kusalā nākusalā na ca kammavipākā; sabbañ-ca rūpaṃ, asaṅkhatā ca dhātu—ime dhammā neva ācayagāmi na apacayagāmino.*

19. Cf. Nidd I 188: *Dasavatthukā sammādiṭṭhi: atthi dinnaṃ, atthi yiṭṭhaṃ, atthi hutaṃ, atthi sukatadukkaṭānaṃ kammānaṃ phalaṃ vipāko, atthi ayaṃ loko, atthi paro loko, atthi mātā, atthi pitā, atthi sattā opapātikā, atthi loke samaṇabrāhmaṇā sammaggatā sammāpaṭipannā ye imañ-ca lokaṃ parañ-ca lokaṃ sayaṃ abhiññā sacchikatvā pavedentī ti.*

Unlike the Niddesa's explanation of right view endowed with ten grounds in accordance with mundane right view, the Tibetan version (Sav 246a) explains it in accordance with supramundane right view; see Intro § 4.4 and the translation in Appendix II. No such explanation of right view endowed with ten grounds can be found in any Pali text. *Dasavatthukā micchādiṭṭhi* is explained at Vibh 391 as the opposite of the mundane right view version, as given above.

20. Vibh 328: *Atthi dinnaṃ ... pavedentī ti: yā evarūpa paññā ... sammādiṭṭhi: idaṃ vuccati kammassakataṃ ñāṇaṃ. Ṭhapetvā saccānulomikaṃ ñāṇaṃ sabbā pi sāsavā kusalā paññā kammassakataṃ ñāṇaṃ. ... Rūpaṃ aniccan-ti ... viññāṇaṃ aniccan-ti vā. Yā evarūpā anulomikā khanti ... dhammanijjhānakhanti: idaṃ vuccati saccānulomikaṃ ñāṇaṃ. Catūsu maggesu paññā maggasamaṅgissa ñāṇaṃ. Catūsu phalesu paññā phalasamaṅgissa ñāṇaṃ. Maggasamaṅgissa ñāṇaṃ dukkhe p'etaṃ ñāṇaṃ ... dukkhanirodhagāminiyā paṭipadāya p'etaṃ ñāṇaṃ.*

Wisdom with regard to the wholesome-indeterminate[21] in the sensuous sphere is "wisdom with regard to the sensuous sphere". Wisdom with regard to the wholesome-indeterminate in the material sphere is called "wisdom with regard to the material sphere". Wisdom with regard to the wholesome-indeterminate in the immaterial sphere is called "wisdom with regard to the immaterial sphere". Wisdom with regard to the paths and the fruits is called "wisdom with regard to the unincluded".[22]

Furthermore, there are four kinds of wisdom, namely, knowledge of the Dhamma, inferential knowledge, knowledge of others' minds, and conventional knowledge.

The wisdom with regard to the four paths and the four fruits is called "knowledge of the Dhamma". [**445b**]

Endowed with this [present] knowledge of the Dhamma, the meditator has knowledge regarding [the truths in] the past and future. The knowledge of the truths in the present is also knowledge of [the truths in] the past and future. This is called "inferential knowledge".[23]

Knowledge of the minds of others—this is called "knowledge of others' minds".[24]

Putting aside these three knowledges, the remaining wisdom is called "conventional knowledge".[25]

---

21. 善有記慧. Saṅghapāla failed to notice the negative prefix *a-* of *avyākata* because of the junction with preceding *kusala*, so elsewhere; see fn. 1650. The Tibetan (Sav 246b) has *rnam par smin pa lung ma bstan pa = vipāka-avyākata* "result-indeterminate".

22. Vibh 329: *Kāmāvacarakusalāvyākate paññā kāmāvacarā paññā. Rūpāvacarakusalāvyākate paññā rūpāvacarā paññā. Arūpāvacarakusalāvyākate paññā arūpāvacarā paññā. Catūsu maggesu ca catūsu phalesu paññā apariyāpannā paññā.*

23. The Tibetan version (Sav 246b) is clearer: "Endowed with that Dhamma knowledge in the present, he directs/applies the method to the past and future thus: 'Whosoever in the past directly knew the truths, he directly knew just these truths. ....'

24. 他心智, *gzhan gyi sems shes pa*. This corresponds to *paracittañāṇa* as in Nidd I 100 (*Ñatvā ti paracittañāṇena vā ñatvā pubbenivāsānussatiñāṇena vā ñatvā*), etc., or perhaps *paracittavijānana*, as found in Mil 359, etc., instead of the usual form *pariye ñāṇaṃ*; see next fn.

25. Vibh 329: *Catūsu maggesu catūsu phalesu paññā dhamme ñāṇaṃ. So iminā dhammena ñātena diṭṭhena pattena viditena pariyogāḷhena atītānāgatena nayaṃ neti: Ye hi keci atītamaddhānaṃ samaṇā vā brāhmaṇā vā dukkhaṃ abbhaññaṃsu dukkhasamudayaṃ ... paṭipadaṃ abbhaññaṃsu, imaññeva te dukkhaṃ abbhaññaṃsu, ... abbhaññaṃsu. Ye hi keci anāgatamaddhānaṃ ... paṭipadaṃ abhijānissantī ti. Yā tattha paññā ... sammādiṭṭhi—idaṃ vuccati anvaye ñāṇaṃ. Tattha katamaṃ pariye ñāṇaṃ? Idha bhikkhu parasattānaṃ parapuggalānaṃ cetasā ceto paricca pajānāti. Sarāgaṃ vā cittaṃ sarāgaṃ citan-ti pajānāti, ... avimuttaṃ cittan-ti pajānātī ti. Yā tattha ... sammādiṭṭhi—idaṃ vuccati pariye ñāṇaṃ. Ṭhapetvā dhamme ñāṇaṃ anvaye ñāṇaṃ pariye ñāṇaṃ, avasesā paññā sammutiñāṇaṃ.* Sv 1019: *Dhamme ñāṇan-ti ekapaṭivedhavasena catusaccadhamme ñāṇaṃ catusaccabbhantare*

Furthermore, there are four kinds of wisdom, namely, there is wisdom that is for accumulation and not for disaccumulation; there is wisdom that is for disaccumulation and not for accumulation; there is wisdom that is for accumulation and for disaccumulation; and there is wisdom that is neither for accumulation nor for disaccumulation.

Herein, wisdom with regard to the wholesome in the sensuous sphere is for accumulation and not for disaccumulation. Wisdom with regard to the four paths is for disaccumulation and not for accumulation. Wisdom with regard to the wholesome in the material sphere and the immaterial sphere is for accumulation and for disaccumulation. Wisdom with regard to the result (*vipāka*) in the four planes and the functional-indeterminate in the three planes is neither for accumulation nor for disaccumulation.[26]

Furthermore, there are four kinds of wisdom, namely, there is wisdom that is for disenchantment (*nibbidā*) but not for penetration (*paṭivedha*); there is wisdom that is for penetration but not for disenchantment; there is wisdom that is for disenchantment and for penetration; there is wisdom that is neither for disenchantment nor for penetration.

Herein, the wisdom whereby one is passionless towards sense-pleasures, but does not penetrate the direct knowledges and the four truths—this is called "wisdom that is for disenchantment but not for penetration".

---

nirodhasacce dhamme ñāṇañ-ca. ... Anvaye ñāṇan-ti cattāri saccāni paccakkhato disvā yathā idāni, evaṃ atīte pi anāgatepi im-eva pañcakkhandhā dukkhasaccaṃ, ... ayam-eva maggo maggasaccan-ti evaṃ tassa ñāṇassa anugatiyaṃ ñāṇaṃ. ... Pariye ñāṇan-ti paresaṃ cittaparicchede ñāṇaṃ. ... Moh 269: ... *Maggānubhāvanibbattaṃ pana atītānāgatesu saccapaṭivedhanayasaṅgahaṇavasena pavattaṃ paccavekkhaṇañāṇaṃ anvaye ñāṇaṃ nāma. Tassa ca yehi nayehi ariyā atītamaddhānaṃ catusaccadhammaṃ jāniṃsu, tepi imaññeva catusaccaṃ evam-eva jāniṃsu, anāgatamaddhānam-pi jānissantī ti evaṃ jānanavasena pavatti ākāro veditabbo. Sarāgādivasena paracittaparicchedañāṇaṃ pariye ñāṇaṃ nāma. Dhammanvayapariyañāṇāni pana ṭhapetvā sabbalokiyapaññāñāṇan-ti sammatattā sammutimhi ñāṇan-ti sammutiñāṇaṃ nāma.*

26. Vibh 310: *Ācayagāminī paññā, apacayagāminī paññā, nevācayagāmināpacayagāminī paññā.* Vibh 330: *Kāmāvacarakusale paññā ācayāya no apacayāya. Catūsu maggesu paññā apacayāya no ācayāya. Rūpāvacara-arūpāvacarakusale paññā ācayāya ceva apacayāya ca. Avasesā paññā neva ācayāya no apacayāya.* Cf. Vibh 326: *Catūsu bhūmīsu vipāke tīsu bhūmīsu kiriyābyākate paññā nevācayagāmināpacayagāminī paññā.* See also fn. 1651.

Moh 399 Be, § 797. *Kāmāvacarakusale paññā ti ayañ-hi ekantena vaṭṭasmiṃ cutipaṭisandhiṃ ācinateva, tasmā ācayāya no apacayāya ti vuttā. Lokuttaramaggapaññā pana yasmā cutipaṭisandhiṃ apacinateva, tasmā apacayāya no ācayāyā ti vuttā. Rūpāvacarārūpāvacarapaññā cutipaṭisandhim-pi ācinati, vikkhambhanavasena kilese ceva kilesamūlake ca dhamme apacinati, tasmā ācayāya ceva apacayāya cā ti vuttā. Sesā neva cutipaṭisandhiṃ ācinati na apacinati, tasmā neva ācayāya no apacayāya ti vuttā.*

The wisdom whereby one is passionless towards sense-pleasures and penetrates the direct knowledges, but does not penetrate the four truths—this is wisdom that is for penetration but not for disenchantment.

The wisdom in the four paths is for disenchantment and for penetration. The other wisdoms are neither for disenchantment nor for penetration.[27]

Furthermore, there are four kinds of wisdom, namely, discrimination of meaning, discrimination of the Dhamma, discrimination of language, and discrimination of discernment.

Knowledge of meaning—this is called, "discrimination of meaning". Knowledge of Dhamma—this is called "discrimination of the Dhamma". Knowledge of speech and language [of the Dhamma]—this is called "discrimination of language". Knowledge of the knowledges—this is called "discrimination of discernment.[28]

Furthermore, knowledge of cause and result (*hetu-phala*)—this is called "discrimination of meaning". Knowledge in regard to cause—this is called "discrimination of the Dhamma". Knowledge of the speech and language of the Dhamma is "discrimination of language". Knowledge of the knowledges—this is called "discrimination of discernment".[29]

---

27. Vibh 330: *Yāya paññāya kāmesu vītarāgo hoti, na ca abhiññāyo paṭivijjhati na ca saccāni: ayaṃ vuccati paññā nibbidāya no paṭivedhāya. Sveva paññāya kāmesu vītarāgo samāno abhiññāyo paṭivijjhati, na ca saccāni: ayaṃ vuccati paññā paṭivedhāya no nibbidāya. Catūsu maggesu paññā nibbidāya ceva paṭivedhāya ca. Avasesā paññā neva nibbidāya no paṭivedhāya.*

28. Vibh 293, 331: *Atthapaṭisambhidā, dhammapaṭisambhidā niruttipaṭisambhidā paṭibhānapaṭisambhidā. Atthe ñāṇaṃ atthapaṭisambhidā dhamme ñāṇaṃ dhammapaṭisambhidā. Tatra dhammaniruttābhilāpe ñāṇaṃ niruttipaṭisambhidā. Ñāṇesu ñāṇaṃ paṭibhāṇapaṭisambhidā. Imā catasso paṭisambhidā.* Mp I 119 (cf. Paṭis I 119): *Tattha atthesu ñāṇaṃ atthapaṭisambhidā, dhammesu ñāṇaṃ dhammapaṭisambhidā, atthadhammaniruttābhilāpe ñāṇaṃ niruttipaṭisambhidā, ñāṇesu ñāṇaṃ paṭibhānapaṭisambhidā.* Paṭis-a I 3, Vibh-a 385, Ud-a 136: *Atthappabhedassa sallakkhaṇavibhāvanavavatthānakaraṇasamatthaṃ atthe pabhedagataṃ ñāṇaṃ atthapaṭisambhidā. ... dhamme pabhedagataṃ ñāṇaṃ dhammapaṭisambhidā. ... niruttābhilāpe pabhedagataṃ ñāṇaṃ niruttipaṭisambhidā. ... paṭibhāne pabhedagataṃ ñāṇaṃ paṭibhānapaṭisambhidā.*

29. Vibh 293: *Hetumhi ñāṇaṃ dhammapaṭisambhidā, hetuphale ñāṇaṃ atthapaṭisambhidā, tatra dhammaniruttābhilāpe ñāṇaṃ niruttipaṭisambhidā, ñāṇesu ñāṇaṃ paṭibhānapaṭisambhidā.* Paṭis-a I 36: *Tatthā pi paccayuppanno attho dukkhasaccaṃ viya pākaṭo suviññeyyo cā ti paṭhamaṃ atthapaṭisambhidāñāṇaṃ uddiṭṭhaṃ, tassa atthassa hetudhammavisayattā tadanantaraṃ dhammapaṭisambhidāñāṇaṃ, tadubhayassa niruttivisayattā tadanantaraṃ niruttipaṭisambhidāñāṇaṃ, tesu tīsu pi ñāṇesu pavattanato tadanantaraṃ paṭibhānapaṭisambhidāñāṇaṃ.* Cf. Nidd I 234: *Idhekaccassa adhigatā honti cattāro satipaṭṭhānā ... cha abhiññāyo, tassa attho ñāto dhammo ñāto nirutti ñātā, atthe ñāte attho paṭibhāyati, dhamme ñāte dhammo paṭibhāyati, niruttiyā ñātāya nirutti paṭibhāyati; imesu tīsu ñāṇesu ñāṇaṃ paṭibhānapaṭisambhidā.* Peṭ 33: *Yaṃ kho muni nānappakārassa*

Furthermore, the knowledge of suffering and cessation—this is called "discrimination of meaning". The knowledge of origination and the path—this is called "discrimination of the Dhamma". Knowledge of the speech and language of the Dhamma—this is called "discrimination of language". Knowledge of the knowledges—this is called "discrimination of discernment".[30]

Furthermore, knowledge of the Dhamma, namely: suttas, recitations, expositions, verses, inspired utterances, sayings, birth-stories, marvels, extensive dialogues—this is called "discrimination of the Dhamma".[31] Knowledge of the meaning of what is spoken, "This is the meaning of what is spoken"—this is called "discrimination of meaning". Knowledge of the speech and language of the Dhamma—this is called "discrimination of language". Knowledge of the knowledges is called "discrimination of discernment".[32]

Furthermore, knowledge of the eye [of Dhamma]—this is called "discrimination of the Dhamma". Knowledge of the eye [of Dhamma] in the sense of vision—this is called "discrimination of meaning".[33] Knowledge of

---

nānāniruttiyo devanāgayakkhānaṃ dameti dhamme vavatthānena vatvā kāraṇato aññaṃ pāraṃ gamissatī ti netaṃ ṭhānaṃ vijjati: dhammapaṭisambhidā. Yato panimā niruttito satta satta niruttiyo nābhisambhuneyyā ti netaṃ ṭhānaṃ vijjati: niruttipaṭisambhidā. Nirutti kho pana abhisamaggaratānaṃ sāvakānaṃ tamatthamaviññāpaye ti netaṃ ṭhānaṃ vijjati: atthapaṭisambhidā. Mahesakkhā devaputtā upasaṅkamitvā pañhe pucchiṃsu. Kāyikena vā mānasikena vā paripīḷitassa hatthakuṇī ti vā pāde vā khañje dandhassa so attho na paribhājiyatī ti netaṃ ṭhānaṃ vijjati: paṭibhānapaṭisambhidā.

30. Vibh 293: *Dukkhe ñāṇaṃ atthapaṭisambhidā. Dukkhasamudaye ñāṇaṃ dhammapaṭisambhidā. Dukkhanirodhe ñāṇaṃ atthapaṭisambhidā. Dukkhanirodhagāminiyā paṭipadāya ñāṇaṃ dhammapaṭisambhidā. ...*

31. Vibh 294: *Idha bhikkhu dhammaṃ jānāti suttaṃ geyyaṃ veyyākaraṇaṃ gāthaṃ udānaṃ itivuttakaṃ jātakaṃ abbhutadhammaṃ vedallaṃ: ayaṃ vuccati dhammapaṭisambhidā. So tassa tasseva bhāsitassa atthaṃ jānāti: ayaṃ imassa bhāsitassa attho, ayaṃ imassa bhāsitassa attho ti: ayaṃ vuccati atthapaṭisambhidā. ...*

32. Both 樂說 and Tibetan *spobs pa* mean "eloquence", which is a meaning that *paṭibhāna* can also have in Pali. However, in the passages quoted above the authors of the late canonical texts and the *Peṭaka* interpreted *paṭibhāna* as "discernment" or "perspicaciousness".

33. 眼智 "eye-knowledge" presumably refers to the *dhammacakkhu*, "the eye of Dhamma". Cf. Paṭis II 150: *Cakkhuṃ udapādīti dassanaṭṭhena.* Paṭis II 149ff.: *Cakkhuṃ dhammo, ñāṇaṃ dhammo, paññā dhammo, vijjā dhammo, āloko dhammo. Ime pañca dhammā dhammapaṭisambhidāya ārammaṇā ceva honti gocarā ca. Ye tassā ārammaṇā te tassā gocarā. Ye tassā gocarā te tassā ārammaṇā. Tena vuccati dhammesu ñāṇaṃ dhammapaṭisambhidā.* Vibh 296: *Yasmiṃ samaye akusalaṃ cittaṃ uppannaṃ hoti somanassasahagataṃ diṭṭhigatasampayuttaṃ, rūpārammaṇaṃ vā ... dhammārammaṇaṃ vā yaṃ yaṃ vā panārabbha, tasmiṃ samaye phasso hoti ... avikkhepo hoti: ime dhammā akusalā. Imesu dhammesu ñāṇaṃ dhammapaṭisambhidā. Tesaṃ vipāke ñāṇaṃ atthapaṭisambhidā.*

the speech and language of the Dhamma—this is called "discrimination of language". Knowledge of the knowledges—this is called "discrimination of discernment". [**445c**]

Furthermore, there are four kinds of wisdom, namely, knowledge of suffering, knowledge of the origination of suffering, knowledge of the cessation of suffering, and knowledge of one who possesses the path [leading to the cessation of suffering].

Knowledge about (*ārabbha*) suffering is knowledge of suffering. Knowledge about the origination of suffering is knowledge of the origination of suffering. [Knowledge about the cessation of suffering is] knowledge of the cessation of suffering.[34] Knowledge about the practice [leading to the cessation of suffering] is knowledge of one who possesses the path [leading to the cessation of suffering].

The [tenth] chapter of the Path to Freedom, the Exposition of Wisdom, is finished.

Yāya niruttiyā tesaṃ dhammānaṃ paññatti hoti, tatra dhammaniruttābhilāpe ñāṇaṃ niruttipaṭisambhidā. Yena ñāṇena tāni ñāṇāni jānāti: imāni ñāṇāni idam atthajotakānī ti, ñāṇesu ñāṇaṃ paṭibhāṇapaṭisambhidā.

34. The explanation of this knowledge, which is mentioned in the introductory sentence above, is not in the Chinese text. The Tibetan text gives the introductory sentence and then "and so on, in detail".

Cf. D III 227: *Dukkhe ñāṇaṃ, samudaye ñāṇaṃ, nirodhe ñāṇaṃ, magge ñāṇaṃ.* Vibh 328: *Maggasamaṅgissa ñāṇaṃ dukkhepetaṃ ñāṇaṃ, dukkhasamudayepetaṃ ñāṇaṃ, dukkhanirodhepetaṃ ñāṇaṃ, dukkhanirodhagāminiyā paṭipadāyapetaṃ ñāṇaṃ. Tattha katamaṃ dukkhe ñāṇaṃ? Dukkhaṃ ārabbha yā uppajjati paññā pajānanā ... pe ... amoho dhammavicayo sammādiṭṭhi idaṃ vuccati dukkhe ñāṇaṃ. Dukkhasamudayaṃ ārabbha ... dukkhanirodhagāminiṃ paṭipadaṃ ārabbha yā ... sammādiṭṭhi idaṃ vuccati dukkhanirodhagāminiyā paṭipadāya ñāṇaṃ.*

Chapter 11

The Five Skills

1. Introduction

Now, the beginner meditator who desires release from ageing and death, who desires to abandon the cause of saṃsāra, desires to abandon the darkness of ignorance, desires to cut through the rope of craving and desires to obtain noble wisdom, should give rise to five skills in five areas, namely, the skill in the aggregates, skill in the sense bases, skill in the elements, skill in dependent arising, and skill in the noble truths.[1]

Skill in the Aggregates

2. What is skill in the aggregates

Q. What is the skill in the aggregates?

A. The five aggregates are the aggregate of matter (*rūpa*), the aggregate of feeling (*vedanā*), the aggregate of perception (*saññā*), the aggregate of formations (*saṅkhārā*), and the aggregate of consciousness (*viññāṇa*).

Aggregate of Matter

3. What is the aggregate of matter?

Q. What is the aggregate of matter?

A. The four great primaries and the matter dependent on the great primaries.[2]

---

1. The characters 方便 usually correspond to *upāya*, but the Tibetan *mkhas pa* = Pali *kosalla/kusala* and Skt *kauśalya*, "skill", "skilfulness", or "proficiency". Cf. 安定方便, "skill in absorption", *appanākosalla*, at 414b18, and 作意方便, "skill in attending", *manasikāra-kosalla*, at 413b22. See also Skilling 1994: 176 n. 1.

Cf. Nidd-a I 99: *Khandhakusalā ti pañcasu khandhesu salakkhaṇasāmaññalakkhaṇesu chekā, ñātatīraṇapahānavasena kusalā ti attho.* Nidd I 69: *Kusalā ti ye te khandhakusalā dhātukusalā āyatanakusalā paṭiccasamuppādakusalā satipaṭṭhānakusalā sammappadhānakusalā iddhipādakusalā indriyakusalā balakusalā bojjhaṅgakusalā maggakusalā phalakusalā nibbānakusalā, ...*

2. M I 185: *Katamo cāvuso, rūpupādānakkhandho? Cattāri ca mahābhūtāni, catunnañ-ca mahābhūtānaṃ upādāya rūpaṃ.* Cf. S II 3, M I 52: *... upādāya rūpaṃ. Idaṃ vuccati rūpaṃ.* Cf. Dhs 124, para. 584: *... vuccati sabbaṃ rūpaṃ.*

4. Four great primaries

Q. What are the four great primaries?

A. The earth element, the water element, the fire element, and the wind element.

Q. What is the earth element?

A. That which has the intrinsic nature of hardness and the characteristic of hardness—this is called "earth element".

Q. What is the water element?

A. Water moistens matter and makes it cohere —this is called "water element".

Q. What is the fire element? Fire heats and matures matter—this is called "fire element".

Q. What is the wind element?

A. Wind supports matter—this is called "wind element".[3]

The beginner meditator overcomes the hindrances in two ways, namely, through defining [the elements] briefly and through defining in detail, as was taught fully in the [section on] defining of the four elements.

5. Dependent matter

Q. What is matter dependent on the four great primaries?

A. (1) The sense base of eye, (2) sense base of ear, (3) sense base of nose, (4) sense base of tongue, (5) sense base of body, (6) sense base of forms, (7) sense base of sounds, (8) sense base of odours, (9) sense base of tastes, (10) female faculty, (11) male faculty, (12) life faculty, (13) bodily intimation, (14) verbal intimation, (15) space element, (16) lightness of matter, (17)

"Matter dependent on the great primaries" is used here as translation for *upādāya rūpaṃ* instead of the usual "matter derived from the great primaries". According to Karunadasa (2015b: 170), the usual translation "derived" or "evolved" for *upādāya* with the four elements is "not consonant with Buddhist philosophy, because it presupposes the dichotomy between substance and quality. ... a distinction rejected by the Abhidhamma ". The Chinese has 所造, "created by", "sprung from", while the Tibetan version (179a) has las *byung ba* "arisen from", "occurring due to". For *upādārūpa*, the Chinese has 所造色, "created matter" while the Tibetan has *kun nas bslang ba'i gzugs*, "originated matter", "produced matter".

3. Cf. Vism XI.41/p.351–2: *Yo imasmiṃ kāye thaddhabhāvo vā, kharabhāvo vā ayaṃ paṭhavidhātu; yo ābandhanabhāvo vā, dravabhāvo vā ayaṃ āpodhātu; yo paripācanabhāvo vā uṇhabhāvo vā, ayaṃ tejodhātu; yo vitthambhanabhāvo vā samudīraṇabhāvo vā, ayaṃ vāyodhātū ti ...*

softness of matter, (18) malleability of matter, (19) growth of matter, (20) continuity of matter, (21) birth of matter (*jātirūpa*), (22) ageing of matter, (23) impermanence of matter, (24) solid food,[4] (25) material basis (*vatthurūpa*), and (26) torpor of matter (*middharūpa*).[5]

6. Sense bases

Q. What is the sense base of eye?[6]

A. That by which forms are seen. Dependent upon forms impinging on it, eye-consciousness arises.[7]

Furthermore, the eye sensitivity (*cakkhu-pasāda*) that is located in the flesh demarcated as the three discs of the white of the eye, iris, and pupil; is based inside the five layers of flesh, blood, wind, phlegm, and serum;[8] is half a mustard-seed in size, like the head of a louse; produced by former kamma;[9]

---

4. Cf. Vism XIV.36/p.444: *Cakkhu, sotaṃ, ghānaṃ, jivhā, kāyo, rūpaṃ, saddo, gandho, raso, itthindriyaṃ purisindriyaṃ, jīvitindriyaṃ, hadayavatthu, kāyaviññatti, vacīviññatti, ākāsadhātu, rūpassa lahutā, rūpassa mudutā, rūpassa kammaññatā, rūpassa upacayo, rūpassa santati, rūpassa jaratā rūpassa aniccatā, kabaliṅkāro āhāro.*

5. The Tibetan quotation (179a) is identical except that it does not start with a question but with "Matter dependent on the four great primaries is [of] twenty-six [kinds], namely, eye, ear, nose, ..." and ends with "torpor", *gnyid*, instead of "torpor of matter". It also adds tangibles (*phoṭṭhabba*) as the 10th sense base, making it a list of 27 items instead of 26. This is an addition that does not fit; see Introduction § 4.4. The sense base of touches is not found in the list in Vism; see Ñāṇamoli's fn. to Vism XIV.36 in PoP. Cf. fn. 1698. On *middharūpa*, see Introduction § 5 idea 1.

6. In the Pali, the explanations of sense-bases are at Vism XIV.37–57/p.445–447 and As 395–20.

7. M III 285: *Cakkhuñ ca, bhikkhave, paṭicca rūpe ca uppajjati cakkhuviññāṇaṃ.*

8. Cf. Vism XIV.47/p.445: *Cakkhu cettha yadetaṃ loke nīlapakhuma-samākiṇṇakaṇhasukkamaṇḍalavicittaṃ nīluppaladalasannibhaṃ cakkhūti vuccati. Tassa sasambhāracakkhuno setamaṇḍalaparikkhittassa kaṇhamaṇḍalassa majjhe abhimukhe ṭhitānaṃ sarīrasaṇṭhānuppattipadese sattasu picupaṭalesu āsittatelaṃ picupaṭalāni viya satta akkhipaṭalānibyāpetvā dhāraṇanhāpanamaṇḍanabījanakiccāhi catūhi dhātīhi khattiyakumāro viya sandhāraṇabandhanaparipācanasamudīraṇakiccāhi catūhi dhātūhi katūpakāraṃ utucittāhārehi upatthambhiyamānaṃ āyunā anupāliyamānaṃ vaṇṇa-gandharasādīhi parivutaṃ pamāṇato ūkāsiramattaṃ cakkhuviññāṇādīnaṃ yathārahaṃ vatthudvārabhāvaṃ sādhayamānaṃ tiṭṭhati.*

9. S IV 132: *Cakkhuṃ ... mano purāṇakammaṃ abhisaṅkhato abhisañcetayito vedaniyo daṭṭhabbo.* Spk II 402: *Cakkhu ... purāṇakamman-ti na cakkhu purāṇaṃ, kammam-eva purāṇaṃ, kammato pana nibbattattā paccayanāmena evaṃ vuttaṃ. Abhisaṅkhatan-ti paccayehi abhisamāgantvā kataṃ.*

In the following sense organs the Chinese text does not have 所成, "accomplished" (*bhūta*, etc.) or "made of" (-*maya*) as here, but 所造, "made by/of,

and is dependent on the four great primaries, [in which] the heat element is predominant (*adhika*)[10]—this sensitive matter is called "the sense base of the eye". [**446a**]

A. was taught by Venerable Sāriputta: "The eye sensitivity by which one sees forms, small or subtle, is comparable to [the head of] a louse".[11]

Q. What is the sense base of ear?

A. That by which sounds are heard. Dependent upon sounds impinging on it, ear-consciousness arises. This is called "the sense base of ear".

Furthermore, the sensitive matter that is inside the two ear-holes, is fringed by tawny hair, is based in the membrane that is [coiling] like the stalk of a runner bean [plant], is produced by former kamma, and is dependent on the four great primaries, [in which] the space element[12] is predominant—this is called "the sense base of ear".[13]

---

dependent on" (*kata, upādāya*), which is the same as if used with the four elements in this section.

10. 四大, can correspond to *cattāri mahābhūtāni*, as well as *mahābhūta*. Cf. Vism XIV.42/p.444, As 312, Moh 82: *Keci pana tejādhikānaṃ bhūtānaṃ pasādo cakkhu, vāyu-pathavī-āpādhikānaṃ bhūtānaṃ pasādā sotaghānajivhā, kāyo sabbesam-pī ti vadanti. Apare tejādhikānaṃ pasādo cakkhu, vivara-vāyu-āpa-pathavādhikānaṃ sotaghānajivhākāyā ti vadanti. ...* Cf. Vism-mhṭ: II 90: *Kecī ti mahāsaṅghikesu ekacce. Tesu hi vasudhammo evaṃ vadati cakkhumhi tejo adhikaṃ, sote vāyu, ghāne pathavī, jivhāya āpo, kāye sabbe pi samā ti. Cakkhādīsu tejādi-adhikatā nāma tannissayabhūtānaṃ tadadhikatāyā ti dassento tejādhikānaṃ bhūtānaṃ pasādo cakkhu ti ādim-āha. ...* Abhidh-av 67: *Keci panāhu: Tejādhikānaṃ bhūtānaṃ, pasādo pana cakkhu ti; / Ākāsānilatoyubbi-adhikānaṃ tu sesakā.* Abhidh-av-pṭ II 126: *Kecī ti mahāsaṅghiyesu ekacce. Cakkhādīsu tejādi-adhikatā nāma tannissayabhūtānaṃ tadadhikatāyā ti dassento tejādhikānan-ti ādim-āha. Tattha tejādhikānan-ti pamāṇavasena catunnaṃ dhātūnaṃ samānabhāva pi kiccavasena tejodhātu-adhikānaṃ. Evaṃ sesesu pi. Ākāsa ... pe ... sesakā ti ākāsādhikānaṃ bhūtānaṃ pasādo sotaṃ, vāyu-adhikānaṃ ghānaṃ, toyādhikānaṃ jivhā, phoṭṭhabbasaṅkhātapathavādhikānaṃ kāyo ti attho.*

Instead of attributing it to Vasudhamma of the Mahāsaṅghikas, as the Vism-mhṭ does, the *Visuddhimagga Sannē* (a 13th century word-by-word-commentary based on an older word-by-word-commentary; see Hettiaratchi 1950: 80–84) attributes this to Vasudhamma the Abhayagirivāsin; see Cousins 2012: 110.

11. Also quoted in Vism XIV.48/p.446, Dhs–a 307, Abhidh-av 66: *Vuttam pi c' etaṃ Dhammasenāpatinā: Yena cakkhuppasādena rūpāni samanupassati, parittaṃ sukhumaṃ c' etaṃ ūkāsirasamūpaman-ti.* The original source of this verse cannot be traced. The Chinese text has 牖柯, yu-ka, a transliteration of Sanskrit *yūkā* or Pali *ūkā*, "louse". At 445c28 there is 蟣子頭, "louse-nit-head".

12. This cannot be correct as the space element is not one of the four great primaries, but rather is dependent on them. The parallel passage attributed to "others" in the Vism instead has *vivara*, "opening", while the Abhidh-av has *ākāsa*, see fn. 1677.

13. Cf. Vism XIV.42/p.44 at fn. 1677. Cf. Vism XIV.49/p.446, Abhidh-av 66: *Sasambhārasotabilassa anto tanutambalomācite aṅgulivedhakasaṇṭhāne padese sotaṃ*

Q. What is the sense base of nose?
A. That by which odours are sensed. Dependent upon odours impinging on it, nose-consciousness arises. This is called "the sense base of nose".

Furthermore, the sensitive matter that is in the centre of the nasal passages where the three [passages] meet, is based in a small aperture that is shaped like a Koviḷāra [flower], is produced by former kamma, and is dependent on the four great primaries, [in which] the wind element is predominant—this is called "the sense base of nose".[14]

Q. What is the sense base of tongue?
A. That by which tastes are known. Dependent upon tastes impinging on it, tongue-consciousness arises. This is called "the sense base of tongue".

Furthermore, the sensory matter that is based in the flesh on top of the tongue, that is two fingers in size, is shaped like a blue lotus flower [petal],[15] is produced by former kamma, and is dependent on the four great primaries [in which] the water element is predominant—this is called "the sense base of tongue".

Q. What is the sense base of body?
A. That by which tangibles are sensed. Dependent upon the impinging of tangibles on it, body-consciousness arises. This is called the "sense base of body". Furthermore, it is the sensitive matter that is in the entire feeling-body—except for body hair, head hair, nails, teeth, and other parts without feeling—is produced by former kamma, and is dependent on the four great primaries [in which] the earth element is predominant—this is called "the sense base of body".

That which is seen [by the eye] as forms—this is called "sense base of forms".

That which impinges [the ear] as sounds—this is called "sense base of sounds".

That which impinges [the nose] as odours—this is called "sense base of odours".

That which impinges [the tongue] as tastes—this is called "sense base of tastes".[16]

---

vuttappakārāhi dhātūhi katūpakāraṃ utucittāhārehi upatthambhiyamānaṃ āyunā anupāliyamānaṃ vaṇṇādīhi parivutaṃ sotaviññāṇādīnaṃ yathārahaṃ vatthudvārabhāvaṃ sādhayamānaṃ tiṭṭhati.

14. Cf. Vism XIV.50/p.446: *Sasambhāraghānabilassa anto ajapadasaṇṭhāne padese ghānaṃ yathāvuttappakārupakārupatthambhanānupālanaparivāraṃ* .... The *koviḷāra* is the Orchid Tree, *Bauhinia variegata.*

15. Cf. Vism XIV.51/p.446: *Sasambhārajivhāmajjhassa upari uppaladalaggasaṇṭhāne padese jivhā yathāvuttappakārupakārupatthambhanānupālanaparivārā ...*

16. No exact parallel can be traced, but compare Vism XIV.54–57/p.446f.

7. Other kinds of dependent matter

The state (*bhāva*) of a female is the "female faculty".[17]

The state of a male is the "male faculty".

That which maintains the matter produced by kamma—this is called "life faculty".

That which, by the body, causes the manifestation of activities reckoned as activity—this is called "bodily intimation".

That which, by speech, causes the manifestation of activities reckoned as activity—this is called "verbal intimation".

That which delimits matter is called "space element".

The state of lightness of matter—this is called "lightness of matter".

The state of softness of matter—this is called "softness of matter".

The state of malleability of matter—this is called "malleability of matter". These [last] three kinds are non-indolence of the body.[18]

The increase of the sense bases—this is called "growth of matter".[19]

The growth of matter—this is called "continuity of matter".

The generation of matter—this is called "birth of matter".

The maturing of matter—this is called "ageing of matter".

The disintegration of matter—this is called "impermanence of matter".

The vital essence (*ojā*) which sustains beings[20]—this is called "solid food".

The [mind] element and mind-consciousness-element arise dependent on matter—this is called "material basis" (*vatthurūpa*).[21]

The torpor of the elements—this is called torpor of matter.

These twenty-six [kinds of] dependent matter and the four great primaries make up the thirty kinds of matter.[22] [**446b**]

---

17. In the Pali the explanations of these other kinds of dependent matter are at Vism XIV.57–71/p.447–450 and As 320–331.

18. 身不懈怠性. The characters 懈怠 correspond to *thīna* or *kosajja*, not to *middha*, "torpor", which is below as the last item in this list of dependent kinds of matter. Perhaps 不懈怠 corresponds to *alīna*, "non-sluggishness" or "activeness".

19. Cf. Dhs 144: *Yo āyatanānaṃ ācayo, so rūpassa upacayo—idaṃ taṃ rūpaṃ rūpassa upacayo.* As 326: *āyatanānan-ti aḍḍhekādasannaṃ rūpāyatanānaṃ. Ācayo ti nibbatti. So rūpassa upacayo ti yo āyatanānaṃ ācayo punappunaṃ nibbattamānānaṃ, so va rūpassa upacayo nāma hoti; vaḍḍhī ti attho. Yo rūpassa upacayo sā rūpassa santatī ti yā evaṃ upacitānaṃ rūpānaṃ vaḍḍhi, tato uttaritaraṃ pavattikāle sā rūpassa santati nāma hoti; pavattī ti attho.* See also Vism XIV.66–67/p.449.

20. Cf. Vism XIV.70/p.450: *Ojālakkhaṇo kabaḷīkāro āhāro, rūpāharaṇaraso ... Yāya ojāya sattā yāpenti, tassā etaṃ adhivacanaṃ.* D III 211, A V 51, Khp 2: *Sabbe sattā āhāraṭṭhitikā.*

21. 處色. Vism XIV.60/p.447: *Manodhātumanoviññāṇadhātūnaṃ nissayalakkhaṇaṃ hadayavatthu, tāsaññeva dhātūnaṃ ādhāraṇarasaṃ, ... manodhātumanoviññāṇadhātūnañ-ceva taṃsampayuttadhammānañ-ca vatthubhāvaṃ sādhayamānaṃ tiṭṭhati.*

22. According to the Mahāvihāra tradition, there are twenty-eight kinds of matter,

8. Difference between the four great primaries and dependent matter

Q. What is the difference between the four great primaries and the matter that is dependent on the four great primaries?

A. The four great primaries are co-arisen (*sahajāta*) dependent on the four entities. Matter that is dependent on the four great primaries is born dependent on the four great primaries.[23] Matter that is dependent on the four great primaries is neither dependent on the four great primaries nor is it dependent on the matter that is dependent on the four great primaries.

The four great primaries should be understood to be like three sticks leaning against [each other].[24] Matter that is dependent on the four great primaries should be understood as the shadow of the three sticks leaning against [each other].

This is the difference.

9. Five ways of knowing matter

Thereupon, the meditator should know these thirty kinds of matter in detail in five ways: through producing, clusters, birth, diversity, and unity.

10. Producing

Q. How [should it be known] through producing (*samuṭṭhāna*)?[25]

A. Nine kinds of matter are produced through the condition[26] of kamma, namely, the sense bases of eye, ear, nose, tongue and body, the female faculty, male faculty, life faculty, and the material basis (*vatthurūpa*).

---

see Abhidh-av 71, v. 695: *Bhūtā rūpāni cattāri, upādā catuvīsati, aṭṭhavīsati rūpāni, sabbān' eva bhavanti hi.* The Pali has "matter" in the plural, *rūpāni*, lit. "matters" or "materialities", which sounds awkward in English.

23. Paṭṭh I 67: *ekaṃ mahābhūtaṃ sahajātā tayo mahābhūtā, tayo mahābhūte sahajātaṃ ekaṃ mahābhūtaṃ, dve mahābhūte sahajātā dve mahābhūtā, mahābhūte sahajātaṃ cittasamuṭṭhānaṃ rūpaṃ kaṭattārūpaṃ upādārūpaṃ; bāhiraṃ... āhārasamuṭṭhānaṃ... utusamuṭṭhānaṃ...*

24. Cf. Vism XVIII 78/p.535, Yam-a 107: *Aññamaññaṃ uppādanupatthambhanabhāvena upakārako dhammo aññamaññapaccayo aññamaññūpatthambhakaṃ tidaṇḍakaṃ viya.* Cf. *Abhidharmakośa* I.51d.

25. Cf. Abhidh-av 72–73: *Samuṭṭhānan-ti cattāri rūpasamuṭṭhānāni utucittāhāra-kammānīti. Kammaṃ utu ca cittañ-ca, āhāro rūpahetuyo; / Eteheva ca rūpāni, jāyan-ti na panaññato. ...*

26. Cf. Abhidh-av-pṭ 58: *Catusamuṭṭhito kammacitta-utuāhārasaṅkhātehi catūhi paccayehi samuṭṭhito nibbatto...*

Two kinds of matter are produced by the condition of mind (*citta*), namely, bodily intimation, and verbal intimation.

One [kind of] matter is produced by the conditions of season and mind, namely, the sense base of sound.

Four kinds of matter are produced by the conditions of season, mind and food, namely, lightness of matter, softness of matter, malleability of matter, and torpor of matter.

Twelve kinds of matter are produced by [all] the four conditions,[27] namely, the sense bases of form, odour and taste, the space element, growth of matter, continuity of matter, birth of matter, solid food, and the four elements.

Two kinds of matter are not produced [by conditions], namely, ageing of matter and impermanence of matter. However, with birth as condition, there is ageing; and with ageing as condition, there is impermanence.

Thus should it be known in detail through producing.

11. Clusters

Q. How [should it be known] through clusters (*kalāpa*)?

A. Nine clusters are produced by kamma. Nine clusters are produced by mind. Six clusters are produced by season. Three clusters are produced by food.[28]

Q. What are the nine clusters that are produced by kamma?

A. They are the eye-decad, ear-decad, nose-decad, tongue-decad, body-decad, female faculty-decad, male faculty-decad, [material] basis-decad, and life-faculty-ennead.[29]

Q. What is the "eye-decad"?

---

27. The four conditions are the abovementioned kamma, season, mind, and nutriment. Cf. the section on contemplating the four elements by way of conditions at 439c.

28. Cf. As 82: *Tattha catubbidho kāyo upādinnako, āhārasamuṭṭhāno, utusamuṭṭhāno, cittasamuṭṭhānoti. Tattha cakkhāyatanādīni jīvitindriyapariyantāni aṭṭha kammasamuṭṭhānarūpānipi, kammasamuṭṭhānāneva catasso dhātuyo vaṇṇo gandho raso ojā ti aṭṭha upādinnakakāyo nāma. Tāneva aṭṭha āhārajāni āhārasamuṭṭhānikakāyo nāma. Aṭṭha utujāni utusamuṭṭhānikakāyo nāma. Aṭṭha cittajāni cittasamuṭṭhānikakāyo nāma.*

29. Abhidh-s VI § 46: *Tattha jīvitaṃ avinibbhogarūpañ ca cakkhunā saha cakkhudasakan ti pavuccati. Tathā sotādīhi saddhiṃ sotadasakaṃ ghānadasakaṃ jivhādasakaṃ kāyadasakaṃ itthibhāvadasakaṃ pumbhāvadasakaṃ vatthudasakañ ceti yathākkamaṃ yojetabbaṃ. Avinibbhogarūpam eva jīvitena saha jīvitanavakan ti pavuccati. Ime nava kammasamuṭṭhānakalāpā.*

A. Eye-sensitivity (*cakkhu-pasāda*) with the four great primaries as its basis (*vatthu*).[30]

Furthermore, it is the colour, odour, taste, vital essence,[31] life faculty, and eye-sensitivity that are dependent on the four great primaries. These ten

---

30. 眼清淨四界是其處. Cf. As 316: *Tattha cakkhupasādassa paccayāni cattāri mahābhūtāni, vaṇṇo gandho raso ojā, jīvitindriyaṃ cakkhupasādo ti idaṃ ekantato avinibhuttānaṃ dasannaṃ nipphannarūpānaṃ vasena cakkhudasakaṃ nāma.* Vism XVII.156/553: *Tattha vaṇṇo gandho raso ojā catasso cā pi dhātuyo cakkhupasādo jīvitan-ti ayaṃ dasarūpaparimāṇo rūpapuñjo cakkhudasako nāma.* Vibh 70/§ 156: *katamaṃ cakkhāyatanaṃ? Yaṃ cakkhu catunnaṃ mahābhūtānaṃ upādāya pasādo attabhāvapariyāpanno anidassano sappaṭigho...* Paṭis-a I 246: *Oḷārikan-ti cakkhusotaghāna-jivhākāyarūpasaddagandharasaṃ phoṭṭhabbasaṅkhātā pathavītejovāyo cā ti dvādasavidhaṃ rūpaṃ ghaṭṭanavasena gahetabbato oḷārikaṃ. Sesaṃ pana āpodhātu itthindriyaṃ purisindriyaṃ jīvitindriyaṃ hadayavatthu ojā ākāsadhātu kāyaviññatti vacīviññatti rūpassa lahutā mudutā kammaññatā upacayo santati jaratā aniccatā ti soḷasavidhaṃ rūpaṃ ghaṭṭanavasena agahetabbato sukhumaṃ.*

31. Instead of "vital essence", *ojā*, the Chinese text has 觸, corresponding to *phoṭṭhabba*, "tangible", which cannot be correct because the sense base of the body is not given in the list of dependent kinds of matter at 445c (wherein *ojā* is included as coarse food ["The vital essence which sustains beings—this is called "solid nutriment"] at 446a27), and nor is it in the explanations of these. "Tangibles" is given in the Tibetan quotation of the list of dependent kinds of matter; see Intro. §4.4, and Skilling, 1994: 180–81. The same mistake is found in Ch. 8 § 166; see fn. 1514.

After *rasa*, "tastes", the Tibetan adds *gzi brjid*, which corresponds to Skt *ojas* in the sense of "lustre/splendour"; see Skilling, 1994: 184, n. 1. Vism and As (see preceding fn) also have *ojā* in their lists. The characters for *ojā*, as used at 446a27, are 氣味. Perhaps a corruption occurred during transmission of the text because 味, "tastes", precedes 觸 in this list, i.e. 味觸. The original could have had 味氣味, which could have been misunderstood and "corrected" during transmission. However, since in the "by way groups" section at 439b20 there is also *phoṭṭhabba* instead of *ojā*, it is more likely that Saṅghapāla or a copyist held the view that *phoṭṭhabbā* is dependent matter and corrected the text. Not knowing the Theravada Abhidhamma viewpoint, he assumed that there had to be *phoṭṭhabbā* here and that *ojā* was a corruption. The Sarvāstivādins held that, although the other sense bases are dependent matter, the sense base of tangibles is sometimes primary matter (because of the characteristic of tangible solidity of the earth element, etc.) and sometimes secondary/dependent matter; see *Abhidharmakośabhāṣya* I.10d, 23b, 35a–b; II.22a–c. The Sarvāstivāda Vaibhāṣikas, whose works such as the **Mahāvibhāṣa* were popular in China, held that tangibles are only dependent matter; see Abhidh-k-bh II.22c; Karunadasa 2015a: 32–35, 146–47 and 2015b 173, 178–179; Ronkin 2005: 57; Skilling, 1994: 181. The Theravādins held that tangibles are primary matter consisting of the earth, fire, and wind elements, but not the water element, which is intangible due to not having the characteristic of coolness (*sīta*), etc., and is therefore included as a subtle matter (*sukhumarūpa*) in the sense base of mental states (*dhammāyatana*). Other schools associated coolness with the water element; see Karunadasa 2015a: 35

states occur together and are inseparable (*avinibbhoga*) from each other. This is called "cluster". This is called "eye-decad".[32]

---

and 2015b 173, 178–79. On coolness, see also fn. 1510.

See Dhs 133, § 595: *Katamaṃ taṃ rūpaṃ upādā? Cakkhāyatanaṃ, ... rasāyatanaṃ, itthindriyaṃ, purisindriyaṃ, jīvitindriyaṃ, kāyaviññatti, vacīviññatti, ākāsadhātu, rūpassa lahutā, rūpassa mudutā, rūpassa kammaññatā, rūpassa upacayo, rūpassa santati, rūpassa jaratā, rūpassa aniccatā, kabaḷīkāro āhāro.* Dhs 144, § 646: *Katamaṃ taṃ rūpaṃ no upādā? Phoṭṭhabbāyatanaṃ, āpodhātu.* § 647: *Katamaṃ taṃ rūpaṃ phoṭṭhabbāyatanaṃ? Paṭhavīdhātu tejodhātu vāyodhātu kakkhaḷaṃ ... lahukaṃ, yaṃ phoṭṭhabbaṃ anidassanaṃ sappaṭighaṃ kāyena anidassanena sappaṭighena phusi vā phusati vā phusissati vā ....* Dhs 156, § 763. *Phoṭṭhabbāyatanaṃ āpodhātu—idaṃ taṃ rūpaṃ bāhiraṃ mahābhūtaṃ.* § 764. ... *Rūpāyatanaṃ ... pe ... kabaḷīkāro āhāro—idaṃ taṃ rūpaṃ bāhiraṃ na mahābhūtaṃ.* Dhs 146, § 652: ... *rasāyatanaṃ phoṭṭhabbāyatanaṃ ākāsadhātu āpodhātu rūpassa upacayo rūpassa santati kabaḷīkāro āhāro—idaṃ taṃ rūpaṃ upādiṇṇaṃ.* Dhs 147, § 666. ... *cittasamuṭṭhānaṃ rūpāyatanaṃ ... phoṭṭhabbāyatanaṃ ākāsadhātu āpodhātu rūpassa lahutā ... kabaḷīkāro āhāro—idaṃ taṃ rūpaṃ cittasamuṭṭhānaṃ.* Dhs 147, § 896. *Phoṭṭhabbāyatanaṃ—idaṃ taṃ rūpaṃ no upādā oḷārikaṃ.* 897. ... *Āpodhātu—idaṃ taṃ rūpaṃ no upādā sukhumaṃ.* M-ṭ II 63: *Āpodhātu sukhumarūpaṃ.* Vism-mhṭ II 108: *Kimidaṃ phoṭṭhabbaṃ nāmā ti? Pathavītejovāyodhātuttayaṃ. Kasmā panettha āpodhātu aggahitā, nanu sītatā phusitvā gayhati, sā ca āpodhātu ti? Saccaṃ gayhati, na pana sā āpodhātu. Kiñcarahī ti? Tejodhātu eva.* ... Abhidh-s 196: *Āpodhātuyā sukhumabhāvena phusituṃ asakkuṇeyyattā vuttaṃ āpodhātu vivajjitaṃ bhūtattayasaṅkhātan-ti. Kiñcāpi hi sītatā phusitvā gayhati, sā pana tejo yeva. Mande hi uṇhatte sītabuddhi sītatāsaṅkhātassa kassaci guṇassa abhāvato. Tayidaṃ sītabuddhiyā anavaṭṭhitabhāvato viññāyati pārāpāre viya. ... Vuttañhetaṃ porāṇehi—Davatāsahavuttīni, tīṇi bhūtāni samphusaṃ;* ... Abhi-av-pṭ II 3: *Phusīyatī ti ghaṭṭīyati. Kiṃ taṃ phoṭṭhabbaṃ nāmā ti āha pathavītejavāyavoti. Iminā dhātuttayam-eva kāyaviññāṇaviññeyyabhāvasaṅkhātaphoṭṭhabbaṃ nāma, na aññan-ti dasseti. Kasmā panettha āpodhātu na gahitā, nanu sītatā phusitvā gayhati, sā ca āpodhātu evāti? Saccaṃ gayhati, na pana āpodhātu, kiñcarahi tejodhātu eva.* ... Moh 95: *Tattha āpodhātuvivajjitabhūtattayaṃ phoṭṭhabbāyatanaṃ phoṭṭhabbadhātu kāyaviññeyyaṃ, kāyaviññāṇaviññeyyan-ti ca vuccati, sukhumarūpaṃ dhammāyatanaṃ dhammadhātū ti, tadeva pasādasahitaṃ manoviññeyyaṃ, manoviññāṇaviññeyyan-ti ca vuttaṃ. Sesaṃ suviññeyyam-eva. Kasmā panettha āpodhātuvivajjitānañ-ñeva bhūtānaṃ phoṭṭhabbatā vuttā, nanu āpodhātu pi sītavasena phusitvā veditabbā ti? Na sītassā pi tejodhātuttā. Uṇham-eva hi sītan-ti byapadissati.* ...

In the definition of the sense base of tangibles in Ch. 11 § 32, the water element is not found in the readings of the old editions listed in the footnote in the Taishō edition, although the Taishō reads it in the main text.

32. Sav 179b: "Because these ten states are an inseparable conglomeration...'". See Skilling, 1994: 183.

There is variation in the characters for "occur together". In 446b20, c07, 共生, in b22, b24, c10 共起 are used, both meaning "arising together", *saha-jāta, saha-vattana*, which might correspond to *sahavutti* of Abhidh-s (see below), while in c09, 隨起, "arising sequentially" is used. The Tibetan parallel of 446b20–24, has only *rjes su 'jug par byed pa*, corresponding to *anu-vattana, anuvattati; rjes su* = *anu*, not *saha*.

Their arising is birth; their decay is called ageing; their disintegration is impermanence; what delimits them is the space element.[33] These four states (*dhamma*) and that cluster occur together.

This eye-decad gives birth to a second eye-decad, dependent upon [the first in its] ageing phase; the accrual (*ācaya*) of these two kinds of decads is called "accumulation" (*upacaya*). The continuance (*anupabandhana*) of these [states] is called "continuity".[34] These six states [and] that [cluster] occur together.

Furthermore, the second eye-decad, dependent upon [the first in its] ageing phase, gives birth to a third decad. These second and third eye-decads are called "cluster". The continuance of these states is called "continuity".

The disintegration of the first decad, the decay of the second decad, and the arising of the third decad occur in a single moment (*eka-khaṇa*). The interval between the eye-decads arisen thus cannot be known; because of the quickness of the moment, it cannot be known in the present world. [**446c**] There are meditators who see the eye-continuity like a flowing stream, like the flame of a lamp.[35]

This is called the "eye-decad".

In the same way, the ear-decad, the nose-decad, the tongue-decad, the body-decad, female-faculty-decad, male-faculty-decad, [material] basis-decad,[36] and the life-faculty-ennead should be understood in detail.[37]

Cf. Abhidh-s 42, §45: *Ekuppādā ekanirodhā ekanissayā sahavuttino ekavīsati rūpakalāpā nāma.* Abhidh-s 211 *Sahavuttino ti visuṃ visuṃ kalāpagatarūpavasena sahavuttino, na sabbakalāpānaṃ aññamaññaṃ sahuppattivasena.*

33. Vism-mhṭ II 100: *Ayaṃ hi ākāsadhātu taṃ taṃ rūpakalāpaṃ paricchindantī viya hoti. Tenāha rūpapariyantappakāsanarasā ti.*

34. Abhidh-av 71: *Pavattilakkhaṇā rūpassa santati, anuppabandhanarasā, anupaccheda-paccupaṭṭhānā, anuppabandharūpapadaṭṭhānā.* Vism-mhṭ II 102: ... *Tattha yo āyatanānan-ti yo aḍḍhekādasannaṃ rūpāyatanānaṃ ādicayattā ācayo ti vutto. So eva upacayo paṭhamuppādabhāvato upa-saddo paṭhamatthoti katvā. Yo pana tattheva uppajjamānānaṃ upari cayattā upacayo, sā eva santati anupabandhavasena uppattibhāvato. Atha vā yo āyatanānaṃ ācayo paṭhamabhāvena upalakkhito uppādo, so pana tattheva uppajjamānānaṃ upari cayattā upacayo, vaḍḍhī ti attho. Upacayo vaḍḍhibhāvena upalakkhito uppādo, sā eva santati pabandhākārena uppattibhāvato.*

35. Abhidh-s VI 10: *Catu-samuṭṭhāna-rupā-kalāpa-santati kāmaloke dīpa-jālā viya nadī soto viya.* Vibh-mṭ 44: *Yattha yattha hi ārammaṇe arūpadhammā uppajjanti, tattha tattheva te bhijjanti, na aññaṃ saṅkamanti, ārammaṇadhammā ca yathāsakaṃ khaṇato uddhaṃ na tiṭṭhantī ti. Svāyamattho padīpādi-udāharaṇena veditabbo.*

36. The *vatthudasaka* is not found in the Chinese text here, but is listed above at 448b18, and it is found here in the Sav as *dngos po bcu ldan*.

After this sentence the Tibetan skips over the rest of this method and resumes at 446c23.

37. Vism-mhṭ 107: *Kammato jātan-ti ettha yaṃ ekantakammasamuṭṭhānaṃ aṭṭhindriyāni, hadayañ-cā ti navavidhaṃ rūpaṃ, yañ-ca navavidhe catusamuṭṭhāne kammasamuṭṭhānaṃ*

Q. What are the nine clusters produced by mind (*citta*)?
A. Bare-octad, bare-body intimation-ennead, bare-speech intimation-decad, bare-lightness-ennead, lightness-body intimation-decad, lightness-speech intimation-undecad, bare-torpor-ennead,[38] torpor-body intimation-decad, and torpor-speech intimation-undecad.[39]

Q. What is the bare-octad produced by mind?
A. The four elements and the colour, odour, taste, and vital essence[40] dependent on the elements. These eight states occur together and are inseparable. These eight are called the "bare-octad".

The arising of these is birth; the decay of these is ageing; their disintegration is impermanence; what delimits them is the space element. These four states and that [cluster] occur sequentially.
A. the time of disintegration of that [first] bare-octad, a second mind occurs together with a second bare-octad.

The disintegration of the first bare [-octad] and the arising of the second bare [-octad] occur in a single moment.[41] These are not [occurring] mutually *aññamañña*) as a cluster. Through the three occurring together, they become

---

navavidham-evarūpan-tievaṃaṭṭhārasavidham-pikammatouppajjanatokammajaṃ. Abhidh-s 42: *Tattha jīvitaṃ avinibbhogarūpañ-ca cakkhunā saha cakkhudasakan-ti pavuccati. Tathā sotādīhi saddhiṃ sotadasakaṃ ghānadasakaṃ jivhādasakaṃ kāyadasakaṃ itthibhāvadasakaṃ pumbhāvadasakaṃ vatthudasakañ-ce ti yathākkamaṃ yojetabbaṃ. Avinibbhogarūpam-eva jīvitena saha jīvitanavakan-ti pavuccati. Ime nava kammasamuṭṭhānakalāpā.*

38. In accordance with the variant reading given below, see fn. 1711, this and the next occurrences of "eye" have been changed to "torpor".

39. Cf. Vism-mhṭ 107: *Viññattidvayaṃ, saddo, ākāsadhātu, lahutādittayaṃ cittasamuṭṭhānāni avinibbhogarūpānīti etaṃ pañcadasavidhaṃ rūpaṃ cittajaṃ.* Abhidh-s 42 VI § 47: *Avinibbhogarūpaṃ pana suddhaṭṭhakaṃ, tadeva kāyaviññattiyā saha kāyaviññattinavakaṃ, vacīviññattisaddehi saha vacīviññattidasakaṃ, lahutādīhi saddhiṃ lahutādekādasakaṃ, kāyaviññattilahutādidvādasakaṃ, vacīviññattisaddalahutāditerasakañ-ce ti cha cittasamuṭṭhānakalāpā.*

The variant reading in Taishō has "ten" instead of "seven" and has been taken here. EKS had 'bare-speech intimation-heptad' but, as LC notes, this is impossible because no *kalāpa* can have less than the basis eight: "it should be a *dasaka*, i.e. one more than the ennead for body intimation, because it should be 'bare-speech intimation-sound-decad'. 'Lightness-speech intimation-undecad' is a group of eleven precisely because it includes 'sound'".

40. 色香味觸. The text has "tangible", *phoṭṭhabba*, instead of "vital essence"; see fn. 1698.

41. Since two sentences further down it is said that there are "three ... produced together" presumably this should, in accordance with the parallel above, be read as "the disintegration of the first bare [octad], the decay of the second bare [octad], and the arising of the third bare [octad] occur in a single moment".

a cluster.[42] In the same way, the bare-lightness-ennead and the bare-torpor-ennead [should be understood]. The six intimation clusters[43] do not disintegrate first and do not arise second, do not occur in one moment. Why? One mind does not produce two intimations.

The rest should be understood in the way it was taught fully before.

Q. What are the six clusters produced by season?
A. Bare-octad, bare-sound-ennead, bare-lightness-ennead, lightness-sound-decad, bare-torpor[44]-ennead, torpor-sound-decad.[45] There are two external clusters: bare-octad and sound-ennead.

Q. What are the three clusters that are produced by food?
A. Bare octad, bare-lightness-ennead, and bare-torpor-ennead.

Of the clusters that are produced by season and food: continuity [of matter] and [matter as] basis [produced by] kamma[46] should be understood as identical. The rest is as was taught above.

---

42. 446c11–12; 此非展轉為聚, 以與三所. It is not clear what is meant here with "three". The text might be corrupt and it might stand for "two". There is a variant reading in the previous sentence which has "third consciousness" instead of "second consciousness".

起所聚. The characters 為聚 can mean "mutually/reciprocally" (*aññamañña*), "successive/in sequence" (*paramparā*).

43. Bare-body intimation, bare-speech intimation, lightness-body intimation, lightness-speech–intimation, eye-body intimation, eye-speech intimation.

44. Taishō reads 眼, "eye", but this is a corruption of 眠, "torpor", *middha*. LC: "It would make perfect sense for 'torpor' to be produced by mind, nutriment, and season. Eye groups should not be produced by mind, nutriment, and season". *Middharūpa*, torpor of matter, is the last kind of matter given in the list of kinds of matter, which includes lightness, *lahutā*, at 445c25. Two sentences further down, at 446c18, a footnote mentions that one edition reads 眠, *middha*, instead of 眼, eye, and in 446c21 the text itself reads 眠, *middha*. The characters for eye and torpor—眼 and 眠—are quite similar and easily would have been confused by a copyist, as can also be seen in the footnote at 445c25 where it is shown that several editions wrongly read 眼色 = *cakkhurūpa*, instead of 眠色 = *middharūpa*.

45. Abhidh-s 43 §48–49. *Suddhaṭṭhakaṃ saddanavakaṃ lahutādekādasakaṃ saddalahutādidvādasakañ-ce ti cattāro utusamuṭṭhānakalāpā. Suddhaṭṭhakaṃ lahutādekādasakañ-ce ti dve āhārasamuṭṭhānakalāpā.* Vism-mhṭ 107: *Ākāsadhātu, lahutādittayaṃ, āhārasamuṭṭhānāni avinibbhogarūpānī ti etaṃ dvādasavidhaṃ rūpaṃ āhārajaṃ. Ettha saddaṃ pakkhipitvā terasavidhaṃ rūpaṃ ututo samuṭṭhitaṃ utujaṃ.*

46. From here on, the text of this paragraph is difficult to follow and appears to be corrupted due to a copyist trying to correct the text.

業處, *kamma-vatthu*, "kamma-basis" probably is the dependent matter of *vatthurūpa*, "material basis". As a cluster this is the "basis decad", *vatthudasaka*, given in the introduction of this section as one of the nine clusters that are produced by

The life [faculty]-ennead[47] cluster is produced in the sensuous sphere, in [matter as] basis [produced by] kamma.

[In the material sphere] there are five[48] clusters through which there is life: nose, tongue, body, the male, and female faculties. Accordingly, the three [clusters] beginning with lightness, and [the cluster of] torpor do not exist in the material sphere.

The life [faculty]-ennead cluster [occurs in] the Brahmā deities [who are beings] without perception (*asaññā*). In their bodies, there are all of the sense bases, through which they obtain life [at rebirth].[49]

---

kamma, and corresponding to the *hadayavatthudasaka* "heart-basis-decad" of Vism. Elsewhere in Vim 處色 (= *vatthu* + *rūpa*) is used for *vatthurūpa*, which is produced from kamma and is the continuity of kamma-produced matter. No exact parallel in the Pali can be traced but there are related passages: As 22: *Evaṃ parittāya rūpasantatiyā tīṇi santatisīsāni honti vatthudasakaṃ, kāyadasakaṃ, itthiyā itthindriyavasena purisassa purisindriyavasena bhāvadasakan-ti. Tattha vatthurūpaṃ, tassa nissayāni cattāri mahābhūtāni, taṃnissitā vaṇṇagandharasojā, jīvitan-ti idaṃ vatthudasakaṃ nāma. ...* Abhidh-av-pṭ II 138: *... nipphanna-upādāyarūpanissayaṃ dhātudvayaṃ pañcavokārabhave rūpapaṭibaddhavuttittā. ... Hotu tāva dhātudvayanissayo vatthu, upādāyarūpañ-ca, taṃ panetaṃ kammasamuṭṭhānaṃ paṭiniyatakiccaṃ hadayappadese ṭhitamekan-ti daṭṭhabbaṃ. Kathametaṃ viññāyatī ti? Vuccate vatthurūpabhāvato kammasamuṭṭhānaṃ cakkhu viya. Yañ-hi viññāṇassa vatthubhūtaṃ rūpaṃ, taṃ kammasamuṭṭhānaṃ yathā cakkhupasādo, ...*

47. 命九天聚, lit. "life ennead divine cluster". The placing of "divine", 天, after "life ennead" is odd. The fn. in Taishō says that one edition has 無 "without" instead of 天 "divine". In the next fn. it says that 4 other editions leave out 天 from 命九天聚. Elsewhere 命根九 "life-faculty-ennead" is used as the name of this cluster. As 天 does not fit in both cases, it has not been translated.

48. Read 五, "five", instead of 八, "eight". LC: "It should be five groups. The error has obviously arisen by the addition of five and the three following. However, it is four of the six season-born groups which do not occur in *rūpadhātu*, i.e. those with lightness and *middha*. Nutriment-born groups are not found there".

49. (無有)命九聚無想梵天, 於其身一切入, 以是得活入. Possibly this refers to inoperative sense-faculties since there is no sensitive matter, *pasādarūpa*. Cf. 447a09: "At the moment of birth of a deity who is a being without perception, nine kinds of matter are produced, namely, the life faculty ennead", 無想天眾生於其生刹那九色起命根九.

Cf. Moh 73 Be: *asaññīnaṃ pana sabbāni pi vatthuviññāṇāni na santi. Tesaṃ hi jīvitanavakam-eva rūpaṃ paṭisandhi, pavattiyaṃ bhavaṅgaṃ, maraṇakāle cuti ca hutvā pavattati.* Vibh 419: *Asaññasattānaṃ devānaṃ upapattikkhaṇe eko khandho pātubhavati: rūpakkhandho; dve āyatanāni pātubhavanti: rūpāyatanaṃ, dhammāyatanaṃ; dve dhātuyo pātubhavanti: rūpadhātu, dhammadhātu; ekaṃ saccaṃ pātubhavati: dukkhasaccaṃ; ekindriyaṃ pātubhavati: rūpajīvitindriyaṃ.* Cf. Vibh-mhṭ 108. Yam III 170–173: *Asaññasattānaṃ arūpānaṃ tesaṃ tattha jīvitindriyaṃ uppajjittha, no ca tesaṃ tattha cakkhundriyaṃ ... manindriyaṃ uppajjittha.* Abhidh-s 44, § 59. *Asaññasattānaṃ pana cakkhusotavatthusaddā pi na labbhanti, tathā sabbāni pi cittajarūpāni, tasmā tesaṃ*

Thus should it be known through birth.
Thus, [one should know] through clusters.

12. Birth

Q. How [should it be known] through birth?

A. Now, when a male or female enters the womb, at the moment of birth (*upapattikkhaṇa*) thirty kinds of matter are produced, namely, the [material] basis-decad, body-decad, the female faculty-decad or the male faculty-decad. In the case of one who is neither a male nor a female (*napuṃsaka*), twenty kinds of matter are produced, namely, the [material] basis-decad and the body-decad.[50]

When a male or a female fully possessed of the sense-faculties and the sense bases is spontaneously born (*opapātika*)[51] in the sensuous sphere, seventy kinds of matter are produced at the moment of birth, namely, the [material] basis-decad, the body-decad, the eye-decad, the ear-decad, the nose-decad, the tongue-decad, the female faculty-decad, or the male faculty-decad.

---

paṭisandhikāle jīvitanavakam-eva, pavattiyañ-ca saddavajjitaṃ utusamuṭṭhānarūpaṃ atiricchati. Cf. Kv 396.

50. Cf. Vism XVII.155–156 / pp. 552–53: *Tiṃsa nava ceva rūpīsu, / sattati ukkaṃsatotha rūpāni; / Saṃsedupapātayonisu, atha vā avakaṃsato tiṃsa. Rūpībrahmesu tāva opapātikayonikesu cakkhusotavatthudasakānaṃ jīvitanavakassa cā ti catunnaṃ kalāpānaṃ vasena tiṃsa ca nava ca paṭisandhiviññāṇena saha rūpāni uppajjanti. Rūpī brahme pana ṭhapetvā aññesu saṃsedajaopapātikayonikesu ukkaṃsato cakkhusotaghānajivhākāya-vatthubhāvadasakānaṃ vasena sattati, tāni ca niccaṃ devesu. Tattha vaṇṇo gandho raso ojā catasso cāpi dhātuyo cakkhupasādo jīvitan-ti ayaṃ dasarūpaparimāṇo rūpapuñjo cakkhudasako nāma. Evaṃ sesā veditabbā. Avakaṃsato pana jaccandhabadhira-aghānakanapuṃsakassa jivhākāyavatthudasakānaṃ vasena tiṃsa rūpāni uppajjanti. Ukkaṃsāvakaṃsānaṃ pana antare anurūpato vikappo veditabbo.* Abhidh-s 77 v. 746: *Gabbhaseyyaka-sattassa, paṭisandhikkhaṇe pana tiṃsa rūpāni jāyante, sabhāvass' eva dehino.* Abhidh-s v. 747: *Abhāva-gabbhaseyyānaṃ; aṇḍajānañ ca vīsati / bhavanti pana rūpāni, kāyavatthuvasena tu.* Cf. Vibh-a 169–70: *Evaṃ pavattamāne c' etasmiṃ nāmarūpe yasmā abhāvaka-gabbhaseyyakānaṃ aṇḍajānañ ca paṭisandhikkhaṇe vatthu-kāyavasena rūpato dve santatisīsāni tayo ca arūpino khandhā pātubhavanti, tasmā tesaṃ vitthārena rūparūpato vīsati-dhammā tayo ca arūpino khandhā ti ete tevīsati-dhammā viññāṇapaccayā nāmarūpan-ti veditabbā.*

51. The characters 化生 correspond to Pali *opapātika* = Skt *upapāduka*, "spontaneously reborn". *Rdzus skyes* in the Tibetan quotation confirms this. Cf. Vibh 418: *Kāmadhātuyā upapattikkhaṇe kassa ekādasāyatanāni pātubhavanti? Kāmāvacarānaṃ devānaṃ, paṭhamakappikānaṃ manussānaṃ, opapātikānaṃ petānaṃ, opapātikānaṃ asurānaṃ, opapātikānaṃ tiracchānagatānaṃ, nerayikānaṃ paripuṇṇāyatanānaṃ upapattikkhaṇe ekādasāyatanāni pātubhavanti ...*

When a male or female is spontaneously born blind in a bad destination, at the moment of birth sixty kinds of matter are produced, namely, [all] except the eye-decad.

Likewise, when one is born deaf [**447a**], sixty kinds of matter are produced, namely, [all] except the ear-decad.

In one born blind and deaf, fifty kinds of matter are produced namely, [all] except the eye-decad and the ear-decad.

When one who is neither a male nor a female, who is fully possessed of the sense-faculties and the sense bases, is spontaneously born in a bad destination, or is a human at the beginning of an aeon, at the moment of birth, sixty kinds of matter are produced, namely, [all] except the female-and-male faculty [decad].[52]

In one who is [born] blind, and who is neither a male nor a female, fifty kinds of matter are produced, namely, [all] except the eye faculty-decad and the neither-female-nor-male faculty [decad].

In one who is [born] deaf, and who is neither a male nor a female, fifty kinds of matter are produced, namely, [all] except the ear-decad and the neither-female-nor-male faculty [decad].

In one [born] blind and deaf, who is neither a male nor a female, forty kinds of matter are produced: the [material] basis-decad, the body-decad, the nose-decad, and the tongue-decad.

At the moment of birth of a Brahmā deity, forty-nine[53] kinds of matter are produced, namely, the [material] basis-decad, the eye-decad, the ear-decad, the body-decad, and the life-faculty-ennead.

A. the moment of birth of a deity who is a being without perception (*asaññasatta*), nine kinds of matter are produced, namely, the life-faculty-ennead.

Thus should it be known through birth.

13. Diversity

Q. How [should it be known] through diversity?

A. All kinds of matter are of two kinds, namely, coarse or subtle.

---

52. The Tibetan text instead has *'dod pa bcu ldan, kāma-dasaka*, "sensual-decad", or perhaps "sexual-decad", here and in the following.

53. 天於其生剎那四十九色起. The Tibetan text (180b): "At the moment of birth of Brahmās, 39 kinds of matter arise: ...". The number 39 is confirmed by the Abhidh-s (p. 38,8 Ch. VI § 27), which says that the body-decad is not found in the Brahmaloka; see Skilling 1994: 183, n. 1. Cf. Vism XVII.156: *Rūpībrahmesu tāva opapātikayonikesu cakkhusotavatthudasakānaṃ jīvitanavakassa cā ti catunnaṃ kalāpānaṃ vasena tiṃsa ca nava ca paṭisandhiviññāṇena saha rūpāni uppajjanti.*

Herein, twelve kinds of matter[54] are coarse in the sense of being with impact; the other eighteen kinds of matter are subtle in the sense of being without impact.

14. Two kinds of matter

Furthermore, there are two kinds of matter, namely, internal and external.

Herein, five kinds of matter—the five sense bases of the eye, etc.—are internal in the sense of having [an external] sense object (*visaya*); the other twenty-five are external matter, in the sense of not having a sense object.

Furthermore, there are two kinds of matter, namely, faculty and non-faculty.[55]

Herein, eight kinds of matter are faculty in the sense of authority—the five internal [sense-faculties], the female faculty, male faculty, and life faculty—the other twenty-two kinds of matter are non-faculty in the sense of non-authority.[56]

54. 於是十二色大內外色入以有對義. The text is corrupt: "twelve kinds of matter are coarse—the internal and external sense base of forms—in the sense...". "Internal and external matter sense base" probably is an intrusion from the next pair of kinds of matter. Tibetan (Sav 180b): "All matter is of two kinds: coarse in the sense of having impact, and subtle in the sense of having no impact. Herein the coarse kinds of matter are twelve: eye, ..., tastes, earth element, fire element, wind element. The subtle kinds of matter are eighteen: the others, i.e. the life faculty, etc". The 12 kinds in the Tibetan correspond to the ones given in the Vism and the Paṭis-a, where the sense base of tangibles is defined as the elements of earth, fire, and water. Below, at 447a28, the 12 coarse kinds of matter are again not defined, but the water element is given separately, implying that the other three elements are included in the coarse kinds of matter, while the water element is subtle matter.

Vism XIV.73/p.450: *Cakkhādīni nava āpodhātuvajjitā tisso dhātuyo cā ti dvādasavidhaṃ ghaṭṭanavasena gahetabbato oḷārikaṃ, sesaṃ tato viparītattā sukhumaṃ.* Paṭis-a I 246: *Oḷārikan-ti cakkhusotaghānajivhākāyarūpasaddagandharasaṃ phoṭṭhabba-saṅkhātā pathavītejovāyo cā ti dvādasavidhaṃ rūpaṃ ghaṭṭanavasena gahetabbato oḷārikaṃ. Sesaṃ pana āpodhātu itthindriyaṃ purisindriyaṃ jīvitindriyaṃ hadayavatthu ojā ākāsadhātu kāyaviññatti vacīviññatti rūpassa lahutā mudutā kammaññatā upacayo santati jaratā aniccatā ti soḷasavidhaṃ rūpaṃ ghaṭṭanavasena agahetabbato sukhumaṃ.*

55. Lit. "life faculty and non-life faculty", *jīvitindriya, ajīvitindriya*. Cf. *anindriya-baddharūpa*, "matter not bound up with faculties", below at § 31.

The Tibetan text has "... matter as faculty (*dbang po'i gzugs, indriyarūpa*) and matter as non-faculty (*dbang po min pa'i gzugs, anindriya-rūpa*)". See also Skilling 1994: 197.

56. Cf. Dhs 125–27, § 585. Cf. Vism 381 (§ 73): *Pasādarūpaṃ eva itthindriyādittayena saddhiṃ adhipatiyaṭṭhena indriyaṃ, sesaṃ tato viparītatā anindriyaṃ*: "Just the matter of the [5] sense bases together with the three starting with the femininity faculty are faculty, in the sense of authority; the other [22 faculties] are non-faculty for the opposite reason [that is, because they do not exercise authority]". Cf. Abhidh-s VI. 7

15. Three kinds of matter

All matter is of three kinds, namely, clung-to kinds of matter (*upādiṇṇa-rūpa*), not-clung-to kinds of matter (*anupādiṇṇa-rūpa*), and differentiated kinds of matter (*vibhatta-rūpa*).[57]

Herein nine kinds of matter are clung-to—the eight faculties and the material basis—in the sense of being produced through the result of kamma (*kammavipāka*).

Nine kinds of matter are not-clung-to—the sense base of sounds, body intimation, speech intimation, lightness of matter, softness of matter, malleability of matter, ageing of matter, impermanence of matter, and torpor—in the sense of not being produced through the result of kamma.

The other twelve kinds of matter are differentiated in the sense of being both [clung-to and not-clung-to].

Furthermore, matter is of three kinds: visible (*sanidassana*) and with impact (*sappaṭigha*), invisible and with impact, and invisible and without impact.[58]

(Be 35,2; transl. in Bodhi 2007a: 245–46): *Pasāda-bhāva-jīvita-saṅkhataṃ aṭṭhavidham-pi indriyarūpaṃ itaraṃ anindriyarūpaṃ.*

57. As Skilling (1994: 189, n.2) suggests, the Chinese translation's 有壞, "perishable", is a mistranslation of *vibhatta*, "separated" or "distinct", or "divided", with the translator misinterpreting it as *vibhūta* or *vipatta*. In the Dhammasaṅgaṇī passage that this passage is related to (see below), these distinct matters are given as the "or whatever other matter there is, made of kamma, [i.e.] the sense base of forms, ... odours, ... tastes, ... touches, the space element, water element, growth of matter, continuity of matter, solid food—this is that matter that is clung to".

The Tibetan has *rnam par phye ba*, which corresponds to Sanskrit *vibhakta*. Instead of "produced through the result of kamma", = *kammavipākajā*, 業報所成, the Tibetan has "produced by kamma", = *kammajā*, *las las skyes pa*.

Dhs 146, § 652ff: *Cakkhāyatanaṃ sotāyatanaṃ ghānāyatanaṃ jivhāyatanaṃ kāyāyatanaṃ itthindriyaṃ purisindriyaṃ jīvitindriyaṃ, yaṃ vā panaññam-pi atthi rūpaṃ kammassa katattā rūpāyatanaṃ gandhāyatanaṃ rasāyatanaṃ phoṭṭhabbāyatanaṃ ākāsadhātu āpodhātu rūpassa upacayo rūpassa santati kabaḷīkāro āhāro—idaṃ taṃ rūpaṃ upādiṇṇaṃ. ... Saddāyatanaṃ kāyaviññatti vacīviññatti rūpassa lahutā rūpassa mudutā rūpassa kammaññatā rūpassa jaratā rūpassa aniccatā, yaṃ vā panaññam-pi atthi rūpaṃ na kammassa katattā rūpāyatanaṃ ... āhāro — idaṃ taṃ rūpaṃ anupādiṇṇaṃ. ...*

58. D III 217: *Tividhena rūpa-saṅgaho. Sanidassana-sappaṭighaṃ rūpaṃ, anidassana-sappaṭighaṃ rūpam, anidassana-appaṭighaṃ rūpaṃ.* Spk III 997: *Sanidassan' ādisu attānaṃ ārabbha pavattena cakkhu-viññāṇa-saṅkhātena saha nidassanenā ti sanidassanaṃ. Cakkhu-paṭihananasamatthato saha-paṭighenā ti sappaṭighaṃ. Tam atthato rūp'āyataṇam eva. Cakkhu-viññāṇa-saṅkhātaṃ nāssa nidassanan ti anidassanaṃ. Sot' ādi-paṭihananasamatthato saha-paṭighenā ti sappaṭighaṃ. Taṃ atthato cakkhāyatanan' ādīni nava āyatanāni. Vuttappakāraṃ nāssa nidassanan ti anidassanaṃ. Nāssa paṭigho ti appaṭighaṃ. Taṃ atthato ṭhapetvā das' āyatanāni avasesaṃ sukhuma-rūpaṃ.* Vism-mhṭ II 107: *Sanidassanakammajādīnaṃ*

Herein, one [kind of] matter is visible and with impact, that is, the sense base of forms, in the sense of being visible and being touchable.[59]

Eleven kinds of matter are invisible and with impact, that is, except the sense base of forms, [any] other coarse kinds of matter, in the sense of not being visible but being touchable.

Eighteen kinds of matter are invisible and without impact, that is, [any] other subtle kinds of matter, in the sense of not being visible and not being touchable.

16. Four kinds of matter

Furthermore, all matter is of four kinds, namely, matter as intrinsic nature (*sabhāva-rūpa*), matter as alteration (*vikāra-rūpa*), matter as characteristic (*lakkhaṇa-rūpa*), and matter as delimiting (*pariccheda-rūpa*).[60]

Herein nineteen kinds of matter are matter as intrinsic nature— the twelve coarse kinds of matter, the female faculty, male faculty, life faculty, water element, solid food, material basis, and torpor of matter—in the sense of being produced (*nipphanna*).[61]

Seven kinds of matter are matter as alteration, namely, body intimation, speech intimation, [**447b**] lightness of matter, softness of matter, malleability

---

tikānan-ti sanidassanattikassa, kammajādittikānañ-ca. Oḷārike ti dvādasavidhe oḷārikarūpe. Rūpan-ti rūpāyatanaṃ. Daṭṭhabbabhāvasaṅkhātena saha nidassanenā ti sanidassanaṃ, paṭihananabhāvasaṅkhātena saha paṭighenā ti sappaṭighaṃ ...

59. 可觸. The Tibetan has *gegs*, "impede, obstruct". The translation "touchable" is used here lacking any better term. The corresponding Pali term is probably *paṭihanana*, as in the commentary quoted in the preceding fn.

60. The translator apparently misunderstood *vikāra* as *viggaha* and rendered it as 形, "shape, physical appearance", but this is not in accordance with the explanation, as well as the Vism parallel, and the Tibetan translation's *rnam par 'gyur ba = vipariṇāma*. See Skilling 1994: 192–193 & 193 n. 3. Cf. Vism XIV.77/p.451: *Nipphannarūpaṃ panettha rūparūpaṃ nāma, ākāsadhātu paricchedarūpaṃ nāma, kāyaviññatti ādi kammaññatāpariyantaṃ vikārarūpaṃ nāma, jātijarābhaṅgaṃ lakkhaṇarūpaṃ nāmāti.* Cf. Abhidh-s 39: *Iti ca aṭṭhārasavidhampetaṃ rūpaṃ sabhāvarūpaṃ salakkhaṇarūpaṃ nipphannarūpaṃ rūparūpaṃ sammasanarūpan-ti ca saṅgahaṃ gacchati. Ākāsadhātu paricchedarūpaṃ nāma. Kāyaviññatti vacīviññatti viññattirūpaṃ nāma. Rūpassa lahutā mudutā kammaññatā viññattidvayaṃ vikārarūpaṃ nāma. Rūpassa upacayo santati jaratā aniccatā lakkhaṇarūpaṃ nāma.* Nāmar v. 556. *Iti lakkhaṇarūpaṃ tu, tividhaṃ bhinnakālikaṃ; Sabhāvarūpadhammesu, taṃtaṃkālopalakkhitaṃ.* 557. *Yena lakkhīyati rūpaṃ, bhinnākāraṃ khaṇe khaṇe; Vipassanānayatthāya, tamiccāha tathāgato.* 558. *Iccevaṃ saparicchedā, savikārā salakkhaṇā; Akicchā paṭivedhāya, dayāpannena tādinā.* 559. *Rūpadhammā sabhāvena, vijjamānā ti bhāsitā; Ajjhattikādibhedena, bahudhā bhijjare kathaṃ; ...*

61. Vism XIV.73: ... *sabhāveneva pariggahetabbato nipphannaṃ.* Vism XIV.77: *Nipphannarūpaṃ panettha rūparūpaṃ nāma ...*

of matter, growth of matter, and continuity of matter—in the sense of transforming matter as intrinsic nature.

Three [kinds of matter] are matter as characteristic—birth of matter, ageing of matter, and impermanence of matter—in the sense of characteristic of the conditioned (*saṅkhata*).[62]

One [kind of] matter is matter as delimiting—namely, the space element—in the sense of delimiting clusters. Herein, matter as intrinsic nature is delimited; the rest is not delimited.[63]

Thus, one should analyse through diversity.

17. Unity

Q. How should one analyse through unity?

A. [All matter is not a cause (*hetu*), is without a cause, is dissociated from a cause,][64] is with a condition, is conditioned, is mundane, is subject to

---

62. ... 以有為相義, lit. "in the sense of conditioned characteristic"; 有為 = *saṅkhata*. The Tibetan (181b) has: "In the sense of [characteristic of the] conditioned (*'dus byas kyi don* = *'dus byas kyi mtshan nyid kyi don?*), three are matter as characteristic (*mtshan nyid kyi gzugs*): birth of matter, ageing of matter, and impermanence of matter". Cf. Skilling 1994: 193. The birth, ageing, and impermanence of matter are equated here to the three characteristics of the conditioned (*saṅkhatalakkhaṇāni*), i.e. *jātirūpa* to *uppāda*, *rūpassa jaratā* to *ṭhitassa aññathatta*, and *rūpassa aniccatā* to *vaya*. Cf. Nāmar-p v. 28: *Nipphannaṃ rūparūpaṃ khaṃ, paricchedotha lakkhaṇaṃ; / Jāti-ādittayaṃ rūpaṃ, vikāro lahutādikaṃ. / Yathā saṅkhatadhammānaṃ, lakkhaṇaṃ saṅkhataṃ tathā; / Paricchedādikaṃ rūpaṃ, tajjātimanatikkamā. Paṭṭhānuddesadīpanīpāṭhā* p. 503: *Lakkhaṇarūpāni saṅkhatabhūtānaṃ rūpakalāpānaṃ saṅkhatabhāvajānanatthāya lakkhaṇamattattā kalāpamuttāni.*

63. Cf. Skilling 1994: 193–194. Cf. Nāmar-p v. 679: *Ākāsadhātu rūpānaṃ paricchedakalakkhaṇā; Taṃtaṃrūpakalāpānaṃ pariyanto ti vuccati.*

64. 一切色非因非無因因不相應, lit. "All matter is neither a cause nor without a cause [and] dissociated from cause ...." Tibetan (181b): "... is not without a cause (*rgyu med pa ma yin pa*), has a cause (*rgyu can* = *hetuka*), is dissociated (*mi ldan pa*), ...". Here the term *hetu* is used in a special sense which the Pali commentaries call *hetuhetu*, "cause-cause" or *mūlahetu*, "root-cause" (as *kusalahetu*, etc.), which the suttas call *kusala-* & *akusala-mūla*. The roots or causes are the non-greed, non-hatred, and non-delusion, and their opposites that give rise to wholesome, unwholesome, and indeterminate dhammas. Matter itself cannot be a karmic root-cause. *Hetu* in this sense is probably unique to the Theravāda Abhidhamma and therefore the Chinese and Tibetan translators did not understand it. Saṅghapāla also did not understand the parallel passage in the consciousness aggregate section at 448b20: "The six kinds of consciousness are not causes, are without [causes for their] arising", see fn. 1820.

See As 303 § 594 (on Dhs 133 § 594: *Sabbaṃ rūpaṃ na hetum-eva, ahetukam-eva, hetuvippayuttam-eva, ...*): *Na hetumevā ti sādhāraṇahetupaṭikkhepaniddeso. Tattha hetuhetu paccayahetu uttamahetu sādhāraṇahetūti catubbidho hetu. Tesu tayo kusalahetū,*

contaminations, subject to fetters, ties, torrents,[65] yokes hindrances, holding, clinging, and affliction, is indeterminate, is without object, is not a mental factor, is dissociated from mind, is restricted, connected to the sensuous sphere, is not fixed, is not leading out, is not accompanied by pleasure, is not accompanied by pain, is not accompanied by neither-pain-nor-pleasure, is neither accumulating nor disaccumulating, is neither training nor non-training, and is neither to be abandoned through seeing nor through contemplative practice (*bhāvanā*).[66]

---

tayo akusalahetū, tayo abyākatahetūti ayaṃ hetuhetu nāma. ... Imasmiṃ panatthe hetuhetu adhippeto.... As-mṭ 142: *Hetuhetūti mūlahetu, hetupaccayahetūti vā ayamattho.* As-anuṭ 150: *Yadi pi hino ti etena patiṭṭhāti kusalādiko dhammoti alobhādayo kevalaṃ hetupadavacanīyā, kāraṇabhāvasāmaññato pana mahābhūtādayo pi hetu-saddābhidheyyā ti mūlaṭṭhavācinā dutiyena hetu-saddena visesetvā āha hetuhetū ti. Suppatiṭṭhitabhāvasādhanato kusalādidhammānaṃ mūlatthena upakārakadhammā tayo kusalahetū ti ādinā paṭṭhāne ca te yeva hetupaccayo ti vuttā ti āha mūlahetu paccayahetū ti vā ayam-attho ti.* Dhs 242–43: § 1442: *... Alobho ... adoso ... amoho kiriyahetu, kāmāvacarakiriyato ahetuke cittuppāde ṭhapetvā, cattāro ñāṇavippayutte cittuppāde ṭhapetvā, tīsu bhūmīsu kiriyesu uppajjati— ime dhammā hetū.* 1442. ... *Ṭhapetvā hetū, catūsu bhūmīsu kusalaṃ, akusalaṃ, catūsu bhūmīsu vipāko, tīsu bhūmīsu kiriyābyākataṃ, rūpañ-ca, nibbānañca— ime dhammā na hetū.* ... 1444. ... *Vicikicchāsahagato moho, uddhaccasahagato moho, dvepañcaviññāṇāni, tisso ca manodhātuyo, pañca ca ahetukamanoviññāṇadhātuyo, rūpañ-ca, nibbānañca— ime dhammā ahetukā.* ... 1446. ... *Vicikicchāsahagato moho, ... nibbānañ-ca—ime dhammā hetuvippayuttā.* Vibh 63: ... *Rūpakkhandho ahetuko. Cattāro khandhā siyā sahetukā, siyā ahetukā. Rūpakkhandho hetuvippayutto. Cattāro khandhā siyā hetusampayuttā, siyā hetuvippayuttā. Rūpakkhandho na vattabbo hetu ceva sahetuko cā ti pi, sahetuko ceva na ca hetū ti pi. ... Rūpakkhandho na vattabbo hetu ceva hetusampayutto cā ti pi, hetusampayutto ceva na ca hetū ti pi. ... Rūpakkhandho na hetu ahetuko.* ... Dhs 188–190, § 1059: *Katame dhammā hetū? Tayo kusalahetū, tayo akusalahetū, tayo abyākatahetū, nava kāmāvacarahetū cha rūpāvacarahetū, cha arūpāvacarahetū, cha apariyāpannahetū.* 1060. *Tattha katame tayo kusalahetū? Alobho, adoso, amoho.* ... 1068. *Tattha katame tayo abyākatahetū? Kusalānaṃ vā dhammānaṃ vipākato kiriyābyākatesu vā dhammesu alobho adoso amoho ....*

65. The Tibetan translator misunderstood *oghaniya* as *moghaniya* "stupefying" or *mohaniya* "deluding", *rmongs par bya ba*, due to misinterpreting *ganthaniyamoghaniyaṃ* in the manuscript as *ganthaniya-moghaniyaṃ* instead of as *ganthaniyam-oghaniyaṃ*.

66. See Dhs 124–25, Vibh 12: *Sabbaṃ rūpaṃ na hetu, ahetukaṃ, hetuvippayuttaṃ, sappaccayaṃ, saṅkhataṃ, rūpiyaṃ, lokiyaṃ, sāsavaṃ, saṃyojaniyaṃ, ganthaniyaṃ, oghaniyaṃ, yoganiyaṃ, nīvaraṇiyaṃ, parāmaṭṭhaṃ, upādāniyaṃ, saṃkilesikaṃ, abyākataṃ, anārammaṇaṃ, acetasikaṃ, cittavippayuttaṃ, nevavipākanavipākadhammadhammaṃ, asaṃkiliṭṭhasaṃkilesikaṃ, na savitakkasavicāraṃ, na avitakkavicāramattaṃ, avitakka-avicāraṃ, na pītisahagataṃ, na sukhasahagataṃ, na upekkhāsahagataṃ, neva dassanena na bhāvanāya pahātabbaṃ, neva dassanena na bhāvanāya pahātabbahetukaṃ, neva ācayagāmi na apacayagāmi, nevasekkhanāsekkhaṃ, parittaṃ, kāmāvacaraṃ, na rūpāvacaraṃ, na arūpāvacaraṃ, pariyāpannaṃ, no apariyāpannaṃ, aniyataṃ, aniyyānikaṃ, uppannaṃ, chahi viññāṇehi viññeyyaṃ, aniccaṃ, jarābhibhūtaṃ.*

Thus, one should know in detail through unity.
This is called the aggregate of matter.

Aggregate of Feeling

18. What is the aggregate of feeling?

Q. What is the aggregate of feeling?

A. By way of characteristic, there is one feeling: the one experienced by the mind.[67]

By way of basis (*vatthu*), there are two feelings, namely, bodily feeling and mental feeling.

By way of intrinsic nature (*sabhāva*), there are three feelings, namely, pleasant feeling, painful feeling, and neither pleasant nor painful feeling.[68]

By way of states (*dhamma*), there are four feelings, namely, wholesome feelings, unwholesome feelings, resultant (*vipāka*) feelings, and functional (*kiriya*) feelings.

By way of faculties, there are five feelings, namely, pleasure faculty, pain faculty, joy faculty, distress faculty, and equanimity faculty.[69]

By way of black and white (*kaṇhasukka*) [kamma], there are six feelings, namely, pleasant feeling subject to contaminations (*sāsava*), pleasant feeling not subject to contaminations (*anāsava*), painful feeling subject to contaminations, painful feeling not subject to contaminations, neither pleasant nor painful feeling subject to contaminations, and neither pleasant nor painful feeling not subject to contaminations.[70]

---

67. Tibetan (Sav 182a): "... which is experienced (*anubhavana*) as the object of mind (*cittārammaṇa*)". Cf. Vism XIV.81 & 125: ... *yaṃ kiñci vedayitalakkhaṇaṃ, sabbaṃ taṃ ekato katvā vedanākkhandho; ....*

Vism-mhṭ II 255: *Vedanā anubhavanalakkhaṇato, lokiyasāsavādibhāvato ca ekavidhā.* Vism XIV.125/p.460: *Idāni yaṃ vuttaṃ yaṃ kiñci vedayitalakkhaṇaṃ, sabbaṃ taṃ ekato katvā vedanākkhandho veditabbo ti, etthā pi vedayitalakkhaṇaṃ nāma vedanāva. Yathāha vedayati vedayatī ti kho āvuso, tasmā vedanā ti vuccatī ti. Sā pana vedayitalakkhaṇena sabhāvato ekavidhā pi jātivasena tividhā hoti kusalā, akusalā, abyākatā cā ti.*

Sv-ṭ I 252: *Vedanānan-ti ettha vedanāggahaṇena avasiṭṭha-upādānakkhandhānam-pi saṅgaho khandhalakkhaṇena ekalakkhaṇattā.*

68. S IV 231–32: *Kāyikā ca cetasikā ca. Imā vuccanti bhikkhave dve vedanā. ... Sukhā vedanā dukkhā vedanā adukkhamasukhā vedanā. Imā vuccanti bhikkhave tisso vedanā.*

69. Ibid. 232: *Sukhindriyaṃ dukkhindriyaṃ somanassindriyaṃ domanassindriyaṃ upekkhindriyaṃ. Imā vuccanti bhikkhave pañca vedanā.*

70. Instead of *sāsava*, 有漏, and *nirāsava*, 無漏, the Tibetan (Sav 182a) has *zang zing dang bcas pa & zang zing med pa*, corresponding to *sāmisa & nirāmisa*, "worldly & non-worldly". Possibly Saṅghapāla did not find a satisfactory translation for *sāmisa &*

By way of sense door (*dvāra*),[71] there are seven feelings, namely, feeling born of eye contact, feeling born of ear-contact, feeling born of nose-contact, feeling born of tongue-contact, feeling born of body-contact, feeling born of mind-element contact, and feeling born of mind-consciousness-element contact.[72]

In detail, there are 108 feelings: six feelings [of joy] arisen dependent on desire [of the household-life] (*gehasita*);[73] six feelings [of joy] arisen dependent on renunciation (*nekkhammasita*); six feelings of distress arisen dependent on desire [of the household-life]; six feelings of distress arisen dependent on renunciation; six feelings of equanimity arisen dependent on desire [of the household-life]; and six feelings of equanimity arisen dependent on renunciation.[74] Six times six are thirty-six, and in the three divisions of time, three times thirty-six [are 108 feelings].

This is called the aggregate of feeling.

---

nirāmisa and chose 有漏, and 無漏, which according to DDB can also correspond to *samala & nimmala, lokika & lokuttara.*

71. Cf. Paṭis-a I 362, Nidd-a I 228: *Dvārato vedanā vuttā, cakkhusamphassajādikā; ...* Vibh-a 178: *Cakkhusamphassajāvedanā ti ādinā hi nayena pāḷiyaṃ imā cakkhusamphassajādikā dvārato chaḷeva vedanā vuttā.*

72. Cf. Vibh 15, etc.: *Sattavidhena vedanākkhandho: cakkhusamphassajā vedanā, sotasamphassajā vedanā, ghānasamphassajā vedanā, jivhāsamphassajā vedanā, kāyasamphassajā vedanā, manodhātusamphassajā vedanā, manoviññāṇadhātusamphassajā vedanā.*

73. The Pali term *geha* means "household-life", but in the Pali commentaries it is primarily taken as sensual desire, perhaps due to its similarity to *gedha*. The Chinese translation gives this latter sense, "dependent upon desire", 依愛, while the Tibetan has both senses, "dependent on desire/longing (*āsa*) of the household-life", *khyim gyi re ba la brten pa*. Cf. Sv-ṭ II 332: *Gehasitan-ti kāmaguṇanissitaṃ. Kāmaguṇā hi kāmarāgassa gehasadisattā idha gehan-ti adhippetā.* Ps V 21, Vibh-a 508: *Gehasitānī-ti kāmaguṇanissitāni.*

74. See also Ch. 8 § 16 & fn. 755. Cf. M III 216: *Chattiṃsa sattapadā veditabbā ti. ... Cha gehasitāni somanassāni, cha nekkhammasitāni somanassāni, cha gehasitāni domanassāni, cha nekkhammasitāni domanassāni, cha gehasitā upekkhā, cha nekkhammasitā upekkhā. Tattha katamāni cha gehasitāni somanassāni? Cakkhuviññeyyānaṃ rūpānaṃ iṭṭhānaṃ kantānaṃ manāpānaṃ manoramānaṃ lokāmisapaṭisaṃyuttānaṃ paṭilābhaṃ vā paṭilābhato samanupassato pubbe vā paṭiladdhapubbaṃ atītaṃ niruddhaṃ vipariṇataṃ samanussarato uppajjati somanassaṃ. ...* Cf. S IV 232: *Cha gehasitāni somanassāni, ... cha nekkhammasitā upekkhā, imā vuccanti ... chattiṃsa vedanā. Katamañ-ca ... aṭṭhasataṃ vedanā? Atītā chattiṃsa vedanā, anāgatā chattiṃsa vedanā, paccuppannā chattiṃsa vedanā ...* Cf. Vibh 381/§ 947. *Tattha katamāni cha gehasitāni somanassāni? Manāpiyesu rūpesu gehasitaṃ cetasikaṃ sātaṃ cetasikaṃ sukhaṃ cetosamphassajaṃ sātaṃ sukhaṃ vedayitaṃ cetosamphassajā sātā sukhā vedanā, ... Tattha katamāni cha gehasitāni domanassāni? Amanāpiyesu rūpesu gehasitaṃ cetasikaṃ asātaṃ ... dukkhā vedanā, ... Tattha katamā cha gehasitā upekkhā? Upekkhāṭṭhāniyesu rūpesu gehasitaṃ cetasikaṃ neva sātaṃ nāsātaṃ ...*

Aggregate of Perception

19. What is the aggregate of perception?

Q. What is the aggregate of perception?

A. By way of characteristic, there is one perception, [namely,] that which is known as object by the mind.[75]

By way of black and white, there are two perceptions, namely, inverted perception (*viparīta-saññā*) and non-inverted perception.

By way of unwholesomeness (*akusala*), there are three perceptions, namely, perception of sensual desire, perception of ill will, and perception of harming.

By way of wholesomeness (*kusala*), there are three perceptions, namely, perception of renunciation, perception of non-ill-will, and perception of non-harming.[76]

By way of the door of not knowing the grounds of selfhood,[77] there are four perceptions, [**447c**] namely, the perception of beauty in what is foul, the perception of happiness in what is suffering, the perception of permanence in what is impermanent, and the perception of self in what is without self.

By way of the door of knowing the grounds of selfhood, there are four perceptions, namely, perception of the foul, perception of suffering, perception of impermanence, and perception of without self.[78]

---

adukkhamasukhā vedanā, ... Cf. Sv III 775, Paṭis-a III 696, Ps I 279: *Sāmisaṃ vā sukhan-ti ādīsu sāmisā sukhā nāma pañcakāmaguṇāmisasannissitā cha gehasitasomanassavedanā. Nirāmisā sukhā nāma cha nekkhammasitasomanassavedanā. Sāmisā dukkhā nāma cha gehasitadomanassavedanā. Nirāmisā dukkhā nāma cha nekkhammasitadomanassavedanā. Sāmisā adukkhamasukhā nāma cha gehasita-upekkhāvedanā. Nirāmisā adukkhamasukhā nāma cha nekkhammasita-upekkhāvedanā.*

75. 以心知事. Tibetan: "that which is perceived as object by the mind". Cf. As 110: *Nīlādibhedaṃ ārammaṇaṃ sañjānātī ti saññā.* Abhidh-s 105: *Nīlādibhedaṃ ārammaṇaṃ sañjānāti saññaṃ katvā jānātī ti saññā, sā sañjānanalakkhaṇā.* M-a II 343: *Yaṃ sañjānātī ti yaṃ ārammaṇaṃ saññā sañjānāti, viññāṇam-pi tadeva vijānātī ti attho. ... Saññā hi nīlādivasena ārammaṇaṃ sañjānanamattam-eva, aniccaṃ dukkhaṃ anattā ti lakkhaṇapaṭivedhaṃ pāpetuṃ na sakkoti. Viññāṇaṃ nīlādivasena ārammaṇañceva sañjānāti, aniccādilakkhaṇapaṭivedhañ-ca pāpeti* ... Vism XIV.81 & 129: ... *yaṃkiñci sañjānanalakkhaṇaṃ, sabbaṃ taṃ ekato katvā saññākkhandho;* .... Vism-mhṭ II 112: *Nīlādibhedassa ārammaṇassa sañjānanaṃ, nīlaṃ pītaṃ dīghaṃ rassan-ti ca ādinā saññuppādavasena jānanaṃ gahaṇaṃ lakkhaṇaṃ etassā ti sañjānanalakkhaṇaṃ.*

76. D III 215: *Tisso akusala-saññā. Kāma-saññā, vyāpāda-saññā vihiṃsā saññā. Tisso kusala-saññā. Nekkhamma-saññā, avyāpāda-saññā, avihiṃsā-saññā.*

77. 以不知義性處門. The characters 義性處 correspond to *attabhāvavatthu*, a term only found in the *Peṭaka* and *Netti*; see Appendix V.

78. A II 52 and Paṭis II 79: *Anicce bhikkhave niccan ti saññāvipallāso cittavipallāso*

According to the Vinaya,[79] there are five perceptions: [perception of appropriateness (*kappiya*) with regard to the inappropriate, perception of inappropriateness with regard to the appropriate, perception of inappropriateness with regard to inappropriate, perception of appropriateness with regard to appropriate, and perception of doubt with regard to inappropriate and the appropriate.]

By way of object, there are six perceptions: perception of forms, perception of sounds, perception of odours, perception of tastes, perception of tangibles, and perception of mental states.[80]

By way of door, there are seven perceptions: perception born of eye contact, perception born of ear-contact, perception born of nose-contact, perception born of tongue-contact, perception born of body-contact, perception born of mind-element-contact, and perception born of mind-consciousness-element -contact.[81]

---

diṭṭhivipallāso, adukkhe bhikkhave dukkhan ti saññāvipallāso ..., anattani bhikkhave attā ti saññāvipallāso ..., asubhe bhikkhave subhan ti saññāvipallāso cittavipallāso diṭṭhivipallāso ... Anicce bhikkhave aniccan ti na saññāvipallāso ...

79. No statement like this can be found in the Pali Vinaya or in any other Pali texts. The most likely location of this kind of enumerative statement would be the Parivāra; so possibly Upatissa took it from the Parivāra of the Abhayagiri school, or an equivalent text.

The text is corrupt. It has "... five perceptions: the perception of beauty in what is foul, the perception of foulness in what is foul, the perception of foulness in what is beautiful, the perception of beauty in what is beautiful, and uncertain perception". The part on the four distortions is an intrusion from above. The Tibetan text (Sav 182b) instead has: "... (1) perception of appropriateness regarding the inappropriate, (2) perception of inappropriateness regarding the appropriate, (3) perception of inappropriateness regarding the inappropriate, (4) perception of appropriateness regarding the appropriate, (5) perception of doubt (*vimati*) regarding the inappropriate, and (6) perception of doubt regarding the appropriate". Probably the last two should be taken as one, i.e. perception of doubt regarding the inappropriate and appropriate. This concerns the appropriateness of the things that a monk accepts, uses, eats, etc., and the doubt about their appropriateness that he might have, for example, when a monk is uncertain (*vematika*) whether something is appropriate or allowable (*kappiya*), e.g. when he is uncertain whether something is money or not, but nevertheless accepts it and therefore falls into an offence. Cf. Dhs 205: *Tattha katamaṃ kukkuccaṃ? Akappiye kappiyasaññitā, kappiye akappiyasaññitā...* Vin V 118: *Apare pi dve puggalā bālā yo ca akappiye kappiyasaññī, yo ca kappiye akappiyasaññī. Dve puggalā paṇḍitā yo ca akappiye akappiyasaññī, yo ca kappiye kappiyasaññī.* Cf. A I 84.

80. Vibh 102, 104: *Rūpasaññā ... dhammasaññā loke piyarūpaṃ etth'esā taṇhā pahīyamānā pahīyati, ettha nirujjhamānā nirujjhati.*

81. The Tibetan has instead: "By way of elements (*khams kyi dbang gis* = *dhātuso*) there are seven kinds, ...".

Thus should the various kinds of perception be known.
This is called the aggregate of perception.[82]

Aggregate of Formations

20. What is the aggregate of formations?

Q. What is the aggregate of formations?
A. (1) Contact, (2) volition, (3) thinking, (4) exploring, (5) rapture, (6) faith, (7) energy, (8) mindfulness, (9) concentration, (10) wisdom, (11) life faculty, (12) restraining, (13) non-greed, (14) non-hate,[83] (15) conscience, (16) shame, (17) tranquillity, (18) motivation, (19) resolve, (20) equanimity, (21) attention, (22) greed, (23) hatred, (24) delusion, (25) conceit, (26) [wrong] views, (27) agitation, (28) worry, (29) doubt, (30) sloth, (31) consciencelessness, (32) shamelessness, and, except for feeling and perception, all [other] mental properties (*cetasika dhamma*)—[these] are the aggregate of formations.[84]

21. Meaning and similes

Herein: (1) Contact is the mind touching an object. It is like a sunbeam touching a wall.[85] Perception is its footing.

---

82. Cf. Vibh-a 19: *Cakkhusamphassajā saññā ti ādīni atītādivasena niddiṭṭha-saññaṃ sabhāvato dassetuṃ vuttāni. Tattha cakkhusamphassato, cakkhusamphassasmiṃ vā jātā cakkhusamphassajā nāma. Sesesu pi es'eva nayo. Ettha ca purimā pañca cakkhuppasādādivatthukā va. Manosamphassajā hadayavatthukā pi avatthukā pi. Sabbā catubhūmikā-saññā.*

83. The Tibetan (Sav 183a) adds *ma rmongs pa* = *amoha*, non-delusion, making a list of 33 items instead of 32.

84. Cf. Dhs 17, 27: *Phasso cetanā vitakko vicāro pīti cittassekaggatā saddhindriyaṃ vīriyindriyaṃ satindriyaṃ samādhindriyaṃ paññindriyaṃ jīvitindriyaṃ sammādiṭṭhi sammāsaṅkappo sammāvāyāmo sammāsati sammāsamādhi saddhābalaṃ vīriyabalaṃ satibalaṃ samādhibalaṃ paññābalaṃ hiribalaṃ ottappabalaṃ alobho adoso amoho anabhijjhā abyāpādo sammādiṭṭhi hirī ottappaṃ kāyapassaddhi cittapassaddhi kāyalahutā cittalahutā kāyamudutā cittamudutā kāyakammaññatā cittakammaññatā kāyapāguññatā cittapāguññatā kāyujukatā cittujukatā sati sampajaññaṃ samatho vipassanā paggāho avikkhepo; ye vā pana tasmiṃ samaye aññe pi atthi paṭiccasamuppannā arūpino dhammā ṭhapetvā vedanākkhandhaṃ ṭhapetvā saññākkhandhaṃ ṭhapetvā viññāṇakkhandhaṃ—ayaṃ tasmiṃ samaye saṅkhārakkhandho hoti.* Dhs 80: *Phasso cetanā vitakko vicāro pīti cittassekaggatā vīriyindriyaṃ samādhindriyaṃ jīvitindriyaṃ micchādiṭṭhi micchāsaṅkappo micchāvāyāmo micchāsamādhi vīriyabalaṃ samādhibalaṃ ahirikabalaṃ anottappabalaṃ lobho moho abhijjhā micchādiṭṭhi ahirikaṃ anottappaṃ samatho paggāho avikkhepo; ye vā pana ... saṅkhārakkhandho hoti ... pe ... ime dhammā akusalā.*

85. S II 103: *Seyyathā pi bhikkhave kuṭāgāraṃ vā kuṭāgārasālā vā uttarāya vā dakkhiṇāya vā pācīnāya vā vātapānā suriye uggacchante vātapānena rasmi pavisitvā kvāssa patiṭṭhitā ti? ...*

(2) Volition is mental activity.[86] It is like a house builder placing a foundation in the earth. The doors of kamma are its footing.[87]

(3) Thinking is verbal formation.[88] It is like mentally reciting discourses. Perception is its footing.

(4) Exploring is mental investigation of objects. It is like reflecting upon the meaning [of something].[89] Thinking is its footing.

(5) Rapture is mental gladness. It is like a man winning something. Exultation is its footing.[90]

---

86. 思者是心動. The character 動 usually corresponds to *iñjanā, calana, īraṇā, īhā, spanda* "movement, motion, activity", and the like (see DDB s.v. 動) and here could be an interpretation *vyāpāra/byāpāra*, "occupation, interest, action, activity, performance, concern" or of *vipphāra*, "pervasive force, intervention". Cf. Abhidh-av-pṭ v.77: *Cetanā cittavipphārā, sāyaṃ byāpāralakkhaṇā; Kammantāyūhanarasā, saṃvidhānan-ti gayhati.* Vism-mhṭ II 140: *Abhisandahati pabandhati pavatteti. Cetanābhāvo byāpārabhāvo. Āyūhanaṃ cetayanaṃ īriyanaṃ. Saṃvidahanaṃ vicāraṇaṃ.* See Ñāṇamoli, PoP, VI.42 fn. 6: "There seems to be an association of meaning between *vipphāra, vyāpāra, vipphandana, īhaka,* and *paripphandana* (perhaps also *ābhoga*) in the general senses of interestedness, activity, concern, interference, intervention, etc".

Vism XIV.135/p.463: *Cetayatī ti cetanā. Abhisandahatī ti attho. Sā cetanābhāvalakkhaṇā, āyūhanarasā, saṃvidahanapaccupaṭṭhānā sakiccaparakiccasādhikā ...*

87. 事門 literally means "object-door", *ārammaṇa-dvāra*, but this does not make sense. The character 事 here is in the sense of kamma or action (cf. 和合事, "proper acts", *sāmīcikamma* at 428c18, and 事非事, *kammākammāni*, "legal acts and non-legal acts" at 461b14, etc.) and 事門 corresponds to *kammadvāra*, "door of action". In Pali texts *cetanā* is said to proceed by way of the doors of action of the body, speech, and mind. As 82: *tīṇi kammadvārāni ... Kāyakammadvāraṃ, vacīkammadvāraṃ, manokammadvāran-ti.* Vibh-a 144: *... tāni tīṇi kammadvārāni dassento tattha katamo kāyasaṅkhāro? Kāyasañcetanā-ti ādim-āha. Tattha kāyasañcetanā ti kāyaviññattiṃ samuṭṭhāpetvā kāyadvārato pavattā aṭṭha kāmāvacarakusalacetanā ...* Dhs 110: *... Sā cetayitalakkhaṇā, cetanābhāvalakkhaṇā ti attho. Āyūhanarasā.*

88. The Ming edition reads "mental" 心 instead of "verbal" 口, but, given the simile of reciting discourses in the mind, and Pali explanations of *vitakkavicārā* as "verbal formation", 口 fits. Cf. M I 301, S IV 293: *Assāsapassāsā kho, āvuso visākha, kāyasaṅkhāro, vitakkavicārā vacīsaṅkhāro, saññā ca vedanā ca cittasaṅkhāro ti. ... ... Pubbe kho, āvuso visākha, vitakketvā vicāretvā pacchā vācaṃ bhindati, tasmā vitakkavicārā vacīsaṅkhāro.* Cf. Paṭis I 99: *Dutiyaṃ jhānaṃ samāpannassa vitakkavicārā vacīsaṅkhārā paṭippassaddhā honti.*

89. Cf. 415c15: "With thinking one thinks (*cinteti*); with exploring one reflects upon (*anucinteti*)".

90. A similar definition of rapture, as one of the first jhāna factors, in Ch. 8: "To please and to pervade are its salient characteristic; delight is its essential function; ...; exultation is its near cause".

(6) Faith[91] is mental clarity (*pasāda*). It is like a spell[92] for clearing water. The four factors of stream-entry[93] are its footing.[94]

(7) Energy is mental vigour. It is like a strong ox bearing a burden. The eight bases of application [of energy][95] are its footing.

(8) Mindfulness is guarding of mind.[96] It is like holding a bowl with oil.[97] The four establishments of mindfulness are its footing.[98]

(9) Concentration is one-pointedness of mind. It is like the [unflickering] flame of lamp inside a palace.[99] The four jhānas are its footing.[100]

(10) Wisdom is mental vision. It is like a man with eyes. The four noble truths are its footing.[101]

---

91. 心 = *citta* or *hadaya*, "mind", "heart", so in the enumeration above. The explanation, however, is in accordance with the explanation of *saddhā*, "faith", in Vism XIV.140/p.464. The Tibetan quotation has *dad* pa, which corresponds to *saddhā* or *pasāda*. The character 心 does not have the meaning of *saddhā* or *pasāda* elsewhere in Chinese.

92. Vism XIV.140 has "water-clearing gem": ...*sā saddahanalakkhaṇā, okappanalakkhaṇā vā, pasādanarasā udakappasādakamaṇi viya, pakkhandanarasā vā oghuttaraṇo viya.*

93. The four are: associating with good people, hearing the true Dhamma, reasoned attention, and practising the Dhamma in accordance with the Dhamma. See D III 227: *Cattāri sotāpattiyaṅgāni: sappurisasaṃsevo, saddhammassavanaṃ, yonisomanasikāro, dhammānudhammappaṭipatti.* Cf. Peṭ 128: *Avippaṭisāralakkhaṇā saddhā, saddahanā paccupaṭṭhānaṃ. Tassa cattāri sotāpattiyaṅgāni padaṭṭhānaṃ. Evañ-hi vuttaṃ bhagavatā saddhindriyaṃ bhikkhave, kuhiṃ daṭṭhabbaṃ, catūsu sotāpattiyaṅgesu kusalesu dhammesu.*

94. This section on the five faculties (*indriya*), i.e. items 6 to 10, is discussed in Hayashi 2003.

95. Peṭ 128: *Sūrā-apaṭikkhepanalakkhaṇaṃ vīriyindriyaṃ, vīriyindriyārambho paccupaṭṭhānaṃ. Tassa atītā cattāro sammappadhānā padaṭṭhānaṃ.* Cf. Hayashi 2003: 101. Vism XIV.137: 461. *Vīrabhāvo vīriyaṃ ... vīriyārambhavatthupadaṭṭhānaṃ vā, sammā āraddhaṃ sabbasampattīnaṃ mūlaṃ hotī ti daṭṭhabbaṃ.*

八事處 corresponds to the *aṭṭha ārambhavatthūni* of D III 256 & A IV 333: *Aṭṭha ārambhavatthūni. Idhāvuso, bhikkhunā kammaṃ kātabbaṃ hoti. Tassa evaṃ hoti kammaṃ kho me kātabbaṃ bhavissati, ...*

96. Vism XIV.144, Nidd-a 44: ... *Sā panesā apilāpanalakkhaṇā, asammosanarasā, ārakkhapaccupaṭṭhānā, ... cakkhudvārādīnaṃ rakkhaṇato dovāriko viya ca daṭṭhabbā.*

97. See S V 169. Cf. J 96: *Samatittikaṃ anavasekaṃ / telapattaṃ yathā parihareyya / Evaṃ sacittamanurakkhe / patthayāno disaṃ agatapubbanti.*

98. Peṭ 129–29: *Sati saraṇalakkhaṇā, asammohapaccupaṭṭhānā. Tassa atītā cattāro satipaṭṭhānā padaṭṭhānaṃ. Yathā vuttaṃ bhagavatā satindriyaṃ bhikkhave, kuhiṃ daṭṭhabbaṃ, catūsu satipaṭṭhānesu.*

99. This simile is also at Ch. 6 § 2/406c27. See fn. 476.

100. Peṭ 129–29: *Ekaggalakkhaṇo samādhi, avikkhepapaccupaṭṭhāno, tassa cattāri ñāṇāni padaṭṭhānaṃ. Yathā vuttaṃ bhagavatā samādhindriyaṃ, bhikkhave, kuhiṃ daṭṭhabbaṃ, catūsu jhānesu.*

101. Vism XIV.143, Nidd-a 57: *Pajānātī ti paññā. Kiṃ pajānāti? Idaṃ dukkhan-ti ādinā*

(11) Life faculty is life of immaterial things.[102] It is as water is to a lotus. Name-and-matter are its footing.

(12) Refraining (*nivāraṇa*)[103] is the mind abstaining from evil.[104] It is like a

---

nayena ariyasaccāni. Sā yathāsabhāvapaṭivedha-lakkhaṇā, akkhalitapaṭivedhalakkhaṇā vā kusalissāsakhitta-usupaṭivedho viya, visayobhāsanarasā padīpo viya, asammohapaccupaṭṭhānā araññagatasudesako viya. Th-a III 25: *dassanalakkhaṇaṃ paññan-ti.*

102. For the life faculty as a dependent matter see § 7. Cf. Vism XIV.138: *Taṃ hi rūpadhammānaṃ jīvitaṃ, idaṃ arūpadhammānan-ti.* Vibh 123: *... jīvitindriyaṃ duvidhena: ... Yo tesaṃ rūpīnaṃ dhammānaṃ āyu ... rūpajīvitindriyaṃ Yo tesaṃ arūpīnaṃ dhammānaṃ āyu ... arūpajīvitindriyaṃ.* Paṭis-a I 85: *... sabbacittasahajaṃ sahaja-arūpānupālanaṃ arūpajīvitindriyaṃ.*

103. Elsewhere in Vim 蓋 corresponds to *nīvaraṇa, āvaraṇa*, "hindrance, obstruction", but the Tibetan version has *sdom pa* = *saṃvara*, "restraint" (e.g., *so sor thar pa'i sdom pa* = *pātimokkha-saṃvara*). Since the corresponding Pāli words both contain the root √ *var*, probably the original had *nivāraṇa*, which was misunderstood as *nīvaraṇa*. Cf. PED s.v. *nivāraṇa* & *nivāreti*. Cf. Dhp-a III 4 (on Dhp 77 *pāpā cittaṃ nivāraye*): *Pāpā cittan-ti kāyaduccaritādipāpakammato vā akusalacittuppādato vā sabbathāmena cittaṃ nivāraye.* Sn-a I 269: *Yatatto, yasmā anuttarāya viratiyā sabbapāpehi uparatacitto ti vuttaṃ hoti.* Sn 104: *Yāni sotāni lokasmiṃ, sati tesaṃ nivāraṇaṃ; / Sotānaṃ saṃvaraṃ brūmi, paññāyete pidhiyyare.*

LC: "If this is not the equivalent of *virati*, then three path factors, i.e. right speech, action, and livelihood, will be impossible for Vim, since they are otherwise not in the list of *saṅkhāras*, as they are in Vism. That seems very unlikely. The position of a single *virati* is mentioned in Abhidh-av and attributed to the Abhayagirivāsins in the 12th century *ṭīkā*. Given that the Theriya tradition of the Mahāvihāra generally holds that there is a single *virati* in *lokuttara* skilful *citta*, it would not be a great step to hold the same for jhāna. This would imply *virati* from the hindrances. Since there are no *viratis* in *rūpāvacara citta*, this would have to be true for *upacārajhāna*. It could easily be extended to all *kusala-kāmāvacara-citta*. It would then be *niyata* and appropriate in this list of *cetasikas* which are *niyata*, i.e. necessarily present in one or more *cittuppāda*. The most obvious variation is the absence of the six pairs, but in the northern abhidharma systems we do meet a single *praśrabdhi* which is explained as possessing a number of the qualities associated with the six pairs. So perhaps it is not such a great difference. See: Abhidh-av p. 22: *Lakkhaṇādito pana etā tisso pi viratiyo kāyaduccaritādivatthūnaṃ avītikkamalakkhaṇā, kāyaduccaritādivatthuto saṅkocanarasā, akiriyapaccupaṭṭhānā, saddhāhiriottappa-appicchatādiguṇapadaṭṭhānā. Keci pana imāsu ekekaṃ niyataṃ viratiṃ icchanti.* Abhidh-av-ṭ I 311: *Kecī ti Abhayagirivāsino. Imāsū ti imāsu tīsu viratīsu. Ekekaṃ niyataṃ viratim icchantī ti aññaṃ ekaṃ catutthaniyataviratim icchanti. Atha vā niddhāraṇatthe bhummavasena imāsaṃ antare ekaṃ niyataṃ viratim icchantī ti attho. Ubhayathā pi pana tesaṃ icchā na yujjati aparāya viratiyā dhammasenāpatinā pi adesitattā, visayassa ca sadā sannihitattābhāvena niyatāya eva ekissā abhāvato. Ten'eva hi abhayagirivāsino yeva ca keci imāsaṃ tividhattaṃ aniyatattam eva ca icchanti. Vuttañ hi tehi: karuṇāmuditā sammāvācākammanta-ājivā yebhuyyato aniyatā honti gocarabhedato ti. Ettha pana yebhuyyato ti vacanaṃ lokuttaracittesu sabbadā ekato yeva ca labbhamānataṃ sandhāya vuttaṃ.*"

104. 心惡止離. Usually 惡 corresponds to *pāpa* but also to *akusala* and *dussīla*. When taken as two words 止離 means "stopping and avoiding/abstaining from". Cf. 400c09

man who wishes to live, avoiding poison.[105] The four jhānas are its footing.

(13) Non-greed is the mind giving up attachment. It is like being freed from a debt.[106] Renunciation (*nekkhamma*)[107] is its footing.

(14) Non-hatred is the mind without ill will.[108] It is [supple] like cat leather.[109] The four immeasurables are its footing.

(15) Conscience (*hiri*) is scrupulousness (*lajjā*) with regard to doing wrong. It is like detesting excrement and urine. Having oneself as authority (*attādhipateyyā*) is its footing.

(16) Shame (*ottappa*) is fear of doing wrong. It is like fearing a superior. Having the world as authority (*lokādhipateyyā*) is its footing.[110] [**448a**]

(17) Tranquillity is the stilling of movement of mind. It is like a man taking a bath in cool water in the heat of summer. Rapture is its footing.

(18) Motivation (*chanda*) is the desire to do good. It is like a faithful benefactor (*dāyaka*). The four bases of supernormal power (*iddhipāda*) are its footing.

(19) Resolve is the inclination of the mind. It is like water flowing down a slope. Thinking and exploring are its footing.

(20) Equanimity is the mind not being dejected or elated.[111] It is like a man holding a pair of scales [in balance]. The balancing of [the faculties of] energy [and so on][112] is its footing.

是戒能離惡, "that virtue avoids/abstains from evil/unwholesomeness".

105. Cf. Dhp V 123: *Visaṃ jīvitukāmo va, pāpāni parivajjaye*, and M II 260.

106. Peṭ 127: *Icchāpaṭisaṃharaṇalakkhaṇo alobho, tassa adinnādānā veramaṇī padaṭṭhānaṃ*. Cf. Hayashi 2003: 62. Cf. D I 69–72, M I 275:. ... *Seyyathā pi ... āṇaṇyaṃ yathā ārogyaṃ yathā bandhanāmokkhaṃ yathā bhujissaṃ yathā khemantabhūmiṃ; evam-eva bhikkhu ime pañca nīvaraṇe pahīne attani samanupassati*. A III 354: *Asokaṃ virajaṃ khemaṃ, etaṃ āṇaṇyamuttaman-ti*.

107. Cf. Peṭ 121: *Attāsayavañcanālakkhaṇo lobho, tassa adinnādānaṃ padaṭṭhānaṃ*. Cf. Hayashi 2003: 62 and p. 75 note 20.

108. Cf. Peṭ 121: *Abyāpādalakkhaṇo adoso*.

109. Cf. M I 128–29: ... *sabbāvantaṃ lokaṃ biḷārabhastāsamena cetasā vipulena mahaggatena appamāṇena averena abyāpajjhena pharitvā viharissāmā ti*. Th 1138: *biḷārabhastaṃ va yathā sumadditaṃ*.

110. Spk III 978: *Hirī ca ottappañ cā ti yaṃ hiriyati hiriyitabbena ottappati ottappitabbenā ti evaṃ vitthāritāni hiri-ottappāni. Api c' ettha ajjhatta-samuṭṭhānā hirī, bahiddhā samuṭṭhānaṃ ottappaṃ. Attādhipateyyā hirī, lokādhipateyyaṃ ottappaṃ. Lajjā sabhāva-saṇṭhitā hirī, bhaya-sabhāva-saṇṭhitaṃ ottappaṃ*.

111. 不去來 "not going away and coming" can correspond to gatāga, but here probably to *onata-unnata*, "dejected and elated". Cf. Spk III 121: *Upekkhā dhurasamādhīti ... unnatonatākārassa abhāvena dvinnam-pi yugapadesānaṃ samatā ti attho*; Th 662: *Unnatā sukhadhammena, dukkhadhammena conatā ...*; A IV 282: ... *tulādhāro ... tulaṃ paggahetvā jānāti ettakena vā onataṃ ... unnatan-ti*.

112. 彼精進等足處. The character 等 usually denotes "etcetera" in Vim but is also used for 等, "evenness", *samatta*. Cf. "the one who maintains the mind and mental

(21) Attention is the regulating of the mind.[113] It is like a man holding a rudder. Wholesomeness and unwholesomeness are its footing.

(22) Greed is mental attachment. It is like a goose.[114] Lovable and desirable forms are its footing.[115]

(23) Hatred is mental irritation. It is like an angry viper. The ten grounds for anger[116] are its footing.

(24) Delusion is the mind without vision. It is like a blind man.[117] The four distortions (*vipallāsa*) are its footing.[118]

(25) Conceit (*māna*) is haughtiness of mind. It is like wrestling.[119] The three kinds [of conceit][120] are its footing.

(26) [Wrong] views (*diṭṭhi*) is grasping of the mind. It is like the blind men stroking the elephant.[121] The utterance of another [person] and unreasoned attention[122] are its footing.

(27) Agitation is non-stillness of mind. It is like water that is boiling.[123] Overly exerted energy (*accāraddhaviriya*) is its footing.

---

properties evenly and [maintains] the means for concentration evenly, like the hand holding a pair of scales" at 407a05.

113. 作意者是心令起法則, lit. "Attention is the mind giving rise to dhamma-regularity".

114. 鵝鳥 = *haṃsa*, "goose". A gosling becomes attached or "fixed" to the first large moving creature it sees when it hatches and will follow it. When it sees a human instead of the parent, it will follow the human. The goose is also known for its lifelong fidelity to its partner.

115. Peṭ 121: *Ajjhosānalakkhaṇā taṇhā, tassā piyarūpasātarūpaṃ padaṭṭhānaṃ. Attāsayavañcanālakkhaṇo lobho, tassa adinnādānaṃ padaṭṭhānaṃ.*

116. *Dasa āghātavatthūni*. See fn. 809.

117. It 84: *Mūḷho atthaṃ na jānāti, mūḷho dhammaṃ na passati, / Andhaṃ tamaṃ tadā hoti, yaṃ moho sahate naraṃ.*

118. Peṭ 121: *andhakāratimisā appaṭivedhalakkhaṇā avijjā, tassā vipallāsapadaṭṭhānaṃ.*

119. 如共相撲, or lit. "like wrestling together". This would refer to wrestling an opponent to a lower position and gain and maintain a superior position oneself.

Cf. As 255: *Tattha maññatī ti māno. So unnatilakkhaṇo, sampaggaharaso, ketukamyatāpaccupaṭṭhāno, diṭṭhivippayuttalobhapadaṭṭhāno, ummādo viya daṭṭhabboti.*

120. A III 444: ... *tayo mānā pahātabbā? Māno, omāno, atimāno.* Nidd I 79: *Tividhena māno: seyyohamasmī ti māno, sadisohamasmī ti māno, hīnohamasmī ti māno.*

121. Ud 68: *Tena hi bhaṇe jaccandhānaṃ hatthiṃ dassehī ti. ... Yehi bhikkhave jaccandhehi hatthissa sīsaṃ diṭṭhaṃ ahosi, te evam āhaṃsu: ediso deva hatthī seyyathā pi kumbho 'ti ...* Ud-a 341: *yathā ekeko jaccandho sīsādikaṃ ekekaṃ yeva hatthissa aṅgaṃ phusitvā hatthī mayā diṭṭho ti saññaṃ uppādesi, tathā karohī ti.*

122. Cf. Ch. I § 13/400a10. See fn. 194. Cf. A I 87, M I 294: *Dve me bhikkhave paccayā micchādiṭṭhiyā. Katame dve? Parato ghoso, ayoniso ca manasikāro.*

123. Cf. SN 46:55/S V 122f.

(28) Worry is mental decline. It is like desiring the foul. The falling away from goodness through doing evil is its footing.[124]

(29) Doubt is the grasping of the mind to various [views]. It is like a man travelling to a distant land who is confused at a junction of two roads.[125] Unreasoned attention (*ayoniso manasikāra*) is its footing.

(30) Sloth is indolence and sluggishness of the mind. It is like a torpid viper. The eight grounds of laziness[126] are its footing.

(31) Consciencelessness is the mind having no scruples with regard to doing wrong. It is like an outcaste (*caṇḍāla*). Irreverence is its footing.[127]

(32) Shamelessness is the mind's non-fear of doing wrong. It is like a wicked king. The six [kinds of] irreverence are its footing.[128]

This is called the aggregate of formations.

---

124. In the enumeration at the start of this section there is戲 ("play"), which elsewhere in Vim and Chinese Buddhist texts is used for *kela*, "merriment", "unsettledness", while here there is悔, which corresponds to *kukkucca*. At Ch. 8 § 23/p.416b20, the definition of the latter is "'worry': This is vexation of mind, non-concentration", 悔者心恨不定.

125. S III 108–9: *Dvidhāpatho ti kho Tissa vicikicchāyetaṃ adhivacanaṃ. Vāmamaggo ti kho Tissa aṭṭhaṅgikassetaṃ micchāmaggassa adhivacanaṃ, seyyathīdaṃ micchādiṭṭhiyā ... micchāsamādhissa. Dakkhiṇamaggo ti kho Tissa ariyassetaṃ aṭṭhaṅgikassa maggassa adhivacanaṃ, ...*

126. *Aṭṭha kusītavatthūni*, A IV 331–33, D III 255f. 懈怠 is used for the hindrance of *thīna* at 416b09, etc.

127. Outcastes, or dalits, do dirty jobs such as removing excrement and dead animals from Indian towns and are therefore considered as not being ashamed of touching dirty things. In other Pali texts *ahiri* is likened to a shameless village pig and *anotappa* to a reckless moth flying into a fire. Abhidh-av-pṭ I 315: *Tesu hi alajjanākārena pāpānaṃ karaṇarasaṃ ahirikaṃ. Anuttāsākārena anottappaṃ. Vuttappakāreneva pāpato asaṅkocanapaccupaṭṭhānāni attani, paresu ca agāravapadaṭṭhānāni. Gāmasūkarassa viya asucito kilesāsucito ajigucchanaṃ ahirikena hoti. Salabhassa viya aggito pāpato anuttāso anottappena hoti.* Cf. Vism-mhṭ II 149.

128. See D III 243: *Cha agāravā. Idhāvuso, bhikkhu satthari ... dhamme ... saṅghe ... sikkhāya ... appamāde ... paṭisanthāre agāravo viharati appatisso.*

Aggregate of Consciousness

22. What is the aggregate of consciousness?

Q. What is the aggregate of consciousness?

A. It is eye-consciousness, ear-consciousness, nose-consciousness, tongue-consciousness, body-consciousness, mind-element, and mind-consciousness-element.[129]

Herein, eye-consciousness: dependent upon the condition of eye and forms,[130] consciousness is produced—this is called eye-consciousness.

Ear-consciousness: dependent upon the condition of ear and sounds, consciousness is produced—this is called ear-consciousness.

Nose-consciousness: dependent upon the condition of nose and odours, consciousness is produced—this is called nose-consciousness.

Tongue-consciousness: dependent upon the condition of tongue and flavours, consciousness is produced—this is called tongue-consciousness.

Body-consciousness: dependent upon the condition of body and tangibles, consciousness is produced—this is called body-consciousness.[131]

Mind-element: dependent upon the [material] base (*vatthu*) and the five [sense] objects (*ārammaṇa*), dependent upon [these] two objects [are] the five consciousnesses, immediately before and after [these five], consciousness is produced—this is called mind-element.[132]

Mind-consciousness-element: putting aside these six kinds of consciousness, the remaining mind (*citta*)—this is called mind-consciousness-element.[133]

---

129. For the last two items, the Tibetan text has mind faculty, *manindriya*, and mind-consciousness, *manoviññāṇa: yid kyi dbang po dang yid kyi rnam par shes pa.*

130. 依眼緣色生識. Probably 依 & 緣 simply express *paṭicca* "dependent upon" or *paccayā* "with ... as condition" rather than *paccayaṃ paṭicca* "dependent upon the condition of ...".

131. Cf. M I 260: *Yaṃ yadeva ... paccayaṃ paṭicca uppajjati viññāṇaṃ, tena teneva viññāṇaṃ tveva saṅkhyaṃ gacchati. Cakkhuñca paṭicca rūpe ca uppajjati viññāṇaṃ, cakkhuviññāṇaṃ tveva saṅkhyaṃ gacchati; ... manañ-ca paṭicca dhamme ca uppajjati viññāṇaṃ, manoviññāṇaṃ tveva saṅkhyaṃ gacchati.*

132. 意界者依處五事依二事五識若前後次第生識此謂意界. Supposedly this refers to the mind-consciousness arising immediately after the cessation of the sense-consciousnesses; see Ch. 11 § 37–38. Cf. Vibh 89: *Cakkhuviññāṇadhātuyā ... kāyaviññāṇadhātuyā uppajjitvā niruddhasamanantarā uppajjati cittaṃ mano ... viññāṇakkhandho tajjāmanodhātu sabbadhammesu vā pana paṭhamasamannāhāro uppajjati cittaṃ ... tajjāmanodhātu ayaṃ vuccati manodhātu.*

133. Yam I 199: *Manodhātuṃ ṭhapetvā avaseso mano, na manodhātu. Manodhātu mano ceva manodhātu ca.* Spk II 131: *sabbam-pi manoviññāṇaṃ manoviññāṇadhātū ti.* Dhs 209, 253: *Cakkhuviññāṇaṃ, sotaviññāṇaṃ, ghānaviññāṇaṃ, jivhāviññāṇaṃ, kāyaviññāṇaṃ,*

23. Three ways of knowing consciousness

These seven kinds of consciousness should be known in detail in three ways: through bases (*vatthu*) and objects (*ārammaṇa*), and through objects and through states (*dhamma*).

24. Bases and objects

Q. How [should it be known] through bases (*vatthu*) and objects (*ārammaṇa*)?
A. The five kinds of consciousness have different bases and different objects. The mind-element and mind-consciousness-element are one as to basis.[134]

Five-fold is the object of mind-element; six-fold is the object of mind-consciousness-element.

Five kinds of consciousness are internal as to state; internal as to basis; external as to object.[135] [**448b**]

Mind-element is internal as to state; external as to basis and object.

Mind-consciousness-element is internal as to state; external as to basis; internal and external as to object.

The six kinds of consciousness have a pre-arising basis and have a pre-arising object.[136]

A. the moment of [name-and-matter] entering the body (*okkantikkhaṇa*), the mind-consciousness-element has a co-arising condition.[137]

---

manodhātu, manoviññāṇadhātu—ime dhammā cittā.

134. Vibh 319: *Asambhinnavatthukā, asambhinnārammaṇā ti asambhinnasmiṃ vatthusmiṃ asambhinne ārammaṇe uppajjanti. Nānāvatthukā nānārammaṇā ti aññaṃ cakkhuviññāṇassa vatthu ca ārammaṇañ-ca,..., aññaṃ kāyaviññāṇassa vatthu ca ārammaṇañ-ca. Na aññamaññassa gocaravisayaṃ paccanubhontī ti cakkhuviññāṇassa gocaravisayaṃ sotaviññāṇaṃ na paccanubhoti, sotaviññāṇassa gocaravisayam-pi cakkhuviññāṇaṃ na paccanubhoti. ...* Cf. S V 217/M I 295: *Pañcimāni ... indriyāni nānāvisayāni nānāgocarāni na aññamaññassa gocaravisayaṃ paccanubhonti. ... Cakkhundriyaṃ, sotindriyaṃ, ghānindriyaṃ, jivhindriyaṃ, kāyindriyaṃ. Imesaṃ kho, brāhmaṇa, pañcannaṃ indriyānaṃ nānāvisayānaṃ nānāgocarānaṃ na aññamaññassa gocaravisayaṃ paccanubhontānaṃ mano paṭisaraṇaṃ, mano'va nesaṃ gocaravisayaṃ paccanubhotī ti.*

135. Vibh 319, § 762: *Ajjhattikavatthukā, bāhirārammaṇā ti pañcannaṃ viññāṇānaṃ vatthu ajjhattikā ārammaṇā bāhirā.*

136. Vibh 319, § 762: *Purejātavatthukā, purejātārammaṇā ti purejātasmiṃ vatthusmiṃ purejāte ārammaṇe uppajjanti.* Vibh-a 403: *Purejātavatthukā purejātārammaṇā ti sahuppattipaṭikkhepo. Na hi te sahuppannaṃ vatthuṃ vā ārammaṇaṃ vā paṭicca uppajjanti, sayaṃ pana pacchājātā hutvā purejātesu vatthārammaṇesu uppajjanti.*

137. 意識界於入體剎那共生處. Cf. Paṭṭh I.4/§ 6: *Sahajātapaccayo ti cattāro khandhā arūpino aññamaññaṃ sahajātapaccayena paccayo. Cattāro mahābhūtā aññamaññaṃ sahajātapaccayena paccayo. Okkantikkhaṇe nāmarūpaṃ aññamaññaṃ sahajātapaccayena paccayo.* Cf. Vism XIV.60/p.447: *Manodhātumanoviññāṇadhātūnaṃ*

In the immaterial [sphere, the mind-consciousness-element] has no pre-arising basis and [material] objects at all.[138]

Thus should it be known through bases and objects.

25. Objects

Q. How [should it be known] through objects?

A. Each of the five kinds of consciousness has its [own] domain. They are not produced one by one, in succession; they are not produced simultaneously; they arise unmixed.[139]

---

nissayalakkhaṇaṃ hadayavatthu, tāsaññeva dhātūnaṃ ādhāraṇarasaṃ, ... manodhātumanoviññāṇadhātūnañceva taṃsampayuttadhammānañ-ca vatthubhāvaṃ sādhayamānaṃ tiṭṭhati.

138. 初以生處於無色有無處一切事, lit. ""pre-/first through arising basis, in immaterial(s) have without basis all objects". The first clause 初以生處 presumably is to be read as 以初生處 "through/with/on account of pre-arising basis". The passage appears corrupt. At rebirth the material basis is kamma-produced and arises together with the four mental aggregates and therefore these cannot have a pre-arising condition. In the *āruppadhātu* beings have objects, i.e. their own and others' mental states, but there is also no pre-arising condition.

Paṭṭh-a 414/§ 61: *Purejātapaccaye vatthuṃ purejātapaccayā ti vatthuṃ paṭicca vatthunā purejātapaccayataṃ sādhentena uppajjantī ti attho. Vipākābyākataṃ ekaṃ khandhan-ti ettha yaṃ vipākābyākatassa vatthu okkantikkhaṇe sahajātapaccayo hoti, taṃ purejātapaccayabhājaniyattā idha na gahetabbaṃ. Ye pi kusalādayo āruppe purejātapaccayaṃ na labhanti, tepi purejātapaccayabhājaniyato yeva idha na gahetabbā. Ārammaṇaṃ pana niyamato purejātapaccayabhāvaṃ na labhati. Rūpāyatanādīni hi cakkhuviññāṇādīnaṃ yeva purejātapaccayataṃ sādhenti, manoviññāṇadhātuyā atītānāgatāni pi ārammaṇaṃ honti yeva. Tasmā idha na gahitaṃ.* Paṭṭh-a 370/§ 10: *Okkantikkhaṇe ti pañcavokārabhave paṭisandhikkhaṇe. Tasmiñ-hi khaṇe nāmarūpaṃ okkantaṃ viya pakkhandantaṃ viya paralokato imaṃ lokaṃ āgantvā pavisantaṃ viya uppajjati, tasmā so khaṇo okkantikkhaṇo ti vuccati. Ettha ca rūpan-ti hadayavatthumattam-eva adhippetaṃ. Tañ-hi nāmassa, nāmañ-ca tassa aññamaññaṃ sahajātapaccayaṭṭhaṃ pharati. Cittacetasikā ti pavattiyaṃ cattāro khandhā. ... Rūpino dhammā arūpīnaṃ dhammānan-ti hadayavatthu catunnaṃ khandhānaṃ. ... Sahajātapaccayenā ti paṭisandhiṃ sandhāya vuttaṃ. ...* Paṭṭh I.4/§ 6: *Cittacetasikā dhammā cittasamuṭṭhānānaṃ rūpānaṃ sahajātapaccayena paccayo. Mahābhūtā upādārūpānaṃ sahajātapaccayena paccayo. Rūpino dhammā arūpīnaṃ dhammānaṃ kiñci kāle sahajātapaccayena paccayo, kiñci kāle na sahajātapaccayena paccayo.* Paṭṭh I.6/§ 10: *Yaṃ rūpaṃ nissāya manodhātu ca manoviññāṇadhātu ca vattanti, taṃ rūpaṃ manodhātuyā taṃsampayuttakānañ-ca dhammānaṃ purejātapaccayena paccayo. Manoviññāṇadhātuyā taṃsampayuttakānañ-ca dhammānaṃ kiñci kāle purejātapaccayena paccayo, kiñci kāle na purejātapaccayena paccayo.*

139. Vibh 319, § 762: *Asambhinnavatthukā, asambhinnārammaṇā ti asambhinnasmiṃ vatthusmiṃ asambhinne ārammaṇe uppajjanti. Na apubbaṃ acarimaṃ uppajjantī ti na ekakkhaṇe uppajjanti.* Dhs §764: *na abbokiṇṇā uppajjantī ti na paṭipāṭiyā uppajjanti. Na*

Through the five kinds of consciousness, no state whatever is known, except the first instance.[140]

Through the mind-element, no state whatever is known; except [that to which] the mind is adverting.[141]

Through the six kinds of consciousness, there is no establishing of postures whatever;[142] through activation (*javana*), there is the establishing of them.[143]

Through the six kinds of consciousness there is no initiation of bodily and verbal kamma;[144] [through activation, these are initiated].

Through the six kinds of consciousness, there is no undertaking of wholesome and unwholesome states;[145] through activation, these are undertaken.

Through the six kinds of consciousness, one does not enter upon [an attainment] or emerge from [an attainment];[146] through activation, one enters upon and through the *bhavaṅga*, one emerges from.

---

apubbaṃ acarimaṃ uppajjantī ti na ekakkhaṇe uppajjanti.

140. Vibh 320, § 766: *Pañcahi viññāṇehi na kañci dhammaṃ paṭivijānātī ti pañcahi viññāṇehi na kañci dhammaṃ paṭivijānāti. Aññatra abhinipātamattā ti aññatra āpāthamattā.* Vibh-a 405: *Na kañci dhammaṃ paṭivijānātī ti manopubbaṅgamā dhammā ti evaṃ vuttaṃ ekam-pi kusalaṃ vā akusalaṃ vā na paṭivijānāti. Aññatra abhinipātamattā ti ṭhapetvā rūpādīnaṃ abhinipātamattaṃ. ...*

The Vim has 初起, which would correspond to *paṭhamābhinipāta*; cf. As 107: *Kasmā panettha phassova paṭhamaṃ vutto ti? Cittassa paṭhamābhinipātattā. Ārammaṇasmiñhi cittassa paṭhamābhinipāto hutvā phasso ārammaṇaṃ phusamāno uppajjati, tasmā paṭhamaṃ vutto. Phassena pana phusitvā vedanāya vedayati, saññāya sañjānāti, cetanāya ceteti. ....* Sv 722 ... *tasmiṃ ārammaṇe cittacetasikānaṃ paṭhamābhinipāto taṃ ārammaṇaṃ phusanto uppajjamāno phasso ...*

141. 意轉, *mano āvajjana* or *mano pavattana*, "which proceed in the mind". Cf. Vibh 320, § 766: *Pañcannaṃ viññāṇānaṃ samanantarā pi na kañci dhammaṃ paṭivijānātī ti pañcannaṃ viññāṇānaṃ samanantarā manodhātuyā pi na kañci dhammaṃ paṭivijānāti.*

142. Vibh 321, § 766: *Pañcahi viññāṇehi na kañci iriyāpathaṃ kappetī ti pañcahi viññāṇehi na kañci iriyāpathaṃ kappeti—gamanaṃ vā ṭhānaṃ vā nisajjaṃ vā seyyaṃ vā. Pañcannaṃ viññāṇānaṃ samanantarā pi na kañci iriyāpathaṃ kappetī ti pañcannaṃ viññāṇānaṃ samanantarā manodhātuyā pi na kañci iriyāpathaṃ kappeti—gamanaṃ vā ṭhānaṃ vā nisajjaṃ vā seyyaṃ vā.*

143. Vibh-a 405: *Na hi pañcadvārikajavanena ... sabbo pi panesa pabhedo manodvārikajavane yeva labbhati.*

144. Vibh 321, § 766: *Pañcahi viññāṇehi na kāyakammaṃ na vacīkammaṃ paṭṭhapetī ti pañcahi viññāṇehi na kāyakammaṃ na vacīkammaṃ paṭṭhapeti. ... paṭṭhapetī ti pañcannaṃ viññāṇānaṃ samanantarā manodhātuyā pi na kāyakammaṃ na vacīkammaṃ paṭṭhapeti.*

145. Vibh 321, § 766: *Pañcahi viññāṇehi na kusalākusalaṃ dhammaṃ samādiyatī ti pañcahi viññāṇehi na kusalākusalaṃ dhammaṃ samādiyati. ... samādiyatī ti pañcannaṃ viññāṇānaṃ samanantarā manodhātuyā pi na kusalākusalaṃ dhammaṃ samādiyati.*

146. Vibh 321, § 766: *Pañcahi viññāṇehi na samāpajjati na vuṭṭhātī ti pañcahi viññāṇehi na*

Through the six kinds of consciousness, there is no passing away or arising;[147] through the *bhavaṅga* or through the object there is passing away.

Through result (*vipāka*), mind-consciousness-element is produced.[148]

Through the six kinds of consciousness, one does not sleep, awake, or see dreams;[149] through the *bhavaṅga,* one sleeps; through the mind's adverting one awakens; through activation, one sees dreams.[150]

Thus should it be known through objects.

26. States

Q. How [should it be known] through states?

A. The five kinds of consciousness are with[out][151] thinking and exploring. The mind-element is with thinking and exploring. The mind-consciousness-element is with either thinking or exploring, without thinking and with a slight degree of exploring, or without thinking and exploring.

The five kinds of consciousness are accompanied by equanimity. Body-consciousness is accompanied either by pleasure or by pain. The mind-consciousness-element is accompanied by joy, distress, or equanimity.

---

samāpajjati na vuṭṭhāti. ... vuṭṭhātī ti pañcannaṃ viññāṇānaṃ samanantarā manodhātuyā pi na samāpajjati na vuṭṭhāti.

147. Vibh 321, § 766: *Pañcahi viññāṇehi na cavati na uppajjatī ti pañcahi viññāṇehi na cavati na uppajjati. ... uppajjatī ti pañcannaṃ viññāṇānaṃ samanantarā manodhātuyā pi na cavati na uppajjati.*

148. *Paṭisandhi* and *cuti* are resultant mind-consciousness-element.

149. Vibh 321, § 766: *Pañcahi viññāṇehi na supati na paṭibujjhati na supinaṃ passatī ti pañcahi viññāṇehi na supati na paṭibujjhati na supinaṃ passati. ... passatī ti pañcannaṃ viññāṇānaṃ samanantarā manodhātuyāpi na supati na paṭibujjhati na supinaṃ passati.*

150. Vibh-a 405: *...na kiñca supinaṃ passatī ti imesu tīsu ṭhānesu saha javanena vīthicittaṃ paṭikkhittaṃ. ... Tena cittena ñatvā kiṃ ayaṃ imasmiṃ ṭhāne āloko ti jānāti.*

Cf. Vibh-a 406: *Na supati na paṭibujjhati na supinaṃ passatī ti sabbenāpi ca pañcadvārikacittena neva niddaṃ okkamati, na niddāyati, na paṭibujjhati, na kiñca supinaṃ passatī ti imesu tīsu ṭhānesu saha javanena vīthicittaṃ paṭikkhittaṃ. Niddāyantassa hi mahāvaṭṭiṃ jāletvā dīpe cakkhusamīpe upanīte paṭhamaṃ cakkhudvārikaṃ āvajjanaṃ bhavaṅgaṃ na āvaṭṭeti, manodvārikam-eva āvaṭṭeti. Atha javanaṃ javitvā bhavaṅgaṃ otarati. Dutiyavāre cakkhudvārikaṃ āvajjanaṃ bhavaṅgaṃ āvaṭṭeti. Tato cakkhuviññāṇādīni javanapariyosānāni pavattanti. Tadanantaraṃ bhavaṅgaṃ pavattati. Tatiyavāre manodvārika-āvajjanena bhavaṅge āvaṭṭite manodvārikajavanaṃ javati. Tena cittena ñatvā 'kiṃ ayaṃ imasmiṃ ṭhāne āloko'ti jānāti. ... ...*

151. LC: "It should be 'without thinking and exploring'. Perhaps the translator has made an error because *vitakka* and *vicāra* do accompany the five sense *viññāṇa* (in a very weak form) in the northern abhidharma systems. The original must have had 'without' because otherwise it could have simply referred to the 'six kinds of consciousness' as elsewhere".

The five kinds of consciousness are resultant. The mind-element is either resultant or functional (*kiriya*). Mind-consciousness-element is either wholesome, unwholesome, or resultant-functional.

The six kinds of consciousness are not causes, are without [causes for their] arising,[152] are mundane states, subject to contaminations, are subject to fetters, ties, torrents, yokes, hindrances, to holding [to views], clinging, affliction, and are neither removed through seeing nor through development (*bhāvanā*). They are neither accumulating nor disaccumulating. They are neither training nor non-training. They are restricted (*paritta*), are of the sense-plane, are not fixed, and are not leading out (*aniyyānika*). They are [cognized by] the mind-consciousness-element. They all break up.[153]

Thus should it be known through states.

---

152. 無因無起, lit. "without cause, without arising", = *ahetu* & *anuppāda*. The character 起, "arising", corresponds to *uppāda, vuṭṭhāna*, and the like. LC: "'Without cause' must be a rendering of *na hetum eva*, i.e., not any of the nine *hetus*. Then 'without arising' must render Pali *ahetukam eva*, i.e., entirely without any *hetu*. This does not have a parallel in the northern abhidharma and so has been misunderstood by the Chinese translator". Cf. 447b05: "All matter is neither a cause (*hetu*) nor without a cause; it is dissociated from a cause, ...".

Cf. Dhs 244: *Dvepañcaviññāṇāni, tisso ca manodhātuyo, pañca ca ahetukamanoviññāṇadhātuyo, rūpañ-ca, nibbānañ-ca, ime dhammā na hetū ahetukā. Hetū dhammā na vattabbā, na hetū sahetukātipi, na hetū ahetukā ti pi.* Vibh-a 402: *Na hetumevā ti sādhāraṇahetupaṭikkhepaniddeso. Tattha hetuhetu, paccayahetu, uttamahetu, sādhāraṇahetū ti catubbidho hetū ti-ādinā nayena yaṃ vattabbaṃ siyā, taṃ sabbaṃ rūpakaṇḍe sabbaṃ rūpaṃ na hetum-evā ti ādīnaṃ atthavaṇṇanāyaṃ (As § 594) vuttam-eva. Ahetukam-evā ti ādīsu byañjanasandhivasena makāro veditabbo; ahetukā evā ti attho. Sesapadesu pi eseva nayo. Apica hetū dhammā nahetū dhammā ti ādīsu (Dhs Dukamātikā 1) dhammakoṭṭhāsesu pañcaviññāṇāni hetū dhammā ti vā sahetukā dhammā ti vā nahonti. Ekantena pana na hetū yeva, ahetukā yevā ti imānipi nayenettha sabbapadesu attho veditabbo.* Vism-mhṭ II 106 to Vism XIV.72: *Sampayuttadhammarāsi hinoti etena patiṭṭhahatīhi hetu, mūlaṭṭhena lobhādiko, alobhādiko ca, tādiso hetu na hotī ti nahetu. Nāssa hetu atthī ti ahetukaṃ, sahetukapaṭiyogibhāvato hetunā saha na uppajjatī ti attho. Ahetukam-eva hetunā vippayuttatāya hetuvippayuttaṃ.*

153. Vibh 318, § 761: *pañca viññāṇā na hetum-eva, ahetukam-eva, hetuvippayuttam-eva, sappaccayam-eva, saṅkhatam-eva, arūpam-eva, lokiyam-eva, sāsavam-eva, saṃyojaniyam-eva, ganthaniyam-eva, oghaniyam-eva, yoganiyam-eva, nīvaraṇiyam-eva, parāmaṭṭham-eva, upādāniyam-eva, saṃkilesikam-eva, abyākatam-eva, sārammaṇam-eva, acetasikam-eva, vipākam-eva, upādinnupādāniyam-eva, asaṃkiliṭṭhasaṃkilesikam-eva, na savitakkasavicāram-eva, na avitakkavicāramattam-eva, avitakka-avicāram-eva, na pītisahagatam-eva, neva dassanena na bhāvanāya pahātabbam-eva, neva dassanena na bhāvanāya pahātabbahetukam-eva, nevācayagāmināpacayagāmim-eva, nevasekkhanāsekkham-eva, parittam-eva, kāmāvacaram-eva, na rūpāvacaram-eva, na arūpāvacaram-eva, pariyāpannam-eva, no apariyāpannam-eva, aniyatam-eva, aniyyānikam-eva, uppannaṃ manoviññāṇaviññeyyam-eva, aniccam-eva, jarābhibhūtam-eva.*

This is called the "aggregate of consciousness".
This is called the "five aggregates".

27. Four ways of knowing the five aggregates

Furthermore, the five aggregates should be known in detail in four ways: through word meaning, through characteristic, through analysis and through inclusion.

28. Word meaning

Q. How [should it be known through] through word meaning?
A. Matter has the meaning of materializing. Feeling has the meaning of experiencing. Perception has the meaning of perceiving. Formations has the meaning of forming. Consciousness has the meaning of cognising.[154] Aggregate has the meaning of aggregation of [similar] kinds [of states].[155]
Thus should it be known through word meaning.

29. Characteristic

Q. How through characteristic?
A. The characteristic of matter is the materializing of itself.[156] It is like seeing

---

154. Cf. S III 86–7: *Ruppatī ti kho ... tasmā rūpan-ti vuccati. ... Vedayatī ti kho ... tasmā vedanā ti vuccati. ... Sañjānātī ti kho ... tasmā saññā ti vuccati. ... Saṅkhatamabhisaṅkharontī ti kho ... tasmā saṅkhārā ti vuccati. ... Vijānātī ti kho ... tasmā viññāṇan-ti vuccati. ...*

155. See fn. 1501 and @和合, which @@. 種類集. The Tibetan (Sav 183a) has "coming together/aggregation of similar types/kinds", *rigs mthun pa'i tshogs pa.* Elsewhere in Vim 集 corresponds to *samudaya*, "origination", but in Chinese texts it usually corresponds to *samuccaya, sañcaya*, etc. In the discussion of the aggregate of matter above, *tshogs pa* corresponds to *kalāpa*, "group". Cf. Vibh 1: *Yaṃ kiñci rūpaṃ atītānāgatapaccuppannaṃ ... santike vā, tadekajjhaṃ abhisaññūhitvā abhisaṅkhipitvā ayaṃ vuccati rūpakkhandho.* Abhidh-s 228: *Atītānāgatapaccuppannādibhedabhinnā te te sabhāgadhammā ekajjhaṃ rāsaṭṭhena khandhā. Tenāha bhagavā* (Vibh 1): *tadekajjhaṃ abhisaṃyūhitvā abhisaṅkhipitvā ayaṃ vuccati rūpakkhandho ...* Vism XIV.195/p.473: *Tadekajjhaṃ abhisaṃyūhitvā abhisaṅkhipitvā ti taṃ atītādīhi padehi visuṃ visuṃ niddiṭṭhaṃ rūpaṃ sabbaṃ ruppanalakkhaṇasaṅkhāte ekavidhabhāve paññāya rāsiṃ katvā rūpakkhandha ti vuccatī ti ayamettha attho. Etena sabbam-pi rūpaṃ ruppanalakkhaṇe rāsibhāvūpagamanena rūpakkhandhoti dassitaṃ hoti. Na hi rūpato añño rūpakkhandho nāma atthi.* Cf. As 6.

156. 色者自色相, or "Matter is its own material characteristic". Tibetan (Sav 183a): "The characteristic of matter is materializing. It is like being eaten up/prepared/built by matter", *gzugs kyi mtshan nyid ni gzugs par bya ba ste bzos pa'i gzugs bzhin no.* Cf. S III 86: *Ruppatī ti kho ... tasmā rūpan-ti vuccati. Kena ruppati? Sītenapi ruppati, uṇhenapi ruppati, jighacchāyapi ruppati,* ... Nidd-a I 12: *Tattha ruppatī ti kuppati ghaṭṭīyati pīḷīyati,*

a thorn [stuck in the flesh].[157] The four great primaries are its footing. [**448c**]

The characteristic of feeling is experiencing. It is like the disease of leprosy.[158] Contact is its footing.

The characteristic of perception is to grasp the aspects (*ākāra*) [of an object].[159] It is like creating an image (*bimba*).[160] Contact is its footing.

The characteristic of formations is [the propelling of] aggregation.[161] It is like the propelling of a wheel.[162] Contact is its footing.

The characteristic of consciousness is cognising (*vijānana*). It is likened to the cognising of taste.[163] Name-and-matter are its footing.

Thus should it be known through characteristic.

30. Analysis

Q. How through analysis?[164]

A. Three kinds of aggregates are analysed: the five aggregates (*pañcakkhandhā*), the five aggregates subject to clinging (*pañcupādānakkhandhā*), and the five aggregates of the Dhamma (*pañcadhammakkhandhā*).

Herein, the five aggregates are all conditioned phenomena (*saṅkhata-dhamma*).

The five aggregates subject to clinging are all states subject to contaminations (*sāsava*).[165]

---

bhijjatī ti attho.

157. 如見刺, or "like seeing a splinter/dart/spear".

158. Tibetan (Sav 183a): "it is like experiencing the itching of a leprous sore".

159. Paṭis-a II 514: *ākāraggāhikā saññā.* Spk II 293: ... *ārammaṇassa ākārasaṇṭhāna-gahaṇavasena saññā pākaṭā hoti.* Nāmar-p v. 78: *Ākāragahaṇaṃ saññā, sā sañjānana-lakkhaṇā; Nimittuppādanarasā, upalakkhāti gayhati.*

160. Tibetan (Sav 183a): "like a creation (*nimmita* ?) of supernormal power (*abhiññā*)".

161. 和合 also means "compounding", "cohering", "connecting", etc. (*saṅgaha, sannipāta, saṃyutta, saññoga*, etc.) Cf. 450a08: "the characteristic of the aggregates is aggregation...;" 行者和合為相. Cf. S III 86–7: *Rūpaṃ rūpattāya saṅkhatam abhisaṅkharonti, ... viññāṇaṃ viññāṇattāya saṅkhatam abhisaṅkharonti.* Tibetan (Sav 183a): "the characteristic of formations is impelling/propelling/forcing aggregation/accumulation (*'du ba*), like the impelling/hurling of a wheel".

162. Cf. A I 111: *Atha kho ... rathakāro yaṃ taṃ cakkaṃ chahi divasehi niṭṭhitaṃ taṃ pavattesi. Taṃ pavattitaṃ samānaṃ yāvatikā abhisaṅkhārassa gati tāvatikaṃ gantvā ciṅgulāyitvā bhūmiyaṃ papati ...*

163. This clause is not in the Tibetan. Cf. S III 87: *Ambilam pi vijānāti, ... aloṇikam pi vijānāti. Vijānātī ti kho ... tasmā viññāṇan ti vuccati.*

164. 分別 corresponds to *vibhaṅga, vibhajana, pariccheda.* 以分別 earlier in Vim this corresponds to *paricchedato.*

165. Cf. S III 47: *Katame ca ... pañcakkhandhā? Yaṃ kiñci ... rūpaṃ ... viññāṇaṃ atītānāgatapaccuppannaṃ ... ayaṃ vuccati viññāṇakkhandho. ... Katame ca ...*

The five aggregates of the Dhamma are the aggregate of virtue, the aggregate of concentration, the aggregate of wisdom, the aggregate of freedom, and the aggregate of knowledge and discernment of freedom.[166]

Herein [the sense of] the five aggregates subject to clinging is intended.[167] Thus should it be known through analysis.

31. Inclusion

Q. How through inclusion?

A. There are three kinds of inclusion (*saṅgaha*): inclusion in the sense bases, inclusion in the elements, and inclusion in the truths.[168]

Herein the aggregate of matter is included in eleven sense bases. Three aggregates are included in the sense base of mental states. The aggregate of consciousness is included in the sense base of mind.[169]

The aggregate of matter is included in eleven elements. Three aggregates are included in the element of mental states. The aggregate of consciousness is included in seven elements.[170]

The aggregate of virtue, the aggregate of concentration, the aggregate of wisdom, the aggregate of the knowledge and discernment of freedom are included in the sense base of mental states and element of mental states. The aggregate of freedom is included in the sense base of mental

---

pañcupādānakkhandhā? Yaṃ kiñci ... rūpaṃ ... viññāṇaṃ atītānāgatapaccuppannaṃ ... sāsavaṃ upādāniyaṃ, ayaṃ vuccati viññāṇupādānakkhandho.

166. Cf.DIII279:*pañcadhammakkhandhā:sīlakkhandho,samādhikkhandho,paññākkhandho, vimuttikkhandho, vimuttiñāṇadassanakkhandho.* Paṭis-a III 652: ... *Paññākkhandhan-ti maggapaññañ-ca sekkhāsekkhānaṃ lokiyapaññañ-ca. Vimuttikkhandhan-ti phalavimuttiṃ. Vimuttiñāṇadassanakkhandhan-ti paccavekkhaṇañāṇaṃ.*

167. Elsewhere in Vim this phrase is used to denote the preferred item, i.e. the primary sense intended according to the author. 可樂, *mngon par 'dod*, corresponds to *adhippeta*, "is desired", "is preferred", "is intended".

168. This section is partly based on the methodology of the *Dhātukathā*, of which the *mātikā* is: *Saṅgaho asaṅgaho, saṅgahitena asaṅgahitaṃ, asaṅgahitena saṅgahitaṃ, saṅgahitena saṅgahitaṃ ... Pañcakkhandhā, dvādasāyatanāni, aṭṭhārasa dhātuyo, cattāri saccāni, bāvīsatindriyāni ...*

169. Cf. Dhāt 33: *Cakkhāyatanena ye dhammā ... phoṭṭhabbadhātuyā ye dhammā khandhasaṅgahena saṅgahitā āyatanasaṅgahena asaṅgahitā dhātusaṅgahena asaṅgahitā, te dhammā katihi khandhehi katihāyatanehi katihi dhātūhi asaṅgahitā? Te dhammā catūhi khandhehi dvīhāyatanehi aṭṭhahi dhātūhi asaṅgahitā. Cakkhuviññāṇadhātuyā ye dhammā... manoviññāṇadhātuyā ye dhammā khandhasaṅgahena saṅgahitā āyatanasaṅgahena asaṅgahitā dhātusaṅgahena asaṅgahitā ... pe ... te dhammā catūhi khandhehi ekādasahāyatanehi dvādasahi dhātūhi asaṅgahitā.*

170. The Tibetan has "seven consciousness elements", *rnam par shes pa'i khams bdun.* On the seven consciousness elements in Theravāda Abhidhamma, see fn. 1852.

states, the sense base of mind, the element of mental states, and the mind-consciousness-element.

The five aggregates are included in the truths or not included in the truths. The five aggregates subject to clinging are included in the truth of suffering and in the truth of origination.[171]

The aggregates of virtue, concentration, and wisdom are included in the truth of the path. The aggregate of freedom is not included in the truths. The aggregate of knowledge and discernment of freedom is included in the truth of suffering.

There are states included in the aggregates and not in the truths. There are states included in the truths and not in the aggregates. There are states included in the truths and in the aggregates. There are states included neither in the truths nor in the aggregates.

Herein, matter not bound up with faculties[172] and the [states] associated with the paths and with the fruits of recluseship (*sāmaññaphala*)[173] are included in the aggregates and not in the truths. Nibbāna is included in the truths and not in the aggregates. Three truths are included in the aggregates and in the truths. Concept (*paññatti*) is not included in the aggregates and neither in the truths.[174]

Thus, in these ways there is skill in knowledge of analysis of the aggregates.

This is called "skill in the aggregates".

The skill in the aggregates is finished.

---

171. Read 集諦 instead of 習諦. The Tibetan has "origination of suffering", *kun 'byung gi bden pa*.

172. According to Paṭis-a, see below, there are "others" who say that *anindriyabaddharūpa* cannot be an object of *vipassanā*. Does the *Vimuttimagga* implicitly approve of this view when it says that *anindriyabaddharūpa* is not included in the Truths, but just in the aggregates? This tenet is disagreed with in the Kv.

Paṭis-a I 290: *Aññe pana anindriyabaddhā rūpādayo avipassanūpagā ti vadanti. ... Tasmā paresaṃ cakkhādivavatthānam-pi anindriyabaddharūpādivavatthānam-pi icchitabbam-eva, tasmā tebhūmakasaṅkhārā avipassanūpagā nāma natthi.* Paṭis-a I 114: *Keci pana avipassanūpagānaṃ ñātapariññā-ti vadanti. Abhiññeyyena ñātapariññāya vuttattā taṃ na sundaraṃ.* Vism XIV.19/p.440: *attano khandhe gahetvā āraddhā vipassanā paññā ajjhattābhinivesā. Parassa khandhe bāhiraṃ vā anindriyabaddharūpaṃ gahetvā āraddhā bahiddhābhinivesā.* Kv 546f: ... *yathā indriyabaddhaṃ dukkhaṃ pariññātaṃ na puna uppajjati, evam-evaṃ anindriyabaddhaṃ dukkhaṃ pariññātaṃ na puna uppajjatī ti? Na hevaṃ vattabbe. Tena hi indriyabaddhaññeva dukkhan-ti. ...* Cf. Dhs 241: *Anindriyabaddharūpañ-ca nibbānañ-ca ṭhapetvā, sabbe dhammā siyā ajjhattā, siyā bahiddhā, siyā ajjhattabahiddhā. Anindriyabaddharūpañ-ca nibbānañ-ca bahiddhā.*

173. Cf. Vism XIV.89/p.512: *tattha maggasampayuttā dhammā sāmaññaphalāni ca yad aniccaṃ taṃ dukkhan-ti vacanato saṅkhāradukkhatāya dukkhaṃ, na ariyasaccaṃ.*

174 The Tibetan (184a) text adds a list of the 11 types of designation. For a discussion of this passage as found at Ch. 11 § 36, see fn. 1863.

Skill in the Sense Bases

32. What is the skill in the sense bases?

Q. What is the skill in the sense bases?
A. The twelve sense bases are the sense base of eye, form, ear, sound, nose, odour, tongue, taste, body, tangibles, mind, and mental states.[175]

Herein, the sense base of eye is the element of sensitivity[176] by which one sees forms.[177]

The sense base of form is the element of colour-luminosity (*vaṇṇanibhā*)[178] that is the sense object (*visaya*) of the eye.

---

175. D III 102: *Chayimāni bhante ajjhattikabāhirāni āyatanāni, cakkhuñ-ceva rūpā ca, sotañ-ceva saddā ca, ghānañ-ceva gandhā ca, jivhā ceva rasā ca, kāyo c eva phoṭṭhabbā ca, mano ceva dhammā ca.* Vibh 70/§ 155: *Dvādasāyatanāni cakkhāyatanaṃ, sotāyatanaṃ, ghānāyatanaṃ, jivhāyatanaṃ, kāyāyatanaṃ, manāyatanaṃ, rūpāyatanaṃ, saddāyatanaṃ, gandhāyatanaṃ, rasāyatanaṃ, phoṭṭhabbāyatanaṃ, dhammāyatanaṃ.*

176. The Chinese and Tibetan have 界清淨 & *khams rab tu dang ba* which correspond to *dhātu-pasāda*, "element-sensitivity" or "sensitivity of the elements". The Vibhaṅga parallels below indicate that the sentient matter dependent on the 4 great primaries is intended. But see Peṭ 113: *cakkhuno pasādo cakkhudhātu*, "the sensitivity of the eye is the eye element" and Spk II 130: ... *cakkhupasādo cakkhudhātu, rūpārammaṇaṃ rūpadhātu, cakkhupasādavatthukaṃ cittaṃ cakkhuviññāṇadhātu*, "... eye-sensitivity is the eye element ...", which suggest that it is to be taken as a *kammadhāraya* compound the "sensitivity which is an element" or "element of sensitivity", or the original could have had two nominatives, "the element, the sensitivity".

177. Cf. Vibh 70, § 156: *Tattha katamaṃ cakkhāyatanaṃ? Yaṃ cakkhu catunnaṃ mahābhūtānaṃ upādāya pasādo attabhāvapariyāpanno anidassano sappaṭigho, yena cakkhunā anidassanena sappaṭighena rūpaṃ sanidassanaṃ sappaṭighaṃ passi vā passati vā passissati vā passe vā, cakkhumpetaṃ cakkhāyatanampetaṃ cakkhudhātupesā* ... Vism XV.14: *cakkhāyatanaṃ jātivasena cakkhupasādamattam-eva.*

178. 色形楱 or 色形模, perhaps "material form"; 色形 = *vaṇṇa/rūpa* + *saṇṭhāna*; the Taishō text adds the character 摸, "touch" (corresponding to *parimajjati* or *parāmasati*), while the fourth edition in the footnote reads 模, "form, shape", which is a better fit. In the parallel at Ch. 11 § 40/p. 449c28 there is just 色形. The Tibetan does not have a corresponding word. Probably the original had *vaṇṇanibhā*, "colour-luminosity" or "the luminosity which is colour", of which *nibhā* was understood by the translator as *nirbhā* in the sense of "appearance", 形, rather than "luminosity". According to the *Atthasālinī* (As 317), only colour-luminosity is objectively visible, not shape (*saṇṭhāna*), which is an expression (*vohāra*) superimposed on differences in colour-luminosity; see Karunadasa 2015a 43–46, 2015b: 186.

Cf. Dhs 139, Vibh 70, § 162: *Yaṃ rūpaṃ catunnaṃ mahābhūtānaṃ upādāya vaṇṇanibhā sanidassanaṃ sappaṭighaṃ nīlaṃ ... dīghaṃ rassaṃ aṇuṃ thūlaṃ ... yaṃ rūpaṃ sanidassanaṃ sappaṭighaṃ cakkhunā anidassanena sappaṭighena passi vā passati vā passissati vā passe vā, rūpampetaṃ rūpāyatanam-petaṃ rūpadhātupesā. Idaṃ vuccati*

The sense base of ear is the element of sensitivity by which one hears sounds.

The sense base of sound is the element of noise (*ghosa*) that is the sense object of the ear.

The sense base of nose is the element of sensitivity by which one smells odours. [**449a**]

The sense base of odour is the element of odour that is the sense object of the nose.

The sense base of tongue is the element of sensitivity by which one tastes tastes.[179]

The sense base of taste is the element of flavour (*rasa*)[180] that is the sense object of the tongue.

The sense base of body is the element of sensitivity by which one touches [tangibles].[181]

---

rūpāyatanaṃ. As 316: *Vaṇṇo va nibhā vaṇṇanibhā*. Vin I 26: *seyyathā pi mahā-aggikkhandho, purimāhi vaṇṇanibhāhi abhikkantataro ca paṇītataro ca.*

179. 知味, lit. "know/experience taste"; Tibetan: *ro myong bar byed pa* : "experience taste" or "taste" = Skt *(ā)svādayati* "to taste" = Pali *sāyati.*

180. 氣味 corresponds to *ojā*, "vital essence", elsewhere in Vim, but this cannot be the case here. The Tibetan (Sav 184a) just has *ro*, which corresponds to *rasa.*

181. 以是觸細滑 = "through which one touches the smooth" or "... the fine and smooth". The Tibetan (Sav 184b) just has "that by which one touches a tangible", *gang gis reg bya la reg pa* = *yena phoṭṭhabbaṃ phusati,* which corresponds to Vibh 71: *yena kāyena anidassanena sappaṭighena phoṭṭhabbaṃ anidassanaṃ sappaṭighaṃ phusi vā phusati vā phusissati vā phuse vā.* In its discussion of sense base of tangibles (see next fn), Dhs 144 gives *saṇhaṃ pharusaṃ*, "smooth and rough", and perhaps that pair was originally here, or in the definition of sense base of tangibles. Since none of the definitions of the other sense bases specifies the characteristics of what is sensed, the Chinese text likely is corrupt here.

The sense base of tangibles is the earth element, fire element, wind element,[182] hardness, softness, coolness, and warmth,[183] which are the sense object of the body.

The sense base of mind is the seven consciousness elements.[184]

---

182. Taishō includes the water element, 水界, but the footnote says that it is not found in other editions. The Pali parallels only have three elements since the Theravāda Abhidhamma does not include the water element in the sense base of tangibles but in the sense base of mental states; see fn. 1273. The *Vimuttimagga* includes the water element among the 18 subtle kinds of matter (*sukhumarūpa*) at 447a28 which implies that it does not include the water element in sense base of tangibles; see fn. 1721.

The Tibetan (Sav 184b) has all the four elements but, oddly, it places the water element after the wind element (*reg bya'i skye mched ni sa'i khams dang me'i khams dang rlung gi khams dang chu'i khams*), i.e. as the 4th element, while it should come 2nd. This misplacement suggests that the water element was not in the original but was added by the translator or a scribe. Cf. Dhs 144, Vibh 72: *Pathavīdhātu tejodhātu vāyodhātu kakkhaḷaṃ mudukaṃ saṇhaṃ pharusaṃ sukhasamphassaṃ dukkhasamphassaṃ garukaṃ lahukaṃ, yaṃ phoṭṭhabbaṃ anidassanaṃ sappaṭighaṃ kāyena anidassanena sappaṭighena phusi vā phusati ... idaṃ taṃ rūpaṃ phoṭṭhabbāyatanaṃ.* As 332: *Kakkhaḷan-ti thaddhaṃ. Mudukan-ti athaddhaṃ. Saṇhan-ti maṭṭhaṃ. Pharusan-ti kharaṃ. ... Ettha ca kakkhaḷaṃ mudukaṃ saṇhaṃ pharusaṃ garukaṃ lahukan-ti padehi pathavīdhātu eva bhājitā. Yadāyaṃ kāyo āyusahagato ca hoti usmāsahagato ca viññāṇasahagato ca tadā lahutaro ca hoti mudutaro ca kammaññataro cā ti suttepi lahumudubhūtaṃ pathavīdhātum-eva sandhāya vuttaṃ. Sukhasamphassaṃ dukkhasamphassan-ti padadvayena pana tīṇipi mahābhūtāni bhājitāni. Pathavīdhātu hi sukhasamphassā-pi atthi dukkhasamphassāpi. Tathā tejodhātuvāyodhātuyo. ... Sukhasamphassā tejodhātu sītasamaye aṅgārakapallaṃ āharitvā gattaṃ sedente assādetvā ... Uṇhasamaye aṅgārakapalle ābhate apanehi nan-ti vattabbaṃ hoti. Sītasamaye bījanena bījante apehi, mā bījā ti vattabbaṃ hoti. ...* Vism XV.14: *Phoṭṭhabbāyatanaṃ pathavīdhātutejodhātuvāyodhātuvasena tippabhedaṃ.* Cf. Vism XV.30.

183. 堅軟冷煖. The Tibetan puts "warmth" (*uṇha*) before "coolness", (*sra ba dang 'jam pa dang dro ba dang bsil ba*, cf. Skilling 1994: 180 n. 2), which could be the original order since at Ch. 8 § 164 & 170 (439b09 & 440a02) coolness, *sīta*, is given as a nature of and the characteristic of the wind element. Instead of the Dhammasaṅganī's *saṇhaṃ pharusaṃ*, "smooth and rough" (see preceding fn), the Vim gives the characteristics of the fire element (i.e. warmth) and wind element (i.e. coolness). According to Dhs, "hardness, softness" are the earth element, with "softness" being "non-hardness", *athaddha*.

184. In the Pali commentaries a sevenfold division of the consciousness element is found which takes the *manodhātu* as a consciousness element along with the *manoviññāṇadhātu*; see Abhidh-av-pṭ I 348: *Channaṃ viññāṇānan-ti cakkhuviññāṇādīnaṃ pañcannaṃ, manoviññāṇassa ca. Sattaviññāṇadhātūnan-ti cakkhuviññāṇadhātādīnaṃ pañcannaṃ, manodhātumanoviññāṇadhātudvayassā ti sattannaṃ viññāṇadhātūnaṃ.* Vism-mhṭ 46: *Viññāṇadhātu yadi pi chaviññāṇadhātuvasena vibhattā, tathā pi viññāṇadhātuggahaṇena tassā purecārikapacchācārikattā manodhātu gahitā va hotī ti vuttattā āha viññāṇadhātu ... pe ... sattaviññāṇasaṅkhepo yevā ti* (= Vism XV.30/p.487). This sevenfold division is based on Vibh 71: *Sattavidhena manāyatanaṃ: cakkhuviññāṇaṃ, sotaviññāṇaṃ, ghānaviññāṇaṃ, jivhāviññāṇaṃ, kāyaviññāṇaṃ, manodhātu,*

The sense base of mental states is the three immaterial aggregates, the eighteen subtle kinds of matter, and nibbāna.[185]

These are the twelve sense bases.

33. Five ways of knowing the sense bases

Furthermore, these twelve sense bases should be known in detail in five ways: through word meaning, sense object, condition, occurrence of process of mind,[186] and inclusion.

34. Word meaning

Q. How [should it be known] through word meaning?
A. "Eye" has the meaning of "seeing". "Form" has the meaning of "manifestation". "Ear" has the meaning of "hearing". "Sound" has the meaning of "noise" (*ghosa*). "Nose" has the meaning of "smelling". "Odour" has the meaning of "odour". "Tongue" has the meaning of "tasting". "Taste" has the meaning of "flavour" (*rasa*). "Body" has the meaning of "staying upright". "Tangibles" has the meaning of "touchability". "Mind" has the meaning of "knowing". "Mental state" has the meaning of "without soul" (*nijjīva*).

"Base" has the meaning of "entrance to [material and] immaterial states";[187] has the meaning of "ground" (*vatthu*); and it has the meaning of "basis" (*ṭhāna* or *adhiṭṭhāna*).[188]

---

manoviññāṇadhātu and Dhs 209: *Cakkhuviññāṇaṃ, sotaviññāṇaṃ, ghānaviññāṇaṃ, jivhāviññāṇaṃ, kāyaviññāṇaṃ, manodhātu, manoviññāṇadhātu—ime dhammā cittā.*

185. Cf. Vibh 72, § 167: *katamaṃ dhammāyatanaṃ? Vedanākkhandho, saññākkhandho, saṅkhārakkhandho, yañ-ca rūpaṃ anidassana-appaṭighaṃ dhammāyatanapariyāpannaṃ, asaṅkhatā ca dhātu.* Dhs 179, § 984: *Itthindriyaṃ purisindriyaṃ... pe ... kabaḷīkāro āhāro. Idaṃ vuccati rūpaṃ anidassana-appaṭighaṃ dhammāyatanapariyāpannaṃ.* Dhs 148, § 675: *Itthindriyaṃ ... pe ... kabaḷīkāro āhāro idaṃ vuccati rūpaṃ sukhumaṃ.* As 79: ... *pannarasa sukhumarūpāni, nibbānapaññattī ti ime dhammāyatane pariyāpannā ca, ...* Vism XV.34: *Dhammadhātu tiṇṇaṃ arūpakkhandhānaṃ soḷasannaṃ sukhumarūpānaṃ asaṅkhatāya ca dhātuyā vasena vīsati dhammā ti saṅkhaṃ gacchati.* (See Ñāṇamoli's footnote on the sixteen subtle material qualities in this passage in PoP.) Vism XV.14: *Dhammāyatanaṃ vedanāsaññāsaṅkhārakkhandhasukhumarūpanibbānānaṃ sabhāvanānattabhedato anekappabhedanti.* Moh 175: *Sabbam-pi viññāṇaṃ manāyatanaṃ nāma. Cetasikasukhumarūpanibbānāni dhammāyatanaṃ nāma.*

On nibbāna being the object of mind or consciousness, see fn. 1883.

186. 夾勝心起; see note below.

187. 無色法門 corresponds to *arūpa-dhamma-dvāra* or *-mukha*, lit. "non-material-thing/state entrance". There is no parallel to this in Vism XV.3–7.

188. Cf. Vism XV.4–5: *Api ca nivāsaṭṭhānaṭṭhena ākaraṭṭhena samosaraṇaṭṭhānaṭṭhena sañjātidesaṭṭhena kāraṇaṭṭhena ca āyatanaṃ veditabbaṃ.*

Thus should it be known through word meaning.

35. Sense object

Q. How through sense object (*visaya*)?

A. The eye and ear do not [directly] meet with the sense object.[189] The nose, tongue, and body [directly] meet with the sense object. The mind is concurrent with the sense object.[190]

Furthermore, some say: "The ear meets together with the sense object. Why? Because one does not hear sounds if there is a nearby obstruction, as when a spell (*mantra*) is spoken".

It is also said: "The eye within its own range (*gocara*) meets with the sense object.[191] Why? Because one cannot see the other side of a wall".

Thus, one should know through sense object.

36. Condition

Q. How through condition?

A. Depending on eye, forms, light, and attention, eye-consciousness arises.

Herein, the eye is a condition for eye-consciousness as four conditions: pre-arising-condition, support-condition, faculty-condition, and presence-condition.

Forms are a condition as three conditions: pre-arising-condition, object-condition, and presence-condition.

Light is a condition as three conditions: pre-arising-condition, support-condition, and presence-condition.

---

189. The character 至 corresponds here to *sampatta* or *sampāpuṇāti*, "reaches", "arrives at", or "meets". What is meant is that unlike the other three sense organs, the eye and ear do not come in direct contact with their objects, only do so at a distance; see the discussion of this in Karunadasa 2015a 43–48, 2015b 185–189. See also As 313f.: ... *visesavantesu ca etesu cakkhusotāni asampattavisayaggāhakāni attano nissayaṃ anallīnanissaye eva visaye viññāṇahetuttā. Ghānajivhākāyā sampattavisayaggāhakā, nissayavasena ceva sayañ-ca attano nissayaṃ allīne yeva visaye viññāṇahetuttā. Aṭṭhakathāyaṃ pana āpāthagatattāva ārammaṇaṃ sampattaṃ nāma. Candamaṇḍalasūriyamaṇḍalānañ-hi dvācattālīsayojanasahassamatthake ṭhitānaṃ vaṇṇo cakkhupasādaṃ ghaṭṭeti. So dūre ṭhatvā paññāyamāno pi sampatto yeva nāma. Taṃ gocarattā cakkhu sampattagocaram-eva nāma. Dūre rukkhaṃ chindantānampi, rajakānañ-ca vatthaṃ dhovantānaṃ dūratova kāyavikāro paññāyati. Saddo pana dhātuparamparāya āgantvā sotaṃ ghaṭṭetvā saṇikaṃ vavatthānaṃ gacchatī ti vuttaṃ. Tattha kiñcāpi āpāthagatattā ārammaṇaṃ sampattan-ti vuttaṃ,* ... The first part of this is also found in Vism XIV.46/p.445.

190. 意俱境界 or "the mind [is] together (*saha*) with the object".

191. In both cases 境界 is used. Presumably, 境 stands for *gocara* and 界 for *visaya*. In Vim 境界 sometimes corresponds to *gocara* and sometimes to *visaya*.

Attention is a condition as two conditions: continuity-condition (*anantara- or samanantara-paccaya*) and absence-condition (*natthi-paccaya*).

Depending on ear, sounds, [ear-] cavity, and attention, there is the arising of ear-consciousness. One should analyse through this [same] analysis [of conditions].

Depending on nose, odours, wind, and attention, there is the arising of nose-consciousness.

Depending on tongue, tastes, water, and attention, there is the arising of tongue-consciousness.

Depending on body, tangibles, and attention, there is the arising of body-consciousness.

Depending on mind, mental states, resolve (*adhimutti*),[192] and attention, there is the arising of mind consciousness.[193]

Herein, "mind" (*mano*) is the *bhavaṅga* mind (*citta*).

"Mental states" is the mental states object (*dhammārammaṇa*). There are four kinds:

The six internal sense bases (*āyatana*) of past, present, and future are the first kind.

The [other] faculties (*indriya*) [and the ones] which are not faculties—excluding the five external sense bases past, present, and future—are the second kind.[194]

---

192. The *bhavaṅga* is not mentioned here unlike in the parallel at Vism XV.39. The text has 解脫 corresponding to *adhimokkha* or *adhimutti*; see DDB s.v. 解脫 and 447c11 where 解脫 corresponds to Tibetan *mos pa = adhimokkha, adhimutti.* Below, in the explanation, 專心, "focus/inclination of mind", *ninna, ekaggatā*, is used instead, and then, in the analysis of the next condition, again 解脫 is used.

193. Vism XV.39/488f.: *tenāhu pubbācariyā: cakkhurūpālokamanasikāre paṭicca uppajjati cakkhuviññāṇaṃ. sotasaddavivaramanasikāre paṭicca uppajjati sotaviññāṇaṃ. ghānagandhavāyumanasikāre paṭicca uppajjati ghānaviññāṇaṃ. jivhārasa-āpamanasikāre paṭicca uppajjati jivhāviññāṇaṃ. kāyaphoṭṭhabbapathavīmanasikāre paṭicca uppajjati kāyaviññāṇaṃ. bhavaṅgamanadhammamanasikāre paṭicca uppajjati manoviññāṇan ti.*

Vibh-a 358 = Sv I 195: *tathā cakkhu nissayapaccayo, rūpaṃ ārammaṇapaccayo, āvajjanaṃ anantarasamanantara-anantarūpanissayanatthivigatapaccayo, āloko upanissayapaccayo, vedanādayo sahajātādipaccayā. evam etesaṃ paccayānaṃ samavāye ālokanavilokanaṃ paññāyati.* As 282f.: *tattha asambhinnattā cakkhussa, āpāthagatattā rūpānaṃ, ālokasannissitaṃ, manasikārahetukaṃ catūhi paccayehi uppajjati cakkhuviññāṇaṃ, saddhiṃ sampayuttadhammehi. tattha matassā-pi cakkhu sambhinnaṃ hoti.*

194. 非入根, lit. "non-sense base faculty", *anāyatana-indriya*, which does not make sense. LC: "This is the second kind of *dhammārammaṇa*. The third kind is the *dhammadhātu* which includes all *cetasika* and nibbāna. I think the fourth kind is *paññatti*. The first kind was the six internal *āyatanas*, i.e. *citta* plus the five *pasādarūpa*. So what can the second kind be? It cannot be the five external sense bases because they are not *dhammārammaṇa*. Possibly the second kind was meant to list the

The sense base of mental states is the third kind.

The fourth kind is the eleven kinds of concept (*paññatti*), namely, (1) living beings (*sattā*), (2) directions (*disā*), (3) [region], (4) time (*kāla*), (5) transgression (*āpatti*), (6) asceticism (*dhuta*), (7) totality sign (*kasiṇa-nimitta*), (8) the object of the attainment of the base of nothingness (*akiñcāyatanasamāpattiārammana*), (9) the attainment of cessation (*nirodhasamāpatti*), (10) existing (*vijjamāna*), and (11) not existing (*avijjamāna*).[195] **[449b]**

---

remaining kinds of *rūpa*, i.e. not visible object, etc. (because they are *rūpārammaṇa*, etc.) and not eye, etc. (because already covered as part of the first kind). The problem with this is that those kinds of *rūpa* are part of the *dhammadhātu/dhammāyatana*, but note that the passage from As 80 precisely removes from consideration whether the items listed are or are not included in the *dhammāyatana* (*ime dhammāyatane pariyāpannā ca, apariyāpannā ca*). So the second kind should be referring to: 'all *rūpa* which is *anidassana* and *appaṭigha* excluding the five external sense bases' or 'the remaining *indriya rūpa* and all *anindriya rūpa* excluding the five external sense bases'".

Cf. Vism XIV.73 *Pasādarūpam-eva itthindriyādittayena saddhiṃ adhipatiyaṭṭhena indriyaṃ, sesaṃ tato viparītattā anindriyaṃ.* Abhidh-av 75, v. 735. *Cakkhu-āyatanādīni, pañca ajjhattikāni tu;/ Tevīsatividhaṃ sesaṃ, bāhiran-ti pavuccati.* 736: *Cakkhusotindriyādīni, indriyāni panaṭṭha tu; / Sesañ-ca tu vīsaṃ rūpaṃ, anindriyamudīritaṃ.*

195. The third item is missing and is supplied from the Tibetan parallel (Sav 184a), which does not define *paññatti* here, probably since it already did so above at Ch. 11 § 31 (see fn. 1863 and Intro. § 4.4): "Furthermore, designation is eleven states, namely, (1) beings, (2) directions, (3) region (*yul* = *visaya, desa*), (4) time, (5) transgression, (6) factor of asceticism (*dhutaṅga*), (7) sign of totality, (8) the object of the attainment of the base of nothingness, (9) attainment of cessation, (10) correct conception (*bhūta-saṅkappa/kappa/vitakka* = *vijjamāna*), (11) incorrect conception". Both in the Chinese and Tibetan the last two items are 實思, *yang dag pa'i rnam par rtog pa* and 不實思惟, *yang dag ma yin pa'i rnam par rtog pa*, lit. "conception of the real and conception of the not real", which could be due to a misunderstanding of *vijjamāna* "existing" (see the Pali parallel in Abhidh-av below) as Sanskrit *vidya* + *mānya(na)* (although the Skt word *vidyamāna* has the same sense as Pali *vijjamāna*). 思惟, *rnam par rtog pa* corresponds to *manyanā, manasikāra, cintā, saṅkappa*, etc. Dhammapāla says that the 6th item, the "factor of asceticism," cannot be *paññatti* and rejects this Abhayagirivāsin idea (Vism-mhṭ I 103); see Intro. § 5 idea 18 and fn. 451. Instead of *sems can*, "being(s)", the Tibetan reads *sems pa*, "volition". This must be due to a Tibetan copyist altering *sems can* to *sems pa.*

Cf. Dhs-mṭ 179–180: *Yadi ca satta-ratha-ghaṭādi-disā-kāla-kasiṇa-ajaṭākāsakasiṇu-gghāṭimākāsa-ākiñcaññāyatanavisaya-nirodhasamāpatti-ādippakārā upādāpaññatti avijjamānapaññatti, eteneva vacanena tassā avijjamānatā vuttā ti na sā atthīti vattabbā. ... Yasmā pana yesu rūpādīsu cakkhādīsu ca tathā tathā pavattamānesu satto itthī ratho ghaṭo ti ādikā vicittasaññā uppajjati, saññānulomāni ca adhivacanāni, tehi rūpacakkhādīhi añño sattarathādisaññāvalambito vacanattho vijjamāno na hoti, tasmā sattarathādi-abhilāpā avijjamānapaññattī ti vuccanti, ...* Abhidh-av 83: *Tattha samūhapaññatti nāma rūpārūpadhammesu ekassa vā bahūnaṃ vā nāmaṃ gahetvā samūhamevopādāya*

This is called "the mental states object".[196]
"Resolve" is the mind following [the object] resolutely.[197]

---

vuccati. Kathaṃ? Accha-taraccha-ghaṭa-paṭādippabhedā—ayaṃ samūhapaññatti nāma. Asamūhapaññatti pana disākāsakālanimittābhāvanirodhādibhedā. Yadā pana sā vijjamānaṃ paramatthaṃ jotayati, tadā vijjamānapaññattī ti pavuccati. Yadā avijjamānaṃ samūhāsamūhabhedaṃ nāmamattaṃ jotayati, tadā avijjamānapaññattī ti pavuccati. Abhidh-av-pṭ II 201: *Ayaṃ samūhapaññatti nāma samūhassa paññāpanato. Disākāsādīsu disā-ggahaṇena candasūriyāvattanamupādāya paññāpiyamānaṃ puratthimādidisāpaññattiṃ dasseti. Ākāsa-ggahaṇena asamphuṭṭhadhamme upādāya paññāpiyamānaṃ kūpaguhādi-ākāsapaññattiṃ dasseti. Kāla-ggahaṇena candavattanādikamupādāya paññāpiyamānaṃ pubbaṇhādikālapaññattiṃ dasseti. Nimitta-ggahaṇena bahiddhā pathavīmaṇḍalādikaṃ, ajjhattikañ-ca bhāvanāvisesaṃ upādāya paññāpiyamānaṃ kasiṇanimittādikaṃ dasseti. Abhāva-ggahaṇena bhāvanābalena appavattanasabhāvaṃ ākāsānañcāyatanajhānaṃ upādāya pavattaṃ ākiñcaññāyatanajhānārammaṇaṃ abhāvapaññattiṃ dasseti. Nirodha-ggahaṇena bhāvanābalena niruddhaṃ nevasaññānāsaññāyatanaṃ nissāya paññattaṃ nirodhapaññattiṃ dasseti. Ādi-ggahaṇena khayādisabhāvaṃ taṃ taṃ dhammamupādāya paññāpiyamānaṃ aniccalakkhaṇādikaṃ saṅgaṇhāti. Sāpi hi disākāsādikā viya dhammasamūhamupādāya apaññattabhāvato asamūhapaññattiyevāti. Sāti ayaṃ dvidhā upādāpaññatti. Tajjāpaññatti vacanatthaṃ amuñcitvā pavattito upādāpaññattiyaṃ yeva saṅgayhatī ti vuttaṃ vijjamānaṃ paramatthaṃ jotayatī ti. Evañ-ca katvā upari cha paññattiyo pi ettheva saṅgahaṃ gacchantī ti vuttaṃ. Vijjamānan-ti sabhāvena upalabbhamānaṃ. Avijjamānan-ti ṭhapetvā lokasaṅketaṃ sabhāvavasena anupalabbhamānaṃ.* As 80: *Dhammārammaṇe cha ajjhattikāni āyatanāni, tīṇi lakkhaṇāni, tayo arūpino khandhā, pannarasa sukhumarūpāni, nibbānapaññattī ti.* Dhs-mṭ 159: *Tīṇi lakkhaṇānīti aniccadukkha-anattatā. Nāmakasiṇasattapaññattiyo tisso paññattiyo.*

A. to *satta* being *paññatti*, see also S I 135: *Kiṃ nu satto ti paccesi, māra diṭṭhigataṃ nu te; Suddhasaṅkhārapuñjoyaṃ, nayidha sattupalabbhati. Yathā hi aṅgasambhārā, hoti saddo ratho ti; Evaṃ khandhesu santesu, hoti satto ti sammuti.* Paṭis-a I 67: *saṅkhāre upādāya satto ti paññattimattasambhavato vā phalopacārena saṅkhārā sattā ti vuttā ti veditabbaṃ. Na hi koci satto paccayaṭṭhitiko atthi aññatra saṅkhārehi, vohāravasena pana evaṃ vuccati.* Pm-vn 138: *Devayakkhamanussādi-nānābhedā salakkhikā; Sattapaññatti nāmāyaṃ, svāyaṃ satto ti sammato. ....* Mil 24–27: *... nāgaseno ti ... sīhaseno ti vā, api ca kho, mahārāja, saṅkhā samaññā paññatti vohāro nāmamattaṃ yadidaṃ nāgaseno ti, na hettha puggalo upalabbhatī ti. ... rūpañ-ca ... viññāṇañ-ca paṭicca nāgaseno ti saṅkhā ... nāmamattaṃ pavattati, paramatthato panettha puggalo nūpalabbhati.*

A. to *āpatti*, see Vjb 555: *... ettha āpatti nāma kiṃ paramatthasabhāvā, udāhu na vattabbasabhāvāti? Na vattabbasabhāvā. Vuttañ-hi ... vibhaṅge ... pārājikan-ti nāmañceva āpatti cā ti ... vacanato sammutimattaṃ, tasmā kusalattikavinimuttā na vattabbadhammabhūtā ekaccā sammuti evā ti vuttaṃ.*

196. Cf. Nidd-a II 72: *Manatī ti mano, vijānātī ti attho. Attano lakkhaṇaṃ dhārentī ti dhammā. Mano ti sahāvajjanabhavaṅgaṃ. Dhammā ti nibbānaṃ muñcitvā avasesā dhammārammaṇa-dhammā. Manoviññāṇan-ti javanamanoviññāṇaṃ.* Cf. the definition of *dhammārammaṇa* in As 80 in fn. 1863.

197. The variant reading 如理 = *yoniso, yathāvat, anurūpa, yuttarūpa* has been translated here, instead of 如昱, "like a bright light". Cf. Vism XIV.151/p.466, As 132: *Adhimuccanaṃ*

"Attention" is the adverting of the mind at the mind sense door.[198]

"Mind consciousness" is the activation mind (*javana-citta*).[199]

Herein, the mind is a condition for mind consciousness as support-condition.

Mental states are a condition as object-condition.

Resolve is a condition as support-condition.

Attention is a condition as two conditions: continuity-condition and absence-condition.[200]

Thus should it be known through condition.

37. Occurrence of the process of mind

Q. How through the occurrence of the process of mind?[201]

---

adhimokkho. So sanniṭṭhānalakkhaṇo, asaṃsappanaraso, nicchayapaccupaṭṭhāno, sanniṭṭheyyadhammapadaṭṭhāno, ārammaṇe niccalabhāvena indakhīlo viya daṭṭhabbo. Vibh-a 209: *Adhimokkhaniddese pana adhimuccanavasena adhimokkho. Adhimuccati vā tena ārammaṇe cittaṃ nibbicikicchatāya sanniṭṭhānaṃ gacchatī ti adhimokkho.*

198. Vism XIV.152/p.466, As 132: *Kiriyā kāro, manasmiṃ kāro manasikāro. Purimamanato visadisaṃ manaṃ karotī tipi manasikāro. Svāyaṃ ārammaṇapaṭipādako vīthipaṭipādako javanapaṭipādakotī tippakāro. ... Javanapaṭipādakoti manodvārāvajjanassa.*

199. Abhidh-av-pṭ 86: *taṃ manoviññāṇaṃ taṃ manoviññāṇasaṅkhātaṃ javanacittaṃ.* Nidd-a I 108, Abhidh-av-pṭ 99: *viññāṇan-ti javanacittaṃ.*

200. 有緣 = *atthi-paccaya*, "presence-condition". Above, in the analysis of the eye condition at 449a21, the definition of attention correctly is 非有緣, "non-presence-condition", or "absence-condition". Presumably the character 非 was lost here. Cf. Vibh-a 358: *Tathā cakkhu nissayapaccayo, rūpaṃ ārammaṇapaccayo, āvajjanaṃ anantara-samanantara-anantarūpanissaya-natthi-vigatapaccayo.*

201. 夾勝心起. *Vīthicitta-ppavattana* or *-ppavatti.* The character 夾 can mean "to hold between", "lined (garment)", "narrow lane", and this roughly corresponds to the Pali & Skt meanings of *vīthi* as "track", "street", "line". In Vim, 勝 usually corresponds to *visesa*, "distinctive", and a few times to "endeavour", *padhāna*". The translator might have added 勝to denote the active state of mind during the process in contrast to the inactive state in *bhavaṅga*; see Kim 2015: 235. Kim (2015: 239f.) suggests that 夾 corresponds to *visayappavatti* as used in Abhidh-s. However, for *visaya* the binome 境界 is used in Vim and there is no reason why there would be a sudden change to the unusual character 夾, which is used only in this section of Vim. Ñāṇamoli (PoP XVII.137) rendered *vīthicitta* as "cognitive series consciousness". The process is described at Vism XIV.110–123/pp.457–59. Cf. As 279 *Suttānusārena gamanakālo viya vīthicittappavatti.* Abhidh-s IV.6: *Ettha ca vīthicittappavattiyā sukhaggahaṇatthaṃ ambopamādikaṃ āharanti.* Abhidh-av 138: *Iti vīthippavattānaṃ, dvārālambaṇasaṅgaho.* Moh 75: *nāpi appavattamāne visaye pañcadvārikavīthicittāni pavattantī ti. Ayaṃ pañcadvāre visayappavattibhedena cittappavattiniyamo.*

For a detailed description of the process, see Cousins 1981: 22–46 and Bodhi 2007a: 149–184 (on Abhidh-s ch. IV).

A. At the eye sense door, putting aside the process [of mind], there are three kinds [of object]: great, medium, and slight.[202]

Herein, seven [kinds of] mind (*citta*) occur in a process with a great object. Immediately after [the sense object process, the bhavaṅga mind] arises.[203] Without interruption, following upon the *bhavaṅga* mind are the: (1) adverting mind (*āvajjana-citta*), (2) seeing mind (*dassana-citta*), (3) receiving mind (*sampaṭicchana-citta*), (4) investigation mind (*santīraṇa-citta*), (5) determining mind (*voṭṭhabbana-citta*), (6) activation mind (*javana-citta*), and (7) that-same-object mind (*tadārammaṇa-citta*).

Herein, the bhavaṅga mind is the mind with [the five sense-] faculties.[204] It is like [a spider with] stretched threads.[205] The adverting mind has a form-

---

202. Cf. Bodhi 2007a: 152–60 (on Abhidh-s IV.5–9). Cf. Vism XIV.121–122. Cf. Abhidh-av-pṭ II.37/§387–91: *Tathā hi visayaṃ āhu, catudhā ettha paṇḍitā; Mahantātimahantato, parittātiparittato ti. ... Ārammaṇantarāpāthe, dvikkhattuṃ calite mano; Cittantarassa hetuttaṃ, yānaṃ calanamīritan-ti.*

203. 無間生阿毘地獄, "immediate birth [in] Avīci hell". This is due to a misunderstanding of *avīcikaṃ*, "without interval", i.e. the bhavaṅga mind occurs without interval.

Cf. Vism XXI.129/p.669: *Tato bhavaṅgaṃ āvaṭṭetvā uppannassa tassa kiriyacittassānantaraṃ avīcikaṃ cittasantatiṃ anuppabandhamānaṃ tatheva saṅkhāre ārammaṇaṃ katvā uppajjati paṭhamaṃ javanacittaṃ, ...* Vism-mhṭ II 479: *Visadisacittapavattisaṅkhātāya vīciyā abhāvena avīcikā, cittasantati. Kiriyamanodhātuyā hi bhavaṅge āvaṭṭite kiriyamayacittapavattivipākacittuppattiyā savīcikā santarā, na evaṃ manodvārāvajjanenā ti vuttaṃ avīcikaṃ cittasantatiṃ anuppabandhamānan-ti.* Vism XIV.122/p.459-60: *Javanāvasāne pana sace pañcadvāre atimahantaṃ, manodvāre ca vibhūtamārammaṇaṃ hoti, atha kāmāvacarasattānaṃ kāmāvacarajavanāvasāne iṭṭhārammaṇādīnaṃ purimakammajavanacittādīnañ-ca vasena yo yo paccayo laddho hoti, tassa tassa vasena aṭṭhasu sahetukakāmāvacaravipākesu tīsu vipākāhetukamanoviññāṇadhātūsu ca aññataraṃ paṭisotagataṃ nāvaṃ anubandhamānaṃ kiñci antaraṃ udakamiva bhavaṅgassārammaṇato aññasmiṃ ārammaṇe javitaṃ javanamanubandhaṃ dvikkhattuṃ sakiṃ vā vipākaviññāṇaṃ uppajjati. Tadetaṃ javanāvasāne bhavaṅgassa ārammaṇe pavattanārahaṃ samānaṃ tassa javanassa ārammaṇaṃ ārammaṇaṃ katvā pavattattā tadārammaṇan-ti vuccati ...*

204. 於是有分心者是於此有根心. Herein, 有根心 could be *bhavindriya-citta*, "existence faculty mind" or *sa-indriya-citta* "having/with faculties mind". DDB gives 有根 as "accompanied by faculties, ... Skt *sêndriya*". If so, then this might be related to sense-faculties mentioned in the parallel at Vism XIV.115/p.458: *Evaṃ pavatte pana bhavaṅgasantāne yadā sattānaṃ indriyāni ārammaṇagahaṇakkhamāni honti, tadā cakkhussāpāthagate rūpe rūpaṃ paṭicca cakkhupasādassa ghaṭṭanā hoti, tato ghaṭṭanānubhāvena bhavaṅgacalanaṃ hoti, atha niruddhe bhavaṅge tadeva rūpaṃ ārammaṇaṃ katvā bhavaṅgaṃ vicchindamānā viya āvajjanakiccaṃ sādhayamānā kiriyamanodhātu uppajjati.*

205. The text literally has "drawing/pulling thread", 牽縷. Probably this is related to the simile of the spider in As and Abhidh-av quoted below, where the bhavaṅga mind is compared to a spider at the centre of the web. The operation of the mind process is compared to the time when the spider goes along whichever thread of the web has

object (*rūpārammaṇa*) process at the eye sense door as condition. Through the condition of mutuality (*aññamañña-paccaya*) of the [four] elements, dependent upon the [material] basis (*vatthu* = *vatthurūpa*),[206] there is the arising of the bhavaṅga mind, which sees a form-object. Immediately after the bhavaṅga mind, adverting gives rise to the adverting mind, which depends on the eye and the corresponding adverting. Immediately after the adverting mind, the obtaining of vision gives rise to the seeing mind [in the sense of] seeing [the object] with the mind. Immediately after the seeing mind, receiving gives rise to the receiving mind in the sense of receiving [the object]. Immediately after the receiving mind, investigating gives rise to the investigation mind in the sense of investigating [the object]. Immediately after the investigation mind, determining gives rise to the determining mind in the sense of determining [the object] with a functional-causeless[207]

---

been disturbed. Nothing precisely corresponds to the act of 'drawing' the thread. The five threads do, however, correspond to the five senses. So perhaps what is meant is a combination of the bhavaṅga mind proper with the disturbance of bhavaṅga when an object impacts the sensitive matter of one of the sense organs. Perhaps the translator misunderstood *anusāra*, "going along", or perhaps it is an idiomatic Chinese expression for a spider spreading (*pasāreti*) its threads.

Cf. As 279: *Tattha suttan-ti, eko panthamakkaṭako pañcasu disāsu suttaṃ pasāretvā jālaṃ katvā majjhe nipajjati. Paṭhamadisāya pasāritasutte pāṇakena vā paṭaṅgena vā makkhikāya vā pahaṭe nipannaṭṭhānato calitvā nikkhamitvā suttānusārena gantvā tassa yūsaṃ pivitvā puna-āgantvā tattheva nipajjati. Dutiyadisādīsu pahaṭakālepi evam-eva karoti. Tattha pañcasu disāsu pasāritasuttaṃ viya pañcapasādā. Majjhe nipannamakkaṭako viya cittaṃ. Pāṇakādīhi suttaghaṭṭanakālo viya ārammaṇena pasādassa ghaṭṭitakālo. Majjhe nipannamakkaṭakassa calanaṃ viya pasādaghaṭṭanakaṃ ārammaṇaṃ gahetvā kiriyamanodhātuyā bhavaṅgassa āvaṭṭitakālo. Suttānusārena gamanakālo viya vīthicittappavatti. Sīse vijjhitvā yūsapivanaṃ viya javanassa ārammaṇe javitakālo. Puna āgantvā majjhe nipajjanaṃ viya cittassa hadayavatthum-eva nissāya pavattanaṃ.*

Abhidh-av 54f: v 476. *Panthamakkaṭako nāma, disāsu pana pañcasu; Tattha suttaṃ pasāretvā, jālamajjhe nipajjati. ...* 483. *Manodhātukriyācittaṃ, bhavaṅgāvaṭṭanaṃ mataṃ; Tassā suttānusāraṃva, vīthicittapavattanaṃ.*

206. 以緣展轉諸界，依處有分心成起. Perhaps: "through the condition of the (material) base which depends on the reciprocity of the elements". Also at 449b29 below.

Cf. Vibh-a 42: *Manodvāre pana dhammārammaṇe āpāthagate eko evaṃ pariggahaṃ paṭṭhapeti: etaṃ dhammārammaṇaṃ kiṃ nissitanti? Vatthunissitanti. Vatthu kiṃ nissitanti? Mahābhūtāni nissitanti. So cattāri mahābhūtāni upādārūpañ-ca rūpan-ti pariggaṇhāti, tadārammaṇe dhamme arūpan-ti pariggaṇhāti.*

207. 由業心, although literally corresponding to *hetuka-kiriya-citta,* here corresponds to *kiriyāhetuka-citta.* Saṅghapāla also misunderstood the long *ā* in *kiriyāvyākate;* see fn. 1650. Cf. Vism XIV.120/p.459: *Santīraṇānantaraṃ pana tam-eva visayaṃ vavatthāpayamānā uppajjati kiriyāhetukamanoviññāṇadhātu upekkhāsahagatā ti evaṃ ekasseva kiriyaviññāṇassa voṭṭhabbanavasena pavatti veditabbā.*

mind. Immediately after the determining mind, activation [gives rise to the activation mind] in the sense of activating, not in [the sense of] means.[208] Immediately after the activation mind, [that-same-object] gives rise to a resultant that-same-object mind. Following that, [the mind] enters again into the bhavaṅga mind.[209]

38. Simile of the mango

Q. What is the simile?

A. The king is sleeping in his upper chamber with the gate closed. A hunchbacked woman massages the king's feet and the queen sits. The chief minister (*mahāmacca*) and courtiers are lined up in front of him. A deaf doorkeeper is standing leaning [with his back] against the door. At that time the gardener, who is holding mango fruits, knocks at the door. Hearing the sound, the king awakens, and orders the hunchbacked woman: "Go and open the door". The hunchbacked woman, immediately upon being ordered, speaks to the doorkeeper by way of sign language. The deaf doorkeeper grasps the meaning and immediately opens the door. Seeing the mango fruits, the king seizes a knife. The hunchbacked woman accepts the fruits, enters [the room], and presents them to the chief minister. The chief minister presents them to the queen. The queen cleans them, [sees] whether they are ripe or unripe, puts them each in one place, and then offers them to the king. Getting them, the king eats them. Having eaten them, he immediately talks of the merits or demerits of them. Then he goes to sleep again.

Herein, the bhavaṅga mind should be understood as the sleeping king. The king's gardener, who is holding mangos and knocks at the door, as the form-object process at the eye sense door. The awakening of the king by the knocking at the door, and his ordering the hunchbacked woman to

---

208. 不以方便, "not as means" or "not as functional". The characters 方便 correspond to *payoga*, "application", or to *upāya*, "means", or, at 448b19, to *kiriyā, kriyā*. Cf. 以方便義 at 455b18. There is no definition of the following that-same-object mind. Cf. Vism XIV.121/p.459: *imesu yaṃ yaṃ laddhapaccayaṃ hoti, taṃ taṃ javatī ti evaṃ pañcapaññāsāya kusalākusalakiriyavipākaviññāṇānaṃ javanavasena pavatti veditabbā*. Cf. 448b18–20: 識果報意界, 設果報設方便, 意識界設善設不善, 設果報設方便. Cf. As 270: *Sace pana balavārammaṇaṃ āpāthagataṃ hoti kiriyamanodhātuyā bhavaṅge āvaṭṭite cakkhuviññāṇādīni uppajjanti. Javanaṭṭhāne pana paṭhama-kāmāvacara-kusalacittaṃ javanaṃ hutvā chasattavāre javitvā tadārammaṇassa vāraṃ deti. Tadārammaṇaṃ patiṭṭhāha-mānaṃ taṃsadisam-eva mahāvipākacittaṃ patiṭṭhāti. Idaṃ dve nāmāni labhati paṭisandhicittasadisattā mūlabhavaṅgan-ti ca, yaṃ javanena gahitaṃ ārammaṇaṃ tassa gahitattā tadārammaṇan-ti ca. Imasmiṃ ṭhāne cakkhuviññāṇaṃ sampaṭicchanaṃ santīraṇaṃ tadārammaṇan-ti cattāri vipākacittāni gaṇanūpagāni honti.*

209. Cf. Vism XIV.115–123/pp.458–59 and the Vīthiparicheda in Abhidh-s chapter IV.

open the door, as the arising of the bhavaṅga mind through the condition of mutuality of the [four] elements, dependent upon the [material] basis. [**449c**] The hunchbacked woman's instructing the deaf doorkeeper by way of sign language to open the door, as the adverting mind. The opening of the door by the deaf doorkeeper and the seeing of the mangoes, as eye-consciousness. The seizing of the knife by the king, and the hunchbacked woman accepting the fruits and presenting them to the chief minister, as the receiving mind. The chief minister holding the fruits and presenting them to the queen, as the investigation mind. The queen cleaning [the fruits and seeing] whether they are ripe or unripe, and placing each in one place and offering them to the king, should be understood as the determining mind. The eating of the fruits by the king, as the activation mind. His talking about the merits (*guṇa*) or demerits of the fruits, as the resultant that-same-object mind. The king's going to sleep again should be understood as the entering [again] into the bhavaṅga mind.[210]

Herein, in an eye sense door process with a middling object, [after] the activation mind, [the mind] immediately enters into the bhavaṅga mind.

In a process with a slight object, [after] the determining mind, [the mind] immediately enters into the bhavaṅga mind. Accordingly [the processes] at the other sense doors should be understood.

There is no [five sense door] object process at the mind sense door.[211]

---

210. The Pali version of the mango simile is found at As 279, Abhidh-av-pṭ II 60: *Dovāriko ti, eko rājā sayanagato niddāyati. Tassa paricārako pāde parimajjanto nisīdi. Badhiradovāriko dvāre ṭhito. Tayo paṭihārā paṭipāṭiyā ṭhitā. Atheko paccantavāsī manusso paṇṇākāraṃ ādāya āgantvā dvāraṃ ākoṭesi. Badhiradovāriko saddaṃ na suṇāti. Pādaparimajjako saññaṃ adāsi. Tāya saññāya dvāraṃ vivaritvā passi. Paṭhamapaṭihāro paṇṇākāraṃ gahetvā dutiyassa adāsi, dutiyo tatiyassa, tatiyo rañño. Rājā paribhuñji. Tattha so rājā viya javanaṃ daṭṭhabbaṃ. Pādaparimajjako viya āvajjanaṃ. Badhiradovāriko viya cakkhuviññāṇaṃ. Tayo paṭihārā viya sampaṭicchanādīni tīṇi vīthicittāni. Paccantavāsino paṇṇākāraṃ ādāya āgantvā dvārākoṭanaṃ viya ārammaṇassa pasādi-aghaṭṭanaṃ. Pādaparimajjakena saññāya dinnakālo viya kiriyamanodhātuyā bhavaṅgassa āvaṭṭitakālo. Tena dinnasaññāya badhiradovārikassa dvāravivaraṇakālo viya cakkhuviññāṇassa ārammaṇe dassanakiccasādhanakālo. Paṭhamapaṭihārena paṇṇākārassa gahitakālo viya vipākamanodhātuyā ārammaṇassa sampaṭicchitakālo. Paṭhamena dutiyassa dinnakālo viya vipākamanoviññāṇadhātuyā ārammaṇassa santīraṇakālo. Dutiyena tatiyassa dinnakālo viya kiriyamanoviññāṇadhātuyā ārammaṇassa vavatthāpitakālo. Tatiyena rañño dinnakālo viya voṭṭhabbanena javanassa niyyāditakālo. Rañño paribhogakālo viya javanassa ārammaṇarasānubhavanakālo.*

211. LC: "I.e. the term *vīthi* is restricted to the sequence from five sense door adverting to investigating". Cf. Abhidh-s ch. IV.

Cf. Vism XIV.152/p.466, As 133: *Purimamanato visadisaṃ manaṃ karotī ti pi manasikāro. Svāyaṃ ārammaṇapaṭipādako vīthipaṭipādako javanapaṭipādako ti tippakāro. Tattha ārammaṇapaṭipādako manasmiṃ kāroti manasikāro. So sāraṇalakkhaṇo,*

Through the condition of attention, without impetus (*asaṅkhārena*) there is grasping of the object at the mind sense door.[212]

Herein, with regard to a great object, three [kinds of] mind are produced [following] the bhavaṅga mind: adverting mind, activation mind, and that-same-object mind.

With regard to middling and slight objects, two [kinds of] mind are produced: adverting mind and activation mind.[213]

Herein, agreeable or disagreeable middling objects are to be known through various conditions and various feelings.[214] The various kinds

---

sampayuttānaṃ ārammaṇe sampayojanaraso, ārammaṇābhimukhabhāvapaccupaṭṭhāno, saṅkhārakkhandhapariyāpanno. Ārammaṇapaṭipādakattena sampayuttānaṃ sārathi viya daṭṭhabbo. Vīthipaṭipādako ti pana pañcadvārāvajjanass' etaṃ adhivacanaṃ. Javana-paṭipādako ti manodvārāvajjanassa.

212. 以解脱行 = "by/with freedom from formations", but this does not fit here. This is a misunderstanding of *asaṅkhārena,* "effortless".

This passage seems to be related to passages in the *Atthasālinī*; As 268: *Asaṅkhārikaṃ kusalaṃ asaṅkhārikam-pi sasaṅkhārikam-pi vipākaṃ deti. Sasaṅkhārikaṃ sasaṅkhārikam-pi asaṅkhārikam-pi vipākaṃ deti. Ārammaṇena vedanā parivattetabbā. Javanena tadārammaṇaṃ niyāmetabbaṃ.* As 274: *Sasaṅkhārikatihetukakusalenāpi upekkhāsahagatehi asaṅkhārikasasaṅkhārikakusalacittehipi kamme āyūhite taṃsadisavipākacittehi ādinnāya paṭisandhiyā eseva nayo. Upekkhāsahagatadvaye pana paṭhamaṃ iṭṭhamajjhattārammaṇavasena pavattiṃ dassetvā pacchā iṭṭhārammaṇavasena dassetabbā.* As 275: *Duhetukena hi somanassasahagata-asaṅkhārikacittena kamme āyūhite taṃsadiseneva duhetukavipākacittena gahitapaṭisandhikassa vuttanayeneva cakkhudvāre iṭṭhārammaṇe āpāthamāgate tayo moghavārā. Duhetukasomanassasahagata-asaṅkhārika-javanāvasāne taṃsadisam-eva mūlabhavaṅgasaṅkhātaṃ tadārammaṇaṃ.* See also the views of the three theras at As 284–88. Cf. As 155: *Tassattho saha saṅkhārenā ti sasaṅkhāro. Tena sasaṅkhārena sappayogena sa-upāyena paccayagaṇenā ti attho. Yena hi ārammaṇādinā paccayagaṇena paṭhamaṃ mahācittaṃ uppajjati, teneva sappayogena sa-upāyena idaṃ uppajjati. ...* Moh 75: *Yadā pana vuttanayena saddārammaṇādīni sotadvārādīsu ghaṭṭenti, tadāpi cakkhudvāre viya paccekañ-ca chacattālīseva bhavanti. Kevalaṃ hettha āvajjanānantaraṃ cakkhuviññāṇaṭṭhāne sotaviññāṇādidvayāni yathākkamaṃ savanādikiccāni sādhayamānāni uppajjantī ti. Evaṃ pañcadvāre atimahante pañcārammaṇe catupaññāsa kāmāvacaracittāneva sambhavanti. Keci panettha sasaṅkhārikajavanāni pañcadvāre na uppajjanti pubbappayogāsambhavā manodvāreyevetāni uppajjantī ti vadanti.* Moh 31: *Ettha ca pañcadvāre uppannāni javanāni kāyavacīkammāni na honti, manokammāni eva. Tāni ca na kammapathappattāni, kevalaṃ kusalādīni honti. Manodvāre paṭutarappavattāni eva hi kammapathappattāni manokammāni honti, rūpārūpajavanāni pana ekantaṃ bhāvanāmayaṃ manokammam-eva manodvāre eva ca pavattanti.*

213. Cf. Abhidh-s Ch. IV/p.24: *Manodvāre pana yadi vibhūtamārammaṇaṃ āpāthamā-gacchati, tato paraṃ bhavaṅgacalanamanodvāra-āvajjanajavanāvasāne tadārammaṇapākāni pavattanti, tato paraṃ bhavaṅgapāto. Avibhūte panārammaṇe javanāvasāne bhavaṅgapātova hoti, natthi tadārammaṇuppādoti.*

214. Cf. As 269: *Ārammaṇena vedanā parivattetabbā. Javanena tadārammaṇaṃ*

of wholesomeness and unwholesomeness are to be known through the condition of reasoned attention and unreasoned attention.

Thus should it be known through the occurrence of the process of mind.

39. Inclusion

Q. How through inclusion?

A. There are three kinds of inclusion, namely, inclusion in the aggregates, inclusion in the elements, and inclusion in the truths.

Herein, ten sense bases are included in the aggregate of matter. The sense base of mind is included in the aggregate of consciousness. The sense base of mental states, except for nibbāna, is included in four aggregates.[215]

Eleven sense bases are included in eleven elements. The sense base of mind is included in seven elements.

The five internal sense bases are included in the truth of suffering. The five external sense bases are either included or not included in the truth of suffering. The sense base of mind is either included or not included in the truth of suffering. The sense base of mental states is either included or not included in the four truths.[216]

Thus, one should know through inclusion.

---

niyāmetabbaṃ ... As 277: *Idaṃ pana javanaṃ kusalatthāya vā akusalatthāya vā ko niyāmetī ti? Āvajjanañ c'eva voṭṭhabbanañ ca.*

215. The Dhātukathā and its commentary also exclude the *asaṅkhatadhātu* from the *dhammāyatana* when it is included in the aggregates, i.e. in the first four aggregates including the aggregate of matter, here consisting of the 18 kinds of subtle matter (see Ch. 11 § 15), and not including the aggregate of consciousness since it is included in the sense base of mind of which *dhamma*-s are the object. In the Abhidhamma, nibbāna can be the object of the sense base of mind, but is not included in the aggregates. In Ch. 11 § 32 the subtle matters and the *asaṅkhatadhātu* are included in the *dhammāyatana*. See Dhāt 5: *Manāyatanaṃ ekena khandhena ekenāyatanena sattahi dhātūhi saṅgahitaṃ. .... Dhammāyatanaṃ, asaṅkhataṃ khandhato ṭhapetvā, catūhi khandhehi ekenāyatanena ekāya dhātuyā saṅgahitaṃ.* Dhāt-a 118: *Asaṅkhataṃ khandhato ṭhapetvā ti ettha pana yasmā asaṅkhataṃ dhammāyatanaṃ nāma nibbānaṃ, tañ-ca khandhasaṅgahaṃ na gacchati; tasmā khandhato ṭhapetvā ti vuttaṃ. Catūhi khandhehī ti rūpavedanāsaññāsaṅkhāra-kkhandhehi. Nibbānavajjañ-hi dhammāyatanaṃ etehi saṅgahitaṃ. Viññāṇakkhandhena pana ṭhapetvā dhammāyatanadhammadhātuyo sesāyatanadhātūhi ca taṃ na saṅgayhati.* Dhs 211 § 1211–12: *Vedanākkhandho, saññākkhandho, saṅkhārakkhandho—ime dhammā cittasaṃsaṭṭhasamuṭṭhānānuparivattino. ... Cittañ-ca, sabbañ-ca rūpaṃ, asaṅkhatā ca dhātu—ime dhammā no cittasaṃsaṭṭhasamuṭṭhānānuparivattino.*

216. 法入或四諦所攝或非苦諦所攝 means "the sense base of mental states is either included in the four truths or not included in the truth of suffering", which is a copyist's mistake. In the inclusion method, the text instead has "the mental states element is included in the four truths, or not included in the four truths".

Thus, in these ways, one gives rise to knowledge with regard to the sense bases.

This is called "skill in the sense bases".

The skill in the sense bases is finished.

Skill in the Elements

40. What is skill in the elements?

Q. What is skill in the elements?

A. The eighteen elements are the eye element, form element, eye-consciousness element; ear element, sound element, ear-consciousness element; nose element, odour element, nose-consciousness element; tongue element, taste element, tongue-consciousness element; body element, touch element, body-consciousness element; and mind-element, mental states element, mind-consciousness-element.[217]

Herein, eye sensitivity is the eye element. Colour-luminosity[218] is the form element. Eye-consciousness is the eye-consciousness element. In the same way, the other [elements] should be understood.[219]

The mind-element is the adverting at the five sense doors to the object and the receiving of the result.[220] **[450a]**

The mental states element is just the mental states sense base.[221]

217. Vibh 87: *Aṭṭhārasa dhātuyo: cakkhudhātu rūpadhātu cakkhuviññāṇadhātu sotadhātu saddadhātu sotaviññāṇadhātu ghānadhātu gandhadhātu ghānaviññāṇadhātu jivhādhātu rasadhātu jivhāviññāṇadhātu kāyadhātu phoṭṭhabbadhātu kāyaviññāṇadhātu manodhātu dhammadhātu manoviññāṇadhātu.*

218. 色形 = *vaṇṇanibhā.* See fn. 1846.

219. See the start of the sense base skill section above at 448c–449a.

220. Cf. Vism XV.34/p.488: "The mind-element is reckoned as three things on account of the five sense door adverting, and the receiving of the wholesome and the unwholesome result", *manodhātu pana pañcadvārāvajjanakusalākusalavipākasampaṭicchanavasena tayo dhammā ti saṅkhaṃ gacchati.* Cf. Abhidh-av-pṭ II 22: *pañcadvāre āvajjanakāle pañcadvārāvajjanassa ca ārammaṇaṃ hotiti.* Abhidh-s 23: *... tam-eva rūpārammaṇaṃ āvajjantaṃ pañcadvārāvajjanacittaṃ uppajjitvā nirujjhati, tato tassānantaraṃ tam-eva rūpaṃ passantaṃ cakkhuviññāṇaṃ, sampaṭicchantaṃ sampaṭicchanacittaṃ, ...* Vism XIV.118: *cakkhuviññāṇādīnaṃ anantarā tesaññeva visayaṃ sampaṭicchamānā kusalavipākānantaraṃ kusalavipākā, akusalavipākānantaraṃ akusalavipākā manodhātu uppajjati. Evaṃ dvinnaṃ vipākaviññāṇānaṃ sampaṭicchanavasena pavatti veditabbā.*

221. See Ch. 11 § 32/449a05 in the sense bases section above. The *dhammāyatana* and *dhammadhātu* are identical; see Peṭ 99: *Yathā sā dhammadhātu tathā dhammāyatanaṃ pariyesitabbaṃ. Yāyeva hi dhammadhātu tadeva dhammāyatanaṃ anūnaṃ anadhikaṃ.* Abhidh-s 231: *Cetasikānaṃ, soḷasasukhumarūpānaṃ, nibbānassa ca vasena ekūnasattati dhammā āyatanesu dhammāyatanaṃ, dhātūsu dhammadhātū ti ca saṅkhaṃ gacchanti.*

[The (kinds of) mind occurring by way of] the six consciousness elements and the other [kinds of] mind (*citta*) are the mind-consciousness-element.[222]

The rest was taught in detail under [skill in the] sense bases.

41. Inclusion

Herein, ten elements are included in the aggregate of matter. The mental states element, except for nibbāna, is included in four aggregates. Seven elements are included in the aggregate of consciousness. Eleven elements are included in eleven sense bases. Seven elements are included in the sense base of mind.[223]

Moh 25: *Te puna āyatanato duvidhā honti: manāyatanaṃ dhammāyatanan-ti. Sañjātisamosaraṇaṭṭhānaṭṭhena hettha cittaṃ manāyatanaṃ, sesā pana aṭṭhatiṃsa dhammā dhammāyatananti. Evaṃ āyatanato duvidhā honti. Te puna dhātuvasena duvidhā: manoviññāṇadhātu dhammadhātū ti. Nissattanijjīvaṭṭhena hettha cittaṃ manoviññāṇadhātu, sesā dhammadhātū ti.*

222. The text is corrupt: "At five door adverting object, mind-element receives result. Mind-element just mental states sense base except* mental states element six consciousness elements other/remaining mind(s) mind-consciousness-element. (* variant reading: except = other). 於五門轉事意界受果報, 意界唯法入, *除法界六識界, 餘心意識界 (* 除＝餘). This refers to the seven consciousness elements, i.e. the five physical consciousness elements, the mind-element, and the mind-consciousness-element; see fn. 1852. In Vibh 88–89, the *manodhātu* is defined as the *citta* & *viññāṇa* arisen dependent upon the adverting to the five physical consciousnesses, while the *manoviññāṇadhātu* is defined as the *citta* & *viññāṇa* arisen dependent upon the *manodhātu*: *Cakkhuviññāṇadhātuyā uppajjitvā niruddhasamanantarā uppajjati cittaṃ mano mānasaṃ ... viññāṇaṃ viññāṇakkhandho tajjāmanodhātu; ... kāyaviññāṇadhātuyā uppajjitvā niruddhasamanantarā uppajjati ... tajjāmanodhātu, sabbadhammesu vā pana paṭhamasamannāhāro uppajjati ... tajjāmanodhātu—ayaṃ vuccati manodhātu. ... Cakkhuviññāṇadhātuyā uppajjitvā niruddhasamanantarā uppajjati manodhātu, manodhātuyā uppajjitvā niruddhasamanantarā uppajjati ... tajjāmanoviññāṇadhātu; ... kāyaviññāṇadhātuyā uppajjitvā niruddhasamanantarā uppajjati manodhātu, manodhātuyāpi uppajjitvā niruddhasamanantarā uppajjati ... tajjāmanoviññāṇadhātu, manañ-ca paṭicca dhamme ca uppajjati ... tajjāmanoviññāṇadhātu—ayaṃ vuccati manoviññāṇadhātu.*

According to the *Vibhaṅga-mūlaṭīkā*, if only the minds ending in the activation mind by way of the six sense-doors would be taken as *manoviññāṇadhātū*, then, due to not taking into account the decease minds, relinking minds, and bhavaṅga minds, the explanation is incomplete. Therefore the meaning is to be understood "by way of the six sense-door minds or also as the other [kinds of mind] of common characteristics explained as 'mind-consciousness-element'". Vibh-mṭ 48: *Yadi pana channaṃ dvārānaṃ vasena javanāvasānāneva cittāni idha manoviññāṇadhātū ti dassitānīti ayamattho gayheyya, cutipaṭisandhibhavaṅgānaṃ aggahitattā sāvasesā desanā āpajjati, tasmā yathāvuttena nayena attho veditabbo. Chadvārikacittehi vā samānalakkhaṇāni aññānipi manoviññāṇadhātū ti dassitānīti veditabbāni.*

223. See fn. 1883.

Eleven elements are included in the truth of suffering. Five elements are included in the truth of suffering, or not included in the truth of suffering. The mental states element is included in the four truths, or not included in the four truths. The mind-consciousness-element is included in the truth of suffering or not included in the truth of suffering.[224]

Q. What is the range (*gocara* or *visaya*) of the elements?

A. Just these states are the range: the aggregates, sense bases, and elements.

It is taught that the characteristic of the aggregates is aggregation of similar (*sabhāga*) states.[225]

It is taught that the characteristic of the sense bases is entrance (*dvāra, mukha*).[226]

It is taught that the characteristic of the elements is intrinsic nature (*sabhāva*).[227]

---

224. This differs from the classification in the Dhātukathā. Dhāt 8–9: *Dukkhasaccaṃ pañcahi khandhehi dvādasahāyatanehi aṭṭhārasahi dhātūhi saṅgahitaṃ. ... Na kehici khandhehi na kehici āyatanehi na kāhici dhātūhi asaṅgahitaṃ. Samudayasaccaṃ ... maggasaccaṃ ekena khandhena ekenāyatanena ekāya dhātuyā saṅgahitaṃ. ... Catūhi khandhehi ekādasahāyatanehi sattarasahi dhātūhi asaṅgahitaṃ. Nirodhasaccaṃ na kehici khandhehi ekenāyatanena ekāya dhātuyā saṅgahitaṃ. ... Pañcahi khandhehi ekādasahāyatanehi sattarasahi dhātūhi asaṅgahitaṃ.*

225. "Aggregation" = 和合, which also means "compounding", "cohering", "connecting", etc. (*saṅgaha, sannipāta, saṃyutta, saññoga,* etc.). The Tibetan (184b) has: "aggregation of similar states", *ris mthun pa'i ches rnams tshogs pa*. Cf. M I 190: *Yato ca kho, āvuso, ajjhattikañceva cakkhuṃ aparibhinnaṃ hoti, bāhirā ca rūpā āpāthaṃ āgacchanti, tajjo ca samannāhāro hoti. Evaṃ tajjassa viññāṇabhāgassa pātubhāvo hoti. Yaṃ tathābhūtassa rūpaṃ taṃ rūpupādānakkhandhe saṅgahaṃ gacchati, yā tathābhūtassa vedanā sā vedanupādānakkhandhe saṅgahaṃ gacchati, yā tathābhūtassa saññā sā saññupādānakkhandhe saṅgahaṃ gacchati, ye tathābhūtassa saṅkhārā te saṅkhārupādānakkhandhe saṅgahaṃ gacchanti, yaṃ tathābhūtassa viññāṇaṃ taṃ viññāṇupādānakkhandhe saṅgahaṃ gacchati. So evaṃ pajānāti evañ-hi kira imesaṃ pañcannaṃ upādānakkhandhānaṃ saṅgaho sannipāto samavāyo hoti.* Peṭ 112f.: *Tattha katamo khandhattho? Samūhattho khandhattho, puñjattho khandhattho, rāsattho khandhattho. Taṃ yathā dabbakkhandho vanakkhandho dārukkhandho aggikkhandho udakakkhandho vāyukkhandho iti evaṃ khandhesu sabbasaṅgaho va evaṃ khandhattho.* Vibh-a 2f.: *Tatrāyaṃ khandha-saddo sambahulesu ṭhānesu dissati rāsimhi, guṇe, paṇṇattiyaṃ, ruḷhiyan ti. ... svāyam idha rāsito adhippeto. Ayañ hi khandhaṭṭho nāma piṇḍaṭṭho pūgaṭṭho ghaṭaṭṭho rāsaṭṭho. tasmā rāsilakkhaṇā khandhā ti veditabbā. Koṭṭhāsaṭṭho ti pi vattuṃ vaṭṭati; lokasmiñ hi iṇaṃ gahetvā codiyamānā dvīhi khandhehi dassāma, tīhi khandhehi dassāmā' ti vadanti. Iti koṭṭhāsalakkhaṇā khandhā ti pi vattuṃ vaṭṭati.*

226. Cf. Vism XV.4–5: *Apica nivāsaṭṭhānaṭṭhena ākaraṭṭhena samosaraṇaṭṭhānaṭṭhena sañjātidesaṭṭhena kāraṇaṭṭhena ca āyatanaṃ veditabbaṃ.*

227. Cf. Vism XV.21: *attano sabhāvaṃ dhārentī ti dhātuyo.* A-a II 277: *Tattha dhātuyoti sabhāvā. Nijjīvanissattabhāvappakāsako hi sabhāvaṭṭho dhātvaṭṭho nāma.* Paṭis-a II 521:

Furthermore, the Fortunate One taught the truth of suffering by way of the aggregates method (*dvāra*) to one with sharp faculties; he taught the truth of suffering by way of the sense bases method to one with average faculties;[228] and he taught the truth of suffering by way of the elements method to one with dull faculties.

Furthermore, he taught the aggregates by teaching matter in brief and by analysis of name (*nāma*) [in full] to one who has the characteristic of attachment to name (*nāma*); he taught the sense bases by analysis of matter [in full] and by teaching name in brief to one who has the characteristic of attachment to matter; and he taught the elements by analysis of name-and-matter [in full] to one who has the characteristic of attachment to name-and-matter.[229]

Furthermore, he taught the aggregates by teaching the grounds of selfhood (*attabhāvavatthu*);[230] he taught the sense bases by teaching the bases and objects (*vatthu & ārammaṇa*); and he taught the elements by teaching the bases and objects and by teaching the process of mind (*cittavīthi, cittappavatti*).[231]

In these ways, [arises] skill in defining the elements.

This is called "skill in the elements".

The skill in the elements is finished.

---

sabhāvaṭṭhena, nissattaṭṭhena vā dhātū ti.

228. In the Pali, the term *majjhindriya* is only found in the *Netti.* Nett 100: *iti tesaṃ mudumajjhādhimattatā ayaṃ mudindriyo ayaṃ majjhindriyo ayaṃ tikkhindriyo ti. Tattha bhagavā tikkhindriyaṃ saṃkhittena ovādena ovadati, majjhindriyaṃ bhagavā saṃkhittavitthārena ovadati, mudindriyaṃ bhagavā vitthārena ovadati. ...* The Tibetan version is different.

229. 於名著相人 lit. means "towards name attachment characteristic person"; 為著色相人, "for attachment matter characteristic person"; and於名色著相人 "towards name and matter attachment characteristic person". However, the character相, "characteristic" or "sign", is often confused with 想, "perception". The latter is supported by the Tibetan (Sav 184b–185a): "Furthermore, to one who perceives beauty (*sdug pa'i 'du shes can = subhasaññī*) in the immaterial aggregates ...".

230. See Appendix V.

231. This refers to the "occurrence of the process of mind", *vīthicittapavatti*, as described in detail in the sense base skill section, and briefly in this section as adverting of the mind at the sense bases, etc. The Tibetan (Sav 185a) has *nges pa skyed pa. Negs pa* can mean "record/register [in one's mind], fix [in the mind]" and *skyed pa* can mean *pavatti*, so possibly the Tibetan translator understood *cittavīthi* or *vīthipavatti* as the process of registration.

Skill in Dependent Arising

42. What is skill in dependent arising?

Q. What is skill in dependent arising?

A. With ignorance as condition, formations; with formations as condition, consciousness; with consciousness as condition, name-and-matter; with name-and-matter as condition, the six sense bases; with the six sense bases as condition, contact; with contact as condition, feeling; with feeling as condition, craving; with craving as condition, clinging; with clinging as condition, existence; with existence as condition, birth; with birth as condition, ageing and death, sorrow, lamentation, pain, distress, and grief.[232] In this way, there is the origination of this entire mass of suffering.

But through the cessation of ignorance, there is the cessation of the formations; through the cessation of the formations, there is the cessation of consciousness; through the cessation of consciousness, there is the cessation of name-and-matter; through the cessation of name-and-matter, there is the cessation of the six sense bases; through the cessation of the six sense bases, there is the cessation of contact; through the cessation of contact, there is the cessation of feeling; through the cessation of feeling, there is the cessation of craving; through the cessation of craving, there is the cessation of clinging; through the cessation of clinging, there is the cessation of existence; through the cessation of existence, there is the cessation of birth; through the cessation of birth, there is the cessation of ageing and death, sorrow, lamentation, pain, distress, and grief. In this way, there is the cessation of this entire mass of suffering.[233]

---

232. "Distress and grief", *domanassupāyāsa*, are translated by one character, 惱.

233. Ud 1; S II 1: *Katamo ca ... paṭiccasamuppādo? Avijjāpaccayā ... saṅkhārā; saṅkhārapaccayā viññāṇaṃ; viññāṇapaccayā nāmarūpaṃ; nāmarūpapaccayā saḷāyatanaṃ; saḷāyatanapaccayā phasso; phassapaccayā vedanā; vedanāpaccayā taṇhā; taṇhāpaccayā upādānaṃ; upādānapaccayā bhavo; bhavapaccayā jāti; jātipaccayā jarāmaraṇaṃ sokaparidevadukkhadomanassupāyāsā sambhavanti. Evametassa kevalassa dukkhakkhandhassa samudayo hoti. Ayaṃ vuccati ... paṭiccasamuppādo. Avijjāya tveva asesavirāganirodhā saṅkhāranirodho; saṅkhāranirodhā viññāṇanirodho; viññāṇanirodhā nāmarūpanirodho; nāmarūpanirodhā saḷāyatananirodho; saḷāyatananirodhā phassanirodho; phassanirodhā vedanānirodho; vedanānirodhā taṇhānirodho; taṇhānirodhā upādānanirodho; upādānanirodhā bhavanirodho; bhavanirodhā jātinirodho; jātinirodhā jarāmaraṇaṃ sokaparidevadukkhadomanassupāyāsā nirujjhanti. Evametassa kevalassa dukkhakkhandhassa nirodho hotī ti.*

43. Explanation of the twelve factors

Herein "ignorance" (*avijjā*) is non-knowledge (*aññāṇa*) of the four truths.[234]

"Formations" (*saṅkhārā*) are bodily, verbal, and mental actions (*kamma*).

"Consciousness" (*viññāṇa*): the mind (*citta*) at the moment of entering the womb is called consciousness.[235]

"Name-and-matter": [name] is the mental properties (*cetasika dhamma*) that arise together (*sahajāta*) with the relinking mind (*paṭisandhi-citta*) and [matter is] the embryonic matter (*kalala-rūpa*).[236]

"Six sense bases" are the six internal sense bases.[237]

---

234. Peṭ 116: *Tattha katamā avijjā? Yaṃ catūsu ariyasaccesu aññāṇanti.* Peṭ 118: *Tattha avijjā nāma catūsu ariyasaccesu yathābhūtaṃ aññāṇaṃ, ayaṃ avijjā.* Cf. Spk II 78, etc.

235. Tibetan (Sav 185b): "the mind of the time/occasion of relinking (*paṭisandhi-samaya/kāla*)". 入胎 means "enters the womb" and corresponds to *gabbhāvakkanti.*

236. Cf. Paṭis-a III 571: *Pañcakkhandhā ti ettha paṭisandhicittena paṭisandhikkhaṇe labbhamānāni rūpāni rūpakkhandho, sahajātā vedanā vedanākkhandho, saññā saññākkhandho, sesacetasikā saṅkhārakkhandho, paṭisandhicittaṃ viññāṇakkhandho.* Vibh-a 21–2: *gabbhaseyyakasattānañ-hi paṭisandhikkhaṇe pañcakkhandhā apacchāapure ekato pātubhavanti. Tasmiṃ khaṇe pātubhūtā kalalasaṅkhātā rūpasantati parittā hoti. ... Evaṃ parittāya rūpasantatiyā tīṇi santatisīsāni honti—vatthudasakaṃ, kāyadasakaṃ, ... Tattha vatthurūpaṃ, tassa nissayāni cattāri mahābhūtāni, taṃnissitā vaṇṇagandharasojā, jīvitanti—idaṃ vatthudasakaṃ nāma ... Evaṃ gabbhaseyyakānaṃ paṭisandhiyaṃ ukkaṭṭhaparicchedena samatiṃsa kammajarūpāni rūpakkhandho nāma hoti. Paṭisandhicittena pana sahajātā vedanā vedanākkhandho, saññā saññākkhandho, saṅkhārā saṅkhārakkhandha. Paṭisandhicittaṃ viññāṇakkhandho ti.* Cf. Vin III 73: *Manussaviggaho nāma yaṃ mātukucchismiṃ paṭhamaṃ cittaṃ uppannaṃ paṭhamaṃ viññāṇaṃ pātubhūtaṃ, yāva maraṇakālā etthantare eso manussaviggaho nāma.* Sp II 437: *Paṭhamaṃ cittan-ti paṭisandhicittaṃ. Uppannan-ti jātaṃ. Paṭhamaṃ viññāṇaṃ pātubhūtan-ti idaṃ tasseva vevacanaṃ. Mātukucchismiṃ paṭhamaṃ cittan-ti vacanena cettha sakalāpi pañcavokārapaṭisandhi dassitā hoti. Tasmā tañ-ca paṭhamaṃ cittaṃ taṃsampayuttā ca tayo arūpakkhandhā tena saha nibbattañ-ca kalalarūpan-ti ayaṃ sabbapaṭhamo manussaviggaho. Tattha kalalarūpan-ti itthipurisānaṃ kāyavatthubhāvadasakavasena samatiṃsa rūpāni, napuṃsakānaṃ kāyavatthudasakavasena vīsati. Tattha itthipurisānaṃ kalalarūpaṃ jāti-uṇṇāya ekena aṃsunā uddhaṭatelabindumattaṃ hoti acchaṃ vippasannaṃ.* Cf. the Sanskrit version of the Mahānidānasutta (D II 63) as quoted in Abhidh-k-vy 669: *vijñānaṃ ced ānanda mātuḥ kukṣiṃ nāvakrāmed api tu tan nāmarūpaṃ kalalatvāya saṃmūrchet. na bhadanta. vijñānaṃ ced ānandāvakrāmya kṣipram evāpakrāmed api tu tan nāmarūpam itthavtāya prajñāyeta. no bhadanta. vijñānaṃ ced ānanda daharasya kumārasya kumārikāyā vā ucchidyeta vinaśyen na bhaved api tu tan nāmarūpaṃ vṛddhiṃ vipulatām āpadyeta. no bhadanta. tad anenāpi paryāyeṇa veditavyaṃ. yad vijñānasya pratyayaṃ nāmarūpaṃ. nāmarūpapratyayaṃ ca vijñānam iti vistaraḥ.*

237. Peṭ 115: *Tattha chaḷāyatanan-ti cha ajjhattikāni āyatanāni, cakkhu ajjhattikaṃ āyatanaṃ yāva mano ajjhattikaṃ āyatanaṃ. Phasso ti cha phassakāyā cakkhusamphasso yāva manosamphasso ti phasso. Cha vedanākāyā vedanā. Taṇhā ti cha taṇhākāyā taṇhā. Upādānan-ti cattāri upādānāni kāmupādānaṃ diṭṭhupādānaṃ sīlabbatupādānaṃ*

"Contact" is the six groups of contact.
"Feeling" is the six groups of feeling.
"Craving" is the six groups of craving.
"Clinging" is the four kinds of clinging.
"Existence" is kamma-produced (*kammanibbatta*) [**450b**] sensuous existence, material existence, and immaterial existence.[238]
"Birth" is the arising of the aggregates in an existence.[239]
"Ageing" is the maturing of the aggregates.
"Death" is the disintegration of the aggregates.

44. Simile of the seed

Q. Why "with ignorance as condition, formations; ... with birth as condition, ageing, and death"?[240]

A. For a long time, the five aggregates subject to clinging have been attached to, cherished, and held on to as "this is mine", ["this I am"] and "this is my self" by the uninstructed worldling due to not knowing the four noble truths.[241]

Thus, the desire (*icchā, abhinandi*) for, and attachment to, existence, and the desire for the origination (*samudaya*) of existence are the volition [to obtain a new existence].[242] [Because of] that volition and tendency, [which

---

attavādupādānan-ti upādānaṃ.

238. A I 223: *Kāmadhātuvepakkañ-ca, ... Rūpadhātuvepakkañ-ca, ... arūpadhātuvepakkañ-ca, ānanda, kammaṃ nābhavissa, api nu kho arūpabhavo paññāyethā ti? No hetaṃ, bhante. Iti kho, ānanda, kammaṃ khettaṃ, viññāṇaṃ bījaṃ, taṇhā sneho. Avijjānīvaraṇānaṃ sattānaṃ taṇhāsaṃyojanānaṃ paṇītāya dhātuyā viññāṇaṃ patiṭṭhitaṃ evaṃ āyatiṃ punabbhavābhinibbatti hoti. Evaṃ kho, ānanda, bhavo hotī ti.* Peṭ 115: *Bhavo ti tayo bhavā kāmabhavo rūpabhavo arūpabhavo.*

239. S II 2: *Yā tesaṃ tesaṃ sattānaṃ tamhi tamhi sattanikāye jāti sañjāti okkanti nibbatti abhinibbatti khandhānaṃ pātubhāvo āyatanānaṃ paṭilābho. Ayaṃ vuccati ... jāti.* Peṭ 115: *Yā paṭhamaṃ khandhānaṃ paṭhamaṃ dhātūnaṃ paṭhamaṃ āyatanānaṃ uppatti jāti sañjāti okkanti abhinibbatti khandhānaṃ pātubhāvo, ayaṃ jāti.*

240. Both the Chinese and Tibetan text abbreviate the formula, but the Chinese does not indicate this while the Tibetan does.

241. Cf. S II 94: *Yañ-ca kho etaṃ bhikkhave vuccati cittaṃ iti pi mano iti pi viññāṇaṃ iti pi tatrāssutavā puthujjano nālaṃ nibbindituṃ .... Taṃ kissa hetu? Dīgharattaṃ hetaṃ bhikkhave assutavato puthujjanassa ajjhositaṃ mamāyitaṃ parāmaṭṭhaṃ etaṃ mama eso 'hamasmi eso me attā ti.*

242. 如是有樂著樂和合為有思惟. The Tibetan translation is somewhat different. 非智所處 and *dngos po yongs su mi shes pa* correspond to *apariññātavatthuka*; see It-a I 84: ... *anupacchinnabhavamūlassa apariññātavatthukassa puthujjanassa ayam-īdisī kaṭasivaḍḍhanā.* Thī-a 288: *Dīgho bālānaṃ saṃsāro ti kilesakammavipākavaṭṭa-bhūtānaṃ khandhāyatanādīnaṃ paṭipāṭipavattisaṅkhāto saṃsāro apariññātavatthukānaṃ andhabālānaṃ dīgho buddhañāṇenapi aparicchindaniyo.* Ps I 26: *puthujjano*

is due to] not fully knowing the ground (*vatthu*) to obtain [a new] existence, there is the establishing [of consciousness] in [a new] existence. It is like a seed [planted] in a ploughed, prepared field.[243] Without that [seed of] consciousness, there is the cessation of existence. This is "with ignorance as condition, formations".

---

apariññātavatthuko, apariññāmūlikā ... Ps-ṭ I 66: *Apariññātavatthuko ti tīhi pariññāhi apariññātakkhandho.* Cf. S II 65–66: *Yañ-ca ... cetetiyañ-ca pakappetiyañ-ca anuseti, ārammaṇam-etaṃ hoti viññāṇassa ṭhitiyā. Ārammaṇe sati patiṭṭhā viññāṇassa hoti. Tasmiṃ patiṭṭhite viññāṇe virūḷhe āyatiṃ punabbhavābhinibbatti hoti. Āyatiṃ punabbhavābhinibbattiyā sati āyatiṃ jāti jarāmaraṇaṃ sokaparidevadukkhadomanassupāyāsā sambhavanti. ... Tasmiṃ patiṭṭhite viññāṇe virūḷhe nāmarūpassa avakkanti hoti. Nāmarūpapaccayā saḷāyatanaṃ; ... sokaparidevadukkhadomanassupāyāsā sambhavanti.* S II 100: *Kabaḷīkāre ... phasse ... manosañcetanāya, ... viññāṇe ce bhikkhave āhāre atthi rāgo atthi nandī atthi taṇhā, patiṭṭhitaṃ tattha viññāṇaṃ virūḷhaṃ. Yattha patiṭṭhitaṃ viññāṇaṃ virūḷhaṃ, atthi tattha nāmarūpassa avakkanti. ...* S III 53: *Rūpupayaṃ vā, ... saṅkhārupayaṃ vā ... viññāṇaṃ tiṭṭhamānaṃ tiṭṭheyya, saṅkhārārammaṇaṃ saṅkhārappatiṭṭhaṃ nandūpasecanaṃ vuddhiṃ virūḷhiṃ vepullaṃ āpajjeyya.* Cf. Abhidh-k-bh III.4: *manaḥsaṃcetanayā punarbhavasyākṣepaḥ ākṣiptasya punaḥ karmaparibhāvitād vijñānavījād-abhinirvṛtti-r-ityanayoranutpannasya bhavasyākaraṇe prādhānyam.* Abhidh-k-vy 319: *... karmaparibhāvitād vijñānabījād abhinirvṛttir iti / bījād ivāṃkurasya punarbhavasyotpāda ity arthaḥ.* Abhidh-k-bh III.6: *yattarhi sūtra uktaṃ vijñāne āhāre asti nandī asti rāga iti yatrāsti nandī asti rāgaḥ pratiṣṭhitaṃ tatra vijñānamadhirūḍham iti.*

243. S I 134 *Yathā aññataraṃ bījaṃ, khette vuttaṃ virūhati; pathavīrasañcāgamma, sinehañ-ca tadūbhayaṃ. Evaṃ khandhā ca dhātuyo, cha ca āyatanā ime; hetuṃ paṭicca sambhūtā, hetubhaṅgā nirujjhare ti.* Sn 238. *Khīṇaṃ purāṇaṃ navaṃ natthi sambhavaṃ, virattacittāyatike bhavasmiṃ; te khīṇabījā avirūḷhichandā, nibbanti dhīrā yathāyaṃ padīpo.* S III 54–55: *Imāni cassu ... pañca bījajātāni akhaṇḍāni ... sukhasayitāni, pathavī ca assa, āpo ca assa; api numāni ... pañca bījajātāni vuddhiṃ virūḷhiṃ vepullaṃ āpajjeyyunti? ... Seyyathā pi ... pathavīdhātu, evaṃ catasso viññāṇaṭṭhitiyo daṭṭhabbā. ... āpodhātu, evaṃ nandirāgo daṭṭhabbo. ... pañca bījajātāni, evaṃ viññāṇaṃ sāhāraṃ daṭṭhabbaṃ. Rūpupayaṃ, ... viññāṇaṃ tiṭṭhamānaṃ tiṭṭheyya, saṅkhārārammaṇaṃ saṅkhārappatiṭṭhaṃ nandūpasecanaṃ vuddhiṃ virūḷhiṃ vepullaṃ āpajjeyya. Yo ... evaṃ vadeyya: ahamaññatra rūpā aññatra vedanāya aññatra saññāya aññatra saṅkhārehi viññāṇassa āgatiṃ vā gatiṃ vā cutiṃ vā upapattiṃ vā vuddhiṃ vā virūḷhiṃ vā vepullaṃ vā paññāpessāmī ti, netaṃ ṭhānaṃ vijjati. Rūpadhātuyā ... Viññāṇadhātuyā ce ... bhikkhuno rāgo pahīno hoti. Rāgassa pahānā vocchijjatārammaṇaṃ patiṭṭhā viññāṇassa na hoti. Tadappatiṭṭhitaṃ viññāṇaṃ avirūḷhaṃ anabhisaṅkhaccavimuttaṃ.* Spk II 271: *Catasso viññāṇaṭṭhitiyo ti kammaviññāṇassa ārammaṇabhūtā rūpādayo cattāro khandhā. Te hi ārammaṇavasena patiṭṭhābhūtattā pathavīdhātusadisā. Nandirāgo sinehanaṭṭhena āpodhātusadiso. Viññāṇaṃ sāhāran-ti sappaccayaṃ kammaviññāṇaṃ. Tañ-hi bījaṃ viya pathaviyaṃ ārammaṇapathaviyaṃ viruhati.* Peṭ 108: *Puna sā yaṃ kiñci kammaṃ ācayagāmi sabbaṃ taṃ avijjāvasena abhisaṅkhariyati taṇhāvasena ca allīyati aññāṇavasena ca tattha ādīnavam-pi na jānāti. Tadeva viññāṇabījaṃ bhavati, sā yeva taṇhāsineho bhavati. Sāyeva avijjā sammoho ti. Evam-pi avijjāpaccayā saṅkhārā vattabbā.* Abhidh-k-bh III.7: *api ca kṣetrabhāvena bhagavatā catasro vijñānasthitayo deśitāḥ / vījabhāvena ca sopādānaṃ vijñānaṃ kṛtsnameveti ...*

The formations that are produced [due to] that ignorance, the volition to enter existence, and the desire for the sign-object of existence is [kamma] accumulation (*āyuhana*). [When there is] adverting (*āvajjana*) to existence, there arises relinking consciousness. In existence, the process of mind goes on uninterruptedly.[244] Therefore, "with formations as condition, consciousness".

45. Simile of the sun and the simile of the two bundles of reeds

A. without the sun, there is neither establishing of a ray of light on the ground nor any increase in it, so without consciousness there is no name-and-matter; there is no body (*sarīra*) [for name-and-matter] to be established in nor growth of it.[245] It is as bundles of reeds that are leaning against each

---

244. 彼無明所起行思入有著於有相事成為聚於轉有起相續識. If taking 行思 as *abhisaṅkhāra-cetanā* (see Tibetan), and 所起 as qualifying 無明, this can be translated as "[Due to] that ignorance which is produced, [there is] the preparation-volition [to] enter existence, the desire for the existence-sign-object is [karmic] accumulation. ..." The Tibetan has *mngon par 'du byed pa'i sems pa* = "volition of preparation/formation" corresponds to *abhisaṅkhārikā cetanā*. Cf. Paṭis-a II 514: *abhisaṅkhārikā cetanā* and Nidd-a II 456: *Abhisaṅkhārasahagataviññāṇassā ti kusalākusalacetanāsampayuttacittassa.* 入有, *srid par zhugs shing*, "entering/going into/approaching existence", perhaps corresponds to *bhavanikanti*, understanding *nikanti* as *nir-krama*, or to *bhavūpagamana*. 有相事, *srid pa mtshan mar dmigs pa* = *bhava-nimitta-ārammaṇa*. The action- and destination-signs are said to be the object of the relinking consciousness in the *kamma, kammanimitta, gati, gatinimitta*; see the "three links" section at § 50–52 of this chapter. 隨心, lit. "following/sequent/mind", *anu* + *citta*. Probably this denotes the *vīthicitta* since 隨心 can correspond to *cittānuvṛtti* (see DDB). The Tibetan, see next fn., has *nges pa'i sems pa, niyama-* or *viniścita-citta*, "ascertaining mind", which might be a translation of *vīthicitta*, or *cittavīthi*, understanding it as *vṛtticitta.*

Cf. Paṭis-a III 571: *Nikantikkhaṇe ti attano vipākaṃ dātuṃ paccupaṭṭhitakamme vā tathā paccupaṭṭhitakammena upaṭṭhāpite kammanimitte vā gatinimitte vā uppajjamānānaṃ nikantikkhaṇe. Nikantī ti nikāmanā patthanā. Āsannamaraṇassa hi mohena ākulacittattā avīcijālāya pi nikanti uppajjati, kiṃ pana sesesu nimittesu. ... Bhavanikanti pana paṭisandhi-anantaraṃ pavattabhavaṅgavīthito vuṭṭhitamattasseva attano khandhasantānaṃ ārabbha sabbesam-pi uppajjati.* Vism-mhṭ II 372: *Bhavesu vijjamānadosapaṭicchādanapatthanā daḷhaggāhabhāvena saṅkhārabhavānaṃ hetubhūtā janakasahāyatāya bhavanikanti taṃsahajāta-āsannakāraṇattā abhisaṅkhārikā, apassayabhūtā.* S IV 168: *Nimittassādagadhitaṃ vā ... viññāṇaṃ tiṭṭhamānaṃ tiṭṭhati ... tasmiṃ ce samaye kālaṃ karoti, ṭhānametaṃ vijjati, yaṃ dvinnaṃ gatīnaṃ aññataraṃ gatiṃ upapajjeyya nirayaṃ vā tiracchānayoniṃ vā.*

245. Cf. SN 12:64/S II 103: *Seyyathā pi ... kūṭāgāraṃ ... vā uttarāya vā ... vātapānā sūriye uggacchanta vātapānena rasmi pavisitvā kvāssa patiṭṭhitā ti? ... Evaṃ eva viññāṇe ce ... āhāre natthi rāgo ... appatiṭṭhitaṃ tattha viññāṇaṃ avirūḷhaṃ. ... Yattha appatiṭṭhitaṃ viññāṇaṃ avirūḷhaṃ, natthi tattha nāmarūpassa avakkanti. Yattha natthi nāmarūpassa avakkanti, natthi tattha saṅkhārānaṃ vuddhi. ....* S II 66: *Yañ-ca ... ceteti yañ-ca pakappeti yañ-ca*

other are mutually depending on each other. Therefore, "with consciousness as condition, name-and-matter".[246]

Dependent upon the [material] basis (*vatthu*) born together with name, the sense base of mind arises and grows.[247] Dependent upon name [born together with] the life [faculty] and the four great primaries, and with food and season as condition, the other five sense bases arise and grow. There is no [arising of these sense bases] other than with these conditions.[248] Therefore, "with name-and-matter as condition, six sense bases".

By the coming together (*saṅgati, sannipāta*) of the sense-faculties, sense objects (*visaya*) and consciousness,[249] contact arises. Therefore, "with the six sense bases as condition, contact".

Through contact there is feeling—painful, pleasurable, and neither painful nor pleasurable. Without contact, [there is no feeling].[250] Therefore,

---

anuseti, ārammaṇametaṃ hoti viññāṇassa ṭhitiyā. Ārammaṇe sati patiṭṭhā viññāṇassa hoti. Tasmiṃ patiṭṭhite viññāṇe virūḷhe nāmarūpassa avakkanti hoti. Nāmarūpapaccayā saḷāyatanaṃ; .... A I 76: *Channaṃ ... dhātūnaṃ upādāya gabbhassāvakkanti hoti; okkantiyā sati nāmarūpaṃ, nāmarūpapaccayā saḷāyatanaṃ, ...* Vibh-a 192: *Okkanti nāmarūpan-ti yā gabbhe rūpārūpadhammānaṃ okkanti, āgantvā pavisanaṃ viya—idaṃ nāmarūpaṃ.*

246. S II 114: *Seyyathā pi āvuso dve naḷakalāpiyo aññamaññaṃ nissāya tiṭṭheyyuṃ, evam eva kho āvuso nāmarūpapaccayā viññāṇaṃ ...* Abhidh-k-vy 668: *tadyathāyuṣman śāriputra dve naḍakalāpyāv ākāśe ucchrite syātāṃ. te anyonyaniśrite anyonyaṃ niśritya tiṣṭheyātām. tatra kaścid ekām apanayet. dvitīyā nipatet. dvitīyām apanayet. ekā nipatet. evam āyuṣman śāriputra nāmaṃ ca rūpaṃ cānyonyaniśritaṃ.*

247. 依處餘名共生起意入增長. "Other" 餘, is before "name", but this does not fit and likely is an intrusion from the next clause. The Tibetan does not have it: "The sense base of mind occurs dependent upon the material basis born together with name". This passage is related to the discussion of the dependent arising of the six sense bases in Vism XVII. 203–219/pp. 563–65, particularly, § 209/p.563: *Āruppato hi aññasmim-pi pañcavokārabhave taṃ vipākanāmaṃ hadayavatthuno sahāyaṃ hutvā chaṭṭhassa manāyatanassa yathā āruppe vuttaṃ, tatheva avakaṃsato sattadhā paccayo hoti. Itaresaṃ pana taṃ pañcannaṃ cakkhāyatanādīnaṃ catumahābhūtasahāyaṃ hutvā sahajātanissayavipākavippayutta-atthi-avigatavasena chahākārehi paccayo hoti. ...* Cf. Vism XIV.60/p.447. *Manodhātumanoviññāṇadhātūnaṃ nissayalakkhaṇaṃ hadayavatthu, ... manodhātumanoviññāṇadhātūnañ-ceva taṃsampayuttadhammānañ-ca vatthubhāvaṃ sādhayamānaṃ tiṭṭhati.* Cf. Vibh 138 etc.: *nāmapaccayā chaṭṭhāyatanaṃ.*

248. The text literally has, "not other/except for these conditions", 非餘此緣. Tibetan (186a): "Without these, there is no [arising]". This is related to Vism XVII. 207/p.563, "For there is a specific sense base when a specific kind of name-and-matter exists, not otherwise": *Tassa tassa hi nāmassa rūpassa ca bhāve taṃ taṃ āyatanaṃ hoti, na aññathā.*

249. This refers to the arising of contact due to the coming together of sense-faculty, sense-object, and consciousness, i.e. to the 18 elements—the internal and external sense bases and the consciousnesses arising dependent on them.

250. Sav 186a: "Without contact [it] is not", *reg pa med par ma yin no.*

"with contact as condition, feeling".

When the foolish worldling (*bāla puthujjana*) feels pleasure, he is attached to it and seeks even more [of it]. When he feels pain, to counter that [pain], he looks for pleasure. If he feels neither pain nor pleasure, he feels equanimity.[251] Therefore, "with feeling as condition, craving".

Through craving, he clings strongly to the object of craving. Therefore, "with craving as condition, clinging".

The clinging to existence (*bhavupādāna*) creates the object (*ārammaṇa*) for the seed of existence.[252] Therefore, "with clinging as condition, existence".

According to his particular kamma, there is birth in the [rebirth] destinations (*gati*). Therefore, "with existence as condition, birth".

Through birth, there is ageing and death. Therefore, "with birth as condition, ageing and death".

46. Simile of the seed and sprout

A. the rice seed is the condition for the husk,[253] so ignorance should be understood as the condition for the formations. As the seed is the condition for the sprout,[254] so formations are the condition for consciousness. As the sprout is the condition for the leaf, so consciousness is the condition for name-and-matter. As the leaf is the condition for the stalk, so name-and-matter is the condition for six sense bases. As the stalk is the condition for the plant, so six sense bases are the condition for contact. As the plant is the

251. Cf. Vibh-a 180: *Dukkhī sukhaṃ patthayati, sukhī bhiyyo pi icchati, / upekhā pana santattā sukham icc' eva bhāsitā.* S IV 205: *Sukhaṃ vediyamānassa, vedanaṃ appajānato; / So rāgānusayo hoti, anissaraṇadassino. / Dukkhaṃ vedayamānassa, vedanaṃ appajānato; / Paṭighānusayo hoti, anissaraṇadassino. / Adukkhamasukhaṃ santaṃ, bhūripaññena desitaṃ; / Tañcāpi abhinandati, neva dukkhā pamuccati.* Cf. S IV 208: *So dukkhāya vedanāya phuṭṭho samāno kāmasukhaṃ abhinandati. Taṃ kissa hetu? Na hi so ... pajānāti assutavā puthujjano aññatra kāmasukhā dukkhāya vedanāya nissaraṇaṃ, ...*

252. 彼有取作事為有種. Tibetan (186a): "The actions associated with clinging are the seed of existence". Mp II 349: *Ekabījī ti ekasseva bhavassa bījaṃ etassa atthī ti ekabījī.* Nett-ṭ 146: *Ekaṃ eva bhavabījaṃ paṭisandhiviññāṇaṃ ekabījaṃ, taṃ assa atthīti ekabījī.* Cf. Khp-a 194, Sn-a I 278: *ye ca taṇhāpahāneneva āyatike bhavasmiṃ virattacittā, te khīṇāsavā bhikkhū kammaṃ khettaṃ viññāṇaṃ bījan-ti (A I 223) ettha vuttassa paṭisandhiviññāṇassa kammakkhayeneva khīṇattā khīṇabījā.*

253. The text has 穀, *dhañña*, unhusked rice here, while below, under "craving is the condition for clinging", where it should be the same, it instead has 米, husked rice, *sāli*. The Tibetan term for the former, *sbun ma*, is "husk", while for the latter it has *'bras bu*, "fruit".

254. Cf. Vibh-a 196: *Bīje sati aṅkuro viya.* Mhv xv.43: *Bījamhā nikkhamma aṅkuro.* See also Abhidh-k-bh III.36, 150|22–23: *tadyathā vījādaṅkurakāṇḍapatrādīnāṃ prabhavo bhavatyevaṃ kleśāt kleśakarmavastūnām.*

condition for the flower, so contact is the condition for feeling. As the flower is the condition for nectar, so feeling is the condition for craving. As nectar is the condition for the ear of rice, so craving is the condition for clinging. As the ear of rice is the condition for the seed, so clinging is the condition for existence. As the seed is the condition for the sprout, so existence is the condition for birth. Thus, there is the arising of a succession (*santati*) of seeds of which the past end (*pubbanta*) cannot be known and the future end (*aparanta*) also cannot be known. [**450c**]

Similarly, birth has ignorance as its first cause (*nidāna*) of the succession. Its past end cannot be known and its future end also cannot be known.[255] If one asks, "What is the condition of ignorance"? The answer is, "Only ignorance is the condition for ignorance".[256] The latent tendencies (*anusaya*)

---

255. Cf. Nett 79 (... *bījaṅkuro viya* ...) in the next note. Cf. Mil 50: *Rājā āha bhante nāgasena, atītassa ... anāgatassa ... paccuppannassa addhānassa kiṃ mūlanti? Atītassa ca, ... anāgatassa ca ... paccuppannassa ca addhānassa avijjā mūlaṃ. Avijjāpaccayā saṅkhārā, ... Evam-etassa kevalassa dukkhakkhandhassa addhānassa purimā koṭi na paññāyatī ti. ... Yathā, mahārāja, puriso parittaṃ bījaṃ pathaviyaṃ nikkhipeyya, tato aṅkuro uṭṭhahitvā anupubbena vuḍḍhiṃ virūḷhiṃ vepullaṃ āpajjitvā phalaṃ dadeyya. Tato bījaṃ gahetvā puna ropeyya, tato pi aṅkuro uṭṭhahitvā anupubbena vuḍḍhiṃ virūḷhiṃ vepullaṃ āpajjitvā phalaṃ dadeyya. Evam-etissā santatiyā atthi anto ti? Natthi bhante ti. Evam-eva kho ... addhānassā-pi purimā koṭi na paññāyatī ti.* Cf. S II 178: *Anamataggāyaṃ bhikkhave saṃsāro pubbākoṭi na paññāyati avijjānīvaraṇānaṃ sattānaṃ taṇhāsaṃyojanānaṃ sandhāvataṃ saṃsarataṃ.* See also Abhidh-k-bh III.19: *ityanadibhavacakrakam... punaḥ kleśakarmāṇi tebhyaḥ punarjanmetyanādibhavacakrakaṃ veditavyam ... dṛṣṭaṃ cāṅkurādīṣu vījādīnāṃ sāmarthyaṃ deśakālapratiniyamādagnyādīnāṃ ca pākajādiṣviti nāsti nirhetukaḥ ... hetvadhīnatvājjanmano vījakṣayādivaṅkurasyeti ya eṣa skandhasaṃtāno janmatrayāvastha ūpadiṣṭaḥ.* and Abhidh-k-bh III.26–27: *yadi khalu dvādaśāṅga eva pratītyasamutpāda evaṃ satyavidyāyā anupadiṣṭahetukatvādādimān saṃsāraḥ prāpnoti jarāmaraṇasya cānupadiṣṭaphalatvādantavān / aṅgāntaraṃ vā punarupasaṃkhyātavyaṃ tasyāpyanyasmāditya navasthāprasaṅgaḥ nopasaṃkhyātavyam / yasmādupadarśito 'tra bhagavatā kleśāt kleśaḥ kriyā caiva tato vastu tataḥ punaḥ / vastukleśāśca jāyante bhavāṅganāmayaṃ nayaḥ ...*

256. Cf. S IV 50: *Avijjā kho bhikkhu eko dhammo yassa pahānā bhikkhuno avijjā pahīyati vijjā uppajjatī ti.* (Cf. D II 215, A V 116) Nett 79: *Vuttaṃ hi avijjāpaccayā saṅkhārā, saṅkhārapaccayā viññāṇaṃ. Evaṃ sabbo paṭiccasamuppādo. Iti avijjā avijjāya hetu, ayonisomanasikāro paccayo. Purimikā avijjā pacchimikāya avijjāya hetu. Tattha purimikā avijjā avijjānusayo, pacchimikā avijjā avijjāpariyuṭṭhānam. Purimiko avijjānusayo pacchimikassa avijjāpariyuṭṭhānassa hetubhūto paribrūhanāya bījaṅkuro viya samanantarahetutāya. Yaṃ pana yattha phalaṃ nibbattati, idaṃ tassa paramparahetutāya hetubhūtaṃ. Duvidho hi hetu: samanantarahetu paraṃparahetu ca. Evaṃ avijjāya pi duvidho hetu: samanantarahetu paramparahetu ca.* Vism XVII.279–289/p.577: *Iti yasmā āsavasamudayā ete dhammā honti, tasmā ete sijjhamānā avijjāya hetubhūte āsave sādhenti. Āsavesu ca siddhesu paccayabhāve bhāvato avijjāpi siddhāva hotī ti. Evaṃ tāvettha sokādīhi avijjā siddhā hotī ti veditabbā. Yasmā pana evaṃ paccayabhāve bhāvato avijjāya siddhāya*

are the condition for the obsessions (*pariyuṭṭhāna*). The obsessions are the condition for the latent tendencies. The former [are the conditions] for the former and the latter [are the conditions] for the latter.[257]

Furthermore, all the afflictions are the condition for ignorance. As the Buddha taught: "With the origination of the contaminations, there is the origination of ignorance".[258]

47. In a single mind-moment

Furthermore, [dependent arising occurs by way of] a single mental property (*cetasika*) thus:[259]

---

puna avijjāpaccayā saṅkhārā, saṅkhārapaccayā viññāṇan-ti evaṃ hetuphalaparamparāya pariyosānaṃ natthi. Tasmā taṃ hetuphalasambandhavasena pavattaṃ dvādasaṅgaṃ bhavacakkaṃ aviditādīti siddhaṃ hoti.

Likewise *taṇhā* has as its condition *taṇhā*, see D II 309: *dhammataṇhā loke piyarūpaṃ sātarūpaṃ etthesā taṇhā uppajjamānā uppajjati...*

257. 初為初後為後. Tibetan (Sav 186b): "The former is the condition for the former and the latter is the condition for the latter". Cf. Netti 79, *purimikā avijjā pacchimikāya avijjāya hetu*, two notes above. Cf. Paṭṭh I.2.4: *Purimā purimā kusalā dhammā pacchimānaṃ pacchimānaṃ kusalānaṃ dhammānaṃ anantarapaccayena paccayo.*

258. M I 54: ... *Āsavasamudayā avijjāsamudayo, āsavanirodhā avijjānirodho. ... Tayo me āvuso āsavā: kāmāsavo bhavāsavo avijjāsavo. Avijjāsamudayā āsavasamudayo, avijjānirodhā āsavanirodho.*

259. 一心法 = *eka-cittadhamma* or *eka-cetasika*. The conclusion of this section at 450c13 has, 於一剎那 "within a single moment", *eka-citta-khaṇa*. The Tibetan (Sav 186b) has "by way of a single mind state it is ..." or "the mode of single mind state is ...", *sems gcig pa'i tshul* = *eka-citta/cetasikassa vidhi/naya/-to,* while at the conclusion (187b) it has "through a single moment", *skad cig gcig gis.*

This passage refers to the *abhidhammabhājanīya* method of explaining *paṭiccasamuppāda* as taking place within a single mind moment, which is mentioned in the Vibhaṅga commentary (Vibh-a 199–212, translated in Ñāṇamoli 1996 I 244–261) with regard to a Vibhaṅga passage (Vibh 144–148) that describes dependent arising taking place at the occasion of the arising of an unwholesome mind. There are similarities with the description in Vim. A description of dependent origination taking place in a moment is also found in the *Abhidharmakośabhāṣya* III.24: "How is [dependent origination] momentary? In a single moment too, there are twelve factors, namely, if one would kill a living being due to greed, that which is delusion is ignorance; the intention is formations; the cognition (*prativijñapti*) of the object is consciousness; the four aggregates that co-exist with consciousness are name-and-matter; the sense-faculties established in name-and-matter are the six sense bases; the falling onto the six sense bases is contact; the experiencing of contact is feeling; the greed is craving; the obsessions (*paryavasthāna* = *pariyuṭṭhāna*) associated with that are clinging; the bodily and verbal karma produced by that is existence; the emergence of those dharmas is birth; [their] maturing is ageing; and [their] dissolution is death."

When seeing a form with the eye, the foolish person gives rise to greed (*rāga, taṇhā*). At this time, the mind is deluded with regard to beauty and pleasure (*subha-sukha*)—this is called "ignorance".

The volition (*cetanā*) that is due to desire is "with ignorance as condition, formations".[260]

Vibh-a 199–212/§ 932–1009: ... *yasmā na kevalaṃ ayaṃ paccayākāro nānācittesuyeva hoti, ekacittepi hotiyeva, tasmā abhidhammabhājanīyavasena ekacittakkhaṇikaṃ paccayākāraṃ nānappakārato dassetuṃ avijjāpaccayā saṅkhāro ti ādinā nayena mātikaṃ tāva ṭhapesi....* Vibh 144–148/§ 248–255: *Katame dhammā akusalā? Yasmiṃ samaye akusalaṃ cittaṃ uppannaṃ hoti somanassasahagataṃ diṭṭhigatasampayuttaṃ rūpārammaṇaṃ vā saddārammaṇaṃ vā ... dhammārammaṇaṃ vā yaṃ yaṃ vā panārabbha. ... ... Tasmiṃ samaye avijjāpaccayā saṅkhāro, saṅkhārapaccayā viññāṇaṃ, viññāṇapaccayā nāmarūpaṃ, nāmarūpapaccayā chaṭṭhāyatanaṃ, chaṭṭhāyatanapaccayā phasso, ... dukkhakkhandhassa samudayo hoti. Tattha katamā avijjā? Yaṃ aññāṇaṃ adassanaṃ ... moho akusalamūlaṃ. ... Yā cetanā sañcetanā sañcetayitattaṃ, ayaṃ vuccati avijjāpaccayā saṅkhāro. ... Yaṃ cittaṃ mano ... viññāṇakkhandho tajjāmanoviññāṇadhātu, idaṃ vuccati saṅkhārapaccayā viññāṇaṃ. ... Tattha katamaṃ viññāṇapaccayā nāmarūpaṃ? ... Vedanākkhandho, saññākkhandho, saṅkhārakkhandha, idaṃ vuccati nāmaṃ. ... Cakkhāyatanassa ... kāyāyatanassa upacayo, yaṃ vā panaññam-pi atthi rūpaṃ cittajaṃ cittahetukaṃ cittasamuṭṭhānaṃ, idaṃ vuccati rūpaṃ. Iti idañ-ca nāmaṃ, idañ-ca rūpaṃ. Idaṃ vuccati viññāṇapaccayā nāmarūpaṃ. Nāmarūpapaccayā chaṭṭhāyatananti. ... saṅkhārakkhandho, idaṃ vuccati nāmaṃ. ... Yaṃ rūpaṃ nissāya manoviññāṇadhātu vattati, idaṃ vuccati rūpaṃ. ... Idaṃ vuccati nāmarūpaṃ. ... Yo phasso phusanā ..., ayaṃ vuccati chaṭṭhāyatanapaccayā phasso. ... Yaṃ cetasikaṃ sātaṃ ... cetosamphassajā sātā sukhā vedanā, ayaṃ vuccati phassapaccayā vedanā. ... Yo rāgo ... nandirāgo cittassa sārāgo, ayaṃ vuccati vedanāpaccayā taṇhā. ... Yā diṭṭhi diṭṭhigataṃ ... vipariyāsaggāho, idaṃ vuccati taṇhāpaccayā upādānaṃ. ... Ṭhapetvā upādānaṃ, vedanākkhandho saññākkhandho saṅkhārakkhandho viññāṇakkhandho, ayaṃ vuccati upādānapaccayā bhavo. ... Yā tesaṃ tesaṃ dhammānaṃ jāti sañjāti nibbatti abhinibbatti pātubhāvo, ayaṃ vuccati bhavapaccayā jāti. ... Atthi jarā, atthi maraṇaṃ. Tattha katamā jarā? Yā tesaṃ tesaṃ dhammānaṃ jarā jīraṇatā āyuno saṃhāni, ayaṃ vuccati jarā. ... Yo tesaṃ tesaṃ dhammānaṃ khayo vayo bhedo paribhedo aniccatā antaradhānaṃ, idaṃ vuccati maraṇaṃ. Iti ayañ-ca jarā, idañ-ca maraṇaṃ. Idaṃ vuccati jātipaccayā jarāmaraṇaṃ. Evametassa kevalassa dukkhakkhandhassa samudayo hotī ti.* Abhidh-k-bh III.24/133|01–08: *sa caiṣa pratītyasamutpādaś caturvidha ucyate | kṣaṇikaḥ prakarṣikaḥ sāṃbandhikaḥ āvasthikaś ca | kathaṃ kṣaṇikaḥ | ekasmin khalv api kṣaṇe dvādaśāṅgāni bhavanti | tadyathā lobhavaśena prāṇinaṃ jīvitād vyaparopayet | yo mohaḥ sā 'vidyā | yā cetanā te saṃskārāḥ | vastuprativijñaptirvijñānam | vijñānasahabhuvaś catvāraḥ skandhā nāmarūpam | nāmarūpe vyavasthāpitāni indriyāṇi ṣaḍāyatanam | ṣaḍḍāyatanābhinipātaḥ sparśaḥ | sparśānubhavanaṃ vedanā | yo lobhaḥ sa tṛṣṇā | tatsaṃprayuktāni paryavasthānāni upādānam | tatsamutthitaṃ kāyavākkarma bhavaḥ | teṣāṃ dharmāṇām utsarjanaṃ jātiḥ parīpāko jarā bhaṅgo maraṇam iti |*

260. 思著是無明緣行. On this and the next factor of dependent origination, see the simile of the seeds above in § 44. The Tibetan version is different.

The mind (*citta*) that is due to desire[261] is "with formations as condition, consciousness".

The mental properties (*cetasika dhamma*) associated with consciousness[262] and the dependent kinds of matter (*upādārūpa*) due to that are "with consciousness as condition, name-and-matter".

With delight (*nandi*) born of craving as condition, with delight, and with matter [born of] delight as condition, there is sensitivity of the sense-faculties[263] is "with name-and-matter as condition, the six sense bases".

Ignorance-contact (*avijjāsamphassa*) is "with the six sense bases as condition, contact".[264]

---

261. 心著此行緣識. The character 著 covers a wide range of corresponding terms such as *ajjhosāna, abhinivesa, gedha, anuyoga*, etc. The Tibetan has *chags = gedha, lobha* or *rāga*.

262. The text has 知, "knowing", *vijjā, jānati,* which might be due to a corruption in the manuscript that Saṅghapāla translated, i.e. it had *ñāṇa* or *viññā* instead of *viññāṇa*. Sav 186b: "The mental factors associated with that and the dependent kinds of matter due to that are ...".

263. 從愛生喜緣喜故喜色緣故緣諸根清淨. The first clauses might be corrupt. The Tibetan version makes more sense at first, but is wrong in the last clause by interpreting *pasāda* as "no lucidity", *rab tu dang ba ma yin pa*.

Cf. Paṭis I 52: *Idha paṭisandhi viññāṇaṃ, okkanti nāmarūpaṃ, pasādo āyatanaṃ*. Cf. Paṭis I 112: *Kathaṃ tiṇṇaṃ cittānaṃ vipphārattā indriyānaṃ pasādavasena nānattekattaviññāṇacariyāpariyogāhaṇe paññā cetopariyañāṇaṃ? ... So imesu catūsu iddhipādesu cittaṃ paribhāvetvā paridametvā, muduṃ karitvā kammaniyaṃ evaṃ pajānāti, idaṃ rūpaṃ somanassindriyasamuṭṭhitaṃ, ...* Paṭis-a I 51: *Indriyānaṃ pasādavasenā ti cakkhādīnaṃ channaṃ indriyānaṃ pasādavasena, indriyānaṃ patiṭṭhitokāsā cettha phalūpacārena indriyānan-ti vuttā yathā vippasannāni kho te, āvuso, indriyāni parisuddho chavivaṇṇo pariyodāto ti. Indriyapatiṭṭhitokāsesupi hadayavatthu eva idhādhippetaṃ. Pasādavasenā ti ca anāvilabhāvavasena.* Cf. Paṭis I 52: *Idha paṭisandhi viññāṇaṃ, okkanti nāmarūpaṃ, pasādo āyatanaṃ.*

264. The term *avijjāsamphassa* occurs only in two suttas and their commentaries: S III 96: *... assutavā puthujjano ... rūpaṃ attato samanupassati. Yā kho pana sā ... samanupassanā saṅkhāro so. So pana saṅkhāro kiṃnidāno ...? Avijjāsamphassajena ... vedayitena phuṭṭhassa assutavato puthujjanassa uppannā taṇhā; tatojo so saṅkhāro. Iti kho ... so pi saṅkhāro, anicco saṅkhato paṭiccasamuppanno; sā pi taṇhā ....; vedanā ...; phasso ...; avijjā aniccā saṅkhatā paṭiccasamuppannā. Evam-pi kho ... jānato evaṃ passato anantarā āsavānaṃ khayo hoti.* Cf. S III 46: *... assutavā puthujjano ... viññāṇaṃ attato samanupassati, ... Iti ayañceva samanupassanā asmī ti cassa avigataṃ [adhigataṃ v.l.] hoti. Asmī ti kho pana ... avigate pañcannaṃ indriyānaṃ avakkanti hoti—cakkhundriyassa ... kāyindriyassa. Atthi ... mano, atthi dhammā, atthi avijjādhātu. Avijjāsamphassajena ... vedayitena phuṭṭhassa assutavato puthujjanassa asmī ti pissa hoti ... bhavissanti pissa hoti. Tiṭṭhanti kho pana ... tattheva [tatheva v.l.] pañcindriyāni. Athettha sutavato ariyasāvakassa avijjā pahīyati, vijjā uppajjati. Tassa avijjāvirāgā vijjuppādā asmīti pissa na hoti ...* Cf. A III 411, Kv 370: *Api ca kho ... nete kāmā kāmaguṇā nāmete ariyassa vinaye vuccanti: Saṅkapparāgo purisassa kāmo, / nete*

Pleasure (*sāta*) is "with contact as condition, feeling".[265]

Greed (*rāga*) is "with feeling as condition, craving".[266]

The clinging to beauty and pleasure [that occurs] due to greed[267] is "with craving as condition, clinging".

The volition [that occurs] due to greed is "with clinging as condition, existence".

The manifestation of those states[268] is "with existence as condition, birth".

[The alteration of] what persists is "ageing".[269]

---

kāmā yāni citrāni loke. / saṅkapparāgo purisassa kāmo, / tiṭṭhanti citrāni tatheva loke; / athettha dhīrā vinayanti chandan-ti. Cf. S I 22, Sn-a II 539, Sn 173.

Spk explains *avijjāsamphassa* as "contact associated with ignorance". Spk II 269: *Avijjāsamphassajenā ti avijjāsampayuttaphassato jātena.*

It is also found in the *Abhidharmakośabhāṣya*: "In a sūtrānta it is said that unreasoned attention is the cause for ignorance, and it is shown at the time of contact: 'Dependent on the eye and forms there arises muddled attention born from delusion.' At the time of feeling it inevitably is with ignorance, as [is said] in a sūtrānta: 'Craving arises dependent on feeling born from ignorance contact'. Hence, when at the moment of contact there is unreasoned attention, by [this] being the condition, the ignorance that occurs together with feeling is effected." Abhidh-k-bh III.27: *ayoniśo manaskāro heturavidyāyā uktaḥ sūtrāntare / sa cāpi sparśakāle nirdiṣṭaḥ cakṣuḥ pratītya rūpāṇi cotpadyate āvilo manaskāro mohaja iti vedanākāle cāvaśyamavidyayā bhavitavyam / avidyāsaṃsparśajaṃ veditaṃ pratītyotpannā tṛṣṇe ti sūtrāntarāt / ataḥ sparśakāle bhavann-ayoniśomanaskāro vedanāsahavarttinyā avidyāyāḥ pratyayabhāvena siddha.* Abhidh-k-vy 289: *... avidyāsaṃprayuktāt sparśāj jātaṃ avidyāsaṃsparśajaṃ veditaṃ / yatra veditam avidyāsaṃsparśajam / avaśyaṃ tatrāvidyā saṃprayujyate / na hi veditam asaṃprayuktam avidyayā tṛṣṇāhetur bhavatī ti ...*

265. 喜觸緣受欲. The term *bde ba* usually corresponds to *sukha*, but elsewhere in the Tibetan version it is found in *bde ba'i ngo bo* "pleasant form" or *sātarūpa*. Given the Tibetan and parallel in Vibh (*Yaṃ cetasikaṃ sātaṃ ... cetosamphassajā sātā sukhā vedanā, ayaṃ vuccati phassapaccayā vedanā*) 喜 likely corresponds to *sāta* here.

266. 欲 "greed" corresponds to *rāga*. Cf. the Vibh parallel above. The Tibetan (Sav 187a) has greed, *'dod chags pa.*

267. 著 can correspond to *rāga* and *lobha*, "greed", *nikanti*, "attachment", *rati*, "delight/liking". The Tibetan has greed, *chags pa = rāga, lobha.* Since in the next factor, "greed for existence", *bhavarāga*, is implied, "greed" has been chosen as translation here.

268. Vibh 145: *Yā tesaṃ tesaṃ dhammānaṃ jāti sañjāti nibbatti abhinibbatti pātubhāvo, ayaṃ vuccati bhavapaccayā jāti. ... Yā tesaṃ tesaṃ dhammānaṃ jarā jīraṇatā āyuno saṃhāni, ayaṃ vuccati jarā. ... Yo tesaṃ tesaṃ dhammānaṃ khayo vayo bhedo paribhedo aniccatā antaradhānaṃ, idaṃ vuccati maraṇaṃ. ...*

269. 住已 = *ṭhatvā* or *ṭhita.* The Tibetan has "alteration of what persists/continues/ remains/stays", *gnas pa gzhan du gyur pa nyid,* which corresponds to Pali *thiṭassa aññathatta* & Skt *sthityanyathātva,* "alteration of what has remained". This makes better sense in this context of momentariness and the three characteristics of

Momentary dissolution is "death".[270]

Thus, in a single moment (*eka-khaṇa)* there is the twelve factored dependent arising.[271]

48. Questions on kamma, afflictions, results, etc.

Q. How many of the twelve factors of dependent arising are afflictions? How many [factors] are kamma? How many [factors] are result (*vipāka*)? How many [factors] are past? How many are future? How many are present? How many are conditions? How many have arisen?[272] What is dependent arising? What are dependently arisen states? What are the differences between these two? What is the profound nature of dependent arising?

---

conditioned states (*uppāda, ṭhiti, bhaṅga*). Cf. Spk II 266: *Ṭhitassa aññathattaṃ paññāyatī ti dharamānassa jīvamānassa jarā paññāyati. Ṭhitī ti hi jīvitindriyasaṅkhātāya anupālanāya nāmaṃ. Aññathattan-ti jarāya. Tenāhu porāṇā: Uppādo jāti akkhāto, bhaṅgo vutto vayoti ca; / Aññathattaṃ jarā vuttā, ṭhitī ca anupālanā ti. Evaṃ ekekassa khandhassa uppādajarābhaṅgasaṅkhātāni tīṇi lakkhaṇāni honti yāni sandhāya vuttaṃ tīṇimāni ... saṅkhatassa saṅkhatalakkhaṇānī ti. ... Tattha saṅkhārānaṃ uppādakkhaṇe saṅkhāro pi uppādalakkhaṇam-pi kālasaṅkhāto tassa khaṇo pi paññāyati. Uppādopī ti vutte saṅkhāro pi jarālakkhaṇam-pi kālasaṅkhāto tassa khaṇo pi paññāyati. Bhaṅgakkhaṇe saṅkhāro pi taṃlakkhaṇam-pi kālasaṅkhāto tassa khaṇo pi paññāyati.* Nett 22: *Tattha jarā ca maraṇañ-ca imāni dve saṅkhatassa saṅkhatalakkhaṇāni. Jarāyaṃ ṭhitassa aññathattaṃ, maraṇaṃ vayo.* Mp II 252: *Uppādo ti jāti. Vayo ti bhedo. Ṭhitassa aññathattaṃ nāma jarā. Tattha saṅkhatan-ti tebhūmakā dhammā. Maggaphalāni pana asammasanūpagattā idha na kathīyanti. Uppādādayo saṅkhatalakkhaṇā nāma. Tesu uppādakkhaṇe uppādo, ṭhānakkhaṇe jarā, bhedakkhaṇe vayo.* Spk II 267: *Apare pana vadanti arūpadhammānaṃ jarākhaṇo nāma na sakkā paññāpetuṃ, sammāsambuddho ca vedanāya uppādo paññāyati, vayo paññāyati, ṭhitāya aññathattaṃ paññāyatī ti vadanto arūpadhammānam pi tīṇi lakkhaṇāni paññāpeti, tāni atthikkhaṇaṃ upādāya labbhantī ti vatvā: Atthitā sabbadhammānaṃ, ṭhiti nāma pavuccati. / Tass'eva bhedo maraṇaṃ, sabbadā sabbapāṇinan ti.*

270. Vism VIII.2/p.229: ... *saṅkhārānaṃ khaṇabhaṅgasaṅkhātaṃ khaṇikamaraṇaṃ.* Abhidh-s 23: *uppādaṭhitibhaṅgavasena khaṇattayaṃ ekacittakkhaṇaṃ nāma.* Paṭis-a II 503: *Tattha aniccan-ti pañcakkhandhā. Kasmā? Uppādavayaññathattabhāvā. Aniccatā ti tesaṃ yeva uppādavayaññathattaṃ, hutvā abhāvo vā, nibbattānaṃ tenevākārena aṭṭhatvā khaṇabhaṅgena bhedoti attho.* Paṭis-a I 143: *Pavatte rūpārūpadhammānaṃ bhedo khaṇikamaraṇaṃ nāma.* Vism-mhṭ I 287: *Saṅkhārānaṃ khaṇabhaṅgasaṅkhātan-ti saṅkhatadhammānaṃ udayavayaparicchinnassa pavattikhaṇassa bhaṅgo nirodhoti saṅkhaṃ gataṃ. Khaṇikamaraṇan-ti yathāvuttakhaṇavantaṃ tasmiṃ yeva khaṇe labbhamānaṃ maraṇaṃ.* II 446: *Maraṇamevā ti bhaṅgam-eva. Tenā ti bhaṅgadassanena khaṇe khaṇe bhaṅgam-eva passato hi nimittasaññitaṃ saṅkhāragataṃ aniccatāya vuttanayena sappaṭibhayaṃ hutvā upaṭṭhāti.*

271. Tibetan: "Thus, one should understand it as a succession of twelve factors taking place together in a single moment".

272. 幾因緣幾已起. These two questions are not answered below and are not found

A. Three [factors] are afflictions: ignorance, craving, and clinging. Two [factors] are kamma: formations and existence. The other seven [factors] are result.[273]

Herein, the afflictions that are the cause for the production of further existence (*punabbhavābhinibbatti*) are like the colours (*citra, rūpa*) of a painter. Kamma [with its] requisites (*sambhāra*)[274] is like the action of painting with the colours. The afflictions that cause the production of [further] existence and are the condition for the obtaining of birth are like the different colours.[275]

Two [factors] are past: ignorance and the formations. Two [factors] are future: birth and ageing-and-death. The other eight [factors] are present.[276]

---

in the Tibetan (187a).

273. Cf. Vism XVII.298/p.581: *ettha pana saṅkhārabhavā kammavaṭṭaṃ, avijjā-taṇhupādānāni kilesavaṭṭaṃ, viññāṇanāmarūpasaḷāyatanaphassavedanā vipākavaṭṭanti.* Cf. Abhidh-k III.20–21: *sa pratītyasamutpādo dvādaśāṅgastrikāṇḍakaḥ|pūrvāparāntayordve dve madhye'ṣṭau paripūriṇaḥ || pūrvakleśā daśā'vidyā saṃskārāḥ pūrvakarmaṇaḥ | saṃdhiskandhāstu vijñānaṃ nāmarūpamataḥ param.* 26: *kleśāstrīṇi dvayaṃ karma sapta vastu phalaṃ tathā|phalahetvabhisaṃkṣepo dvayormadhyānumānataḥ ||*

274. 其事不自生 = "his action is not self-produced", which does not make sense in this context. The characters 自生 correspond to *sayambhū, sayaṃkata*, "self-produced". This must be a misinterpretation of *evam-evasasambhārakakammaṃ* or *sahakammasambhāraṃ kammaṃ*, (see the Pali parallel in next fn.) as *asayaṃ-saṃkhāra-kammaṃ*.

275. The last line is cryptic. It could also be translated as "The defilements that cause rearising—[that is] with existence as condition, there is the obtaining of birth—are like ..."

Cf. S II 101: *Seyyathā pi ... rajako vā cittakārako vā sati rajanāya vā ... mañjiṭṭhāya vā suparimaṭṭhe vā phalake bhittiyā vā dussapaṭṭe vā itthirūpaṃ vā purisarūpaṃ vā abhinimmineyya sabbaṅgapaccaṅgaṃ; evam-eva kho ... kabaḷīkāre ce āhāre atthi rāgo atthi nandī atthi taṇhā, patiṭṭhitaṃ tattha viññāṇaṃ virūḷhaṃ. Yattha patiṭṭhitaṃ viññāṇaṃ virūḷhaṃ, atthi tattha nāmarūpassa avakkanti. Yattha ... tattha saṅkhārānaṃ vuddhi. Yattha ... tattha āyatiṃ punabbhavābhinibbatti.* Spk II 114: *rajakacittakārā viya hi sahakammasambhāraṃ kammaṃ, phalakabhittidussapaṭā viya tebhūmakavaṭṭaṃ. Yathā rajakacittakārā parisuddhesu phalakādīsu rūpaṃ samuṭṭhāpenti, evam-eva sasambhārakakammaṃ bhavesu rūpaṃ samuṭṭhāpeti.* Spk-ṭ II 115: *Kāraṇañcettha saṅkhārā veditabbā. Te hi āyatiṃ punabbhavābhinibbattiyā hetū, taṇhā-avijjāyo, kālagati-ādayo ca kammassa sambhārā. Keci pana kilesavaṭṭakammagatikālā cā ti adhippāyena kālagati-ādayo ca kammassa sambhārā ti vadanti. ... Tathā cāha sasambhārakakammaṃ bhavesu rūpaṃ samuṭṭhāpetī ti. Rūpan-ti attabhāvaṃ.*

276. Cf. Vism XVII.285/p.578: *Atītapaccuppannānāgatā cassa tayo kālā. Tesu pāḷiyaṃ sarūpato āgatavasena avijjā, saṅkhārā cā ti dve aṅgāni atītakālāni. Viññāṇādīni bhavāvasānāni aṭṭha paccuppannakālāni. Jāti ceva jarāmaraṇañ-ca dve anāgatakālānīti veditabbāni.* Abhidh-k-bh III.20: *kathameṣu trikāṇḍeṣu dvādaśāṅgāni vyavasthāpyante / pūrvāparāntayordve dve madhye 'ṣṭau avidyā saṃskārāśca pūrvānte jātirjarāmaraṇaṃ cāparānte / śeṣāṇyaṣṭau madhye / kiṃ punaretānyaṣṭāṅgāni sarvasyāṃ jātau bhavanti* . Cf. Abhidh-k-bh III.25: *pūrvāparāntamadhyeṣu saṃmohavinivṛttaye ...*

Thus, the beginningless cycle of saṃsāra[277] is to be understood by the apprehension of the three divisions of time.

The twelve factors of dependent arising should not be taught [separately], nor should dependent arising be taught separately from these twelve [factors]. Then what is dependent arising? When these twelve states (*dhamma*) are a succession (*anukkamma*) of reciprocal causes (*aññamañña-kāraṇa?*),[278] it is called "dependent arising" (*paṭiccasamuppāda*). When the twelve factors of dependent arising have arisen, [it is called "dependently arisen] states" (*paṭiccasamuppannā dhammā*).[279]

What is the difference between these two? With regard to dependent arising: the formations (*saṅkhārā*) change.[280] Not having fully come into being (*aparinipphanna*), they are not to be spoken of (*navattabba*); they are not to be spoken of as conditioned (*saṅkhata*) or as unconditioned (*asaṅkhata*). By arising, dependently arisen states are formations that have fully come into being (*parinipphanna*) and are conditioned (*saṅkhata*).[281] This is the difference between these two states.

---

277. 無始生死相續. Tibetan: *thog ma dang tha ma med pa 'khor ba'i lam*. Cf. Vmv I 130: *anādimato saṃsāravaṭṭassa* and Th-a II 107, Ud-a 391 (Ee), Nett-a 143: *anādimatisaṃsāra*. In the Vism (XVII.285), this passage on the three times is located at the end of a section proving that the "wheel of becoming is without a known beginning", *bhavacakkaṃ aviditādīti*.

278. Cf. Ud-a 37: *aññamaññaṃ paṭicca paṭimukhaṃ katvā kāraṇasamavāyaṃ appaṭikkhipitvā sahite uppādetī ti paṭiccasamuppādo*. Tibetan: "When the twelve factors are a succession of reciprocal causes, reasons, associated factors, and specific conditions, it is dependent arising".

279. In the *Abhidharmakośabhāṣya*, in answer to the question on the difference between *pratītyasamutpāda* and *pratītyasamutpanna*, it is said that *samutpāda* is the cause and *samutpanna* is the result. The factor that is a cause is *pratītyasamutpāda* and when it arises from this, the factor that is result is *pratītyasamutpanna*. "Thus all the factors, being cause as well as result, fulfill both ways". Abhidh-k-bh III.28: *heturatra samutpādaḥ samutpannaṃ phalaṃ matam / hetubhūtamaṅgapratītya-samutpādaḥ samutpadyate 'smād-iti kṛtvā phalabhūtamaṅgapratītyasamutpannam/ evaṃ sarvāṇyaṅgānyubhayayathā sidhyanti / hetuphalabhavāt*.

280. The character 異 corresponds to *aññathā*, *pṛthak*, *vikāra*, *vipariṇāma*, *itara*, etc. The Tibetan (187b) has *rnam par 'gyur ba*, which can correspond to *vipariṇāma* and *vikāra*.

281. Cf. As 343: *Parinipphannan-ti pannarasa rūpāni parinipphannāni nāma, dasa aparinipphannāni nāma. Yadi aparinipphannā, asaṅkhatā nāma bhaveyyuṃ. Tesaṃ yeva pana rūpānaṃ kāyavikāro kāyaviññatti nāma ... nibbatti upacayo nāma, pavatti santati nāma, jīraṇākāro jaratā nāma, hutvā abhāvākāro aniccatā nāmāti. Sabbaṃ parinipphannaṃ saṅkhatam-eva hotī ti.* Vibh-a 29: *Pañcapi pana khandhā parinipphannā va honti, no aparinipphannā; saṅkhatāva no asaṅkhatā; apica nipphannāpi hontiyeva. Sabhāvadhammesu hi nibbānamevekaṃ aparinipphannaṃ anipphannañ-ca. Nirodhasamāpatti pana nāmapaññatti ca kathanti? Nirodhasamāpatti lokiyalokuttarā ti vā saṅkhatāsaṅkhatā ti vā*

What is the profound nature of dependent arising? By whatever modes (*ākāra*) and characteristics (*lakkhaṇa*), ignorance is the condition for formations,[282] the noble ones, independent of another (*aparapaccaya*),[283] penetrate with the eye of wisdom those modes, characteristics, and natures (*sabhāva*). Thus, all this is called the profound nature of dependent arising.[284] **[451a]**

49. Seven ways of knowing dependent arising

Furthermore, this dependent arising should be known through seven ways thus: (1) through the three links, (2) the four collections, (3) the twenty modes, (4) the wheel, (5) way, (6) analysis, and (7) through inclusion.

50. Three links

Q. How [should it be known] through the three links (*sandhito*)?[285]

A. Herein the interval between the formations and consciousness is the first link; the interval between feeling and craving is the second link; the interval between existence and birth is the third link.

With past kamma and afflictions (*kammakilesa*) as condition, present results—this is the first link. With present results as condition, present

---

parinipphannāparinipphannā ti vā na vattabbā.

282. Cf. Peṭ 105: *Sā pi avijjā saṅkhārānaṃ paccayo catūhi kāraṇehi sahajātapaccayatāya samanantarapaccayatāya abhisandanapaccayatāya patiṭṭhānapaccayatāya* ... Paṭis I 50: *Avijjā saṅkhārānaṃ uppādaṭṭhiti ca pavattaṭṭhiti ca nimittaṭṭhiti ca āyūhanaṭṭhiti ca saññogaṭṭhiti ca palibodhaṭṭhiti ca samudayaṭṭhiti ca hetuṭṭhiti ca paccayaṭṭhiti ca. Imehi navahākārehi avijjā paccayo, saṅkhārā paccayasamuppannā. Ubho pete dhammā paccayasamuppannā ti ....*

283. S II 17: *Dukkham-eva uppajjamānaṃ uppajjati, dukkhaṃ nirujjhamānaṃ nirujjhatī ti—na kaṅkhati na vicikicchati, aparapaccayā ñāṇam-evassa ettha hoti. Ettāvatā kho, kaccāna, sammādiṭṭhi hoti.* Sn 55: *Diṭṭhīvisūkāni upātivatto, patto niyāmaṃ paṭiladdhamaggo; Uppannañāṇomhi anaññaneyyo.*

284. Cf. S II 92; D II 55: *Gambhīro cāyaṃ ānanda paṭicca-samuppādo gambhīrāvabhāso ca.*

285. Paṭis-a I 243: *Tisandhin-ti tayo sandhayo assā ti tisandhi, taṃ tisandhiṃ. Atītahetupaccuppannaphalānamantarā eko hetuphalasandhi, paccuppannaphala-anāgatahetūnamantarā eko phalahetusandhi, paccuppannahetu-anāgataphalānamantarā eko hetuphalasandhi. Paṭiccasamuppādapāḷiyaṃ sarūpato āgatavasena pana avijjāsaṅkhārā eko saṅkhepo, viññāṇanāmarūpasaḷāyatanaphassavedanā dutiyo, taṇhupādānabhavā tatiyo, jātijarāmaraṇaṃ catuttho. Avijjāsaṅkhārā ti dve aṅgāni atītakālāni, viññāṇādīni bhavāvasānāni aṭṭha paccuppannakālāni, jātijarāmaraṇan-ti dve anāgatakālāni. Saṅkhāra-viññāṇānaṃ antarā eko hetuphalasandhi, vedanātaṇhānamantarā eko phalahetusandhi, bhavajātīnamantarā eko hetuphalasandhi.* Cf. Vism XVII.289.

afflictions—this is the second link. With present afflictions as condition, future results—this is the third link.

The first and the third are the cause-result-link (*hetu-phala-sandhi*) and the existence-link (*bhava-sandhi*). The second link is the result-cause link (*phala-hetu-sandhi*), [which is] not an existence-link.[286]

51. Existence-link

Q. What is the meaning of "existence-link"?

A. Upon decease (*cuti*), immediately the non-transmigrating (*asaṅkanti*?)[287] aggregates, sense bases, and elements, due to the condition of past kamma-affliction, produce further existence in the [rebirth] destinations (*gati*). This is called the "existence-link".

Q. How does this happen?

A. The worldling, affected by ignorance (*avijjāgata*) and fettered by craving, performs meritorious and demeritorious kamma. If he dies at this time, he experiences pain. Lying on his deathbed, he does not see this world; he does not see that world. He has lost mindfulness (*muṭṭhasati*) and cannot regain it. Then he experiences the arising of suffering. There is decline of intellect,

286. 第二節果因節非有節. Presumably, this means that the *phala-hetu-sandhi* only applies to the present life, as is implied in the preceding, and is not a link between existences. 非有節 could also be translated as "non-existence link". Tibetan: "Furthermore, the first and third are the cause-result (*hetuphala*) link. The second is the result link. The existence link does not exist".

287. 未度陰入界, lit. "the not yet crossed over/liberated (*saṅkamana*, *taraṇa*, *nittharaṇa*, etc.) aggregates ..." Tibetan: "Immediately upon passing away, there is production of further existence in the non-transmigrating aggregates, sense bases, elements. This is the 'existence link'".

This is related to the discussion at Vism XVII.161–164, Vibh-a 162f.: ... *Kadāci pañcakkhandhāya kāmāvacaracutiyā rūpāvacaracutiyā vā anantarā catukkhandhā āruppapaṭisandhi. Evaṃ atītārammaṇacutiyā atītanavattabbapaccuppannārammaṇā paṭisandhi ... Iti hetaṃ laddhapaccayaṃ rūpārūpadhammamattaṃ uppajjamānaṃ bhavantaraṃ upetī ti vuccati, na satto, na jīvo. Tassa nāpi atītabhavato idha saṅkanti atthi, nāpi tato hetuṃ vinā idha pātubhāvo. ... Taṃ santativasena taṇhāya nāmiyamānaṃ saṅkhārehi khippamānaṃ orimatīrarukkhavinibaddharajjumālambitvā mātikātikkamako viya purimañ-ca nissayaṃ jahati, aparañ-ca kammasamuṭṭhāpitaṃ nissayaṃ assādayamānaṃ vā anassādayamānaṃ vā ārammaṇādīhiyeva paccayehi pavattati. Ettha ca purimaṃ cavanato cuti, pacchimaṃ bhavantarādipaṭisandhānato paṭisandhī ti vuccati. Tadetaṃ nāpi purimabhavā idha āgataṃ, nāpi tato kammasaṅkhāranativisayādihetuṃ vinā pātubhūtan-ti veditabbaṃ. ... Etthāha nanu evaṃ asaṅkantipātubhāve sati ye imasmiṃ manussattabhāve khandhā, tesaṃ niruddhattā phalapaccayassa ca kammassa tattha agamanato aññassa aññato ca taṃ phalaṃ siyā? ...* Abhid-av-pṭ II 101: *Asaṅkanti pātubhāve ti saṅkanti pātubhāvarahite, asaṅkantivasena vā pātubhāve, asaṅkamitvāva pātubhāve ti attho.*

mindfulness, and wisdom. There is decline of bodily strength and energy. The sense-faculties gradually perish. From the body, either upwards or downwards, the life faculty perishes. It perishes and withers like a withered talipot palm leaf.[288] Then he is like one who is asleep and dreaming. Through kamma, four things appear [to him]: kamma, kamma-sign (*kamma-nimitta*), destination (*gati*), and destination-sign.

52. Kamma, kamma-sign, destination, and destination-sign

Q. What is kamma?

A. What has been done—meritorious or demeritorious, heavy or light, much or little, what is proximate, [or] what has been formerly done—that kamma appears then and there (*teneva*) [i.e. at the time of death].[289]

Kamma-sign: that kamma done which is dependent upon the basis (*vatthu*), that basis appears then and there, [i.e.] the kamma-sign accompanying kamma appears at that time, or [it appears] according to kamma [presently] being done.[290]

---

288. Cf. Vism XVII.163/p.554, Vibh-a 163: *Atītabhavasmiṃ hi sarasena upakkamena vā samāsannamaraṇassa asayhānaṃ sabbaṅgapaccaṅgasandhibandhanacchedakānaṃ māraṇantikavedanāsatthānaṃ sannipātaṃ asahantassa ātape pakkhittaharitatālapaṇṇamiva kamena upasussamāne sarīre niruddhesu cakkhādīsu indriyesu hadayavatthumatte patiṭṭhitesu kāyindriyamanindriyajīvitindriyesu taṅkhaṇāvasesahadayavatthusannissitaṃ viññāṇaṃ garukasamāsevitāsannapubbakatānaṃ aññataraṃ laddhāvasesapaccayasaṅkhārasaṅkhātaṃ kammaṃ, tadupaṭṭhāpitaṃ vā kammanimittagatinimittasaṅkhātaṃ visayaṃ ārabbha pavattati.*

289. The text literally has "... little, according to the closeness of what has been formerly done", 如近其初所造, which is due to a misunderstanding of *yadāsannaṃ*, see parallel below. Cf. Paṭis-a III 575: *Aparam-pi catubbidhaṃ kammaṃ yaggarukaṃ yabbahulaṃ yadāsannaṃ kaṭattā vā pana kammanti. Tattha kusalaṃ vā hotu akusalaṃ vā, garukāgarukesu yaṃ garukaṃ mātughātādikammaṃ vā mahaggatakammaṃ vā, tadeva paṭhamaṃ vipaccati. Tathā bahulābahulesupi yaṃ bahulaṃ hoti susīlyaṃ vā dussīlyaṃ vā, tadeva paṭhamaṃ vipaccati. Yadāsannaṃ nāma maraṇakāle anussaritakammaṃ vā katakammaṃ vā. Yañ-hi āsannamaraṇe anussarituṃ sakkoti kātuṃ vā, teneva upapajjati. Etehi pana tīhi muttaṃ punappunaṃ laddhāsevanaṃ kaṭattā vā pana kammaṃ nāma hoti. Tesaṃ abhāve taṃ paṭisandhiṃ ākaḍḍhati.*

290. Tibetan (188a): "The sign of kamma: that kamma which is done depending upon the basis, in that (*de'i*) basis [it] appears. At that very time it occurs in accordance with the kamma done". Cf. Vism-mhṭ 312: *Kammanimittaṃ nāma yaṃ vatthuṃ ārammaṇaṃ katvā āyūhanakāle kammaṃ āyūhati, taṃ atīte kappakoṭisatasahassamatthakepi hi kamme kate vipaccanakāle āgantvā kammaṃ vā kammanimittaṃ vā upatiṭṭhati.* Vibh-a 155: ... *kammaṃ āyūhati. Tattha atīte kappakoṭisatasahassamatthakasmim-pi kamme kate tasmiṃ khaṇe kammaṃ vā kammanimittaṃ vā āgantvā upaṭṭhāti.* Abhidh-av-ṭ II 63: ... *āyūhati, taṃ dānūpakaraṇādikaṃ, pāṇaghātopakaraṇādikañ-ca.* Abhidh-av-ṭ I 275: *kammakaraṇakāle*

Destination: A good destination appears through the condition of merit; a bad destination appears through the condition of demerit.

Destination-sign: When three objects come together at the time of entry into the womb, he obtains rebirth.[291]

With regard to one who is spontaneously born (*opapātika*): depending on wherever there is birth, his particular site of rearising (*upapatti-vatthu?*) appears: a celestial palace (*vimāna*), seat, mountain, tree, or river. According to that particular destination, and together with grasping, the sign appears. He, at that time, whether he is going, standing, sitting or lying down, sees that [sign] and grasps it.

A. that time [of death], the kamma previously done, the kamma-sign, the destination, and the destination-sign become the object of the activation mind, which arises and ceases. At the end of life, at departure, the activation mind immediately ceases together with the life faculty and there is the decease [mind] (*cuti-citta*). Immediately after this, the [relinking-] mind arises through the activation mind.

It is only that kamma, kamma-sign, destination, or destination-sign which becomes the object of the resultant mind-basis which passes over (*otāreti, atikkamati*) to the future existence.[292] Like the lighting of a lamp by a lamp,[293] or like a flame rising from a fire, the relinking mind (*paṭisandhi-citta*) arises like a companion. [**451b**]

In the womb of the mother, dependent upon the impurity (*asuci*) of the mother and father, there is the arising of thirty kinds of matter produced by kamma:[294] the decads of material basis (*vatthurūpa*), body, and gender. Those

---

cetanāya gahitamārammaṇaṃ kammanimittaṃ nāma taṃ dānūpakaraṇādikaṃ pāṇaghātopakaraṇādikañ-ca.

291. I.e. the union of mother and father, the mother being in season, and the *gandhabba* being present; see M I 265: *Yato ca kho ... mātāpitaro ca sannipatitā honti, mātā ca utunī hoti, gandhabbo ca paccupaṭṭhito hoti evaṃ tiṇṇaṃ sannipātā gabbhassāvakkanti hoti.*

292. 作事果報心處度於後有. The characters 心處 might correspond to *hadaya-vatthu*. Although 心 usually corresponds to *citta* in Vim, in the list of parts of the body at 432c24 it corresponds to *hadaya*. Otherwise, it could mean "mind [which dependent on this] basis" or "mind as basis". Compare "enters into the bhavaṅga" 度後分 at 458a06.

293. Cf. Mil 71: *Rājā āha: bhante nāgasena, na ca saṅkamati paṭisandahati cāti. Āma mahārāja, na ca saṅkamati paṭisandahati cāti. Katham bhante nāgasena na ca saṅkamati paṭisandahati ca, opammaṃ karohī ti. Yathā mahārāja kocid eva puriso padīpato padīpaṃ padīpeyya, kin nu kho so mahārāja padīpo padīpamhā saṅkanto ti. Na hi bhante ti. Evam eva kho mahārāja na ca saṅkamati paṭisandahati cāti.*

294. The decads of physical basis, body, and sex. Cf. Vibh-a 22: *Evaṃ parittāya rūpasantatiyā tīṇi santatisīsāni honti—vatthudasakaṃ, kāyadasakaṃ, itthiyā*

[decads], at the moment of decay,[295] are without [the decads arising from] the relinking mind, [so] there is the arising of forty-six kinds of matter: the thirty produced by kamma, and the two times eight kinds of matter produced by food and season.[296] Without [the decads arising from] the relinking mind, matter, at the moment of decay, [is produced] together with a second mind, and there is the arising of fifty-four kinds of matter: the thirty produced by kamma and the three times eight kinds of matter produced by food, season, [and mind (*citta*)].[297]

---

itthindriyavasena purisassa purisindriyavasena bhāvadasakanti. Tattha vatthurūpaṃ, tassa nissayāni cattāri mahābhūtāni, taṃnissitā vaṇṇagandharasojā, jīvitan-ti idaṃ vatthudasakaṃ nāma. Kāyapasādo, tassa nissayāni cattāri mahābhūtāni, tannissitā vaṇṇagandharasojā, jīvitan-ti idaṃ kāyadasakaṃ nāma. Itthiyā itthibhāvo, purisassa purisabhāvo, tassa nissayāni cattāri mahābhūtāni, tannissitā vaṇṇagandharasojā, jīvitanti—idaṃ bhāvadasakaṃ nāma. Evaṃ gabbhaseyyakānaṃ paṭisandhiyaṃ ukkaṭṭhaparicchedena samatiṃsa kammajarūpāni rūpakkhandho nāma hoti. Paṭis-a III 571: *Nāmarūpapaccayāpi viññāṇan-ti ettha tasmiṃ paṭisandhikkhaṇe tayo vipākahetū sesacetasikā ca nāmaṃ, hadayavatthu rūpaṃ. Tato nāmarūpapaccayato pi paṭisandhiviññāṇaṃ pavattati. Viññāṇapaccayāpi nāmarūpan-ti etthā pi nāmaṃ vuttappakāram-eva, rūpaṃ pana idha sahetukamanussapaṭisandhiyā adhippetattā gabbhaseyyakānaṃ vatthudasakaṃ kāyadasakaṃ bhāvadasakan-ti samatiṃsa rūpāni, saṃsedajānaṃ opapātikānañ-ca paripuṇṇāyatanānaṃ cakkhudasakaṃ sotadasakaṃ ghānadasakaṃ jivhādasakañ-cā ti samasattati rūpāni. Taṃ vuttappakāraṃ nāmarūpaṃ paṭisandhikkhaṇe paṭisandhiviññāṇapaccayā pavattati.*

295. On the moment of decay, *jarākhaṇa*, see fn. 1937.

296. The text has 食節所成, "produced by food and relinking", but 節 "relinking", must be a corruption of 時, "season", as found below in 食時所成.

297. Cf. Abhidh-av-pṭ II 173: *Tassa gabbhaseyyakasattassa tiṃsa rūpānīti kāyabhāva-vatthudasakavasena samatiṃsa kammajarūpāniyeva. Tadā hi neva cittajarūpamatthi paṭisandhicittassa rūpasamuṭṭhāpakattābhāvato, nāpi utujaṃ purimuppanna-utuno abhāvā. Utu hi ṭhānappattaṃ rūpaṃ samuṭṭhāpeti, na ca āhārajaṃ tasmiṃ kāye ajjhohaṭassa abhāvato, tasmā kammasamuṭṭhānāniyeva tiṃsa rūpāni paṭisandhikkhaṇe nibbattanti.* Vism XVII.193–194, Vibh-a 170–171: *Pavatte pana sabbattha rūpappavattidese paṭisandhicittassa ṭhitikkhaṇe paṭisandhicittena saha pavatta-ututo utusamuṭṭhānaṃ suddhaṭṭhakaṃ pātubhavati. Paṭisandhicittaṃ pana rūpaṃ na samuṭṭhāpeti. ... Paṭisandhicittato pana uddhaṃ paṭhamabhavaṅgato pabhuti cittasamuṭṭhānakaṃ suddhaṭṭhakaṃ. Saddapātubhāvakāle paṭisandhikkhaṇato uddhaṃ pavatta-ututo ceva cittato ca saddanavakaṃ. Ye pana kabaḷikārāhārūpajīvino gabbhaseyyakasattā tesaṃ, yañcassa bhuñjatī mātā, annaṃ pānañ-ca bhojanaṃ; Tena so tattha yāpeti, mātukucchigato naro ti. Vacanato mātarā ajjhoharitāhārena anugate sarīre, opapātikānaṃ sabbapaṭhamaṃ attano mukhagataṃ kheḷaṃ ajjhoharaṇakāle āhārasamuṭṭhānaṃ suddhaṭṭhakan-ti idaṃ āhārasamuṭṭhānassa suddhaṭṭhakassa utucittasamuṭṭhānānañ-ca ukkaṃsato dvinnaṃ navakānaṃ vasena chabbīsatividhaṃ, pubbe ekekacittakkhaṇe tikkhattuṃ uppajjamānaṃ vuttaṃ kammasamuṭṭhānaṃ sattatividhan-ti channavutividhaṃ rūpaṃ tayo ca arūpino khandhā ti samāsato navanavuti dhammā.* Vibh-a 23: *Yadi hi cittaṃ ṭhānakkhaṇe vā bhaṅgakkhaṇe vā rūpaṃ samuṭṭhāpeyya, paṭisandhicittam-pi rūpaṃ samuṭṭhāpeyya. Na*

Thus, the arising of consciousness has name-and-matter as condition, and name-and-matter has consciousness as condition.[298]

Thus, there is the existence-link.

Thus should it be known through the three links.

53. Four collections

Q. How [should it be known] through the four collections (*saṅkhepato*)?

A. (1) Ignorance and the formations are collected (*saṅgahita*) in past kamma-affliction.

(2) Consciousness, name-and-matter, the six sense bases, contact, and feeling are collected in present result.

(3) Craving, clinging, and existence are collected in present kamma-affliction.

(4) Birth and ageing-and-death are collected in future result.

Thus should it be known through the four collections.[299]

54. Twenty modes

Q. How [should it be known] through the twenty modes (*ākārehi*)?

A. (1) By grasping ignorance, past craving, and clinging, it is grasped through the affliction-characteristic.

(2) By grasping the formations and past existence, it is grasped through the kamma-characteristic.

(3) By grasping consciousness, name-and-matter, the six sense bases, contact, and feeling, together with present birth and ageing-and-death, it is grasped through the result-characteristic.

(4) By grasping craving, clinging, and present [ignorance],[300] it is grasped through the affliction-characteristic.

---

pana cittaṃ tasmiṃ khaṇadvaye rūpaṃ samuṭṭhāpeti. Yathā pana ahicchattakamakulaṃ pathavito uṭṭhahantaṃ paṃsucuṇṇaṃ gahetvāva uṭṭhahati, evaṃ cittaṃ purejātaṃ vatthuṃ nissāya uppādakkhaṇe aṭṭha rūpāni gahetvāva uṭṭhahati. Cf. Vism XX.30–42/p.615ff.

298. Cf. S II 104: *Paccudāvattati kho idaṃ viññāṇam nāmarūpamhā nāparaṃ gacchati, ettāvatājāyetha vājīyetha vāmīyetha vācavetha vā upapajjetha vā yad idaṃ nāmarūpapaccayā viññāṇaṃ, viññāṇapaccayā nāmarūpaṃ, nāmarūpapaccayā saḷāyatanaṃ, ... pe ...*

299. Cf. Vism XVII.290/p.579: *Sandhīnaṃ ādipariyosānavavatthitā panassa cattāro saṅgahā honti. Seyyathidaṃ avijjāsaṅkhārā eko saṅgaho. Viññāṇanāmarūpasaḷāyatanaphassavedanā dutiyo. Taṇhupādānabhavā tatiyo. Jātijarāmaraṇaṃ catutthoti. Evamidaṃ catubhedasaṅgahan-ti veditabbaṃ.*

300. "Ignorance" is missing in the text, but is found in the Tibetan (... *da ltar gyi ma rig pa bzung ba* ...). Likewise, in the next sentence "result-characteristic" is missing from the text, but is found in the Tibetan (... *tsor ba bzung ba yin te rnam par smin pa'i mtsan nyid yin pas so*).

(5) By grasping existence and present formations, it is grasped through the kamma-characteristic.

(6) By grasping birth, ageing-and-death, future consciousness, name-and-matter, six sense bases, contact, and feeling, it is grasped [through the result-characteristic.]

These twenty-four states become twenty by grasping them in their entirety.[301]

A. it is said in the Abhidhamma: "In former-kamma-existence, delusion is ignorance, [kamma] accumulation (*āyūha*) is formations, attachment is craving, seeking[302] is clinging, volition is existence—these five states [in former-kamma-existence are the conditions for relinking here.][303]

[Relinking is consciousness, descent is name-and-matter, sensitivity is sense bases, what is touched is contact, and what is felt is feeling—these five states] in former-kamma-existence are the conditions for rearising-existence (*upapattibhava*) here.

---

301. Cf. Paṭis I 52: ... *Itime catusaṅkhepe tayo addhe tisandhiṃ vīsatiyā ākārehi paṭiccasamuppādaṃ jānāti passati aññāti paṭivijjhati.* Cf. Vism VII.22/p.200: *Tattha avijjāsaṅkhārā eko saṅkhepo, viññāṇanāmarūpasaḷāyatanaphassavedanā eko, taṇhupādānabhavā eko, jātijarāmaraṇaṃ eko. Purimasaṅkhepo cettha atīto addhā, dve majjhimā paccuppanno, jātijarāmaraṇaṃ anāgato. Avijjāsaṅkhāraggahaṇena cettha taṇhupādānabhavā gahitāva hontī ti ime pañca dhammā atīte kammavaṭṭaṃ, viññāṇādayo pañca etarahi vipākavaṭṭaṃ, taṇhupādānabhavaggahaṇena avijjāsaṅkhārā gahitāva hontī ti ime pañca dhammā etarahi kammavaṭṭaṃ, jātijarāmaraṇāpadesena viññāṇādīnaṃ niddiṭṭhattā ime pañca dhammā āyatiṃ vipākavaṭṭaṃ. Te ākārato vīsatividhā honti. Saṅkhāraviññāṇānañcettha antarā eko sandhi, vedanātaṇhānamantarā eko, bhavajātīnamantarā ekoti, iti bhagavā etaṃ catusaṅkhepaṃ tiyaddhaṃ vīsatākāraṃ tisandhiṃ paṭiccasamuppādaṃ sabbākārato jānāti passati aññāti paṭivijjhati.* Cf. Paṭis-a I 243: *Kathaṃ pana dvādasahi paṭiccasamuppādaṅgehi ime vīsati ākārā gahitā hontī ti? Avijjā saṅkhārāti ime dve atītahetuyo sarūpato vuttā. Yasmā pana avidvā paritassati, paritassito upādiyati, tassupādānapaccayā bhavo, tasmā tehi dvīhi gahitehi taṇhupādānabhavāpi gahitāva honti. Paccuppanne viññāṇanāmarūpasaḷāyatanaphassavedanā sarūpato vuttāyeva. Taṇhupādānabhavā paccuppannahetuyo sarūpato vuttā. Bhave pana gahite tassa pubbabhāgā taṃsampayuttā vā saṅkhārā gahitāva honti, taṇhupādānaggahaṇena ca taṃsampayuttā. Yāya vā mūḷho kammaṃ karoti, sā avijjā gahitāva hoti. Anāgate jāti jarāmaraṇan-ti dve sarūpena vuttāni, jātijarāmaraṇaggahaṇeneva pana viññāṇādīni pañca anāgataphalāni gahitāneva honti. Tesaṃ yeva hi jātijarāmaraṇānī ti evaṃ dvādasahi aṅgehi vīsati ākārā gahitā honti.*

302. 覓是取. Elsewhere in Vim 覓 corresponds to *esana* and *pariyesana*, "seeking/going after". The Paṭis parallel has *upagamana* "approaching/coming near to/undertaking/entering".

303. A section of five of the twenty states is missing from the Chinese text, probably due to haplography. It is here supplied from the abridged version in the Tibetan and in the Pali parallel.

[Here] the delusion of not understanding the [maturing of the] sense bases is ignorance;[304] [kamma] accumulation is formations; attachment is craving; seeking is clinging; volition is existence—these five states in kamma-existence here are the conditions for relinking in the future.[305]

In future [existence], the relinking is consciousness; descent is name-and-matter; sensitivity (*pasāda*) is sense base; what is touched is contact; what is felt is feeling—these five states in the future rearising-existence (*upapattibhava*) have their condition in the kamma done here."[306]

Thus should it be known through the twenty modes.

55. Wheel

Q. How [should it be known] through the wheel (*cakkato*)?

A. With ignorance as condition, the formations; with formations as condition, consciousness; ... with birth as condition, ageing and death. Thus, there is the origination of this entire mass of suffering.

304. 不了諸入癡是無明. The Paṭis parallel (see next fn.) has ... *paripakkattā āyatanānaṃ moho avijjā*, while the Tibetan has "due to the maturing of the sense bases, etc., ignorance". Probably Saṅghapāla did not understand the term *paripakkattā*, "maturing". Cf. Vism XVII.296: *idha paripakkattā āyatanānan-ti paripakkāyatanassa kammakaraṇakāle sammoho dassito.*

305. 生時, "(re-) birth-time", *upapatti-* or *jāti-samaya* or *-kāla*, is found here and at the start of the next sentence, but this term is not found elsewhere in the Vim. The Tibetan has *nying mtshams sbyor ba = pratisandhi*. The Paṭis and Vism parallels have *paṭisandhi*, "relinking". Cf. Vism-mhṭ II 308: *upapattikkhaṇeti paṭisandhikkhaṇe.* Vibh-mṭ 70 (on Vibh 411): *Tāni hi rūpabhave pañcavokāre upapattikkhaṇe uppajjanti. Kāmadhātuyaṃ paṭisandhikkhaṇe uppajjamānānan-ti yojanā.*

306. = Paṭis I 52: *Purimakammabhavasmiṃ moho avijjā, āyūhanā saṅkhārā, nikanti taṇhā, upagamanaṃ upādānaṃ, cetanā bhavo. Ime pañca dhammā purimakammabhavasmiṃ idha paṭisandhiyā paccayā. Idha paṭisandhi viññāṇaṃ, okkanti nāmarūpaṃ, pasādo āyatanaṃ, phuṭṭho phasso, vedayitaṃ vedanā. Ime pañca dhammā idhupapattibhavasmiṃ purekatassa kammassa paccayā. Idha paripakkattā āyatanānaṃ moho avijjā, āyūhanā saṅkhārā, nikanti taṇhā upagamanaṃ upādānaṃ, cetanā bhavo. Ime pañca dhammā idha kammabhavasmiṃ āyatiṃ paṭisandhiyā paccayā. Āyatiṃ paṭisandhi viññāṇaṃ, okkanti nāmarūpaṃ, pasādo āyatanaṃ, phuṭṭho phasso, vedayitaṃ vedanā. Ime pañca dhammā āyatiṃ upapattibhavasmiṃ idha katassa kammassa paccayā.*

See Ñāṇamoli's note on the parallel at Vism XVII.292–297/p.579–81. Cf. Paṭis-a: I 241: *Nikanti taṇhā ti yā kammaṃ karontassa tassa phale upapattibhave nikāmanā patthanā, sā taṇhā nāma. Upagamanaṃ upādānan ti yaṃ kammabhavassa paccayabhūtaṃ imasmiṃ nāma kamme kate kāmā sampajjantī ti vā idaṃ katvā asukasmiṃ nāma ṭhāne kāme sevissāmī ti vā attā ucchinno suucchinno hotī ti vā sukhī hotiṃ vigatapariḷāho ti vā sīlabbataṃ sukhena paripūratī ti vā pavattaṃ upagamanaṃ daḷhagahaṇaṃ, idaṃ upādānaṃ nāma.*

Herein, the not knowing of this entire mass of suffering is ignorance;[307] with ignorance as condition, the formations again.[308]

Thus, it should be known through the wheel.

56. Way

Q. How [should it be known] through way (*naya*)?

A. There are two ways, namely, one beginning with ignorance and one beginning with ageing and death. When questioned about that which begins with ignorance, one should answer in the regular order (*anuloma*); and when questioned about that which begins with ageing and death, the answer should be in the reverse order (*paṭiloma*).

Furthermore, that which begins with ignorance is the threshold (*mukha*) to the future (*aparanta*), [**451c**] the future knowledge of the path. That which begins with ageing and death is the threshold to the past (*pubbanta*), the past knowledge of the path.[309]

Thus should it be known through way.

57. Analysis

Q. How [should it be known] through analysis?

A. There are two kinds of dependent arising: mundane dependent arising and supramundane dependent arising.

Herein, that which begins with ignorance [until suffering] is mundane dependent arising.

Q. What is supramundane dependent arising?

A. [Beginning with] suffering; with suffering as proximate cause, faith;[310] with faith as proximate cause, gladness; with gladness as proximate cause,

---

307. S II 4: *Katamā ca ... avijjā? Yaṃ kho ... dukkhe aññāṇaṃ, dukkhasamudaye aññāṇaṃ, dukkhanirodhe aññāṇaṃ, dukkhanirodhagāminiyā paṭipadāya aññāṇaṃ. ayaṃ vuccati ... avijjā. Iti kho ... avijjāpaccayā saṅkhārā; saṅkhārapaccayā viññāṇaṃ ...pe... evametassa kevalassa dukkhakkhandhassa samudayo hoti. Avijjāya tveva asesavirāganirodhā saṅkhāranirodho; saṅkhāranirodhā viññāṇanirodho ...pe... evametassa kevalassa dukkhakkhandhassa nirodho hotī ti.*

308. Tibetan (189a): "Likewise, again 'with ignorance as condition, formations', and so on. Again, in this manner, there is an endless turning of the wheel of dependent arising".

309. No parallel can be traced in Pali texts.

310. This is the supramundane conditioned arising scheme as described in the Upanisā Sutta at S II 31/SN 12:23: *... jātūpanisaṃ dukkhaṃ, dukkhūpanisā saddhā, saddhūpanisaṃ pāmojjaṃ, pāmojjūpanisā pīti, pītūpanisā passaddhi, passaddhūpanisaṃ sukhaṃ, sukhūpaniso samādhi, samādhūpanisaṃ yathābhūtañāṇadassanaṃ, yathābhūtañāṇadassanūpanisā nibbidā, nibbidūpaniso virāgo, virāgūpanisā vimutti, vimuttūpanisaṃ khayeñāṇaṃ.*

rapture; with rapture as proximate cause, tranquillity; with tranquillity as proximate cause, pleasure; with pleasure as proximate cause, concentration; with concentration as proximate cause, knowledge and vision according to reality; with knowledge and vision according to reality as proximate cause, disenchantment; with disenchantment as proximate cause, dispassion; with dispassion as proximate cause, freedom; and with freedom as proximate cause, knowledge of destruction. This is called supramundane dependent arising.[311]

It is also said:[312] "There are four kinds of dependent arising: with kamma-affliction as cause; seed as cause; preparation as cause; and shared kamma as cause".[313]

Q. What is meant by "kamma-affliction as cause"?
A. It is that which begins with ignorance.

Q. What is meant by "seed as cause"?
A. It is like the succession of seed and sprout.[314]

Q. What is meant by "preparation (*abhisaṅkhāra*) as cause"?
A. It is like the [supernormal] creation of forms.[315]

Q. What is meant by "shared kamma (*sādhāraṇakamma*) as cause"?
A. It is like the earth, Himalaya, sea, sun, and moon.[316]

---

311. Cf. Nett 67: *Es'ev' anto dukkhassā ti paṭiccasamuppādo. So duvidho: lokiyo ca lokuttaro ca. Tattha lokiyo: avijjāpaccayā saṅkhārā yāva jarāmaraṇā; lokuttaro: sīlavato avippaṭisāro jāyati yāva nāparaṃ itthattāyā.* Cf. S II 32, A IV 336, V 312f.

312. 復說, see Introduction§ 4.8. The Tibetan (189b) has "it is also said in others", *gzhan dag tu yang gsungs pa*, which probably corresponds to *apare pana vadanti* or *apare vadanti*, "others say", or perhaps it is a misunderstanding of *aparam-pi vutta*, "again it is also said" to which the Chinese appears to correspond.

313. This section seems to be related to the five *niyāma*: Moh 78: *Pañcavidho hi niyāmo: bījaniyāmo utuniyāmo kammaniyāmo dhammaniyāmo cittaniyāmoti, tattha aṅkurapaṇṇadaṇḍapupphaphalādikkamena tesaṃ tesaṃ bījānaṃ aññoññavisadi-sarukkhatiṇagacchalatādisantāne attanā sadisaphaladānaṃ bījaniyāmo nāma.*

314. See § 44 of this chapter.

315. Cf. Sn-a I 361: *manomayiddhiyā abhisaṅkharitvā nimmitabuddhaṃ māpesi.* Dhp-a II 194: *ime pana iddhiyā abhisaṅkharitvā nimmitakāle gatā bhavissantī ti.* Mp I 363: *Satthā tassā caritavasena iddhiyā ekaṃ itthirūpaṃ nimminitvā...*

316. Cf. Kv-a 100: *paṭhavīsamuddasūriyacandimādayo hi sabbesaṃ sādhāraṇakammavipāko ti tesaṃ laddhi.* Paṭis-a I 290: ... *Itarathā hi sakasantānapariyāpannāpi rūpādayo dhammā sabbe na saṅgaṇheyyuṃ. Yasmā anindriyabaddharūpādayo pi vipassanūpagā, tasmā tesaṃ kammasambhūtapadena saṅgaho veditabbo. Te pi hi sabbasattasādhāraṇakammapaccaya-utusamuṭṭhānā. Aññe pana anindriyabaddhā rūpādayo avipassanūpagā ti vadanti.*

Furthermore, some say: "Shared kamma is not a cause. Matter,[317] mind (*citta*), states (*dhamma*), and season (*utu*) are causes. There is no shared kamma. As the Fortunate One taught in a verse,

"Kamma is not shared with another;
It is the treasure another cannot steal.
The merit that is done by a man
Is the good reward he gains by himself."[318]
Thus should it be known through analysis.

58. Inclusion

Q. How [should it be known] through inclusion?
A. There are four kinds of inclusion: inclusion in the aggregates, inclusion in the sense bases, inclusion in the elements, and inclusion in the truths.

Herein, ignorance, formations, contact, craving, clinging, and existence are included in the aggregate of formations. Consciousness is included in the aggregate of consciousness. Name-and-matter is included in four aggregates. The six sense bases are included in two aggregates. Feeling is included in the aggregate of feeling. Birth, ageing, and death are included in the aggregate of matter and in the aggregate of formations.[319]

---

317. 諸色 perhaps can mean "(dependent) kinds of matter", as at 439c17.

318. Kv 751: *Asādhāraṇam aññesaṃ, acoraharaṇo nidhi. / Kayirātha macco puññāni, sace sucaritaṃ care.* Cp: Kh 7: *asādhāraṇamaññesaṃ, acorāharaṇo nidhi. / Kayirātha dhīro puññāni, yo nidhi anugāmiko.*

Cf. Spk I 37: *Kammassakā hi sattā, attano kammānurūpaṃ eva gatiṃ gacchanti, n'eva pitā puttassa kammena gacchati, na putto pitu kammena, na matā puttassa, na putto mātuyā, na bhātā bhaginiyā, na ācariyo antevāsino, na antevāsī ācariyassa kammena gacchati.*

319. The Tibetan text includes *nāmarūpa* in the five aggregates instead of four, by excluding *viññāṇa*. According to the Dhātukathā, etc., *nāmarūpa* is included in four aggregates. See the discussion of this adaptation in the Introduction § 4.4. Dhāt 14 § 64: *Viññāṇapaccayā nāmarūpaṃ catūhi khandhehi ekādasahāyatanehi ekādasahi dhātūhi saṅgahitaṃ.* Moh 326: *Paṭiccasamuppādesu nāmarūpaṃ viññāṇavajjitehi catūhi khandhehi, ekādasahi āyatanadhātūhi ca saṅgahitaṃ. Ettha hi pavattiyaṃ nāmarūpassā-pi gahitattā saddāyatanam-pi gahitan-ti veditabbaṃ.* Vibh 136: *Vedanākkhandho, saññākkhandho, saṅkhārakkhandho—idaṃ vuccati nāmaṃ.* Vibh 144: *Vedanākkhandho, saññākkhandho, saṅkhārakkhandho—idaṃ vuccati viññāṇapaccayā nāmaṃ.* Vibh 149: *... saṅkhārakkhandho—idaṃ vuccati viññāṇapaccayā nāmaṃ viññāṇahetukaṃ.* Vibh 153: *... viññāṇapaccayā nāmaṃ viññāṇasampayuttaṃ.* M-a IV 78: *Cakkhudvāre cakkhupasādo ceva rūpārammaṇañ-ca rūpaṃ, sampayuttā tayo khandhā nāmaṃ. Taṃ nāmarūpaṃ cakkhuviññāṇassa paññāpanāya hetu ceva paccayo ca.* Cf. M I 52, S II 3, Peṭ 116: *Vedanā, saññā, cetanā, phasso, manasikāro—idaṃ vuccati nāmaṃ.* Cf. Paṭis I 183: *Katamo nāmakāyo? Vedanā, saññā, cetanā, phasso, manasikāro ...* Cf. Vibh-a 169: *Suttantasmiñhi tattha katamaṃ nāmaṃ? Vedanā saññā cetanā phasso manasikāro ti*

Ignorance, formations, contact, feeling, craving, clinging, existence, birth, ageing, and death are included in the sense base of mental states. Consciousness is included in the sense base of mind. Name-and-matter is included in the five internal sense bases. The six sense bases are included in the six internal sense bases.[320]

Ignorance, formations, contact, feeling, craving, clinging, existence, birth, ageing, and death are included in the element of mental states. Consciousness is included in the mind-consciousness-element. Name-and-matter is included in the five elements. The six sense bases are included in the twelve [elements].

Ignorance, craving, and clinging are included in the truth [of origination].[321] The other nine are included in the truth of suffering. The path factors of supramundane dependent arising are included in the truth of the path. The cessation of dependent arising is included in the truth of cessation.

Thus should it be known through inclusion.

Thus should it be known by way of the skill in dependent arising.

This is called "skill in dependent arising".

The skill in dependent arising is finished. *[452a]*

---

vuttaṃ. Idha vedanākkhandho saññākkhandho saṅkhārakkhandho ti. Tattha hi yampi cakkhuviññāṇapaccayā nāmaṃ uppajjati, uppannañ-ca cittassa ṭhiti arūpīnaṃ dhammānaṃ āyūti evaṃ aññadhammasannissayena aggahetabbato pākaṭaṃ, taṃ dassento cetanāphassamanasikāravasena saṅkhārakkhandhaṃ tidhā bhinditvā dvīhi khandhehi saddhiṃ desesi. Idha pana tattha vuttañ-ca avuttañ-ca sabbaṃ nāmaṃ saṅgaṇhanto tayo khandhā vedanākkhandho saññākkhandho saṅkhārakkhandho ti āha. Dhs 226, § 1316. *Vedanākkhandho, saññākkhandho, saṅkhārakkhandho, viññāṇakkhandho, asaṅkhatā ca dhātu—idaṃ vuccati nāmaṃ.*

320. In contrast, the Tibetan includes *nāmarūpa* in the sense base and element of mind and the six external sense bases and elements. On this adaptation, see Introduction § 4.4. Cf. Dhāt 14, § 65: *Nāmarūpapaccayā saḷāyatanaṃ dvīhi khandhehi chahāyatanehi dvādasahi dhātūhi saṅgahitaṃ. ... Tīhi khandhehi chahāyatanehi chahi dhātūhi asaṅgahitaṃ.* Moh 326: *Saḷāyatanaṃ dvīhi khandhehi, pasādaviññāṇabhūtehi chahi āyatanehi, dvādasahi dhātūhi saṅgahitaṃ.* Moh 146: *Pasādarūpacittasaṅkhātāni cha ajjhattikāni āyatanāni. ... Sesarūpacetasikanibbānapaññattisaṅkhātāni cha bāhirāyatanāni, idha pana paññattiyo pi labbhanti.*

321. The Chinese text is corrupt here. It literally has: "The six sense bases are included in the twelve truths. Ignorance, craving, and clinging are included in the ten truths", 六入十二諦所攝, 無明愛取十諦所攝. However, the six senses, as in the Tibetan, belong to the preceding element section. Here they are implied in the "other nine". The character 集, "origination", must have been lost and replaced with "ten", 十, by a copyist who could not make sense of the text.

Skill in the Noble Truths

59. What is skill in the noble truths?

Q. What is skill in the noble truths?
A. The four noble truths are the noble truth of suffering, the noble truth of the origination of suffering, the noble truth of the cessation of suffering, and the noble truth of the path leading to the cessation of suffering.

60. Truth of suffering

Q. What is the noble truth of suffering?
A. "Birth is suffering; ageing is suffering; death is suffering; sorrow is suffering; lamentation is suffering; pain is suffering; distress [and grief] are suffering; association with those who are not dear is suffering; separation from those who are dear is suffering; not getting what is wished for is suffering; in brief the five aggregates subject to clinging are suffering".[322]

"Birth is suffering" is the arising of the aggregates of various orders of beings. The origination of all suffering is the meaning.[323]

"Ageing is suffering": Being born, the elements mature. Decline in strength, appearance (*vaṇṇa, saṇṭhāna*), sense-faculties, memory, and wisdom is the meaning.[324]

"Death is suffering" is giving rise to fear with regard to the exhaustion of life is the meaning.

"Sorrow is suffering" is the consuming[325] of the mind on reaching a state of suffering. Burning inside is the meaning.[326]

---

322. D II 304 ff; Vibh 99: *Cattāri ariyasaccāni: dukkhaṃ ariyasaccaṃ dukkhasamudayo ariyasaccaṃ dukkhanirodho ariyasaccaṃ dukkhanirodhagāmini paṭipadā ariyasaccaṃ. Tattha katamaṃ dukkhaṃ ariyasaccaṃ? Jāti pi dukkhā jarā pi dukkhā maraṇaṃ pi dukkhaṃ sokaparidevadukkhadomanassupāyāsā pi dukkhā appiyehi sampayogo dukkho piyehi vippayogo dukkho yam p'icchaṃ na labhati tam pi dukkhaṃ: saṅkhittena pañcupādānakkhandhā pi dukkhā.*

In this list as well as in the explanation the Chinese just has 惱, *domanassa*, but not *upāyāsa*, while the Tibetan lists and explains both *yid mi bde ba* = *domanassa*, and *'khrug pa* = *upāyāsa*. Moreover, in the Chinese list (physical) *dukkha* is given after *domanassa* instead of preceding it, however in the explanation it precedes it.

323. Cf. D II 305; Vibh 99: *Yā tesaṃ tesaṃ sattānaṃ tamhi tamhi sattanikāye jāti sañjāti okkanti abhinibbatti khandhānaṃ pātubhāvo āyatanānaṃ paṭilābho, ayaṃ vuccati bhikkhave jāti.*

324. Cf. D II 305; Vibh 99: *āyuno saṃhāni indriyānaṃ paripāko.*

325. 思惟, the Pali has *parijjhāyana*, "consuming", "burning". Tibetan: *yongs su 'chang ba* = *pari-dhāraṇa*. Both the Chinese and Tibetan translators misinterpreted *jhāyana* in *parijjhāyana* [or *pariḍayhana*] as "considering" or "bearing in mind".

326. Cf. Paṭis I 37, Vibh 99: *antosoko antoparisoko cetaso parijjhāyanā.* The Tibetan has:

"Lamentation is suffering" is the suffering that leads to verbal expression.[327] Burning inside and outside is the meaning.

"Pain is suffering" is the suffering of the body. Because of this, one suffers physically is the meaning.

"Distress is suffering" is the suffering of the mind. Because of this, one suffers mentally is the meaning.[328]

"Association with those who are not dear is suffering" is being united with disagreeable beings. This gives rise to suffering is the meaning.

"Separation from those who are dear is suffering" is being parted and separated from agreeable beings. This gives rise to sorrow[329] is the meaning.

"Not getting what is wished for": [When] desiring separation from those who are disagreeable and desiring association with those who are agreeable, and not getting it. The losing of what is wished for is the meaning.

"In brief, the five aggregates subject to clinging are suffering": There is no separation from the suffering of these five aggregates subject to clinging, therefore in brief, the five aggregates subject to clinging are suffering.[330]

Q. What are the five aggregates subject to clinging?[331]

A. The matter aggregate subject to clinging, the feeling aggregate subject to clinging, the perception aggregate subject to clinging, the formations aggregate subject to clinging, the consciousness aggregate subject to clinging. These are to be known according to the full explanation in the [section on] skill in the aggregates.

61. Kinds of suffering

Herein, suffering is of two kinds thus: suffering as basis (*vatthuka-dukkha, vatthu-dukkha*) and suffering as intrinsic nature (*sabhāva-dukkha*).

Birth is suffering, death is suffering, association with those who are not dear is suffering, separation from those who are dear is suffering, not getting what is wished for is suffering; in brief, the five aggregates subject to clinging are suffering—this is called "suffering as basis".[332]

"inner and outer burning", but this likely is a mistake.

327. Cf. Vibh 99: *paridevitattaṃ vācā palāpo.*

328. The Tibetan (191a) includes an explanation of *upāyāsa* that is missing in the Chinese: "Grief is extensive fear (*'jigs pa rgyas pa*) when there is suffering. It is suffering in the sense of being deluded."

329. Tibetan (191a): "... sorrow and lamentation (*sokaparideva*)", ... *mya ngan dang smre sngags 'don pa.*

330. Cf. the explanations of these terms at M III 248ff, and Vibh 99.

331. This question and answer are not in the Tibetan.

332. Vibh-a 104: *Sokassa dukkhaṭṭho veditabbo ti ettha pana ayaṃ sabhāvadukkhattā c'eva*

Sorrow, lamentation, pain, distress, and grief are suffering—this is called "suffering as intrinsic nature".[333]

Suffering is of three kinds: the suffering of suffering, the suffering of change, and the suffering of formations.[334]

Herein bodily and mental suffering—this is called "suffering of suffering".[335]

The change of the basis (*vatthu*) of pleasant feeling that is subject to contaminations—this is called "the suffering of change".[336]

The five aggregates subject to clinging—this is called "the suffering of formations".

This is called the noble truth of suffering.

---

dukkhassa ca vatthubhāvena dukkho ti vutto. Vibh-a 93: *Tattha kāyikacetasikā dukkhavedanā sabhāvato ca nāmato ca dukkhattā dukkhadukkhaṃ nāma. ... Ṭhapetvā dukkhadukkhaṃ sesaṃ dukkhasaccavibhaṅge āgataṃ jāti ādi sabbam-pi tassa tassa dukkhassa vatthubhāvato pariyāyadukkhaṃ nāma.* Vibh-a 95: *Idāni jātiyā dukkhaṭṭho veditabbo ti ayañ-hi jāti sayaṃ na dukkhā, dukkhuppattiyā pana vatthubhāvena dukkhā ti vuttā. Kataradukkhassa panāyaṃ vatthū ti? Yaṃ taṃ bālapaṇḍitasuttādīsu bhagavatā pi upamāvasena pakāsitaṃ āpāyikaṃdukkhaṃ, yañ-ca sugatiyaṃ manussaloke gabbhokkantimūlakādibhedaṃ dukkhaṃ uppajjati, tassa sabbassā-pi esā vatthu.* Vibh-a 97: *Iti imassa sabbassā-pi dukkhassa ayaṃ jāti vatthum-eva hotī ti.* Sn-a I 41: *Sohaṃ jātidukkhavatthukehi sabbadukkhehi parimutto...*

333. For Pali passages, see fn. 2000. 自性 = *sabhāva*. The Tibetan has *rang rtags* = "own sign" or "intrinsic character", with the v.l. *rang brtags*. Elsewhere in the Tibetan quotations *rang bzhin* and *rang gi ngo bo* are used for *sabhāva*.

334. Cf. D III 216: *Tisso dukkhatā: Dukkhadukkhatā, saṅkhāradukkhatā, viparināmadukkhatā.* Vibh-a 93: *Tattha kāyikacetasikā dukkhavedanā sabhāvato ca nāmato ca dukkhattā dukkhadukkhaṃ nāma. Sukhavedanā vipariṇāmena dukkhuppattihetuto vipariṇāmadukkhaṃ nāma. Upekkhāvedanā c'eva avasesā ca tebhūmakā saṅkhārā udayabbayapīḷitattā saṅkhāradukkhaṃ nāma.* Nidd-a I 77: ... *Vipariṇāmadukkhan-ti sukhavedanā vipariṇāmadukkhassa hetuto vipariṇāmadukkhaṃ.* Abhidh-k-bh 6.3: *tisro hi duḥkhatā duḥkhaduḥkhatā saṃskāraduḥkhatā vipariṇāmaduḥkhatā ca / tābhiryathāyogamaśeṣataḥ sarva sāsravāḥ saṃskārā duḥkhāḥ /... duḥkhāyāḥ duḥkhasvabhāvenaiva duḥkhatā ... aduḥkhāsukhāvedanāyāḥ saṃskāreṇaiva duḥkhatā / pratyayābhisaṃskaraṇādyadanityaṃ tadduḥkham iti.*

335. The Tibetan has "pain/suffering of body and of speech", *lus kyi dang ngag gi sdug bsngal, = kāyika-vācika dukkha.* This cannot be correct since there is no suffering of speech, since feeling only applies to body and mind.

336. Cf. S IV 216: *Sukhā vedanā, dukkhā vedanā, adukkhamasukhā vedanā, imā tisso vedanā vuttā mayā. Vuttaṃ kho panetaṃ, bhikkhu, mayā yaṃ kiñci vedayitaṃ, taṃ dukkhasminti. Taṃ kho panetaṃ, bhikkhu, mayā saṅkhārānaṃ yeva aniccataṃ ... vipariṇāmadhammataṃ sandhāya bhāsitaṃ ...* Cf. S II 53, M III 208.

62. Truth of the origination of suffering

Q. What is the noble truth of the origination of suffering?
A. "This craving, causing further existence (*punabbhava*), accompanied by delight and greed, delighting everywhere, namely, [**452b**] the craving for sense-pleasure, the craving for existence, and the craving for annihilation".

Herein, "this craving causing further existence": The fostering of craving for existence causes existence and birth".

"[This] craving", as the origination of suffering, means just craving unaccompanied [by delight and greed], which is taught as the origination of suffering.

"Accompanied by delight and greed (*nandirāga*)": When just craving causes delight (*nandi*), it is called delight. When it causes staining (*rañjana*), it is called greed (*rāga*). [It means] delight arising together with greed.[337]

"Delighting everywhere": Wherever self-hood (*attabhāva*) is produced, there it delights. Wherever there is a likeable object (*piyarūpa*), there it delights.[338]

"Namely, the craving for sense-pleasure, the craving for existence, and the craving for annihilation": Putting aside craving for existence and the craving for annihilation, [all] other cravings are craving for sense-pleasure. The craving for existence is accompanied by the view of eternalism and the craving for annihilation is accompanied by the view of annihilationism.[339]

This is called the "noble truth of the origination of suffering".

---

337. Cf. Nidd-a I 38: *Nandī ca sā rañjanaṭṭhena rāgo cā ti nandirāgo. Tattha ekasmiṃ ārammaṇe sakiṃ uppannā taṇhā nandī, puna-ppunaṃ uppajjamānā nandirāgo ti vuccati.* This explanation and the preceding ones are missing from the Tibetan.

338. Tibetan (191b): adds "Furthermore, wherever there is a likeable object or pleasant object (*piyarūpa sātarūpa*), there it delights".

Cf. Paṭis I 39: *Yāyaṃ taṇhā ponobhavikā ... vibhavataṇhā, sā kho panesā taṇhā kattha uppajjamānā uppajjati, kattha nivisamānā nivisati? Yaṃ loke piyarūpaṃ sātarūpaṃ, etthesā taṇhā uppajjamānā uppajjati, ettha nivisamānā nivisati. Kiñca loke piyarūpaṃ sātarūpaṃ? Cakkhu loke piyarūpaṃ sātarūpaṃ, etthesā taṇhā uppajjamānā uppajjati.* Cf. D II 308, etc.

339. S V 421; Vin I 10: Vibh 101–3; D II 308–10: *Katamañ ca bhikkhave dukkhasamudayaṃ ariyasaccaṃ? Yāyaṃ taṇhā ponobhavikā nandi-rāga-sahagatā tatratatrābhinandinī, seyyathīdaṃ kāma-taṇhā bhava-taṇhā vibhava-taṇhā.* Cf. Paṭis-a I 158/ Vibh-a 110f/Sv 799/ Vism XVI.61: *Yāyaṃ taṇhā ti yā ayaṃ taṇhā. Ponobbhavikā ti punabbhavakaraṇaṃ punobbhavo, ... Ahinandanasaṅkhātena nandirāgena sahagatā ti nandirāgasahagatā, nandirāgena saddhiṃ atthato ekattam eva gatā ti vuttaṃ hoti. Tatratatrābhinandinī ti yatra yatra attabhāvo nibbattati tatratatrābhinandinī, rūpādīsu vā ārammaṇesu tatratatrābhinandinī; rūpābhinandinī saddagandharasaphoṭṭhabbadhammābhinandinī ti attho. ... Kāmataṇhā ti kāme taṇhā kāmataṇhā; pañcakāmaguṇikarāgass' etaṃ adhivacanaṃ. Bhave taṇhā bhavataṇhā; bhavapatthanāvasena uppannassa sassatadiṭṭhisahagatassa rūpārūpabhavarāgassa ca jhānanikantiyā cetaṃ adhivacanaṃ. Vibhave taṇhā vibhavataṇhā; ucchedadiṭṭhisahagatassa rāgass'etaṃ adhivacanaṃ.*

63. Truth of the cessation of suffering

Q. What is the noble truth of the cessation of suffering?
A. "The remainderless [fading away,] cessation, relinquishing, renouncing, being delivered from, and dislodging of that very craving".[340]

This is called "the noble truth of the cessation of suffering".

Q. Isn't this also the cessation of the origination [of suffering]? Then why did the Fortunate One teach the cessation of the cause of suffering?
A. The cessation of the cause of suffering is the cessation without rearising (*anuppāda-nirodha*) in the sense of having to be realized (*sacchikātabbaṃ*). Therefore the cessation of the origination was taught by the Fortunate One as the cessation of suffering.[341]

[This is called "the noble truth of the cessation of suffering".][342]

64. Truth of the path leading to the cessation of suffering

Q. What is the noble truth of the path leading to the cessation of suffering?
A. It is the noble eightfold path, namely, right view, right intention, right speech, right action, right livelihood, right effort, right mindfulness, and right concentration.

Right view is the knowledge of the four truths.[343]

Right intention is the three wholesome intentions.[344]

Right speech is the abstaining from the four wrong [verbal] conducts.

---

340. Ibid. 310–11: *... dukkha-nirodhaṃ ariya-saccaṃ? Yo tassā yeva taṇhāya asesa-virāga-nirodho cāgo paṭinissaggo mutti anālayo ...*

341. This question and answer is not in the Tibetan (Sav 191b). Cf. Paṭis II 217: *Evaṃ hetunirodhā dukkhanirodho. Evaṃ atthi maggabhāvanā, atthi phalasacchikiriyā, atthi kilesappahānaṃ, atthi dhammābhisamayo ti.* Paṭis-a III 688: *Hetunirodhā dukkhanirodhoti kilesānaṃ bījabhūtassa santānassa anuppādanirodhā anāgatakkhandhabhūtassa dukkhassa hetubhūtānaṃ kilesānaṃ anuppādanirodho hoti. Evaṃ dukkhassa hetubhūtakilesānaṃ anuppādanirodhā dukkhassa anuppādanirodho hoti.* Cf. Vism XVI.18/p.495, Vibh-a 84, etc.: *dukkhassa vā anuppādanirodhapaccayattā dukkhanirodhanti.* Vism XVI.62/p.506f., Vibh-a 112, etc.: *... ettha yo tasseva dukkhassā ti vattabbe yasmā samudayanirodheneva dukkhaṃ nirujjhati, no aññathā. ...*

342. Although this conclusion is found in the preceding and following sections, it is missing from the Chinese here. The Tibetan (191b) has it.

343. D II 311: *Yaṃ kho ... dukkhe ñāṇaṃ, ... dukkhanirodhagāminiyā paṭipadāya ñāṇaṃ, ayaṃ vuccati ... sammādiṭṭhi. ...*

344. D III 215: *Tayo kusalasaṅkappā nekkhammasaṅkappo, abyāpādasaṅkappo, avihiṃsāsaṅkappo.* D II 311: *Nekkhammasaṅkappo abyāpādasaṅkappo avihiṃsāsaṅkappo, ayaṃ vuccati bhikkhave, sammāsaṅkappo.*

Right action is abstaining from the three wrong [physical] conducts.[345]
Right livelihood is abstaining from wrong livelihood.[346]
Right effort is the four right efforts.[347]
Right mindfulness is the four establishments of mindfulness.
Right concentration is the four jhānas.

Furthermore, knowledge and vision of nibbāna due to the development of the noble path—this is right view.

The thinking (*vitakka*) [directed] just towards nibbāna—this is right intention.

The abandoning of wrong speech—this is right speech.

The abandoning of wrong action—this is right action.

The abandoning of wrong livelihood—this is right livelihood.

The abandoning of wrong effort—this is right effort.

The mindfulness [directed] towards nibbāna—this is right mindfulness.

The one-pointedness of mind (*cittekaggatā*) [directed] towards nibbāna—this is right concentration.[348]

---

345. Dhs 63: ... *catūhi vacīduccaritehi ārati virati paṭivirati veramaṇī ... ayaṃ tasmiṃ samaye sammāvācā hoti. ... tīhi kāyaduccaritehi ārati ... sammākammanto hoti.* Mp II 90: *Kāyaduccaritan-ti pāṇātipātādi tividhaṃ akusalaṃ kāyakammaṃ. Cattāri vacīduccaritan-ti musāvādādi catubbidhaṃ akusalaṃ vacīkammaṃ.* Nidd-a I 61: *Tattha kāyaduccaritan-ti pāṇātipāta-adinnādānamicchācāracetanā veditabbā. Vacīduccaritan-ti musāvāda-pisuṇavācāpharusavācāsamphappalāpacetanā veditabbā.* D II 311: *Musāvādā veramaṇī pisuṇāya ... pharusāya ... samphappalāpā veramaṇī, ayaṃ vuccati ... sammāvācā. Pāṇātipātā ... adinnādānā ... kāmesumicchācārā veramaṇī, ayaṃ ... sammākammanto.* Cf. M III 74.

346. Dhs 63: ... *micchāājīvā ārati virati paṭivirati veramaṇī ... ayaṃ tasmiṃ samaye sammāājīvo hoti.* Cf. M III 74.

347. Cf. D III 225: *saṃvarapadhānaṃ pahānapadhānaṃ bhāvanāpadhānaṃ anurakkhaṇāpadhānaṃ*, Cf. D II 312, A II 15.

348. Cf. Vism XVI.76–83/p.509f.: *Saṅkhepato hi catusaccapaṭivedhāya paṭipannassa yogino nibbānārammaṇaṃ avijjānusayasamugghātakaṃ paññācakkhu sammādiṭṭhi. ... Tathā sampannadiṭṭhino taṃsampayuttaṃ micchāsaṅkappanighātakaṃ cetaso nibbānapadābhiniropanaṃ sammāsaṅkappo. ... Tathā passato vitakkayato ca taṃsampayuttāva vacīduccaritasamugghātikā micchāvācāya virati sammāvācā nāma. Sā ... micchāvācāppahānapaccupaṭṭhānā. Tathā viramato taṃsampayuttāva micchākammantasamucchedikā pāṇātipātādivirati sammākammanto nāma. So ... micchākammantappahānapaccupaṭṭhāno. Yā panassa tesaṃ sammāvācākammantānaṃ visuddhibhūtā taṃsampayuttāva kuhanādi-upacchedikā micchājīvavirati, so sammāājīvo nāma. So ... micchājīvāppahānapaccupaṭṭhāno. Athassa yo tassā sammāvācākammantājīvasaṅkhātāya sīlabhūmiyaṃ patiṭṭhitassa tadanurūpo taṃsampayuttova kosajjasamucchedako vīriyārambho, esa sammāvāyāmo nāma. So ... micchāvāyāmappahānapaccupaṭṭhāno. Tassevaṃ vāyamato taṃsampayuttova micchāsativiniddhunano cetaso asammoso sammāsati nāma. ... Evaṃ anuttarāya satiyā saṃrakkhiyamānacittassa taṃsampayuttāva micchāsamādhividdhaṃsikā cittekaggatā sammāsamādhi nāma.*

Cf. Paṭis-a I 195: *Lokuttaramagge pana catusaccappaṭivedhāya pavattassa ariya-*

Herein, the faculty of wisdom, the power of wisdom, the basis of supernormal power of examination, and the enlightenment factor of the investigation of the Dhamma are included in internal right view.[1]

The faculty of energy, the power of energy, the basis of supernormal power of energy, the basis of supernormal power of motivation, the enlightenment factor of energy, and the fourfold right effort are included in internal right effort.[2]

The faculty of mindfulness, the power of mindfulness, the enlightenment factor of mindfulness, and the four establishments of mindfulness are included in internal right mindfulness.

The faculty of concentration, the power of concentration, the basis of supernormal power of mind, the faculty of faith, the power of faith, the enlightenment factor of concentration, the enlightenment factor of rapture, the enlightenment factor of tranquillity, and the enlightenment factor of equanimity are included in internal right concentration.[3]

Thus, the thirty-seven states that are aids to enlightenment (*bodhipakkhiyā dhammā*) are included in the noble eightfold path.

This is called "the noble truth of the path leading to the cessation of suffering".

This is called "the four noble truths".

---

sāvakassa nibbānārammaṇaṃ ... cittekaggatā sammāsamādhi. Esa lokuttaro ariyo aṭṭhaṅgiko maggo.

Cf. Paṭis I 69f. (quoted Vism XXII.45/p.681ff.): *Sotāpattimaggakkhaṇe dassanaṭṭhena sammādiṭṭhi micchādiṭṭhiyā vuṭṭhāti, tadanuvattakakilesehi ca khandhehi ca vuṭṭhāti, bahiddhā ca sabbanimittehi vuṭṭhāti. Tena vuccati dubhato vuṭṭhānavivaṭṭane paññā magge ñāṇaṃ. Abhiniropanaṭṭhena sammāsaṅkappo micchāsaṅkappā vuṭṭhāti, ... Pariggahaṭṭhena sammāvācā micchāvācāya vuṭṭhāti, ... Samuṭṭhānaṭṭhena sammākammanto micchākammantā vuṭṭhāti, ... Vodānaṭṭhena sammāājīvo micchāājīvā vuṭṭhāti, ... Paggahaṭṭhena sammāvāyāmo micchāvāyāmā vuṭṭhāti, ... Upaṭṭhānaṭṭhena sammāsati micchāsatiyā vuṭṭhāti, ... Avikkhepaṭṭhena sammāsamādhi micchāsamādhito vuṭṭhāti, ... magge ñāṇaṃ.*

1. Tibetan (192a) "... are included (*pariyāpanna*) in internal right view" .... Cf. D II 303, M I 62, Vibh 200: *Santaṃ vā ajjhattaṃ dhammavicayasambojjhaṅgaṃ atthi me ajjhattaṃ dhammavicayasambojjhaṅgo ti.*

2. Due to a translator's or copyist's mistake, the Tibetan (Sav 192a) adds the enlightenment factor of tranquillity here, and leaves it out from right concentration.

Cf. D II 303, M I 62, Vibh 200: *Santaṃ vā ajjhattaṃ vīriyasambojjhaṅgaṃ atthi me ajjhattaṃ vīriyasambojjhaṅgo ti pajānāti. ... santaṃ vā ajjhattaṃ satisambojjhaṅgaṃ atthi me ajjhattaṃ satisambojjhaṅgo ti pajānāti ...*

3. Cf. D II 215: *Ajjhattaṃ kāye kāyānupassī viharanto tattha sammā samādhiyati, sammā vippasīdati.* Sv 237: *Tattha sammāsamādhiyatī ti tasmiṃ ajjhattakāye samāhito ekaggacitto hoti.* D II 304, M I 62, Vibh 200: *Santaṃ vā ajjhattaṃ samādhisambojjhaṅgaṃ atthi me ajjhattaṃ samādhisambojjhaṅgo ti pajānāti.*

65. Why four noble truths are taught

Q. Why are four noble truths taught and not three or five?
A. [This is] all doubt. Since they are mundane and supramundane causes and results (*hetuphala*), they are four. [**452c**]

Q. How?

[A.] Suffering is mundane result. Origination is mundane cause. Cessation is supramundane result. The path is supramundane cause. Therefore, four and not three or five are taught.[4]

Furthermore, because of the four phrases, "to be understood", "to be abandoned", "to be realized", and "to be practised", there are four.[5]

66. Eleven ways of knowing the four noble truths

The distinctions of these four noble truths should be known in eleven ways: through word meaning, through characteristic, through sequence, through collection, through simile, through analysis, through enumeration, through oneness, through diversity, through successive explanation, and through inclusion.

67. Word meaning

Q. How through word meaning (*vacanattha*)?
A. The noble truths are expounded by the noble one; therefore, they are called "noble truths". Because he penetrated them, they are noble truths.[6]

---

4. The Chinese text is corrupt and has been translated in accordance with the Tibetan parallel. The Chinese has no character indicating where the answer starts and it shifts over from 世間 and 出世間, *lokiya* and *lokuttara* 世諦 and 出世諦, *lokiya-* and *lokuttara-sacca* or *samutti-* and *paramattha-sacca*. Literally: "How? Mundane truth result is suffering. The origination of suffering is mundane truth cause and result. Cessation is supramundane truth result. The path is supramundane truth cause", ... 為世間出世間果因故成四,問云何世諦果苦集世諦因果,滅出世諦果,道出世諦因.

5. Cf. S V 435: *Imesaṃ kho ... catunnaṃ ariyasaccānaṃ atthi ariyasaccaṃ pariññeyyaṃ, atthi ariyasaccaṃ pahātabbaṃ, atthi ariyasaccaṃ sacchikātabbaṃ, atthi ariyasaccaṃ bhāvetabbaṃ. Katamañ-ca ... ariyasaccaṃ pariññeyyaṃ? Dukkhaṃ ... ariyasaccaṃ pariññeyyaṃ, dukkhasamudayaṃ ariyasaccaṃ pahātabbaṃ, dukkhanirodhaṃ ariyasaccaṃ sacchikātabbaṃ, dukkhanirodhagāminī paṭipadā ariyasaccaṃ bhāvetabbaṃ.* Cf. S V 422. Cf. Vism XVI.27–28/p.487, Paṭis-a I 197, Vibh-a 86: *Kasmā pana cattāreva ariyasaccāni vuttāni anūnāni anadhikānī ti ce? ... Tathā pariññeyyapahātabbasacchikātabbabhāvetabbānaṃ, ... vasenā pi cattāreva vuttānī ti.*

6. There is no indication in the Chinese text as well as the Tibetan that a plural "noble ones" is intended. Cf. Th-a II 205: *Cattāri ariyasaccānī ti ādinā tehi desitaṃ dhammaṃ dasseti. Tattha cattārī ti gaṇanaparicchedo. Ariyasaccānī ti paricchinnadhammadassanaṃ. Vacanatthato pana ariyāni ca avitathaṭṭhena saccāni cā ti ariyasaccāni, ariyassa vā*

"Truth" has the meaning of realness (*tatha*), has the meaning of non-unrealness (*avitatha*), has the meaning of non-otherwiseness (*anaññatha*).[7]

"Suffering" has the meaning of hurting.[8] "Origination" has the meaning of cause.[9] "Cessation" has the meaning of ceasing [with no rearising].[10] "Path" has the meaning of seeing the ultimate.[11]

Thus should it be known through word meaning.

---

bhagavato saccāni tena desitattā, ariyabhāvakarāni vā saccānīti ariyasaccāni. Spk III 299 (on S V 435): *Tathāgato ariyo, tasmā ariyasaccānī ti yasmā ariyena tathāgatena paṭividdhattā desitattā ca tāni ariyasantakāni honti, tasmā ariyassa saccattā ariyasaccānīti attho.* Vism XVI.20: *Yasmā panetāni buddhādayo ariyā paṭivijjhanti, tasmā ariyasaccānī ti vuccanti. Yathāha cattārimāni ... ariyasaccāni. Katamāni ... imāni kho ... cattāri ariyasaccāni. Ariyā imāni paṭivijjhanti, tasmā ariyasaccānī ti vuccantī ti* (S V 435). *Api ca ariyassa saccāni ti pi ariyasaccāni. Yathāha sadevake ... loke ... pe ... manussāya tathāgato ariyo, tasmā ariyasaccānī ti vuccantī ti* (S V 433). Abhidh-s 232: *Ariyānaṃ vā saccāni tehi paṭivijjhitabbattā, ariyassa vā sammāsambuddhassa saccāni tena desitattā ti ariyasaccāni.*

7. S V 430–31, Paṭis II 103: *Cattārimāni bhikkhave tathāni avithatāni anaññathāni. ... Idaṃ dukkhan ti bhikkhave tatham etaṃ avitatham etaṃ anaññatatham etam. ...* Paṭis II 104: *Cattāro dukkhassa dukkhaṭṭhā tathā avitathā anaññathā. Dukkhassa pīḷanaṭṭho, saṅkhataṭṭho, santāpaṭṭho, vipariṇāmaṭṭho ... Samudayassa āyūhanaṭṭho, nidānaṭṭho, saṃyogaṭṭho palibodhaṭṭho ... Nirodhassa nissaraṇaṭṭho, vivekaṭṭho, asaṅkhataṭṭho, amataṭṭho ... Maggassa niyyānaṭṭho, hetuṭṭho, dassanaṭṭho, ādhipateyyaṭṭho—ime cattāro maggassa maggaṭṭhā tathā avitathā anaññathā. Evaṃ maggo tathaṭṭhena saccaṃ.* Spk III 298: *Sabhāva-vijahanaṭṭhena tathaṃ. Dukkhaṃ hi dukkham eva vuttaṃ sabhāvassa amoghatāya avitathaṃ. Na dukkhaṃ adukkhaṃ nāma hoti. Añña-sabhāvānupagamena anaññathaṃ. Na hi dukkhaṃ samudayādisabhāvaṃ upagacchati. Samudayādīsu pi es' eva nayo ti.* It-a I 179: *Bhūtato aviparītasabhāvato salakkhaṇato sāmaññalakkhaṇato ca passati.* Cf. Ap-a 383, D III 273.

8. The Taishō ed. reads 果 but has the v.l. 苦 = *dukkha, pīḷana, ābādha,* which matches *mnar ba,* meaning "affliction, torment, oppression" in the Tibetan parallel at 192b and *pīḷanaṭṭho* in Paṭis II 104 in the preceding fn. At 194a *mnar ba* corresponds to 逼, "to harass, press" at 453a24.

9. The Chinese has 因 = *hetu, kāraṇa, nidāna,* while the Tibetan has *bskyed pa = uppāda, pabhava, janana.* In the following "characteristics" method the Chinese again has 因, while the Tibetan has *rgyu = hetu, nidāna.*

10. 隨滅, lit. *anu-nirodha*. Tibetan: *rjes su 'gog pa = anu-nirodha.* The term *anunirodha* is not found in Pali texts. Perhaps the Vim originally had *anuppādā-nirodha* or *anuppatti-nirodha* from which *-ppāda* or *-patti* was lost due to an early scribal error. Cf. Vism-mhṭ II 208: *Yathā niruddhā na santi, evaṃ anuppannāpīti abhāvasāmaññato nirodhasadisatāya anuppatti eva nirodho anuppattinirodho.* Paṭis-a I 324: *Nirodhetī ti anuppādanirodhena nirodheti.*

11. 見第一. Tibetan (192b): *dam pa'i don goms par byed pa:* "cultivation of the ultimate goal", *paramatthabhāvanā?* Ps IV 107: *Diṭṭhisampanno ti maggadiṭṭhiyā sampanno sotāpanno ariyasāvako.* Nidd I 20: *uttamadiṭṭhippatto bhāvitamaggo pahīnakileso paṭividdhākuppo sacchikatanirodho, dukkhaṃ tassa pariññātaṃ.* Compare "the path has ... the characteristic of seeing (*dassana*)", § 68 end.

68. Characteristics

Q. How through characteristic (*lakkhaṇa*)?

A. Suffering has the characteristic of disadvantage (*ādīnava*).[12] Origination (*samudaya*) has the characteristic of cause (*hetu*). Cessation has the characteristic of non-arising (*anuppāda*). The path has the characteristic of means (*upāya*).[13]

Furthermore, suffering has the characteristic of harassment (*pīḷana*),[14] the characteristic of distress (*domanassa*),[15] the characteristic of the conditioned (*saṅkhata*), and the characteristic of change.[16]

Origination has the characteristic of accumulation (*āyuhana*), the characteristic of source (*nidāna*), the characteristic of bondage, and the characteristic of obstruction.[17]

---

12. Cf. Mp V 21: *Ādīnavamaddasā ti dukkhasaccaṃ addasa.* Paṭis II 242: *Ādīnavato ti dukkhānupassanā.* Ud-a 282: *Appassādā kāmā bahudukkhā bahupāyāsā, ādīnavo ettha bhiyyo ti ādinā nayena kāmānaṃ ādīnavaṃ okāraṃ saṃkilesaṃ kathesi. Tattha ādīnavan-ti dosaṃ.* J-a IV 312: *Ādīnavan-ti evarūpaṃ dosaṃ.*

13. Cf. Nett 8: *Cattāri saccāni dukkhaṃ samudayaṃ nirodhaṃ maggaṃ. Ādīnavo ca phalañ-ca dukkhaṃ, assādo samudayo, nissaraṇaṃ nirodho, upāyo āṇatti ca maggo. Imāni cattāri saccāni.* Nett-a 56 Be: *Avasesapaccayasamavāye dukkhassa uppattikāraṇattā samudayo. Sabbagatisuññattā natthi ettha saṃsāracārakasaṅkhāto dukkharodho, etasmiṃ vā adhigate saṃsāracārakasaṅkhātassadukkharodhassaabhāvotipinirodho,anuppādanirodhapaccayattā vā. ... Saha vipassanāya ariyamaggo desanā ca desanāphalādhigamassa upāyoti katvā upāyo āṇatti ca maggo ti vuttaṃ.* Nidd-a II 3: *Samudayañcā ti paccayañ-ca. Atthaṅgamañcā ti uppannānaṃ abhāvagamanañ-ca, anuppannānaṃ anuppādaṃ vā. Assādañcā ti ānisaṃsañ-ca. Ādīnavañcā ti dosañ-ca. Nissaraṇañcā ti nikkhamanañ-ca.* Spk II 154: *Catūsu hi dhātūsu assādo samudayasaccaṃ, ādīnavo dukkhasaccaṃ, nissaraṇaṃ nirodhasaccaṃ, nirodhappajānano maggo maggasaccaṃ.* Paṭis-a III 537–38: *Samudayan-ti paccayaṃ. Atthaṅgaman-ti uppannānaṃ abhāvagamanaṃ, anuppannānaṃ anuppādaṃ vā. ...*

14. Compare the commentary on these terms at Vism XXII.99–102/p.691–92. Cf. Vism XXI.7/p.640: *abhiṇhapaṭipīḷanākāro dukkhalakkhaṇaṃ.* Cf. Vism XVI.50–51: *Dukkhaṃ nāma kāyikaṃ dukkhaṃ, taṃ kāyapīḷanalakkhaṇaṃ, ... Domanassaṃ nāma mānasaṃ dukkhaṃ. Taṃ cittapīḷanalakkhaṇaṃ, ...*

15. 憂 = *domanassa*. The Tibetan has *kun du gdung ba* (also at 453a24) corresponding to *santāpa*, as in the parallel at Paṭis II 104: *Dukkhassa pīḷanaṭṭho, saṅkhataṭṭho, santāpaṭṭho, vipariṇāmaṭṭho ... Samudayassa āyūhanaṭṭho, nidānaṭṭho, saṃyogaṭṭho palibodhaṭṭho ... Nirodhassa nissaraṇaṭṭho, vivekaṭṭho, asaṅkhataṭṭho, amataṭṭho ... Maggassa niyyānaṭṭho, hetuṭṭho, dassanaṭṭho, ādhipateyyaṭṭho.* Khp-a 109: *pīḷanasaṅkhatasantāpavipariṇāmaṭṭhena vā dukkhamariyasaccaṃ, āyūhananidānasaṃyogapalibodhaṭṭhena samudayaṃ, nissaraṇa-vivekāsaṅkhata-amataṭṭhena nirodhaṃ, niyyānikahetudassanādhipateyyaṭṭhena maggaṃ.*

16. Also at 457a26. At 401b25 有邊 stands for *pariyanta*. Saṅghapāla misunderstood or read *vipariṇāma*, "change", as *parimāṇa*, "limit". See Paṭis II 104 quoted below. The Tibetan version has *yongs su 'gyur ba* = *vipariṇāma, pariṇāma.*

17. 著 usually corresponds to terms that denote attachment and bondage

Cessation has the characteristic of escape (*nissaraṇa*), the characteristic of seclusion, the characteristic of the unconditioned and the characteristic of the deathless (*amata*).

The path has the characteristic of leading out (*niyyāna*), the characteristic of causing to reach (*sampāpaka*),[18] the characteristic of seeing, and the characteristic of authority.

Thus should it be known through various characteristics.

69. Sequence

Q. How through sequence (*kama*)?

A. The truth of suffering is taught first, because it has the sense of being gross and the sense of being evident.[19]

Because of this, suffering is born, therefore the origination [of suffering] is taught second.

The cessation of origination is the cessation of suffering, therefore cessation is taught third.

This is the means for real cessation, therefore the way is taught fourth.[20]

It is like a skilful physician who at first diagnoses the disease and then seeks the source of the disease. For the destruction of the disease, he

---

(*gaha, baddha, yuta, pariveṭhita,* etc.) not to ones denoting obstruction. Apparently Saṅghapāla understood *palibodha* as Skt *paribaddha*, "bound, obstructed". The Tibetan has the obscure *yongs su spags pa; yongs su* = *pari* and *spags pa* = "removes/shifts".

18. Cf. Sv I 224: *tassa ca sampāpakaṃ ariyamaggaṃ ayaṃ dukkhanirodhagāminī paṭipadā ti.* Sv-ṭ I 187: *Kāraṇan-tī tividhaṃ kāraṇaṃ sampāpakaṃ nibbattakaṃ ñāpakanti. Tattha ariyamaggo nibbānassa sampāpakaṃ kāraṇaṃ...* Paṭis-a III 579: *Maggo ceva hetu cā ti tassa tassa kiccassa karaṇāya paṭipadaṭṭhena maggo, sampāpakaṭṭhena hetu. Tena maggassa paṭipadaṭṭho sampāpakaṭṭho ca vutto hoti. Ayaṃ maggo ayaṃ paṭipadāti ādīsu hi paṭipadā maggo, maggassa niyyānaṭṭho hetuṭṭhoti ādīsu sampāpako hetu.*

19. Instead of "evident", 證, = *viññeyya?*, the Tibetan text has *rkyen* = *paccaya*, "condition".

Cf. Vism XVI.29, Paṭis-a I 197: *Kamato ti ayam-pi desanākkamova. Ettha ca oḷārikattā sabbasattasādhāraṇattā ca suviññeyyan-ti dukkhasaccaṃ paṭhamaṃ vuttaṃ, tasseva hetudassanatthaṃ tadanantaraṃ samudayasaccaṃ, hetunirodhā phalanirodhoti ñāpanatthaṃ tato nirodhasaccaṃ, tadadhigamupāyadassanatthaṃ ante maggasaccaṃ. Bhavasukhassādagadhitānaṃ vā sattānaṃ saṃvegajananatthaṃ paṭhamaṃ dukkhamāha. Taṃ neva akataṃ āgacchati, na issaranimmānādito hoti, ito pana hotī ti ñāpanatthaṃ tadanantaraṃ samudayaṃ. Tato sahetukena dukkhena abhibhūtattā saṃviggamānasānaṃ dukkhanissaraṇagavesīnaṃ nissaraṇadassanena assāsajananatthaṃ nirodhaṃ. Tato nirodhādhigamatthaṃ nirodhasampāpakaṃ maggan-ti evamettha kamato vinicchayo veditabbo.*

20. Tibetan (193a): "this is the means for the cessation of origination", *kun 'byung 'gog pa'i thabs.*

prescribes medicine in accordance with the disease.[21]

Herein, the disease is to be understood as suffering; the source of the disease as origination; the ending of the disease as cessation; and the medicine as the path.[22]

Thus should it be known through sequence.

70. Collection

Q. How through collection (*saṅkhepa, samāsa*)?

A. Occurrence (*pavatti*) is suffering; causing occurrence is origination; non-occurrence is cessation; and causing non-occurrence is the path.[23]

The grounds for afflictions (*kilesa-vatthu*)[24] are suffering; afflictions are origination; the abandoning of afflictions is cessation; and the means for abandoning[25] is the path.

The defining (*vavatthāna*) of suffering removes [the views] headed by identity-view (*sakkāya-diṭṭhi-pamukha*); the defining of origination removes

---

21. Literally: "It is like a clever physician who at first sees the source of the disease and then inquires as to the contributory causes (*paccaya*)", but this disagrees with the following explanation, the Tibetan version and the Pali parallels.

22. Cf. Vism XVI.87/p.512, Paṭis-a I 197: *Rogo viya vā dukkhasaccaṃ, roganidānam-iva samudayasaccaṃ, rogavūpasamo viya nirodhasaccaṃ, bhesajjamiva maggasaccaṃ.* Vism XIX.2/p.598: *yathā nāma kusalo bhisakko rogaṃ disvā tassa samuṭṭhānaṃ pariyesati.* Cf. A III 238: *Seyyathā pi bho puriso ābādhiko dukkhito bāḷhagilāno, tassa kusalo bhisakko ṭhānaso ābādhaṃ nīhareyya, evam eva kho bho yato yato tassa bhoto gotamassa dhammaṃ suṇāti yadi suttaso ... tato tato sokaparideva dukkhadomanassupāyāsā abbhatthaṃ gacchanti.* A IV 340: *Bhisakko ti bhikkhave tathāgatass' etaṃ adhivacanaṃ arahato sammāsambuddhassa.* It 101: *Aham-asmi bhikkhave brāhmaṇo ... anuttaro bhisakko sallakatto.* Peṭ 123–24: *Tattha dve rogā sattānaṃ avijjā ca bhavataṇhā ca. Etesaṃ dvinnaṃ rogānaṃ nighātāya bhagavatā dve bhesajjāni vuttā samatho ca vipassanā ca. ... Avijjārogassa vipassanā bhesajjaṃ, avijjāvirāgā paññāvimutti arogaṃ.*

23. Cf. Paṭis-a I 197, Vibh-a 85: *pavattipavattakanivattinivattakalakkhaṇāni paṭipāṭiyā.* Vism XVI.28/p.497: *Apica pavattim-ācikkhanto bhagavā sahetukaṃ ācikkhi, nivattiñca sa-upāyaṃ. Iti pavattinivattitadubhayahetūnaṃ etaparamato cattāreva vuttāni.*

24. Cf. Nett-a 198: *Dasa vatthuke kilesapuñje ti. Dasavidhakāraṇe kilesasamūhe ti attho. Tattha kilesāpi kilesavatthu, kilesānaṃ paccayadhammā pi kilesavatthu. Tesu kāraṇabhāvena purimasiddhā kilesā parato paresaṃ kilesānaṃ paccayabhāvato kilesā pi kilesavatthu. Ayonisomanasikāro, ayonisomanasikāraparikkhatā ca dhammā kilesuppattihetubhāvato kilesappaccayā pi kilesavatthu ti daṭṭhabbaṃ.* Cf. Th 932 *Kilesehābhibhūtā te, tena tena vidhāvitā; / Narā kilesavatthūsu, sasaṅgām-eva ghosite.* Th-a III 77 *Kilesavatthūsū ti paṭhamaṃ uppannaṃ kilesā pacchā uppajjanakānaṃ kāraṇabhāvato kilesāva kilesavatthūni, tesu kilesavatthūsu samūhitesu, ...*

25. *Pahānupāya.* Cf. Ps I 176: *Tato tassa pahānupāyaṃ vicinanto atthi paṇītan-ti pajānāti, ettāvatānena maggasaccavavatthānaṃ kataṃ hoti.*

[the views] headed by the view of annihilationism (*uccheda-diṭṭhi*); the defining of cessation removes [the views] headed by the view of eternalism (*sassata-diṭṭhi*); and the defining of the path removes [the views] headed by wrong views.[26]

Thus should it be known through collection.

71. Simile

Q. How through simile (*upamā*)?

A. Suffering should be regarded as being like a poisonous tree; origination as the seed [of the poisonous tree]; cessation as the burning of the seed; and the path as the fire [burning the seed].[27]

Suffering should be regarded as being like the near shore, which is dreadful and fearful; origination as the torrent (*ogha*); cessation as the further shore that is free from dread and fear; and the path as the boat that enables one to cross over [to the further shore].[28] **[453a]**

---

26. Lit. "closes the door of identity view", 關身見門. The Taishō text reads 開 "opens", but gives the variant reading 關 "closes". The Tibetan has: "destroys the entrance/door". Cf. Paṭis-a II 463: ... *sakkāyadiṭṭhisamugghāteneva ca dvāsaṭṭhi diṭṭhiyo samugghātaṃ gacchanti, tasmā sakkāyadiṭṭhippamukhena dvāsaṭṭhi diṭṭhigatānī ti vuttā, sakkāyadiṭṭhippamukhena sakkāyadiṭṭhidvārena dvāsaṭṭhi diṭṭhigatāni hontī ti attho. Sakkāyadiṭṭhippamukhānī ti pāṭho sundarataro. Sakkāyadiṭṭhi pamukhā ādi etesan-ti sakkāyadiṭṭhippamukhāni. Kāni tāni? Dvāsaṭṭhi diṭṭhigatāni.* Nett-a 195 ... *sakkāyadassanamukhena ucchedādi-antadvayaṃ, majjhimañ-ca paṭipadaṃ niddhāreti. Tattha ime vuccanti ucchedavādino ti ime rūpādike pañcakkhandhe attato upagacchantā rūpādīnaṃ aniccabhāvato ucchijjati attā vinassati na hoti paraṃ maraṇā ti evaṃ abhinivisanato ucchedavādino ti vuccanti. Ime vuccanti sassatavādino ti ime rūpavantaṃ vā attanān-ti ādinā rūpādivinimutto añño koci attā ti upagacchantā so nicco dhuvo sassato ti abhinivisanato sassatavādino ti vuccanti. Ucchedasassatavādā ubho antā, ayaṃ saṃsārapavattī ti ādi saccaniddhāraṇaṃ, taṃ suviññeyyaṃ. Ucchedasassataṃ samāsato vīsativatthukā sakkāyadiṭṭhīti attā ucchijjati attā nicco ti ca ādippavattanato ucchedasassatadassanaṃ saṅkhepato vīsativatthukā sakkāyadiṭṭhi eva hoti. Sabbo pi hi attavādo sakkāyadiṭṭhi-antogadho evā ti.*

27. Paṭis-a I 197: *Visarukkharukkhamūlamūlūpacchedatadupacchedūpāyehi, ... yojetvā-petāni upamāto veditabbānī ti.* Vism XV.42: *Sabbānatthāvahassa khandhasantānassa hetuto visarukkhabījāni viya.*

28. Cf. Paṭis-a I 197: *orimatīramahoghapārimatīrataṃsampāpakavāyāmehi ca yojetvāpetāni upamāto veditabbānīti.* S IV 174–5: *Mahā udakaṇṇavo ti bhikkhave catunnaṃ oghānaṃ adhivacanaṃ, kāmoghassa bhavoghassa diṭṭhoghassa avijjoghassa. Orimantīraṃ sāsaṅkaṃ sappaṭibhayan ti kho bhikkhave sakkāyassetaṃ adhivacanaṃ. Kullan ti kho bhikkhave ariyassetaṃ aṭṭhaṅgikassa maggassa adhivacanaṃ, seyyathidaṃ sammādiṭṭhiyā .... Hatthehi ca pādehi ca vāyāmo ti kho bhikkhave viriyārambhassetaṃ adhivacanaṃ. Tiṇṇo pāraṅgato thale tiṭṭhati brāhmaṇo ti kho bhikkhave arahato etaṃ adhivacanan ti.* Cf. M I 134: ... *ayaṃ kho mahāudakaṇṇavo, orimaṃ tīraṃ sāsaṅkaṃ sappaṭibhayaṃ, pārimaṃ tīraṃ*

Suffering should be regarded as being like the carrying of a burden;[29] origination as the taking up of the burden; cessation as the laying down of the burden; and the path as the means for laying down the burden.[30]

Thus should it be known through simile.

72. Analysis

Q. How is it to be known through analysis (*vibhaṅga*)?

A. There are four kinds of truth: truth of speech (*vācā-sacca*), manifold individual truth (*puthu-pacceka-sacca*), ultimate truth (*paramattha-sacca*), and noble truth (*ariya-sacca*).

Herein, the speaking of true words and not of untrue [words]—this is called "truth of speech".

The great many wrong views (*diṭṭhigati*)—this is manifold individual truth.[31]

"That truth which is false (*musa, mosa*), bhikkhu, has a delusive nature

---

khemaṃ appaṭibhayaṃ; natthi ca nāvā santāraṇī uttarasetu vā apārā pāraṃ gamanāya. Yaṃnūnāhaṃ tiṇakaṭṭhasākhāpalāsaṃ saṃkaḍḍhitvā, kullaṃ bandhitvā, taṃ kullaṃ nissāya hatthehi ca pādehi ca vāyamamāno sotthinā pāraṃ uttareyyan-ti.

29. 擔擔 and Tibetan *khur khur ba* both correspond to *bhārabharaṇa, bhārabharita* or the like.

30. Paṭis-a I 197: *Etesu pana bhāro viya dukkhasaccaṃ daṭṭhabbaṃ, bhārādānamiva samudayasaccaṃ, bhāranikkhepanamiva nirodhasaccaṃ, bhāranikkhepanūpāyo viya maggasaccaṃ. ... upamāto veditabbānīti.* S III 25–6: *Katamo ca bhikkhave bhāro? Pañcupādānakkhandhā tissa vacanīyaṃ. ... Katamo ca bhikkhave bhārahāro? Puggalo tissa vacanīyaṃ. Yvāyaṃ āyasmā evaṃ nāmo evaṃ gotto. ... Katamañ ... bhārādānaṃ? Yāyaṃ taṇhā ponobhavikā nandirāga-sahagatā tatra tatrābhinandinī, ... Katamañ ... bhāranikkhepanaṃ? Yo tassā-yeva taṇhāya asesa-virāga-nirodho cāgo paṭinissaggo mutti anālayo.* M I 139–40: *Kathañ ca bhikkhave bhikkhu ariyo pannaddhajo pannabhāro visaṃyutto hoti? Idha bhikkhave bhikkhuno asmimāno pahīno hoti ucchinnamūlo tālavatthukato anabhāvakato āyatiṃ anuppādadhammo.*

31. 各各諦. The Tibetan (193b) has *so sor bden pa* = *pacceka-sacca*. Cf. D III 270: *Kathañcāvuso, bhikkhu paṇunnapaccekasacco hoti? Idhāvuso, bhikkhuno yāni tāni puthusamaṇabrāhmaṇānaṃ puthupaccekasaccāni, sabbāni tāni nunnāni honti paṇunnāni cattāni vantāni muttāni pahīnāni paṭinissaṭṭhāni.* Sv III 1051: *Puthusamaṇabrāhmaṇānan-ti bahūnaṃ samaṇabrāhmaṇānaṃ. ... Puthupaccekasaccānī ti bahūni pāṭekkasaccāni, idam-eva dassanaṃ saccaṃ, idam-eva dassanaṃ saccan-ti evaṃ pāṭiyekkaṃ gahitāni bahūni saccānīti attho. Nunnānīti nihatāni. Paṇunnānīti suṭṭhu nihatāni.* A II 40, V 30: *Kathañ-ca ... panuṇṇapaccekasacco hoti? Idha ... yāni tāni puthusamaṇabrāhmaṇānaṃ puthupaccekasaccāni, seyyathidaṃ—sassato lokoti vā, ... na na hoti tathāgato paraṃ maraṇā ti vā; sabbāni tāni nuṇṇāni ... paṭinissaṭṭhāni.* Sn-a II 540, Nidd-a II 283: *... Evaṃ sante attano satthārādīni nissitā tattheva esa vādo subho ti evaṃ subhaṃ vadānā hutvā puthū samaṇabrāhmaṇā sassato loko ti ādīsu paccekasaccesu niviṭṭhā.*

(*mosadhamma*). That truth which is not false and does not have a non-delusive nature is nibbāna"—this is absolute truth.[32]

The truth to be developed by the noble one(s) is noble truth.

Herein, [the sense of] noble truth is intended.

Thus should it be known through analysis.

73. Enumeration

Q. How is it to be known through enumeration (*gaṇanā*)?

A. Leaving aside craving, the truth of suffering is the wholesome, unwholesome, and indeterminate states of the three planes. The truth of origination is craving. The truth of cessation is the abandoning of craving. The truth of the path is the noble eightfold path.

Furthermore, leaving aside craving and the other (*avasesa*) afflictions, the truth of suffering is the wholesome, unwholesome, and indeterminate states of the three planes. The truth of origination is craving and the other afflictions. The truth of cessation is the abandoning of these. The truth of the path is the [noble eightfold] path.

Furthermore, leaving aside craving, the other afflictions, and all unwholesomeness, the truth of suffering is the wholesome and indeterminate states[33] of the three planes. The truth of origination is craving together with the other afflictions and all unwholesome states. The truth of cessation is the abandoning of these. The truth of the path is the [noble eightfold] path.

Furthermore, leaving aside craving, the other afflictions, and all unwholesomeness and wholesomeness of the three planes: the truth of suffering is the indeterminate states of the three planes. The truth of origination is craving together with the other afflictions and all unwholesomeness and wholesomeness in the three planes. The truth of cessation is the abandoning of these. The truth of the path is the [noble eightfold] path.[34]

---

32. M III 245: *Tañhi, bhikkhu, musā yaṃ mosadhammaṃ, taṃ saccaṃ yaṃ amosadhammaṃ nibbānaṃ. Tasmā evaṃ samannāgato bhikkhu iminā paramena saccādhiṭṭhānena samannāgato hoti. Etañhi, bhikkhu, paramaṃ ariyasaccaṃ yadidaṃ—amosadhammaṃ nibbānaṃ.* Vism-mhṭ II 194, Vibh-mṭ 53: *Idam-eva saccaṃ, moghamaññan-ti (M I 140, etc.) pavattā diṭṭhi saccan-ti abhinivisanavuttiyā diṭṭhisaccaṃ. Amosadhammattā nibbānaṃ paramatthasaccaṃ. Amosadhammaṃ nibbānaṃ, tadariyā saccato vidūti (Sn 763) hi vuttaṃ, tassa pana taṃsampāpakassa ca maggassa pajānanā paṭivedho avivādakāraṇan-ti dvayampi, ekaṃ hi saccaṃ na dutiyam-atthi, yasmiṃ pajā no vivade pajānanti imissā (Sn 890) gāthāya saccan-ti vuttaṃ.*

33. 善有記 = *kusalāvyakata*; see fn. 1650.

34. Vibh 106/§ 206: ... *Taṇhā—ayaṃ vuccati dukkhasamudayo. ... Avasesā ca kilesā, avasesā ca akusalā dhammā, tīṇi ca kusalamūlāni sāsavāni, avasesā ca sāsavā kusalā*

Herein, in the sense of desiring satisfaction in existence,[35] craving is origination. In the sense of fetter of existence, the other afflictions are origination. In the sense of having to be abandoned and in the sense of giving rise to existence, all unwholesome states are origination. In the sense of causing existence, the wholesome states of the three planes are origination.

Therefore, craving and the other afflictions are origination. All unwholesome and wholesome states of the three planes are the truth of suffering or the truth of origination.

The characteristics of harassment, distress, being conditioned (*saṅkhata*), and change are the truth of suffering.

The characteristics of accumulation (*āyuhana*), source (*nidāna*), obstruction, and bondage are the truth of origination.[36]

Thus should it be known through enumeration.

74. Oneness

Q. How through oneness (*ekatta*)?

A. These four truths are one in four ways: in the sense of truth; in the sense of realness; in the sense of doctrine; and in the sense of emptiness.[37]

---

dhammā, sāsavā ca kusalākusalānaṃ dhammānaṃ vipākā, ye ca dhammā kiriyā neva kusalā nākusalā na ca kammavipākā, sabbañ-ca rūpaṃ—idaṃ vuccati dukkhaṃ. ... Taṇhāya pahānaṃ—ayaṃ vuccati dukkhanirodho. ... Idha bhikkhu yasmiṃ samaye lokuttaraṃ jhānaṃ bhāveti ... tasmiṃ samaye aṭṭhaṅgiko maggo hoti sammādiṭṭhi ... sammāsamādhi. Tattha katamā sammādiṭṭhi? .... Ayaṃ vuccati dukkhanirodhagāminī paṭipadā. Avasesā dhammā dukkhanirodhagāminiyā paṭipadāya sampayuttā. ... ... Taṇhā ca, avasesā ca kilesā, avasesā ca akusalā dhammā, tīṇi ca kusalamūlāni sāsavāni, avasesā ca sāsavā kusalā dhammā—... Sāsavā kusalākusalānaṃ dhammānaṃ vipākā, ye ca dhammā kiriyā neva kusalā nākusalā na ca kammavipākā, sabbañ-ca rūpaṃ—... Taṇhāya ca, avasesānañ-ca kilesānaṃ, avasesānañ-ca akusalānaṃ dhammānaṃ, tiṇṇañ-ca kusalamūlānaṃ sāsavānaṃ, avasesānañ-ca sāsavānaṃ kusalānaṃ dhammānaṃ pahānaṃ ...

35. *Bhavassādagadhita?* Cf. Sv-ṭ II 365: *bhavesu sukhaggahaṇavasena bhavassādo hotī ti.* Vism-mhṭ II 363: *... bhavārāmā. Tasmiṃ bhave ratā abhiratā ti bhavaratā. Bhave sammodaṃ āpannā ti bhavasammuditā. Tīhipi padehi bhavassādagadhitatāva vuttā.*

36. These characteristics are also given at 452c12. Cf. Paṭis II 104: *Dukkhassa pīḷanaṭṭho, saṅkhataṭṭho, santāpaṭṭho, vipariṇāmaṭṭho ... Samudayassa āyūhanaṭṭho, nidānaṭṭho, saṃyogaṭṭho palibodhaṭṭho.*

37. Instead of "in the sense of emptiness", 以空義, the Tibetan text (194a) has "in the sense of method (*naya*)", *rigs pa'i don gyis* = *nayaṭṭhena* as the fourth way.

Cf. Paṭis II 106: *Tathaṭṭhena, anattaṭṭhena, saccaṭṭhena, paṭivedhaṭṭhena, abhijānanaṭṭhena, parijānanaṭṭhena, dhammaṭṭhena, tathaṭṭhena, ñātaṭṭhena, sacchikiriyaṭṭhena, phassanaṭṭhena, abhisamayaṭṭhena—imehi dvādasahi ākārehi cattāri saccāni ekasaṅgahitāni. Yaṃ ekasaṅgahitaṃ taṃ ekattaṃ. Ekattaṃ ekena ñāṇena paṭivijjhatī ti—cattāri saccāni ekappaṭivedhāni.* Paṭis-a III 594: *Ekappaṭivedhānī ti ekena maggañāṇena*

Thus should it be known through oneness.

75. Diversity

Q. How is it to be known through diversity (*nānatta*)?

A. There are two truths: mundane and supramundane truth.[38]

Mundane truth is subject to contaminations, is subject to fetters, ties, [**453b**] torrents, yokes, hindrances, to holding, clinging, and affliction.[39] It is suffering and origination.

Supramundane truth is not subject to contaminations, is not subject to fetters, ties, torrents, yokes, hindrances, holding, clinging, and affliction. It is cessation and the path.

Three truths are conditioned (*saṅkhata*). The truth of cessation is unconditioned.[40]

Three truths are immaterial (*arūpa*). The truth of suffering is material and immaterial.[41]

The truth of origination is unwholesome. The truth of the path is wholesome. The truth of cessation is indeterminate. The truth of suffering is wholesome, unwholesome, and indeterminate.[42]

The truth of suffering is to be understood; the truth of origination is to be abandoned; the truth of cessation is to be realized; and the truth of the path is to be practiced.[43]

Thus should it be known through diversity.

---

paṭivedho, ekato vā paṭivedho etesan-ti ekappaṭivedhāni. Anattaṭṭhenā ti catunnam-pi saccānaṃ attavirahitattā anattaṭṭhena. Vuttañhetaṃ visuddhimagge: paramatthato hi sabbāneva saccāni vedakakārakanibbutagamakābhāvato suññānīti veditabbāni. Tenetaṃ vuccati, ... Dhuvasukha-attavirahito, maggo iti suññatā tesū ti. Saccaṭṭhenā ti avisaṃvādakaṭṭhena. Cf. Paṭis-a I 198: *Sabbāneva panetāni saccāni paramatthena vedakakārakanibbutagamakābhāvato suññānī ti veditabbāni. Tenetaṃ vuccati: ... Dhuvasukha-attavirahito, maggo iti suññatā tesu. ... Sabbāneva saccāni aññamaññasabhāgāni avitathato attasuññato dukkarapaṭivedhato ca.*

38. Vibh 116: *Dve saccā lokiyā; dve saccā lokuttarā.*

39. Cf. Dhs 3–6: *lokiyaṃ, sāsavaṃ, saṃyojaniyaṃ, ganthaniyaṃ, oghaniyaṃ, yoganiyaṃ, nīvaraṇiyaṃ, parāmaṭṭhaṃ, upādāniyaṃ, saṅkilesikaṃ.* Cf. Dhs § 584–85 and Vibh 12.

40. Vibh 116: *Tīṇi saccāni saṅkhatā; nirodhasaccaṃ asaṅkhataṃ.*

41. Vibh 116: *Tīṇi saccāni arūpāni; dukkhasaccaṃ siyā rūpaṃ siyā arūpaṃ.*

42. Vibh 112: *Samudayasaccaṃ akusalaṃ; maggasaccaṃ kusalaṃ; nirodhasaccaṃ avyākataṃ dukkhasaccaṃ siyā kusalaṃ siyā akusalaṃ siyā avyākataṃ.*

43. See fn. 2021.

76. Successive explanation

Q. How through successive explanation?[44]

A. Through one kind (*ekavidhena*), the body endowed with consciousness (*saviññāṇaka-kāya*) is suffering; the conceit "I am" (*asmimāna*) is origination; its abandoning is cessation; and mindfulness of the body is the path.[45]

Through two kinds, name-and-matter are suffering; ignorance and craving for existence are origination; the abandoning of these is cessation; and calm and insight are the path.

Through three kinds, the three states of suffering[46] are the truth of suffering; the three roots of unwholesomeness are origination; the abandoning of these is cessation; and virtue, concentration, and wisdom are the path.

Through four kinds, the four grounds of selfhood[47] are suffering; the four distortions (*vipallāsa*) are origination; the abandoning of the distortions is cessation; and the four establishments of mindfulness (*satipaṭṭhānā*) are the path.

Through five kinds, the five destinations[48] are suffering; the five hindrances[49] are origination; the abandoning of the hindrances is cessation; and the five faculties (*indriya*) are the path.[50]

---

44. This type of explanation is closest to the type found in the *Peṭakopadesa* and the Dasuttarasutta of the Dīgha Nikāya.

Tibetan (Sav 194b) *mthar chags kyis rgyas par bshad pa* = "serial extensive explanation"; Chinese 次第廣 = "serial extensive explanation", "sequential detailed explanation", "successive explanation", "serial extension", "successive increase". The Vism parallel (XVI.92/p.514) is *ekavidhādi*, "As to singlefold and so on", but the Chinese and Tibetan suggest *anukkama* + *vitthāra* or similar terms.

45. Cf. DN III 272f.: *Katamo eko dhammo bhāvetabbo? Kāyagatāsati sātasahagatā. ... Katamo eko dhammo pahātabbo? Asmimāno.*

46. The text literally has "the suffering of suffering is the truth of suffering", 苦苦是苦諦. The Tibetan (Sav 194b) has: "the three kinds of suffering are the truth of suffering", *sdug bsngal gsum ni sdug bsngal bden pa.* 苦苦 "suffering of suffering" = *dukkhadukkhatā*, but since the individual items are not listed elsewhere in this section in the Chinese, the text is corrupt and should be amended to 三苦是苦諦. On the three kinds of suffering, see fn. 2002.

47. *Attabhāvavatthu.* See fn. 1746. The Tibetan (194b) includes an explanation of *attabhāvavatthu* that is quite different from the one in the *Peṭaka* and *Netti*; see Introduction § 4.4. Cf. Peṭ 121: *Tattha pañcakkhandhā cattāri attabhāvavatthūni bhavanti. Yo rūpakkhandho, so kāyo attabhāvavatthu. Yo vedanākkhandho, so vedanā attabhāvavatthu. Yo saññākkhandho ca saṅkhārakkhandho ca, te dhammā attabhāvavatthu. Yo viññāṇakkhandho, so cittaṃ attabhāvavatthu. Iti pañcakkhandhā cattāri attabhāvavatthūni.*

48. D III 234: *pañca gatiyo: nirayo, tiracchāna-yoni, pettivisayo, manussā, devā.*

49. D III 234: *pañca nīvaraṇāni. Kāmacchanda-nīvaraṇaṃ vyāpāda-nīvaraṇaṃ, thīna-middha-nīvaraṇaṃ, uddhacca-kukkucca-nīvaraṇaṃ, vicikicchā-nīvaraṇaṃ.*

50. D III 239: *pañcindriyāni: saddhindriyaṃ, vīriyindriyaṃ, satindriyaṃ, samādhindriyaṃ,*

Through six kinds, the six bases of contact are suffering;[51] the six groups of craving[52] are origination; the abandoning of the groups of craving is cessation; and the six states for escaping[53] are the path.

Through seven kinds, the seven stations of consciousness are suffering; the seven latent tendencies are origination; the abandoning of the seven latent tendencies is cessation; and the seven factors of enlightenment are the path.[54]

Through eight kinds, the eight worldly states are suffering; the eight kinds of wrongness are origination; the abandoning of the eight kinds of wrongness is cessation; and the eight kinds of rightness are the path.[55]

Through nine kinds, the nine abodes of beings[56] are suffering; the nine states rooted in craving[57] are origination; the abandoning of these is

---

paññindriyaṃ. The Tibetan does not list these.

51. The Tibetan lists the six bases of contact. Cf. A I 176: *cakkhu phassāyatanaṃ, sotaṃ phassāyatanaṃ, ghānaṃ phassāyatanaṃ, jivhā phassāyatanaṃ, kāyo phassāyatanaṃ, mano phassāyatanaṃ—imāni cha phassāyatanānīti.*

52. The Tibetan lists the six groups of craving. S II 3: *Katamā ca bhikkhave taṇhā? Cha-y-ime bhikkhave taṇhākāyā. Rūpataṇhā saddataṇhā gandhataṇhā rasataṇhā phoṭṭhabbataṇhā dhammataṇhā.*

53. Cf. D III 247–50, 289, A III 290–92: *Cha nissaraṇīyadhātuyo ... nissaraṇaṃ h' etaṃ āvuso vyāpādassa, yadidaṃ mettā ceto-vimutti ... vihesāya, yadidaṃ karuṇā ceto-vimutti ... aratiyā, yadidaṃ muditā ceto-vimutti ... rāgassa, yadidaṃ upekhā ceto-vimutti ... sabba-nimittānaṃ, yadidaṃ animittā ceto-vimutti ... vicikicchā-kathaṃkathā-sallassa, yadidaṃ asmīti-mānasamugghāto.* Cf. the *ṣaḍ niḥsaraṇīyā dhātavaḥ* in the Daśottarasūtra of the Dīrghāgama.

Sv III 1036: *Nissaraṇiyā dhātuyo ti nissaṭadhātuyo va. ... Yadidaṃ mettācetovimuttī ti yā ayaṃ mettācetovimutti, idaṃ nissaraṇaṃ byāpādassa, byāpādato nissaṭā ti attho. Yo pana mettāya tikacatukkajjhānato vuṭṭhito saṅkhāre sammasitvā tatiyamaggaṃ patvā puna byāpādo natthī ti tatiyaphalena nibbānaṃ passati, tassa cittaṃ accantaṃ nissaraṇaṃ byāpādassa. ... Animittā cetovimuttī ti arahattaphalasamāpatti. ... Asmimānasamugghāto ti arahattamaggo. ...*

The Tibetan (Sav 194b–195a) has a different term for the last item—*kun du chags par bya ba'i chos* = *saṃrañjanīya dhamma*—with an equally unusual explanation; see Introduction § 4.4 and the footnote to the Tibetan translation in Appendix II.

54. *Satta viññāṇaṭṭhitiya*, D III 253; see fn. 2439. *Satta anusayā*, D III 254; fully given in Ch. 12 § 61. *Satta sambojjhaṅgā*, D III 251–2. The Tibetan (Sav 195a) lists the seven stations in an abridged manner, and also lists the seven tendencies, but not the *bojjhaṅga.*

55. *Aṭṭha loka-dhammā*, D III 254; fully given in Ch. 12 § 62. *Aṭṭha micchattā* (= *micchādiṭṭhi ... micchā samādhi*), D III 254. *Aṭṭha sammattā* (= *sammā-diṭṭhi ... sammā-samādhi*), D III 255.

56. *Nava sattāvāsā*, D III 263, 288. See fn. 2440.

57. Vibh 390; A IV 400–1: *Taṇhaṃ paṭicca pariyesanā, pariyesanaṃ paṭicca lābho, lābhaṃ paṭicca vinicchayo, vinicchayaṃ paṭicca chandarāgo, chandarāgaṃ paṭicca ajjhosānaṃ, ajjhosānaṃ paṭicca pariggaho, pariggahaṃ paṭicca macchariyaṃ, macchariyaṃ*

cessation; and the nine states rooted in reasoned attention[58] are the path.

Through ten kinds, the formations in the ten directions are suffering;[59] the ten fetters[60] are origination; the abandoning of the fetters is cessation;[61] and the ten perceptions are the path.[62]

Thus should it be known through successive explanation.

77. Inclusion

Q. How through inclusion (*saṅgaha*)?

A. There are three kinds of inclusion, namely, inclusion in the aggregates, inclusion in the sense bases, and inclusion in the elements.[63]

---

paṭicca ārakkhādhikaraṇaṃ, daṇḍādāna-satthādānakalahaviggahavivādā tuvaṃtuvaṃ-pesuññamusāvādā aneke pāpakā akusalā dhammā sambhavanti. Ime kho bhikkhave nava taṇhāmūlakā dhammā ti.

58. There are two versions, with the first five items the same and the last four different. In the Dasuttarasutta, the last four are seeing things as they are, disentchantment, dispassion, and freedom, while in the Paṭisambhidāmagga these are seeing the four noble truths as they are. D III 288: *Nava yonisomanasikāramūlakā dhammā, yonisomanasikaroto pāmojjaṃ jāyati, pamuditassa pīti jāyati, pītimanassa kāyo passambhati, passaddhakāyo sukhaṃ vedeti, sukhino cittaṃ samādhiyati, samāhite citte yathābhūtaṃ jānāti passati, yathābhūtaṃ jānaṃ passaṃ nibbindati, nibbindaṃ virajjati, virāgā vimuccati.* Paṭis I 86: *Nava yonisomanasikāramūlakā dhammā: aniccato yonisomanasikaroto pāmojjaṃ jāyati, pamuditassa pīti jāyati, pītimanassa kāyo passambhati, passaddhakāyo sukhaṃ vedeti, sukhino cittaṃ samādhiyati, samāhitena cittena idaṃ dukkhan-ti ... ayaṃ dukkhasamudayo ti ... ayaṃ dukkhanirodho ti ... ayaṃ dukkhanirodhagāminī paṭipadā ti yathābhūtaṃ pajānāti.* ... Paṭis-a I 303: *Yonisomanasikāramūlakā ti yonisomanasikāro mūlaṃ patiṭṭhā etesan-ti yonisomanasikāramūlakā. Yonisomanasikāraṃ muñcitvāyeva hi pāmojjādayo nava na honti.*

59. Cf. Nidd I 410: *Ye puratthimāya disāya saṅkhārā, ... ye dasasu disāsu saṅkhārā, te pi eritā ... dukkhe patiṭṭhitā atāṇā ... asaraṇībhūtā.*

60. Dhs 197, Vibh 391: *Dasa saṃyojanāni: kāmarāgasaṃyojanaṃ, ..., avijjāsaṃyojanaṃ.* In the Chinese text they are listed below at Ch. 12 § 67.

61. Cf. It 18: *dukkhassantakaro hoti, sabbosaṃyojanakkhayā ti.* Th 181–2: *akuppā me vimuttī ti sabbasaṃyojanakkhayā'ti.*

62. This could correspond to two lists of 10 perceptions. Most likely it is the one in the Dasuttarasutta, also found in the AN and in Sarvāstivāda works. A somewhat different list of 10 perceptions, which is added in the Tibetan translation, is given in the Girimānandasutta. On this and the anomalies in the Tibetan version, see Introduction § 4.4.

D III 291, A V 105 (also A I 41): *Asubhasaññā, maraṇasaññā, āhāre paṭikkūlasaññā, sabbaloke anabhiratasaññā, aniccasaññā, anicce dukkhasaññā, dukkhe anattasaññā, pahānasaññā, virāgasaññā, nirodhasaññā.* A V 115: *Aniccasaññā, anattasaññā, asubhasaññā, ādīnavasaññā, pahānasaññā, virāgasaññā, nirodhasaññā, sabbaloke anabhiratasaññā, sabbasaṅkhāresu anicchāsaññā, ānāpānassati.*

63. Peṭ 111: *Buddhānaṃ bhagavantānaṃ sāsanaṃ tividhena saṅgahaṃ gacchati,*

Herein, the truth of suffering is included in the five aggregates;[64] the truth of origination and the truth of the path are included in the aggregate of formations; cessation is not included in the aggregates.

The truth of suffering is included in the twelve sense bases. Three truths are included in the sense base of mental states (*dhammāyatana*).

The truth of suffering is included in the eighteen elements. Three truths are included in the element of mental states (*dhammadhātu*).[65]

Thus, one should know through inclusion.

Through this method, knowledge with regard to the noble truths arises.

This is called "skill in the noble truths".

The skill in the noble truths is finished.

[The eleventh chapter of the Path to Freedom, the Exposition of the Five Skills, is finished.]

---

khandhesu dhātūsu āyatanesu ca.

64. Cf. S III 196: *Rūpaṃ kho rādha dukkhaṃ, ... viññāṇaṃ dukkhaṃ.* Vibh-a 50: *Yad aniccaṃ taṃ dukkhan ti vacanato pana tad eva khandhapañcakaṃ dukkhaṃ. Kasmā? Abhiṇhasampatipīḷanato. Abhiṇhasampatipīlanākāro dukkha-lakkhaṇaṃ.* Nett 42: *Pañcakkhandhā dukkhaṃ.* Dhp 202: *natthi khandhādisā dukkhā.*

65. Dhāt 8f.: *Dukkhasaccaṃ pañcahi khandhehi dvādasahāyatanehi aṭṭhārasahi dhātūhi saṅgahitaṃ. Katihi asaṅgahitaṃ? Na kehici khandhehi na kehici āyatanehi na kāhici dhātūhi asaṅgahitaṃ. Samudayasaccaṃ ... maggasaccaṃ ekena khandhena ekenāyatanena ekāya dhātuyā saṅgahitaṃ. Katihi asaṅgahitaṃ? Catūhi khandhehi ekādasahāyatanehi sattarasahi dhātūhi asaṅgahitaṃ. Nirodhasaccaṃ na kehici khandhehi ekenāyatanena ekāya dhātuyā saṅgahitaṃ. Katihi asaṅgahitaṃ? Pañcahi khandhehi ekādasahāyatanehi sattarasahi dhātūhi asaṅgahitaṃ.*

Chapter 12

Exposition of the Truths (*Saccaniddesa*)

1. Introduction

[**453c**] Now, the meditator has received clarification about the aggregates, elements, sense bases, dependent arising, and the truths, and has heard about virtue, the kinds of asceticism, and the jhānas, but because of being a worldling he is not yet liberated from the fear of bad destinations. He has contemplated the fearfulness of the bad destinations and of the beginningless saṃsāra,[1] has contemplated that the opportunity might be lost, has contemplated the simile of the three hundred spear strikes,[2] has contemplated the simile of the man desirous of [quenching] his burning head,[3] but he has not yet analysed the four noble truths. In order to analyse the noble truths he should exert himself, should be motivated, should apply energy, and he should try to accomplish it wholeheartedly and mindfully.

2. Procedure of defining the four noble truths

Q. How should he apply himself?

A. The meditator should at first hear the four noble truths in brief or in detail, or in brief and in detail. Through hearing, through [grasping] the meaning, and through rehearsing, he should bear them in mind. Then the meditator enters a quiet place, sits down, and composes his mind, not letting

---

1. Cf. S II 92: *Etassa, Ānanda, dhammassa ananubodhā appaṭivedhā evamayaṃ pajā tantākulakajātā guḷāguṇṭhikajātā, muñjababbajabhūtā apāyaṃ duggatiṃ vinipātaṃ saṃsāraṃ nātivattati.* S V 431: *Catunnaṃ ... ariyasaccānaṃ ananubodhā appaṭivedhā evamidaṃ dīghamaddhānaṃ sandhāvitaṃ saṃsaritaṃ mamañceva tumhākañ-ca.*

2. M III 165–66; S II 100: ... *Ekissā pi bhante sattiyā haññamāno tato nidānaṃ dukkhaṃ domanassaṃ paṭisaṃvediyetha ko pana vāda tīhi sattasatehi haññāmāno ti? Evam eva kvāhaṃ bhikkhave viññāṇāhāro daṭṭhabbo ti vadāmi.* S I 128; Thī 58, 141: *Sattisūlūpamā kāmā khandhānaṃ adhikuṭṭanā.*

3. A II 93: *Seyyathā pi bhikkhave ādittacelo vā ādittasīso vā, tass' eva celassa vā sīsassa vā nibbāpanāya adhimattaṃ chandañ ca vāyāmañ ca ussāhañ ca ussoḷhiñ ca appaṭivāniñ-ca satiñ ca sampajaññañ-ca kareyya, evam eva kho bhikkhave tena puggalena tesaṃ yeva kusalānaṃ dhammānaṃ paṭilābhāya adhimatto chando ca ...* S V 440: *Ādittaṃ bhikkhave celaṃ vā sīsaṃ vā anajjhupekkhitvā amanasikaritvā anabhisametānaṃ catunnaṃ ariyasaccānaṃ yathābhūtaṃ abhisamayāya adhimatto chando ca vāyāmo ca ussāho ca ussoḷhī ca appaṭivānī ca sati ca sampajaññañ ca karaṇīyaṃ.* S III 143: ... *careyyādittasīso va, patthayaṃ accutaṃ padan-ti.*

it go here and there, and defines (*vavattheti, vavatthapeti*) the four noble truths.

3. Defining the truth of suffering

First, he should define the truth of suffering through the aggregates, the sense bases, or the elements.

The aggregates should be defined through the specific characteristics (*salakkhaṇa*)[4] and through the [general] characteristics of the aggregates, in the way it was taught in detail under the skill in the aggregates.[5] The sense bases should be defined through the characteristics of the sense bases, in the way it was taught in detail under the skill in the sense bases. The elements should be defined through the characteristics of the elements, in the way it was taught in detail under the skill in the elements.

Thus, the meditator, having defined: "The aggregates, sense bases, and elements are mere aggregates, sense bases, and elements, without a being, without a soul", and having gained the delimitation of the formations (*saṅkhāra-pariccheda*), defines in brief the two divisions, namely, name-and-matter.[6]

---

4. 以自相以陰相應令起 (453c11). 自相 and *salakkhaṇa*, lit. means "own characteristic". *Salakkhaṇa* is the "specific characteristic" such as hardness of earth, etc. as opposed to the "general characteristic" (*sāmaññalakkhaṇa*) of impermanence, suffering, and not self. On the important role of the terms *svalakṣaṇa* and *sāmānyalakṣaṇa* in the Sarvāstivāda Abhidharma, see Dhammajoti 2009: 18–22. See also fn. 643, 1477, 1505. Cf. Nidd-a I 199: *Khandhakusalā ti pañcasu khandhesu salakkhaṇasāmaññalakkhaṇesu cheka.* J-a II 34: *Sabbe khandhāyatanadhātudhamme salakkhaṇasāmaññalakkhaṇavasena attano ñāṇassa vidite...* Sv-ṭ II 377: *Salakkhaṇasāmaññalakkhaṇānan-ti phusanāditaṃ-taṃlakkhaṇānañceva aniccatādisāmaññalakkhaṇānañ-ca vasena ti yojanā.* It-a II 152: *khandhādivibhāgatosalakkhaṇatosāmaññalakkhaṇatotividhehinayehidhammānaṃñāpakā avabodhakā.* Cf. Vism XX.3–4/p.606f.: *Tattha ruppanalakkhaṇaṃ rūpaṃ, vedayitalakkhaṇā vedanā ti evaṃ tesaṃ tesaṃ dhammānaṃ paccattalakkhaṇasallakkhaṇavasena pavattā paññā ñātapariññā nāma. Rūpaṃ aniccaṃ, vedanā aniccā ti ādinā nayena tesaṃ yeva dhammānaṃ sāmaññalakkhaṇaṃ āropetvā pavattā lakkhaṇārammaṇikavipassanā paññā tīraṇapariññā nāma.* ... Vism XVII.303/p.582: *Yasmā panettha salakkhaṇasāmaññalakkhaṇavasena dhammānaṃ adassanato andho viya avijjā.*

See also the *Śrāvakabhūmi, Yogasthāna* III, Shukla ed. 385: *Kharalakṣaṇā pṛthivī yāvatsamudīraṇalakṣaṇo vāyuḥ vijānanalakṣaṇaṃ vijñānaṃ ... svalakṣaṇaṃ paryeṣate. Sarvva ete dhātavaḥ anityatayā samasamāḥ yāvannirātmatayetyevaṃ sāmānyalakṣaṇaṃ paryeṣate*; see Wayman 1961: 115.

5. See Ch. 11 § 29.

6. Cf. Mp II 278: ... *Tattha cattāro arūpakkhandhā nāmaṃ, rūpakkhandho rūpan-ti nāmañ-ca rūpañcā ti dve yeva dhammā honti, tato uddhaṃ satto vā jīvo vā natthīti ....*

Herein, the ten sense bases and the ten elements of the aggregate of matter are matter. The four aggregates, the sense base of mind, and the seven elements[7] are name. The sense base of mental states and the element of mental states are name or matter.[8]

Name is other than matter; matter is other than name. Matter is empty of name; name is empty of matter. Name does not mix with matter; matter does not mix with name.[9] It is like the drum and its sound [which do not mix with each other. Nevertheless,] matter occurs only in dependence upon name, and name occurs [only] in dependence upon matter.[10] It is like the blind and the cripple going on a journey [in dependence upon each other].[11]

Q. What are the differences between name-and-matter?

A. Name has no body; matter has a body. Name has [an object] which is known; matter does not have [an object] which is known.[12] Name proceeds quickly; matter proceeds slowly. Name has no accumulation (*ācaya, āyuhana*); matter has accumulation. Name thinks, knows, intends, cognizes; matter is without these [activities]. Matter walks, leans, sits, lies down, bends, and stretches; name is without these [activities]. Name knows, "I go", "I lean", "I sit", "I lie down", "I bend", "I stretch"; matter is without these [activities]. Matter drinks, eats, chews, tastes; name is without these [activities]. Name knows, "I drink", "I eat", "I chew", "I taste"; matter is without these [activities]. Matter

---

7. The mental states element and the six consciousness elements.

8. 法入法界或名或色. Cf. Vibh 146: *Nāmarūpapaccayā chaṭṭhāyatanan-ti. Atthi nāmaṃ, atthi rūpaṃ. Tattha katamaṃ nāmaṃ? Vedanākkhandho, saññākkhandho, saṅkhārakkhandho, idaṃ vuccati nāmaṃ. Tattha katamaṃ rūpaṃ? Yaṃ rūpaṃ nissāya manoviññāṇadhātu vattati, idaṃ vuccati rūpaṃ. Iti idañ-ca nāmaṃ, idañ-ca rūpaṃ. Idaṃ vuccati nāmarūpaṃ. Tattha katamaṃ nāmarūpapaccayā chaṭṭhāyatanaṃ? Yaṃ cittaṃ mano mānasaṃ hadayaṃ paṇḍaraṃ mano manāyatanaṃ manindriyaṃ viññāṇaṃ viññāṇakkhandho tajjāmanoviññāṇadhātu, ...* Cf. S V 184: *Nāmarūpasamudayā cittassa samudayo; nāmarūpanirodhā cittassa atthaṅgamo.*

9. 名者以色不離色者以名不離: "name is not separate (不離) from matter, and matter is not separate from name", but the Pali parallel has *asamissa*, "not mixed with", which fits better given the preceding clauses. At 456b1,7 不雜 corresponds to *amissa*, "not mixed with". A Chinese copyist probably mistook 雜 for the similar 離.

10. Cf. Vism XVIII.33/p.595: *Yathā ca daṇḍābhihataṃ bheriṃ nissāya sadde pavattamāne aññā bherī añño saddo, ... rūpaṃ paṭicca nāmaṃ pavattati.*

11. Vism XVIII.35/p.596: *Yathā jacchandho ca pīṭhasappī ca disā pakkamitukāmā assu. ... na ca tesaṃ aññamaññaṃ nissāya uppatti vā pavatti vā na hoti.* Abhidh-av vv. 1220–21: *Nāmaṃ nissāya rūpan tu, rūpaṃ, nissāya nāmakaṃ, pavattati sadā sabbaṃ, pañcavokāra-bhūmiyaṃ; imassa pana atthassa, āvibhāvattham eva ca, jaccandha-pīṭhasappīnaṃ, vattabbā upamā idha.*

12. 名者有所知色者無所知. The binome所知 corresponds to that which is cognitively known or experienced; *ñeyya* or *paṭisaṃvidita.*

claps the hands, frolics, laughs, cries, and says all sorts of words; name is without these [activities]. Name knows, "I clap", "I frolic", "I laugh", "I cry", "I say all sorts of words"; matter is without these [activities].[13]

These are the differences between name-and-matter. [**454a**]

Thus, the meditator, having defined, "name-and-matter are merely name-and-matter; [they are] without a being, without a soul," and having gained the delimitation of the formations, then [defines] everything in brief.

The definition of the truth of suffering, vision according to reality (*yāthāvadassana*), purity of view (*diṭṭhivisuddhi*),[14] and the definition of name-and-matter—these are epithets for the definition of the truth of suffering, which is to be realized.

4. Defining the truth of origination

The meditator, who has thus defined the truth of suffering, [but still] has the perception of a being, then should contemplate the source (*nidāna*) of suffering.

Q. What is the source and what is the origination of suffering?

A. The meditator knows that: "Suffering has birth as its source;[15] birth has existence as its source; existence has clinging as its source; clinging has

13. Not traced in Vism, but see Abhidh-av v. 1219: *Bhuñjāmīti pivāmīti, khādāmīti tatheva ca; / Rodāmīti hasāmīti, rūpassetaṃ na vijjati.*

14. 如實知見清淨. The characters 如實知見 corresponds to *ñāṇadassanavisuddhi* elsewhere in Vim, e.g. 400b15, so this can also mean "purity of knowledge and vision according to reality", *yathābhūtañāṇadassanavisuddhi.*

Cf. Vism XVIII.2/p.587: *Yaṃ pana vuttaṃ diṭṭhivisuddhi, kaṅkhāvitaraṇavisuddhi, maggāmaggañāṇadassanavisuddhi, paṭipadāñāṇadassanavisuddhi, ñāṇadassana-visuddhī ti imā pana pañca visuddhiyo sarīran ti, tattha nāmarūpānaṃ yāthāvadassanaṃ diṭṭhivisuddhi nāma.* Vism XVIII.37: *nāmarūpānaṃ yāthāvadassanaṃ diṭṭhivisuddhī ti.* Paṭis-a I 257: *Nāmarūpapariggahe sati paccayapariggahasambhavato dhammaṭṭhitiñāṇavacaneneva vuttena diṭṭhivisuddhisaṅkhātena nāmarūpavavatthāpanena dukkhasaccassa vavatthānaṃ kataṃ hoti.* Nidd-a II 102: *... so idaṃ nāmaṃ, idaṃ rūpan ti dvedhā vavatthapeti. Evaṃ vavatthapetvā nāmarūpato uddhaṃ añño satto ... natthī ti passati. ... evamādinā nayena nāmarūpānaṃ yāthāvadassanasaṅkhātena diṭṭhivisuddhibhūtena ñāṇena nāmarūpaṃ pariggahetvā puna tassa paccayam-pi parigganhanto vuttanayena nāmarūpaṃ pariggahetvā ko nu kho imassa hetū ti pariyesanto ahetuvādavisamahetuvādesu dosaṃ disvā rogaṃ disvā tassa nidānaṃ samuṭṭhānam-pi pariyesanto vejjo viya tassa hetuñca paccayañ-ca pariyesanto avijjā taṇhā upādānaṃ kamman-ti ime cattāro dhamme nāmarūpassa uppādapaccayattā hetū ti. ...* A-ṭ III 116: *Taruṇavipassanā ti nāmarūpapariggahe ñāṇaṃ, paccayapariggahe ñāṇaṃ, sammasane ñāṇaṃ, maggāmagge vavatthapetvā ṭhitañāṇan-ti catunnaṃ ñāṇānaṃ adhivacanaṃ.* S-a II 53: *Taruṇavipassanā ti saṅkhāraparicchede ñāṇaṃ kaṅkhāvitaraṇe ñāṇaṃ sammasane ñāṇaṃ maggāmagge ñāṇan-ti catunnaṃ ñāṇānaṃ adhivacanaṃ.*

15. Cf. Paṭis II 110: *Jarāmaraṇaṃ kiṃnidānaṃ, kiṃsamudayaṃ, kiṃjātikaṃ, kiṃpabhavan-ti evaṃ esanaṭṭhena saccaṃ. Jarāmaraṇaṃ jātinidānaṃ, jātisamudayaṃ,*

craving as its source; craving has feeling as its source; feeling has contact as its source; contact has the six sense bases as its source; the six sense bases have name-and-matter as its source; name-and-matter has consciousness as its source; consciousness has the formations as its source; the formations have ignorance as its source. Thus, with ignorance as condition, formations; with formations as condition, consciousness; ... with birth as condition, ageing, death, sorrow, lamentation, pain, distress, and grief. Thus is there the origination of this entire mass of suffering".

Thus, the meditator defines in detail the links of dependent arising.

Then he does it in brief: "With feeling as condition, craving".

The definition of the origination of suffering, knowledge of the stability of the Dhamma (*dhammaṭṭhiti-ñāṇa*), knowledge of the apprehending of conditions (*paccayapariggaha-ñāṇa*), and the purity of overcoming doubt (*kaṅkhāvitaraṇa-visuddhi*)—these are epithets for the knowledge of the definition of the truth of origination.[16]

---

jātijātikaṃ, jātippabhavan-ti evaṃ pariggahaṭṭhena saccaṃ. Jarāmaraṇañ-ca pajānāti, jarāmaraṇasamudayañ-ca pajānāti, jarāmaraṇanirodhañ-ca pajānāti, jarāmaraṇa-nirodhagāminiṃ paṭipadañ-ca pajānāti evaṃ paṭivedhaṭṭhena saccaṃ. ... M I 67: *Ime ca ... cattāro upādānā. Kiṃnidānā kiṃsamudayā kiṃjātikā kiṃpabhavā? Ime cattāro upādānā taṇhānidānā taṇhāsamudayā taṇhājātikā taṇhāpabhavā. ...* S II 107: *Idha ... bhikkhu sammasamāno sammasati antaraṃ sammasaṃ yaṃ kho idaṃ anekavidhaṃ nānappakārakaṃ dukkhaṃ loke uppajjati jarāmaraṇaṃ. Idaṃ kho dukkhaṃ kiṃnidānaṃ kiṃsamudayaṃ kiṃjātikaṃ kiṃpabhavaṃ, kismiṃ sati jarāmaraṇaṃ hoti, kismiṃ asati jarāmaraṇaṃ na hotī'ti? So sammasamāno evaṃ jānāti yaṃ kho idaṃ anekavidhaṃ nānappakārakaṃ dukkhaṃ loke uppajjati jarāmaraṇaṃ. Idaṃ kho dukkhaṃ upadhinidānaṃ upadhisamudayaṃ upadhijātikaṃ upadhipabhavaṃ, upadhismiṃ sati jarāmaraṇaṃ hoti, upadhismiṃ asati jarāmaraṇaṃ na hotī'ti. So jarāmaraṇañ-ca pajānāti jarāmaraṇasamudayañ-ca pajānāti jarāmaraṇanirodhañ-ca pajānāti yā ca jarāmaraṇanirodhasāruppagāminī paṭipadā tañ-ca pajānāti. ...*

16. See fn. 2095. Cf. Nidd-a II 103: ... *Evaṃ rūpakāyassa paccayapariggahaṃ katvā puna cakkhuñca paṭicca rūpe ca uppajjati cakkhuviññāṇan-ti-ādinā nayena nāmakāyassa pi paccayaṃ pariggaṇhāti, evaṃ pariggaṇhanto atītānāgatā pi dhammā evam-eva vattantī ti sanniṭṭhānaṃ karoti. Tassa yā sā pubbantaṃ ārabbha ahosiṃ nu kho ahaṃ atītamaddhānaṃ, ... chabbidhā vicikicchā vuttā, sā sabbā pi pahiyyati. Evaṃ paccayapariggahaṇena tīsu addhāsu kaṅkhaṃ vitaritvā ṭhitaṃ ñāṇaṃ kaṅkhāvitaraṇavisuddhī ti pi dhammaṭṭhitiñāṇan ti pi yathābhūtañāṇan-ti pi sammādassanan-ti pi vuccati.* Cf. Mp II 279: ... *iti ime ca arūpadhammā chasaṭṭhi ca rūpadhammā ti sabbe pi samodhānetvā nāmañ-ca rūpañcā ti dveva dhammā honti, tato uddhaṃ satto vā jīvo vā natthīti nāmarūpavasena pañcakkhandhe vavatthapetvā tesaṃ paccayaṃ pariyesanto avijjāpaccayā taṇhāpaccayā kammapaccayā āhārapaccayā ti evaṃ paccayaṃ disvā, atīte pi imehi paccayehi idaṃ vaṭṭaṃ pavattittha, anāgate pi etehi paccayehi pavattissati, etarahi pi etehi yeva pavattatī ti tīsu kālesu kaṅkhaṃ vitaritvā anukkamena paṭipajjamāno arahattaṃ pāpuṇāti.* Abhidh-av-pṭ 85 978: *Iti nānappakārena, paccayānaṃ pariggaho; / Sappaccayanāmarūpaṃ, vavatthānan-ti veditaṃ.* 979. *Idappaccayatāñāṇaṃ, paccayākāradassanaṃ; / Dhammaṭṭhiti yathābhūta-ñāṇadassana-*

5. Defining the truth of cessation

The meditator, having defined the truth of the origination of suffering and having transcended doubt with regard to the three times,[17] then contemplates the cessation of suffering.

Q. The cessation of what is the cessation of suffering?
A. For the cessation of suffering the meditator knows thus: "Through the cessation of birth, this suffering ceases; through the cessation of birth, existence ceases; through the cessation of existence, clinging ceases; through the cessation of clinging, craving ceases; ... through the cessation of ignorance, the formations cease. Thus, through the cessation of ignorance, the formations cease; through the cessation of the formations, consciousness ceases; ... through the cessation of birth, ageing, death, sorrow, lamentation, pain, distress, and grief cease. Thus is there the cessation of this entire mass of suffering".

The meditator, having thus contemplated in detail the cessation of the links of dependent arising, then contemplates them in brief: "With feeling as condition, craving. Owing to its cessation, suffering ceases".

Thus, he defines the truth of cessation.

6. Defining the truth of the path leading to the cessation of suffering

The meditator, having thus defined the truth of cessation, then contemplates the path leading to the cessation of suffering: "What is the path and what is the way (*paṭipadā*) leading to the cessation of craving?" The meditator knows: "The contemplation of the disadvantage in the five aggregates subject to clinging: This is the path; this is the way leading to the cessation of craving".

The definition of the truth of the path is to be understood as was taught in detail under the skill in the [noble] truths.

7. Comprehension of the five aggregates by way of the three characteristics

The meditator, having defined sequentially the four truths, then sequentially contemplates and analyses by way of comprehending (*sammasana*) the five aggregates subject to clinging through one hundred and eighty methods (*pariyāya, naya*). Whatever matter—past, future, or present, internal or external, great or small, coarse or subtle, far or near—all matter he defines in

---

nāmakaṃ. 980. Kālattayavibhāgesu, kaṅkhāsaṃklesasodhanaṃ; / Kaṅkhāvitaraṇā nāma, visuddhī ti pavuccatī ti.

17. See preceding footnote.

detail as impermanent, [**454b**] he defines in detail as suffering, he defines in detail as without self. And so for any feeling, any perception, any formations, any consciousness.[18]

For each aggregate twelve methods.[19] For five aggregates, twelve times five is sixty. The sixty [kinds of] seeing of impermanence, sixty [kinds of] seeing of suffering, and sixty [kinds of] seeing of without self are one hundred and eighty.

Furthermore, there are one hundred and eighty methods: six internal sense bases; six external sense bases; six groups of consciousness (*viññāṇakāyā*); six groups of contact; six groups of feeling; six groups of perception; six groups of volition; six groups of craving; six [kinds of] thinking; six [kinds of] exploring. These ten sixes are sixty. Sixty kinds of seeing of impermanence, sixty [kinds of] seeing of suffering, and sixty [kinds of] seeing of without self: three times sixty are one hundred and eighty.

Furthermore, he analyses and contemplates the formations as impermanent thus: "The ages, years, seasons, months, fortnights, days, nights, hours, seconds, and moments [revolve]. By revolving, states and formations are renewed like the revolving of the continuity (*santati*) of the lamp and the flame".[20]

He analyses and contemplates the formations as suffering thus: "Through experiencing the suffering of the bad destinations, hunger and thirst, fear, searching, separation from dear ones, ageing, disease, death, sorrow,

---

18. Paṭis I 53–4: *Kathaṃ atītānāgatapaccuppannānaṃ dhammānaṃ saṅkhipitvā vavatthāne paññā sammasane ñāṇaṃ? Yaṃ kiñci rūpaṃ atītānāgatapaccuppannaṃ ajjhattaṃ vā bahiddhā vā oḷārikaṃ vā sukhumaṃ vā hīnaṃ vā paṇītaṃ vā yaṃ dūre santike vā, sabbaṃ rūpaṃ aniccato vavattheti, ekaṃ sammasanaṃ; dukkhato vavattheti, ekaṃ sammasanaṃ; anattato vavattheti, ekaṃ sammasanaṃ. ...*

19. Paṭis-a I 248: *Keci pana sabbaṃ rūpaṃ, sabbaṃ vedanaṃ, sabbaṃ saññaṃ, sabbe saṅkhāre, sabbaṃ viññāṇan ti padam pi pakkhipitvā ekekasmiṃ khandhe dvādasa dvādasa katvā pañcasu saṭṭhi, anupassanāto asītisatasammasanānī ti vadanti.* LC: "In other words, 'some' (? = Vim) include the totality of each aggregate to get a twelfth item, i.e. the eleven *atītānāgatapaccuppannaṃ ajjhattaṃ vā bahiddhā vā oḷārikaṃ vā sukhumaṃ vā hīnaṃ vā paṇītaṃ vā yaṃ dūre santike vā,* + 1 *sabbaṃ rūpaṃ,* etc". Cf. Vism XX.13–14/p.610 and the Chachakkasutta, MN 148.

20. 以迴轉法行成新故如燈焰相續成轉. An alternative translation is: "... Through the revolving/recurring (*āvaṭṭana?*) of states, formations are renewed ...".

Cf. Mil 40: *Yathā mahārāja kocid eva puriso padīpaṃ padīpeyya, kiṃ so sabbarattiṃ dīpeyyā ti. Āma bhante sabbarattiṃ padīpeyya ti. Kin-nu kho mahārāja yā purime yāme acci sā majjhime yāme accī ti. Na hi bhante ti. Yā majjhime yāme acci sā pacchime yāme accī ti. Na hi bhante ti. Kin-nu kho mahārāja añño so ahosi purime yāme padīpo, añño majjhime yāme padīpo, añño pacchime yāme padīpo ti. Na hi bhante, taṃ yeva nissāya sabbarattiṃ padīpito ti. Evam eva kho majārāja dhammasantati sandahati, añño uppajjati añño nirujjhati, apubbaṃ acarimaṃ viya sandahati, tena na ca so na ca añño pacchimaviññāṇasaṅgahaṃ gacchatī ti.*

lamentation, pain, distress, and grief. This is the characteristic of the continuity of the formations".[21]

He analyses and contemplates the formations as without self thus: "When—by way of the aggregates, the sense bases, the elements, dependent arising, the truths, the results of kamma, and conditions (*paccaya*)—[the formations] have originated, they originate [further formations]. As intrinsic natures that are without a being, disinterested (*nirīhaka*), unconcerned (*abyāpāra*), the formations arise".[22]

He contemplates matter as impermanent in the sense of destruction (*khaya*), as suffering in the sense of fearfulness (*bhaya*), as without self in the sense of insubstantiality (*asāraka*). Thus, he analyses in brief and in detail. In the same way, he contemplates that feeling, perception, the formations, and consciousness as impermanent in the sense of destruction, as suffering in the sense of fear, and as without self in the sense of insubstantiality.[23] Thus, he analyses in brief and in detail.

Herein, having analysed through impermanence, he dispels the perception of permanence; having analysed through suffering, he dispels the perception of happiness; having analysed through without self, he dispels the perception of self.

Q. How does he analyse in detail through impermanence?

A. When seeing all the formations as they are, as delimited by non-existence (*abhāva*),[24] as delimited by destruction, the mind emerges from the sign [of

---

21. 此行相應相續. Lit.: "These formations [are] associated with continuity".

22. 從陰入界因緣諦業果報因緣令生所生無眾生不動無事自性行成起. This refers to the causal regularity or "such-naturedness" (*evaṃdhammatā*) of formations, i.e. when the formations are originated through ignorance, they in turn automatically originate consciousness without any "self" being involved; see § 13 below. Compare 455b12: "By seeing the formations first and last as intrinsic natures (*sabhāva*) that are devoid [of a soul] and indifferent, there is no clinging to a self" and 455b25ff.: "Why are all formations unconcerned and indifferent? They persist without having been originated by another [being]. They persist as intrinsic natures and conditions that come together and aggregate as dependently arisen [states]. Through such-naturedness, when they are originated, they originate." See fn. 2143. On *dhamma* as *sabhāva*, see Vism VIII.246: *dhammā ti sabhāvā*, and Ñāṇamoli's note on it in PoP. Cf. Vism-mhṭ II 389: *Tesu ime dhammā satipi suññanirīha-abyāpārabhāve dhammasabhāvato ādhipaccavasena pavattantī ti anattalakkhaṇavibhāvanatthaṃ indriyāni gahitāni.*

23. Paṭis I 52: *Rūpaṃ ... viññāṇaṃ ... atītānāgatapaccuppannaṃ aniccaṃ khayaṭṭhena, dukkhaṃ bhayaṭṭhena anattā asārakaṭṭhenā ti saṅkhipitvā vavatthāne paññā sammasane ñāṇaṃ.*

24. Cf. Paṭis-a I 247: ... *ekādasahi okāsehi paricchinditvā sabbaṃ rūpaṃ aniccato vavattheti aniccan-ti sammasati. Kathaṃ? Parato vuttanayena. Vuttañhetaṃ rūpaṃ atītānāgatapaccuppannaṃ aniccaṃ khayaṭṭhena-ti. Tasmā esa yaṃ atītaṃ rūpaṃ, taṃ yasmā*

permanence] and leaps into the signless element (*animitta-dhātu*). Thus, he analyses in detail through impermanence.

Q. How does he analyse in detail through suffering?
A. When the mind is stirred with fear towards all formations, it emerges from the desired, and leaps into the desireless element (*appaṇihita-dhātu*). Thus, he analyses in detail through suffering.

Q. How does he analyse in detail through without self?
A. When seeing all states as alien (*parato*), the mind emerges from adherence (*abhinivesa*) and leaps into the emptiness element. Thus, he analyses in detail through without self.[25]

Thus, he analyses the three [planes of] existence, the five destinations, the seven stations of consciousness, and the nine abodes of beings, contemplating them in terms of destruction, fear, and insubstantiality. [**454c**]

The analysis of the truths is finished.

---

atīte yeva khīṇaṃ, nayimaṃ bhavaṃ sampattan-ti aniccaṃ khayaṭṭhena, yaṃ anāgataṃ rūpaṃ anantarabhave nibbattissati, tam-pi tattheva khīyissati, na tato paraṃ bhavaṃ gamissatī ti aniccaṃ khayaṭṭhena, yaṃ paccuppannaṃ rūpaṃ, taṃ idheva khīyati, na ito gacchatī ti aniccaṃ khayaṭṭhena, yaṃ ajjhattaṃ rūpaṃ, tam-pi ajjhattam-eva khīyati, na bahiddhābhāvaṃ gacchatī ti aniccaṃ khayaṭṭhena, yaṃ bahiddhā oḷārikaṃ sukhumaṃ hīnaṃ paṇītaṃ dūre santike, tam-pi ettheva khīyati, na dūrabhāvaṃ gacchatī ti aniccaṃ khayaṭṭhenā ti sammasati.

25. Paṭis II 48: *Sabbasaṅkhāre paricchedaparivaṭumato samanupassanatāya animittāya ca dhātuyā cittasampakkhandanatāya, sabbasaṅkhāresu manosamuttejanatāya appaṇihitāya ca dhātuyā cittasampakkhandanatāya, sabbadhamme parato samanupassanatāya suññatāya ca dhātuyā cittasampakkhandanatāya ... Aniccato manasikaroto khayato saṅkhārā upaṭṭhanti, dukkhato manasikaroto bhayato saṅkhārā upaṭṭhanti, anattato manasikaroto suññato saṅkhārā upaṭṭhanti.*

Paṭis-a II 159: *Sabbasaṅkhāre paricchedaparivaṭumato samanupassanatāyā ti sabbesaṃ saṅkhārānaṃ udayabbayavasena paricchedato ceva parivaṭumato ca samanupassanatāya. Lokaniyyānaṃ hotī ti pāṭhaseso. Aniccānupassanā hi udayato pubbe saṅkhārā natthī ti paricchinditvā tesaṃ gatiṃ samannesamānā vayato paraṃ na gacchanti, ettheva antaradhāyantī ti parivaṭumato pariyantato samanupassati. Sabbasaṅkhārā hi udayena pubbantaparicchinnā, vayena aparantaparicchinnā. Animittāya ca dhātuyā cittasampakkhandanatāyā ti vipassanākkhaṇepi nibbānaninnatāya animittākārena upaṭṭhānato animittasaṅkhātāya nibbānadhātuyā cittapavisanatāya ca lokaniyyānaṃ hoti. Manosamuttejanatāyā ti cittasaṃvejanatāya. Dukkhānupassanāya hi saṅkhāresu cittaṃ saṃvijjati. Appaṇihitāya ca dhātuyā ti vipassanākkhaṇepi nibbānaninnatāya appaṇihitākārena upaṭṭhānato appaṇihitasaṅkhātāya nibbānadhātuyā. ... Parato samanupassanatāyā ti paccayāyattattā avasatāya avidheyyatāya ca nāhaṃ na maman-ti evaṃ anattato samanupassanatāya. Suññatāya ca dhātuyā ti vipassanākkhaṇepi nibbānaninnatāya suññatākārena upaṭṭhānato suññatāsaṅkhātāya nibbānadhātuyā. Iti imāni tīṇi vacanāni aniccadukkhānattānupassanānaṃ vasena vuttāni.*

8. Grasping the Sign

The meditator, having analysed the three characteristics in the five aggregates subject to clinging, arouses the wish to enter [the stream] and desires to abandon the formations. At that time, the present internal five aggregates subject to clinging are grasped by way of the characteristics. He penetrates rise and fall: "Thus, these states, which have not arisen [before], now arise; and having arisen, they fall away".[26] Thus, he penetrates.

9. Grasping the aggregates in three ways

Herein, in grasping the sign there are three kinds: grasping the sign of afflictions, grasping the sign of concentration, and grasping the sign of insight.

[**Q.** What is grasping the sign of afflictions?]

[**A.**] Herein, the foolish worldling, through the distorted perception of pleasure and permanence in objects seen, heard, sensed, or known, arouses the mind[27] by delighting [in them] and grasps the sign in these afflictions which are due to adherence.[28] It is like a moth flying into the flame of a lamp.[29]

---

26. Cf. Paṭis-a I 256: *Tass' evaṃ pākaṭibhūta-sacca-paṭiccasamuppāda-nayalakkhaṇa-bhedassa: Evaṃ kira nām'ime dhammā anuppannapubbā uppajjantī, uppannā nirujjhantī ti niccanavā 'va hutvā saṅkhārā upaṭṭhahanti.*

27. 所初心, lit. "begin/first mind".

28. 初心以好取相於此著煩惱. The characters 著煩惱, = *abhinivesa-kilesa?*, could mean "defilements which are due to adherence", "defilements which are adherence", or "adherence defilements", or perhaps "defilements adhered to". Cf. Vism XXII.121/pp. 695f: *Tasmā tāya saṃyogābhinivesassa pahānaṃ hoti, kāmasaṃyogādikassa kilesābhinivesassa kilesappavattiyā pahānaṃ hotī ti attho.* Vism-mhṭ II 509: *Niviṭṭhabhāvena ogāḷhabhāvena pavattasaṃyojanādikilesā eva kilesābhiniveso.*

Cf. Ud-a 270: *Āyasmā hi sāriputto anupasantakilesānaṃ sattānaṃ rāgādikilesajanita-santāpadarathapariḷāhadukkhañceva kilesābhisaṅkhāranimittaṃ jātijarābyādhimaraṇas okaparidevādidukkhañ-ca paccakkhato disvā atītānāgatepi nesaṃ vaṭṭamūlakadukkhaṃ parituletvā karuṇāyamāno attanāpi puthujjanakāle anubhūtaṃ kilesanimittaṃ vā anappakaṃ dukkhaṃ anussaritvā īdisassa nāma mahādukkhassa hetubhūtā kilesā idāni me suppahīnā ti attano kilesavūpasamaṃ abhiṇhaṃ paccavekkhati.* Th-a III 192: *Saññāya vipariyesāti ādikā gāthā tena yācitena āyasmatā ānandena vuttā. Vipariyesā ti vipallāsena asubhe subhan-ti pavattena viparītaggāhena. Nimittan-ti kilesajanakanimittaṃ.* As 399, Nidd-a II 390: *Nimittaggāhīti itthipurisanimittaṃ vā subhanimittādikaṃ vā kilesavatthubhūtaṃ nimittaṃ chandarāgavasena gaṇhāti, diṭṭhamatte yeva na saṇṭhāti.*

29. Cf. Ud 72: *Upātidhāvanti na sāram enti, navaṃ navaṃ bandhanaṃ brūhayanti, patanti pajjotam iv' ādhipātā, diṭṭhe sute iti h' eke niviṭṭhā ti.* Cf. Ud-a 355–6: *Tattha upātidhāvanti na sāramentī ti sīlasamādhipaññāvimutti ādibhedaṃ sāraṃ na enti, catusaccābhisamayavasena na adhigacchanti. Tasmiṃ pana sa-upāye sāre tiṭṭhante yeva vimuttābhilāsāya taṃ upentā viya hutvā pi diṭṭhivipallāsena atidhāvanti atikkamitvā gacchanti, pañcupādānakkhandhe niccaṃ subhaṃ sukhaṃ attā ti abhinivisitvā gaṇhantā ti attho. Navaṃ navaṃ bandhanaṃ*

This is called grasping the sign of afflictions.

Q. What is grasping the sign of concentration?

A. Herein, the meditator, wishing to gain concentration, arouses the mind with mindfulness and clear knowing (*sati-sampajañña*) and grasps the sign of one of the thirty-eight meditation subjects, fastening the mind [to it] for the purpose of undistractedness (*avikkhepa*), as if he were fastening an elephant [to a post].[30]

This is called grasping the sign of concentration.

Q. What is grasping the sign of insight?[31]

A. One who has the [wrong] view of permanence arouses the mind with wisdom and analyses the specific characteristics (*salakkhaṇa*)[32] of matter, feeling, perception, formations, and consciousness respectively. Desiring release [from the aggregates],[33] he develops that sign as if he were holding a poisonous snake.[34]

---

brūhayantī ti tathā gaṇhantā ca taṇhādiṭṭhisaṅkhātaṃ navaṃ navaṃ bandhanaṃ brūhayanti vaḍḍhayanti. Patanti pajjotamivādhipātakā, diṭṭhe sute itiheke niviṭṭhā ti evaṃ taṇhādiṭṭhibandhanehi baddhattā eke samaṇabrāhmaṇā diṭṭhe attanā cakkhuviññāṇena diṭṭhidassaneneva vā diṭṭhe anussavūpalabbhamatteneva ca sute itiha ekantato evametanti niviṭṭhā diṭṭhābhinivesena sassatanti ādinā abhiniviṭṭhā, ekantahitaṃ vā nissaraṇaṃ ajānantā rāgādīhi ekādasahi aggīhi ādittaṃ bhavattayasaṅkhātaṃ aṅgārakāsuṃ yeva ime viya adhipātakā imaṃ pajjotaṃ patanti, na tato sīsaṃ ukkhipituṃ sakkontī ti attho. Vibh-a 146: *Salabho viya dīpasikhābhinipātaṃ.*

30. Cf. Th 1141: *Ārammaṇe taṃ balasā nibandhisaṃ nāgaṃ va thambhamhi daḷhāya rajjuyā taṃ me suguttaṃ satiyā subhāvitaṃ anissitaṃ sabbabhavesu hehisi.*

31. Nidd II 359: *ñāṇacaritassa bhagavā puggalassa ācikkhati vipassanānimittaṃ aniccākāraṃ dukkhākāraṃ anattākāraṃ.* Mp III 390: *Tattha ca nimittaṃ gaṇhāhīti tasmiñca samabhāve sati yena ādāse mukhabimbeneva nimittena uppajjitabbaṃ, taṃ samathanimittaṃ vipassanānimittaṃ magganimittaṃ phalanimittañ-ca gaṇhāhi nibbattehīti evamassa satthā arahatte pakkhipitvā kammaṭṭhānaṃ kathesi.*

32. See fn. 1505.

33. The character 捨 can correspond to "equanimity" (*upekkhā*) or to "abandoning/relinquishing/release" (*cāga/pahāna/muñcana*), etc., therefore 樂欲捨 could also mean "desiring equanimity". "Knowledge of desire for release", *muñcitukamyatāñāṇa* is 樂解脫智 at 456c28, while "knowledge of equanimity towards the formations", *saṅkhārupekkhāñāṇa*, is 行捨智 at 461b27. The explanation of the simile in the As, see next fn., indicates that equanimity could be the intended meaning. However, according to the explanation of the simile in Vism XXI.49–50, the man who has grabbed a snake instead of a fish desires release from the snake. It does not mention equanimity.

34. Cf. As 173: *Yathā cetāsaṃ atthato ekībhāvo, evaṃ saṅkhārupekkhāvipassanupekkhānampi. Paññā eva hi esā kiccavasena dvidhā bhinnā. Yathā hi purisassa sāyaṃ gehaṃ paviṭṭhaṃ sappaṃ ajapadadaṇḍaṃ gahetvā pariyesamānassa taṃ thusakoṭṭhake nipannaṃ*

This is called "grasping the sign of insight".

Herein, [the sense of] grasping of the sign of insight is intended.

Q. How does one grasp the sign of matter, feeling, perception, the formations, and consciousness?

A. "The sign of matter": One contemplates matter by way of the earth element or the water element or the fire element or the wind element, or by way of the sense base of eye [... ear ... nose ... tongue] or the sense base of body.

"The sign of feeling": One contemplates feeling by way of pleasant, painful, or neither pleasant nor painful [feelings].

"The sign of perception": One contemplates perception by way of the perception of forms [... sounds ... odours ... tastes ... tangibles,] or perception of mental states.

"The sign of the formations": One contemplates the formations through contact, volition, thinking, exploring, or attention.

"The sign of consciousness": One contemplates consciousness by way of eye-consciousness [ear ... nose ... tongue ... body ...] or mind consciousness.

Thus, the meditator contemplates them and grasps well their signs through defining (*vavatthāna*) them well. Defining them thus he grasps the signs of matter, feeling, perception, the formations, and consciousness.[35]

10. Grasping of the sign of mind

Furthermore, in two ways one grasps the sign of mind (*citta*): through object (*ārammaṇato*) and through attending (*manasikārato*).

Q. How does one grasp the sign of mind through the object?

---

disvā sappo nu kho no'ti avalokentassa sovatthikattayaṃ disvā nibbematikassa sappo, na sappo ti vicinane majjhattatā hoti; evam-eva yā āraddhavipassakassa vipassanāñāṇena lakkhaṇattaye diṭṭhe saṅkhārānaṃ aniccabhāvādivicinane majjhattatā uppajjati, ayaṃ vipassanupekkhā. Yathā pana tassa purisassa ajapadadaṇḍakena gāḷhaṃ sappaṃ gahetvā kintāhaṃ imaṃ sappaṃ aviheṭhento attānañ-ca iminā aḍaṃsāpento muñceyyan-ti muñcanākāram-eva pariyesato gahaṇe majjhattatā hoti; evam-eva yā lakkhaṇattayassa diṭṭhattā, āditte viya tayo bhave passato, saṅkhāraggahaṇe majjhattatā, ayaṃ saṅkhārupekkhā. Iti vipassanupekkhāya siddhāya saṅkhārupekkhā pi siddhāva hoti. Vism XXI.49–50/p.652–53: *Evañ-hi passatānena tilakkhaṇaṃ āropetvā saṅkhārā pariggahitā nāma honti. Kasmā panāyamete evaṃ pariggaṇhātī ti? Muñcanassa upāyasampādanatthaṃ. Tatrāyaṃ upamā eko kira puriso macche gahessāmī ti ... antoudake sappaṃ gīvāya gahetvā ... sappoti sañjānitvā bhīto ādīnavaṃ disvā gahaṇe nibbinno muñcitukāmo hutvā muñcanassa upāyaṃ karonto ... Sappaṃ muñcitukāmatā viya muñcitukamyatāñāṇaṃ, muñcanassa upāyakaraṇaṃ viya paṭisaṅkhānupassanāñāṇena saṅkhāresu tilakkhaṇāropanaṃ. ....*

35. Cf. Paṭis I 92: *Rūpanimittaṃ ... vedanānimittaṃ ... saññānimittaṃ... saṅkhāranimittaṃ... viññāṇanimittaṃ... cakkhunimittaṃ ... jarāmaraṇanimittaṃ bhayato sampassamāno animitte adhimuttattā phussa phussa vayaṃ passati—animitto vihāro. ...*

A. One should contemplate "through this object my mind arises"; "through this object of matter my mind arises"; "through this object of feeling my mind arises"; "through this object of perception my mind arises"; "through this object of formations my mind arises"; and "through this object of consciousness my mind arises"—thus one should contemplate them. Thus, one grasps the sign of mind through the object.

Q. How does one grasp the sign of mind through attending?
A. "Through my attending to matter, my mind arises"—thus one should contemplate. "Through my attending to feeling ... perception ... and formations, my mind arises"—thus should one contemplate. Having attended thus one grasps the sign of mind.[36]

Q. How is that sign well grasped?
A. Through these modes (*ākāra*) and through these characteristics, the sign of matter, feeling, perception, formations, and consciousness is contemplated. [**455a**] If one can repeatedly contemplate that sign through these modes and through these characteristics, it is called a "well grasped sign".

11. Knowledge of rise and fall

"One penetrates rise and fall": one penetrates: "There is arising; there is falling away; there is arising and falling away'".

Accordingly, the matter that has arisen is present. The characteristic of production [of matter] (*nibbatti*) is arising. The characteristic of change [of matter] (*vipariṇāma*) is falling away. When both of these [characteristics] are seen with the eye of wisdom, there is penetration of rise and fall.

The feeling [perception, the formations, and consciousness] that have arisen are present. The characteristic of the production of feeling, perception, the formations, and consciousness is arising. The characteristic of change in them is falling away. When both of these are seen with the eye of wisdom, there is penetration of rise and fall.

Furthermore, in three ways, one penetrates the characteristics of arising, and in three ways, one penetrates the characteristics of falling away: through cause (*hetuto*), through condition (*paccayato*), and through essential nature (*sarasato*).

Q. How does one penetrate the characteristics of arising through cause?

---

36. Cf. S V 184: *Nāmarūpasamudayā cittassa samudayo; nāmarūpanirodhā cittassa atthaṅgamo. Manasikārasamudayā dhammānaṃ samudayo; manasikāranirodhā dhammānaṃ atthaṅgamo ti.*

A. Craving, ignorance, and kamma are the causes for the arising of the aggregates. By seeing this with the eye of wisdom, one penetrates the characteristics of arising through cause.[37]

Q. How does one penetrate the characteristics of arising through condition?
A. Food is the condition for the arising of the aggregate of matter. Contact is the condition for the arising of three aggregates. Name-and-matter is the condition for the arising of the aggregate of consciousness.[38] By seeing this with the eye of wisdom, one penetrates the characteristics of arising through condition.

Q. How does one penetrate the characteristics of arising through essential nature?[39]
A. Like the uninterrupted succession of the flame of a lamp,[40] the formations arise one after another, ever anew. By seeing this with the eye of wisdom, one penetrates the characteristics of arising through essential nature.

Accordingly, by seeing arising through cause, the truth of origination is seen through characteristics. By the understanding (*avabodha*) of arising through condition, and by seeing arising through intrinsic function, the truth of suffering is seen through characteristics.

By way of the moment (*khaṇato, khaṇavasena*), one cannot obtain understanding (*avabodha*).[41]

Thus, in three ways one penetrates the characteristics of arising.

Q. How does one penetrate falling away in three ways?

---

37. Cf. Paṭis I 55: *Avijjāsamudayā rūpasamudayo ti paccayasamudayaṭṭhena rūpakkhandhassa udayaṃ passati, taṇhāsamudayā rūpasamudayo ti paccayasamudayaṭṭhena rūpakkhandhassa udayaṃ passati, kammasamudayā rūpasamudayo ti paccayasamudayaṭṭhena rūpakkhandhassa udayaṃ passati.* S III 59–61: *Āhārasamudayā rūpasamudayo; ... Phassasamudayā vedanāsamudayo;. ... Phassasamudayā saññāsamudayo;. ... Phassasamudayā saṅkhārasamudayo; ... Nāmarūpasamudayā viññāṇasamudayo; ....*

38. Cf. Paṭis I 57: *Rūpakkhandho āhārasamudayo, vedanā saññā saṅkhārā tayo khandhā phassasamudayā, viññāṇakkhandho nāmarūpasamudayo.*

39. 以自味. *Yāthāvasarasato* "according to intrinsic nature" in Vism XXI.4/p.640: *Udayabbayam pana pariggahetvā santatiyā vikopitāya aniccalakkhaṇaṃ yāthāvasarasato upaṭṭhāti. Abhiṇhasampaṭipīḷanaṃ manasikatvā iriyāpathe ugghāṭite dukkhalakkhaṇaṃ yāthāvasarasato upaṭṭhāti. Nānādhātuyo vinibbhujitvā ghanavinibbhoge kate anattalakkhaṇaṃ yāthāvasarasato upaṭṭhāti.*

40. Vibh-mṭ 44: *Yattha yattha hi ārammaṇe arūpadhammā uppajjanti, tattha tattheva te bhijjanti, na aññaṃ saṅkamanti, ārammaṇadhammā ca yathāsakaṃ khaṇato uddhaṃ na tiṭṭhantī ti. Svāyamattho padīpādi-udāharaṇena veditabbo.*

41. 以剎那不可得覺. See the discussion of this in the Introduction § 5, idea 21.

A. Through the falling away of cause, through the falling away of condition, and through essential nature.[42]

Herein, through the falling away of craving, ignorance, and kamma, there is the falling away of the aggregates.[43] Seeing this with the eye of wisdom, one penetrates the characteristics of falling away through the falling away of cause.

Through the falling away of food, there is the falling away of the aggregate of matter; through the falling away of contact, there is the falling away of three aggregates; through the falling away of name-and-matter, there is the falling away of the aggregate of consciousness.[44] When seeing this with the eye of wisdom, one penetrates the characteristics of falling away through the falling away of condition.

Like the uninterrupted succession of the flame of a lamp, the formations fall away one after another. By seeing this with the eye of wisdom, one penetrates the characteristics of falling away through essential nature.

Accordingly, by seeing the falling away of causes, the truth of cessation is seen through characteristics. By the understanding (*avabodha*) of the characteristics of non-arising (*anuppāda*) through the falling away of condition and by seeing falling away through essential nature, the truth of suffering is first seen through characteristics. By way of the moment, one cannot obtain understanding.

12. Obtaining the higher knowledge

Q. How does one see the truth of suffering through rise and fall?
A. One obtains vision through the characteristics.

Q. How will higher knowledge arise? How does one see arising and falling away through cause?
A. Through the characteristics of the truth of suffering one obtains vision [but] one does not yet fully see[45] the suffering until one has seen according to

42. 以自味滅 = "through the falling away of essential nature", but the explanations below do not have 滅 "falling away".

43. Cf. Paṭis I 55–57: *Avijjānirodhā rūpanirodho ti paccayanirodhaṭṭhena rūpakkhandhassa vayaṃ passati, taṇhānirodhā rūpanirodho ti paccayanirodhaṭṭhena rūpakkhandhassa vayaṃ passati, kamma-nirodhā rūpanirodho, paccayanirodhaṭṭhena rūpakkhandhassa vayaṃ passati.*

44. Cf. Paṭis I 57: *Nāmarūpanirodhā viññāṇanirodho ti paccayanirodhaṭṭhena viññāṇakkhandhassa vayaṃ passati.* S III 59–61: ... *āhāranirodhā rūpanirodho. ... phassanirodhā vedanānirodho. ... phassanirodhā saññānirodho. ... phassanirodhā saṅkhāranirodho. ... nāmarūpanirodhā viññāṇanirodho.*

45. 成滿, or "pervasive", or "complete". Elsewhere in Vim this corresponds to forms of *pharati* and *pūreti*. This passage could also be translated as "... [but] the vision

reality the danger of the formations and the mind emerges from the sign of formations and crosses over to the formationless (*visaṅkhāra*).[46] [**455b**] When one has seen according to reality the danger of the formations, the mind emerges from the sign of formations and crosses over to the formationless, where one fully sees suffering because one has gone to the end [of suffering].[47]

It is like a flying bird surrounded by a fire. It is not yet free from [danger and] fear if it has not yet reached the open sky. When it sees the danger of the surrounding fire, it flies into the sky and then fully sees the fearfulness of the surrounding fire.[48] Thus should it be understood.

Herein, by the seeing of arising through cause and through condition, there is penetration (*paṭivedha*) of the arising-characteristic of dependent arising: "When this exists, this is. Owing to the arising of this, this arises".[49]

By the seeing of falling away through cause and through condition, there is penetration of the cessation-characteristic of dependent arising:[50] "When

---

of that suffering is not yet full until ..." Cf. 455c10–11 below.

46. Vism XXII.5/p.672: *Sabbaṃ nimittārammaṇam-pi sabbaṃ pavattārammaṇam-pi palibodhato upaṭṭhāti. Athassa sabbasmiṃ nimittapavattārammaṇe palibodhato upaṭṭhite anulomañāṇassa āsevanante animittaṃ appavattaṃ visaṅkhāraṃ nirodhaṃ nibbānaṃ ārammaṇaṃ kurumānaṃ* ... XXII.6 ... *taṃ saṅkhārārammaṇaṃ muñcitvā gotrabhucittena visaṅkhāre paratīrabhūte nibbāne patati.* Spk III 144: *uppādaṃ anāvajjitattā anuppādaṃ āvajjitattā satisambojjhaṅgo tiṭṭhati, pavattaṃ, appavattaṃ, nimittaṃ, animittaṃ saṅkhāre anāvajjitattā, visaṅkhāraṃ āvajjitattā satisambojjhaṅgo tiṭṭhatī ti.* Vism-mhṭ II 216: *Vivaṭṭānupassanāya hi saṅkhārehi patilīyamānamānasassa uppajjamānaṃ maggañāṇaṃ visaṅkhāraṃ dukkhanissaraṇaṃ ārammaṇaṃ katvā dukkhaṃ paricchindati, dukkhagatañ-ca taṇhaṃ pajahati, nirodhañ-ca sacchikaroti phusati.*

47. 謂往邊故. Elsewhere 邊 corresponds to *pariyanta*. Cf. Nidd I 20: *So pāraṃ gato pārappatto antagato antappatto koṭigato koṭippatto pariyantagato ... nibbānappatto.*

48. In the original text the bird would at first not have been aware of the danger and therefore not fearful, but then, having seen the danger, it becomes fearful and flies away to the open sky. Cf. the simile of the house on fire at Vism XXI.94–95, and the simile of the bird surrounded by fire in the desire-for-release-knowledge topic below.

49. Ud 1: *Imasmiṃ sati idaṃ hoti, imass' uppādā idaṃ uppajjati, yadidaṃ: avijjāpaccayā saṅkhārā.*

50. 故以見滅因緣生相成通達. Lit. "the characteristic of cessation of dependent arising birth" or "... cessation of birth/production of dependent arising". The characters 因緣生 are elsewhere in Chinese texts used to translate *pratītya-samutpanna/paṭicca-samuppanna*, but not in Vim (*paṭicca-samuppannā dhammā* = 因緣所起法 or 因緣法), but it is not found in the preceding characteristic of arising (因緣起相) and 生 could be a corruption.

Cf. Paṭis I 55 in fn 24 above, and Ud-a 38: *Imasmiṃ sati idaṃ hotī ti imasmiṃ avijjādike paccaye sati idaṃ saṅkhārādikaṃ phalaṃ hoti. Imassuppādā idaṃ uppajjatī ti imassa avijjādikassa paccayassa uppādā idaṃ saṅkhārādikaṃ phalaṃ uppajjatī ti attho. Imasmiṃ asati idaṃ na hoti, imassa nirodhā idaṃ nirujjhatī ti avijjādīnaṃ abhāve saṅkhārādīnaṃ*

this does not exist, this is not. Owing to the cessation of this, this ceases".[51]

Having seen arising through essential nature and through rise and fall, there is penetration. Knowing the arising of dependently arisen states, of conditioned states, one also knows their falling away and knows their persistence (*ṭhiti*).

13. Four states

Thus, by seeing rise and fall, four methods (*naya*) are known: (1) the method of unity (*ekatta*), (2) the method of diversity (*nānatta*), (3) the method of unconcern (*avyāpāratā*), and (4) the method of such-naturedness (*evaṃdhammatā*).[52]

---

abhāvassa avijjādīnaṃ nirodhe saṅkhārādīnaṃ nirodhassa ca dutiyatatiyasuttavacanena etasmiṃ paccayalakkhaṇe niyamo dassito hoti imasmiṃ sati eva, nāsati. Imassuppādā eva, nānuppādā. Anirodhā eva, na nirodhāti. Tenetaṃ lakkhaṇaṃ antogadhaniyamaṃ idha paṭiccasamuppādassa vuttan-ti daṭṭhabbaṃ. Nirodho ti ca avijjādīnaṃ virāgādhigamena āyatiṃ anuppādo appavatti. Tathā hi vuttaṃ avijjāya tveva asesavirāganirodhā saṅkhāranirodho ti ādi. Nirodhanirodhī ca uppādanirodhībhāvena vutto imassa nirodhā idaṃ nirujjhatī ti. Ud 2: *Imasmiṃ asati idaṃ na hoti, imassa nirodhā idaṃ nirujjhati, yadidaṃ: avijjānirodhā saṅkhāranirodho ...*

51. Vism XX.101/p.632: *Paccayato cassa udayadassanena anulomo paṭiccasamuppādo pākaṭo hoti, imasmiṃ sati idaṃ hotī ti avabodhato. Paccayato vayadassanena paṭilomo paṭiccasamuppādo pākaṭo hoti, imassa nirodhā idaṃ nirujjhatī ti avabodhato. Khaṇato pana udayabbayadassanena paṭiccasamuppannā dhammā pākaṭā honti saṅkhatalakkhaṇāvabodhato. Udayabbayavanto hi saṅkhatā, te ca paṭiccasamuppannā ti.*

52. Cf. Vism XVII.309/p.585; Vibh-a 198–9: *Yasmā panettha ekattanayo, nānattanayo, abyāpāranayo, evaṃdhammatānayoti cattāro atthanayā honti, tasmā nayabhedatopetaṃ bhavacakkaṃ viññātabbaṃ yathārahaṃ. Tattha avijjāpaccayā saṅkhārā, saṅkhārapaccayā viññāṇan-ti evaṃ bījassa aṅkurādibhāvena rukkhabhāvappatti viya santānānupacchedo ekattanayo nāma. Yaṃ sammā passanto hetuphalasambandhena santānassa anupacchedāvabodhato ucchedadiṭṭhiṃ pajahati. Micchā passanto hetuphalasambandhena pavattamānassa santānānupacchedassa ekattagahaṇato sassatadiṭṭhiṃ upādiyati. Avijjādīnaṃ pana yathāsakaṃlakkhaṇavavatthānaṃ nānattanayo nāma. Yaṃ sammā passanto navanavānaṃ uppādadassanato sassatadiṭṭhiṃ pajahati. Micchā passanto ekasantānapatitassa bhinnasantānasseva nānattaggahaṇato ucchedadiṭṭhiṃ upādiyati. Avijjāya saṅkhārā mayā uppādetabbā, saṅkhārānaṃ vā viññāṇaṃ amhehīti evamādibyāpārābhāvo abyāpāranayo nāma. Yaṃ sammā passanto kārakassa abhāvāvabodhato attadiṭṭhiṃ pajahati. Micchā passanto yo asatipi byāpāre avijjādīnaṃ sabhāvaniyamasiddho hetubhāvo, tassa aggahaṇato akiriyadiṭṭhiṃ upādiyati. Avijjādīhi pana kāraṇehi saṅkhārādīnaṃ yeva sambhavo khīrādīhi dadhi ādīnaṃ viya, na aññesan-ti ayaṃ evaṃdhammatānayo nāma. Yaṃ sammā passanto paccayānurūpato phalāvabodhā ahetukadiṭṭhiṃ akiriyadiṭṭhiñca pajahati. Micchā passanto paccayānurūpaṃ phalappavattiṃ aggahetvā yato kutoci yassa kassaci asambhavaggahaṇato ahetukadiṭṭhiñceva niyatavādañ-ca upādiyatī ti.* Vism XX.102/p.632: *Paccayato cassa udayadassanena ekattanayo pākaṭo hoti hetuphalasambandhena*

Herein, by seeing the formations that are being grasped as a single continuity (*eka-santāna*) through arising, there is no clinging to diversity. By seeing the formations that are adverted to first and last[53] through falling away, there is no clinging to unity. By seeing the formations first and last as intrinsic natures (*sabhāva*) that are devoid [of a soul] and indifferent,[54] there

---

santānassa anupacchedāvabodhato. Atha suṭṭhutaraṃ ucchedadiṭṭhiṃ pajahati. Khaṇato udayadassanena nānattanayo pākaṭo hoti navanavānaṃ uppādāvabodhato. Atha suṭṭhutaraṃ sassatadiṭṭhiṃ pajahati. Paccayato cassa udayabbayadassanena abyāpāranayo pākaṭo hoti dhammānaṃ avasavattibhāvāvabodhato. Atha suṭṭhutaraṃ attadiṭṭhiṃ pajahati. Paccayato pana udayadassanena evaṃdhammatānayo pākaṭo hoti paccayānurūpena phalassa uppādāvabodhato. Atha suṭṭhutaraṃ akiriyadiṭṭhiṃ pajahati.

53. This refers to the delimitation of formations, see next topic, § 14.

54. 自性離無動諸行. As to 自性離 "intrinsic nature devoid of/separate from": If 離 qualifies 性離, then it should come before it (i.e. 離性離), and it would contradict the statement later in this discussion that formations "persist as intrinsic natures and conditions". Probably characters that denote "soul", *jīva*, or "being", *satta*, got lost here; see the Mil and Vism-mhṭ parallels below, or there perhaps was something similar to *īhābhogavivajjitā* or *īhābyāpārarahita* "devoid of interest and concern"; see Pali passages below. 無動 corresponds to *nirīhaka*, "inactive, indifferent, desireless, without endeavour", which occurs along with *abyāpāra* and *nijjīva* in Vim (at 455b28 later in this section) and in Pali texts. Ñāṇamoli renders *nirīhaka* & *abyāpāra* as "incurious" and "uninterested"; see PoP XVIII.309, fn. 47. Cf. Mil 413: ... *sattavināsaṃ navasattapātubhāvaṃ saṅkhārasassatabhāvaṃ yo karoti, so paṭisaṃvedeti, añño karoti, añño paṭisaṃvedeti, kammaphaladassanā ca kiriyaphaladiṭṭhi ca iti evarūpāni ceva aññāni ca vivādapathāni apanetvā saṅkhārānaṃ sabhāvaṃ paramasuññataṃ nirīhanijjīvataṃ accantaṃ suññataṃ ādiyitabbaṃ.* Vism-mhṭ II 389: *Tesu ime dhammā satipi suññanirīha-abyāpārabhāve dhammasabhāvato ādhipaccavasena pavattantī ti anattalakkhaṇavibhāvanatthaṃ indriyāni gahitāni.* Cf. Abhidh-av 762–63: *Hetuhetusamuppannā, īhābhogavivajjitā; ... Saṅkhārādisabhāvā ti, ...* Vism XV.15: *Tathā nirīhakato abyāpārato ca. Na hi cakkhurūpādīnaṃ evaṃ hoti aho vata amhākaṃ sāmaggiyaṃ viññāṇaṃ nāma uppajjeyyā ti, na ca tāni viññāṇuppādanatthaṃ dvārabhāvena vatthubhāvena ārammaṇabhāvena vā īhanti, na byāpāramāpajjanti, atha kho dhammatāvesā, yaṃ cakkhurūpādisāmaggiyaṃ cakkhuviññāṇādīni sambhavantī ti. Tasmā nirīhakato abyāpārato ca daṭṭhabbāni.* Vism-mhṭ II 175: *Dhammatāvā ti sabhāvo eva, kāraṇasamatthatā vā īhābyāpārarahitānaṃ dvārādibhāvo dhammatā.* Vism XVIII.32: *Tasmā yathā dāruyantaṃ suññaṃ nijjīvaṃ nirīhakaṃ, atha ca pana dārurajjukasamāyogavasena gacchatipi tiṭṭhatipi. Saīhakaṃ sabyāpāraṃ viya khāyati, evamidaṃ nāmarūpam-pi suññaṃ nijjīvaṃ nirīhakaṃ, atha ca pana aññamaññasamāyogavasena gacchatipi tiṭṭhatipi. Saīhakaṃ sabyāpāraṃ viya khāyatī ti daṭṭhabbaṃ.* Abhidh-av-pṭ II 307: *Yathā dārumayaṃ yantaṃ nijjīvaṃ jīvavirahitaṃ abbhantare vattamānassa jīvassa abhāvato tato yeva nirīhakaṃ nibyāpāraṃ, atha ca pana dārurajjusamāyoge paccayavisesavasena taṃ dāruyantaṃ gacchatipi tiṭṭhatipi, sajīvaṃ sabyāpāraṃ viya gamanādikiccaṃ sādhentamiva khāyati, tathā idaṃ nāmarūpam-pi kiñcāpi nijjīvaṃ nirīhakañ-ca, atha ca pana aññamaññasaṅkhatapaccayavisesassa samāyoge sajīvaṃ sabyāpāraṃ gacchantaṃ tiṭṭhantañ-ca khāyatī ti.*

is no clinging to a self.[55] By seeing the formations that are adverted to first and last as dependently arisen states, there is no clinging to unconcern.

The uninstructed worldling, through not understanding unity, gives rise to the doctrine of annihilationism (*ucchedavāda*). Through not understanding diversity, he gives rise to the doctrine of eternalism (*sassatavāda*). Through not understanding unconcern, he gives rise to the doctrine of a self (*attavāda*). Through not understanding such-naturedness, he gives rise to the doctrine of inefficacy of kamma (*akiriyavāda*).[56]

Herein, in [the sense of] general words (*sāmañña-vacana*), there is unity; in [the sense of] specific words, there is diversity.[57] In [the sense of] inclusion (*saṅgaha*), there is unity; in the sense of analysis (*vibhaṅga*) there is diversity.[58] In the sense of affliction, there is unity; in the sense of means (*upāya*), there is diversity.[59] In [the sense of] result of craving, there is unity; in [the sense of] result of kamma, there is diversity.

The meditator, seeing unity thus, does not cling to the [annihilationistic] view of diversity; and seeing diversity, he does not cling to the eternalistic view of unity. When seeing unity, he dispels the view that "the one who acts is other than the one who experiences". When seeing diversity, he dispels the view that "the one who acts is the [same as the] one who experiences".[60]

---

55. In line with the results of the other three methods, this should be "no clinging to such-naturedness". However, it is not incorrect since further on it is said that "through not understanding unconcern, he effects the doctrine of a self" and "through the understanding of unconcern and such-naturedness, the characteristic of without self is penetrated".

56. See fn. 2133.

57. Cf. M-ṭ I 135: *Tathā arahan-ti sāmaññato adhiṭṭhānaṃ, taṃ avikappetvā visesavacanaṃ vītarāgattā vītadosattā vītamohattā ti. Iminā nayena sesapadesupi sāmaññavisesaniddhāraṇā veditabbā.* Vism-mhṭ I 449: *Nānattekattato ti visesasāmaññato. Dhammānaṃ hi aññamaññaṃ visadisatā nānattaṃ, samānatā ekattaṃ.*

58. The construction in the first part of this paragraph (of which no parallel can be traced in the Pali) is corrupt. In accordance with the required oppositions of unity and diversity, as in the latter part, read it as: 以平等語言成一相, 以勝語言成種種相, 以攝成一相, 以分別義成種種.

59. Cf. Paṭis I 102: *Nānattekattan-ti kāmacchando nānattaṃ, nekkhammaṃ ekattaṃ. ... Nīvaraṇā nānattaṃ, paṭhamaṃ jhānaṃ ekattaṃ ... pe ... sabbe kilesā nānattaṃ, arahattamaggo ekattaṃ.*

60. ... 餘作餘覺 ... 彼作彼覺 .... Cf. S II 20: *So karoti so paṭisaṃvedayatī ti kho, kassapa, ādito sato sayaṃkataṃ dukkhan-ti iti vadaṃ sassataṃ etaṃ pareti. Añño karoti añño paṭisaṃvedayatī ti kho, kassapa, vedanābhitunnassa sato paraṃkataṃ dukkhan-ti iti vadaṃ ucchedaṃ etaṃ pareti.* Sp II 35: *... so karoti so paṭisaṃvedayatī ti kho, ... iti evaṃ vadanto āditova sassataṃ dīpeti, sassataṃ gaṇhāti. Kasmā? Tassa hi taṃ dassanaṃ etaṃ pareti, kārakañ-ca vedakañ-ca ekam-eva gaṇhantaṃ etaṃ sassataṃ upagacchatī ti attho. ... añño karoti añño paṭisaṃvediyatī ti kho pana, kassapa, ādimhiyeva evaṃ sati, pacchā kārako*

When seeing unity, he dispels the view of annihilationism. When seeing diversity, he dispels the view of eternalism.

The meditator, through [seeing] rise and fall, sees unity and diversity.

Q. How does he know such-naturedness through arising?
A. Seeing the arising of formations, he sees that they are unconcerned.

Q. Why are all formations unconcerned and indifferent?
A. They persist without having been originated by another [being]. They persist as intrinsic natures and conditions[61] that come together and aggregate as dependently arisen [states]. When, through such-naturedness, they are originated, they [in turn] originate [other formations].[62]

---

idheva ucchijjati, tena kataṃ añño paṭisaṃvediyatī ti evaṃ uppannāya ucchedadiṭṭhiyā saddhiṃ sampayuttāya vedanāya abhitunnassa viddhassa sato paraṃkataṃ dukkhan-ti ayaṃ laddhi hotī ti. ... S I 134: *Nayidaṃ attakataṃ bimbaṃ, nayidaṃ parakataṃ aghaṃ, ...*

61. 住自性因緣, lit. "remain/persist intrinsic nature [and] condition". The next paragraph shows that 自性 and 因緣 are two separate words. This reflects the *Peṭakopadesa's* idea that *hetu* as *sabhāva* is the internal, producing, particular cause, while *paccaya* is the external, contributory, shared condition; see Ronkin 2005: 98–99. Peṭ 104: *Sabhāvo hetu, parabhāvo paccayo. ... Ajjhattiko hetu, bāhiro paccayo. ... Nibbattako hetu, paṭiggāhako paccayo. Nevāsiko hetu, āgantuko paccayo. Asādhāraṇo hetu, sādhāraṇo paccayo. Eko yeva hetu, aparāparo paccayo.* Cf. Paṭis-a I 18: *Atthato pana attano sabhāvaṃ dhārentī ti vā, paccayehi dhārīyantī ti vā, ... sakasakalakkhaṇe dhārentī ti vā, ... yathāyogaṃ dhammā ti vuccanti. Idha pana attano paccayehi dhārīyantī ti dhammā, paccayasamuppannā dhammā tiṭṭhanti uppajjanti ceva pavattanti ca etāyā ti dhammaṭṭhiti, paccayadhammānametaṃ adhivacanaṃ.*

62. 和合集為因緣如是以止法生令生. This means that the formations, when originated due to ignorance, etc., in turn automatically originate consciousness, etc. without any being or self being involved; see next fn.

Read 以如是止法 ("through such-naturedness" instead of 如是以止法 "such/thus through naturedness"), so too at 455c03–04.

Cf. Abhidh-av 762–63: *Hetuhetusamuppannā, īhābhogavivajjitā; / Paccayāya ca paccetu-mabyāpārā tato matā. Avijjādīnamevātha, sambhave sambhavanti ca; / Saṅkhārādisabhāvā ti, ṭhitevaṃdhammatāya te.* Nāmar-p vv. 760–764: *Paccayapaccayuppanna-santānabhedato pana. / Nānābhūtānam ekantaṃ, bījarukkhādayo viya / tathā pi tesaṃ dhammānaṃ, vatthulakkhaṇabhedato. / Dīpavaṭṭisikhānaṃ va, natthi ekantam ekatā / hetuhetusamuppannā, īhābhogavivajjitā. / paccayāya ca paccetum abyāpārā tato matā / avijjādīnam evātha, sambhave sambhavanti ca. / Aṅkhārādisabhāvā ti, ṭhit'evaṃdhammatāya te. / ittham ekattanānattā, abyāpāro tathāparo. / Etth' evaṃdhammatā ceti, nayā vuttā catubbidhā.* Vibh-a 198: *Avijjāya saṅkhārā mayā uppādetabbā, saṅkhārānaṃ vā viññāṇaṃ amhehī ti evamādibyāpārābhāvo abyāpāranayo nāma; yaṃ sammā passanto kārakassa abhāvāvabodhato attadiṭṭhiṃ pajahati, micchā passanto yo asatipi byāpāre avijjādīnaṃ sabhāvaniyamasiddho hetubhāvo tassa aggahaṇato akiriyadiṭṭhiṃ upādiyati. Avijjādīhi pana kāraṇehi saṅkhārādīnaṃ yeva sambhavo khīrādīhi dadhi ādīnaṃ viya, na aññesan-ti ayaṃ evaṃdhammatānayo nāma; yaṃ sammā*

Herein, in the sense of soullessness (*nijjīva*) and in the sense of indifference, unconcern should be understood. In the sense of intrinsic nature and in the sense of condition, such-naturedness should be understood.[63] The manifestation of emptiness is unconcern. The manifestation of the kamma that has been done is such-naturedness. **[455c]** The manifestation of unconcern is called "states (*dhamma*)".[64] The manifestation of such-naturedness is called "formations".

Herein, through the understanding of unity, the characteristic of suffering is penetrated; through the understanding of diversity, the characteristic of impermanence is penetrated; and through the understanding of unconcern and through the understanding of such-naturedness, the characteristic of without self is penetrated.

Q. Should the meditator [who wishes] to observe the rise and fall of all formations without remainder[65] do so by observing one place?

A. At the first [one] place of formations he grasps their characteristics and penetrates rise and fall. Then, he pervades all formations without remainder. It is like a man who, having tasted the water in one place at the sea, promptly knows all seawater to be salty. Thus should it be known.

---

passanto paccayānurūpato phalāvabodhato ahetukadiṭṭhiñca akiriyadiṭṭhiñ-ca pajahati, micchā passanto paccayānurūpaṃ phalappavattiṃ aggahetvā yato kutoci yassa kassaci asambhavaggahaṇato ahetukadiṭṭhiñceva niyatavādañ-ca upādiyatī ti.

63. LC: "The Pali term *avyāpāra* means 'inactivity'. The point is that by means of this method one sees that the movement between the links of conditioned origination does not require any activity on one's part. It is an automatic and, as it were, mechanical process. There is no 'doer'. That is why seeing it makes *anattā* clear. But if one does not see that each link naturally has its own activity by which it functions as a cause for the next, one may come to a false vision which denies all causality. The Pali term *evaṃdhammatānaya* is translated by CPD as 'the way of such natural regularity'. Here the point is that by means of this method one sees that the movement between the links of conditioned origination follows definite rules. It is lawful; not random. Just as curds, etc. and not something different arise due to such causes as milk. So seeing it means that one recognizes causality. But if one does not understand the way in which results conform to conditions, one will think in terms of randomness or determinism. Cf. Sn 575: *na hi so upakkamo atthi, yena jātā na miyyare. / jaram-pi patvā maraṇaṃ, evaṃdhammā hi pāṇino*". Cf. Paṭis-a I 121: *Bhūtan ti jātaṃ. Saṅkhatan ti paccayehi saṅgamma kataṃ. Paṭiccasamuppannan ti te te paccaye paṭicca sammā saha ca uppannaṃ. Paṭhamena sañjātattadīpanena aniccatā, dutiyena aniccassā-pi sato paccayānubhāvadīpanena parāyattatā, tatiyena parāyattassā-pi sato paccayānaṃ abyāpārattadīpanena evaṃdhammatā dīpitā hoti.*

64. 如是止法令現無事名法. Cf. As-anuṭ 37: *nissattanijjīvaṭṭhena dhammā ti abyāpārato suññatāmukhena avataraṇaṃ,*

65. 無餘處 = *anavasesa/niravasesa* + *ṭhāṇa* "without remainder place".

He pervades formations in two ways: through object and through non-delusion.

Herein, grasping the characteristics of the formations, he penetrates rise and fall. Those formations are pervaded through that object. Therefore, because of the abandoning of non-knowledge, the remaining formations are pervaded through non-delusion.

Thus is there knowledge of rise and fall (*udayabbayañāṇa*).

14. Knowledge of delimitation of formations

With regard to the knowledge of delimitation of formations (*saṅkhāra-paricchedañāṇa*): Because of the first extremity (*anta*) of arising of all formations, there is delimitation. Because of the last extremity of falling away of all formations, there is delimitation.

Because of the first extremity of arising, there is separation. Because of the last extremity of falling away, there is separation.[66] Because of arising, following their arising they are without former [ones]. Because of falling away, following their falling away they are without later [ones].[67]

Therefore, the knowledge of rise and fall is the knowledge of delimitation of formations.

The knowledge of rise and fall is finished.

15. Knowledge of the contemplation of dissolution

The meditator, rightly contemplating the characteristics of arising and falling away, having analysed well the formations, and wishing to obtain cessation and calm, does not attend to [arising], does not contemplate arising, but sees only the dissolution of mind.[68]

---

66. Cf. Vism II 425 (on Vism XX.103/p.632): *Pubbantāparantaviveko atītānāgata-bhāvasuññatā. Na hi saṅkhārā khaṇattayato pubbe, pacchā ca vijjanti, tasmā pubbantāparantavivekāvabodhato ti ādi-antavantatā paṭivedhato ti attho.*

67. Cf. Paṭis II 48: *Sabbasaṅkhāre paricchedaparivaṭumato samanupassanatāya animittāya ca dhātuyā cittasampakkhandanatāya, ...* Paṭis-a III 560: *Sabbasaṅkhāre paricchedaparivaṭumato samanupassanatāyā ti sabbesaṃ saṅkhārānaṃ udayabbayavasena paricchedato ceva parivaṭumato ca samanupassanatāya. ... Aniccānupassanā hi udayato pubbe saṅkhārā natthī ti paricchinditvā tesaṃ gatiṃ samannesamānā vayato paraṃ na gacchanti, ettheva antaradhāyantī ti parivaṭumato pariyantato samanupassati. Sabbasaṅkhārā hi udayena pubbantaparicchinnā, vayena aparantaparicchinnā.* Vism XXI.68/p.657: *Tattha paricchedaparivaṭumato ti udayabbayavasena paricchedato ceva parivaṭumato ca. Aniccānupassanaṃ hi udayato pubbe saṅkhārā natthī ti paricchinditvā tesaṃ gatiṃ samannesamānaṃ vayato paraṃ na gacchanti, ettheva antaradhāyantī ti parivaṭumato samanupassati.*

68. Since the same character 滅 can correspond to *vaya*, *nirodha*, or *bhaṅga*, it is

Through [seeing] the arising and dissolution of the mind [that has arisen] dependent upon the object of matter (*rūpārammaṇa*), he sees the dissolution of the mind [that sees]. Likewise: Through ... the object of feeling .... Through the object ... of perception .... Through ... the object of formations .... Through [seeing] the arising and dissolution of the mind [that has arisen] dependent upon the object of consciousness, he sees the dissolution of the mind [that sees].[69]

16. Three ways of seeing dissolution

Furthermore, he sees dissolution in three ways: through clusters, through pairs, and through analysis.

17. Clusters

Q. How through clusters (*kalāpa*)?

A. He sees through clusters the dissolution of the mind and mental properties that have arisen [dependent] on the basis of [seeing the impermanence of] the various postures.[70]

---

often unclear which Pali term it corresponds to in this section. The same applies to the character 生, corresponding to *udaya, jāti, pabhava, nibbatta,* etc.

Cf. Vism XXI.17/p.642: *Atha vā so evaṃ viratto yathā diṭṭhaṃ saṅkhāragataṃ ... nirodhatova manasikaroti, nirodhamevassa passati, no samudayan-ti attho.*

69. Literally: "Through the object of matter, through the arising and dissolution (or, rise and fall) of the mind which depends on that object, he sees the dissolution of the mind". As happens several times in this section, the Chinese text is not consistent. With the object of consciousness the Chinese has "arising and dissolution of mind" 心生滅, instead of just "dissolution of mind", 心滅.

Cf. Vism XXI.11–13/p.641f.: *Kathaṃ ārammaṇapaṭisaṅkhā bhaṅgānupassane paññā vipassane ñāṇaṃ? Rūpārammaṇatā cittaṃ uppajjitvā bhijjati, taṃ ārammaṇaṃ paṭisaṅkhā tassa cittassa bhaṅgaṃ anupassati.* (Paṭis I 57–58) ... *Tattha rūpārammaṇatā cittaṃ uppajjitvā bhijjatī ti rūpārammaṇaṃ cittaṃ uppajjitvā bhijjati. Atha vā rūpārammaṇabhāve cittaṃ uppajjitvā bhijjatī ti attho. Taṃ ārammaṇaṃ paṭisaṅkhā ti taṃ rūpārammaṇaṃ paṭisaṅkhāya jānitvā, khayato vayato disvā ti attho. Tassa cittassa bhaṅgaṃ anupassatī ti yena cittena taṃ rūpārammaṇaṃ khayato vayato diṭṭhaṃ, tassa cittassa aparena cittena bhaṅgaṃ anupassatī ti attho. Tenāhu porāṇā ñātañ-ca ñāṇañ-ca ubho pi vipassatī ti.*

70. Sv III 768, Ps I 252: ... *catuiriyāpathapariggaṇhanena kāye kāyānupassī viharati. Samudayadhammānupassī vā ti ādīsu pana avijjāsamudayā rūpasamudayo ti ādinā nayena pañcahākārehi rūpakkhandhassa samudayo ca vayo ca nīharitabbo. Tañ hi sandhāya idha samudayadhammānupassī vā ti ādi vuttaṃ. Atthi kāyo ti vā pan'assā ti ādi vuttasadisam eva. Idha pana catuiriyāpathapariggāhikā sati dukkhasaccaṃ, tassā samuṭṭhāpikā purimataṇhā samudayasaccaṃ, ubhinnaṃ appavatti nirodhasaccaṃ, dukkhaparijānano samudayapajahano nirodhārammaṇo ariyamaggo maggasaccaṃ.*

Furthermore, having seen the impermanence of matter, feeling, perception, formations, and consciousness, he then sees through clusters the dissolution of the mind and the mental properties that have arisen dependent upon the object of [seeing] impermanence. In the same way, with the object of suffering and the object of without self.[71]

Thus, one should see through clusters.

18. Pairs

Q. How through pairs (*yamaka*)?

A. Having contemplated impermanence [thinking] "matter is impermanent", he sees the arising and dissolution of the mind[72] that occurs following[73] the object of impermanence.[74]

Likewise: Having contemplated "feeling ... "perception ... "formations ... "consciousness is impermanent", he sees the arising and the dissolution of the mind that occurs following the object of impermanence. In the same way, with the object of suffering and the object of without self.

Thus should he contemplate through pairs.

19. Analysis

Q. How through analysis (*vibhaṅga*)?

A. Having contemplated "matter is impermanent", he sees the arising and dissolution of the mind that occurs following the object of impermanence.

---

71. Cf. Vism XX. 78/p.626: ... *rūpaṃ aniccaṃ dukkhamanattā ti pavattaṃ cittaṃ aparena cittena aniccaṃ dukkhamanattā ti sammasanto kalāpato sammasatī ti vuttaṃ,* ... Cf. Paṭis I 57–8.

72. In this method and the next, the text has "arising and dissolution of the mind", 心生滅, not "dissolution of the mind", 心滅, as in the first method. In conformity with the topic, the latter is preferable, but because the text consistently has the former, it is left in this way.

73. 隨無常事起. Or "along with", or "subsequent to" = *anuvattati*? According to the Abhidhamma no two minds can arise at the same time. Cf. 446c09: 此四法彼隨起. Perhaps it corresponds to *aparena* in Vism XX. 78–79. See preceding and following fn.

74. Cf. Vism XX. 79/p.626: ... *Yamakato ti idha bhikkhu ādānanikkheparūpaṃ aniccaṃ dukkhamanattā ti sammasitvā tam-pi cittaṃ aparena cittena aniccaṃ dukkhamanattā ti sammasati.* ... S IV 67–68: *Dvayaṃ ... paṭicca viññāṇaṃ sambhoti. ... Manañ-ca paṭicca dhamme ca uppajjati manoviññāṇaṃ. Mano anicco vipariṇāmī aññathābhāvī. Dhammā aniccā .... Itthetaṃ dvayaṃ calañceva vyayañ-ca aniccaṃ vipariṇāmi aññathābhāvi. Manoviññāṇaṃ aniccaṃ ... Yo pi hetu yo pi paccayo manoviññāṇassa uppādāya, so pi hetu so pi paccayo anicco ... Aniccaṃ kho pana ... paccayaṃ paṭicca uppannaṃ manoviññāṇaṃ, kuto niccaṃ bhavissati? ...*

[**456a**] [By seeing the dissolution of the mind, he again sees dissolution.][75] Thus, through analysis, he reflects on the dissolution of many mind [-moments].[76] Likewise, having contemplated the impermanence of feeling ... perception ... formations ... consciousness, he sees the arising and dissolution of the mind that occurs following the object of impermanence. By seeing the dissolution of the mind, he again sees dissolution. Thus, through analysis, he sees the dissolution of many mind [-moments]. Likewise, he contemplates suffering and without self.

Having thus analysed, he now just contemplates dissolution. That object of the cessation of suffering becomes the focus [of contemplation]. Constantly investigating the momentariness of formations, he obtains sharpness [of faculties].[77]

The meditator, through this knowledge, which is independent of another (*aparapaccaya*), sees the entire world through its intrinsic nature (*sabhāva*) as [unenduring as] a mustard seed on the point [of an awl],[78] and that in a single mind-moment (*citta-khaṇa*) there is birth and the change of ageing and death.[79]

A. this time, the meditator knows in accordance with what is taught in verse thus:

---

75. This is supplied from the parallel sentence on the consciousness aggregate below. On the contemplation of dissolution of the mind, see § 15 above.

76. 如是以分別觀見多心滅. Perhaps the original text intended: "through analysis of many mind [-moments] (*cittakkhaṇāni?*) he reflects on dissolution" or "through analysis he much reflects on the dissolution of mind".

77. Cf. 432a04: "'Momentary death' means: 'The momentary dissolution of formations'" and the explanation of "contemplating death through momentariness" at 432b26ff: "... a being's life-span lasts a single mind-moment. ..."

78. See fn. 2173 to the last verse below. Cf. Sn 625: *Vāri pokkharapatte va, āragge-r-iva sāsapo, yo na lippati kāmesu, tam-ahaṃ brūmi brāhmaṇaṃ.*

79. 生老死變 = "birth ageing death change".

Cf. Paṭis-a 104/Vism XXII.116/p.695 *Vipariṇāmānupassanā ti rūpasattaka-arūpasattakādivasena taṃ taṃ paricchedaṃ atikkamma aññathā pavattidassanaṃ. Uppannassa vā jarāya ceva maraṇena ca dvīhākārehi vipariṇāmadassanaṃ.* Paṭis-a 254: *Yaṃ pana nibbattilakkhaṇavipariṇāmalakkhaṇāni passanto khandhānaṃ udayabbayaṃ passati, idamassa khaṇato udayabbayadassanaṃ. Uppattikkhaṇe yeva hi nibbattilakkhaṇaṃ, bhaṅgakkhaṇe ca vipariṇāmalakkhaṇaṃ.* Vism XX.19: *Jarāya ceva maraṇena cā ti dvedhā pariṇāmapakatitāya vipariṇāmadhammato.* XX.95: *... jātassa nāmarūpassa nibbattilakkhaṇaṃ jātiṃ uppādaṃ abhinavākāraṃ udayo ti, vipariṇāmalakkhaṇaṃ khayaṃ bhaṅgaṃ vayo ti samanupassati.* Paṭis II 178: *Katamaṃ vipariṇāmasuññaṃ? Jātaṃ rūpaṃ sabhāvena suññaṃ. Vigataṃ rūpaṃ vipariṇatañceva suññañ-ca. Jātā vedanā sabhāvena suññā. Vigatā vedanā vipariṇatā ceva suññā ca ...* Paṭis-a 632: *Jarābhaṅgavasena virūpo pariṇāmo vipariṇāmo, tena vipariṇāmena suññaṃ vipariṇāmasuññaṃ.*

The pair of name-and-matter depend on each other,
When one breaks up, both conditions break up.[80]
[Since] they originate from a cause, [81]
The aggregates are impermanent, of the nature of breaking up.
Suffering is of the nature to arise and to fall away.[82]

The five states of forms, odors, and the rest,
Arise not from the eye nor from forms,
Yet are not separate from both of them,
They originate from a cause and are conditioned,[83]
Just as the sound of a drum struck by a stick.

The five states of forms, odors, and the rest,
Arise not from the ear nor from sounds,
Yet are not separate from both of them,
They originate from a cause and are conditioned,
Just as the sound of a drum struck by a stick.

The five states of forms, odors, and the rest,
Arise not from the nose nor from odors,

---

80. Cf. Vism XVIII.32/p.535: *Yathā hi dvīsu naḷakalāpīsu aññamaññaṃ nissāya ṭhapitāsu ekā ekissā upatthambho hoti, ekissā patamānāya itarāpi patati, evam-evaṃ pañcavokārabhave nāmarūpaṃ aññamaññaṃ nissāya pavattati, ekaṃ ekassa upatthambho hoti. Maraṇavasena ekasmiṃ patamāne itaram-pi patati. Tenāhu porāṇā: Yamakaṃ nāmarūpañ-ca, ubho aññoññanissitā, / Ekasmiṃ bhijjamānasmiṃ, ubho bhijjanti paccayā ti.* The verse by the *porāṇā* is also found at Abhidh-av v. 1215.

81. 及彼因所生 "and they/that originated/produced from a cause", *te ca hetu-pabhavā/-samuṭṭhāna?* This clause and the following verse on the aggregates and suffering cannot be found in Pali parallels of the preceding verse and apparently belong to the following. Cf. S I 134: *Evaṃ khandhā ca dhātuyo, ... / Hetuṃ paṭicca sambhūtā, hetubhaṅgā nirujjhare ti.* Paṭis I 51: *... viññāṇaṃ hetu, nāmarūpaṃ hetusamuppannaṃ ...*

82. Or "Suffering, of the nature to arise and fall away" referring to the aggregates as suffering. Cf. S II 17: *Dukkham-eva uppajjamānaṃ uppajjati, dukkhaṃ nirujjhamānaṃ nirujjhatī ti.*

83. Vism XVIII.33/p.535: *Yathā ca daṇḍābhihataṃ bheriṃ nissāya sadde pavattamāne aññā bherī, añño saddo, bherisaddā asammissā, bherī saddena suññā, saddo bheriyā suñño, evam-evaṃ vatthudvārārammaṇasaṅkhātaṃ rūpaṃ nissāya nāme pavattamāne aññaṃ rūpaṃ, aññaṃ nāmaṃ, nāmarūpā asammissā, nāmaṃ rūpena suññaṃ, rūpaṃ nāmena suññaṃ, apica kho bheriṃ paṭicca saddo viya rūpaṃ paṭicca nāmaṃ pavattati. Tenāhu porāṇā:*

Na cakkhuto jāyare phassapañcamā, / Na rūpato no ca ubhinnamantarā; / Hetuṃ paṭiccappabhavanti saṅkhatā, / Yathā pi saddo pahaṭāya bheriyā. / Na sotato ... saddato ... ghānato ... gandhato ... jivhāto ... rasato ... kāyato ... phassato ... / Na vatthurūpā pabhavanti saṅkhatā, / Na cāpi dhammāyatanehi niggatā; / Hetuṃ paṭiccappabhavanti saṅkhatā, / Yathā pi saddo pahaṭāya bheriyā ti.

Yet are not separate from both of them,
They originate from a cause and are conditioned,
Just as the sound of a drum struck by a stick.

The five states of forms, odors, and the rest,
Arise not from the tongue nor from taste,
Yet are not separate from both of them,
They originate from a cause and are conditioned,
Just as the sound of a drum struck by a stick.

The five states of forms, odors, and the rest,
Arise not from the body nor from touch,
Yet are not separate from both of them,
They originate from a cause and are conditioned,
Just as the sound of a drum struck by a stick.

They do not originate from the material basis (*vatthurūpa*),
Nor do they emerge from the sense base of mental states.
They originate from a cause and are conditioned,
Just as the sound of a drum struck by a stick.

Their root is weak; weak are their former causes, weak their conditions,
Weak are their originators, weak their common grounds,
Weak are their connections, and weak their associates,
[Being dependent] on each other, they are always weak.

Being of a reciprocal nature, they are unsettled, [**456b**]
They cannot establish each other,
They cannot originate, nor do they have an originator,
Like a town of gandhabbas are their former originators.[84]

---

84. Cf. Nidd I 43: *Kathaṃ sarasaparittatāya appakaṃ jīvitaṃ? Assāsūpanibandhaṃ jīvitaṃ, ... viññāṇūpanibandhaṃ jīvitaṃ. Mūlam-pi imesaṃ dubbalaṃ, pubbahetūpi imesaṃ dubbalā. Ye paccayā tepi dubbalā, yepi pabhāvikā tepi dubbalā. Sahabhūmi imesaṃ dubbalā, sampayogāpi imesaṃ dubbalā, sahajāpi imesaṃ dubbalā, yāpi payojikā sāpi dubbalā, aññamaññaṃ ime niccadubbalā, aññamaññaṃ anavaṭṭhitā ime. Aññamaññaṃ paripātayanti ime, aññamaññassa hi natthi tāyitā, na cāpi ṭhapenti aññamaññaṃ ime. Yo pi nibbattako so na vijjati.* (Verses:) *Na ca kenaci koci hāyati, / gandhabbā ca ime hi sabbaso; / Purimehi pabhāvikā ime, yepi pabhāvikā te pure matā; / Purimāpi ca pacchimā pi ca, aññamaññaṃ na kadāci maddasaṃsū-ti.*

Nidd-a I 152: *Idāni nesaṃ dubbalakāraṇaṃ dassento mūlam-pi imesaṃ dubbalanti ādim-āha. Tattha mūlam-pī ti patiṭṭhaṭṭhena mūlabhūtam-pi. Assāsapassāsānañ-hi karajakāyo mūlaṃ. Mahābhūtādīnaṃ avijjākammataṇhāhārā. Imesan-ti vuttappakārānaṃ assāsādīnaṃ jīvitindriyapavattikāraṇavasena vuttānaṃ. Etesu hi ekekasmiṃ asati jīvitindriyaṃ na tiṭṭhati. Dubbalan-ti appathāmaṃ. Pubbahetū pī ti atītajātiyaṃ imassa vipākavaṭṭassa hetubhūtā kāraṇasaṅkhātā avijjāsaṅkhārataṇhupādānabhavā pi. Imesaṃ dubbalā ye paccayā te pi dubbalā ti ye ārammaṇādisādhāraṇapaccayā. Pabhāvikā ti padhānaṃ hutvā uppādikā bhavataṇhā.*

They do not arise by themselves,
Nor persist by their own strength.
They arise in compliance to other states,
When arisen they are subject to contaminations.

They are not self-produced by their own strength,
Nor by their own causes, nor by their own objects,
They are conditioned, their grounds are not self-produced,
Their activities (*ākāra, byāpāra*) are not self-produced,
Conditioned, weak in themselves, they arise.[85]

Immediately it goes nowhere,
And from nowhere it comes;
It is not born in another land—
The mind is without a self.[86]

Life and selfhood;
Happiness and suffering,
are joined in one mind [-moment];
quickly the moment [passes by].

Deities [who are living] 80,000 aeons,[87]
Live [joined in just] one [mind] and not to a second,
[They do] not [live] joined in two mind [-moments].[88]

Sahabhūmīti sahabhavikāpi rūpārūpadhammā. Sampayogāpīti ekato yuttāpi arūpadhammā. Sahajāpīti saddhiṃ ekacitte uppannāpi. Yā pi payojikā ti cutipaṭisandhivasena yojetuṃ niyuttā ti payojikā, vaṭṭamūlakā taṇhā. Vuttañ-hetaṃ taṇhādutiyo puriso ti. Niccadubbalā ti nirantarena dubbalā. Anavaṭṭhitā ti na avaṭṭhitā, otaritvā na ṭhitā. ... Na cāpi ṭhapenti aññamaññan-ti aññe aññaṃ ṭhapetuṃ na sakkonti. Yo pi nibbattako so na vijjatī ti yo pi imesaṃ uppādako dhammo, so idāni natthi. ... Gandhabbā ca ime hi sabbasoti sabbe hi ime khandhā sabbākārena bhaṅgaṃ pāpuṇituṃ yuttā. Purimehi pabhāvitā imeti pubbahetupaccayehi ime vattamānakā uppādikā. Yepi pabhāvikā ti yepi ime vattamānakā uppādakā pubbahetupaccayā. ...

85. Vism XVIII.35–36/p.596: ... *Tattha jaccandho pi nittejo dubbalo na sakena tejena sakena balena gacchati, pīṭhasappīpi nittejo dubbalo na sakena tejena sakena balena gacchati, na ca tesaṃ aññamaññaṃ nissāya gamanaṃ nappavattati, evam-evaṃ nāmam-pi nittejaṃ na sakena tejena uppajjati, na tāsu tāsu kiriyāsu pavattati. Rūpam-pi nittejaṃ na sakena tejena uppajjati, na tāsu tāsu kiriyāsu pavattati, na ca tesaṃ aññamaññaṃ nissāya uppatti vā pavatti vā na hoti. Tenetaṃ vuccati: Na sakena balena jāyare, / No pi sakena balena tiṭṭhare; / Paradhammavasānuvattino, / Jāyare saṅkhatā attadubbalā. / Parapaccayato ca jāyare, / Para-ārammaṇato samuṭṭhitā; / Ārammaṇapaccayehi ca, / Paradhammehi cime pabhāvitā.*

86. Untraced. On the sense bases not coming from and going to anywhere, cf. Vism XV.15, quoted at fn. 2172.

87. 山海 = "mountains, seas". This is due to mistaking Pali *maru* (= Sanskrit *marut*) "deity" as Sanskrit *maru* "mountain".

88. 一住不再無二心相應 = Nidd I 42: *tveva te pi jīvanti, dvīhi cittehi saṃyutā (v.l.*

Of those who have passed away,
And of those who are remaining,
The aggregates ceased are all alike:
Gone, [and not reuniting again].
Those [aggregates] that have broken up incessantly,
And those that will break up in the future,
Those that are breaking up in the meantime:
They are not different with regard to characteristics.
When it is not produced, it is not born,
Only in the present it lives,
In the ultimate sense the world [dies]
When the mind breaks up.

[When broken up, states] do not become a treasure,[89]
In the future there is no pile of them,
Even those that are produced, persist
Like a mustard seed [on the point of an awl].
States that are born are foredoomed by their dissolution;
Being of the nature to fall apart [they persist],[90]
Not mixing with the former ones.

Invisible is their coming and going,
Invisible is their arising.[91]
Unarisen states are like lightning in the sky,
In a moment they arise and pass away.[92]

---

samohitā); see below. Nidd-a I 150: *Na tveva te pi jīvanti, dvīhi cittasamohitā ti tepi devā dvīhi cittehi samohitā ekato hutvā yuganaddhena cittena na tu eva jīvanti, ekenekena cittena jīvantī ti attho.* Vism-mht II 411: *Dvīhi cittehi samohitā ti evaṃ cirajīvino pi te dvīhi cittehi sahitā hutvā na tiṭṭhanti. Idaṃ vuttaṃ hoti tesam-pi santāne jīvitādīni dvīhi cittehi saha na tiṭṭhanti, ekena cittena saha uppannāni teneva saha nirujjhanato yāva dutiyā na tiṭṭhantī ti.*

89. Saṅghapāla did not understand *anidhānagatā* and mistranslated it as "do not go and come", 無去來. Cf. Vism-mhṭ 412: *Anidhānagatā bhaggā ti ye bhaggā, na te katthaci nidhānaṃ gatā, atha kho abhāvam-eva gatā.*

90. Ammend世間以法初不雜 to 世間法以初不雜 = *palokadhammā tiṭṭhanti, purāṇehi amissitā.*

91. 不見去來不見生. The Pali parallel has: "Invisibly they come; breaking up, invisibly they go" *dassanato āyanti, bhaṅgā gacchanti dassanaṃ*; see next fn. Vism XV.15/ p. 484: *Daṭṭhabbato ti ettha pana sabbāneva saṅkhatāni āyatanāni anāgamanato aniggamanato ca daṭṭhabbāni. Na hi tāni pubbe udayā kutoci āgacchanti, na pi uddhaṃ vayā kuhiñci gacchanti, atha kho pubbe udayā appaṭiladdhasabhāvāni, uddhaṃ vayā paribhinnasabhāvāni, pubbantāparantavemajjhe paccayāyattavuttitāya avasāni pavattanti. Tasmā anāgamanato aniggamanato ca daṭṭhabbāni.*

92. The last five verses have a partial parallel in Nidd I 42 (quoted in Vism

Thus, the meditator, who is constantly seeing dissolution, attains concentration. Just as smoke arises when sticks are rubbed together for fire, so do the states that are aids to enlightenment (*bodhipakkhiya*) arise moment by moment.

When brilliance, knowledge, rapture, tranquillity, pleasure, exertion, resolve, establishing of mindfulness, equanimity, and longing[93] arise, if the meditator is unwary (*avyatta*) regarding these states, he will give rise to distraction (*vikkhepa*) or overestimation (*adhimāna*).

Q. How does he dispel distraction?

A. When the meditator gives rise to rapture with regard to the Dhamma, that rapture calms [his mind] again. Thus, calming his mind again, he is [not] seized by agitation with regard to [higher meditative] states (*dhammuddhaccaviggahita*).[94] When his mind is [not] seized by agitation

---

XX.72/p.624–625): *Jīvitaṃ attabhāvo ca, sukhadukkhā ca kevalā; Ekacittasamāyuttā, lahuso vattate khaṇo. / Cullāsītisahassāni, kappā tiṭṭhanti ye marū; Na tveva te pi jīvanti, dvīhi cittehi saṃyutā (= Se. Be: samohitā; Ee: samāhitā). / Ye niruddhā marantassa, tiṭṭhamānassa vā idha; Sabbe pi sadisā khandhā, gatā appaṭisandhikā. / Anantarā ca ye bhaggā, ye ca bhaggā anāgatā; Tadantare niruddhānaṃ, vesamaṃ natthi lakkhaṇe. / Anibbattena na jāto, paccuppannena jīvati; Cittabhaggā mato loko, paññatti paramatthiyā. / Yathā ninnā pavattanti, chandena pariṇāmitā; Acchinnadhārā vattanti, saḷāyatanapaccayā. / Anidhānagatā bhaggā, puñjo natthi anāgate; Nibbattāyeva tiṭṭhanti, āragge sāsapūpamā. / Nibbattānañ-ca dhammānaṃ, bhaṅgo nesaṃ purakkhato; Palokadhammā tiṭṭhanti, purāṇehi amissitā. / Adassanato āyanti, bhaṅgā gacchanti dassanaṃ; Vijjuppādova ākāse, uppajjanti vayanti cā ti. Evaṃ ṭhitiparittatāya appakaṃ jīvitaṃ.*

A prose passage about formations continually arising and passing away in Vism XX.104 mentions the similes of the town of gandhabbas, mustard seed, and lightning flash. Cf. Vism-mhṭ II 426.

93. Cf. Vism XX.105: ... *āraddhavipassakassa dasa vipassanupakkilesā uppajjanti. ... Obhāso, ñāṇaṃ, pīti, passaddhi, sukhaṃ, adhimokkho, paggaho, upaṭṭhānaṃ, upekkhā, nikantī ti.* The order of *paggaha* and *adhimokkha* is different in the Vim than it is in Vism. *Nikanti* is translated into Chinese as "renunciation", 出離, Sanskrit *niṣkrānta.* Spk-ṭ II 170: *Nikanti nāma vipassanāya nikāmanā apekkhā.*

94. *Dhammuddhacca* is agitation caused by the the lesser or subtle defilements (*upakkilesa*) that can arise during the development of insight. Cf. Paṭis II 100f., Vism XX.106: *Aniccato manasikaroto obhāso uppajjati ... nikanti uppajjati, nikanti dhammo ti nikantiṃ āvajjati. Tato vikkhepo uddhaccaṃ. Tena uddhaccena viggahitamānaso. Jarāmaraṇaṃ anattato upaṭṭhānaṃ yathābhūtaṃ nappajānāti. Jarāmaraṇaṃ aniccato upaṭṭhānaṃ yathābhūtaṃ nappajānāti, jarāmaraṇaṃ dukkhato upaṭṭhānaṃ yathābhūtaṃ nappajānāti. Tena vuccati dhammuddhaccaviggahitamānaso hoti. So samayo, yaṃ taṃ cittaṃ ajjhattam-eva santiṭṭhati sannisīdati ekodi hoti samādhiyati. Tassa maggo sañjāyatī ti.* ... Paṭis-a III 585: *Dhammuddhaccaviggahitaṃ mānasaṃ hotī ti ettha mandapaññānaṃ vipassakānaṃ upakkilesavatthuttā vipassanupakkilesasaññitesu obhāsādīsu dasasu dhammesu bhantatāvasena uddhaccasahagatacittuppattiyā vikkhepasaṅkhātaṃ uddhaccaṃ*

with regard to states, his mind abandons [the perception of] permanence through concentration [attained through] the contemplation of dissolution. Abandoning [the perception of] permanence, he penetrates. Thus, he dispels [agitation with regard to higher] states.

Q. How does the meditator dispel overestimation?

A. The meditator who gives rise to the state of brilliance, and so on,[95] thinks that he has attained to supramundane states (*lokuttaradhamma*). He thinks that he has attained what he has not attained and does not endeavour any more. Thus, he gives rise to overestimation.

The meditator who is wary (*vyatta*) knows that these [ten lesser] afflictions are distractions to concentration. He knows that mundane states have formations as object, and likewise, he knows that supramundane states have nibbāna as object. [**456c**]

Having known thus by this knowledge he dispels distraction and overestimation. Seeing only dissolution, he practises it well and practises it much.

The knowledge of the contemplation of dissolution (bhaṅgañāṇa) is finished.

---

dhammuddhaccaṃ, tena dhammuddhaccena viggahitaṃ virūpaggahitaṃ virodhamāpāditaṃ mānasaṃ cittaṃ dhammuddhaccaviggahitaṃ mānasaṃ hoti, tena vā dhammuddhaccena kāraṇabhūtena tammūlakataṇhāmānadiṭṭhuppattiyā viggahitaṃ mānasaṃ hoti. ... Hoti so āvuso samayo ti iminā maggāmaggavavatthānena taṃ dhammuddhaccaṃ paṭibāhitvā puna vipassanāvīthiṃ paṭipannakālaṃ dasseti. Mp III 143 (on A II 157): *Dhammuddhaccaviggahitan-ti samathavipassanādhammesu dasavipassanupakkilesasaṅkhātena uddhaccena viggahitaṃ, suggahitan-ti attho.* A III 285: *Yasmiṃ, mahānāma, samaye ariyasāvako dhammaṃ anussarati nevassa tasmiṃ samaye rāgapariyuṭṭhitaṃ ... na mohapariyuṭṭhitaṃ cittaṃ hoti; ujugatamevassa tasmiṃ samaye cittaṃ hoti dhammaṃ ārabbha. Ujugatacitto kho pana, mahānāma, ariyasāvako labhati atthavedaṃ, labhati dhammavedaṃ, labhati dhammūpasaṃhita pāmojjaṃ. Pamuditassa pīti jāyati, pītimanassa kāyo passambhati, passaddhakāyo sukhaṃ vediyati, sukhino cittaṃ samādhiyati. ... dhammasotaṃ samāpanno dhammānussatiṃ bhāveti.* A I 253: *... santi adhicittamanuyuttassa bhikkhuno oḷārikā upakkilesā kāyaduccaritaṃ ... majjhimasahagatā upakkilesā kāmavitakko ... sukhumasahagatā upakkilesā ... anavaññattipaṭisaṃyutto vitakko, tamenaṃ sacetaso bhikkhu ... anabhāvaṃ gameti. Tasmiṃ pahīne tasmiṃ byantīkate athāparaṃ dhammavitakkāvasissati. So hoti samādhi na ceva santo ... sasaṅkhāraniggayhavāritavato hoti. So ... samayo yaṃ taṃ cittaṃ ajjhattaṃ yeva santiṭṭhati sannisīdati ekodi hoti samādhiyati. So hoti samādhi santo ....* Mp II 362: *Dhammavitakkāvasissantī ti dhammavitakkā nāma dasavipassanupakkilesavitakkā.*

95. Or "at first gives rise to brilliance in the dhamma", but see Nidd II-a 106: *Paṇḍito pana bhikkhu obhāsādīsu uppannesu vikkhepaṃ agacchanto obhāsādayo dhammā na maggo, upakkilesavimuttaṃ pana vīthipaṭipannaṃ vipassanāñāṇaṃ maggo 'ti maggañ-ca amaggañ-ca vavatthapeti.*

20. Knowledge of what is appearing as fearful

Thus, the meditator, contemplating dissolution, owing to discernment of dissolution, becomes fearful; fearful of the cause of the aggregates; fearful of the arising of the aggregates. He fears the three kinds of existence,[96] the five destinations,[97] the seven stations of consciousness,[98] and the nine abodes of beings.[99] He fears them as he would fear a wicked man who holds up a sword,[100] a poisonous snake,[101] or a mass of fire.[102] Thus, owing to his discernment of dissolution, he becomes fearful: fearful of the cause of the aggregates and fearful of the arising of the aggregates.

Through attending in this manner to the impermanence of the three kinds of existence, the five destinations, the seven stations of consciousness and the nine abodes of beings, he gives rise to the perception of fear and through [attending to the] security [from these states],[103] he gives rise to the signless (*animitta*). Through attending to suffering, he fears arising (*uppāda*) and through [attending to] security gives rise to non-arising (*anuppāda*). Through attending to without self, he fears the sign and arising, and through [attending to] security gives rise to the signless and to non-arising.[104]

---

96. D III 216: *Tayo bhava: kāma-bhavo, rūpa-bhavo, arūpa-bhavo.* Cf. Vism XXI.33/p.646: *Yasmā panassa kevalaṃ sabbabhavayonigatiṭhitinivāsagatā saṅkhārā byasanāpannā sappaṭibhayā hutvā bhayato upaṭṭhahanti, tasmā bhayatupaṭṭhānan-ti vuccati.* Paṭis-a I 21: *Bhayatupaṭṭhāne paññā ti uppādapavattanimitta-āyūhanāpaṭisandhīnaṃ bhayato upaṭṭhāne pīḷāyogato sappaṭibhayavasena gahaṇūpagamane paññā ti attho. Bhayato upaṭṭhātī ti bhayatupaṭṭhānaṃ ārammaṇaṃ, tasmiṃ bhayatupaṭṭhāne. Atha vā bhayato upatiṭṭhatī ti bhayatupaṭṭhānaṃ paññā taṃ bhayatupaṭṭhānan-ti vuttaṃ hoti.*

97. D III 234: *pañca gatiyo: nirayo, tiracchāna-yoni, pettivisayo, manussā, devā.*

98. *Satta viññāṇaṭṭhitiya.* See D III 253 at fn. 2439.

99. *Sattāvāsā.* See D III 253 at fn. 2440.

100. Cf. S III 115: *Vadhakaṃ rūpaṃ vadhakaṃ rūpan ti yathābhūtaṃ pajānāti. .... vadhakaṃ viññāṇaṃ ...*

101. Cf. S IV 174: *Cattāro āsīvisā uggatejā ghoravisā ti kho bhikkhave catunnetaṃ mahābhūtānaṃ adhivacanaṃ, paṭhavīdhātuyā āpodhātuyā tejodhātuyā vāyodhātuyā.*

102. S II 84–5: *Seyyathā pi ... dasannaṃ va kaṭṭhavāhānaṃ ... mahā aggikkhandho jāleyya. Tatra puriso kālena kālaṃ sukkhāni ceva tiṇāni ... kaṭṭhāni pakkhipeyya. Evañ-hi so bhikkhave mahā aggikkhandho tadāhāro tadupādāno ciraṃ dīghamaddhānaṃ jāleyya. Evam eva kho bhikkhave upādāniyesu dhammesu assādānupassino viharato taṇhā pavaḍḍhati. Taṇhāpaccayā upādānaṃ ... Evam etassa kevalassa dukkhakkhandhassa samudayo hoti.*

103. Security (*khema*), the signless and non-arising are synonyms of nibbāna. See Paṭis I 13–14: *Uppādo bhayaṃ, anuppādo kheman-ti abhiññeyyaṃ. Pavattaṃ bhayaṃ, appavattaṃ kheman-ti .... Nimittaṃ bhayaṃ, animittaṃ kheman-ti ... Anuppādo nibbānan-ti .... Appavattaṃ nibbānan-ti .... Animittaṃ nibbānan-ti abhiññeyyaṃ.*

104. Cf. Paṭis I 58, Vism XX.37/p.648: *Kathaṃ bhayatupaṭṭhāne paññā ādīnave ñāṇaṃ? Uppādo bhayanti—bhayatupaṭṭhāne paññā ādīnave ñāṇaṃ. Pavattaṃ ... nimittaṃ bhayanti...*

The contemplation of disadvantage (*ādīnava*), the contemplation of disenchantment, and the acceptance in conformity (*anulomika-khanti*)—these are epithets for this [knowledge of what is appearing as fearful].[105]

The knowledge of what is appearing as fearful (bhayatupaṭṭhānañāṇa) is finished.

21. Knowledge of desire for release

The meditator, through developing the knowledge of what is appearing as fearful, gives rise to the knowledge of desire for release (*muñcitakamyatāñāṇa*). When he fears the cause of the aggregates, the knowledge of desire for release arises. When he fears the arising of the aggregates, the knowledge of desire for release arises. When he fears the three kinds of existence, the five destinations, the seven stations of consciousness, and the nine abodes of beings, the knowledge of desire for release arises. It is as a bird encircled by a fire desiring to get free of it, and like a man encircled by robbers desiring to get free of them.

Thus, when the meditator fears the cause of the aggregates, the arising of the aggregates, the three kinds of existence, the five destinations, the seven stations of consciousness, and the nine abodes of beings, the desire-for-release-knowledge arises.[106] Through attending to impermanence,

---

Anuppādo kheman-ti santipade ñāṇaṃ. ... Uppādo bhayaṃ, anuppādo kheman-ti santipade ñāṇaṃ. ... Uppādo dukkhan-ti bhayatupaṭṭhāne paññā ādīnave ñāṇaṃ. ... Paṭis II 63, Vism XXI.33/p.646: *Aniccato manasikaroto nimittaṃ bhayato upaṭṭhāti. Dukkhato manasikaroto pavattaṃ bhayato upaṭṭhāti. Anattato manasikaroto nimittañ-ca pavattañ-ca bhayato upaṭṭhāti. ...* Vism XXI.40/p.649, Paṭis-a I 261: *Anuppādo kheman-ti santipade ñāṇanti ādi pana ādīnavañāṇassa paṭipakkhañāṇadassanatthaṃ vuttaṃ. Bhayatupaṭṭhānena vā ādīnavaṃ disvā ubbiggahadayānaṃ abhayam-pi atthi khemaṃ nirādīnavan-ti assāsajananattham-pi etaṃ vuttaṃ. Yasmā vā panassa uppādādayo bhayato sūpaṭṭhitā honti, tassa tappaṭipakkhaninnaṃ cittaṃ hoti, tasmā bhayatupaṭṭhānavasena siddhassa ādīnavañāṇassa ānisaṃsadassanatthampetaṃ vuttan-ti veditabbaṃ.*

105. 觀過患觀厭離軟隨相似忍. The character 軟 = *mudu* "soft", is an intrusion. 厭離 = *nibbidā*.

Cf. Vism XXI.44/p.651: *Taṃ panetaṃ purimena ñāṇadvayena atthato ekaṃ. Tenāhu porāṇā: Bhayatupaṭṭhānaṃ ekam-eva tīṇi nāmāni labhati, sabbasaṅkhāre bhayato addasā ti bhayatupaṭṭhānaṃ nāma jātaṃ. Tesuyeva saṅkhāresu ādīnavaṃ uppādetī ti ādīnavānupassanā nāma jātaṃ. Tesu yeva saṅkhāresu nibbindamānaṃ uppannan-ti nibbidānupassanā nāma jātan-ti. Pāḷiyam-pi vuttaṃ* (Paṭis II 63): *Yā ca bhayatupaṭṭhāne paññā, yañ-ca ādīnave ñāṇaṃ, yā ca nibbidā, ime dhammā ekatthā, byañjanam-eva nānan-ti.*

106. Cf. Paṭis I 61: *Uppādo bhayan-ti muñcitukamyatā paṭisaṅkhā santiṭṭhanā pañña saṅkhārupekkhāsu ñāṇaṃ pavattaṃ bhayan-ti muñcitukamyatā paṭisaṅkhā santiṭṭhanā paññā saṅkhārupekkhāsu ñāṇaṃ ... pe ... 'upāyāso bhayan' ti muñcitukamyatā paṭisaṅkhā santiṭṭhanā paññā saṅkhārupekkhāsu ñāṇaṃ.*

he fears the cause; through attending to suffering, he fears arising; and through attending to without self, he fears both cause and arising. Then the knowledge of desire for release arises.

For a worldling and trainee, there are two ways of directing the mind towards desire for release: He delights in it or sees it with insight. [**457a**] When he sees it with insight, there is higher penetration. When he delights in it, his mind becomes defiled, which is an obstacle to development, an obstruction to penetration.[107]

The reflection-contemplation, equanimity towards the formations, and acceptance in conformity (*anulomika-khanti*)—these are epithets [for the knowledge of desire for release].[108]

The knowledge of desire for release is finished.

---

107. Paṭis I 62: *Puthujjanassa katamehi dvīhākārehi saṅkhārupekkhāya cittassa abhinīhāro hoti? Puthujjano saṅkhārupekkhaṃ abhinandati vā vipassati vā. Sekkho saṅkhārupekkhaṃ abhinandati vā vipassati vā paṭisaṅkhāya vā phalasamāpattiṃ samāpajjati.... Kathaṃ puthujjanassa ca sekkhassa ca saṅkhārupekkhāya cittassa abhinīhāro ekattaṃ hoti? Puthujjanassa saṅkhārupekkhaṃ abhinandato cittaṃ kilissati, bhāvanāya paripantho hoti, paṭivedhassa antarāyo hoti, āyatiṃ paṭisandhiyā paccayo hoti. Sekkhassa pi saṅkhārupekkhaṃ abhinandato cittaṃ kilissati, bhāvanāya paripantho hoti, uttaripaṭivedhassa antarāyo hoti, āyatiṃ paṭisandhiyā paccayo hoti.* Paṭis-a I 270: *Cittaṃ kilissatī ti vipassanānikantisaṅkhātena lobhakilesena cittaṃ kilissati, tāpīyati bādhīyatī ti attho. Bhāvanāya paripantho hotī ti paṭiladdhāya vipassanābhāvanāya upaghāto hoti. Paṭivedhassa antarāyo hotī ti vipassanābhāvanāya paṭilabhitabbassa saccappaṭivedhassa paṭilābhantarāyo hoti.*

108. Cf. Paṭis I.1: *Muñcitukamyatāpaṭisaṅkhāsantiṭṭhanā paññā saṅkhārupekkhāsu ñāṇaṃ.* Paṭis II 63: *Yā ca muñcitukamyatā yā ca paṭisaṅkhānupassanā yā ca saṅkhārupekkhā, ime dhammāekatthā, byañjanam-evanānaṃ.* Paṭis-a I 21: *Muñcitukamyatāpaṭisaṅkhāsantiṭṭhanā paññā saṅkhārupekkhāsu ñāṇan-ti ... Iti pubbabhāge nibbidāñāṇena nibbinnassa uppādādīni pariccajitukāmatā muñcitukamyatā. Muñcanassa upāyakaraṇatthaṃ majjhe paṭisaṅkhānaṃ paṭisaṅkhā. Muñcitvā avasāne ajjhupekkhanaṃ santiṭṭhanā. Evaṃ avatthābhedena tippakārā paññā saṅkhārānaṃ ajjhupekkhanāsu ñāṇaṃ, muñcitukamyatā-paṭisaṅkhāsantiṭṭhanāsaṅkhātānaṃ avatthābhedena bhinnānaṃ tissannam-pi paññānaṃ saṅkhārupekkhataṃ icchantena pana paññā ti ca saṅkhārupekkhāsū ti ca bahuvacanaṃ kataṃ, avatthābhedena bhinnassā pi ekattā ñāṇan-ti ekavacanaṃ katan-ti veditabbaṃ. Vuttañ-ca yā ca muñcitukamyatā yā ca paṭisaṅkhānupassanā yā ca saṅkhārupekkhā, ime dhammā ekaṭṭhā, byañjanam-eva nānan-ti. Keci pana saṅkhārupekkhāsū ti bahuvacanaṃ samathavipassanāvasena saṅkhārupekkhānaṃ bahuttā ti pi vadanti. Saṅkhārupekkhāsū ti ca kiriyāpekkhan-ti veditabbaṃ. Avatthābhedena pana tena nibbidāñāṇena nibbindantassa ukkaṇṭhantassa sabbabhavayonigativiññāṇaṭṭhitisattāvāsagatesu sabhedakesu saṅkhāresu cittaṃ na sajjati na laggati na bajjhati, sabbasaṅkhāragataṃ muñcitukāmaṃ chaḍḍetukāmaṃ hoti.* Vism XXI.79/p.660: *Taṃ panetaṃ purimena ñāṇadvayena atthato ekaṃ. Tenāhu porāṇā: Idaṃ saṅkhārupekkhāñāṇaṃ ekam-eva tīṇi nāmāni labhati, heṭṭhā muñcitukamyatāñāṇaṃ nāma jātaṃ, majjhe paṭisaṅkhānupassanāñāṇaṃ nāma, ante ca sikhāppattaṃ saṅkhārupekkhāñāṇaṃ nāma.*

22. Knowledge of conformity

The meditator, thus developing the knowledge of desire for release, desires to be freed from all formations and attain to nibbāna. By attending to just one characteristic, he gives rise to the gates to liberation (*vimokkhamukha*) [through which] knowledge of conformity (*anuloma-ñāṇa*) arises.[109]

In three ways, knowledge of conformity arises; in three ways, he enters into the certainty of rightness:

Seeing the five aggregates as impermanent, he obtains knowledge of conformity. Seeing, "the cessation of the five aggregates is the permanent nibbāna", he enters into the certainty of rightness.

Seeing the five aggregates as suffering, he obtains knowledge of conformity. Seeing, "the cessation of the aggregates is the happy nibbāna", he enters into the certainty of rightness.

Seeing the five aggregates as without self, he obtains knowledge of conformity. Seeing, "the cessation of the aggregates is the absolute nibbāna", he enters into the certainty of rightness.[110]

Q. Through what knowledge will he enter into the certainty of rightness, and through what knowledge is he entering into the certainty of rightness?

---

109. 唯作一相欲令起解脫門相似智起. Cf. Dhs 224–225: *Yasmiñhi vāre maggavuṭṭhānaṃ hoti, tīṇi lakkhaṇāni ekāvajjanena viya āpātham-āgacchanti, tiṇṇañ-ca ekato pāthagamanaṃ nāma ... Ekalakkhaṇadassanamatteneva hi maggavuṭṭhānaṃ nāma na hoti, tasmā aniccato abhiniviṭṭho bhikkhu na kevalaṃ aniccatova vuṭṭhāti, dukkhato pi anattato pi vuṭṭhātiyeva. Dukkhato anattato abhiniviṭṭhepi eseva nayo.* Cf. Paṭis-a III 550. Paṭis II 66–69: *Katamo vimokkho? Suññato vimokkho, animitto vimokkho, appaṇihito vimokkho. Katamo suññato vimokkho? Aniccānupassanāñāṇaṃ niccato abhinivesā muccatī ti suññato vimokkho. Dukkhānupassanāñāṇaṃ sukhato abhinivesā muccatī ti suññato vimokkho. Anattānupassanāñāṇaṃ attato abhinivesā muccatī ti suññato vimokkho. ... Ye tattha jātā anavajjā kusalā bodhipakkhiyādhammā, idaṃ mukhaṃ. Yaṃ tesaṃ dhammānaṃ ārammaṇaṃ nirodho nibbānaṃ, idaṃ vimokkhamukhaṃ. Vimokkhañ-ca mukhañ-ca vimokkhamukhaṃ, idaṃ vimokkhamukhaṃ.* Cf. Vism XXI.66–67/p.657: *Tatridaṃ tividhānupassanāvasena pavattanato tiṇṇaṃ indriyānaṃ ādhipateyyavasena tividhavimokkhamukhabhāvaṃ āpajjati nāma. Tisso hi anupassanā tīṇi vimokkhamukhānī ti vuccanti.* For the *vimokkhamukha*, see also 459c22ff.

110. Paṭis II 237–40: *Pañcakkhandhe aniccato passanto anulomikaṃ khantiṃ paṭilabhati. Pañcannaṃ khandhānaṃ nirodho niccaṃ nibbānan-ti passanto sammattaniyāmaṃ okkamati. Pañcakkhandhe dukkhato passanto ... nirodho sukhaṃ nibbānan-ti passanto ... Pañcakkhandhe anattato passanto ... nirodho paramatthaṃ nibbānan-ti passanto sammattaniyāmaṃ okkamati.* Cf. Vism XX.18/p.611. Vism-mhṭ II 393: *Khandhānaṃ nirodho niccaṃ nibbānan-ti vacanena saṅkhārānaṃ dukkharogatādipaṭipakkho nibbānassa sukhārogyādibhāvo ādinā nayenā ti ettha nayaggahaṇena dīpitoti.*

A. Through knowledge of conformity, he will enter into the certainty of rightness. Through knowledge of the path he is entering into the certainty of rightness.[111]

Q. What is the meaning of knowledge of conformity?
A. Conformity is the four establishments of mindfulness, the four right efforts, the four bases of supernormal power, the five faculties, the five powers, the seven factors of enlightenment, and the eight noble path factors.[112] Through conformity with these, it is called "knowledge of conformity".

The non-opposition (*apaccanīka*), the seeing of benefit, and the acceptance in conformity[113]—these are epithets for knowledge of conformity.

Knowledge of conformity is finished.

23. Knowledge of change of lineage

Immediately after knowledge of conformity, he emerges from the sign of all formations, makes nibbāna the object, and gives rise to the knowledge of change of lineage (*gotrabhuñāṇa*).[114]

Q. What is the meaning of change of lineage (*gotrabhu*)?
A. The overcoming of the state of the worldling is called "change of lineage". The developing[115] of the state of the non-worldling (*aputhujjanadhamma*) is

---

111. Cf. A III 441, Paṭis II 236: *So vata ... bhikkhu sabbasaṅkhāre aniccato samanupassanto anulomikāya khantiyā samannāgato bhavissatī ti ṭhānametaṃ vijjati. Anulomikāya khantiyā samannāgato sammattaniyāmaṃ okkamissatī ti ṭhānametaṃ vijjati. Sammattaniyāmaṃ okkamamāno sotāpattiphalaṃ vā sakadāgāmiphalaṃ vā anāgāmiphalaṃ vā arahattaṃ vā sacchikarissatī ti ṭhānametaṃ vijjatī ti.*

112. Cf. Vism XXII.33: *Cattāro satipaṭṭhānā, cattāro sammappadhānā, cattāro iddhipādā, pañcindriyāni, pañcabalāni, satta bojjhaṅgā, ariyo aṭṭhaṅgiko maggo ti hi ime sattatiṃsa dhammā bojjhaṅgaṭṭhena bodhī ti laddhamānassa ariyamaggassa pakkhe bhavattā bodhipakkhiyā nāma; pakkhe bhavattā ti, nāma upakārabhāve ṭhitattā.*

113. Vibh-a 411: *Anulomikaṃ khantin-ti ādīni paññāvevacanāni. Sā hi heṭṭhā vuttānaṃ kammāyatanādīnaṃ apaccanīkadassanena anulomanato, tathā sattānaṃ hitacariyāya ..., nibbānassa ca avilomanato anulometī ti anulomikā.* Paṭis II 69: *... sabbe pi akusalā dhammā vimokkhapaccanīkā ... sabbe pi kusalā dhammā vimokkhānulomā ....* Vism-mhṭ I 278: *Anulomapaṭipadaṃ apaccanīkapaṭipadan-ti iminā ñāyappaṭipattiṃ. Paṭipajjitabbassa hi nibbānassa anulomanena, apaccanīkatāya cassā ñāyato.*

114. *Gotrabhūñāṇa.* Cf. Paṭis-a I 26: *Kilesānaṃ samucchindanato ... nibbānārammaṇakaraṇato bahiddhā sabbasaṅkhāranimittehi ca vuṭṭhāti ... Tenevāha: Cattāri pi maggañāṇāni animittārammaṇattā nimittato vuṭṭhahanti, ... Tañ-hi gotrabhuñāṇassa anantaraṃ nibbānaṃ ārammaṇaṃ kurumānaṃ sayaṃvajjhe kilese niravasesaṃ samucchindamānaṃ...*

115. 非凡夫法所除, lit. "overcoming of the state of the non-worldling", a mistranslation. The Tibetan (Sav 196a) lacks this clause, includes a plural *dhamma* in the previous one, and gives an alternative interpretation of *gotrabhu* based on the root

also called "change of lineage". The "lineage" (*gotta*)" is nibbāna.

Furthermore, the planting of the seed of nibbāna is called "change of lineage".[116]

A. is said in the Abhidhamma: "The overcoming of birth is called 'change of lineage'. The entering into non-arising (*anuppādā*) is also called 'change of lineage'".[117] Again, "The overcoming of occurrence and the sign is 'change of lineage'. The entering into the occurrenceless and the signless is called 'change of lineage'".

The first focussing on nibbāna[118] and the wisdom with regard to emergence

---

√*bhuj* "enjoys" : "... the overcoming of the states of the worldling. The 'lineage' (*rigs*) is nibbāna; the enjoying (*spyod*) of this is 'enjoying (*za*) of of lineage'". *Gotrabhu* is first translated as *rigs spyod*, "enjoying of the lineage", with *spyod* for *bhoga, anubhavati,* etc., and then as *rigs za*, with *za* for "to eat". In Pali there is no interpretation of *gotrabhu* based on √*bhuj2*, but the Tibetan could be based on *ābhoga* "enjoyment" (*ā* + √*bhuj2*), a misunderstanding of "bending to" (*ā* + √*bhuj1*) as in *nibbānārammaṇe ... paṭhamābhoga* .... 性除, "lineage" + "discards/overcomes", is based on *gotta* + *abhibhuyyati*, with 除 for *vinodeti, vajjati*, etc. Cf. Vism XXII.5/p.672: *... anulomañāṇassa āsevanante animittaṃ ... nibbānaṃ ārammaṇaṃ kurumānaṃ puthujjanagottaṃ puthujjanasaṅkhaṃ puthujjanabhūmiṃ atikkamamānaṃ ariyagottaṃ ... okkamamānaṃ nibbānārammaṇe paṭhamāvattana-paṭhamābhoga-paṭhamasamannāhārabhūtaṃ maggassa ... paccayabhāvaṃ sādhayamānaṃ sikhāppattaṃ vipassanāya muddhabhūtaṃ apunarāvattakaṃ uppajjati.* Paṭis-a I 26: *Puthujjanagottābhibhavanato ariyagottabhāvanato gotrabhu. Idañ-hi anulomañāṇehi padumapalāsato udakamiva sabbasaṅkhārato patilīyamānacittassa anulomañāṇassa āsevanante animittaṃ nibbānaṃ ārammaṇaṃ kurumānaṃ puthujjanagottaṃ ... apunarāvattakaṃ uppajjati.* Cf. Paṭis-a I 274f.: *Abhibhuyyatī ti gotrabhū ti ca puthujjanagottābhibhavanato gotrabhubhāvo vutto. ...*

116. Paṭis-a I 275: *Gottattho cettha bījattho.*

117. Cf. Paṭis I 65: *Uppādaṃ abhibhuyyitvā anuppādaṃ pakkhandatī ti gotrabhu. Pavattaṃ abhibhuyyitvā appavattaṃ pakkhandatī ti gotrabhu. Nimittaṃ abhibhuyyitvā animittaṃ pakkhandatī ti gotrabhu ...* The Tibetan (Sav 196a) has "the enjoying/partaking of non-arising", *mi skye ba za ba*, instead of "entering into non-arising".

118. 於泥洹是初引路. Presumably 引路 "leading/guiding/directing [on the] road" is a free rendering of *samannāhāra*, "bringing together". In Vim 路 corresponds to *pantha, patha,* "path, road" not to the noble *magga,* which is 道. And if this would refer to the path to nibbāna then the Chinese construction would be different. The Tibetan has: "The first focussing on nibbāna and the wisdom with regard to emergence and turning away is knowledge of the partaking of lineage". Paṭis-a I 275 attributes the idea that the first focussing on nibbāna is a designation for gotrabhu to "others" and says that it does not fit in connection with the fruit (*phala*). Since the Vim passage is in the context of the attainment of the Path and it is also found so in the Vism and other texts, this idea cannot be linked to the Vim. Cf. Vism XXII.5/p.672, quoted above: *... ariyabhūmiṃ okkamamānaṃ nibbānārammaṇe paṭhamāvattanapaṭhamābhogapaṭhamasamannāhārabhūtaṃ ...* Paṭis-a I 275: *Vattanipakaraṇe kira vuttaṃ gottaṃ vuccati nibbānaṃ sabbaparipanthehi guttattā, taṃ paṭipajjatī*

and the turning away from the external—these are epithets for [knowledge of] change of lineage. [119]

The knowledge of change of lineage is finished.

24. Knowledge of the path

Immediately after the knowledge of change of lineage, he, fully knowing suffering, abandoning its origination, realizing its cessation, and developing the path, gives rise to the path-knowledge of stream-entry and all the states that are aids to enlightenment (*bodhipakkhiyā dhammā*). At this time, the meditator, through seclusion,[120] sees the end of existence,[121] the unconditioned, and the deathless element.

25. Comprehension of the truths in a single moment

He comprehends the four noble truths in a single moment, in a single knowledge, simultaneously. There is comprehension through the comprehension of the full understanding of suffering, the comprehension of the abandoning of origination, the comprehension of the realization of cessation and the comprehension of the development of the path.

It is taught in the simile [of the boat] in verse thus: [**457b**]

---

ti gotrabhūti, aṭṭha samāpattiyo pi gottaṃ gotrabhuparipanthehi guttattā, taṃ gottaṃ paṭipajjatī ti gotrabhūti vuttaṃ. Catunnaṃ maggānaṃ yeva gotrabhu nibbānārammaṇaṃ, catassannaṃ phalasamāpattīnaṃ gotrabhu saṅkhārārammaṇaṃ phalasamāpattininnattā ti vadanti. Vuttañhetaṃ visuddhimagge tassa pavattānupubbavipassanassa saṅkhārārammaṇagotrabhuñāṇānantaraṃ phalasamāpattivasena nirodhe cittaṃ appetī ti. ... Aññe pana yo nibbāne paṭhamābhogo paṭhamasamannāhāro, ayaṃ vuccati gotrabhū ti vadanti, taṃ phalaṃ sandhāya na yujjati. Abhidh-av 125, v. 1327: *Gocaraṃ kurumānaṃ taṃ, nibbānārammaṇe pana; Paṭhamāvajjanañceva, paṭhamābhogatāpi ca.*

119. Paṭis I 1: *Bahiddhā vuṭṭhānavivaṭṭane paññā gotrabhuñāṇaṃ.* Cf. PoP XXII.5, fn.1.

120. Cf. Nidd I 27: *Yo sabbasaṅkhārasamatho ... nibbānaṃ, ayaṃ upadhiviveko. ... upadhiviveko ca nirūpadhīnaṃ puggalānaṃ visaṅkhāragatānaṃ.* Nidd-a I 104: *Visaṅkhāragatānan-ti saṅkhārārammaṇaṃ cajitvā vigatasaṅkhāraṃ nibbānaṃ ārammaṇavasena upagatānaṃ.* Nidd-a I 101: *... Tehi duvidhekaṭṭhehi kilesehi cittaṃ vivittaṃ hotī ti maggacittaṃ viviccati, phalacittaṃ vivittaṃ viyuttaṃ apasakkitaṃ suññaṃ hotī ti attho.* Vism-mhṭ II 506: *Kilesasaṅgaṇikādivasena avivekabhūtassa. Vivekaṭṭho upadhivivekatā. Sabbasaṅkhāravivittatā asaṅkhatabhāvoti evaṃ acchariyabbhutasabhāvo pi ariyamaggo saṅkhato eva, ayam-eva ca eko asaṅkhatoti nirodhassa asaṅkhatabhāvo supākaṭo hoti.*

121. Also in the next section, at 457b14. At 401b25, etc, 有邊 stands for *pariyanta*, but here for *bhavapariyanta*. Tibetan version: "At this time, due to that, he sees the end of existence (*bhavapariyanta*), ..." Cf. Nidd I 21: *... bhavapariyante ṭhito, saṃsārapariyante ṭhito, ... antime bhave ṭhito, ... antimadehadharo ...*

It is like a man who abandons this shore,
And crosses over to the far shore
With a boat wherein he ferries goods.
Sailing the boat, he cuts through the stream.[122]

It is like a boat crossing a river, which performs four functions simultaneously in one moment: it abandons this shore, cuts through the stream, reaches the further shore, and carries over the goods. Like the abandoning of this shore is the comprehension by the full knowledge of suffering;[123] like the cutting of the stream is the comprehension by the abandoning of origination; like the crossing over to the further shore is the comprehension by the realization of cessation; and like the boat ferrying the goods is the comprehension by the development of the path.[124]

---

122. Abhidh-av 1387–88: *Yathā ca mahatī nāvā, apubbācarimaṃ pana. Cattāri pana kiccāni, karot'ekakkhaṇe pana. // Jahatī orimaṃ tīraṃ, sotaṃ chindati sā pana. Tathā vahati bhaṇḍañ ca, tīram appeti pārimaṃ.*

除漏 usually would be interpreted as "gets rid of leaks (*āsavā*)", however the Pali has *sotaṃ chindati*, "cuts the stream (of saṃsāra)" and the Tibetan version's *chu bo gcod pa* supports this. In the prose explanation, the boat performs the four functions, not the man, so "gets rid of leaks" does not fit there. However, 除 can correspond to *chindana, chedana*, while 漏 can correspond to the stream/current of saṃsāra. Cf. S IV 292: *Soto ti kho, bhante, taṇhāyetaṃ adhivacanaṃ. Sā khīṇāsavassa bhikkhuno pahīnā ucchinnamūlā tālāvatthukatā anabhāvaṅkatā āyatiṃ anuppādadhammā. Tasmā khīṇāsavo bhikkhu chinnasoto ti vuccati.* Nidd II 30: *Yāni sotāni lokasmiṃ, sati tesaṃ nivāraṇaṃ; / Sotānaṃ saṃvaraṃ brūmi, paññāyete pidhiyyare. Yāni sotāni lokasmin-ti yāni etāni sotāni mayā kittitāni ... pakāsitāni, seyyathidaṃ taṇhāsoto diṭṭhisoto kilesasoto duccaritasoto avijjāsoto.*

123. 智分別苦, lit. "knowledge comprehension suffering". This corresponds to *dukkhaṃ pariññābhisamayena abhisameti* "comprehension of suffering through the comprehension by full knowledge"; see parallels in next footnote. The same applies to the next three comprehensions. The Tibetan has "comprehension of full knowledge of suffering", *sdug bsngal yongs su shes pa'i mngon rtogs.* Both indicate that the original was *dukkhaṃ pariññābhisamaya* or *dukkhapariññābhisamaya* without *abhisameti.*

124. Peṭ 133–34: *Cattāro abhisamayā, pariññābhisamayo pahānābhisamayo sacchikiriyābhisamayo bhāvanābhisamayo. Tattha ariyasāvako dukkhaṃ pariññābhisamayena abhisameti, samudayaṃ pahānābhisamayena abhisameti, nirodhaṃ sacchikiriyābhisamayena abhisameti, maggaṃ bhāvanābhisamayena abhisameti. Kiṃ kāraṇaṃ? Dukkhassa pariññābhisamayo, samudayassa pahānābhisamayo, nirodhassa sacchikiriyābhisamayo, maggassa bhāvanābhisamayo. ... Evaṃ diṭṭhanto yathā nāvā jalaṃ gacchanto cattāri kiccāni karoti, pārimaṃ tīraṃ pāpeti, orimaṃ tīraṃ jahati, bhāraṃ vahati, sotaṃ chindati, evam eva samathavipassanā yuganandhā vattamānā ekakāle ekakkhaṇe ekacitte cattāri kiccāni karoti, dukkhaṃ pariññābhisamayena abhisameti, yāva maggaṃ bhāvanābhisamayena abhisameti.* Paṭis-a I 332: *Saccābhisamayakālasmiñhi maggañāṇassa ekakkhaṇe pariññā, pahānaṃ, sacchikiriyā, bhāvanā ti cattāri kiccāni honti. Yathā nāvā apubbaṃ acarimaṃ ekakkhaṇe*

Or, it is like a lamp, which with its appearance performs four functions simultaneously in one moment: it burns the wick; dispels darkness; consumes oil; and manifests light.

["Like the burning of the wick is the comprehension through the full knowledge of suffering; like the dispelling of darkness is the comprehension through the abandoning of origination; like the consuming of oil is the comprehension through the realization of cessation; and like the manifestation of light is the comprehension through the development of the path".][125]

Or, it is like the sun, which with its appearance performs four functions simultaneously in one moment: it makes forms visible, dispels darkness, eliminates cold, and manifests light.

Like the making visible of forms is the comprehension through full knowledge of suffering; like the dispelling of darkness is the comprehension through abandoning of origination; like the elimination of cold is the comprehension through realization of cessation; and like the manifestation of light is the comprehension through development of the path.[126]

---

cattāri kiccāni karoti, orimaṃ tīraṃ pajahati, sotaṃ chindati, bhaṇḍaṃ vahati, pārimaṃ tīraṃ appeti, evam-eva maggañāṇaṃ apubbaṃ acarimaṃ ekakkhaṇe cattāri saccāni abhisameti, dukkhaṃ pariññābhisamayena abhisameti, ... Vism XXII.96/p.691: *Yathā nāvā apubbaṃ acarimaṃ ekakkhaṇe cattāri kiccāni karoti: orimatīraṃ pajahati, sotaṃ chindati, bhaṇḍaṃ vahati, pārimaṃ tīraṃ appeti, evam eva maggañāṇaṃ ...*

125. The explanation is missing from the Chinese. Perhaps it was lost due to the similarity with the next simile. The Tibetan (196b) has: "Likewise, respectively, the four comprehensions of full knowledge and so forth of the truths of suffering and so forth". Vism attributes these three similes to the former teachers—*vuttaṃ h'etaṃ porāṇehi.* Vism XXII.92/p.690: *Vuttaṃ hetaṃ porāṇehi: Yathā padīpo apubbaṃ acarimaṃ ekakkhaṇena cattāri kiccāni karoti: vaṭṭiṃ jhāpeti, andhakāraṃ vidhamati, ālokaṃ parividaṃseti, sinehaṃ pariyādiyati—evam eva maggañāṇaṃ apubbaṃ acarimaṃ ekakkhaṇena cattāri saccāni abhisameti, ...* Peṭ 134–5: *Yathā dīpo jalanto ekakāle apubbaṃ acarimaṃ cattāri kiccāni karoti, andhakāraṃ vidhamati, ālokaṃ pātukaroti, rūpaṃ nidassiyati, upādānaṃ pariyādiyati, evam eva samathavipassanā ...*

126. The Chinese text adds "such Noble knowledge is like the sun", 如日如是聖智, which does not fit here and must be a marginal note that was copied into the text. The Tibetan gives the same abridged explanation as the one given in the preceding footnote. Cf. Vism XXII.95/p.690: *Yathā suriyo udayanto apubbaṃ acarimaṃ saha pātubhāvā cattāri kiccāni karoti: rūpagatāni obhāseti, andhakāraṃ vidhamati, ālokaṃ dasseti, sītaṃ paṭippassambheti—evam eva maggañāṇaṃ ... Idhā pi yathā suriyo rūpagatāni obhāseti, evaṃ maggañāṇaṃ dukkhaṃ parijānāti; yathā andhakāraṃ vidhamati, evaṃ samudayaṃ pajahati; yathā ālokaṃ dasseti, evaṃ sahajātāni paccayatāya maggaṃ bhāveti; yathā sītaṃ paṭippassambheti, evaṃ kilesapaṭippassaddhiṃ nirodhaṃ sacchikarotī ti evaṃ upamāsaṃsandanaṃ veditabbaṃ.* Peṭ 134: *Tattha samathavipassanā yuganaddhā vattamānā ekakāle ekakkhaṇe ekacitte cattāri kiccāni karoti, dukkhaṃ pariññābhisamayena*

Q. Seeing suffering as it really is, he fully knows suffering, abandons origination, realizes cessation, and develops the path—what is the meaning of this?

[A]. When he is seeing suffering, the four distortions (*vipallāsa*) do not occur.[127]

[Q] That which has been said [above]: "At that time, he, through seclusion, is seeing the end of existence, the unconditioned, the deathless element. He comprehends the four truths in one knowledge, simultaneously"—what is the meaning of this?

[A.] When there is the knowledge of arising and falling away, then there is not yet the seeing of the flood of suffering and the seeing of the disadvantage of all formations as it really is, and the mind [does not yet] emerge from the sign of formations and enter the formationless. However, when he sees the disadvantage of the formations as it really is, the mind emerges from the sign of formations and enters the formationless.[128] Then he sees the flood of suffering and reaches the final goal (*pariyosāna*).

It is also said[129] that if in this manner, through seclusion and through the knowledge of change of lineage, there is comprehension of the truths, the knowledge of change of lineage emerges from the sign of the formations and there is entering into the formationless. When the knowledge of change of lineage emerges from the sign of the formations, there is entering into the formationless, there is entering into nibbāna.

Intentness on the cause [i.e. nibbāna] is his only object. Through intentness on the object, he obtains concentration of mind. If he does not attain concentration, he does not give rise to calm and insight, and does not fully obtain the states that are aids to enlightenment. Therefore [only] through the knowledge of change of lineage there is comprehension of the truths.[130] From the knowledge of change of lineage, the knowledge of the

---

abhisameti ... Yathā vā suriyo udayanto ekakāle apubbaṃ acarimaṃ cattāri kiccāni karoti, andhakāraṃ vidhamati, ālokaṃ pātukaroti, rūpaṃ nidassiyati, sītaṃ pariyādiyati, ...

127. The questions are put in an unusual way here, and there is no indication where the next question starts. 相 "characteristic" in 此相云何 probably is a corruption of 義 "meaning", as used in 此義云何 in the next question. Also the answer to this question literally is "When is not seeing suffering, the four distortions occur", 若不見苦四顛倒生, which does not fit the question. These two questions are not quoted in the Tibetan version.

128. Vism-mhṭ II 207, Spk-ṭ II 365: ... *sabbasaṅkhārehi nibbinnassa visaṅkhāraninnassa gotrabhunā vivaṭṭitamānasassa maggena sacchikaraṇenā ti attho.* Spk III 144: ... *nimittaṃ ... animittaṃ ... Saṅkhāre anāvajjitattā, visaṅkhāraṃ āvajjitattā satisambojjhaṅgo tiṭṭhatī ti.*

129. This indicates a quotation, but since there is no indication where it ends, no quotation marks have been added here.

130. Peṭ 133: ... *maggassa bhāvanābhisamayo. Samathavipassanāya kathaṃ abhisameti?*

path is produced immediately and, at that time, he obtains the concentration on nibbāna. His mind obtains concentration, gives rise to calm and insight, and fulfils the states that are aids to enlightenment. Therefore, only through the knowledge of the path there is comprehension of the truths.[131]

It is like a man leaving a burning city by stepping over the threshold of the gate. When only one foot has left the city, then he is still not called "one who has left". Just so, when the knowledge of change of lineage emerges from that sign of the formations and there is the entering into the formationless, **[457c]** then he is still not called "one gone beyond the afflictions" because the states [that are aids to enlightenment] are not yet fulfilled. Just as a man leaving a burning city who [has stepped] with both his feet over the threshold of the gate is called "one who has left the burning city", just so, from the knowledge of change of lineage immediately the knowledge of the path is produced, and then one is called "one has left the city of the afflictions", because the states [that are aids to enlightenment] are fulfilled. Therefore, through the knowledge of change of lineage, there is comprehension of the truths.[132]

Q. What is the meaning of "comprehension of the truths"?

A. The four noble truths comprehended together in one moment—[this] is called "comprehension of the truths".[133]

Ārammaṇe cittaṃ upanibandhetvā pañcakkhandhe dukkhato passati. Tattha yo upanibandho, ayaṃ samatho. Yā pariyogāhanā, ayaṃ vipassanā. ... ayaṃ samudayo. Yaṃ tassa pahānaṃ, so nirodho samatho vipassanā ca maggo, evaṃ tesaṃ catunnaṃ ariyasaccānaṃ ekakāle ekakkhaṇe ekacitte apubbaṃ acarimaṃ abhisamayo bhavati. Tenāha bhagavā sahasaccābhisamayā ariyasāvakassa tīṇi saṃyojanāni pahīyantī ti.

131. Cf. Vism XXII.6: ... *nibbānaninnapoṇapabbhāramānaso hutvā tatiyena paratīrassa uparibhāgaṃ patto viya idāni pattabbassa nibbānassa āsanno hutvā tassa cittassa nirodhena taṃ saṅkhārārammaṇaṃ muñcitvā gotrabhucittena visaṅkhāre paratīrabhūte nibbāne patati. Ekārammaṇe pana aladdhāsevanatāya vedhamāno so puriso viya na tāva suppatiṭṭhito hoti, tato maggañāṇena patiṭṭhātī ti.* Vism-mhṭ II 484: *Nibbāne ārammaṇakaraṇavasena patati yogāvacaro. Ekārammaṇeti ekavāraṃ yeva ālambite ārammaṇe. Tenāha aladdhāsevanatāyā ti. Tena ekārammaṇe āsevanā upakāravatī, na tathā nānārammaṇeti dasseti.*

132. Cf. Vism XXII.1f.

133. 答四聖諦於一剎那說和合名分別諦. The part 說和合 "teach combine" does not make sense. The Tibetan (196b) has: "The four noble truths are comprehended (*rtogs pa*) altogether (*mnyam du*) in a single moment, ...". Cf. Paṭis-a III 686: *Tattha abhisamayoti saccānaṃ abhimukhena samāgamo, paṭivedhoti attho.* Paṭis-a III 568: *Abhisamayaṭṭhenā ti abhimukhaṃ samāgamanaṭṭhena.* Paṭis-a III 579: *Saccābhisamayāyā ti catunnaṃ saccānaṃ ekābhisamayāya kiccanipphattivasena ekapaṭivedhāya.*

On this occasion,[134] connected with knowledge of the path, the faculties combine in the sense of authority;[135] the powers [combine] in the sense of unshakeability; the factors of enlightenment [combine] in the sense of leading out; the path factors[136] [combine] in the sense of cause; the establishments of mindfulness [combine] in the sense of establishing; right effort [combines] in the sense of exertion; the bases of supernormal power [combine] in the sense of succeeding; the truths [combine] in the sense of reality; calm [combines] in the sense of undistractedness; insight [combines] in the sense of contemplation; coupling [combines] in the sense of inseparability;[137] purity of virtue [combines] in the sense of restraint;[138] purity of mind [combines] in the sense of undistractedness; purity of view [combines] in the sense of vision; liberation [combines] in the sense of release; direct knowledge [combines] in the sense of penetration; freedom [combines] in the sense of giving up; knowledge of destruction [combines] in the sense of cutting off; foundation [combines] in the sense of motivation; attention [combines] in the sense of origination; contact [combines] in the sense of combining; feeling [combines] in the sense of meeting together; concentration [combines] in the sense of being foremost; mindfulness [combines] in the sense of authority; wisdom

---

134. Cf. Paṭis I 181: *... kathaṃ maggaṃ samodhāneti? ... avikkhepaṭṭhena sammāsamādhiṃ samodhāneti. Ayaṃ puggalo imaṃ maggaṃ imasmiṃ ārammaṇe samodhāneti. ... kathaṃ dhamme samodhāneti? Ādhipateyyaṭṭhena indriyāni samodhāneti, akampiyaṭṭhena balāni ..., niyyānaṭṭhena bojjhaṅge ..., hetuṭṭhena maggaṃ ..., upaṭṭhānaṭṭhena satipaṭṭhānaṃ ..., padahanaṭṭhena sammappadhānaṃ ..., ijjhanaṭṭhena iddhipādaṃ ..., tathaṭṭhena saccaṃ ..., avikkhepaṭṭhena samathaṃ ..., anupassanaṭṭhena vipassanaṃ ..., ekarasaṭṭhena samathavipassanaṃ ..., anativattanaṭṭhena yuganaddhaṃ ..., saṃvaraṭṭhena sīlavisuddhiṃ ..., avikkhepaṭṭhena cittavisuddhiṃ ..., dassanaṭṭhena diṭṭhivisuddhiṃ ..., vimuttaṭṭhena vimokkhaṃ ..., paṭivedhaṭṭhena vijjaṃ ..., pariccāgaṭṭhena vimuttiṃ ..., samucchedaṭṭhena khaye ñāṇaṃ ..., paṭippassaddhaṭṭhena anuppāde ñāṇaṃ ..., chandaṃ mūlaṭṭhena ..., manasikāraṃ samuṭṭhānaṭṭhena ..., phassaṃ samodhānaṭṭhena ..., vedanaṃ samosaraṇaṭṭhena ..., samādhiṃ pamukhaṭṭhena ..., satiṃ ādhipateyyaṭṭhena ..., paññaṃ tatuttaraṭṭhena ..., vimuttiṃ sāraṭṭhena ..., amatogadhaṃ nibbānaṃ pariyosānaṭṭhena samodhāneti.* Paṭis II 216: *Lokuttaramaggakkhaṇe ... Ādhipateyyaṭṭhena indriyābhisamayo, ... Paṭis-a III 568: Ekakkhaṇatāya samodhānaṭṭhenā ti ekajjhaṃ samosaraṇaṭṭhena.*

135. 於此時道智和合依義諸根成平等, with 道智和合 corresponding to *magga-ñāṇa-sampayutta* and 成平 to *samodhāneti*. Tibetan (Sav 197b): "At this time, connected with the Path (*lam de dang ldan pa = magga-sampayutta*), the faculties in the sense of authority are combined/converge".

136. 道分, path factor, = *maggaṅga*. The Paṭis has *magga* instead. Cf. fn. 1168.

137. 不相離 elsewhere in Vim corresponds to *avinibbhoga*, "inseparable". The Tibetan text accords with the Pali: *de dag las mi 'da' ba = anativattana*, "non-excess".

138. Cf. Paṭis-a III 545: *assaddhiyasaṃvaraṭṭhena sīlavisuddhīti assaddhiyassa nivāraṇaṭṭhena virati-atthena sīlamalavisodhanato sīlavisuddhi nāma.*

[combines] in the sense of reality;[139] and [the merging into] the deathless, nibbāna, combines in the sense of conclusion.[140]

26. Three fetters

The meditator, thus knowing, thus seeing, abandons the three fetters, namely, personal-identity-view, doubt, holding on to precepts and observances, and the afflictions conjoined with them (*tadekaṭṭha*).[141]

Q. What is personal-identity-view (*sakkāyadiṭṭhi*)?

A. Herein, the uninstructed worldling regards matter as self; the self as possessing matter; matter as within self; self as within matter. He regards feeling ... perception ... formations ... consciousness as self; the self as possessing consciousness; consciousness as within self; self as within consciousness. This is called personal-identity-view.[142] This personal-identity-view is abandoned, and due to that abandoning, the sixty-two views,[143] beginning with personal-identity-view, are abandoned too.

---

139. 真實 = *bhūta*, "real, existent". The Tibetan has: "wisdom [combines] in the sense of [being] constant", *bar med pa'i don gyis shes rab*. Probably both the Chinese and Tibetan translators did not understand *tatuttara* "superior than that"; the Pali has *taduttara/tatuttara* "the highest of all". Paṭis-a I 107: *Paññā taduttaraṭṭhenā ti ariyamaggapaññā tesaṃ kusalānaṃ dhammānaṃ uttaraṭṭhena seṭṭhaṭṭhena abhiññeyyā. Atha vā tato kilesehi, saṃsāravaṭṭato vā uttarati samatikkamatī ti taduttarā, tassā attho taduttaraṭṭho. Tena taduttaraṭṭhena. Tatuttaraṭṭhenā ti pi pāṭho, tato uttaraṭṭhenā ti attho.*

140. 醍醐最後義, 泥洹最後平等義: "the deathless [combines] in the sense of conclusion; nibbāna combines in the sense of conclusion". The Pali and Tibetan place *amatogadhaṃ* and *nibbānaṃ* together.

141. Lit. "... defilements standing in that one (place)". Cf. Paṭis II 94: *Sotāpattimaggena sakkāyadiṭṭhi vicikicchā sīlabbataparāmāso, imāni tīṇi saññojanāni pahīyanti; diṭṭhānusayo vicikicchānusayo, ime dve anusayā byantihonti.* Nidd-a I 101: *Tadekaṭṭhehi cā ti tehi sakkāyadiṭṭhi ādīhi ekato ṭhitehi ca. ... tehi sakkāyadiṭṭhiyādikilesehi cittaṃ vivittaṃ suññaṃ hoti. Ettha tadekaṭṭhan-ti duvidhaṃ ekaṭṭhaṃ pahānekaṭṭhaṃ sahajekaṭṭhañ-ca. ... Rāgadosamohapamukhesu vā diyaḍḍhesu kilesasahassesu sotāpattimaggena diṭṭhiyā pahīyamānāya diṭṭhiyā saha vicikicchā pahīnā, diṭṭhānusayavicikicchānusayehi saha apāyagamanīyā sabbakilesā pahānekaṭṭhavasena pahīyanti. Sahajekaṭṭhā pana diṭṭhiyā saha vicikicchāya ca saha ekekasmiṃ citte ṭhitā avasesakilesā. ... vicikicchāsahagatacitte pahīyamāne tena sahajāto moho uddhaccaṃ ahirikaṃ anottappan-ti ime kilesā sahajekaṭṭhavasena pahīyanti.* See also footnote **148**.

142. Cf. M I 8; III 17; Vibh 364: *Tattha katamā sakkāyadiṭṭhi? Idha assutavā puthujjano ... rūpaṃ ... viññāṇaṃ attato samanupassati, viññāṇavantaṃ vā attānaṃ, attani vā viññāṇaṃ, viññāṇasmiṃ vā attānaṃ: yā evarūpā diṭṭhi diṭṭhigataṃ ... pe ... vipariyesagāho: ayaṃ vuccati sakkāyadiṭṭhi.*

143. On the 62 views given in the Brahmajāla Sutta, see Bodhi 2007b. Vibh 400: *Tattha katamāni dvāsaṭṭhi diṭṭhigatāni brahmajāle* (D I 44–5) *veyyākaraṇe vuttāni bhagavatā?*

Q. What is doubt?
A. The doubt with regard to suffering, origination, cessation, or the path, or with regard to the Buddha, the Dhamma, and the Saṅgha, or with regard to the past, the future, or the past and future,[144] or with regard to dependently arisen states—this is called "doubt".[145] This is also abandoned.

Q. What is holding on to precepts and observances?
A. There are two kinds of holding on to precepts and observances. They are [holding on due to] craving and [holding on due to] delusion.

"Through this precept, through this observance, through this austerity (*tapas*), and through this practice of the holy life (*brahmacariya*), I will be reborn as a deity or shall be reborn among the deities" [146]—this is called "holding on to precepts and observances due to craving".

"Through precepts, through purity [of observances], and through purity of precepts and observances [there is purity]", such a view of recluses or brahmins outside [of the Dhamma]—this is called "holding on to precepts and observances due to delusion". This is also abandoned.

Q. What are the afflictions conjoined with them (*tadekaṭṭha*)?
A. The greed, hatred, and delusion that lead to the bad destinations are called "the afflictions conjoined with them". These are also abandoned.[147] **[458a]**

Cattāro sassatavādā, cattāro ekaccassatikā, cattāro antānantikā, cattāro amarāvikkhepikā, dve adhiccasamuppannikā, soḷasa saññīvādā, aṭṭha asaññīvādā, aṭṭha nevasaññī-nāsaññīvādā, satta ucchedavādā, pañca diṭṭhadhammanibbānavādā. Imāni dvāsaṭṭhi diṭṭhigatāni Brahmajāle veyyākaraṇe vuttāni bhagavatā.

144. This means doubts as to whether or not and how one existed or will exist in the past or future. Cf. S II 26: *Yato kho ... ariyasāvakassa ayañ-ca paṭiccasamuppādo, ime ca paṭiccasamuppannā dhammā yathābhūtaṃ sammappaññāya sudiṭṭhā honti, so vata pubbantaṃ vā paṭidhāvissati ahosiṃ nu kho ahaṃ atītamaddhānaṃ, ... kiṃ hutvā kiṃ ahosiṃ nu kho ahaṃ atītamaddhānanti; aparantaṃ vā upadhāvissati bhavissāmi nu kho ahaṃ ... ayaṃ nu kho satto kuto āgato, so kuhiṃ gamissatī ti, netaṃ ṭhānaṃ vijjati.* Cf. M I 8 and Vism XIX.6/p.599.

145. Cf. Dhs 183, § 1008; Vibh 364–5: *Satthari ... dhamme ... saṅghe ... sikkhāya ... pubbante ... aparante ... pubbantāparante ... idappaccayatā paṭiccasamuppannesu dhammesu kaṅkhati vicikicchati: yā evarūpā kaṅkhā ... vicikicchā ... manovilekho—ayaṃ vuccati vicikicchā.* Cf. Nidd I 414 & Peṭ 131f, which include the four noble truths.

146. 我皆當生一一天處, lit. "I will be reborn in every heaven, one after the other", which is a mistranslation of *devaññataro*, as found in the Vism parallel in the next fn. Tibetan: "... and through this practice of the holy life, [I] will become a deity, [or] otherwise [I will be born] among [the deities]".

147. A III 438: *Cha ... dhamme appahāya abhabbo diṭṭhisampadaṃ sacchikātuṃ. Katame cha? Sakkāyadiṭṭhiṃ, vicikicchaṃ, sīlabbataparāmāsaṃ, apāyagamanīyaṃ rāgaṃ, apāyagamanīyaṃ dosaṃ, apāyagamanīyaṃ mohaṃ.* Kv 80 etc.: *Apāyagamanīyo rāgo ...doso ... moho pahīno, parihāyati sotāpanno sotāpattiphalā ti.* Nidd I 7: *sotāpattimaggaṃ bhāvento*

27. Stream-enterer

During this interval,[148] he is practising for the realization of the fruit of stream-entry.[149] He has not yet attained to stream-entry and stands in the plane of practice for stream-entry,[150] the eighth plane,[151] the plane of vision.[152]

---

pi apāyagamanīye kāme samucchedato parivajjeti? It-a II 36: *Tattha apāyagamanīyā rāgadosamohā paṭhamamaggena, oḷārikā kāmarāgadosā dutiyamaggena, te yeva anavasesā tatiyamaggena, bhavarāgo avasiṭṭhamoho ca catutthamaggena pahīyanti. Evametesu pahīyantesu tadekaṭṭhato sabbe pi kilesā pahīyanteva.* Paṭis I 27: *Sotāpattimaggakkhaṇe dassanaṭṭhena sammādiṭṭhi micchādiṭṭhiyā vuṭṭhāti, tadanuvattakakilesehi ca khandhehi ca vuṭṭhāti ....* Dhs 182f.: *Katame dhammā dassanena pahātabbā? Tīṇi saṃyojanāni ... tadekaṭṭhā ca kilesā; ...* As 355: *Ettha hi diṭṭhivicikicchāsu pahīyamānāsu apāyagamanīyo lobho doso moho māno thīnaṃ uddhaccaṃ ahirikaṃ anottappan-ti sabbe pime pahānekaṭṭhā hutvā pahīyanti.* See also footnote 142.

148. The text has 於此間 "in this interval", *etasmiṃ antare*, instead of the usual 於此時, "at this time". 間 = *antara*. The Tibetan text (197b) has "for so long as", *de 'di srid du*.

149. Cf. A IV 374: *Arahā, arahattāya paṭipanno, ... sotāpanno, sotāpattiphalasacchikiriyāya paṭipanno, puthujjano: ime kho ... nava puggalā santo saṃvijjamānā lokasmin-ti.* S V 202: *... tato mudutarehi sotāpanno hoti, tato mudutarehi sotāpattiphalasacchikiriyāya paṭipanno hoti. Yassa kho ... imāni pañcindriyāni sabbena sabbaṃ sabbathā sabbaṃ natthi, tamahaṃ bāhiro puthujjanapakkhe ṭhito ti vadāmīti.* Pp 15: *Yassa puggalassa sotāpattiphalasacchikiriyāya paṭipannassa paññindriyaṃ adhimattaṃ hoti, paññāvāhiṃ paññāpubbaṅgamaṃ ariyamaggaṃ bhāveti ayaṃ vuccati puggalo dhammānusārī. Sotāpattiphalasacchikiriyāya paṭipanno puggalo dhammānusārī phale ṭhito diṭṭhippatto. ... Yassa puggalassa sotāpattiphalasacchikiriyāya paṭipannassa saddhindriyaṃ adhimattaṃ hoti, saddhāvāhiṃ saddhāpubbaṅgamaṃ ariyamaggaṃ bhāveti ayaṃ vuccati puggalo saddhānusārī. ...*

150. Cf. Nett-a 38: *... paṭipajjamānabhūmi paṭipannabhūmi paṭhamābhūmi...*

151. Spk 234: *Dhammānusārisaddhānusārino pana dvepi sotāpattimaggaṭṭhapuggalā.* Paṭis-a 643: *Aṭṭhamakassā ti arahattaphalaṭṭhato paṭṭhāya gaṇiyamāne aṭṭhamabhūtassa sotāpattimaggaṭṭhassa.*

152. Cf. Vism XIV.13/p.439: *... paṭhamamaggapaññā dassanabhūmi. Avasesamaggattayapaññā bhāvanābhūmī ti ...* Nett 49: *Dassanabhūmi niyāmāvakkantiyā padaṭṭhānaṃ, bhāvanābhūmi uttarikānaṃ phalānaṃ pattiyā padaṭṭhānaṃ.* Peṭ 30: *... ugghaṭitaññū puggalo indriyāni paṭilabhitvā dassanabhūmiyaṃ ṭhito sotāpattiphalañ-ca pāpuṇāti, ...* Peṭ 130: *Tattha yo yathābhūtaṃ pajānāti, esā dassanabhūmi.* Peṭ 134: *Yadā ariyasāvako sotāpanno bhavati avinipātadhammo niyato yāva dukkhassantaṃ karoti, ayaṃ dassanabhūmi.* Peṭ 177: *Tattha ugghaṭitaññū tikkhindriyatāya dassanabhūmimāgamma sotāpattiphalaṃ pāpuṇāti....* Peṭ 184: *Yathāyaṃ samāhito yathābhūtaṃ pajānāti, ayaṃ dassanabhūmi. Sotāpattiphalañ-ca yathābhūtaṃ pajānanto nibbindatī ti, idaṃ tanukañ-ca kāmarāgabyāpādaṃ sakadāgāmiphalañ-ca yaṃ nibbindati virajjati, ayaṃ paṭhamajjhānabhāvanābhūmi ca rāgavirāgā cetovimutti anāgāmiphalañ-ca.*

The Tibetan adds "gone to certainty/of fixed destination", *nges par gyur pa*, = *niyatagata, niyatabhūta*, or just *niyata*. Cf. M I 141: *Evaṃ svākkhāte ... dhamme ... yesaṃ bhikkhūnaṃ tīṇi saṃyojanāni pahīnāni, sabbe te sotāpannā, avinipātadhammā, niyatā*

The wisdom with regard to emergence and turning away from both—these are epithets for the knowledge of the path of stream-entry.[153]

Immediately after stream-entry, on the abandoning of the three fetters, he makes the unconditioned the object. The states associated with the path, which are not different from the means (*upāya*?),[154] give rise to knowledge of the fruit of stream-entry. Two or three fruition minds (*phala-citta*) arise and immediately after [that the mind] enters into the bhavaṅga. When the mind emerges from the bhavaṅga, he reviews the path, the fruit, and nibbāna, and he reviews the abandoned afflictions and the remaining afflictions.[155]

---

sambodhiparāyanā. S III 225: *Yassa kho ... ime dhammā evaṃ paññāya mattaso nijjhānaṃ khamanti, ayaṃ vuccati dhammānusārī, okkanto sammattaniyāmaṃ, sappurisabhūmiṃ okkanto, vītivatto puthujjanabhūmiṃ; abhabbo taṃ kammaṃ kātuṃ, yaṃ kammaṃ katvā nirayaṃ vā tiracchānayoniṃ vā pettivisayaṃ vā upapajjeyya; abhabbo ca tāva kālaṃ kātuṃ yāva na sotāpattiphalaṃ sacchikaroti. Yo ... ime dhamme evaṃ pajānāti evaṃ passati, ayaṃ vuccati sotāpanno avinipātadhammo niyato sambodhiparāyanoti*. Cf. D I 155, II 92, 283, S II 160, 203, V 371.

153. 或定從兩起轉慧 Cf. Paṭis I 1: *Dubhato vuṭṭhānavivaṭṭane paññā magge ñāṇaṃ*. Paṭis II 64: *Yā ca dubhatovuṭṭhānavivaṭṭane paññā yañ-ca magge ñāṇaṃ, ime dhammā ekatthā, byañjanam-eva nānaṃ*. Paṭis-a I 26: *Dubhato vuṭṭhānavivaṭṭane paññā magge ñāṇan-ti ettha dubhato ti ubhato, dvayato ti vā vuttaṃ hoti. Kilesānaṃ samucchindanato kilesehi ca tadanuvattakakkhandhehi ca nibbānārammaṇakaraṇato bahiddhā sabbasaṅkhāranimittehi ca vuṭṭhāti vivaṭṭatī ti dubhato vuṭṭhānavivaṭṭane paññā. Tenevāha (Vism XXII.44): Cattāri pi maggañāṇāni animittārammaṇattā nimittato vuṭṭhahanti, samudayassa samucchindanato pavattā vuṭṭhahantī ti dubhato vuṭṭhānāni hontī ti*. It is difficult to make sense of 定, "concentration" coming before 從兩, "from both". Perhaps Saṅghapāla interpreted "from both" (*dubhato*) to mean "from both vision and concentration" rather than "from both the sign (of all formations) and from occurrence (of defilement)"; see Ch. 12 § 23 & 49. There is no word corresponding to "concentration" in the Tibetan translation.

154. 與道等法無異方便起. Tibetan: "... stream-entry, [and] the states associated with the path, the disassociated unconditioned is made the object, and the knowledge of the fruit of stream-entry arises".

155. Parts of this passage are obscure; and also in the Tibetan. Cf. Khuddas-pṭ 232: *Nibbānaṃ ārammaṇaṃ katvā gotrabhuñāṇe niruddhe tena dinnasaññāya nibbānaṃ ārammaṇaṃ katvā diṭṭhisaṃyojanaṃ sīlabbataparāmāsasaṃyojanaṃ vicikicchāsaṃyojanan-ti tīṇi saṃyojanāni samucchedavasena viddhaṃsento sotāpattimaggo uppajjati. Tadanantaraṃ tasseva vipākabhūtāni dve tīṇi vā phalacittāni uppajjanti anantaravipākattā lokuttarānaṃ. Phalapariyosāne panassa cittaṃ bhavaṅgaṃ otarati. Tato bhavaṅgaṃ vicchinditvā paccavekkhaṇatthāya manodvārāvajjanaṃ uppajjati. So hi iminā vatāhaṃ maggena āgato ti maggaṃ paccavekkhati, tato ayaṃ me ānisaṃso laddho ti phalaṃ paccavekkhati, tato ime nāma me kilesā pahīnā ti pahīnakilese paccavekkhati, tato ime nāma me kilesā avasiṭṭhā ti uparimaggattayavajjhe kilese paccavekkhati, avasāne ayaṃ me dhammo ārammaṇato paṭividdho ti amataṃ nibbānaṃ paccavekkhati. Iti sotāpannassa ariyasāvakassa pañca paccavekkhaṇāni honti*. Abhidh-s 65, v. 59: *Tato paraṃ dve tīṇi phalacittāni*

He is called a stream-enterer; one who is not subject to regress; one of fixed destiny; one with enlightenment as his destination;[156] one endowed with comprehension; one who has come to the fruit;[157] [a son] born of the breast and the mouth of the Fortunate One, born of the Dhamma, created by the Dhamma; an heir to the Dhamma, not an heir to material things.[158] He is called "one endowed with [right] view"; "one endowed with vision"; "one who has reached this True Dhamma"; "one who sees this True Dhamma"; "one who is possessed of trainee's knowledge"; "one who is possessed of the trainee's higher knowledge";[159] "one who has entered the stream of the Dhamma"; "a noble one with penetrative wisdom"; and "one who dwells having opened the gate of the deathless".[160]

---

pavattitvā bhavaṅgapātova hoti, puna bhavaṅgaṃ vocchinditvā paccavekkhaṇañāṇāni pavattanti. Ibid 27/v. 35. *Cattāro pana magguppādā ekacittakkhaṇikā, tato paraṃ dve tīṇi phalacittāni yathārahaṃ uppajjanti, tato paraṃ bhavaṅgapāto.* Vism XXII.19/p.676: *Phalapariyosāne pan'assa cittaṃ bhavaṅgaṃ otarati, tato bhavaṅgaṃ upacchinditvā maggapaccavekkhaṇatthāya uppajjati manodvārāvajjanaṃ, tasmiṃ niruddhe paṭipāṭiyā satta maggapaccavekkhaṇajavanānī ti. Puna bhavaṅgaṃ otaritvā ten'eva nayena phalādīnaṃ paccavekkhaṇatthāya āvajjanādīni uppajjanti. Yesaṃ uppattiyā esa maggaṃ paccavekkhati, phalaṃ paccavekkhati, pahīnakilese paccavekkhati, avasiṭṭhakilese paccavekkhati, nibbānaṃ paccavekkhati.*

156. S II 68: *Yato kho, gahapati, ariyasāvakassa pañca bhayāni verāni vūpasantāni honti, catūhi ca sotāpattiyaṅgehi samannāgato hoti, ariyo cassa ñāyo paññāya sudiṭṭho hoti suppaṭividdho, so ākaṅkhamāno attanāva attānaṃ byākareyya: khīṇanirayomhi khīṇatiracchānayoni khīṇapettivisayo khīṇāpāyaduggativinipāto, sotāpannohamasmi avinipātadhammo niyato sambodhiparāyano ti.* Cf. S V 355, A III 211f.

157. 未來果欲分別, lit. "who desires to comprehend the future fruits", *anāgataphalāni abhisayamaṃ/abhisametuṃ icchati/āsī.* Tibetan: "one endowed with comprehension, who has come to the fruit", *mngon par rtogs pa dang ldan pa'i 'bras bu 'ongs pa, = abhisemetāvī, āgataphala.* Cf. Vin III 189: ... *āgataphalā abhisametāvinī viññātasāsanā* ... "... who has come to the fruit, one who has comprehended, one who has understood the Teaching". Sp III 632: *Sā pana yasmā ariyasāvikāva hoti, tenassa padabhājane āgataphalā ti ādi vuttaṃ. Tattha āgataṃ phalaṃ assā ti āgataphalā paṭiladdhasotāpattiphalā ti attho. Abhisametāvinī ti paṭividdhacatusaccā.* S II 137: ... *ariyasāvakassa diṭṭhisampannassa puggalassa abhisametāvino...* Spk II 128: *Abhisametāvinoti paññāya ariyasaccāni abhisametvā ṭhitassa.* A III 284: ... *ariyasāvako āgataphalo viññātasāsano* ...

158. Cf. S II 221; M III 29: *Sāriputtam eva taṃ sammā vadamāno vadeyya: Bhagavato putto oraso mukhato jāto dhammajo dhammanimmito dhammadāyādo no āmisadāyādo ti.* S III: 83: *Pañcakkhandhe pariññāya, sattasaddhammagocarā, / pasaṃsiyā sappurisā, puttā buddhassa orasā.*

159. Instead of 覺智 and 覺明 read 學智 and 學明.

160. Between "one endowed with right view" and "one endowed with vision", the Chinese adds: "one who is practising well; one who penetrates the Noble Doctrine; one who dwells having reached the door of the deathless", 修行通達聖法至醍醐門住, which is repeated later in different characters that accord more with the parallel

Therefore, it is said in the verse thus:
Superior to being the sole king of earth,
To being the sole king of heaven,
To being the ruler of the whole universe—
Is the fruit of stream-entry.[161]

28. Once-returner

The meditator, established in this plane, endeavours further for the realization of the fruit of once-returning, and contemplates, beginning with seeing rise and fall, as taught above. He practises in the way through which he previously saw the path. Relying on the faculties, the powers, and factors of enlightenment, he comprehends the truths. Thus, he practises towards the abandoning of coarse greed and hatred and the afflictions conjoined with them.[162] Immediately after this path, he realizes the fruit of once-returning.

29. Non-returner

The meditator, established in this plane, endeavours further for the realization of the fruit of non-returning, and contemplates, beginning with seeing rise and fall, as taught above. He practises in the way through which he previously saw the path. Relying on the faculties, the powers, and factors of enlightenment, he comprehends the truths. Thus, he practises towards the abandoning of subtle greed and hatred and the afflictions conjoined with them.[163] Immediately after this path, he realizes the fruit of non-returning.

---

in Pali and Tibetan. This is a marginal note with an alternative translation that was mistakenly copied into the text.

Cf. S II 43: *Yato kho bhikkhave ariyasāvako evaṃ paccayaṃ pajānāti, ... paccaya-nirodhagāminiṃ paṭipadaṃ pajānāti, ayaṃ vuccati bhikkhave ariyasāvako diṭṭhisampanno iti pi, dassanasampanno iti pi, āgato imaṃ saddhammaṃ iti pi, passati imaṃ saddhammaṃ iti pi, sekhena ñāṇena sammanāgato iti pi, sekhāya vijjāya samannāgato iti pi, dhammasotaṃ samāpanno iti pi, ariyo nibbedhikapañño iti pi, amatadvāraṃ āhacca tiṭṭhati iti pī ti.*

161. Cf. Dhp 178: *Paṭhaviyā ekarajjena, saggassa gamanena vā / sabbalokādhipaccena, sotāpattiphalaṃ varaṃ.* The Tibetan translates the second *pada* as "than oneself going to heaven".

162. Paṭis II 94: *Sakadāgāmimaggena oḷārikaṃ kāmarāgasaññojanaṃ paṭighasaññojanaṃ, imāni dve saññojanāni pahīyanti, oḷāriko kāmarāgānusayo paṭighānusayo, ime dve anusayā byantihonti.*

163. Ibid. 94–5: *Anāgāmimaggena aṇusahagataṃ kāmarāgasaññojanaṃ paṭigha-saññojanaṃ, imāni dve saññojanāni pahīyanti, aṇusahagato kāmarāgānusayo paṭighānusayo, ime dve anusayā byantihonti.*

30. Arahant

The meditator, established in this plane, endeavours further for the realization of the fruit of arahantship, and contemplates, beginning with seeing rise and fall, as taught above. He practises in the way through which he previously saw the path. Relying on the faculties, the powers, and factors of enlightenment, he comprehends the truths. Thus, he practises towards the abandoning of desire for material [existence] and desire for immaterial [existence]; and he abandons conceit, agitation, ignorance, and other afflictions without remainder.[164] [**458b**] [Immediately after this path][165] the meditator realizes the fruit of arahantship. He reviews the path; he reviews the fruit, nibbāna, and he reviews the abandoned afflictions.

That bhikkhu is an arahant, one who has eradicated the contaminations, has done what is to be done, has fully lived [the Holy Life], has laid down the burden, has reached the true goal, has destroyed the fetter of existence, and is liberated by right knowledge.[166]

He has abandoned five factors and is endowed with six factors, has a single guard, is not fettered to death,[167] has dispelled individual truths, has [totally] given up searching, has pure intentions, has tranquillized the bodily formation, has a well-liberated mind, and has well-liberated wisdom,[168] has fully lived the Holy Life, is the greatest person, supreme person, one who has attained the supreme attainment, one who has removed the cross-bar; one whose trench has been filled in; one whose pillar has been uprooted; one who has no bolt;[169] a noble one; one whose banner has been lowered;

---

164. Ibid. 95: *Arahattamaggena rūparāgo arūparāgo māno uddhaccaṃ avijjā—imāni pañca saññojanāni pahīyanti, mānānusayo bhavarāgānusayo avijjānusayo—ime tayo anusayā byantihonti. Evaṃ saññojanāni pahīyanti, anusayā byantihonti.*

165. The Tibetan, as in the two preceding paragraphs, has "immediately after that path, he realizes arahantship".

166. D III 83: ... *bhikkhu arahaṃ khīṇāsavo vusitavā katakaraṇīyo ohitabhāro anuppattasadattho parikkhīṇabhavasaṃyojano sammadaññā vimutto* ... Cf. Kv 86.

167. 不為死所繫. Saṅghapāla misunderstood *caturāpasseno*, "one who has the fourfold support", (see next note) as referring to Māra's fetters, *māra-pāsa*, with *passa* in *apassena* being misunderstood as *pāsa*. The Tibetan skips over this word.

168. A V 29f.: *Dasa-y-ime ... ariyāvāsā, ... bhikkhu pañcaṅgavippahīno hoti, chaḷaṅga-samannāgato, ekārakkho, caturāpasseno, paṇunnapaccekasacco, samavayasaṭṭhesano, anāvilasaṅkappo, passaddhakāyasaṅkhāro, suvimuttacitto, suvimuttapañño. Kathañ ca ... bhikkhu pañcaṅgavippahīno hoti? Idha ... bhikkhuno kāmacchando pahīno hoti, ... vicikicchā pahīnā hoti. ...*

169. 此謂除瞋恚者, 度岸者, 離煩惱者, 無結礙者, 得聖翻者, 除擔者, 不相應者: "'one who has removed hatred', 'one who has gone to the further shore', 'one who has left the defilements', 'one who is without obstruction', 'obtained the noble difference' (翻), 'has got rid of the burden', and 'is detached'". These are mistranslations of

one who has put down the burden; one who is detached; the Recluse; the Brahmin; one who has bathed; knower of the highest knowledges; supreme Brahmin; arahant;[170] one who has crossed over; one who is released; one who is tamed; one who is appeased; one who is comforted[171]—these are epithets for the arahant.

31. Three kinds of stream-enterer and the non-returner

Herein, even if a stream-enterer does not endeavour further in this birth,[172] through the three kinds of accomplishment in [right] view,[173] there are

---

the difficult, idiomatic Pali word-plays: *ukkhittapaligho saṅkiṇṇaparikho abbūḷhesiko niraggaḷo ariyo pannaddhajo pannabhāro visaññutto* of M I 138, A III 84, Kv 86, Nidd I 21. The Tibetan translator also had difficulties.

170. M I 280: *Ayaṃ vuccati ... bhikkhu samaṇo iti pi brāhmaṇo iti pi nhātako iti pi vedagū iti pi sottiyo iti pi ariyo iti pi arahaṃ itipi.* A IV 144–45: *Bhikkhuṃ samaṇo brāhmaṇo, sottiyo ceva nhātako; vedagū ariyo arahā ...* Cf. Th 221. The Tibetan has *gtsang ma* "clean, pure, immaculate" = Skt *śuci*, instead of "supreme Brahmin", 最上婆羅門. 最上 is an interpretation of *sottiyo as su-uttara > sottara*? The term *sottiya* = Skt *śrotriya*, "one versed in sacred learning", "a scholar".

171. Paṭis I 131: *ahañ c'amhi, loko ca atiṇṇo ahaṃ c'amhi mutto, loko ca amutto; ahañ c'amhi danto, loko ca adanto; ahaṃ c'amhi santo, loko ca asanto; ahaṃ c'amhi assattho, loko ca anassattho; ahaṃ c'amhi parinibbuto, loko ca aparinibbuto; pahomi khvāhaṃ tiṇṇo tāretuṃ, mutto mocetuṃ, danto dametuṃ, santo sametuṃ, assattho assāsetuṃ, parinibbuto pare ca parinibbāpetun ti.* Ap I 126: *santo ca samayissati.* Cf. Cp-a 282: ... *tiṇṇo tāreyyaṃ mutto moceyyaṃ danto dameyyaṃ santo sameyyaṃ assattho assāseyyaṃ parinibbuto ...* Ud-a 133: *ahaṃ sadevakaṃ lokaṃ tiṇṇo tāressāmi, mutto mocessāmi, danto damessāmi, santo samessāmi, assattho assāsessāmi, parinibbuto ...*

172. Cf. S V 397: ... *So tena buddhe aveccappasādena ... dhamme ... saṅghe ... ariyakantehi sīlehi samannāgato hoti .... So tehi ariyakantehi sīlehi santuṭṭho na uttari vāyamati divā pavivekāya rattiṃ paṭisallānāya.*

173. *Mtha' rjes su thob pa* "reaching conclusion/certainty" in the Tibetan probably corresponds to *niṭṭhaṃ gata*. At the start of the non-returner section *mthar thug pa rjes su thob pa* is used instead. The Chinese instead has 得見 = *sampannadiṭṭhi* or *diṭṭhisampanna* or *dassanasampanna* in both cases. A passage in the AN and Paṭis has both *niṭṭhaṃ gata & sampannadiṭṭhi* with reference to the 3 kinds of *sotāpanna*, the *sakadāgāmi* and the arahant, and the five kinds of anāgāmins. Probably the original Vim passage also had both.

A V 119, Paṭis I 160: *Ye keci ... mayi niṭṭhaṃ gatā sabbe te diṭṭhisampannā. Tesaṃ diṭṭhisampannānaṃ pañcannaṃ idha niṭṭhā, pañcannaṃ idha vihāya niṭṭhā. Katamesaṃ pañcannaṃ idha niṭṭhā? Sattakkhattuparamassa, kolaṃkolassa, ekabījissa, sakadāgāmissa, yo ca diṭṭheva dhamme arahā imesaṃ pañcannaṃ idha niṭṭhā. Katamesaṃ pañcannaṃ idha vihāya niṭṭhā? Antarāparinibbāyissa ... akaniṭṭhagāmino mesaṃ pañcannaṃ idha vihāya niṭṭhā.* ... Paṭis II 464: *Tattha niṭṭhaṃ gatā ti maggañāṇavasena sammāsambuddho bhagavā ti nicchayaṃ gatā, nibbematikā ti attho.*

three kinds of stream-enterer: the one who is reborn seven times [at most] (*sattakkhattuparama*), the one who goes from good family[174] to good family (*kolaṅkola*), and the one who is reborn once (*ekabījin*).

Herein, one with dull faculties is one who is reborn seven times [at most]; one with middling faculties is one who goes from good family to good family; and one with sharp faculties is one who is reborn once.

"One who is reborn seven times [at most]": having gone seven times[175] to a heavenly realm, and returning to this [world], he makes an end of suffering.

"One who goes from good family to good family": having gone to a good family two or three times, he makes an end of suffering.

"One who is reborn once": having produced [rebirth in] a human existence, he makes an end of suffering.[176]

---

174. In accordance with the explanation "he is only reborn in very wealthy families", *mahābhogakulesuyeva nibbattatī ti* in Paṭis-a II 464 (see next footnote) and the expression *kulaputta*, "son of a good/respectable/eminent family", etc., the term *kola* is rendered as "good family" here.

175. 七生者七時往天堂來此作苦邊. This differs from explanations in the Pali, which do not mention returning to this world.

176. A I 233, A IV 380: *So tiṇṇaṃ saṃyojanānaṃ parikkhayā sattakkhattuparamo hoti. Sattakkhattuparamaṃ deve ca manusse ca sandhāvitvā saṃsaritvā dukkhassantaṃ karoti. ... kolaṃkolo hoti, dve vā tīṇi vā kulāni sandhāvitvā saṃsaritvā dukkhassantaṃ karoti. ... ekabījī hoti, ekaṃ yeva mānusakaṃ bhavaṃ nibbattetvā dukkhassantaṃ karoti.* Cf. Pp 16. Vism XXIII.55/p.709: *Visesato panettha paṭhamamaggapaññaṃ tāva bhāvetvā mandāya vipassanāya āgato mudindriyo pi sattakkhattuparamo nāma hoti, sattasugatibhave saṃsaritvā dukkhassantaṃ karoti. Majjhimāya vipassanāya āgato majjhimindriyo kolaṃkolo nāma hoti, dve vā tīṇi vā kulāni sandhāvitvā saṃsaritvā dukkhassantaṃ karoti. Tikkhāya vipassanāya āgato tikkhindriyo ekabījī nāma hoti, ekaññeva mānusakaṃ bhavaṃ nibbattetvā dukkhassantaṃ karoti.* Paṭis-a II 464: *Sattakkhattuparamassā ti sattakkhattuṃparamā sattavāraparamā bhavūpapatti attabhāvaggahaṇaṃ assa, tato paraṃ aṭṭhamaṃ bhavaṃ nādiyatī ti sattakkhattuparamo. Tassa sattakkhattuparamassa sotāpannassa. Kolaṃkolassā ti kulato kulaṃ gacchatī ti kolaṃkolo. Sotāpattiphalasacchikiriyato hi paṭṭhāya nīce kule upapatti nāma natthi, mahābhogakulesuyeva nibbattatī ti attho. ... Ekabījissā ti khandhabījaṃ nāma kathitaṃ. Yassa hi sotāpannassa ekaṃ yeva khandhabījaṃ atthi, ekaṃ attabhāvaggahaṇaṃ, so ekabījī nāma. ... Mudupañño hi sotāpanno satta bhave nibbattento sattakkhattuparamo nāma, majjhimapañño paraṃ chaṭṭhaṃ bhavaṃ nibbattento kolaṃkolo nāma, tikkhapañño ekaṃ bhavaṃ nibbattento ekabījī nāma.* Peṭ 178: *Ugghaṭitaññū tikkhindriyo ca tato vipañcitaññū mudindriyo tato mudindriyehi neyyo. Tattha ugghaṭitaññū tikkhindriyatāya dassanabhūmimāgamma sotāpattiphalaṃ pāpuṇāti, ekabījako bhavati. Ayaṃ paṭhamo sotāpanno. ... Vipañcitaññū mudūhi indriyehi dassanabhūmimāgamma sotāpattiphalaṃ pāpuṇāti, kolaṃkolo ca hoti. ... Tattha neyyo dassanabhūmimāgamma sotāpattiphalaṃ pāpuṇāti, sattakkhattuparamo ca bhavati. ...* S V 204: *Imesaṃ kho ... pañcannaṃ indriyānaṃ samattā paripūrattā arahaṃ hoti, tato mudutarehi antarāparinibbāyī hoti, ... tato mudutarehi sattakkhattuparamo hoti, tato mudutarehi dhammānusārī hoti, tato mudutarehi saddhānusārī hotī.* Cf. A I 234; A IV 380; A V 119; Pp 16; Peṭ 30.

If a once-returner does not endeavour further in this birth, having returned to this world once, he makes an end of suffering.[177]

32. Five kinds of non-returner

If a non-returner does not endeavour further in this birth, having passed away from here, he is born in a Pure Abode.[178]

Through a distinction of faculties [of faith, etc.],[179] through the five kinds of accomplishment in [right] view, there are five kinds of non-returners:[180] one who attains nibbāna in the interval (*antarā-parinibbāyin*), one who attains nibbāna upon landing (*upahacca-parinibbāyin*), one who attains nibbāna without impetus (*asaṅkhāra-parinibbāyin*), one who attains nibbāna with impetus (*sasaṅkhāra-parinibbāyin*), and one who goes upstream, to Akaniṭṭha heaven (*uddhaṃsoto-akaniṭṭhagāmin*).

Herein, "one who attains nibbāna in the interval" is one who immediately [after having arisen or] not yet having reached the middle of his life span, gives rise to the noble path for the abandoning of the remaining fetters.

"One who attains nibbāna upon landing" is one who, having gone beyond the middle of his life span, gives rise to the noble path for the abandoning of the remaining fetters.

"One who attains nibbāna without impetus" is one who, without impetus, gives rise to the noble path for abandoning the remaining fetters.

"One who attains nibbāna with impetus" is one who, with impetus, gives rise to the noble path for abandoning the remaining fetters.

"One who goes upstream, to Akaniṭṭha" is one who goes from Aviha to Atappa; from Atappa he goes to Sudassa; from Sudassa he goes to Sudassī; from Sudassī he goes to Akaniṭṭha, and in Akaniṭṭha he gives rise to the noble path for abandoning the remaining fetters.[181] **[458c]**

---

177. A I 233, Pp 16: *So tiṇṇaṃ saṃyojanānaṃ parikkhayā rāgadosamohānaṃ tanuttā sakadāgāmī hoti sakid eva imaṃ lokaṃ āgantvā dukkhassa antaṃ karoti.*

178. Cf. Pp 16: *Idhekacco puggalo pañcannaṃ orambhāgiyānaṃ saṃyojanānaṃ parikkhayā opapātiko hoti, tattha parinibbāyī anāvattidhammo tasmā lokā, ayaṃ vuccati puggalo anāgāmī.* D III 237: *pañca suddhāvāsā: avihā, atappā, sudassā, sudassī, akaniṭṭhā.*

179. 諸根勝, *dbang po'i bye brag, indriyavisesa*, "distinction/difference of faculties". Cf. Paṭis-a II 562: *Aniccato manasikaroto katamindriyaṃ adhimattaṃ hotī ti ādi indriyavisesena puggalavisesaṃ dassetuṃ vuttaṃ. ... Saddhāvimutto saddhindriyassa adhimattattā hoti, ... Diṭṭhattā pattoti diṭṭhippattoti sotāpattimaggakkhaṇe sampayuttena paññindriyena paṭhamaṃ nibbānassa diṭṭhattā pacchā sotāpattiphalādivasena nibbānaṃ pattoti diṭṭhippatto, ...*

180. Tibetan (199a): "Through a distinction/difference of faculties, there are five kinds of reaching certainty".

181. D III 237: *pañca anāgāmino: antarā-parinibbāyī, upahaccaparinibbāyī, asaṅkhāra-parinibbāyī, sasaṅkhāra-parinibbāyī, uddhaṃsoto-akaniṭṭha-gāmī.* Pp 16–17: *Katamo ca*

The life span in Aviha is 10,000 aeons; in Atappa, 20,000 aeons; in Sudassa, 40,000 aeons; in Sudassī, 80,000 aeons; and in Akaniṭṭha, 160,000 aeons.[182]

In four [of the Pure Abode] planes, there are five kinds of persons [each], and in Akaniṭṭha, which is without the one who goes upstream, there are four persons. Thus, there are twenty-four persons.

33. No further existence for the arahant

Because the arahant has cut off all afflictions without remainder, there is no cause of further existence. There being no cause, the life force (*āyusaṅkhāra*) of the arahant, who has renounced body and life, is exhausted—this is the abandoning of suffering. The non-arising of other suffering—this is the end of suffering.[183]

---

puggalo antarāparinibbāyī? Idhekacco puggalo pañcannaṃ orambhāgiyānaṃ saṃyojanānaṃ parikkhayā opapātiko hoti, tattha parinibbāyī anāvattidhammo tasmā lokā. So upapannaṃ vā samanantarā appattaṃ vā vemajjhaṃ āyuppamāṇaṃ ariyamaggaṃ sañjaneti upariṭṭhimānaṃ saṃyojanānaṃ pahānāya—ayaṃ vuccati puggalo antarāparinibbāyī. Katamo ca puggalo upahaccaparinibbāyī? Idhekacco ... lokā. So atikkamitvā vemajjhaṃ āyuppamāṇaṃ upahacca vā kālakiriyaṃ ariyamaggaṃ sañjaneti .... Katamo ca puggalo asaṅkhāraparinibbāyī? ... So asaṅkhārena ariyamaggaṃ sañjaneti ... Katamo ca puggalo sasaṅkhāraparinibbāyī? ... So sasaṅkhārena ariyamaggaṃ sañjaneti ... Katamo ca puggalo uddhaṃsoto akaniṭṭhagāmī? ... So avihā cuto atappaṃ gacchati, atappā cuto sudassaṃ gacchati, sudassā cuto sudassiṃ gacchati, sudassiyā cuto akaniṭṭhaṃ gacchati; akaniṭṭhe ariyamaggaṃ sañjaneti .... Cf. Spk III 1029–30: *Anāgāmīsu āyuno majjhaṃ anatikkamitvā antarā va kilesa-parinibbānaṃ arahattaṃ patto antarā-parinibbāyī nāma. Majjhaṃ upahacca atikkamitvā patto upahacca-parinibbāyī nāma. Asaṅkhārena appayogena akilamanto sukhena patto asaṅkhāra-parinibbāyī nāma. Sasaṅkhārena sappayogena kilamanto dukkhena patto sasaṅkhāra-parinibbāyī nāma. Ime cattāro pañcasu pi suddh' āvāsesu labbhanti. Uddhaṃsoto-akaniṭṭha-gāmī ti ettha pana catukkaṃ veditabbaṃ. Yo hi avihato paṭṭhāya cattāro devaloke sodhetvā akaniṭṭhaṃ gantvā parinibbāyati, ayaṃ uddhaṃsoto-akaniṭṭha-gāmī nāma.*

182. 萬劫, "ten-thousand aeons" is probably a misunderstanding of *kappasahassa*, "thousand aeons". According to the Vibhaṅga, the life-span in these heavens should be one, two, four, eight, and sixteen thousand respectively. Vibh 425: *Avihānaṃ devānaṃ kittakaṃ āyuppamāṇaṃ? Kappasahassaṃ. Atappānaṃ devānaṃ kittakaṃ āyuppamāṇaṃ? Dve kappasahassāni. Sudassānaṃ devānaṃ kittakaṃ āyuppamāṇaṃ? Cattāri kappasahassāni. Sudassīnaṃ devānaṃ kittakaṃ āyuppamāṇaṃ? Aṭṭha kappasahassāni. Akaniṭṭhānaṃ devānaṃ kittakaṃ āyuppamāṇaṃ? Soḷasa kappasahassāni.*

183. Cf. Ud-a 431: *Na hi khīṇāsavā aparikkhīṇe āyusaṅkhāre paresaṃ upavādādibhayena parinibbānāya cetenti ghaṭayanti vāyamanti, na ca paresaṃ pasaṃsādihetu ciraṃ tiṭṭhanti, atha kho saraseneva attano āyusaṅkhārassa parikkhayaṃ āgamenti. Yathāha: Nābhikaṅkhāmi maraṇaṃ, nābhikaṅkhāmi jīvitaṃ; / Kālañ-ca paṭikaṅkhāmi, nibbisaṃ bhatako yathā ti.* (Th 196, 606). *Bhagavā pissa āyusaṅkhāraṃ oloketvā parikkhīṇabhāvaṃ ñatvā yassadāni tvaṃ, dabba, kālaṃ maññasī ti āha.* S V 263: *Atha kho bhagavā cāpāle cetiye sato sampajāno*

Therefore, these verses are taught:
As, when a hammer strikes iron red-hot,
Of those sparks that fly away,
And gradually are extinguished,
The destination cannot be known.

Just so, of those rightly liberated ones,
Who crossed the bondage and torrent of sensuality,
And who reached unshakeable happiness,
The destination cannot be [made] known.[184]

34. Gradual realization of the fruit

Q. Now,[185] there are teachers[186] who say: "Gradually one develops the path, gradually one abandons the afflictions, and gradually one comprehends the truths".

āyusaṅkhāraṃ ossaji. ... Tulamatulañ-ca sambhavaṃ, bhavasaṅkhāramavassaji muni; / Ajjhattarato samāhito, abhindi kavacamivattasambhavanti.

184. Ud 93: *Ayoghanahatass'eva jalato jātavedaso / anupubbūpasantassa yathā na ñāyate gati, / evaṃ sammāvimuttānaṃ / kāmabandhoghatārinaṃ / paññāpetuṃ gati natthi pattānaṃ acalaṃ sukhan ti.*

Saṅghapāla misunderstood *jalato*, "blazing", as *jala + anta*, "water + inside", 入水, however, a spark falling into water it quenches immediately, not gradually. The Tibetan translators had difficulties with *jātavedaso* (so in Skt), "fire", and translated it as "born feeling", *rigs kyi tshor bas 'bar ba*. And instead of *acalaṃ sukhaṃ* "unshakeable happiness", they read or understood *acalaṃ padaṃ*, "unshakeable state", *mi g.yo go 'phang.*

Ud-a 435: ... *ayoghanahatassā ti ayo haññati etenā ti ayoghanaṃ, kammārānaṃ ayokūṭaṃ ayomuṭṭhi ca. Tena ayoghanena hatassa pahatassa. Keci pana ayoghanahatassā ti ghana-ayopiṇḍaṃ hatassā ti atthaṃ vadanti. Eva-saddo cettha nipātamattaṃ. Jalato jātavedasoti jhāyamānassa aggissa ... ayomuṭṭhikūṭādinā mahatā ayoghanena hatassa saṃhatassa, kaṃsabhājanādigatassa vā jalamānassa aggissa, tathā uppannassa vā saddassa anukkamena upasantassa suvūpasantassa dasasu disāsu na katthaci gati paññāyati paccayanirodhena appaṭisandhikaniruddhattā.* Cf. A IV 70: *So pañcannaṃ orambhāgiyānaṃ saṃyojanānaṃ parikkhayā antarāparinibbāyī hoti. Seyyathā pi ... divasasantatte ayokapāle haññamāne papaṭikā nibbattitvā nibbāyeyya.*

185. The discussion in this section is based on the Anupubbābhisamayakathā section of the Kathāvatthu (Kv 212–220); see Bapat, 1937: 120f. EKS did not translate this section, noting: "The section ... owing to unintelligibility, is untranslated". The text is hard to follow, which is to be expected since the original Kathāvatthu discussion is also difficult to follow without the help of the commentary. This translation is based on a draft that was made by Rodney Bucknell. The Tibetan skips over this part and resumes at § 47.

186. According to the Kathāvatthu commentary—see next footnote—the view of gradual realization was held by the Andhakas, Sarvāstivādins, Saṃmitiyas,

A. Through twelve, or through eight, or through four path knowledges, one realizes the fruit.

35. Flaw one

Q. What is there in this view [of gradual realization] that does not fit?
A. If one gradually develops [the path], gradually abandons the afflictions, then one gradually realizes through gradually realizing the fruit. This is acceptable because the fruit corresponds to the path. If so, then [this view] is acceptable. [And in the case of a] single fruit of stream-entry? If so, then it is not acceptable. [But if] the gradual development of the path is also the gradual abandoning of the afflictions, then yes [it is acceptable].[187]

36. Flaw two

Furthermore, there is a second flaw: If through the seeing of suffering, one sees the suffering that is abandoned and the afflictions that are abandoned, it is acceptable. Because having seen suffering, the suffering that is abandoned, and the afflictions that have been abandoned, one realizes the fruit of stream-entry in four parts. Realization [in this way] is acceptable because one's

---

and Bhadrayānikas. However, the Sarvāstivādins would have been the most likely "teachers".

187. LC: "In the first part of the Anupubbābhisamayakathā, the opponent answers both yes and no to the question as to whether *abhisamaya* is gradual for the first path, but not for the first fruit. In the latter case, he denies that it is gradual. He answers yes and no in the first case because he believes that it is a single path and it consists of the succession of the four knowledges. The fruit, however, is just one of the four knowledges, i.e. the last (cf. Kv-a). The Chinese text seems to be concerned with the issue of precisely this difference between the cases of *magga* and *phala*. Kv 212f.: Q. *Anupubbābhisamayo ti?* A. *Āmantā.* Q. *Anupubbena sotāpattimaggaṃ bhāvetī ti?* A. *Na hevaṃ vattabbe.* Q. *Anupubbena sotāpattimaggaṃ bhāvetī ti?* A. *Āmantā.* Q. *Anupubbena sotāpattiphalaṃ sacchikarotī ti?* A. *Na hevaṃ vattabbe.* Then similarly for the other four paths".

Cf. Kv-a 59: *Tattha yesaṃ: Anupubbena medhāvī, thokaṃ thokaṃ khaṇe khaṇe; / Kammāro rajatasseva, niddhame malamattano ti. (Dhp 239) ādīni suttāni ayoniso gahetvā sotāpattiphalasacchikiriyāya paṭipanno ekacce kilese dukkhadassanena pajahati, ekacce samudayanirodhamaggadassanena, tathā sesāpīti evaṃ soḷasahi koṭṭhāsehi anupubbena kilesappahānaṃ katvā arahattapaṭilābho hotī ti evarūpā nānābhisamayaladdhi uppannā, seyyathā pi etarahi andhakasabbatthikasammitiyabhadrayānikānaṃ; tesaṃ laddhivivecanatthaṃ anupubbābhisamayoti pucchā sakavādissa, paṭiññā itarassa. Anupubbena sotāpattimaggan-ti puṭṭho pana ekassa maggassa bahubhāvāpattibhayena paṭikkhipati. Dutiyaṃ puṭṭho dukkhadassanādivasena paṭijānāti. Tāni vā cattāripi ñāṇāni eko sotāpattimaggoyevā ti paṭijānāti, phalaṃ pana ekam-eva icchati, tasmā paṭikkhipati.*

efforts have been successful. If it were acceptable in this manner, one would realise stream-entry in four parts, become one who is reborn seven times [at most] in four parts, become one who goes from good family to good family in four parts, become one who is reborn once in four parts, is established in the path in four parts,[188] and is established in the fruit in four parts—this does not fit. If it is not acceptable, [then the view that] by seeing suffering, one sees the suffering that is abandoned, and the afflictions that are abandoned—this does not fit.[189]

37. Flaw three

Furthermore, there is a third flaw: If [the view that] by seeing suffering, one sees the suffering that is abandoned, and the afflictions that are abandoned, is acceptable, then through that seeing of suffering, one is established in the path of stream-entry in four parts. The four parts of faith practice or the four parts of Dhamma practice[190] would be acceptable [while] not seeing the other three truths. If this is acceptable, one is established in four paths of stream-entry, and there are four faith practices [and] there are four dhamma

188. The variant reading is followed here. The Taishō text (458c24) omits "stands in the path(s)".

189. LC: "Kv gives the variations: seeing the other three truths, going to realization of the other three fruits, the appropriate defilements for each stage, the special qualities, and variations of each stage. The sequence occurs previously with some variations in the closely related discussion at Kv 103ff. What Kv is saying is: Q. What does the individual on his way to the realization of the fruit of stream-entry abandon by seeing suffering? A. [The individual on his way to the realization of the fruit of stream-entry] abandons the view of *sakkāya*, doubt, misapprehension of precepts and vows, and the defilements that exist together with these in four parts by seeing suffering. Q. Does the stream-enterer [abandon] in four parts [by seeing suffering]? A. ... Q. Does the stream-enterer not [abandon] in four parts [by seeing suffering]?

The implication is that if the four parts require four separate consciousnesses, then at the time of the first consciousness one either has a stream-enterer who has not abandoned the whole of doubt, etc. or one has a non-stream-enterer who has partially abandoned doubt, etc".

Kv 213–216: *Sotāpattiphalasacchikiriyāya paṭipanno puggalo dukkhadassanena kiṃ jahatī ti? Sakkāyadiṭṭhiṃ, vicikicchaṃ, sīlabbataparāmāsaṃ, tadekaṭṭhe ca kilese catubhāgaṃ jahatī ti. Catubhāgaṃ sotāpanno, catubhāgaṃ na sotāpanno, catubhāgaṃ sotāpattiphalappatto paṭiladdho adhigato sacchikato upasampajja viharati, kāyena phusitvā viharati, catubhāgaṃ na kāyena phusitvā viharati, catubhāgaṃ sattakkhattuparamo kolaṅkolo ekabījī buddhe aveccappasādena samannāgato, dhamme ... pe ... saṅghe ... pe ... ariyakantehi sīlehi samannāgato catubhāgaṃ na ariyakantehi sīlehi samannāgato ti? Na hevaṃ vattabbe.*

190. This refers to the *saddhānusārin* and the *dhammānusārin*, who are practising for the fruit of stream-entry. Cf. 458a01ff.

practices—this does not fit. [**459a**] If it is not acceptable, [then the view that] by seeing suffering, one sees the suffering that is abandoned, and the afflictions that are abandoned—this too does not fit.

38. Flaw four

Furthermore, there is a fourth flaw: If [the view that] by seeing the path one is a practitioner (*paṭipannaka*) and by seeing the path one is established in the fruit, is acceptable, then [the view that] by seeing suffering one is a practitioner, and by seeing [suffering] one is established in the fruit, would be acceptable. If it is acceptable that, due to seeing one kind [of truth], one is a practitioner and is established in the fruit, [then] there are many flaws herein—this does not fit. If it is not acceptable, [then the view that] by seeing the path one is a practitioner, and by seeing the path one is established in the fruit—this too does not fit.[191]

39. Flaw five

Furthermore, there is a fifth flaw: If, by seeing the path, one realizes the fruit, [then] without having yet seen suffering, its origination, and its cessation, there is realization of the fruit. [If] this is acceptable, [then] seeing suffering, its origination, and its cessation is pointless.[192]

191. LC: "Kv 216–219: Q. *Sotāpattiphalasacchikiriyāya paṭipanno puggalo dukkhaṃ dakkhanto paṭipannako ti vattabbo ti?* A. *Āmantā.* Q. *Dukkhe diṭṭhe phale ṭhito ti vattabbo ti?* A. *Na hevaṃ vattabbe.* [Similarly for *samudaya* and *nirodha.*] Q. *Sotāpattiphalasacchikiriyāya paṭipanno puggalo maggaṃ dakkhanto paṭipannako ti vattabbo, magge diṭṭhe phale ṭhito ti vattabbo ti?* A. *Āmantā.* [Each of the first three pairs of questions are then asked again and their answer contrasted with that of the fourth. Then the four questions are asked again in negative format, receiving the equivalent answers.] Q. *Sotāpattiphalasacchikiriyāya paṭipanno puggalo dukkhaṃ dakkhanto paṭipannako ti vattabbo, dukkhe diṭṭhe na vattabbaṃ phale ṭhito ti vattabbo ti?* A. *Āmantā.* Q. *Niratthiyaṃ dukkhadassanan ti?* [Similarly for seeing arising and seeing cessation]".

192. LC: "This again concerns the point that in a four-stage *magga* of the kind presented in Kv (as compared to the sixteen stages adopted by the Vaibhāṣikas), the last stage involves the seeing of the truth of the path and it is this that actually produces the fruit of stream-entry. The argument presented here is precisely that of the next section of Kv. If seeing suffering means that one is 'on the way' but when one has seen suffering one is not established in the fruit, then seeing suffering is useless (*niratthiya*). Similarly in the cases of seeing arising and seeing cessation".

40. Flaw six

Furthermore, there is a sixth flaw: If [the view that] through twelve or through eight or through four path knowledges there is realization of the fruit of stream-entry is acceptable, [then] through this realisation, twelve or eight or four fruits of stream-entry would be acceptable, and there would be path knowledges without fruits. If this were acceptable thus as basis, [then] through there being a flaw herein—this does not fit. Moreover, if it were acceptable, would there be realization of the fruit of stream-entry through twelve, or through eight, or through four path knowledges? This too does not fit.[193]

41. Flaw seven

Furthermore, there is a seventh flaw. If [the view that] twelve, or eight, or four path knowledges produce a single fruit of stream-entry is acceptable, [then] this too does not fit [since] many objects (*ārammaṇa*) would produce one result, just as if many mango fruit [trees] were to produce a single fruit.

42. Objection

Q. If in a single knowledge, in a single moment (*khaṇa*), simultaneously there is comprehension of the four truths, [then] a single knowledge would become four graspings of the object. If by seeing [the truth of] suffering one sees four truths, the four truths become the truth of suffering. If these two [arguments] are pointless, then this [view] does not fit: "In a single moment, in a single knowledge, simultaneously, there is comprehension of four truths".

A. It is not the case that a single knowledge becomes four graspings of the object, and it is not the case that the four truths become the truth of suffering. The meditator only [comprehends] the four truths from the beginning; the different characteristics (*ākāra*) are a unity through previous comprehension.

A. this time, through the noble practice of the truth of suffering, through

---

193. LC: "In Kv, this corresponds to the section after the final 'Objection and answer' section. Bapat seems to have missed it, perhaps because the order is different. Upatissa has logically moved the objection of the *paravādin* to the end so as to produce a list of seven flaws. The exponent of *ekābhisamaya* asks if the fruit of stream-entry is realized by means of four [separate] knowledges, to which the reply is affirmative. He then asks if there are four fruits of stream-entry. This again cannot be argued. The implication is again that the two answers are inconsistent.

Kv 218f.: *Catūhi ñāṇehi sotāpattiphalaṃ sacchikarotī ti? Āmantā. Cattāri sotāpattiphalānī ti? Na hevaṃ vattabbe* ... Kv goes on to apply the same analysis with eight, twelve, 44, and 77 knowledges".

penetration of its characteristics, there is penetration of four truths. With regard to their aspects, the four truths are a unity in the sense of realness (*tathaṭṭhena*).[194]

Likewise the five aggregates, which have different characteristics, are a unity. Through previous comprehension of the aggregate of matter as impermanent, one has also seen the five aggregates as impermanent. One [then] sees impermanence in the immaterial aggregates as well, that is, in all five aggregates. It is the same with the faculties and the elements. Thus should it be understood here.[195]

Miscellaneous Topics

Herein, the miscellaneous topics (*pakiṇṇaka dhamma*) to be known are: insight, thinking, rapture, feelings, planes (*bhūmi*), faculties, liberations, afflictions, and the two attainments.

43. Insight

Herein, insight is of two kinds, namely, jhāna insight and bare insight (*sukkha-vipassanā*). [**459b**]

Q. What is jhāna insight?

---

194. Cf. Paṭis II 106: *Tathaṭṭhena, anattaṭṭhena, saccaṭṭhena, paṭivedhaṭṭhena, abhijānanaṭṭhena, parijānanaṭṭhena, dhammaṭṭhena, dhātuṭṭhena, ñātaṭṭhena, sacchikiriyaṭṭhena, phusanaṭṭhena, abhisamayaṭṭhena—imehi dvādasahi ākārehi cattāri saccāni ekasaṅgahitāni. Yaṃ ekasaṅgahitaṃ taṃ ekattaṃ. Ekattaṃ ekena ñāṇena paṭivijjhatī ti—cattāri saccāni ekappaṭivedhāni.* Paṭis I 142: *Tathaṭṭhena ... abhisamayaṭṭhena—imehi dvādasahi ākārehi sabbe dhammā ekasaṅgahitā.*

195. LC: "In the Kathāvatthu, this objection and answer come after Flaw 5. The objector asks if all four truths are seen when suffering is seen. To this the exponent of *ekābhisamaya* replies that they are. The objector then asks if the truth of suffering is all four truths. This of course cannot be argued. The implication is that these two answers are inconsistent. So the exponent of *ekābhisamaya* asks if when the aggregate of materiality is seen, all five aggregates are seen. The answer has to be yes. So he then asks if the aggregate of materiality is all five aggregates. This of course cannot be argued. The implication is that if these two answers are not inconsistent in these cases, they cannot be in the case of the truths. Kv 218: Q (of objector): *Dukkhe diṭṭhe cattāri saccāni diṭṭhāni hontī ti?* A. *Āmantā.* Q (of objector): *Dukkhasaccaṃ cattāri saccānī ti?* A. *Na hevaṃ vattabbe ...* Q. *Rūpakkhandhe aniccato diṭṭhe pañcakkhandhā aniccato diṭṭhā hontī ti?* A. *Āmantā.* Q. *Rūpakkhandho pañcakkhandhā ti?* A. *Na hevaṃ vattabbe ...* [similarly for the remaining aggregates, the 12 bases, the 18 elements, and the 22 faculties]".

A. Having attained concentration, one overcomes the hindrances by the power of concentration (*samādhi-bala).* Through analysing name (*nāma*) by way of the jhāna factors, one sees with insight (*vipassati*) matter. Preceded by calm (*samatha*), one develops insight.

With regard to bare insight: One overcomes the hindrances through the power of analysis (*vibhaṅga-bala?*)[196] Through analysing matter by way of the formations, one sees name with insight. One develops calm preceded by insight.[197]

44. Thinking

Thinking (*vitakka*): When a bare insight practioner has insight up to the first jhāna, insight and the path and fruit are with thinking.[198]

---

196. Cf. Paṭis I 97: *Dvīhi balehīti dve balāni: samathabalaṃ, vipassanābalaṃ. Katamaṃ samathabalaṃ? Nekkhammavasena cittassekaggatā avikkhepo samathabalaṃ. ... Katamaṃ vipassanābalaṃ? Aniccānupassanā vipassanābalaṃ. Dukkhānupassanā ...* The Vim, however, does not use the terms corresponding to *samatha-bala* (= 奢摩力) and *vipassanā-bala* (= 毘婆舍那力) but *samādhi-bala* (定力) and *vibhaṅga-bala* (分別力), or a term related to *vibhaṅga* such as *paricchedana* (Vim 459b01–03). The Paṭis-a mentions that there is a variant reading *samādhibalaṃ* instead of *samathabalaṃ* in the above passage, Paṭis-a I 314: *samādhibalan-ti pi pāṭho.*

197. A II 157; Paṭis II 92–6: *Idh' āvuso bhikkhu samathapubbaṅgamaṃ vipassanaṃ bhāveti, tassa samathapubbaṅgamaṃ vipassanaṃ bhāvayato maggo sañjāyati. So taṃ maggaṃ āsevati bhāveti bahulīkaroti, tassa taṃ maggaṃ āsevato ... saññojanāni pahīyanti, anusayā byantihonti. Puna ca paraṃ āvuso bhikkhu vipassanāpubbaṅgamaṃ samathaṃ bhāveti, tassa vipassanāpubbaṅgamaṃ samathaṃ bhāvayato maggo sañjāyati. So taṃ maggaṃ āsevati ... anusayā byantihonti ... Kathaṃ samathapubbaṅgamaṃ vipassanaṃ bhāveti? Nekkhammavasena cittassa ekaggatā avikkhepo samādhi, tattha jāte dhamme aniccato ... dukkhato ... anattato anupassanaṭṭhena vipassanā. Iti paṭhamaṃ samatho, pacchā vipassanā; tena vuccati samathapubbaṅgamaṃ vipassanaṃ bhāveti ... Kathaṃ vipassanāpubbaṅgamaṃ samathaṃ bhāveti? Aniccato ... anattato anupassanaṭṭhena vipassanā; tattha jātānaṃ dhammānañ ca vossaggārammaṇatā cittassa ekaggatā avikkhepo samādhi. Iti paṭhamaṃ vipassanā pacchā samatho; tena vuccati vipassanā-pubbaṅgamaṃ samathaṃ bhāveti.* Cf. Ps I 108. *Idhekacco paṭhamaṃ upacārasamādhiṃ vā appanāsamādhiṃ vā uppādeti, ayaṃ samatho; so tañ-ca taṃsampayutte ca dhamme aniccādīhi vipassati, ayaṃ vipassanā. Iti paṭhamaṃ samatho, pacchā vipassanā. Tena vuccati samathapubbaṅgamaṃ vipassanaṃ bhāvetī ti.* Paṭis-a III 586: *... tattha jātānaṃ dhammānaṃ vossaggārammaṇatāya nibbāna-patiṭṭhābhāvena hetubhūtena uppādito yo cittassa ekaggatā-saṅkhāto upacārappaṇābhedo avikkhepo, so samādhī ti vipassanāto pacchā uppādito nibbedhabhāgiyo samādhi niddiṭṭho hoti. Tasmā yeva hi iti paṭhamaṃ vipassanā pacchā samatho ti vuttaṃ.*

198. The Chinese is cryptic and has been translated here in accordance with the parallels in the "Rapture" and "Feeling" sections. 覺者燥觀初禪及觀者,觀道及果成有覺, lit.: "Thinking: dry insight first jhāna and (及) insight: insight/reviewing path and fruit are with thinking". The character 及, "and", can mean "reach, come up to"

In [the first] three jhānas, insight as far as change of lineage is with thinking, and the path and fruit are without thinking.

In the plane with thinking (*savitakka-bhūmi*), the path has eight path factors. In the plane without thinking, there are seven factors, excepting [the factor of right] intention.

45. Rapture

Rapture (*pīti*): When the bare insight practitioner has painful practice (*dukkhapaṭipadā*), insight [as far as] knowledge of conformity arises without pain (*niddukkha*?). Change of lineage, the path, and the fruit arise together with rapture.

When the bare insight practitioner has pleasant practice (*sukhapaṭipadā*), in [the first] two jhānas, insight and the path and fruit arise together with rapture. In the third and fourth jhāna, insight and the path and fruit arise without rapture.

In the plane of rapture, path and fruit, and the seven factors of enlightenment arise [together]. In the plane without rapture, there are six factors of enlightenment, excepting the enlightenment factor of rapture.[199]

---

in other texts. 觀 can correspond to *vipassanā, paccavekkhaṇa,* and *vicāra.*

This section is related to the discussion on insight and jhānas at Vism XXI.111–14: ... *vipassanāniyamena hi sukkhavipassakassa uppannamaggopi, samāpattilābhino jhānaṃ pādakaṃ akatvā uppannamaggopi, paṭhamajjhānaṃ pādakaṃ katvā pakiṇṇakasaṅkhāre sammasitvā uppāditamaggo pi paṭhamajjhānikāva honti. Sabbesu satta bojjhaṅgāni aṭṭha maggaṅgāni pañca jhānaṅgāni honti. Tesaṃ hi pubbabhāgavipassanā somanassasahagatāpi upekkhāsahagatāpi hutvā vuṭṭhānakāle saṅkhārupekkhābhāvaṃ patvā somanassasahagatā hoti.* ...

199. The character 喜 is used both for *pīti,* "rapture", and *somanassa,* "joy". The "plane without rapture" is the *nippītika-bhūmi*, i.e. the third jhāna and above.

Cf. Vism XXI.112–114/p.666–67: *Vipassanāniyamena hi sukkhavipassakassa uppannamaggopi, samāpattilābhino jhānaṃ pādakaṃ akatvā uppannamaggopi, paṭhamajjhānaṃ pādakaṃ katvā pakiṇṇakasaṅkhāre sammasitvā uppāditamaggo pi paṭhamajjhānikāva honti. Sabbesu satta bojjhaṅgāni aṭṭha maggaṅgāni pañca jhānaṅgāni honti. Tesaṃ hi pubbabhāgavipassanā somanassasahagatāpi upekkhāsahagatāpi hutvā vuṭṭhānakāle saṅkhārupekkhābhāvaṃ patvā somanassasahagatā hoti. Pañcakanaye dutiyatatiyacatutthajjhānāni pādakāni katvā uppāditamaggesu yathākkameneva jhānaṃ caturaṅgikaṃ tivaṅgikaṃ duvaṅgikañ-ca hoti. Sabbesu pana satta maggaṅgāni honti. Catutthe cha bojjhaṅgāni. Ayaṃ viseso pādakajjhānaniyamena ceva vipassanāniyamena ca hoti. Tesam-pi hi pubbabhāgavipassanā somanassasahagatāpi upekkhāsahagatāpi hoti. Vuṭṭhānagāminī somanassasahagatāva. Pañcamajjhānaṃ pādakaṃ katvā nibbattitamagge pana upekkhācittekaggatāvasena dve jhānaṅgāni bojjhaṅgamaggaṅgāni cha satta ceva. Ayam-pi viseso ubhayaniyamavasena hoti. Imasmiṃ hi naye pubbabhāgavipassanā somanassasahagatā vā upekkhāsahagatā vā hoti. Vuṭṭhānagāminī upekkhāsahagatāva.* ...

46. Feelings

Feelings: When the bare insight practitioner has painful practice, insight as far as knowledge of conformity arise together with equanimity. Change of lineage and the path and fruit arise together with joy (*somanassa*).

When the bare insight practitioner has pleasant practice, in [the first] three jhānas, insight and the path and the fruit arise together with joy. In the fourth jhāna, insight and the path and fruit arise together with equanimity.

47. Noble planes

There are two kinds of planes: the plane of seeing (*dassanabhūmi*) and the plane of practice (*bhāvanābhūmi*).

Herein, the path of stream-entry is the plane of seeing. The other three paths and the four fruits of recluseship are the plane of practice.

When one sees what one has not yet seen—this is "the plane of seeing". When one practices what one has seen thus—this is called "the plane of practice".[200]

Furthermore, there are two planes: the plane of the trainee and the plane of the non-trainee.

---

200. The plane of seeing is the wisdom of the path of stream-entry, the plane of development is the wisdom of the other three paths. Cf. Vism XIV.13/p.439 ... *paṭhamamaggapaññā dassanabhūmi. Avasesamaggattayapaññā bhāvanābhūmī ti* ... Peṭ 130: *Catasso ariyabhūmiyo, cattāri sāmaññaphalāni, tattha yo yathābhūtaṃ pajānāti, esā dassanabhūmi.* Nett 14: *Dassanena tīṇi saṃyojanāni pahiyyanti .... Bhāvanāya satta saṃyojanāni pahiyyanti ....* Ibid. 50: *Dassanabhūmi niyāmāvakkantiyā padaṭṭhānaṃ. Bhāvanābhūmi uttarikānaṃ phalānaṃ pattiyā padaṭṭhānaṃ.* Nett 49: *Dassanabhūmi niyāmāvakkantiyā padaṭṭhānaṃ, bhāvanābhūmi uttarikānaṃ phalānaṃ pattiyā padaṭṭhānaṃ.* Nett-a 38: *Dassanabhūmi paṭhamamaggaphaladhammā. Bhāvanābhūmi avasiṭṭhamaggaphaladhammā.* Peṭ 30: ... *indriyāni paṭilabhitvā dassanabhūmiyaṃ ṭhito sotāpattiphalañ-ca pāpuṇāti,* .... Peṭ 178: ... *dassanabhūmimāgamma sotāpattiphalaṃ pāpuṇāti, ekabījako bhavati.* ... Peṭ 185: *Yathāyaṃ samāhito yathābhūtaṃ pajānāti, ayaṃ dassanabhūmi. Sotāpattiphalañ-ca yathābhūtaṃ pajānanto nibbindatī ti, idaṃ tanukañ-ca kāmarāgabyāpādaṃ sakadāgāmiphalañ-ca yaṃ nibbindati virajjati, ayaṃ paṭhamajjhāna-bhāvanābhūmi ca rāgavirāgā cetovimutti anāgāmiphalañ-ca.*

The explanation of these two planes corresponds with those of the *darśanamārga* and *bhāvanāmārga* in the Sarvāstivāda scheme of the stages of the paths; see Dhammajoti 2009b: 440–453. The *Abhidharmakośabhāṣya*'s explanation links the three supramundane faculties, see the next section, with these two planes and the plane of the non-trainee. The description of the plane of seeing here in Vim, i.e. "when one sees what one has not yet seen", corresponds to the "'I shall-know-what-is-not-known' faculty". See next fn.

Herein, the four paths and the three fruits of recluseship are the plane of the trainee. The fruit of arahantship is the plane of the non-trainee.[201]

48. Three supramundane faculties

With regard to the faculties: There are three supramundane faculties (*lokuttarindriya*),[202] namely, the "I-shall-know-what-is-not-yet-known" faculty (*anaññātaññassāmītindriya*), the perfect-knowledge faculty (*aññindriyaṃ*) and the one-who-has-perfectly-known faculty (*aññātāvindriyaṃ*).

Herein, the stream-enterer's knowledge of the path, which was not yet known before, one now will know, is the "'I shall-know-what-is-not-yet-known' faculty".

Having known the states of the three path knowledges and the three fruit knowledges, one knows them again—is the "perfect-knowledge faculty".

The knowledge of the fruit of arahantship—having known states completely (*asesa*)—is the "one-who-has-perfectly-known faculty".[203]

---

201. Nett-a 38: *Sekkhabhūmi cattāro ariyamaggadhammā heṭṭhimā ca tayo phaladhammā. Asekkhabhūmi aggaphaladhammā.* Cf. S V 302: ... *sekho bhikkhu sekhabhūmiyaṃ ṭhito sekhosmī ti pajāneyya, asekho bhikkhu asekhabhūmiyaṃ ṭhito asekhosmī ti pajāneyyā ti?* ...

202. This term is only found in the Paṭisambhidamagga commentary. Paṭis-a I 90: *Anaññātaññassāmītindriyādīnaṃ tiṇṇam-pi hi lokuttarindriyānaṃ* ...

203. Cf. D III 219: *Tīn'indriyāni. Anaññātaññassāmītindriyaṃ, aññindriyaṃ, aññātāvindriyaṃ.* Sv III 1002: *Anaññātaññassāmī t' indriyan ti: Ito pubbe aññātaṃ aviditaṃ dhammaṃ jānissāmī ti, paṭipannassa uppannaṃ indriyaṃ sotāpattimaggañāṇass' etaṃ adhivacanaṃ. Aññindriyan ti aññābhūtaṃ jānanabhūtaṃ indriyaṃ. Sotāpattiphalato paṭṭhāya chasu ṭhānesu ñāṇass' etaṃ adhivacanaṃ. Aññātāvindriyan ti aññātavīsu jānana-kicca-pariyosāna-pattesu dhammesu indriyaṃ. Arahattaphalass' etaṃ adhivacanaṃ.* Peṭ 66: *Tattha katamaṃ anaññātaññassāmītindriyaṃ? Idha ... bhikkhu anabhisametassa dukkhassa ariyasaccassa abhisamayāya chandaṃ janeti ... Idha ... idaṃ dukkhaṃ ariyasaccan-ti yathābhūtaṃ pajānāti, yā ca maggo, idaṃ aññindriyaṃ. Āsavakkhayā anāsavo hoti, idaṃ vuccati aññātāvindriyaṃ.* (Cf. Nett 170.) Vibh-a 125: *Anaññātaññassāmīti pavatte jānanalakkhaṇe indaṭṭhaṃ kāretī ti anaññātaññassāmītindriyaṃ. Ñātānaṃ yeva dhammānaṃ puna ājānane indaṭṭhaṃ kāretī ti aññindriyaṃ. Aññātāvībhāve indaṭṭhaṃ kāretī ti aññātāvindriyaṃ.* Spk III 237: *Anaññātaññassāmītindriyan-ti anamatagge saṃsāre ajānitapubbaṃ dhammaṃ jānissāmī ti paṭipannassa sotāpattimaggakkhaṇe uppannaṃ indriyaṃ. Aññindriyan-ti tesaṃ yeva ñātadhammānaṃ ājānanākārena sotāpattiphalādīsu chasu ṭhānesu uppannaṃ indriyaṃ. Aññātāvindriyan-ti aññātāvīsu arahattaphaladhammesu uppannaṃ indriyaṃ. Tattha tattha tena tenākārena uppannassa ñāṇassevetaṃ adhivacanaṃ.* Vism XVI.3/p.491, Vibh-a 125: *pubbabhāge anaññātaṃ amataṃ padaṃ catusaccadhammaṃ vā jānissāmīti evaṃ paṭipannassa uppajjanato indriyaṭṭhasambhavato ca anaññātaññassāmītindriyan-ti vuttaṃ. Dutiyaṃ ājānanato indriyaṭṭhasambhavato ca aññindriyaṃ. Tatiyaṃ aññātāvino catūsu saccesu niṭṭhitaññāṇakiccassa khīṇāsavassa uppajjanato indriyaṭṭhasambhavato ca aññātāvindriyaṃ.*

49. Three liberations

With regard to the liberations: There are three liberations, namely, the signless liberation, the desireless liberation, and the emptiness liberation.[204]

According to the path and knowledge of conformity, the not creating of a sign is the signless liberation; the not creating of a desire is the desireless liberation; and the not creating of attachment is the emptiness liberation.[205]

Furthermore, these three liberations occur in different paths through insight; and they occur in one path through attainment.[206]

Abhidh-k-bh II.8, 042|09-13: *darśanamārge anājñātamājñāsyāmīndriyaṃ, bhāvanāmārge ājñendriyam, aśaikṣamārge ājñātāvīndriyamiti. kiṃ kāraṇam? darśanamārge hyanājñātamājñātuṃ pravṛttaḥ. bhāvanāmārge nāstyapūrvamājñeyaṃ tadeva tvājānāti śeṣānuśayaprahāṇārtham. aśaikṣamārge tvājñātmityavagama ājñātāvaḥ. so 'syāstī ti ājñātāvī.*

Śrāvakabhūmi II-5-b: *trīṇīndriyāṇi: anājñātam ājñāsyāmīndriyam ājñendriyam ājñātavata indriyam. eṣām indriyāṇāṃ kathaṃ vyavasthānaṃ bhavati? anabhisamitānāṃ satyānām abhisamayāya prayuktasyānājñātam ājñāsyāmīndriyavyavasthānam. abhisamitavataḥ śaikṣasyājñendriyavyavasthānam. kṛtakṛtyasyāśaikṣasyārhata ājñātāvīndriyavyavasthānam.*

204. The order, which is so in both the Chinese and Tibetan, is unusual. In Pali and Sanskrit works, the order is the opposite: emptiness, desireless, and signless. As the explanation below shows, the *Vimuttimagga* orders the three liberations in accordance with the contemplations of *anicca, dukkha*, and *anattā* that give rise to them.

Cf. Paṭis II 35: *Suññato vimokkho, animitto vimokkho, appaṇihito vimokkho.* Vin III 94: *suññataṃ vimokkhaṃ... animittaṃ vimokkhaṃ... appaṇihitaṃ vimokkhaṃ.... Śrāvakabhūmi* II-5-c: *trīṇi vimokṣamukhāni: tadyathā śūnyatā apraṇihitam ānimittam.* Abhidh-k-bh VIII.24, 450|07–08: *anāsravāstvete trayaḥ samādhayas trīṇi vimokṣamukhānyucyante: śūnyatāvimokṣamukhamapraṇihitamānimittaṃ vimokṣamukhamiti.*

205. Paṭis II 36: ... *iti paṭisañcikkhati: suññamidaṃ attena vā attaniyena vā ti. So tattha abhinivesaṃ na karotī ti suññato vimokkho. Ayaṃ suññato vimokkho. ... So tattha nimittaṃ na karotī ti animitto vimokkho. ... So tattha paṇidhiṃ na karotī ti appaṇihito vimokkho.* ... Paṭis-a III 553: *Abhinivesaṃ na karotī ti anattānupassanāvasena attābhinivesaṃ na karoti. Nimittaṃ na karotī ti aniccānupassanāvasena niccanimittaṃ na karoti. Paṇidhiṃ na karotī ti dukkhānupassanāvasena paṇidhiṃ na karoti. Ime tayo vimokkhā pariyāyena vipassanākkhaṇe tadaṅgavasenāpi labbhanti, nippariyāyena pana samucchedavasena maggakkhaṇe yeva.*

The Tibetan (199b) has *rnam par thar pa'i sgo*, which corresponds to *vimokkhamukha* "gate to liberation". For the three *vimokkhamukha*, see Nett 90: *Tattha suññatavimokkhamukhaṃ paññākkhandho, animittavimokkhamukhaṃ samādhikkhandho, appaṇihitavimokkhamukhaṃ sīlakkhandho.*

206. This is based on Paṭis II 64 f.: *Katihākārehi tayo vimokkhā nānākkhaṇe honti. Katihākārehi tayo vimokkhā ekakkhaṇe honti.* ... Whereas Paṭis uses *khaṇa* "moment", the Chinese text has "path", *magga*, 道, and so a similar passage in Abhidh-s 65: *Tasmā yadi vuṭṭhānagāminivipassanā anattato vipassati, suññato vimokkho nāma hoti maggo.*

Q. How do these occur in different paths through insight? [**459c**]
A. Through the contemplation of impermanence, there is the signless liberation. Through the contemplation of suffering, there is the desireless liberation. Through the contemplation of without self, there is the emptiness liberation.[207]

Q. How is there signless liberation through the contemplation of impermanence?
A. Through attending to impermanence and through [seeing] the destruction of the formations, the mind has great resolve. One obtains the faith faculty and, following upon it (*tadanvaya*), the other four faculties. One knows the sign according to reality and, following upon it, the [knowledge of the] impermanence of all formations arises and causes the arising of fear of the sign [of the formations]. There is knowledge of occurrence (*pavatta* or *uppāda*) from the sign of the formations. The mind emerges from the sign and passes into the signless.[208] Through the signless liberation, the body is

---

Yadi aniccato vipassati, animitto vimokkho nāma. Yadi dukkhato vipassati, appaṇihito vimokkho nāmā ti ca maggo vipassanāgamanavasena tīṇi nāmāni labhati, tathā phalañ-ca maggāgamanavasena maggavīthiyaṃ. Phalasamāpattivīthiyaṃ pana yathāvuttanayena vipassantānaṃ yathāsakaphalamuppajjamānam-pi vipassanāgamanavaseneva suññatādivimokkhoti ca pavuccati, ārammaṇavasena pana sarasavasena ca nāmattayaṃ sabbattha-sabbesam-pi samam-eva ca. "Therefore, with the insight leading to emergence, one sees with insight without self, the path is known as the emptiness liberation; ... desireless liberation. Thus the path receives three names by way of the approach of insight. ... But in the process of the attainment of fruition, for those who see with insight in the manner as said [above], the fruits that arise respectively in each case are called the emptiness liberation, etc., only by way of the approach of insight. But by way of object and essential nature, the three names are just equal to all (paths and fruits) everywhere". See also Bodhi 2007a: 357.

Sv uses *maggasamādhi* "path-concentration": Sv III 1003: ... *Vipassanāgamanena maggasamādhi appaṇihito nāma. Maggāgamanena phalaṃ appaṇihitaṃ nāmā ti ayaṃ āgamanato kathā. Maggasamādhi pana rāgādīhi suññatattā suññato, ... rāgapaṇidhi ādīnaṃ abhāvā appaṇihitoti ayaṃ saguṇato kathā. Nibbānaṃ rāgādīhi suññatattā rāgādinimittapaṇidhīnañ-ca abhāvā suññatañceva animittañ-ca appaṇihitañ-ca. Tadārammaṇo maggasamādhi suññato animitto appaṇihito. Ayaṃ ārammaṇato kathā.*

207. Paṭis II 58: *Aniccato manasikaronto adhimokkhabahulo animittaṃ vimokkhaṃ paṭilabhati. Dukkhato manasikaronto passaddhibahulo appaṇihitaṃ vimokkhaṃ paṭilabhati. Anattato manasikaronto vedabahulo suññataṃ vimokkhaṃ paṭilabhati.*

208. This passage is based on various passages from the Vimokkhakathā chapter of the Paṭisambhidāmagga. Paṭis II 50: *Aniccato manasikaroto adhimokkhabahulassa saddhindriyaṃ ādhipateyyaṃ hoti. Bhāvanāya cattārindriyāni tadanvayā honti, ... Paṭivedhakāle paññindriyaṃ ādhipateyyaṃ hoti. Paṭivedhāya cattārindriyāni tadanvayā honti, ... ekarasā honti. Ekarasaṭṭhena bhāvanā. Dassanaṭṭhena paṭivedho. Evaṃ paṭivijjhanto pi bhāveti, bhāvento pi paṭivijjhati. Dukkhato manasikaroto passaddhibahulassa*

liberated.[209]

Thus is there signless liberation through the contemplation of impermanence.

Q. How is there desireless liberation through contemplation of suffering?

A. Through attending to suffering and through fear of formations, one causes the mind to emerge. The mind has great tranquillity. One obtains the concentration faculty and, following upon it, the other four faculties. One knows occurrence as it is and, following upon it, all formations are seen as suffering. Through fear of occurrence, one causes the arising of knowledge of occurrence. The mind emerges from occurrence and passes into non-

---

samādhindriyaṃ ādhipateyyaṃ hoti. ... Paṭivedhakāle paññindriyaṃ ādhipateyyaṃ hoti. ... Anattato manasikaroto vedabahulassa paññindriyaṃ ādhipateyyaṃ hoti. Bhāvanāya ... Paṭivedhakālepi paññindriyaṃ ādhipateyyaṃ hoti. ... Paṭis II 57: *Aniccato manasikaroto khayato saṅkhārā upaṭṭhanti. Dukkhato manasikaroto bhayato saṅkhārā upaṭṭhanti. Anattato manasikaroto suññato saṅkhārā upaṭṭhanti.* Paṭis II 62f.: *Aniccato manasikaronto nimittaṃ yathābhūtaṃ jānāti passati; tena vuccati sammādassanaṃ. Evaṃ tadanvayena sabbe saṅkhārā aniccato sudiṭṭhā honti. Ettha kaṅkhā pahīyati. Dukkhato manasikaronto pavattaṃ yathābhūtaṃ jānāti passati; ... Evaṃ tadanvayena sabbe saṅkhārā dukkhato sudiṭṭhā honti. ... Anattato manasikaronto nimittañ ca pavattañ ca yathābhūtaṃ jānāti passati; ... Evaṃ tadanvayena sabbe dhammā anattatosudiṭṭhā honti. ...* Paṭis II 63–64: *Aniccato manasikaroto nimittaṃ bhayato upaṭṭhāti. Dukkhato manasikaroto pavattaṃ bhayato upaṭṭhāti. Anattato manasikaroto nimittañ ca pavattañ ca bhayato upaṭṭhāti. ... Aniccato manasikaroto nimittā cittaṃ vuṭṭhāti, animitte cittaṃ pakkhandati. Ḍukkhato manasikaroto pavattā cittaṃ vuṭṭhāti, appavatte cittaṃ pakkhandati. Anattato manasikaroto nimittā ca pavattā ca cittaṃ vuṭṭhāti, animitte appavatte nirodhe nibbānadhātuyā cittaṃ pakkhandati.* Paṭis I 66: *Uppādā vuṭṭhahitvā anuppādaṃ pakkhandatī ti—gotrabhu. Pavattā vuṭṭhahitvā appavattaṃ pakkhandatī ti—gotrabhu. Nimittā ... animittaṃ pakkhandatī ti—gotrabhu. ... .*

209. 身得脫. The binome 得脫 corresponds to *muccati*, while 解脫 to *vimokkha, vimutti*. Because the signless here is nibbāna, this cannot refer to the deliverance from the matter-body, *rūpa-kāya*, and therefore must refer to the deliverance from the name-body, *nāma-kāya*, or from the *kilesa-kāya*. Cf. Pp-a 177: *Kāyenā ti vimokkhasahajātena nāmakāyena.* Spk I 278: *Ubhatobhāgavimuttā ti dvīhi bhāgehi vimuttā, arūpāvacarasamāpattiyā rūpakāyato vimuttā, aggamaggena nāmakāyato ti.* Cf. Abhidh-a 190, Sv 514: *Rūpakāyato avimuttattā. Tañ-hi kilesakāyato va vimuttaṃ, na rūpakāyato; tasmā tato vuṭṭhāya arahattaṃ patto ubhatobhāgavimutto nāma na hoti. Arūpāvacaraṃ pana nāmakāyato ca vimuttaṃ rūpakāyato cā ti tadeva pādakaṃ katvā arahattaṃ patto ubhatobhāgavimutto hotī ti veditabbo.*

Although 身 usually corresponds to *kāya*, "body", perhaps 身 here corresponds to *attā*, "oneself", as in 身性, *attabhāva*, "selfhood", and 身羸, *attakilamatha*, "wearing-out-oneself". It is unlikely that it is a misunderstanding of the three different persons described in this section in Paṭis, the second of which is the *kāyasakkhī*, "one who has realized with the body". See Paṭis 61: *animittavimokkhassa vasena saddhāvimutto, appaṇihitavimokkhassa vasena kāyasakkhī, suññatavimokkhassa vasena diṭṭhippatto.*

occurrence (*appavatta*). Through the desireless liberation, the body is liberated.

Thus is there desireless liberation through the contemplation of suffering.

Q. How is there the emptiness liberation through contemplation of without self?

A. Attending to without self makes manifest the emptiness of the formations. The mind has great knowledge.[210] One obtains the wisdom faculty and, following upon it, the other four faculties. One knows the sign and occurrence as it is and, following upon it, all phenomena (*dhamma*) are seen as without self. Through fear, one causes the arising of the sign and occurrence. Depending on the sign and occurrence, knowledge arises. The mind separates from the sign and occurrence and passes into the signless, non-occurrence, cessation, and nibbāna. Through the emptiness liberation, the body is liberated. Thus is there the emptiness liberation through the contemplation of without self.

Thus, these three liberations occur in different paths through insight.

Q. How do these three liberations occur in one path through attainment?

A. Having attained the signless liberation, there is attainment of the three liberations.

How? When someone's mind is liberated from the sign [and thus attains the signless liberation, then] through liberation from desire and from attachment, it also attains the desireless liberation [and the emptiness liberation], and [thus all] three liberations are attained.[211]

---

210. 厭惡 corresponds to *saṃvega*, "urgency", or *nibbidā*, "disenchantment". Saṅghapāla misunderstood *vedabahulo*, "great knowledge", as *vegabahulo*, "great urgency", 多厭惡. In Sanskrit *vega* can have the meaning of "outburst (of passion), excitement", see MW s.v. "*vega*". However, in Pali *saṃvega* has this meaning, not *vega*. The Pali commentaries explain *veda* as knowledge or joy: Paṭis-a III 561: *Vedabahulan-ti anattānupassanāya bāhirakehi adiṭṭhaṃ gambhīraṃ anattalakkhaṇaṃ passato ñāṇabahulaṃ cittaṃ hoti. Atha vā sadevakena lokena adiṭṭhaṃ anattalakkhaṇaṃ diṭṭhan-ti tuṭṭhassa tuṭṭhibahulaṃ cittaṃ hoti.*

211. The Chinese text is hard to follow. Saṅghapāla translated the ablatives ending in *-ā* or *-to* ("from") with 以. This is based on a Paṭisambhidā passage on three liberations occurring in one moment in the sense of combining: "When paying attention to impermanence, one is liberated from the sign—[this is] the signless liberation. One has no desire for what one has been released from—[this is] the desireless liberation. One is empty of what one does not desire—[this is] the emptiness liberation. There is signlessness through the sign one is empty of—this is the signless liberation". (And so on for the other liberations.) Paṭis II 67–8: *Kathaṃ samodhānaṭṭhena ... tayo vimokkhā ekakkhaṇe honti? Aniccato manasikaronto nimittā muccatī ti—animitto vimokkho. Yato muccati, tattha na paṇidahatī ti—appaṇihito vimokkho. Yattha na paṇidahati, tena suññoti—suññato vimokkho. Yena suñño, tena nimittena animittoti—animitto vimokkho. ...* Paṭis III

How? When his mind is liberated from desire [and thus attains the desireless liberation, then] through liberation from the sign and from attachment, it attains [the signless liberation and] the emptiness liberation, and [thus all] three liberations are attained.

How? When his mind is liberated from attachment [and thus attains the emptiness liberation, then] through liberation from the sign and from desire [it also attains the signless liberation and desireless liberation and thus all three liberations are attained].

Thus, the three liberations occur in one path through attainment.

Q. What is the difference between liberation and the gate to liberation (*vimokkhamukha*)?

A. Only the knowledge of the path. The freedom from the afflictions is called "liberation". In the sense of entry into the door of the deathless, [**460a**] it is called "gate to liberation".

Furthermore, liberation is only path-knowledge; its object, which is nibbāna—this is called "the gate to liberation".[212]

568: *Nimittā muccatī ti niccanimittato muccati. Iminā vimokkhaṭṭho vutto. Yato muccatī ti yato nimittato muccati. Tattha na paṇidahatī ti tasmiṃ nimitte patthanaṃ na karoti.* Cf. Abhidh-s 65 quoted in fn. 2288.

212. Nidd II-a 108: *Taṃ panesa ce santipadaṃ nibbānaṃ santato passati, sabbasaṅkhārapavattaṃ vissajjetvā nibbānaninnaṃ pakkhandaṃ hoti. No ce nibbānaṃ santato passati, punappunaṃ aniccan-ti vā dukkhan-ti vā anattā ti vā tividhānupassanāvasena saṅkhārārammaṇam-eva hutvā pavattati. Evaṃ tiṭṭhamānañ-ca etaṃ tividhavimokkhamukhabhāvaṃ āpajjitvā tiṭṭhati. Tisso hi anupassanā tīṇi vimokkhamukhānī ti vuccanti. Evaṃ aniccato manasikaronto adhimokkhabahulo animittaṃ vimokkhaṃ paṭilabhati, dukkhato manasikaronto passaddhibahulo appaṇihitaṃ vimokkhaṃ paṭilabhati, anattato manasikaronto vedabahulo suññataṃ vimokkhaṃ paṭilabhati. Ettha ca animitto vimokkho ti animittākārena nibbānaṃ ārammaṇaṃ katvā pavatto ariyamaggo. So hi animittāya dhātuyā uppannattā animitto, kilesehi ca vimuttattā vimokkho. Eteneva nayena appaṇihitākārena nibbānaṃ ārammaṇaṃ katvā pavatto appaṇihito, suññatākārena nibbānaṃ ārammaṇaṃ katvā pavatto suññato ti veditabbo.* Paṭis II 68: *Suññato vimokkho, animitto vimokkho, appaṇihito vimokkho. ... ayaṃ appaṇihito vimokkho. ayaṃ vimokkho. Ye tattha jātā anavajjā kusalā bodhipakkhiyādhammā, idaṃ mukhaṃ. Yaṃ tesaṃ dhammānaṃ ārammaṇaṃ nirodho nibbānaṃ, idaṃ vimokkhamukhaṃ. Vimokkhañ-ca mukhañ-ca vimokkhamukhaṃ, idaṃ vimokkhamukhaṃ.*

LC: "For Buddhaghosa, the three *vimokkhas* are names for the *ariyamagga* (Vism 658: *ettha ca animitto vimokkho ti animittākārena nibbānaṃ ārammaṇaṃ katvā pavatto ariyamaggo*). The three *vimokkhamukha* are the three kinds of insight contemplation (Vism XXI.66/p.657: *tatr'idaṃ tividhānupassanāvasena pavattanato tiṇṇaṃ indriyānaṃ ādhipateyyavasena tividhavimokkhamukhabhāvaṃ āpajjati nāma*). That seems to be the initial position in Paṭis (Paṭis II 48: *tīṇi kho pan'imāni vimokkhamukhāni lokaniyyānāya saṃvattanti*). But in the passage we have above, *mukha* (either 'entrance' or 'culmination' or both) means the *bodhipakkhiyadhamma* at the moment of the

50. One hundred and thirty-four afflictions

There are one hundred and thirty-four afflictions, namely, the three roots of unwholesomeness, the three searches, the four contaminations, the four ties, the four torrents, the four yokes, the four clingings, the four kinds of going the wrong way, the five kinds of selfishness, the five hindrances, the six roots of dispute, the seven latent tendencies, the eight worldly states, the nine conceits, the ten grounds for afflictions, the ten courses of unwholesome kamma, the ten fetters, the ten [kinds of] wrongness, the twelve distortions, and the twelve arisings of the unwholesome mind.

51. Three roots of unwholesomeness

The three roots of unwholesomeness (*akusalamūla*) are: greed, hatred, and delusion.[213]

[Of these three,] hatred is reduced by [the first] two paths. It is abandoned without remainder by the path of non-returning. Greed and delusion are reduced by three paths. They are abandoned without remainder by the path of arahantship.

---

maggacitta. Nibbāna, which is the object of the *maggacitta*, is the *vimokkhamukha*. *Vimokkhamukha* is understood by Paṭis-a as a *kammadhāraya* compound here—the emancipation which is supreme. It is difficult to be sure as to what is intended in Paṭis, but given its love of wordplay and its tendency to explain in terms of multiple levels, I would suppose that it intends to suggest two levels of interpretation. On one level the *vimokkhamukha* are the stage immediately prior to the path and the *vimokkha* are precisely the path. On another level the *vimokkhas* arise as the path at that moment and the *vimokkhamukha* is the object of the path at that moment, i.e. nibbāna, which is both the exit from the world and the supreme emancipation. The Chinese text here seems to have two alternative explanations, but it is not clear to me if they can be identified with those in Paṭis."

Cf. Ps II 354, Spk III 99: *Animittā cetovimutti nāma terasa dhammā: vipassanā, cattāro āruppā, cattāro maggā, cattāri ca phalānīti. Tattha vipassanā niccanimittaṃ sukhanimittaṃ attanimittaṃ ugghāṭetī ti animittā nāma. Cattāro āruppā rūpanimittassa abhāvena animittā nāma. Maggaphalāni nimittakaraṇānaṃ kilesānaṃ abhāvena animittāni. Nibbānam-pi animittam-eva, taṃ pana cetovimutti na hoti, tasmā na gahitaṃ. Atha kasmā suññatā cetovimutti na gahitāti? Sā, suññā rāgenāti-ādivacanato sabbattha anupaviṭṭhāva, tasmā visuṃ na gahitā. Ekatthā ti ārammaṇavasena ekatthā. Appamāṇaṃ ākiñcaññaṃ suññataṃ animittan-ti hi sabbānetāni nibbānasseva nāmāni. Iti iminā pariyāyena ekatthā. Aññasmiṃ pana ṭhāne appamāṇā honti, aññasmiṃ ākiñcaññā aññasmiṃ suññatā aññasmiṃ animittā ti iminā pariyāyena nānābyañjanā.*

213. D III 214: *Tīṇi akusalamūlāni: lobho akusala-mūlaṃ, doso akusala-mūlaṃ, moho akusala-mūlaṃ*. Mp II 317: *akusalamūlānīti akusalānaṃ mūlāni, akusalāni ca tāni mūlāni cā ti vā akusalamūlāni.*

52. Three searches

The three searches (*esanā*) are: the search for sense-pleasures, search for existence, and search for the holy life.[214]

Of these three, the search for the holy life is abandoned without remainder by the path of stream-entry. The search for sense-pleasures is abandoned by the path of non-returning. The search for existence is abandoned by the path of arahantship.

53. Four contaminations

The four contaminations are: the contamination of sense-pleasures, contamination of existence, contamination of views, and the contamination of ignorance.[215]

Herein, the contamination of views is abandoned by the path of stream-entry; the contamination of sense-pleasures is abandoned by the path of non-returning; the contamination of existence and the contamination of ignorance are abandoned by the path of arahantship.[216]

54. Four ties

The four ties (*gantha*) are: the bodily tie of covetousness, the bodily tie of ill will, the bodily tie of holding on to precepts and observances, and the bodily tie of the attachment to "this is the truth".[217]

---

214. D III 216: *Tisso esanā: kāmesanā, bhavesanā, brahmacariyesanā.*

215. D II 81, 84, 91, 123, 126: *Paññāparibhāvitaṃ cittaṃ sammad eva āsavehi vimuccati, seyyathīdaṃ kāmāsavā bhavāsavā, diṭṭhāsavā, avijjāsavā.* Dhs 195, § 1096: *Cattāro āsavā—kāmāsavo, bhavāsavo, diṭṭhāsavo, avijjāsavo.* Nett 116: *Tassa evaṃganthitā kilesā āsavanti. Kuto ca vuccati āsavantī ti? Anusayato vā pariyuṭṭhānato vā. Tattha abhijjhākāyaganthena kāmāsavo, byāpādakāyaganthena bhavāsavo, parāmāsakāyaganthena diṭṭhāsavo, idaṃsaccābhinivesakāyaganthena avijjāsavo.* D III 216: *Tayo āsavā. Kāmāsavo, bhavāsavo, avijjāsavo.* As 369: *pañcakāmaguṇiko rāgo kāmāsavo nāma. Rūpārūpabhavesu chandarāgo jhānanikan-ti sassatadiṭṭhisahajāto rāgo bhavavasena patthanā bhavāsavo nāma. Dvāsaṭṭhi diṭṭhiyo diṭṭhāsavo nāma. Aṭṭhasu ṭhānesu aññāṇaṃ avijjāsavo nāma.*

216. Paṭis I 94: *Kāmāsavo, bhavāsavo, diṭṭhāsavo, avijjāsavo. Katthete āsavā khīyanti? Sotāpattimaggena anavaseso diṭṭhāsavo khīyati, apāyagamanīyo kāmāsavo khīyati, apāyagamanīyo bhavāsavo khīyati, apāyagamanīyo avijjāsavo khīyati. Etthete āsavā khīyanti. Sakadāgāmimaggena oḷāriko kāmāsavo khīyati, tadekaṭṭho bhavāsavo khīyati, tadekaṭṭho avijjāsavo khīyati. Etthete āsavā khīyanti. Anāgāmimaggena anavaseso kāmāsavo khīyati, tadekaṭṭho bhavāsavo khīyati, tadekaṭṭho avijjāsavo khīyati. Etthete āsavā khīyanti. Arahattamaggena anavaseso bhavāsavo khīyati, anavaseso avijjāsavo khīyati. Etthete āsavā khīyanti.*

217. According to Niddesa, the ties are all related to views—i.e. attachment towards

Herein, the bodily tie of holding on to precepts and observances and the bodily tie of attachment to "this is the truth" are abandoned by the path of stream-entry. The bodily tie of ill will is abandoned by the path of non-returning. The bodily tie of covetousness is abandoned by the path of arahantship.

55. Four torrents and four yokes

The four torrents (*ogha*) are: the torrent of sense-pleasures, the torrent of existence, the torrent of views, and the torrent of ignorance.[218]

---

one's own views, repulsion to those of others, taking virtues and vows as the essence of practise, and regarding only one's own view as true and others as false. Other commentaries explain them in the sense of knotting the mental body (*nāmakāya*) as well as material body (*rūpakāya*). The Tibetan translator interpreted them differently "the tie of the body of covetousness", *brnab sems kyi tshogs kyi mdud pa,* etc. According to the *Abhidharmasamuccaya* (p. 48) it means the knotting of the mental body: "Knot is to be understood in the sense of knotting of the body that is the intrinsic nature of the concentrated mind. Why? In four ways the mind is disturbed. Because of welcoming wealth and so on, the mind is disturbed. Because of misbehaviour with regard to disputes and so on, ... Because of suffering due to hardship due to precepts and observances, ... Because of investigation of what has been known without reasoned attention, the mind is disturbed." : *samāhitamanaḥsvabhāvasya kāyasya parigranthārthena grantho veditavyaḥ / tena kiṃ bhavati / caturvidhaṃ cittaṃ vikṣipyate / vittādiṣu anunayahetoḥ cittaṃ vikṣipyate / vivādastuṣu apratipattihetoḥ cittaṃ vikṣipyate / duṣkaraśīlavratаduḥkhahetoḥ cittaṃ vikṣipyate / ayoniśo jñeya santīraṇahetoḥ cittaṃ vikṣipyate*.

D III 230: *Cattāro ganthā: abhijjhā kāya-gantho, vyāpādo kāya-gantho, sīlabbata-parāmāso kāyo-gantho, idaṃ-saccābhiniveso kāya-gantho.* Nidd I 246: ... *Attano diṭṭhiyā rāgo abhijjhā kāyagantho, paravādesu āghāto appaccayo byāpādo kāyagantho, attano sīlaṃ vā vataṃ vā sīlabbataṃ vā parāmāso sīlabbataparāmāso kāyagantho, attano diṭṭhi idaṃsaccābhiniveso kāyagantho.* Nidd-a II 349: *Attano diṭṭhiyā rāgo abhijjhākāyaganthoti sayaṃ gahitadiṭṭhiyā rañjanasaṅkhāto rāgo abhijjhā kāyagantho. ... Attano sīlaṃ vā vataṃ vā ti sayaṃ gahitamethunaviratisaṅkhātaṃ sīlaṃ vā govatādivataṃ vā. Sīlabbataṃ vā ti tadubhayaṃ vā. Parāmāsoti iminā suddhīti ādivasena parato āmasati. Attano diṭṭhi idaṃsaccābhiniveso kāyaganthoti sayaṃ gahitadiṭṭhiṃ idam-eva saccaṃ moghamaññan-ti ayoniso abhiniveso idaṃsaccābhiniveso kāyagantho. Ganthā tassa na vijjantī ti tassa khīṇāsavassa dve diṭṭhiganthā sotāpattimaggena na santi. Byāpādo kāyagantho anāgāmimaggena. Abhijjhā kāyagantho arahattamaggena.* Nett 115 (cf. Peṭ 244): *Paṭhame yoge ṭhito abhijjhāya kāyaṃ ganthati, ayaṃ vuccati abhijjhākāyagantho; ....* Sv III 1024: *Ganthana-vasena ganthā. Vaṭṭasmiṃ nāma-kāyañ c'eva rūpa-kāyañ ca ganthati bandhati palibuddhatī ti kāya-gantho. Idaṃ saccābhiniveso ti: Idam eva saccaṃ mogham aññan ti, evaṃ pavatto diṭṭhi-niveso.* Paṭis-a II 415: *Nāmakāyaṃ gantheti cutipaṭisandhivasena vaṭṭasmiṃ ghaṭetī ti kāyagantho.*

218. D III 230: *Cattāro oghā: kāmogho, bhavogho, diṭṭhogho, avijjogho.*

The four yokes (*yoga*) are: the yoke of sense-pleasures, the yoke of existence, the yoke of views, and the yoke of ignorance.[219]

These are abandoned in the manner as was taught above.[220]

56. Four clingings

The four clingings are: the clinging to sense-pleasures, clinging to views, clinging to precepts and observances, and clinging to a doctrine of a self.[221]

Herein, three clingings are abandoned by the path of stream-entry. The clinging to sense-pleasures is abandoned by the path of arahantship.[222]

57. Four kinds of going the wrong way

The four kinds of going the wrong way are: going the wrong way of desire, going the wrong way of anger, going the wrong way of fear, and going the wrong way of delusion.[223]

These four are abandoned by the path of stream-entry.

58. Five kinds of selfishness

The five kinds of selfishness are: selfishness as to dwelling, family, gain, appearance, and doctrine.[224]

These five are abandoned by the path of non-returning.

---

219. D III 230: *Cattāro yogā: kāma-yogo, bhava-yogo, diṭṭhi-yogo, avijjā-yogo.*

220. I.e. in the four contaminations passage as the Tibetan (200b) says.

221. D III 230: *Cattāri upādānāni: kāmūpādānaṃ, diṭṭhūpādānaṃ, sīlabbatūpādānaṃ, attavādūpādānaṃ.* Dhs 212: *Yo kāmesu kāmacchando ... kāmajjhosānaṃ, idaṃ vuccati kāmupādānaṃ. ... katamaṃ attavādupādānaṃ? Idha assutavā puthujjano ... rūpaṃ attato samanupassati, ... viññāṇasmiṃ vā attānaṃ. Yā evarūpā diṭṭhi ... vipariyāsaggāho ...*

222. According to the the Tibetan (200b), two clingings are destroyed by the path of stream-entry and clinging to the doctrine of a self is abandoned by the path of arahantship. This cannot be correct since *attavādupādāna,* which is equivalent to *sakkāyadiṭṭhi,* is abandoned at stream entry. See the discussion of this at the end of Introduction § 4.4 and fn. 42.

223. D III 228, A II 18: *Cattāri agati-gamanāni: chandāgatiṃ gacchati, dosāgatiṃ gacchati, mohāgatiṃ gacchati, bhayāgatiṃ gacchati.* Vibh 375: *Yā evarūpā agati agatigamanaṃ chandagamanaṃ vaggagamanaṃ vārigamanaṃ imāni cattāri agatigamanāni.*

224. D III 234: *pañca macchariyāni: āvāsa-macchariyaṃ, kula-macchariyaṃ, lābha-macchariyaṃ, vaṇṇa-macchariyaṃ, dhamma-macchariyaṃ.*

59. Five hindrances

The five hindrances are: sensual desire, ill will, sloth and torpor (*thīnamiddha*), agitation and worry, and doubt.[225]

Herein, doubt is abandoned by the path of stream-entry; sensual desire, ill will, and worry are abandoned by the path of non-returning; sloth (*thīna*) and agitation are abandoned by the path of arahantship. Torpor (*middha*) follows matter.[226]

60. Six roots of dispute

The six roots of dispute are: wrath, depreciation, jealousy, craftiness, evil desires, and holding on to one's own views.[227]

Herein, craftiness, evil desires, and holding on to one's own views are abandoned by the path of stream-entry. Wrath, depreciation, and jealousy are abandoned by the path of non-returning.

---

225. D III 234: *pañca nīvaraṇāni: kāmacchandha-nīvaraṇaṃ, vyāpāda-nīvaraṇaṃ, thīna-middha-nīvaraṇaṃ, uddhacca-kukkucca-nīvaraṇaṃ, vicikicchā-nīvaraṇaṃ.*

226. 睡眠隨色. 隨 = *anu, anuvattati, anugacchati,* etc. This means that only when the arahant's physical body ends at his passing away, torpor ends. "Material torpor" or "physical torpor" (*middharūpa*) is one of the kinds of dependent matter (see Ch. 11 § 5 & 7). The concept of *middharūpa* is rejected by the Mahāvihāra tradition, see Introduction § 4.1 & 5. The parallel at Vism XXII.71/p.685 has: *thīnamiddha-uddhaccāni catuttha-ñāṇavajjhāni*: "Sloth and torpor and agitation are eliminated by the fourth knowledge". Cf. Abhidh-av-pṭ II 157: *Middharūpaṃ nāmā ti utucittāhāravasena tisamuṭṭhānaṃ middhaṃ nāma rūpaṃ. ... Natthi nīvaraṇā ti sotāpattimaggena vicikicchānīvaraṇassa, ... arahattamaggena thīnamiddhanīvaraṇānañ-ca pahīnattā. Ayañhettha adhippāyo yadi middhaṃ rūpaṃ siyā, appahātabbaṃ bhaveyya.* Sv 1027: *Kāmacchando nīvaraṇapatto arahattamaggavajjho. Kāmarāgānusayo kāmarāgasaṃyojanapatto anāgāmimaggavajjho. Thīnaṃ cittagelaññaṃ. Middhaṃ khandhattayagelaññaṃ. Ubhayam-pi arahattamaggavajjhaṃ. Tathā uddhaccaṃ. Kukkuccaṃ anāgāmimaggavajjhaṃ. Vicikicchā paṭhamamaggavajjhā.* Ps I 116: *Thīnamiddhapariyuṭṭhitā ti cittagelaññabhūtena thinena sesanāmakāyagelaññabhūtena middhena ca pariyuṭṭhita.*

The Tibetan version (200b) instead has: "sloth and torpor and agitation are abandoned by the path of arahantship", however, this cannot be correct since it includes "torpor" (*gnyid*) in the list of dependent matters at Ch. 11 § 5.

227. Vibh 380: *Kodho, makkho, issā, sāṭheyyaṃ, pāpicchatā, sandiṭṭhiparāmāsitā—imāni cha vivādamūlāni.* D III 246–47: *... Yo so āvuso bhikkhu kodhano hoti upanāhī, ... makkhī hoti paḷāsī ... issukī hoti maccharī ... saṭho hoti māyāvī ... pāpiccho hoti micchā-diṭṭhi-parāmāsī hoti ādhāna-gāhī duppaṭinissaggī. Yo so ... duppaṭinissaggī, so satthari ... dhamme ... saṅghe pi agāravo viharati appaṭisso, sikkhāya na paripūra-kārī hoti. Yo so āvuso bhikkhu satthari agāravo viharati ..., so saṅghe vivādaṃ janeti.*

61. Seven latent tendencies

The seven latent tendencies are: the latent tendency of greed for sense-pleasures, [**460b**] the latent tendency of aversion, the latent tendency of conceit, the latent tendency of views, the latent tendency of doubt, the latent tendency of the greed for existence, and the latent tendency of ignorance.[228]

Herein, the latent tendencies of views and doubt are abandoned by the path of stream-entry. The latent tendency of greed for sense-pleasures and the latent tendency of aversion are abandoned by the path of non-returning. The latent tendency of conceit, the latent tendency of greed for existence and the latent tendency of ignorance are abandoned by the path of arahantship.[229]

62. Eight worldly states

The eight worldly states are: gain and loss, blame and praise, fame and obscurity, pleasure and pain.[230]

Herein, the aversion towards the four disagreeable conditions (*aniṭṭha-vatthu*) is abandoned by the path of non-returning. The affection towards the four agreeable conditions is abandoned by the path of arahantship.[231]

---

228. Vibh 382: *Katame satta anusayā? Kāmarāgānusayo, paṭighānusayo, mānānusayo, diṭṭhānusayo, vicikicchānusayo, bhavarāgānusayo, avijjānusayo.* The order is different in D III 254: *kāmarāgānusayo, paṭighānusayo, diṭṭhānusayo, vicikicchānusayo, mānānusayo, bhavarāgānusayo, avijjānusayo.* The order in the Tibetan text is the same as in Vibh.

229. Nidd-a I 103: *Kilesapaṭipāṭiyā hi kāmarāgānusayapaṭighānusayānaṃ tatiyamaggena abhāvo hoti, mānānusayassa catutthamaggena, diṭṭhānusayavicikicchānusayānaṃ paṭhamamaggena, bhavarāgānusayāvijjānusayānaṃ catutthamaggeneva.*

230. The Tibetan version has the same order as in the Pali, while the Chinese has *nindā-pasaṃsā* before *yasa-ayasa*, 利衰毀譽稱譏苦樂.

Cf. D III 260 (Cf. A II 188, IV 156f.): *Aṭṭha loka-dhammā: lābho ca alābho ca yaso ca ayaso ca nindā ca pasaṃsā ca sukhañ ca dukkhañ ca.* Paṭis-a I 113: *Lābhoti pabbajitassa cīvarādi, gahaṭṭhassa dhanadhaññādi lābho. So yeva alabbhamāno lābho alābho. Na lābho alābho ti vuccamāne atthābhāvāpattito pariññeyyo na siyā. Yasoti parivāro. So yeva alabbhamānā yaso ayaso. Nindā ti avaṇṇabhaṇanaṃ. Pasaṃsā ti vaṇṇabhaṇanaṃ. Sukhan-ti kāmāvacarānaṃ kāyikacetasikaṃ. Dukkhan-ti puthujjanasotāpannasakadāgāmīnaṃ kāyikacetasikaṃ, anāgāmi-arahantānaṃ kāyikam-eva.*

231. Vism XXI.51/683: *Lokadhammā ti lokappavattiyā sati anuparamadhammakattā lābho ... Idha pana kāraṇopacārena lābhādivatthukassa anunayassa alābhādivatthukassa paṭighassa cetaṃ lokadhammaggahaṇena gahaṇaṃ katan-ti veditabbaṃ.* Vism XXI.67/685 *Lokadhammesu paṭigho tatiyañāṇavajjho, anunayo catutthañāṇavajjho, yase ca pasaṃsāya ca anunayo catutthañāṇavajjhoti eke. Macchariyāni paṭhamañāṇavajjhāneva. Vibh 386: Lābhe sārāgo, alābhe paṭivirodho, yase sārāgo, ayase paṭivirodho, pasaṃsāya sārāgo, nindāya paṭivirodho, sukhe sārāgo, dukkhe paṭivirodho: imesu aṭṭhasu lokadhammesu cittassa paṭighāto.*

63. Nine conceits

The nine conceits are: the conceit "I am superior" generated towards one who is superior; or the conceit "I am equal" generated towards one who is superior; or the conceit "I am inferior" generated towards one who is superior; or the conceit "I am superior" generated towards one who is equal; or the conceit "I am equal" generated towards one who is equal; or the conceit "I am inferior" generated towards one who is equal; or the conceit "I am superior" generated towards one who is inferior; or the conceit "I am equal" generated towards one who is inferior; or the conceit "I am inferior" generated towards one who is inferior.[232]

These nine conceits are abandoned by the path of arahantship.

64. Ten grounds for afflictions

The ten grounds for afflictions[233] are: greed, hatred, delusion, conceit, views, doubt, sloth, agitation, consciencelessness, and shamelessness.

Herein, views and doubt are abandoned by the path of stream-entry. Hatred is abandoned by the path of non-returning. The other seven are abandoned by the path of arahantship.

65. Ten grounds for anger

The ten grounds for anger are: [Thinking:] "This person acted, ... acts, ... will act for my harm", one gives rise to anger; this person acted, ... acts, ... will act for the harm of those who are dear to me", one gives rise to anger; this person acted, ... acts, ... will act for the benefit of those who are not dear to me", one gives rise to anger; and one gives rise to anger for no reason.[234]

---

232. Vibh 389: *Seyyassa seyyo'hamasmī ti māno, seyyassa sadiso'hamasmīti māno, seyyassa hīno'hamasmī ti māno, sadisassa seyyo'hamasmī ti māno, sadisassa sadiso'hamasmī ti māno, sadisassa hīno'hamasmī ti māno, hīnassa seyyo'hamasmī ti māno, hīnassa sadiso'hamasmī ti māno, hīnassa hīno'hamasmī ti māno—ime navavidhā mānā.*

233. Read 煩惱處 instead of 惱處, as in Ch. 12 § 50. Dhs 214, Vibh 341: *Dasa kilesavatthūni: lobho doso moho māno diṭṭhi vicikicchā thīnaṃ uddhaccaṃ ahīrikaṃ anottappaṃ. Yesaṃ sattānaṃ imāni dasa kilesavatthūni āsevitāni bhāvitāni bahulīkatāni ussadagatāni: ime te sattā mahārajakkhā.* Paṭis-a II 424: *Tattha kilesā eva kilesavatthūni, vasanti vā ettha akhīṇāsavā sattā lobhādīsu patiṭṭhitattā ti vatthūni, kilesā ca te tappatiṭṭhānaṃ sattānaṃ vatthūni cā ti kilesavatthūni. Yasmā cettha anantarapaccayādibhāvena uppajjamānāpi kilesā vasanti eva nāma, tasmā kilesānaṃ vatthūnītipi kilesavatthūni.*

234. A V 150: *Dasayimāni ... āghātavatthūni. ... Anatthaṃ me acarī ti āghātaṃ bandhati; anatthaṃ me caratī ti ... anatthaṃ me carissatī ti ... piyassa me manāpassa anatthaṃ acarī ti ... anatthaṃ caratī ti ... anatthaṃ carissatī'ti ... appiyassa me amanāpassa atthaṃ acarī'ti atthaṃ caratī ti ... atthaṃ carissatī ti āghātaṃ bandhati; aṭṭhāne ca kuppati—imāni kho ...*

These ten grounds for anger are abandoned by the path of non-returning.

66. Ten courses of unwholesome kamma

The ten courses of unwholesome kamma are: taking of life, taking what is not given, sexual misconduct, lying, harsh speech, malignant speech, frivolous speech, covetousness, ill will, and wrong view.[235]

Herein, the taking of life, taking of what is not given, sexual misconduct, lying, and wrong view are abandoned by the path of stream-entry. Malignant speech, harsh speech, and ill will are abandoned by the path of non-returning. Frivolous speech and covetousness are abandoned by the path of arahantship.

67. Ten fetters

The ten fetters are: the fetter of greed for sense-pleasures, the fetter of ill will, the fetter of conceit, the fetter of (wrong) view, the fetter of doubt, the fetter of holding on to precepts and observances, the fetter of greed for existence, the fetter of envy, the fetter of selfishness, and the fetter of ignorance.[236]

---

dasa āghātavatthūnī ti. Paṭis-a II 423: *Tattha āghātavatthūnīti āghātakāraṇāni. Āghātan-ti cettha kopo, so yeva uparūpari kopassa vatthuttā āghātavatthu. Āghātaṃ bandhatī ti kopaṃ bandhati karoti uppādeti. Atthaṃ me nācari, na carati, na carissati. Piyassa me manāpassa atthaṃ nācari, na carati, na carissati. Appiyassa me amanāpassa anatthaṃ nācari, na carati, na carissatī ti.* Ibid 425: *Dasahi āghātavatthūhīti pubbe vuttehi navahi ca aṭṭhāne vā panāghāto jāyatī ti vuttena cā ti dasahi. Anatthaṃ me acarīti ādīnipi hi avikappetvā khāṇukaṇṭakādimhipi aṭṭhāne āghāto uppajjati.* Cf. Mp V 54: *Aṭṭhāne ti akāraṇe. Sacittakapavattiyañ-hi anatthaṃ me acarī ti ādi kāraṇaṃ bhaveyya, khāṇupahaṭādīsu taṃ natthi. Tasmā tattha āghāto aṭṭhāne āghāto nāma.*

235. Read 結, as in the introduction and the Tibetan parallel, instead of 使. Cf. D III 269: *Dasa akusalakammapathā: pāṇātipāto, adinnādānaṃ, kāmesu micchācāro, musāvādo, pisuṇā vācā, pharusā vācā, samphappalāpo, abhijjhā, vyāpādo, micchādiṭṭhi.*

The order of two of the items in the Chinese is different from that in the Pali since *pharusā vācā*, 惡口, comes before *pisuṇā vācā*, 兩舌. This order is found in a Chinese translation of the Saṃyuktāgama at T 99: 142c05 and in the Ekottarāgama at T 125: 780c25a, etc. and in other works such as in the list of 10 good ways of conduct (十善業, *daśakuśalakarmapatha, daśakuśalāni*) in the Sanskrit *Mahāvyutpatti* (§ 92, entries 1685–1698). In the Ekottarāgama, *samphappalāpa*, 綺語, comes before *pharusā vācā*; which is also the order given in the list of the ten *akusala-karmapatha*, 十惡, in DDB, i.e. 妄語, 綺語, 惡口, 兩舌.

236. Dhs 197, Vibh 391: *Dasa saññojanāni: kāmarāgasaññojanaṃ paṭighasaññojanaṃ mānasaññojanaṃ diṭṭhisaññojanaṃ vicikicchāsaññojanaṃ sīlabbataparāmāsasaññojanaṃ bhavarāgasaññojanaṃ issāsaññojanaṃ macchariyasaññojanaṃ avijjāsaññojanaṃ.* The list of ten fetters given here—a combination of the sutta lists of ten and seven fetters—is

Herein, the fetters of (wrong) view, doubt, and holding on to precepts and observances are abandoned by the path of stream-entry. The fetters of greed for sense-pleasures, ill will, envy, and selfishness are abandoned by the path of non-returning. The fetters of conceit, greed for existence, and ignorance are abandoned by the path of arahantship.

68. Ten kinds of wrongness

The ten kinds of wrongness are: wrong view, wrong intention, wrong speech, wrong action, wrong livelihood, wrong effort, wrong mindfulness, wrong concentration, wrong knowledge, and wrong freedom.[237]

Herein, wrong view, wrong speech in the sense of lying, wrong action, wrong livelihood, wrong knowledge, and wrong freedom are abandoned by the path of stream-entry. Wrong intention, wrong speech in the sense of malignant speech, and harsh speech are abandoned by the path of non-returning. Wrong speech in the sense of frivolous speech, wrong effort, wrong mindfulness, and wrong concentration are abandoned by the path of arahantship. [**460c**]

69. Twelve distortions

The twelve distortions are: distortion of perception, distortion of mind, and distortion of view [due to perceiving] permanence in what is impermanent; distortion of perception, distortion of mind, and distortion of view [due to perceiving] happiness in what is suffering; distortion of perception, distortion of mind, and distortion of view [due to perceiving] beauty in what is foul; and distortion of perception, distortion of mind, and distortion of view [due to perceiving] self in what is without self.[238]

---

the one that is normal for the Abhidhamma. Cf. A IV 7f.

237. Vibh 391–2: *Micchādiṭṭhi micchāsaṅkappo micchāvācā micchā-kammanto micchā-ājīvo micchāvāyāmo micchāsati micchāsamādhi micchāñāṇaṃ micchāvimutti. Ime dasa micchattā.*

238. Both the Chinese and Tibetan versions place what corresponds to *asubhe subhan-ti* before *anattani attā ti*, an order which is not found in any Pali works. A II 52, Paṭis II 80: *Anicce bhikkhave niccan-ti saññāvipallāso cittavipallāso diṭṭhivipallāso; dukkhe bhikkhave sukhan-ti saññāvipallāso cittavipallāso diṭṭhivipallāso; anattani bhikkhave attā ti saññāvipallāso cittavipallāso diṭṭhivipallāso; asubhe bhikkhave subhan-ti saññā-vipallāso cittavipallāso diṭṭhivipallāso.* Peṭ 119: *Anicce niccan-ti, dukkhe sukhanti, anattani attā ti, asubhe subhanti, ayaṃ eko vipallāso. ... Kāyo vedanā cittaṃ dhammā ca. Imāni cattāri vipallāsavatthūni. ... Saññā cittaṃ diṭṭhi ca. Imāni tīṇi vipallāsāni. Tattha manāpike vatthumhi indriyavatthe vaṇṇāyatane vā yo nimittassa uggāho, ayaṃ saññāvipallāso. Tattha viparītacittassa vatthumhi sati viññatti, ayaṃ cittavipallāso. Tattha viparītacittassa tamhi*

Herein, the three distortions [due to perceiving] permanence in what is impermanent, the three distortions [due to perceiving] self in what is without self, the distortion of view [due to perceiving] beauty in what is foul and the distortion of view [due to perceiving] happiness in what is suffering, are abandoned by the path of stream-entry. The distortion of perception and the distortion of mind [due to perceiving] beauty in what is foul are abandoned by the path of non-returning. The distortion of perception and the distortion of mind [due to perceiving] happiness in what is suffering are abandoned by the path of arahantship.[239]

70. Twelve arisings of the unwholesome mind

The twelve arisings of the unwholesome mind are: (1) arising of mind accompanied by joy, associated with (wrong) view, without impetus (*asaṅkhāra*); (2) arising of mind (...) with impetus; (3) arising of mind accompanied by joy, disassociated from (wrong) view, without impetus; (4) arising of mind (...) with impetus; (5) arising of mind accompanied by equanimity, associated with (wrong) view, without impetus; (6) arising of mind (...) with impetus; (7) arising of mind accompanied by equanimity, disassociated from (wrong) view, without impetus; (8) arising of mind (...) with impetus; (9) arising of mind accompanied by distress, associated with aversion, without impetus; (10) arising of mind (...) with impetus; (11) arising of mind accompanied by agitation; and (12) arising of mind accompanied by doubt.[240]

---

rūpe asubhe subhan-ti yā khanti ruci upekkhanā nicchayo diṭṭhi nidassanaṃ santīraṇā, ayaṃ diṭṭhivipallāso. Tattha vatthubhedena kāyesu dvādasa vipallāsā bhavanti. .... Mp III 90: *Anicce ... niccan-ti saññāvipallāso ti anicce vatthusmiṃ niccaṃ idan-ti evaṃ gahetvā uppajjanakasaññā, saññāvipallāso ti attho.*

239. The Chinese text's explanation of the Paths at which the twelve distortions are abandoned is in accordance with the Pali, but in the Tibetan the distortion of perceiving a self is only abandoned at arahantship; see the discussion of this in Introduction § 4.4.

See Vibh-a 501: *Vipariyāsesu aniccādīni vatthūni niccan-ti ādinā nayena viparītato esantī ti vipariyāsā, saññāya vipariyāso saññāvipariyāso. Itaresu pi dvīsu eseva nayo. Evamete catunnaṃ vatthūnaṃ vasena cattāro, yesu vatthūsu saññādīnaṃ vasena dvādasa honti. Tesu aṭṭha sotāpattimaggena pahīyanti. Asubhe subhan-ti saññācittavipallāsā sakadāgāmimaggena tanukā honti, anāgāmimaggena pahīyanti. Dukkhe sukhan-ti saññācittavipallāsā arahattamaggena pahīyantī ti veditabbā.*

240. Cf. Dhs 234, § 1369: *Katame dhammā akusalā? Dvādasa akusalacittuppādā. Ime dhammā akusalā.* Vibh 296 (cf. Dhs 80–81): *Katame dhammā akusalā? Yasmiṃ samaye akusalaṃ cittaṃ uppannaṃ hoti somanassasahagataṃ diṭṭhigatasampayuttaṃ sasaṅkhārena ...pe... somanassasahagataṃ diṭṭhigatavippayuttaṃ ...pe... somanassasahagataṃ diṭṭhigatavippayuttaṃ sasaṅkhārena ...pe... upekkhāsahagataṃ diṭṭhigatasampayuttaṃ ... pe... upekkhāsahagataṃ diṭṭhigatasampayuttaṃ sasaṅkhārena ...pe... upekkhāsahagataṃ*

Herein, the four arisings of mind associated with (wrong) view and the arisings of mind accompanied by doubt are abandoned by the path of stream-entry. The two arisings of mind accompanied by distress[241] are reduced in two paths and abandoned without remainder by the path of non-returning. The four arisings of mind disassociated from views and the arising of mind accompanied by agitation are reduced in three paths and are abandoned without remainder by the path of arahantship.

71. Two attainments not shared with the worldling

Two attainments (*samāpatti*): There are two attainments that are not shared with the worldling: the attainment of fruition and the attainment of cessation of perception and feeling.[242]

72. Attainment of fruition

What is the attainment of fruition? Why is it called attainment of fruition? Who enters upon it?[243] Why does one enter upon it? How does one enter upon it? How does one attend? What are the conditions for entering upon it? What are the conditions for its persistence? What are the conditions for emerging from it? Is this attainment mundane or supramundane?[244]

[Q.] What is the attainment of fruition?

[A.] The absorption (*appanā*) of the mind in nibbāna, the fruit of recluseship (*sāmaññaphala*)—this is "attainment of fruition".[245]

---

diṭṭhigatavippayuttaṃ ...pe... upekkhāsahagataṃ diṭṭhigatavippayuttaṃ sasaṅkhārena ...pe... domanassasahagataṃ paṭighasampayuttaṃ ...pe... domanassasahagataṃ paṭighasampayuttaṃ sasaṅkhārena ... upekkhāsahagataṃ vicikicchāsampayuttaṃ ... upekkhāsahagataṃ uddhaccasampayuttaṃ rūpārammaṇaṃ vā ... Abhidh-av 6 f.: *Tattha lobhamūlaṃ pana somanassupekkhādiṭṭhippayogabhedato aṭṭhavidhaṃ hoti, seyyathidaṃ somanassasahagataṃ diṭṭhigatasampayuttaṃ asaṅkhārikam ekaṃ, ... Evaṃ tāva dvādasavidhaṃ akusalacittaṃ veditabbaṃ, ...* Cf. Vism 684: *Akusalacittuppādā ti lobhamūlā aṭṭha, dosamūlā dve, mohamūlā dve ti ime dvādasa.*

241. "Distress" is missing in the Chinese text, but the Tibetan version (202b) includes it: *yid mi bde ba dang ldan pa'i sems bskyed pa gnyis ni ....*

242. No exact parallel can be traced in the Pali.

243. The Chinese text has "practise it and emerge from it", 誰修誰令起, but the answer here and in the next attainment, the Vism parallel, and the Tibetan indicate that just "enter upon", *samāpajjati*, is intended.

244. Cf. Vism XXIII.5/p.699: *kā phalasamāpatti, ke taṃ samāpajjanti, ke na samāpajjanti, kasmā samāpajjanti, kathañcassā samāpajjanaṃ hoti, kathaṃ ṭhānaṃ, kathaṃ vuṭṭhānaṃ, ...?*

245. Cf. Vism XXIII.6/699: *Kā phalasamāpattī ti yā ariyaphalassa nirodhe appanā.* Vism-mhṭ II 515: *Ariyaphalassa nirodhe appanā ti ariyassa phalajhānassa nibbāne ārammaṇabhūte appanākārena pavatti.* D-a I 158: *Ariyaphalaṃ sāmaññaphalaṃ.*

[Q.] Why is it called "attainment of fruition"?

[A.] It is neither wholesome nor unwholesome nor functional (*kiriya*), [and] is born of the result of the supramundane path (*lokuttaramaggavipākajā*), therefore it is called "attainment of fruition".[246]

[Who enters upon it?]

[A.] The arahant and the non-returner, who are perfect (*paripūrakāri*) in concentration.[247]

---

246. 非善非不善非事出世道果報所成. Tibetan: "It is not wholesome, nor unwholesome, nor functional, nor born of/of the nature of (*rang bzhin*) the result of the super[mundane] Path, ..." Possibly "neither wholesome nor unwholesome nor functional" refers to the *lokuttaramagga* since both the *lokuttaramagga* and *phalasamāpatti* are "not included" (*apariyāpanna*) in *kusala*, *akusala*, and *kiriya* states. However, *phalasamāpatti* is conditioned by and born of the *vipāka* of the *lokuttara kusala* states of the *sekha* (i.e. *anāgāmin*) and *avyākata*, *kiriya* states of the *asekha*. See Ud-a 30: *Sā panāyaṃ phalasamāpatti atthato lokuttarakusalānaṃ vipākabhūtā nibbānārammaṇā appanā ti daṭṭhabbā.* Dhs 263: *Tīsu bhūmīsu kusalaṃ, akusalaṃ, tīsu bhūmīsu vipāko, tīsu bhūmīsu kiriyābyākataṃ, sabbañ-ca rūpaṃ: ime dhammā pariyāpannā. ... Cattāro maggā apariyāpannā, cattāri ca sāmaññaphalāni, nibbānañca: ime dhammā apariyāpannā.* Dhs 224: *Sāsavā kusalākusalābyākatā dhammā kāmāvacarā, rūpāvacarā, arūpāvacarā, rūpakkhandho ... pe ... viññāṇakkhandho: ime dhammā pariyāpannā. ... Maggā ca, maggaphalāni ca, asaṅkhatā ca dhātu—ime dhammā apariyāpannā.* Paṭṭh I 137: *Kusalo dhammo abyākatassa dhammassa anantarapaccayena paccayo. Kusalaṃ vuṭṭhānassa... maggo phalassa... anulomaṃ sekkhāya phalasamāpattiyā... nirodhā vuṭṭhahantassa nevasaññānāsaññāyatanakusalaṃ phalasamāpattiyā anantarapaccayena paccayo. ... Abyākato dhammo abyākatassa dhammassa anantarapaccayena paccayo ... Bhavaṅgaṃ āvajjanāya... kiriyaṃ vuṭṭhānassa... arahato anulomaṃ phalasamāpattiyā... nirodhā vuṭṭhahantassa nevasaññānāsaññāyatanakiriyaṃ phalasamāpattiyā anantarapaccayena paccayo.*

247. A I 232f.: *Idha ... puggalo sīlesu paripūrakārī hoti, samādhismiṃ paripūrakārī paññāya na paripūrakāri hoti; so pañcannaṃ orambhāgiyānaṃ saṃyojanānaṃ parikkhayā ... antarāparinibbāyī hoti. Idha ... bhikkhu sīlesu paripūrakārī hoti samādhismiṃ paripūrakārī paññāya paripūrakārī ... so āsavānaṃ khayā anāsavaṃ cetovimuttiṃ paññāvimuttiṃ diṭṭheva dhamme sayaṃ abhiññā sacchikatvā upasampajja viharati.* A III 194: *Idha ... bhikkhu sīlasampanno samādhisampanno paññāsampanno saññāvedayitanirodhaṃ samāpajjeyyāpi vuṭṭhaheyyāpi atthetaṃ ṭhānaṃ. No ce diṭṭheva dhamme aññaṃ ārādheyya, atikkamm-eva kabaḷīkārāhārabhakkhānaṃ devānaṃ sahabyataṃ aññataraṃ manomayaṃ kāyaṃ upapanno saññāvedayitanirodhaṃ samāpajjeyyāpi vuṭṭhaheyyāpi—atthetaṃ ṭhānanti.* Mp III 298: *No ce diṭṭheva dhamme aññaṃ ārādheyyā ti no ce imasmiṃ yeva attabhāve arahattaṃ pāpuṇeyya.*

Vism XXIII.6–7/p.699: *Ke taṃ samāpajjanti, ke na samāpajjantī ti sabbe pi puthujjanā na samāpajjanti. Kasmā? Anadhigatattā. Ariyā pana sabbe pi samāpajjanti. ... Keci pana sotāpannasakadāgāmino pi na samāpajjanti. Uparimā dve yeva samāpajjantī ti vadanti. Idañ-ca tesaṃ kāraṇaṃ, ete hi samādhismiṃ paripūrakārinoti. Taṃ puthujjanassā-pi attanā paṭiladdhalokiyasamādhisamāpajjanato akāraṇam-eva. Kiñcettha kāraṇākāraṇacintāya. Nanu pāḷiyaṃ yeva vuttaṃ katame dasa gotrabhudhammā vipassanāvasena*

Furthermore, some say that all noble persons can enter upon it, as is taught in the Abhidhamma thus: "For the sake of obtaining the path of stream-entry, it overcomes rearising—this is called 'change of lineage'. For the sake of the attainment of the fruit of stream-entry, it overcomes rearising—this is called 'change of lineage'".[248] In the same way all [the paths and fruits should be understood.]

Furthermore, some say that only the noble persons who are perfect in concentration attain it. As the Venerable Nārada said:[249] "Venerable, it is like a well in a desert, with no rope [and bucket] in it for drawing water. Then a man comes to it, who is scorched by the sun, afflicted, wearied, thirsty, and craving [for water]. That man looks into the well and knows that it has water, but he does not dwell touching it with the body. [**461a**] Even so, venerable, I have seen well, according to reality, with right wisdom that the cessation of existence is nibbāna, but I am not an arahant who has destroyed the contaminations".[250]

---

uppajjanti? Sotāpattimaggapaṭilābhatthāya uppādaṃ pavattaṃ ...pe... upāyāsaṃ bahiddhā saṅkhāranimittaṃ abhibhuyyatī ti gotrabhu. Sotāpattiphalasamāpattatthāya sakadāgāmimaggaṃ...pe...arahattaphalasamāpattatthāya...suññatavihārasamāpattatthāya... animittavihārasamāpattatthāya uppādaṃ ...pe... bahiddhā saṅkhāranimittaṃ abhibhuyyatī ti gotrabhū ti (Paṭis I 67). *Tasmā sabbe pi ariyā attano attano phalaṃ samāpajjantī ti niṭṭhamettha gantabbaṃ.* Paṭis-a I 267: *Keci pana sotāpannasakadāgāmino pi ... samāpajjantī ti vadanti. Idañ-ca nesaṃ kāraṇaṃ ete hi samādhismiṃ paripūrakārinoti. Taṃ puthujjanassā-pi attanā paṭiladdhaṃ lokiyasamādhiṃ samāpajjanato akāraṇam-eva. Kiñcettha kāraṇākāraṇacintāya. Nanu idheva pāḷiyaṃ katame dasa saṅkhārupekkhā vipassanāvasena uppajjanti, katame dasa gotrabhudhammā vipassanāvasena uppajjantī ti imesaṃ pañhānaṃ vissajjane sotāpattiphalasamāpattatthāya sakadāgāmiphalasamāpattatthāyā ti visuṃ visuṃ vuttā. Tasmā sabbe pi ariyā attano attano phalaṃ samāpajjantī ti niṭṭhamettha gantabbaṃ.* Paṭis-gp 136 (Sinh. ed.): *Keci panā ti abhayagirivihāravāsino.*

248. Paṭis I 68: *Sotāpattimaggaṃ paṭilābhatthāya uppādaṃ pavattaṃ nimittaṃ āyuhanaṃ paṭisandhiṃ gatiṃ nibbattiṃ uppattiṃ jātiṃ jaraṃ byādhiṃ maraṇaṃ sokaṃ paridevaṃ upāyāsaṃ bahiddhā saṅkhāranimittaṃ abhibhuyyatī ti gotrabhu. Sotāpattiphalasamāpattatthāya uppādaṃ ...*

249. The Chinese adds 諸比丘, corresponding to the vocative plural *bhikkhave*, "bhikkhus!", which does not fit here and can be an intrusion based on quotations of other Sutta passages as in 400a09, 417a27, etc.

250. S II 117–18: *Aññatreva āvuso Nārada saddhāya aññatra ruciyā aññatra anussavā aññatra ākāraparivitakkā aññatra diṭṭhinijjhānakkhantiyā aham etam jānāmi aham etam passāmi bhavanirodho nibbānan-ti. Tenāyasmā Nārado arahaṃ khīṇāsavo ti. Bhavanirodho nibbānan-ti kho me āvuso yathābhūtaṃ sammappaññāya sudiṭṭhaṃ na c'amhi arahaṃ khīṇāsavo. Seyyathā pi āvuso kantāramagge udapāno, tatra nevassa rajju na udakavārako. Atha puriso āgaccheyya ghammābhitatto ghammapareto kilanto tasito pipāsito, so taṃ udapānaṃ olokeyya, tassa udakan-ti hi kho ñāṇaṃ assa na ca kāyena phusitvā vihareyya. Evam eva kho āvuso bhavanirodho nibbānan-ti yathābhūtaṃ sammappaññāya sudiṭṭhaṃ na*

[Q.] Why does one enter upon it?
A. One enters upon it for the sake of a pleasant dwelling in this life (*diṭṭha-dhammasukhavihāra*), as the Fortunate One taught to Ānanda: "At which time, Ānanda, the Tathāgata, due to not attending to all signs; due to the cessation of certain feelings, dwells having entered upon the signless concentration of mind, at that time, Ānanda, the body of the Tathāgata is [more] at ease".[251]

[Q.] How does one enter upon it?
A. The meditator, desirous of the attainment of fruition, goes into seclusion, sits or lies down and sees with insight the formations, beginning with contemplation of rise and fall and [proceeding] until knowledge of change of lineage. Immediately after knowledge of change of lineage, [his mind] becomes fixed in nibbāna, attainment of fruition. Dependent upon whichever jhāna he develops the path, [dependent] on that jhāna that attainment of fruition is produced.

[Q.] How does one attend?
A. The unconditioned, deathless element is attended to as peaceful.[252]

[Q.] What are the conditions for entering upon it? What are the conditions for its persistence? What are the conditions for emerging from it?
A. There are two conditions for entering upon it: the non-attending to all signs and the attending to the signless element.[253]

Three are the conditions of persistence: non-attending to all signs; attending to the signless element; and previous preparation.[254]

Two are the conditions of emergence: attending to all signs and non-attending to the signless element.[255]

[Q.] Is this attainment mundane or supramundane?

---

c'amhi arahaṃ khīṇāsavo ti. Cf. Spk II 122–23 and Peṭ 169.

251. D II 100, S V 153: *Yasmiṃ ānanda samaye tathāgato sabba-nimittānaṃ amanasikārā ekaccānaṃ vedanānaṃ nirodhā animittaṃ cetosamādhiṃ upasampajja viharati, phāsutaro Ānanda tasmiṃ samaye tathāgatassa kāyo hoti.*

252. Cf. Vism XXI.64/p.656: *Taṃ panesa ce santipadaṃ nibbānaṃ santato passati, sabbasaṅkhārapavattaṃ vissajjetvā nibbānaninnaṃ pakkhandaṃ hoti.* Vism XV.42/p.489: *Asaṅkhatā pana dhātu amatato santato khemato ca daṭṭhabbā.*

253. M I 296: *Kati panāvuso, paccayā animittāya cetovimuttiyā samāpattiyā ti? ... Dve āvuso, paccayā animittāya cetovimuttiyā samāpattiyā sabbanmittānañ ca amanasikāro animittāya ca dhātuyā manasikāro ti.*

254. M I 296–97: *Tayo kho, āvuso, paccayā animittāya cetovimuttiyā ṭhitiyā: sabbanimittānañ ca amanasikāro, animittāya ca dhātuyā manasikāro, pubbe ca abhisaṅkhāro.*

255. Ibid. 297: *Dve kho, āvuso, paccayā animittāya cetovimuttiyā vuṭṭhānāya: sabbanimittānañ ca manasikāro, animittāya ca dhātuyā amanasikāro.*

A. This attainment is supramundane, not mundane.[256]

Q. When the non-returner [develops] insight for the attainment of fruition, why does change of lineage not produce the arahant path immediately?
A. If it is without a basis of pleasure (*sukha*), it does not produce [the arahant path] since insight [only] is without strength.[257]

Herein, two distinct fruitions can be discerned. (1) The fruition that is accomplished with path and change of lineage, [i.e.] the fruition that manifests immediately when the realization (*sacchikiriya*) of the path manifests. (2) The fruition that is accomplished without path and change of lineage: When entering upon the attainment of fruition, the fruition is accomplished without path and change of lineage. When emerging from the attainment of cessation, the fruition is accomplished without path and change of lineage.[258]

The attainment of fruition is finished.

---

256. Cf. Ud-a 30: *Sā panāyaṃ phalasamāpatti atthato lokuttarakusalānaṃ vipākabhūtā nibbānārammaṇā appanā ti daṭṭhabbā.*

257. 答非樂處故, 不生觀見無力故. For 樂處 as "place/basis of pleasure" (*sukha-vatthu/ṭhāna*) with reference to the third jhāna, see 419b29. This probably means that without the basis of *sukha* developed through *samādhi* (the pleasant practice, *sukhapaṭipadā*, see 459b09), there is not sufficient insight strength to produce the path and therefore the non-returner cannot enter the attainment of fruition, i.e. he cannot enter as a "dry insight practitioner" (*sukkhavipassaka*). Cf. Vism-mhṭ II 520 (in relation to the attainment of cessation): *Anāgāmino, arahanto ti ettha sukkhavipassakā ca anāgāmino, ... Ubhaye pi cete sati pi vipassanābale samādhibalassa abhāvato nirodhaṃ na samāpajjanti. Anupubbavihārasambhavataññevettha samādhibalaṃ icchitabbaṃ. Purimakā pana tayo sati pi samādhibale vipassanābalassa abhāvato, aparipuṇṇattā ca samāpajjituṃ na sakkonti. Aparipuṇṇatā cassa saṅkhārānaṃ na sammā parimadditattā.*

258. This difficult passage was not translated by EKS, nor is it found in the Tibetan translation of Sav. A footnote in the Taishō edition says that other editions leave out 無道 "without path" in the last clause, which probably is to be read as 無道及性除果 rather than 無道無性除果.

Cf. Moh 76: *Lokuttarajavanesu pana kusalāni ekasantāne ekavāram-eva javanti, tadanantaraṃ yathāsakaṃ phalacittañ-ca dvattivāraṃ, phalasamāpattivīthiyaṃ phalam-eva anantavāram-pi javati, nirodhasamāpattiyaṃ pana anupubbanirodhavasena paṭhamajjhānato yāvākiñcaññāyatanā yathākkamaṃ āvajjanaparikammādivaseneva samāpajjitvā vuṭṭhitassa gotrabhuto anantaraṃ catutthāruppajavane dvikkhattuṃ javitvā niruddhe yathāparicchinnakālañ-ca cittaṃ na uppajjati, vuṭṭhānakāle ca āvajjanaparikammacittaniyāmena anāgāmiphalaṃ, arahattaphalaṃ vā yathārahame-kavāram-eva uppajjati. Tattha ca kusalagotrabhuto anantaraṃ kusalañceva ādito phalattayañ-ca appeti, kiriyāgotrabhuto kiriyaṃ, arahattaphalañ-ca.*

73. Attainment of the cessation of perception and feeling

What is the attainment of the cessation of perception and feeling? Who enters upon it? Endowed with how many kinds of power does one enter upon it? Through the stilling of how many formations is it entered upon? How many preliminary duties are there? Why does one enter upon it? How does one emerge from it? By what does the mind emerge from it? If the mind has emerged, towards what is it inclined? How many [kinds of] contact touch [the mind upon emerging]? Which formations arise first? What is the difference between a dead person and a person who has entered upon the cessation of perception and feeling? Is this attainment conditioned or unconditioned?

Q. What is the attainment of the cessation of perception and feeling?
A. The non-occurrence (*appavatti*) of the mind (*citta*) and mental properties (*cetasikā dhammā*)—this is called the attainment of the cessation of perception and feeling.[259]

Q. Who enters upon that attainment?
A. The arahant and the non-returner who are perfect in concentration.[260]

Q. Who does not enter upon it?
A. The worldling, the stream-enterer, the once-returner, and one who is born in the immaterial sphere. [**461b**]

Herein, the worldling cannot enter upon it since it is not within his range (*visaya*). The stream-enterer and the once-returner cannot enter upon it since they have not yet fully removed the afflictions and the obstacles to concentration. One who is born in the immaterial sphere cannot enter upon it since the [material] basis for emerging from it again is not there.[261]

---

259. Vism XXIII.18/p.702, Paṭis-a I 319: *Tattha kā nirodhasamāpattī ti? Yā anupubbanirodhavasena cittacetasikānaṃ dhammānaṃ appavatti.*

260. A I 232f.: *Idha ... puggalo sīlesu paripūrakārī hoti, samādhismiṃ paripūrakārī paññāya na paripūrakāri hoti; so pañcannaṃ orambhāgiyānaṃ saṃyojanānaṃ parikkhayā ... antarāparinibbāyī hoti. Idha ... bhikkhu sīlesu paripūrakārī hoti samādhismiṃ paripūrakārī paññāya paripūrakārī ... so āsavānaṃ khayā anāsavaṃ cetovimuttiṃ paññāvimuttiṃ diṭṭheva dhamme sayaṃ abhiññā sacchikatvā upasampajja viharati.*

261. Cf. Vism XXIII.18/p.702: *Ke taṃ samāpajjanti, ke na samāpajjantī ti sabbe pi puthujjanā, sotāpannā, sakadāgāmino, sukkhavipassakā ca anāgāmino, arahanto na samāpajjanti. Aṭṭhasamāpattilābhino pana anāgāmino, khīṇāsavā ca samāpajjanti.* Vism XXIII.29/p.705 *Catuvokārabhave pana paṭhamajjhānādīnaṃ uppatti natthi. Tasmā na sakkā tattha samāpajjitunti. Keci pana vatthussa abhāvā ti vadanti.* Cf. Vism-mhṭ 525: *Vatthussa abhāva ti hadayavatthuno abhāva ti vadanti, karajakāyasaṅkhātassa pana vatthuno abhāvā ti attho. Yadi hi āruppe nirodhaṃ samāpajjeyya cittacetasikānaṃ aññassa ca kassaci abhāvato apaññattikova bhaveyya anupādisesāya nibbānadhātuyā parinibbutasadiso. Kiñcāyaṃ upādāya nirodhaṃ samāpanno ti vucceyya, kiṃ vā etāya vatthucintāya. Aṅgavekallatova*

Q. Endowed with how many kinds of power does one enter upon it?

A. It is entered upon through two kinds of power: through the power of calm and through the power of insight.

Herein "through the power of calm" is owing to achieving mastery in the eight attainments.[262]

"Through the power of insight" is owing to achieving mastery in the seven contemplations. Which seven? Contemplation of impermanence, contemplation of suffering, contemplation of without self, contemplation of disenchantment, contemplation of fading away, contemplation of cessation, and contemplation of relinquishment.[263]

The power of calm is for the ceasing of the jhāna-factors and for the unshakeable liberation.[264]

The power of insight is for seeing the disadvantage of occurrence (*pavatti*), and for the liberation which is non-occurrence.[265]

---

natthi āruppe nirodhasamāpattisamāpajjanaṃ.

262. The eight attainments (*aṭṭhasamāpatti*) are the four jhānas and the four immaterial attainments. Cf. Paṭis I 97–98, Vism XXIII.19–22/p.702–703: *Kathaṃ dvīhi balehi samannāgatattā tayo ca saṅkhārānaṃ paṭippassaddhiyā soḷasahi ñāṇacariyāhi navahi samādhicariyāhi vasibhāvatā paññā nirodhasamāpattiyā ñāṇaṃ? ... samathabalaṃ vipassanābalaṃ. Nekkhammavasena cittassa ekaggatā avikkhepo samathabalaṃ. ... neva-saññānāsaññāyatanasamāpattiyā ākiñcaññāyatanasaññāya na kampatī ti samathabalaṃ.*

263. Cf. Paṭis I 97–98, Vism XXIII.19–22/p.702–703: *Aniccānupassanā vipassanābalaṃ. Dukkhānupassanā... anattānupassanā... nibbidānupassanā... virāgānupassanā... nirodhānupassanā... paṭinissaggānupassanā vipassanābalaṃ*. Cf. Ps I 157: *Vipassanāya samannāgatoti sattavidhāya anupassanāya yutto, sattavidhā anupassanā nāma aniccānupassanā ... paṭinissaggānupassanāti.* Paṭis-a I 316: *Vipassanābale pana satta anupassanāva vipassanābalan-ti vuttā, ñāṇacariyāya satta ca anupassanā vuttā, vivaṭṭanānupassanādayo nava ca visesetvā vuttā. Idaṃ nesaṃ nānattaṃ. Satta anupassanā pana akampiyaṭṭhena balāni vasībhāvaṭṭhena cariyā ti veditabbā.*

264. No parallel can be traced. 不動解脫 can correspond to *akuppa vimokkha,* but in Pali texts this is said to be an insight attainment; see Paṭis II 40: *Cattāro ca ariyamaggā, cattāri ca sāmaññaphalāni, nibbānañ-ca: ayaṃ akuppo vimokkho.* The *akuppa cetovimutti* is the *phalasamāpatti*; e.g. M-a II 232: *Akuppā cetovimuttī ti arahattaphalavimutti.* The Tibetan instead has "resolve towards unshakeability", *mi gyo ba la mos pa.* The term *mos pa* corresponds to *adhimokkha,* not to *vimokkha* (= *rnam par thar pa*), and is used in the next sentence to "resolve towards non-occurrence", *mi 'jug pa rnams la mos pa.* Although 解脫 usually corresponds to *vimutti* or *vimokkha*, at 459c04 it corresponds to *adhimokkha* (in 多解脫, "great resolve," *adhimokkhabahula*), so possibly the Tibetan translation is right.

265. Cf. Paṭis-a I 315: *tattha samathabalaṃ anupubbena cittasantānavūpasamanatthaṃ nirodhe ca paṭipādanatthaṃ, vipassanābalaṃ pavatte ādīnavadassanatthaṃ nirodhe ca ānisaṃsadassanatthaṃ.* Paṭis II 64: *dukkhato manasikaroto pavattā cittaṃ vuṭṭhāti, appavatte cittaṃ pakkhandati. anattato manasikaroto nimittā ca pavattā ca cittaṃ vuṭṭhāti, animitte appavatte nirodhe nibbānadhātuyā cittaṃ pakkhandati.* Paṭis I 74: *Uddhacce*

Q. Through the stilling of how many formations is it entered upon?

A. It is entered upon through the stilling of three formations: verbal formations, bodily formations, and mental formations.

Herein, for one who has entered upon the second jhāna, the verbal formations of thinking and exploring are stilled. For one who has entered upon the fourth jhāna, the bodily formations of inhalations and exhalations are stilled. For one who has entered upon the attainment of the cessation of perception and feeling, the mental formations of perception and feeling are stilled.[266]

Q. How many preliminary duties are there?[267]

A. There are four preliminary duties: personal belongings, non-damage, delimiting the duration, and observing legal acts and non-legal acts.

Herein, "personal belongings" (*ekābaddha*): he resolves with regard to the alms-bowl, robes, [and other requisites].

"Non-damage": he resolves "Let there be no arising of any damage to this body through any means".

"Delimiting the duration": estimating the strength of his body, and making a limit of days, he resolves: "When this period has passed, I will emerge".

"Observing legal acts and non-legal acts": he resolves: "When the time-limit has not yet been reached and the Saṅgha assembles for a legal act or non-legal act, by the sound [of the Saṅgha] I will emerge".

Herein, "personal belongings" is for the sake of protecting the robes. "Non-damage" and "limiting the duration" are for the sake of protecting the body. "Observing legal acts and non-legal acts" is for the sake of not hindering the assembling of the Saṅgha.

When he dwells in the base of nothingness [and has emerged from it], he does the preliminary duties, or when he enters upon the first jhāna [and has emerged from it].[268]

---

akampiyaṭṭhena samādhibalaṃ tadā samudāgataṃ. Avijjāya akampiyaṭṭhena paññābalaṃ tadā samudāgataṃ. Paṭis I 98-99: *Uddhacce ca ... na kampati ... samathabalaṃ. ... Avijjāya ...na kampati ... vipassanābalaṃ.* D-a II 512: *Aṭṭha vimokkhe asacchikatvā paññābaleneva nāmakāyassa ca rūpakāyassa ca appavattiṃ katvā vimutto ti attho.*

266. Cf. Paṭis I 98, Vism XXIII.24/p.703: *Tayo ca saṅkhārānaṃ paṭippassaddhiyā ti ... Dutiyaṃ jhānaṃ samāpannassa vitakkavicārā vacīsaṅkhārā paṭippassaddhā honti. Catutthaṃ jhānaṃ samāpannassa assāsapassāsā kāyasaṅkhārā paṭippassaddhā honti. Saññāvedayitanirodhaṃ samāpannassa saññā ca vedanā ca cittasaṅkhārā paṭippassaddhā honti.*

267. Cf. Vism XXIII.34/p.705: *Catubbidhaṃ pubbakiccaṃ karoti: nānā-baddha-avikopanaṃ, saṅghapaṭimānanaṃ, satthupakkosanaṃ addhānaparicchedan ti.*

268. 住無所有處或初作事入初禪: "[When] he dwells in/is established in the base of nothingness or does the preliminary duties [when] he enters upon the first jhāna". This sentence is corrupt. The Vism says that he should do the preliminary duties upon emerging from the base of nothingness and then enter upon the base

Q. Why does one enter upon it?

A. For the sake of a pleasant dwelling in this life, the ultimate immovable concentration (*āneñja-samāpatti* or *-samādhi*) of the noble ones.

Furthermore, it is for the sake of supernormal power due to the intervention of concentration as in the case of the venerable Sañjīva, the arahant,[269] and for the sake of protecting the body as in the case of the Venerable Sāriputta[270] and as in the case of the Venerable Tissa, the Egret's

---

of neither-perception-nor-non-perception, not the first jhāna. Vism XXIII.34/p.705: *... tato viññāṇañcāyatanaṃ samāpajjitvā vuṭṭhāya tattha saṅkhāre tatheva vipassati. Atha ākiñcaññāyatanaṃ samāpajjitvā vuṭṭhāya catubbidhaṃ pubbakiccaṃ karoti.* XXIII.43–47/p.707–08: *So evaṃ ākiñcaññāyatanaṃ samāpajjitvā vuṭṭhāya imaṃ pubbakiccaṃ katvā nevasaññānāsaññāyatanaṃ samāpajjati. ... ... evam-evaṃ katapubbakicco bhikkhu nevasaññā-nāsaññāyatanaṃ samāpajjitvāva parato acittako hutvā nirodhaṃ phusitvā viharati.*

269. This is probably a mistranslation. The Pali parallels indicate that Sañjīva's body was protected due to the intervention of concentration while he was in cessation. The same applies to Sāriputta. Perhaps the original was: "it is for protecting the body by supernormal power through the intervention of concentration like the venerable Sañjīva the arahant, the Venerable Sāriputta, and ...". Others who were protected by it are the theras Mahānāga and Khāṇukoṇḍañña and the *upāsikās* Uttarā and Sāmāvatī; see Vism XII.30–33/p.380 and Paṭis II 212.

Cf. M I 333–34. Vism XII. 32/p.380, Paṭis-a 671: *Sañjīvattheraṃ pana nirodhasamāpannaṃ kālakatoti sallakkhetvā gopālakādayo tiṇakaṭṭhagomayāni saṅkaḍḍhetvā aggiṃ adaṃsu. Therassa cīvare aṃsumattam-pi najjhāyittha. Ayamassa anupubbasamāpattivasena pavattasamathānubhāvanibbattattā samādhivipphārā iddhi.* Vism XXII.37/p.706: *Yaṃ ekābaddhaṃ hoti nivāsanapāvuraṇaṃ vā nisinnāsanaṃ vā, tattha visuṃ adhiṭṭhānakiccaṃ natthi. Samāpattivaseneva naṃ rakkhati āyasmato sañjīvassa viya. Vuttam-pi cetaṃ (Paṭis II 212) āyasmato sañjīvassa samādhivipphārā iddhi, āyasmato sāriputtassa samādhivipphārā iddhī ti.* Vism XII. 32/p.380: *Samādhito pubbe vā pacchā vā taṃkhaṇe vā samathānubhāvanibbatto viseso samādhivipphārā iddhi.*

270. According to Paṭis-a this refers to the Udāna story about Sāriputta not being hurt despite being hit on the head by a yakkha while having entered upon a certain concentration (*aññataraṃ samādhiṃ*, Ud 39–41). Ud-a explains that this concentration is the divine abiding of equanimity, but adds that "some say that it is 'the attainment of cessation of perception and feeling,' but others say that it is 'the attainment of fruition based on the formless attainments,' since just these three attainments are capable of protecting the body". Earlier on, however, with reference to Mahākassapa's attainment of a "certain concentration" (Ud 29), Ud-a says that the *porāṇā* said that it is the attainment of cessation, while "some" say it is the concentration of fruition of arahantship. He had entered upon cessation instead of fruition "out of compassion for beings. ... For even a little veneration for one who has emerged from this attainment is of especially great fruit and benefit".

Paṭis-a III 669: *Samādhivipphāriddhiniddese āyasmato sāriputtassa samādhivipphārā iddhītiādīsu āyasmato sāriputtassa mahāmoggallānattherena saddhiṁ kapotakandarāyaṁ viharato juṇhāya rattiyā navoropitehi kesehi ajjhokāse nisinnassa eko duṭṭhayakkho*

son (Kontaputtatissa).[271]

Q. How is it entered upon? A. The meditator, having gone to a secluded dwelling, sits down or lies down. Desiring cessation, aspiring for cessation, he enters upon the first jhāna. Having entered, he emerges mindfully from it, and immediately after contemplates that jhāna as impermanent, suffering, and without self, until [he reaches] the knowledge of equanimity towards the formations, and likewise for the second, the third, and the fourth jhānas, the base of boundless space, the base of boundless consciousness, and the base of nothingness. Having entered, he emerges mindfully from it, and immediately after contemplates that attainment as impermanent, suffering, and without self, until [he reaches] the knowledge of equanimity towards the formations, and then immediately after enters upon the base of neither-perception-nor-non-perception. [**461c**] Thereupon, he gives rise to the mind of the base of

---

sahāyakena yakkhena vāriyamānopi sīse pahāraṁ adāsi. Yassa meghassa viya gajjato saddo ahosi, thero tassa paharaṇasamaye samāpattiṁ appetvā nisinno hoti. Athassa tena pahārena na koci ābādho ahosi. Ayaṁ tassa āyasmato samādhivipphārā iddhi. Yathāha .... Ud-a 245: *Tattha aññataraṃ samādhin-ti upekkhābrahmavihārasamāpattiṃ. Keci saññāvedayitanirodhasamāpattin-ti vadanti, apare panāhu āruppapādakaṃ phalasamāpattinti. Imā eva hi tisso kāyarakkhaṇasamatthā samāpattiyo. Tattha nirodhasamāpattiyā samādhipariyāyasambhavo heṭṭhā vuttova, pacchimaṃ yeva pana ācariyā vaṇṇenti.* Ud-a 195–96: *sattāhaṃ ekapallaṅkena nisinno hoti aññataraṃ samādhiṃ samāpajjitvā ti ettha keci tāva āhu arahattaphalasamādhi idha aññataro samādhīti adhippetoti. Tañ-hi so āyasmā bahulaṃ samāpajjati diṭṭhadhammasukhavihāratthaṃ, pahoti ca sattāham-pi phalasamāpattiyā vītināmetuṃ. ... Porāṇā panāhu: aññataraṃ samādhiṃ samāpajjitvā ti nirodhasamāpattiṃ samāpajjitvā. ... Kasmā panāyaṃ thero phalasamāpattiṃ asamāpajjitvā nirodhaṃ samāpajji? Sattesu anukampāya. ... Tañ-hi samāpajjitvā vuṭṭhitassa kato appako pi sakkāro visesato mahapphalo mahānisaṃso hotī ti.*

271. 白鷺子底沙: bai-lu-zi-ti-sha = white-heron-son-tissa or *koñca-putta-tissa* (Skt *kruñca-putra-tiṣya*). This is the arahant Kontaputtatissa Thera whose story is told in the *Mahāvaṃsa* (V.212–217). He had attained the six higher knowledges, but there is no mention of cessation. He is also mentioned in Sp I 51 (in Chinese at T 1462: 682a15; see Bapat 1970: 33f.). He lived during Asoka's time. His brother Sumitta Thera entered final nibbāna through self-immolation. The *Dīpavaṃsa* (VII.32) also mentions the arahant sons of Kontī (*kontiputtā*), who had great powers and passed away during the 8th year of King Asoka's reign. The Mhv (v. 212) says that he was raised by a king, and his mother was a *kuntakinnarī* (cf. Mhv-ṭ I 231f.), explained in Sp-ṭ (I 135) as: "konta bird' is a kind of *kinnara* (i.e., a bird with a human head or elf)" (*kontasakuṇiyo nāma kinnarajātiyo*). The *Sīmāvisodhanī* (p. 27) has another story about their mother, called Kontā. The *kontaputtā* brother theras are given as examples of "egg-born" (*aṇḍajā*) at Ps II 36. The *kontī/kuntī/kontinī/kuntinī* bird was noted for its fear to tread with its feet on the ground out of fear of earthquakes (Sn-a I 317, Mp III 57; cf. Ps IV 21) suggesting that it is a shorebird or wader such as a heron or flamingo that stands and sleeps on one leg. The *Divyāvadāna* and *Aśokāvadāna* do not mention the thera.

neither-perception-nor-non-perception two or three times. Having emerged, he causes the dissolution of mind. Having caused the dissolution of mind, he enters upon non-occurrence (*appavatta*) and the unmanifest (*anidassana*?)—this is called "entering upon the attainment of the cessation of perception and feeling".

Q. How does one emerge from it?
A. Herein, one does not attend thus, "I shall emerge" since it [only] happens when the previously delimited time has arrived.[272]

Q. Through what does the mind emerge?
A. The non-returner emerges by the fruition mind of non-returning. The arahant emerges by the fruition mind of arahantship.[273]

Q. If the mind has emerged, towards what is it inclined?
A. The mind is inclined towards seclusion.[274]

Q. How many contacts touch [the mind upon emerging]?
A. Three contacts, namely, emptiness-contact, signless-contact, and desireless-contact.[275]

Q. Which formations arise first?
A. [Mental formations,] then bodily formations, and then verbal formations.[276]

Q. What is the difference between one who is dead and one who has entered upon the cessation of perception and feeling?

---

272. Cf. S IV 294: *Na kho, gahapati, saññāvedayitanirodhasamāpattiyā vuṭṭhahantassa bhikkhuno evaṃ hoti ahaṃ saññāvedayitanirodhasamāpattiyā vuṭṭhahissanti vā ahaṃ saññāvedayitanirodhasamāpattiyā vuṭṭhahāmī ti vā ahaṃ saññāvedayitanirodhasamāpattiyā vuṭṭhito ti vā. Atha khvassa pubbeva tathā cittaṃ bhāvitaṃ hoti, yaṃ taṃ tathattāya upanetī ti.*

273. Abhidh-s 67: *Vuṭṭhānakāle pana anāgāmino anāgāmiphalacittaṃ, arahato arahatta-phalacittaṃ ekavāram-eva pavattitvā bhavaṅgapāto hoti, tato paraṃ paccavekkhaṇañāṇaṃ pavattati.*

274. Vism XXIII.50/p.708: *Vuṭṭhitassa kiṃninnaṃ cittaṃ hotī ti nibbānaninnaṃ. Vuttaṃ hetaṃ (= M I 302, S IV 294) saññāvedayitanirodhasamāpattiyā vuṭṭhitassa kho, āvuso visākha, bhikkhuno vivekaninnaṃ cittaṃ hoti vivekapoṇaṃ vivekapabbhāran-ti.*

275. In MN 44 § 20/M I 302 it is said that these contacts touch upon emerging from cessation: *Saññāvedayitanirodhasamāpattiyā vuṭṭhitaṃ kho, āvuso visākha, bhikkhuṃ tayo phassā phusanti—suññato phasso, animitto phasso, appaṇihito phasso ti.*

276. The Tibetan omits the verbal formations: "Mental formations and then bodily formations".

Cf. M I 302, S IV 294: *Saññāvedayitanirodhasamāpattiyā vuṭṭhahantassa kho, āvuso visākha, bhikkhuno paṭhamaṃ uppajjati cittasaṅkhāro, tato kāyasaṅkhāro, tato vacīsaṅkhāro-ti.*

A. In case of one who is dead, three formations have ceased and stilled, the life span is exhausted, [physical] heat has subsided, and the sense-faculties have broken up. In the case of one who has entered upon the cessation of perception and feeling, three formations have ceased and stilled,[277] the life span is not exhausted, heat has not subsided, and the sense-faculties are clear. This is the difference.

Q. Is this attainment conditioned or unconditioned?
A. This attainment is not to be spoken of as conditioned or unconditioned.

Q. Why is this attainment not to be spoken of as conditioned or unconditioned?
A. Conditioned states are absent in this attainment and an entry upon and an emergence from an unconditioned state cannot be known. Therefore, this attainment is not to be spoken of as conditioned or unconditioned.[278]

The attainment of cessation is finished.

[The miscellaneous topics are finished.]

The twelfth chapter of the Path to Freedom, the Exposition of the Truths, is finished.

---

277. The Tibetan mistakenly says that the three formations have not ceased (*ma 'gags*). Cf. S IV 293f, M I 296: *... kiṃ nānākaraṇan ti? Yvāyaṃ āvuso mato kālakato, tassa kāyasaṅkhārā niruddhā paṭippassaddhā, vacīsaṅkhārā niruddhā paṭipassaddhā, cittasaṅkhārā niruddhā paṭippassaddhā, āyu parikkhīno, usmā vūpasantā, indriyāni viparibhinnāni: yo cāyaṃ bhikkhu saññāvedayitanirodhaṃ samāpanno tassa pi kāyasaṅkhārā niruddhā paṭipassaddhā, vacīsaṅkhārā niruddhā paṭippassaddhā, cittasaṅkhārā niruddhā paṭippassaddhā, āyu aparikkhīno, usmā avūpasantā, indriyāni vippasannāni.*

278. Cf. Vism XXIII.52: *Nirodhasamāpatti saṅkhatā ti ādipucchāyaṃ pana saṅkhatā ti pi asaṅkhatā ti pi lokiyā ti pi lokuttarā ti pi na vattabbā. Kasmā? Sabhāvato natthitāya. Yasmā panassā samāpajjantassa vasena samāpannā nāma hoti, tasmā nipphannā ti vattuṃ vaṭṭati, no anipphannā.* Kv 327: *Nirodhasamāpatti asaṅkhatā ti? Āmantā. Atthi keci nirodhaṃ samāpajjanti ... sañjanentī ti? Āmantā. ... Nirodhā vodānaṃ vuṭṭhānaṃ paññāyatī ti? Āmantā. ... Na vattabbaṃ: nirodhasamāpatti asaṅkhatā ti? Āmantā.* Kv-a 91: *Tattha nirodhasamāpattī ti catunnaṃ khandhānaṃ appavatti. Yasmā pana sā kariyamānā kariyati, samāpajjiyamānā samāpajjiyati, tasmā nipphannā ti vuccati. Saṅkhatāsaṅkhatalakkhaṇānaṃ pana abhāvena na vattabbā saṅkhatā ti vā asaṅkhatā ti vā. Tattha yesaṃ yasmā saṅkhatā na hoti, tasmā asaṅkhatā ti laddhi, ... Nirodhā vodānaṃ vuṭṭhānan-ti phalasamāpatti veditabbā. Asaṅkhatā pana taṃ natthi yeva, tasmā paṭikkhipati. Tena hīti yasmā saṅkhatā na hoti, tasmā asaṅkhatā ti laddhi. Idaṃ pana asaṅkhatabhāve kāraṇaṃ na hotī ti vuttam-pi avuttasadisamevāti.*

Conclusion

Herein, the enumeration of chapters is:

(1) The Introduction,
(2) Virtue,
(3) Asceticism,
(4) Concentration,
(5) The Search for a Good Friend,
(6) The Exposition of Temperament,
(7) The Meditation Subjects,
(8) The Way to Practise,
(9) The Five Direct Knowledges,
(10) The Exposition of Wisdom,
(11) The Five Skills, and
(12) The Exposition of the Truths.

These twelve chapters are the sequence of chapters of the Path to Freedom.

Endless, incomparable, inconceivable,
Measureless, very fortunate, well spoken,
Who is able to know this Dhamma?

Only the meditator who is able to keep up
The excellent, best path for good practice.
Being without doubt about the Teaching,
He dispels ignorance.

Appendix I

Translation of the Vimuktimārgadhutaguṇanirdeśa

On the Tibetan text, see Introduction § 3 and the section "Tibetan translations of the *Vimuttimagga*" in the Bibliography.

***Vimuktimārgadhutaguṇanirdeśa* in the language of India.**
"The Exposition of the Ascetic Qualities from the Path to Freedom" in the Tibetan language.

Homage to Mañjuśrī the Youthful!

1. Introduction[1]

[Der 131b] Now, the meditator who has such pure virtue gives rise to the wish for good qualities [and] aspires to undertake the ascetic qualities and maintain them. The meditator undertakes the ascetic qualities (*dhutaguṇa*) for various reasons: fewness of wishes, contentment, effacement, disaccumulation, arousal of energy, being easy to support, dwelling in knowledge, and elimination of greed. They are the protection of virtue, the accessories of concentration, the manifestation of the lineage of the noble ones, and the manifestation of qualities of supreme purity.

2. Thirteen kinds of asceticism

Herein, in the thirteen ascetic qualities, two are connected to robes, namely, the state of the rag-robe-wearer, and the state of the three-robes-wearer. Five are connected to food: the state of the alms-food-gatherer, the state of the uninterrupted-alms-round-goer, the state of the one-sitting-eater, the state of the food-limiter, and the state of the later-food-denier. Five are connected to lodgings: the state of the wilderness-dweller, the state of the tree-root-dweller, the state of the open-air-dweller, the state the charnel-ground-dweller, and the state of the user-of-any-dwelling. One is connected with energy, namely, the state of the sitter.

Herein, the state (*ngo bo nyid = [sa]bhāvatā*) of the factor of the rag-robe-wearer (*phyag dar khrod pa'i yan lag = paṃsukūlikaṅga*) is the state of the rag-robe-wearer (*phyag dar khrod pa nyid = paṃsukūlikatta*). The word meaning of the others is also to be taught in the same way.

1. There are no headings in the Tibetan translation.

Herein, the state of the rag-robe-wearer is the rejection of robes [offered] by householders. The state of the three-robes-wearer is the rejection of a fourth robe. The state of the alms-food-gatherer is the rejection of going to meals. The state of the uninterrupted-alms-round-goer is the rejection of skipping [houses while] going [on alms round]. [Der 132a] The state of the one-sitting-eater is the rejection of sitting down two times.

The state of the food-limiter is the rejection of a large amount of food. The state of the later-food-denier is the rejection of taking leftover food. The state of the wilderness-dweller is the rejection of dwelling inside a village (*gāmanta*). The state of the tree-root-dweller is the rejection of dwelling under the cover of a roof. The state of the open-air-dweller is the rejection of dwelling under the cover of a roof and under a root of a tree. The state of the charnel-ground-dweller is the rejection of dwelling elsewhere. The state of the user-of-any-dwelling is the rejection of greed for lodgings. The state of the sitter is the rejection of lying down.

3. Rag-robe-wearer

Herein, how to undertake the state of the rag-robe-wearer?

Seeing the disadvantage in seeking for, receiving, and begging others for householders' robes and seeing the benefits of the state of rag-robe-wearer,[2] one says: "From today onwards I reject householders' robes and undertake the state of the rag-robe-wearer." Thus, one undertakes it.

Herein, the benefits of the state of the rag-robe-wearer are: [practicing in] conformity with the dependence;[3] obtaining [robes] independent of others; not doing unsuitable actions; one uses them without attachment; one has no greed [towards them]; [robes are] not taken by robbers; [there is] no [special] time [to accept them]; they involve little work; it has the characteristic of effacement; it is a practice of a good man; it inspires confidence in those with good qualities; later generations imitate the example; it is cultivation of the right practice; it is praised by the Conqueror. Such and others are the benefits of the state of the rag-robe-wearer.

How many kind of rubbish-rag robe are there? Who wears rag robes? By what is the state of the rag-robe-wearer broken?

There are two kinds of rag robes: ownerless ones [Der 132b] and ones which are by their nature rejected by people. Herein, [a robe that] is

---

2. *Gos nar ma la gnas pa*, "continues to dwell in robes" does not fit here (nor the variant reading without *ma la*). There is no corresponding passage in the Chinese parallel and in the parallels in the 12 following *dhutas*, therefore read *mthong nas 'di skad du* instead of *mthong nas gos nar ma la gnas pa 'di skad du*.

3. Cf. Vism II.21/p.64: *paṃsukūlacīvaraṃ nissāya pabbajjā ti (Vin I 96) vacanato nissayānurūpapaṭipattisabbhāvo*. See fn. 414.

patched together[4] from bits that are collected from a rubbish heap or a pile of sweepings or a market place or a road, and is worn—this is an ownerless rubbish-rag robe. [Robe cloth] cut off at the fringes, cut off at the end, gnawed by cattle, gnawed by rats, given as an offering [at a shrine],[5] robes [covering] a corpse, and the garments of members of other [non-Buddhist] sects—these are rag robes which are by their nature rejected by people.

The rag-robe-wearer is one who refuses robes from householders. By the acceptance of the robes from householders, the state of the rag-robe-wearer is broken.

4. Three-robes-wearer

How to undertake the state of the three-robes-wearer?

Seeing the disadvantage of affliction in seeking extra robes, examining them and making them allowable, and seeing the benefits of the state of the three-robes-wearer, one says: "From today onwards I reject a fourth robe and undertake the state of the three-robes-wearer." Thus one undertakes it.

Herein, the benefits of the state of the three-robes-wearer are: it has the characteristic of being the foremost;[6] avoidance of hoarding; having little [maintenance] responsibilities; contentment [with a robe] just for sustaining the body; going gladly like a bird; it is a practice of a good man; and it has the characteristic of effacement. Such and others are the benefits of the state of the three-robes-wearer.

What are the three robes? Who wears three robes? By what is the state of the three-robes-wearer broken?

The double-robe, upper-robe, and under-robe—these are the three robes. The three-robes-wearer is one who rejects a fourth robe. By the acceptance of a fourth robe the state of the three-robes-wearer is broken.

5. Alms-food-gatherer

How to undertake the state of the alms-food-gatherer? [Der 133a]

Seeing the disadvantage of going to [meal-] invitations—the disruption of one's own work, the coming under the influence of another, and meeting and sitting with disagreeable [people]—and seeing the benefits of the state of the alms-food-gatherer, one says: "From today onwards I reject the going to

---

4. Bapat translates *snam sbyar byas* as "garment", *saṅghāti*, but it rather corresponds to *saṅghātita*, "put together". The Chinese has 掩緝, "pieced together".

5. Read *yas stags*? Cf. 施, T 1648: 404c23.

6. *'Gor yang pa'i tshul can nyid.* The meaning of *'gor yang pa* is unclear; *'gor* can also mean "in the beginning". The Chinese text has "It is a practice of good men", which it repeats as the before last benefit.

meals and undertake the state of the alms-food-gatherer." In such a manner one undertakes it.

Herein, the benefits of the state of the alms-food-gatherer are: [Practising in] conformity with the dependence; independence; not having to sustain others; being without indolence; the abandoning of pride; the helping of other beings; curbing craving for tastes; being unobstructed in the [four] cardinal directions; it is a practice of a good man; and it has the characteristic of effacement. Such and others are the benefits of the state of the alms-food-gatherer.

How many kinds of meal are there? Who is the alms-food-gatherer? By what is the state of the alms-food-gatherer broken?

There are three factors of a meal, namely, (1) food, (2) which is considered as suitable, and (3) an invitation for a meal today or tomorrow or whenever it pleases one—this is a meal.[7] The alms-food-gatherer is one who rejects going to meals. By the acceptance of a meal, the state of the alms-food-gatherer is broken.

6. Uninterrupted-alms-round-goer

How to undertake the state of the uninterrupted-alms-round-goer?

Seeing the disadvantage of non-effacement when just going for alms where one always gets food that is abundant and excellent, and seeing the benefits of the state of the uninterrupted-alms-round-goer, one says: "From today onwards I reject always getting [alms] and undertake the state of the uninterrupted-alms-round-goer." In such a manner one undertakes it.

Herein, the benefits of the state of the uninterrupted-alms-round-goer are: impartial mindedness; benefiting all; abandoning of selfishness towards families [Der 133b]; being without the disadvantage of frequenting families; non-delight when being called [for alms]; not [just] choosing excellent food; being freed from being taken in by people; avoidance of going together with [others]; and it has the characteristic of effacement. Such and others are the benefits of the state of the uninterrupted-alms-round-goer.

What is going uninterruptedly? Who rejects skipping [houses]?[8] By what is the state of the uninterrupted-alms-round-goer broken?

Going uninterruptedly is going for alms to houses uninterruptedly beginning from the first house.[9] The one who goes uninterruptedly is one

7. The Tibetan is cryptic and is quite different from the Chinese version. The reading of the Dergé edition is translated here. Bapat's text has: "[which accords with] the five factors of food, which is suitable, an invitation ...".

8. *brnyogs par rgyu ba gang gis spong*. Probably this is a corruption. In accordance with the answer, the parallel sections in this chapter, and in the Chinese version the question should be "Who goes uninterruptedly?"

9. *mthar gyis rgyu ba ni bsod snyoms spyod pa na khyim dang po nas bzung ste khyim*

who rejects the skipping [houses while] going [on alms round]. By skipping [houses while] going [on alms round] the state of the uninterrupted-alms-round-goer is broken.

7. One-sitting-eater

How to undertake the state of the one-sitting-eater?

Seeing the disadvantage of non-effacement when sitting down two times, sitting down to eat again and again, accepting [the food that is] given, and enjoying food, and seeing the benefits of the state of the one-sitting-eater, one says: "From today onwards I reject sitting down two times to eat and undertake the state of the one-sitting-eater." In such a manner one undertakes it.

Herein, the benefits of the state of the one-sitting-eater are: food is digested; no greed [for food]; no eating of leftovers; fewness of wishes; a good complexion; no disruption of one's work; dwelling in comfort; it is a practice of a good man; and it has the characteristic of effacement. Such and others are the benefits of the state of the one-sitting-eater.

How many kinds of eating at one sitting are there? Who eats at one sitting? What is "bounded by food"? By what is the state of the one-sitting-eater broken?

There are three kinds of eating at one sitting: bounded by sitting, bounded by water, and bounded by food. "Bounded by sitting" is, when having eaten, one gets up from one's seat and then does not eat again. "Bounded by water" is when, having eaten and still sitting on the seat, [Der 134a] one receives water [for washing] in one's alms-bowl and then does not eat again. "Bounded by food" is, when eating a morsel there is the perception "the last" and then one does not eat again.

The one-sitting-eater is one who rejects sitting down twice to eat. "Bounded by food" means that anything that is to be swallowed, except water and medicine, is not allowable. By sitting down twice to eat the state of the one-sitting-eater is broken.

8. Food-limiter

How to undertake the state of the food-limiter?[10]

Seeing the disadvantage of non-effacement when eating much food—physical heaviness, arising of satiety, and great desire—and seeing the benefits of the state of the food-limiter, one says: "From today onwards

---

mthar chags su rgyu ba yin no.

10. "One-who-limits-his-food" = *zas chog pa pa*, lit. "food contentment/sufficiency".

I reject much food and undertake the state of the food-limiter." In such a manner one undertakes it.

Herein, the benefits of the state of the food-limiter are: non-arising of satiety; limiting one's food; knowing the harm of eating a large amount of food; diminishing inertia of the body (*kāyaduṭṭhulla*); abandoning of greed; experiencing little illness; removal of the obsessions; it is a practice of a good man and it has the characteristic of effacement. Such and others are the benefits of the state of the food-limiter.

How should one take the limit of food? Who eats limited food? By what is the state of the food-limiter broken?

Taking a small amount of rice or rice-gruel in one's alms-bowl, one reflects on the sign of the limit, one becomes skilled in the sign of not taking [more]. When conversant, one will know one's belly's limit. The one who eats limited food is one who rejects large amounts of food. By [taking] more than the limit of food [of one's belly] the state of the food-limiter is broken.

9. Later-food-denier

How to undertake the state of the later-food-denier?

Seeing the disadvantage of non-effacement when eating leftover food—arising of satiety and dependency on others—and seeing the benefits of the state of the food-limiter, [Der 134b] one says: "From today onwards I reject leftover food and undertake the state of the later-food-denier." In such a manner one undertakes it.

Herein, the benefits of the state of the later-food-denier are: elimination of expectations; being easy to support; non-dependence on others; abandoning of hoarding [food]; not seeking food again; non-greed; non-arising of satiety; it is a practice of a good man and it has the characteristic of effacement. Such and others are the benefits of the state of the later-food-denier.

How many kinds of refusing of later food are there? Who never eats a meal afterwards? By what is the state of the later-food-denier broken?

There are two kinds of refusing of later food: bounded by leftover [food] and bounded by taking.

Herein, "bounded by leftover [food]" is after having eaten and having refused [more], one does not eat. "Bounded by taking" is when, having taken once one's own ordinary portion [of food], one does not take more.

The later-food-denier is one who rejects leftover food. By the eating of leftover food, the state of the later-food-denier is broken.

10. Wilderness-dweller

How to undertake the state of the wilderness-dweller?

Seeing the disadvantage of dwelling inside the village (*gāmanta*)—distraction due to disagreeable sense objects, the arising of desire, dwelling with commotion—and seeing the benefits of the state of the wilderness-dweller, one says: "From today onwards I reject dwelling inside the village and undertake the state of the wilderness-dweller." In such a manner one undertakes it.

Herein, the benefits of the state of the wilderness-dweller are: avoidance of disagreeable sense objects; [one meets good friends who] correctly teach [one in accordance with] the ten topics of discussion; [one enjoys] great beauty [of nature]; encouragement from deities;[11] one has no need for delight in socializing; to attain the pleasure of seclusion when one wishes; it is congenial to meditation practice due to little sound; it is a practice of a good man and [Der 135a] it has the characteristic of effacement. Such and others are the benefits of the state of the wilderness-dweller.

What are the bounds of a wilderness lodging? Who dwells in the wilderness? By what is the state of the wilderness-dweller broken?

Excluding the village, the village surroundings, parks (*ārāma*) and parks' surroundings, [it is within a distance of] 500 bow-lengths—a bow-length being four forearm-lengths of an average man—these are the bounds of a wilderness lodging.

The wilderness-dweller is one who rejects dwelling inside the village. By dwelling inside the village, the state of the wilderness-dweller is broken.

11. Tree-root-dweller

How to undertake the state of the tree-root-dweller?

Seeing the disadvantage of dwelling under the cover of a roof—appropriation, maintenance of what has been built, asking [help] from others, enjoyment [of possessions, *sambhoga*]—and seeing the benefits of the state of the tree-root-dweller, one says: "From today onwards I reject dwelling under the cover of a roof and undertake the state of the tree-root-dweller." In such a manner one undertakes it.

Herein, the benefits of the state of the tree-root-dweller are: [practicing in] conformity with the dependence; effacement; elimination of delight in work; encouragement of deities; abandoning of selfishness on account of dwellings; elimination of greed; it is a practice of a good man and it has the

11. This could refer to deities visiting monks to encourage them to meditate, as is related in suttas in the Devaputta Saṃyutta, etc. The same benefit is also given in the next *dhutaguṇa*.

characteristic of effacement. Such and others are the benefits of the state of the tree-root-dweller.

How much is the extent of a root of a tree? Which trees are to be avoided? Who dwells at the root of a tree? By what is the state of the tree-root-dweller broken?

As far as [the tree's] shadow falls in the middle of the day, and as far as far as [its] leaves fall when there is no wind, so far is the extent of a root of a tree. Old [decaying] trees, hollow trees and sick trees are to be avoided. The tree-root-dweller is one who rejects dwelling under the cover of a roof. By dwelling under the cover of a roof, the state of the tree-root-dweller is broken. [Der 135b]

12. Open-air-dweller

How to undertake the state of the open-air-dweller?

Seeing the disadvantage of non-effacement when dwelling under the coverings of roofs and at the roots of trees, and of the searching for and appropriation of [dwellings], and seeing the benefits of the state of the open-air-dweller, one says: "From today onwards I reject dwelling under roofs and at roots of trees and undertake the state of the open-air-dweller." In such a manner one undertakes it.

Herein, the benefits of the state of the open-air-dweller are: unrelenting effort (*anikkhitta-dhura*?); dispelling of sloth and torpor; one is like a forest deer; one can go in the four directions (*cātuddisa*) and is independent; it is a practice of a good man and it has the characteristic of effacement. Such and others are the benefits of the state of the open-air-dweller.

Who is the open-air-dweller? By what is the state of the open-air-dweller broken?

The open-air-dweller is one who rejects coverings of roofs and roots of trees. By dwelling under the covering of a roof or at the root of a tree, the state of the open-air-dweller is broken.

13. Charnel-ground-dweller

How to undertake the state of the charnel-ground-dweller?

Seeing the disadvantage of other places—non-arising of urgency and much negligence—and seeing the benefits of the state of the charnel-ground-dweller, one says: "From today onwards I reject other places and undertake the state of the charnel-ground-dweller." In such a manner one undertakes it.

Herein, the benefits of the state of the charnel-ground-dweller are: the obtaining of recollection of death; obtaining the sign of foulness; obtaining the respect and esteem of non-humans; the arising of heedfulness; dispelling of sensual desire; much urgency; enduring fear and dread; abandoning of vanity towards life; constantly reflecting on the [true] nature of the body; it is a practice of a good man and it has the characteristic of effacement. Such and others are the benefits of the state of the charnel-ground-dweller. [Der 136a]

In which charnel grounds should one dwell? Who dwells in a charnel ground? By what is the state of the charnel-ground-dweller broken?

Where there is always burning [of bodies] and smoke, or flames and smoke, in such a charnel ground one should dwell at first and then one can dwell in another charnel ground. The charnel-ground-dweller should not make a hut or building in the charnel ground. He should not stand against the wind or downwind [from corpses]. He should not stand in a fearful (*khu 'phrig*) place. He should not consume meals with fish, meat, milk, sesame-preparations, and mung beans. He should not give his alms-bowl [to lay-people]). He should not sit in houses. If a large crowd of people comes, he should take his seat, robes and utensils and go not too far from the burning. If he is staying in a charnel ground enclosed by a stonewall, and he goes back there again by dawn-rise, then he does not have to take his seat, robes and utensils.

The charnel-ground-dweller is one who rejects dwelling in other places. By the acceptance of other places, the state of the charnel-ground-dweller is broken.

14. User-of-any-dwelling

How to undertake the state of the user-of-any-dwelling?

Seeing the disadvantage of the greed for lodgings (*senāsana*) in oneself and another and the trouble caused to another by making him shift [from his dwelling], and seeing the benefits of the state of the user-of-any-dwelling, one says: "From today onwards I reject greed for lodgings and undertake the state of the user-of-any-dwelling." In such a manner one undertakes it.

Herein, the benefits of the state of the user-of-any-dwelling are: respect and esteem for seclusion; contentment with what one gets; abandoning of greed therein; a friendly mind (*pemacitta*); delight in solitude; it inspires confidence; it is a practice of a good man and it has the characteristic of effacement. Such and others are the benefits of the state of the user-of-any-dwelling.

Who is the user-of-any-dwelling? By what is the state of the user-of-any-dwelling broken? [Der 136b]

The user-of-any-dwelling is one who rejects greed for lodgings. "Rejects greed for lodgings" is not taking a lodging [where someone] is already staying and making him shift from it.[12] By the taking of a lodging for which one is greedy, the state of the user-of-any-dwelling is broken.

15. Sitter

How to undertake the state of the sitter?

Seeing the disadvantage of coming under the sway of sloth, torpor, and indolence, and seeing the benefits of the state of the sitter, one says: "From today onwards I reject lying down and undertake the state of the sitter." In such a manner one undertakes it.

Herein, the benefits of the state of the sitter are: one abandons the ground for idleness; dispels selfishness and greed on account of the body; is dispassionate to the pleasure of reclining; has little concern for sleep; it is conducive to meditation practice and benefits the cultivation of meditation subjects;[13] it is a practice of a good man and it has the characteristic of effacement. Such and others are the benefits of the state of the sitter.

Who is a sitter? By what is the state of the sitter broken?

The sitter is one who rejects lying down. When one gives in to [the desire to] lie down, the state of the sitter is broken.

16. Expediencies

Now, the expediencies of the state of the rag-robe-wearer are: when one who always wears rag robes accepts as an expediency robes made of hemp, kapok, cotton, silk and wool, that are offered by householders, the state of the rag-robe-wearer is not broken.

The expediencies of the state of the three-robes-wearer are: extra robe [cloth that can be] kept for ten days, [robe cloth that can be kept for one month] when there is an expectation of a supplement,[14] sheets for protecting

---

12. When a bhikkhu arrives in a monastery he is given a lodging according to seniority and a more junior bhikkhu or novice might be shifted from his dwelling place to another to make place for the senior.

13. Reading *las kyi gnas, kammaṭṭhāna*, instead of *lus kyi gnas, kāyaṭṭhāna*. The compound *sabbakammaṭṭhānānuyogasappāyatā* at Vism II.75/p.79, corresponds to *rnal 'byor dang mthun pa dang las kyi gnas rgya skye ba nyid dang*. *Anuyogasappāyatā*,was translated as *rnal 'byor dang mthun pa*, "conducive to meditation practice" and *kammaṭṭhāna*, perhaps with *anubrūhana* as given later in the sentence in Vism, as *las kyi gnas rgya skye ba nyid*, lit. "extensive inducing of the meditation subjects".

14. Literally: "When there is an expectation of a supplement [of robe material], keeping an extra robe for ten days". Two kinds of robes, the one that can be kept for 10 days and the one that can be kept for a month, were confused as one kind. See the notes to the Chinese version. Vin III 196: ... *dasāhaparamaṃ atirekacīvaraṃ*

the lodging, upper sheets, cloth for covering sores, handkerchiefs, rains bathing cloth and others, which are [not] determined and [not] assigned.[15] When these are accepted as an expediency, the state of the three-robes-wearer is not broken.

The expediencies of the state of the alms-food-gatherer are: [Der 137a] when a designated meal (*uddesa-bhatta*), ticket meal, fortnightly meal, observance day meal, community meal, or monastery meal, is partaken of as an expediency, the state of the alms-food-gatherer is not broken. Only when seeing the disadvantage of illness are they to be partaken of.

The expediencies of the state of the uninterrupted-alms-round-goer are: if at the gate of a house there is an elephant or a horse or a bull or a dog, or if there is a quarrel or something shameful [happening]—if one sees such [things] and others, one may skip [the house] and move on. Or, if the food of a family is unallowable (*akappiya*) to be eaten,[16] or [when a legal act of] overturning the alms-bowl [is in effect],[17] or if the family is agreed upon as trainees,[18] or when one accompanies one's teacher, one's preceptor or a visiting bhikkhu, one may skip [the house] and move on—the state of the uninterrupted-alms-round-goer is not broken.

The expediencies of the state of the sitter are: if, while taking a meal, one sees an elephant, horse, bull, or snake [coming towards one], or lightning and rain [is coming], or if one sees one's preceptor, teacher or a visitor coming, and one stands up as an expediency and then again eats—the state of the sitter is not broken.

There are no expediencies for the states of the food-limiter and the later-food-denier.

---

dhāretabbaṃ, ... Vin III 199: *... māsaparamaṃ tena bhikkhunā taṃ cīvaraṃ nikkhipitabbaṃ ūnassa pāripūriyā satiyā paccāsāya. ...*

15. The Chinese rightly has these participles in the negative. Extra or expediency robes cannot be determined or assigned by a bhikkhu as he would then assume ownership and break the *dhutaguṇa*.

16. *zas bzar mi rung ba'i khyim*. This could refer to certain kinds of inappropriate meat, such as dog-meat, or any meat that is especially killed for the monk that could be offered at the house. The Chinese instead has "sees an outcast (*caṇḍāla*)". As *caṇḍālas* were known to be dog-meat eaters and scavengers, going to their house could lead to problems. See note to the Chinese translation.

17. This is a special disciplinary procedure to show disapproval of the conduct of a layperson; see the note to the Chinese translation.

18. Read *slob ba* "trainee" in accordance with the Dergé edition, instead of Bapat's *slong ba*. The Chinese has 學家, "trainee-families", i.e. "families that have been agreed upon as trainees" (*sekkhasammatāni*) through a legal act. This refers to the third Pāṭidesanīya rule (see Vin IV 180) that forbids monks from accepting and eating the food of overly generous families that have been declared trainees; see fn. 442.

The expediencies of the state of the wilderness-dweller are: if one dwells within a village (*gāmanta*) as an expediency for an act of full admission (*upasampadā*), for the emergence from an offence (*āpattivuṭṭhāna*), for listening to the Dhamma, for the observance-day ceremony, for the invitation ceremony, for [curing one's own] illness, for curing [another's illness], for understanding a discourse one has not understood, as well as other reasons such as these, the state of the wilderness-dweller is not broken.

The expediencies of the state of the tree-root-dweller are: if one enters a house for such a reason as being forced by rain; and before dawn-rise [returns] again, the state of the tree-root-dweller is not broken.

Any of the expediencies of the wilderness-dweller also are applicable[19] to the states of tree-root-dweller, [Der 137b] open-air-dweller, and charnel-ground-dweller.

The expediencies of the state of the user-of-any-dwelling: when there are such reasons, he is allowed [to take] another's lodging.

There are no expediencies with regard to the state of the sitter, but certain ones say: "When [one lies down] as an expediency [during a medical] examination[20] of the nose, the state of the sitter is not broken".

17. Eight and three ascetic qualities

These thirteen ascetic qualities are in brief only eight. As is said in the Abhidhamma: "There are eight ascetic qualities." How is that so? The state of the food-limiter and the state of the one-sitting-eater are included in the state of the later-food-denier.

Why is this so? [The later-food-denier] takes his own, limited portion[21]—therefore the state of the food-limiter is included. He also does not take food two times—therefore the state of the one-sitting-eater is included. The state of the tree-root-dweller, the state of the open-air-dweller and the state of the charnel-ground-dweller are included in the state of the wilderness-dweller. Why is this so? The wilderness-dweller who makes a forest hut or a multi storey dwelling, etc., delights in work, has attachment [for dwellings] and is greedy [for dwellings], which is not befitting for him. Considering thus he dwells under a tree, in the open air or in a charnel ground. Therefore, there are only eight.

19. Lit. "are seen" or "are to be seen", *blta par bya*.

20. In accordance with the Chinese this should be "pouring [medicine] into the nose".

21. *Gzung ba'i thob pa'i mtha' pa'i bdag nyid kyi rang skal len pa yin* ..., which Bapat translates as: "It is towards the end of everybody's taking his share that [the latter] takes his own share". However, there is no "everybody" in the Tibetan and there is no mention of this practice of taking food as the last in the discussion of the later food denier. This paragraph is not found in the Chinese.

These eight are also fulfilled by three: the state of the wilderness-dweller, the state of the rag-robe-wearer, and the state of the alms-food-gatherer. Thus, when one fulfils the three foremost[22] [qualities] of asceticism, all ascetic qualities are fulfilled. Thus, the Fortunate One said about Venerable Nanda: "When shall [I] see Nanda as wilderness-dweller and rag-robe-wearer, subsisting on scraps and not longing for sense-pleasures?"

18. Miscellaneous topics

Herein, what are the factors of asceticism? How many kinds of ascetic states are there? For which persons with which temperaments is the practice of the ascetic qualities advantageous? [Der 138a] How many kinds of [time-] limit are there? Who is one who is ascetic and who is a proponent of asceticism?

Now, what are the factors of asceticism? Those [factors] which remove (*dhunāti*?) the thirteen grounds (*vatthu*) [of afflictions] are the factors of asceticism.[23]

How are the ascetic qualities to be spoken of (*vattabba*)?[24] They are to be spoken of as wholesome.

How many kinds of ascetic states are there? Two: non-greed and non-delusion. As was said by the Fortunate One: "The rag-robe-wearer dependent on fewness of wishes, dependent on contentment, dependent on effacement, dependent on solitude, and dependent on 'this-is-sufficient'-ness, he is called a 'rag-robe-wearer'".

In another way, through cultivating the non-greed that is sanctioned [by the Buddha], the deception of the pursuit of sensual-pleasure is removed. When there is non-delusion with regard to the ascetic qualities, through cultivating the effacement that is sanctioned [by the Buddha], the deception of the pursuit of exhausting oneself is removed. Therefore, there are two ascetic states: non-greed and non-delusion.

---

22. *Sgo*, usually corresponds to *mukha*, "entrance", but also to *pamukha* "heading, foremost, chief".

23. Or "that which is the removing of the thirteen grounds is the factors of asceticism", *gzhi bcu gsum po de dag gi spong ba gang yin pa de ni sbyangs pa'i yan lag yin*. Cf. Vism II.78: *paṭipakkha-niddhunanato aṅgāni* and II.84: *Tattha ca alobhena paṭikkhepavatthūsu lobhaṃ ... dhunāti*. The Chinese version is quite different. See also the Vism's explanation of *dhutaṅga* in the footnote to the translation from the Chinese.

24. This question is not found in the introduction above and is also not found in the Chinese. As Bapat (1964: 77) suggests, it seems to be a later addition. Judging from the Chinese translation, where it is said that the *dhutas* are not to be spoken of (*navattabba*) as wholesome, etc., the answer also seems to have been adapted at some stage during the transmission of the text by a monk who did not agree with it and suited it to the teachings of his school; see Bapat 1964: xxviii–xxix.

Fewness of wishes, contentment, and solitude are non-greed. Effacement and 'this-is-sufficient'-ness are non-delusion.[25] Herein, through non-greed, greed is removed in the thirteen grounds (*vatthu*) to be rejected. Through non-delusion, the non-knowledge of danger is removed in those very grounds.

For which persons with which temperaments is the practising of the ascetic qualities advantageous? For the greed temperament and the delusion temperament, the practising of the ascetic qualities is advantageous.[26] For the hate temperament, they are not.

Why [can] the one with a greed temperament and one with a delusion temperament practise the ascetic qualities and why [can] the one with a hate temperament not? Because the practising of the ascetic qualities is a painful practice. For the one with a greed temperament, greed is arrested in dependence upon painful practice. [Der 138b] The one with a delusion temperament who is undertaking the practice of the ascetic qualities dependent on effacement is always heedful. When he is heedful, delusion is arrested. Thus, the practising of the ascetic qualities is advantageous for the greed temperament and the delusion temperament.

For the one with a hate temperament, painful practice is like the giving of hot broth to someone with a bile disorder, since [more] hatred is produced [due to it]. Therefore, for the one with a hate temperament the practice of the ascetic qualities is not advantageous.

Others say,[27] "The state of the wilderness-dweller and the state of the tree-root-dweller are advantageous for the one with a hate temperament. Why is this so? Because the wilderness-dweller and the tree-root-dweller are without the disadvantage of irritation due to disagreeable [contacts]."

How many kinds of time limit (*dus kyi mthar thug pa*) are there? Three ascetic qualities—the state of the tree-root-dweller, the state of the open-air-dweller and the state of the charnel-ground-dweller—have a limit of eight months. A covered place in the rainy season is allowed by the Fortunate One.

Who is ascetic[28] and who is a proponent of asceticism? There is one who is ascetic who propounds asceticism; there is one who is ascetic and who does not propound asceticism; there is one who is not ascetic and who propounds

25. According to Vism the latter two are both non-greed and non-delusion. Cf. Vism II.84/p.81: *tattha appicchatā ca santuṭṭhitā ca alobho. Sallekhatā ca pavivekatā ca dvīsu dhammesu anupatanti alobhe ca amohe ca.*

26. *Sbyangs pa'i yon tan sten par dga'.* Vism II.86 *Kassa dhutaṅgasevanā sappāyā ti rāgacaritassa ceva mohacaritassa ca? ...*

27. *Gzhan dag na re zhe,* probably corresponds to *apare vadanti,* "others say", because what follows is a quotation ending with the quotation marker *zhes zer ro.*

28. It is impossible to translate this literally. *Dhuta* literally means "one who has shaken off (defilements)".

asceticism; and there is one who is not ascetic nor propounds asceticism.

Herein, one who is ascetic who propounds asceticism is the arahant who has undertaken the ascetic qualities and is endowed with them. The one who is ascetic who does not propound asceticism is the arahant who has undertaken the ascetic qualities but is not endowed with them. One who is not ascetic but who does propound asceticism is the trainee or worldling who has undertaken the ascetic qualities and is endowed with them. [Der 139a] One who is not ascetic nor propounds asceticism is the trainee or worldling who has not undertaken the ascetic qualities and is not endowed with them.

What is the characteristic of the ascetic qualities? What is their essential function? What is their manifestation? The characteristic of the ascetic qualities is fewness of wishes. The function is contentment. The manifestation is effacement. In another way, the characteristic is non-contamination. The function is non-disadvantage. The manifestation is unrelenting effort.

What is the beginning of the ascetic qualities? What is the middle? What is the end?

The beginning of the ascetic qualities is undertaking. The middle is practising. The end of the ascetic qualities is rejoicing.

The "Exposition of the Ascetic Qualities" from the Path to Freedom, [of which it is] the third chapter, is finished.

Translated, proofread, and finalized by the Indian pandit Vidyākaraprabha and the scholar translator and chief editor Venerable Dpal Brtsegs.[29]

29. Similar to translations of most Indic texts into Chinese, translations into Tibetan were done by teams. Vidyākaraprabha, being an Indian scholar (*mkhan po* = *khen po*), was the one familiar with the language and meaning of the Indic text while the *lotsāwa* or scholar-translator Dpal Brtsegs, a native Tibetan speaker, provided the required meaning in Tibetan and made the final decisions regarding the Tibetan translation. Dpal Brtsegs' title *zhu chen gyi lo tsā ba* (= *shu chen gyi lotsāwa*) "scholar-translator and chief-editor/revisor" indicates that he made the final revisions on the draft translation; see Chimpa 2001: 15. See also Gaffney 2000: 6–7: "The process developed for the translation of each text consisted of a collaborative effort between one or more Tibetan translators (*lo-tsā-ba*) and one or more Indian *panditas* (scholars) or *ācāryas* (teachers). The Indian scholars could bring out the full import of the text at any sections where the Tibetans were in doubt as to the intended meaning. By having scholars from both the Indian and Tibetan traditions the Tibetans attempted to create translations that were as faithful as possible to their source texts."

Appendix II

Quotations from the *Vimuttimagga* in the *Saṃskṛtāsaṃskṛtaviniścaya*

Passages in italics without parenthesis are comments by Daśabalaśrīmitra, the compiler of the *Saṃskṛtāsaṃskṛtaviniścaya*. Passages in the Chinese text that are missing in the Tibetan text have been indicated as missing within parenthesis. On the Tibetan text, see Introduction § 3 and the section on the Tibetan translations in the Bibliography. When the variant readings from the Narthang (Snar) and Peking (Bej) editions as given in the endnotes in the Beijing edition of the Dergé (Der) edition are preferable above the ones in the main text, and are supported by the Chinese (Chin) and Pali parallels, these readings have been translated.

2 § 2. Definition of virtue

[Bej 633, Der 243A, Chin 400c] *The Abhidharma of the Noble Sthavira School says:* There are three kinds of virtue, namely, virtue of volition, virtue of restraint, and virtue of non-transgression. Furthermore, there are two kinds of virtue, namely, virtue in the sense of restraining and virtue in the sense of abandoning. Herein, virtue in the sense of restraining is fourfold, [Der 243B] namely, virtue of refraining,[30] virtue of volition, virtue of self-control and virtue of restraint. Virtue in the sense of abandoning is thirty-seven-fold, namely, the virtue of the abandoning of sensual desire through renunciation; the virtue of the abandoning of ill will by non-ill-will; ...[31] of sloth and torpor by the perception of light; the abandoning of agitation by undistractedness; ... of doubt by the defining of states; ... of ignorance by knowledge; ... of discontent by gladness; ... of the hindrances by the first jhāna; ... of thinking and exploring by the second jhāna; ... of rapture by the third jhāna; ... of pleasure and pain by the fourth jhāna; ... of the perception of matter, perception of impact and perception of diversity by the attainment of the base of boundless space; [Bej 634] ... of the perception of the base of boundless space by the attainment of the base of boundless consciousness; ... of perception of the base of boundless consciousness by the attainment of the base of nothingness; ... of the perception of the base of nothingness by the attainment of the base of neither-perception-nor-non-perception; ... of

30. *Rnam par ldog* = Sanskrit *vinirvartate* = Pali *veramaṇī*?
31. The Tibetan text gives "the virtue of the abandoning of" before each item.

the perception of permanence by the contemplation of impermanence; ... of the perception of happiness by the contemplation of suffering; ... of the perception of self by the contemplation of without self; ... of the perception of delight by the contemplation of disenchantment; ... of the perception of greed by the contemplation of dispassion; ... of origination by the contemplation of cessation; [Der 244A] ... of grasping by the contemplation of relinquishing; the perception of beauty by the contemplation of destruction; ... of the perception of accumulation by contemplation of falling away; ... of the perception of steadiness (*brtan pa*) by the contemplation of change; ... of the sign by the contemplation of the signless; ... of desire by the contemplation of the desireless; ... of adherence to an "I" by the contemplation of emptiness; ... of adherence to cowardice[32] by the ascertaining of states by means of higher wisdom; ... of adherence to delusion by knowledge and vision according to reality; ... of adherence to lodging by contemplation of the ocean [of saṃsāra?];[33] [Bej 635] ... of non-reflection by the reflection-contemplation; ... of adherence to fetters by contemplation of turning away;[34] ... of defilements conjoined with views by the path of the fruit of stream-entry; ... of coarse defilements by the path of once-returning; ... of subtle defilements by the path of non-returning; and the virtue of the abandoning of all defilements by the path of arahantship.

4 § 13. Five kinds of concentration

[Bej 656, Der 252A, Chin 408a] *The scripture of the Noble Sthavira School declares five jhānas, namely:* Endowed with thinking and exploring, rapture, pleasure and one-pointedness of mind, the first jhāna is endowed with five factors. Endowed with exploring, rapture, pleasure and one-pointedness of mind, the second jhāna is endowed with four factors. Endowed with rapture, pleasure and one-pointedness of mind, the third jhāna is endowed with three factors. Endowed with pleasure and one-pointedness of mind, the fourth jhāna is endowed with two factors. Endowed with equanimity and one-pointedness of mind, the fifth jhāna is endowed with two factors.

32. *Dpa' zhum pa'i mngon par zhen pa. Dpa' zhum pa* means "cowardice". This is due to a misunderstanding of *sārādāna* in *sārādānābhinivesa* as Sanskrit *śārada,* BHS *śāradya,* Pali *sārajja,* "timidity". Compare Skt *viśārada* and Pali *visārada, vītasārada* "confidence", "undauntedness".

33. There are two readings: (1) *'tsho ba* in Dergé could be due to a corruption of *ādīnava* "disadvantage" as *ājīva,* and *mtsho ba:* "ocean", "great flood", = Skt *arṇava,* in the Peking and Narthang editions, is a more likely a corruption of *ādīnava.*

34. Reading *rnam par ldog pa* instead of *rnam par rtog pa.*

10 § 1. Introduction

[Bej 636, Der 244B, Chin 444c] *The Noble Sthaviras analyse wisdom through nine questions and answers. The nine questions are:* What is wisdom? What is the characteristic of wisdom? What is its essential function? What is its manifestation? What is the footing of wisdom? What are the benefits of wisdom? What is the meaning of wisdom? How many supportive conditions are there for obtaining wisdom? What is the classification of wisdom? *The answers are as follows:*

10 § 2. Definition, characteristic, function, manifestation, and footing of wisdom

"What is wisdom?" Seeing the object as it is by mind—this is called "wisdom". Furthermore, the attending to what is beneficial and non-benefit and practising much the cause-aspect of the mind (*yid kyi rgyu rnam pa = citta-nimitta?*)—this is called "wisdom".

As is said in the Abhidharma: "What is wisdom? *This is not expressed in one [way] but in thirty ways, namely:*[35] (1) That which is wisdom is understanding (*pajānanā*), (2) investigation (*vicaya*), (3) thorough investigation (*pavicaya*), (4) investigation of the Dhamma (*dhammavicaya*), (5) discerning (*sallakkhaṇā*), (6) discrimination (*upalakkhaṇā*), [Bej 637] (7) differentiation (*paccupalakkhaṇā*), (8) intelligence (*rig pa = paṇḍicca*), (9) skill (*kosalla*), (10) coming to a conclusion (*mthar phyin pa, = niṭṭhaṅgata, pariyosāna?*) [Der 245A], (11) ascertainment (*rnam par 'brel pa*), (12 & 13) consideration [and] examination,[36] (14) comprehensiveness (*bhūrī*), (15) perspicacity (*medhā*), (16) reasoning (*pariṇāyikā*), (17) insight (*vipassanā*), (18) clear knowing (*sampajañña*); (19) the goad (or whip, *lcag*) of wisdom, (20) faculty of wisdom, (21) power of wisdom, (22) sword of wisdom, (23) clarity of wisdom,[37] (24) light of wisdom, (25) brilliance of wisdom, (26) lamp of wisdom, (27) reality of wisdom,[38] (28) non-delusion, (29) investigation of the Dhamma, and (30) right view—this is called "wisdom".

What is its characteristic? Penetration due to reasoning (*rigs pas mngon du byed pa*) is [the characteristic of] wisdom. What is the function of wisdom? Thorough investigation (*pavicaya*) is [the function of] wisdom. What is the

35. This is a comment by Daśabalaśrīmitra that is not found in the Pali or Chinese. The numbers in parentheses in this chapter are not in the Tibetan but have been added here for the sake of clarity.

36. *Sems nye bar yongs su rtogs pa,* literally means "mental examination" but it comes in the place of the Pali *cintā upaparikkhā*, and there should be thirty synonyms in this list.

37. *Shes rab du dang ba = paññāpasāda,* but the Pali has *paññāpāsāda* "palace of wisdom", and so the Chinese.

38. *Shes rab de kho na nyid = prajñātattva?*

manifestation of wisdom? Complete non-delusion is the manifestation of wisdom. What is the footing of wisdom? The four noble truths are the footing of wisdom.

Furthermore, elucidating is the characteristic of wisdom. Fathoming the depth is the essential function of wisdom. The dispelling of the darkness of ignorance is its manifestation. The four discriminations are its footing.

10 § 3. Benefits of wisdom

What, in brief, are the benefits?

> Through wisdom one practices virtue, [and] establishes [oneself] in jhāna.
> Through wisdom one develops the paths, sees the fruits.
> Through wisdom there is superior goodness.
> The unexcelled eye of wisdom dispels the decline of wisdom.
> Unexcelled wisdom improves engagement in counter arguments
> [in debate].
> [Wisdom] is not sullied by worldly states.
> Those endowed with wisdom extensively speak good words [Bej 638]
> About this world, the other world,
> Freedom, attainment of fame, happiness,
> The goal and courageous exertion.
> Those endowed with wisdom, completely understanding
> Mind-and-matter as being dependently originated,
> Teach each truth to beings.
> The wise have wisdom as their pasture,
> With wisdom they abandon the evils
> Of greed, hatred, delusion, and birth and death without remainder,
> They conquer what is hardest to conquer.

10 § 4. Meaning of wisdom

If it is asked "What is the meaning of wisdom?" It should be said: Understanding (*pajānana*)—this is wisdom. Also, the abandoning (*pahāna*) of all faults—this is wisdom. [Der 245B]

10 § 5. Qualities needed for obtaining wisdom

How many supportive conditions are there for attaining wisdom? [Chin 445a] There are eleven supportive conditions, namely, (1) examining the meaning of discourses; (2) much discussion (of the Dhamma); (3) dwelling in a supportive abode; (4) reflecting on the truth[s]; (5) putting in order the physical basis that one is living in; (6–7) practice of virtue and jhāna; (8) a mind free from hindrances; (9) avoidance of unwise persons and (10) association with wise persons; and (11) intentness upon that.

10 § 6–7. Two kinds of wisdom

If it is asked: What is the classification of wisdom? It should be said: There are two kinds of wisdom, namely, mundane and supramundane. Herein, mundane wisdom is not associated with the noble paths and fruits, is subject to contaminations, subject to fetters, ties, torrents, hindrances, to holding on to, clinging, and affliction. Supramundane wisdom is associated with the noble paths and fruits, [Bej 639] is not subject to contaminations, is not subject to fetters, ties, torrents, yokes, holding on to, clinging, and affliction.

10 § 8. Three kinds of wisdom

Furthermore, there are three kinds of wisdom, namely, wisdom sprung from thought, wisdom sprung from learning, and wisdom sprung from practice. Herein, when one by oneself obtains knowledge of the ownership of kamma or knowledge in conformity with the truths or [knowledge] in the sphere of crafts or the field of sciences, without having heard it from another—this is called "wisdom sprung from thought". When one acquires wisdom in these very areas, having heard it oneself from another—this is called "wisdom sprung from learning". The wisdom of all attainments (*samāpatti*)[39]—this is called "wisdom sprung from practice".

Furthermore, there are three kinds: skill in increasing, skill in decreasing, and skill in means. Herein, when one is attending to this, unwholesome states are abandoned and wholesome states increase, that which is wisdom [therein], this is skill in increasing. [Der 246A] Furthermore, when one is attending to this state, unwholesome states increase, and wholesome states decrease, that which is wisdom [therein], this is skill in decreasing. All the wisdom of the taking up (*nye bar bzung ste = upādāya*) of those states—this is skill in means.

Furthermore, there are three kinds of wisdom, namely, wisdom leading to accumulation, wisdom leading to disaccumulation, wisdom leading neither to accumulation nor to disaccumulation.[40] Herein, the wisdom with regard to the three planes of stream-entry, once-returning, non-returning—this is wisdom leading to accumulation. [Bej 640] The wisdom with regard to the

39. *Snyoms par 'jug pa thams cad kyi shes rab* ..... or "the wisdom of all those who have entered upon [attainments]". The Pali is *sabbā pi samāpannassa* paññā bhāvanāmayā paññā: "All the wisdom of those who have entered upon [attainments] is ...". The Chinese translation 若入三昧彼慧悉修 accords with the Pali; see fn. 1648.

40. Read *kun 'phel bar bgrod pa ma yin pa 'grib par bgrod pa ma yin*, as in the v.l. below.

four paths of stream-entry, once-returning, non-returning, arahantship—this is wisdom leading to disaccumulation. The wisdom with regard to the four results of the four planes of stream-entry, once-returning, non-returning, arahantship and the functional-indeterminate of the four planes[41]—this is wisdom leading to neither accumulation nor disaccumulation.

10 § 9. Four kinds of wisdom

Furthermore, there are four kinds of wisdom, namely, knowledge of the ownership of kamma, knowledge in conformity with the truths, knowledge of one who possesses the paths, and knowledge of one who possesses the fruits. Herein, knowledge of the ownership of kamma is right view endowed with ten grounds. Herein, the ten grounds are: (1) knowledge of the truth of suffering, (2) knowledge of the truth of origination, (3) knowledge of the truth of cessation, (4) knowledge of the truth of the path, (4) practice of the noble path, (5) knowledge and vision of nibbāna, (6) the faculty of wisdom, (7) the power of wisdom, (8) the basis of supernormal power of scrutiny, (9) the enlightenment factor of investigation of the Dhamma, and (10) faith in the Triple Gem. Knowledge in conformity with the truths: Seeing the five aggregates as "impermanent", "suffering", and "without self", such acceptance in conformity, this is knowledge in conformity with the truths. The wisdom with regard to the four paths is knowledge of one who possesses the paths. Herein the four paths are the path of the fruit of stream-entry, the path of the fruit of once-returning, the path of the fruit of non-returning, and the path of the fruit of arahantship. [Bej 641, Der 246b] The wisdom with regard to the four fruits is knowledge of one who possesses the fruits. Herein the four fruits are the fruit of stream-entry, the fruit of once-returning, the fruit of non-returning, and the fruit of arahantship.

Furthermore, there are four kinds of wisdom, namely, wisdom with regard to the sensuous sphere, wisdom with regard to the material sphere, wisdom with regard to the immaterial sphere, and wisdom with regard to the unincluded. Herein, wisdom with regard to the wholesome and indeterminate in the sensuous sphere is [wisdom with regard to] the sensuous sphere. Wisdom with regard to the wholesome and indeterminate in the material sphere is [wisdom with regard to] the material sphere. Wisdom with regard to the wholesome and indeterminate in the immaterial sphere is [wisdom with regard to] the immaterial sphere. [Wisdom with regard to] the paths and the fruits is [wisdom with regard to] the unincluded.

---

41. This passage was misunderstood. The three planes are the sensual, material and immaterial planes, and the four planes are these three and the unincluded plane (*apariyāpannā bhūmi*); see Introduction § 4.4.

Furthermore, there are four kinds of wisdom, namely, knowledge of the Dhamma, inferential knowledge, knowledge of others' minds, and conventional knowledge. The wisdom with regard to the four paths and the four fruits is [knowledge] of the Dhamma. [Chin 445b]

Endowed with that Dhamma knowledge in the present,[42] he applies the method to the past and future thus: "Whosoever in the past directly knew the truths, he directly knew just these truths. Whosoever in the future will directly know the truths, he will know just these truths"—this is inferential knowledge. Knowledge of the minds of others, this is knowledge of others' minds. Ignoring these three knowledges, the remaining wisdom is conventional knowledge.

Furthermore, there are four kinds of wisdom, namely, there is wisdom that is for disaccumulation and not for accumulation; [Bej 642] there is wisdom that is for accumulation and not for disaccumulation; there is wisdom that is for disaccumulation and for accumulation; and there is wisdom that is neither for accumulation nor for disaccumulation.[43] Herein, the wisdom with regard to the wholesome in the sensuous sphere is for disaccumulation and not for accumulation. The wisdom with regard to the four paths is for accumulation and not for disaccumulation. Wisdom with regard to the wholesome in the material sphere and the immaterial sphere is for accumulation and for disaccumulation. The wisdom with regard to the result in the four planes and the result-indeterminate[44] in the three planes, [Der 247A] this is neither for disaccumulation nor for accumulation.

Furthermore, there are four kinds of wisdom, namely, there is wisdom that is for disenchantment (*skyo* = *nibbidā*) but not for penetration; there is wisdom that is for penetration but not for disenchantment; there is wisdom that is for disenchantment and for penetration; and there is wisdom that is neither for disenchantment nor for penetration. Herein, the wisdom whereby one is passionless towards sense-pleasures, but does not penetrate the direct knowledges and the four truths—this is for disenchantment but not for penetration. The wisdom whereby one is passionless towards sense-pleasures, and penetrates the direct knowledges, but does not penetrate the four truths—this is for penetration but not for disenchantment. The wisdom in the four paths is for disenchantment and for penetration. The other wisdoms are neither for disenchantment nor for penetration.

---

42. *De chos shes pa 'di dang ldan pa.*

43. Except for the first occurrence of the fourth kind (i.e. "neither for accumulation nor for disaccumulation"), the Tibetan translator inverted the meanings of *ācaya* and *apacaya*. *Ācaya* is here *'grib pa* (which, usually, e.g., at 246a = *apacaya*) and *apacaya* here is *nye bar 'phel* or *'phel ba* (usually *ācaya*).

44. *Rnam par smin pa lung ma bstan pa* = *vipāka-avyākata*. This is a corruption, possibly due to a copyist mistakenly replacing *kiriya* with the *vipāka* as found in the preceding clause. The Pali and Chinese have *kiriyābyākata*, "functional-indeterminate".

Furthermore, there are four kinds of wisdom, namely, discrimination of meaning, discrimination of the Dhamma, discrimination of language and discrimination of discernment (or eloquence, *spobs pa*). [Bej 643] Herein, knowledge of meaning is discrimination of meaning. Knowledge of Dhamma is called discrimination of the Dhamma. Knowledge of language and verbal expression is discrimination of language. Knowledge of knowledge is discrimination of discernment.

In another way, knowledge of cause and result is discrimination of meaning. Knowledge in regard to cause is discrimination of the Dhamma. Knowledge of language and verbal expression is discrimination of language. Knowledge of knowledge is discrimination of discernment.

In another way, the knowledge of suffering and cessation is discrimination of meaning. The knowledge of origination and the path is discrimination of the Dhamma. *[The next] two are as before.*

In another way, knowledge of the teachings, namely, the suttas, recitations, expositions, verses, inspired utterances, sayings, birth-stories, marvels, extensive dialogues—this is discrimination of the Dhamma. [Der 247B] When one knows the meaning of what is spoken, "This is the meaning"—this is discrimination of meaning. Knowledge of the language and verbal expression of that teaching (*chos = dhamma*)—this is discrimination of language. Knowledge of knowledge is discrimination of discernment.

In another way, knowledge of the eye [of Dhamma]—this is discrimination of the Dhamma. Knowledge of the eye [of Dhamma] in the sense of vision—this is discrimination of meaning. *[The next] two are as before.* [Chin 445c]

Furthermore, there are four kinds of wisdom, namely, knowledge of suffering, [Bej 644] knowledge of the origination of suffering, knowledge of the cessation of suffering, and knowledge of one who possesses the path [leading to the cessation of suffering]. *And so on.*

11 § 1. Introduction

[Bej 469, Der 179A, Chin 445c] *The scripture of the Noble Sthavira School expounds as follows:*

Now, the beginner meditator who desires release from ageing and death, who aspires to eliminate the cause of saṃsāra, aspires to dispel the darkness of ignorance, and aspires to attain noble wisdom, should give rise to skill in five areas, namely, the skill in the aggregates, skill in the sense bases, skill in the elements, skill in dependent arising, and skill in the noble truths.

11 § 2–4. Skill in the aggregates

Herein, the five aggregates are the aggregate of matter, the aggregate of feelings, the aggregate of perception, the aggregate of formations, and the aggregate of consciousness. Herein, the aggregate of matter is twofold, namely, the great primaries and the matter arisen from (*byung ba*) the great primaries. Herein, the great primaries are four, namely, earth, water, fire, and wind. *[The detailed description of the four elements is missing.]*

11 § 5. Dependent matter

There are twenty-six [kinds] of matter arisen from the great primaries, namely, (1) eye, (2) ear, (3) nose, (4) tongue, (5) body, (6) forms, (7) sounds, (8) odours, (9) tastes, (10) tangibles,[45] (11) female faculty, (12) male faculty, [Bej 470] (13) life faculty, (14) bodily intimation, (15) verbal intimation, (16) space element, (17) lightness of matter, (18) softness of matter, (19) malleability of matter, (20) growth of matter, (21) continuity of matter, (22) birth of matter, (23) ageing of matter, (24) impermanence of matter, (25) solid food, (26) material basis, and (27) torpor. *[The detailed description is missing.]*

11 § 7. Kinds of dependent matter (end)

[Chin 446a] Therefore the four great primaries and the twenty-six [kinds] of matter arisen from them are thirty. [Chin 446b]. *[A section is missing.]*

11 § 9. Five ways of knowing matter

The thirty [kinds of matter] should be known in detail in five ways, [Der 179B] namely, through producing, clusters, birth, diversity, and unity.

11 § 10. Producing

Herein, with regard to producing, there are four, namely, produced by kamma, produced by mind, produced by time, and produced by food. Herein, nine kinds of matter are produced by kamma, namely, eye, ear, nose, tongue, body, female faculty, male faculty, life-faculty, and the material basis.

Two kinds of matter are produced by mind, namely, bodily intimation and verbal intimation. One is produced by season and mind, namely, the sense base of sound. Four are produced by the conditions of season, mind and food, namely, lightness of matter, softness of matter, malleability of matter, and torpor. Twelve are produced by season, kamma, mind, and

45. This is an addition that does not fit, see Introduction § 4.4

food, namely, the sense bases of form, odour, and taste, [Bej 471] the space element, growth of matter, continuity of matter, birth of matter, solid food, and the earth element, water, fire, and wind. Two kinds of matter are not at all produced [by conditions], namely, ageing of matter and impermanence of matter. However, with birth as condition, there is ageing; and with ageing as condition, there is impermanence.

11 § 11. Clusters

Clusters. Nine clusters are kamma-produced, namely, the eye-decad, ear-decad, nose-decad, tongue-decad, body-decad, female faculty-decad, male faculty-decad, material basis-decad, and life-faculty-ennead. Herein, the eye-decad is eye-sensitivity with the four great primaries as its basis. Colour, odour, taste, vital essence, life faculty, and eye-sensitivity [with the four great primaries as its basis]—because these ten states are an inseparable conglomeration, they are called "eye-decad".

The eye-decad: [its] arising is called "birth"; [its] decay is called "ageing"; [its] disintegration is called "impermanence"; [its] delimitation is called "space element". [Der 180A] These four states of that cluster coincide (*rjes su 'jug par byed pa, anuvattati?*). Furthermore, at the time stage of ageing of the eye-decad itself, depending on that eye-decad, a second eye-decad arises. The accrual of these two eye-decads is called "accumulation". Their continuance is called "continuity". The arising of the previous four at the beginning and these two: these six states coincide. Furthermore, at the time stage of ageing of the second eye-decad, [Bej 472] depending on that second eye-decad, the third eye-decad arises. The accrual of the second and third is called "accumulation". Their continuance is called "continuity". The disintegration of the previous decad and the ageing of the second and the arising of the third occur instantly. The interval or space between the thus occurring eye-decads cannot be known because of the quickness of the moment. [Chin 446c] It is seen like the radiance of a lamp. This is called "eye-decad". In the same way, the ear-decad, the nose-decad, the tongue-decad, the body-decad, female-faculty-decad, male-faculty-decad, material basis-decad, and the life-faculty-ennead should be understood in detail.

Likewise, the other kinds of matter should also be understood in detail. I do not say more about this because it may create fear. [The rest of this method is missing.]

11 § 12. Birth

Birth: At the moment of birth in a womb thirty kinds of matter are produced: the material basis-decad, body-decad, and when a woman, the female faculty-decad or, when a man, the male faculty-decad. Of those neither male nor female, twenty kinds of matter are produced, namely, the material basis-decad and the body-decad.[46]

At the occasion of the birth of males or females fully possessed of the sense bases who are spontaneously born in the sensuous sphere, seventy kinds of matter are produced, namely, the material basis-decad, the body-decad, the eye-decad, [Der 180B] the ear-decad, the nose-decad, [Bej 473] the tongue-decad, when being a female, the feminine faculty-decad and when being a male, the masculine faculty-decad. At the occasion of the birth of blind males or females spontaneously born in bad destinations, sixty kinds of matter are produced due to the absence of the eye-decad. [Chin 447a] Likewise, of those who are deaf, sixty kinds of matter are produced due to the absence of the ear-decad. Of those who are blind and deaf, fifty kinds of matter are produced due to the absence of the eye-decad and the ear-decad. At the occasion of the birth of those fully possessed of the sense bases in bad destinations and of humans at the beginning of an aeon, sixty kinds of matter are produced due to the absence of the sexual-decad. At the occasion of the birth of those born blind and who are neither male nor female, fifty kinds of matter are produced due to the absence of the eye-decad and the sexual-decad. At the occasion of the birth of those born deaf and who are neither male nor female, fifty kinds of matter are produced due to the absence of the ear-decad and the sexual-decad. At the occasion of the birth of those born blind and deaf and who are neither male nor female, forty kinds of matter [are produced], namely, the material basis-decad, the body-decad, the nose-decad, and the tongue-ennead. At the occasion of the birth of Brahmās, thirty-nine kinds of matter are produced: the material basis-decad, the eye-decad, the ear-decad, and the life-faculty-ennead. At the occasion of the birth of beings without perception, nine kinds of matter are produced, namely, the life-faculty-ennead.

11 § 13. Diversity

Diversity. All matter is of two kinds: coarse in the sense of being with impact, and subtle in the sense of being without impact. Herein the coarse kinds of matter are twelve: eye, [Bej 474] ear, nose, tongue, body, forms, sounds, odours, tastes, earth element, fire element, and wind element. The subtle kinds of matter are eighteen, i.e., the others—the life faculty, etc.

11 § 14. Two kinds of matter

Furthermore, there are two kinds [of matter], namely, internal and external. Herein, five kinds are internal in the sense of having a sense-object, namely,

46. See also Skilling 1994: 184f.

eye, ear, nose, tongue and body; [Der 181A] twenty-five kinds are external in the sense of not having a sense-object, namely, forms and the rest.

Furthermore, there are two kinds of matter, namely, faculty matter and non-faculty matter. Herein, eight kinds of matter are faculty matter in the sense of authority, namely, the eye, ear, nose, tongue, body, the female faculty, male faculty and life faculty. Twenty-two kinds of matter are non-faculty matter in the sense of non-authority, namely, the other kinds of matter.

11 § 15. Three kinds of matter

Furthermore, all matter is of three kinds, namely, clung-to matter, not-clung-to matter and differentiated matter. Herein, in the sense of being born through kamma, nine kinds of matter are clung-to, namely, the eight [kinds of] faculty matter and the material basis. In the sense of not being produced through the result of kamma, nine kinds of matter are not-clung-to, namely, the [sense base of] sounds, body intimation, speech intimation, lightness of matter, softness of matter, malleability, ageing, impermanence, and torpor. [Bej 475] In the sense of being both [clung-to and not-clung-to], the other twelve kinds of matter are differentiated.

Furthermore, it is of three kinds: matter that is visible and with impact, matter that is invisible and with impact and matter that is invisible and without impact. Herein, in the sense of being visible and impeding, one [kind of] matter is visible and with impact, namely, the sense base of forms. In the sense of not being visible but impeding, eleven kinds of matter are invisible and with impact, namely, except the sense base of forms, namely, any [kinds of] "coarse matter". In the sense of not being visible and not impeding, eighteen kinds of matter are invisible and without impact, namely, any [kinds of] "subtle matter".

11 § 16. Four kinds of matter

Furthermore, all matter is of four kinds, namely, [Der 181B] matter as intrinsic nature, matter as alteration, matter as characteristic, and matter as delimiting. Herein, in the sense of being produced, nineteen kinds of matter are matter as intrinsic nature, namely, the twelve [kinds of] "coarse matter"—the female faculty, male faculty, life faculty, water element, solid food, material basis and torpor of matter. In the sense of transforming matter as intrinsic nature, seven kinds of matter are matter as alteration, namely, body intimation, speech intimation, [Chin 447b] lightness of matter, softness of matter, malleability of matter, [Bej 476] growth of matter, and continuity of matter. In the sense of [characteristic of the] conditioned,[47]

47. *'Dus byas kyi don = 'dus byas kyi mtshan nyid kyi don?*

three are matter as characteristic: birth of matter, ageing of matter and impermanence of matter. In the sense of delimiting clusters, one [kind of] matter is matter as delimiting, namely, the space element. Herein, matter as intrinsic nature is delimited; the rest is not delimited.[48]

11 § 17. Unity

For unity of matter there are many terms: is not without a cause, is with a cause, is dissociated [from a cause,] is with a condition, is conditioned, is mundane, is subject to contaminations, subject to fetters, ties, stupefaction,[49] yokes, hindrances, to holding, clinging, and affliction, is indeterminate, without object, not a mental factor, dissociated from mind, restricted, connected to the sensuous sphere, is not fixed, is not leading out, is not accompanied by pleasure and is not accompanied by pain, is not accumulating and is not disaccumulating, is not training and is not non-training, is not to be abandoned through seeing and is not to be abandoned through contemplative practice (*bhāvanā*). [Der 182A]

Thus the aggregate of matter should be understood.

11 § 18. What is the aggregate of feeling?

Feeling. By way of characteristic it is one, namely, that which is experienced as the object of mind (*cittārammaṇa*). By way of basis, there are two kinds, [Bej 477] namely, bodily and mental. By way of intrinsic nature, there are three kinds, namely, pleasant feeling, painful feeling, and neither pleasant nor painful feeling. By way of states (*dhamma*), there are four kinds, namely, wholesome feelings, unwholesome feelings, resultant feelings, and functional feelings. By way of faculties, there are five kinds, namely, pleasure faculty, pain faculty, joy faculty, distress faculty, and equanimity faculty. By way of black and white [kamma], there are six kinds, namely, worldly (*sāmisa*) painful feeling, unworldly painful feeling, worldly pleasant feeling, unworldly pleasant feeling, worldly neither pleasant nor painful feeling, and unworldly neither pleasant nor painful feeling. By way of sense door, there are seven kinds, namely, feeling born of eye-contact, feeling born of ear-contact, feeling born of nose-contact, feeling born of tongue-contact, feeling born of body-contact, feeling born of mind-contact, and feeling born of mind-consciousness-element contact.

In detail, there are 108 feelings, namely, six of joy dependent on desire of

---

48. Cf. Skilling 1994: 193–194.

49. The Tibetan translator misunderstood *oghaniya* as *moghaniya* "stupefying" or *mohaniya* "deluding", *rmongs par bya ba* due to misinterpreting *ganthaniyamoghaniyaṃ* in the manuscript as *ganthaniya-moghaniyaṃ* instead of *ganthaniyam-oghaniyaṃ*.

the household; six of distress dependent on desire of the household; six of joy dependent on renunciation; six of distress dependent on renunciation; six of equanimity dependent on desire of the household; [Bej 478] six of equanimity dependent on renunciation. Herein, the six divisions of six feelings in three [times] are 108. This is called "the aggregate of feeling".

11 § 19. What is the aggregate of perception?

Perception. By way of characteristic it is one, namely, that which is perceived as the object of mind. [Der 182B] By way of black and white, there are two kinds of perception, namely, inverted and non-inverted. By way of unwholesomeness, there are three kinds, namely, perception of sensual desire, perception of ill will, and perception of harming. By way of wholesomeness, there are three kinds, namely, perception of renunciation, and perception of non-ill-will and perception of non-harming.

By way of the door of not knowing the grounds of selfhood, there are four kinds, [Chin 447c] namely, the perception of beauty in what is foul, the perception of happiness in what is suffering, the perception of permanence in what is impermanent, and the perception of self in what is without self. By way of the door of knowing the grounds of selfhood, there are four kinds, namely, perception of the foul, perception of suffering, perception of impermanence, and perception of without self.

By way of the Vinaya, there are five kinds, namely, (1) perception of appropriateness with regard to the inappropriate, (2) perception of inappropriateness with regard to the appropriate, (3) perception of inappropriateness with regard to the inappropriate, (4) perception of appropriateness with regard to the appropriate, (5) perception of doubt (*vimati*) with regard to the inappropriate, and (6) perception of doubt with regard to the appropriate.

By way of object, there are six perceptions, namely, perception of forms, perception of sounds, perception of odours, [Bej 479] perception of tastes, perception of tangibles, and perception of mental states.

By way of elements (*khams kyi dbang gis = dhātuso*) there are seven kinds, namely, perception that is born of eye-element contact, perception that is born of ear-element contact, perception that is born of nose-element contact, perception that is born of the tongue-element contact, perception that is born of body-element contact, perception that is born of mind-element contact, perception that is born of [mind] consciousness-element contact.

Any perception such as this is the suchness (*de kho na nyid = tathatā?*) of perception.

This is called the aggregate of perception.

11 § 20. What is the aggregate of formations?

Formations are manifold, namely, (1) contact, (2) volition, (3) thinking, (4) exploring, (5) rapture, (6) faith, [Der 183A] (7) energy, (8) mindfulness, (9) concentration, (10) wisdom, (11) life faculty, (12) restraining, (13) non-greed, (14) non-hate, (15) non-delusion, (16) conscience, (17) shame, (18) tranquillity, (19) motivation, (20) resolve, (21) equanimity, (22) attention, (23) greed, (24) hatred, (25) delusion, (26) conceit, (27) [wrong] views, (28) agitation, (29) worry, (30) doubt, (31) sloth, (32) consciencelessness, (33) shamelessness—such and other manifold formations, except for feeling and perception, are the aggregate of formations. *[The detailed description of the formations is missing.]*

11 § 22. What is the aggregate of consciousness?

[Chin 448a] Consciousness. There are seven [kinds of consciousness], namely, eye-consciousness, ear-consciousness, nose-consciousness, tongue-consciousness, body-consciousness, [Bej 480] mind faculty, and mind consciousness—this is the aggregate of consciousness. *[The detailed description of the consciousness aggregate is missing.]*

11 § 27. Four ways of knowing the five aggregates

[Chin 448b] Furthermore, the causes and characteristics of these five aggregates should be known by particularity and diversity in four ways: word meaning, characteristic, analysis, and inclusion.

11 § 28. Word meaning

Herein, with regard to word meaning, there are six, namely, matter has the meaning of materializing. Feeling has the meaning of experiencing. Perception has the meaning of perceiving. Formations has the meaning of forming. Consciousness has the meaning of cognising. Aggregate has the meaning of aggregation of similar types.

11 § 29. Characteristic

Characteristic. There are five characteristics: The characteristic of matter is materializing. It is like being eaten up/built by matter (*bzos pa'i gzugs*). The four great primaries are the footing of matter. [Chin 448c] The characteristic of feeling is experiencing. It is like experiencing the itching of a leprous sore. Contact is the footing of feeling. The characteristic of perception is to grasp the aspects[50] [of an object]. It is like a creation of

50. *Mtshan ma = nimitta, ākāra, vyañjana*

supernormal power.[51] Contact is the footing of perception. The characteristic of formations is the impelling of aggregation. It is like the propelling of a wheel. Contact is the footing of formations. The characteristic of consciousness is cognizing.[52] Name-and-matter is the footing of consciousness.

11 § 30. Analysis

[Der 183B] Analysis is analysis of the aggregates, namely, the five aggregates, the five aggregates subject to clinging, and the five aggregates of the Dhamma. Herein, the five aggregates are all conditioned phenomena. [Bej 481] What are five aggregates subject to clinging? All states subject to contaminations. What are the five aggregates of the Dhamma? The aggregate of virtue, the aggregate of concentration, the aggregate of wisdom, the aggregate of freedom, and the aggregate of knowledge and discernment of freedom. In this context, the five aggregates subject to clinging are intended.

11 § 31. Inclusion

Inclusion. There are three kinds of inclusion, namely, inclusion in the sense bases, inclusion in the elements, and inclusion in the truths.

Herein the aggregate of matter is included in the eleven sense bases, namely, the ten [starting with the] sense base of forms and the single sense base of states. The three immaterial aggregates, namely, feeling, perception, and formations, are included in the sense base of mental states. One is included in the sense base of mind, namely the aggregate of consciousness.

The aggregate of matter is included in eleven elements. The three immaterial aggregates are included in the element of mental states. The aggregate of consciousness is included in the seven consciousness elements.[53]

The four aggregates of virtue, concentration, wisdom, and knowledge and discernment of freedom are included in the sense base of mental states and element of mental states. The aggregate of freedom is included in the sense base of mental states, [the sense base of mind,][54] the element of mental states, and the mind-consciousness-element.

The five aggregates subject to clinging are included in the truth of suffering. Clinging is included in the truth of origination. The three aggregates of virtue, concentration and wisdom are included in the truth of the path.

---

51. *Mngon par shes pa'i rgyu mtshan = abhiññā + nimitta?*

52. The simile of the cognizing of taste, as found in the Chinese, is missing in the Tibetan.

53. *Rnam par shes pa'i khams bdun.* On the seven consciousness elements in Theravāda Abhidhamma, see fn. 1852.

54. The sense base of mind is missing in Sav.

[Bej 482] The aggregate of freedom is included in the truth of cessation. The aggregate of the knowledge and discernment of freedom is included in the truth of suffering. Herein, there are states included in the aggregates but not included in the truths. [Der 184A] There are states included in the truths but not included in the aggregates. There are states included in the truths and included in the aggregates. There are states not included in the truths and not included in the aggregates.

Herein, matter not bound up with faculties and the states associated with the paths and with the fruits of recluseship are included in the aggregates and not in the truths. Nibbāna is included in the truths and not in the aggregates. Three truths are included in the aggregates and in the truths. Concept (*btags yod* = *paññatti*) is not included in the aggregates and not included in the truths. Concept (*btags pa*) is eleven states, namely, (1) volition[55] (2) directions, (3) region, (4) time, (5) transgression, (6) factor of asceticism, (7) sign of totality, (8) the object of the attainment of the base of nothingness, (9) attainment of cessation, (10) correct conception, and (11) incorrect conception.

These are the ways in which knowledge of the skill in the aggregates arises.

This is called "skill in the aggregates".

11 § 32. Skill in the sense bases

Skill in the sense bases. What are the sense bases? There are twelve, namely, the sense base of eye, the sense base of form, the sense base of ear, the sense base of sound, the sense base of nose, the sense base of odour, the sense base of tongue, the sense base of taste, the sense base of body, the sense base of tangibles, [Bej 483] the sense base of mind, and the sense base of mental states.

Herein, the sense base of eye is the element of sensitivity by which forms are delimited. The sense base of form is the element of colour which is the sense object of the eye. The sense base of ear is the element of sensitivity by which one hears sounds. The sense base of sound is the element of noise (*ghosa*) which is the sense object of the ear. The sense base of nose is the element of sensitivity by which one smells odours. [Chin 449a] The sense base of odour is the element of odour which is the sense object of the nose. The sense base of tongue is the element of sensitivity by which one tastes. The sense base of taste is the element of flavour (*rasa*) which is the sense object of the tongue. The sense base of body is the element of sensitivity

55. This is a corruption due to a Tibetan copyist altering *sems can* "living being" to *sems pa*, "volition" or "thought". See fn. 1863 and the discussion of alterations in the Introduction at § 4.4.

by which one touches tangibles. [Der 184B] The sense base of tangibles is the earth element, fire element, wind element, water element, hardness, softness, warmth, and coolness, which are the sense object of the body. The sense base of mind is the seven consciousness elements. The sense base of mental states is the three immaterial aggregates, the ten[56] subtle kinds of matter and nibbāna. *And so forth, the twelve sense bases in detail. [The rest of the description of the twelve sense bases is missing.]*

11 § 39. Skill in the sense bases (end)

[Chin 449c] These are the ways in which knowledge of the skill in the sense bases arises.

This is called "skill in the sense bases".

11 § 40. Skill in the elements

Skill in the elements. What are the eighteen elements? The eye element, form element, eye-consciousness element; ear element, sound element, ear-consciousness element; nose element, odour element, nose-consciousness element; tongue element, taste element, [Bej 484] tongue-consciousness element; body element, touch element, body-consciousness element; mind-element, mental states element, mind-consciousness-element. *And so forth in detail.*

[The detailed description of the skill in the elements and the first part of the section on inclusion is missing.]

11 § 41. Differences between the aggregates, sense bases and element methods

[Chin 450a] Now, what is taught regarding the differences between the aggregates, sense bases and element methods? It is taught that the characteristic of the aggregates is aggregation of similar states. It is taught that the characteristic of the sense bases is entrance (*sgo = mukha, dvāra*). It is taught that the characteristic of the elements is intrinsic nature.

Furthermore, to persons who understand after being told the heading[57] the Fortunate One taught the truth of suffering by way of the aggregate method. To persons who understand after detailed explanation[58] he taught

56. In accordance with the 11 § 13, the Pali and Chinese, this should be "eighteen", *bco brgyad.*

57. Or "by a nod of the head"; *mgo smos pas go ba'i gang zag rnams = ugghaṭitaññū.*

58. *Rnam par spros pas go ba = vipañcitaññū*

the truth of suffering by way of the sense base method. To persons attached to the word[59] he taught the truth of suffering by way of the element method.

Furthermore, to one who perceives beauty in the immaterial aggregates he taught the aggregates [by teaching] matter in brief and [by much] analysing of the immaterial aggregates. [Der 185A] To one who perceives beauty in matter he taught the sense bases [by] much analysing of matter [and by teaching] the immaterial aggregates in brief. To one who perceives beauty in the immaterial [aggregates] together with matter he taught the elements by way of much analysis of the immaterial [aggregates] and matter.

Furthermore, what are taught as the grounds of selfhood, as for these, he taught the aggregates. What are taught as the objects of the bases (*dngos po'i dmigs pa*), as for these, he taught the sense bases. What are taught as the objects of the bases [and] the occurrence of the process [of mind], as for these, he taught the elements. [Bej 485]

These are the ways in which skill in knowledge of the definition of the elements [arises].

This is called "skill in the elements".

The analysis of the aggregates, sense bases and elements according to the system of the Sthavira School. The Analysis of the Conditioned and Unconditioned (= Saṃskṛtāsaṃskṛtaviniścaya) compiled by the Great Pandita, the Auspicious Friend of the One with Ten Powers (= Daśabalaśrīmitra), Chapter 13.

11 § 42. Skill in dependent arising

The skill in dependent arising is as follows: With ignorance as condition, formations; with formations as condition, consciousness; with consciousness as condition, name-and-matter; with name-and-matter as condition, the six sense bases; with the six sense bases as condition, contact; with contact as condition, feeling; with feeling as condition, craving; with craving as condition, clinging; with clinging as condition, existence, with existence as condition, birth; with birth as condition, ageing and death, sorrow, lamentation, pain, distress and grief. Thus there is the origination of this entire great mass of suffering. This is the arising mode (*lugs su byung ba*).

Through the cessation of ignorance, there is the cessation of the formations; through the cessation of the formations, there is the cessation of consciousness; through the cessation of consciousness, there is the cessation of name-and-matter; through the cessation of name-and-matter, there is the cessation of the six sense bases; through the cessation of the six sense bases, there is the cessation of contact; through the cessation of contact, there is the cessation of feeling; through the cessation of feeling, there is the cessation of

59. *Tshig la 'chel ba* = *padaparama* misunderstood as *padaparāmṛṣṭa*?

craving; through the cessation of craving, there is the cessation of clinging; through the cessation of clinging, [Bej 486] there is the cessation of existence; [Der 185B] through the cessation of existence, there is the cessation of birth; through the cessation of birth, there is the cessation of ageing and death, sorrow, lamentation, pain, distress and grief cease. In this way, there is the cessation of this entire great mass of suffering. This is the reversing mode (*lugs las ldog pa*).

11 § 43. Explanation of the twelve factors

Herein non-knowledge of the four truths is ignorance. Bodily, verbal, and mental action is formations. The mind at the time of relinking[60] is consciousness. Name is the mental properties associated with the relinking mind; matter is the embryo (*kalala*)—[this is] name-and-matter. The six internal sense bases are the six sense bases. The six groups of contact are contact. The six groups of feeling are feeling. The six groups of craving are craving. The four kinds of clinging are clinging. Kamma-produced [Chin 450b] sensuous, material and immaterial existence is existence. The arising of the aggregates in existences is birth. The maturing of the aggregates is ageing. The disintegration of the aggregates is death.

11 § 44. Simile of the seed

Now, why is it said "with ignorance as condition, formations" until "with birth as condition, ageing and death"? Now, the uninstructed worldling, due to not knowing the four noble truths, has for a long time cherished and held on to the aggregates subject to clinging as "this is mine" and "this is I" and "this is my self". Thus due to attachment to existence, [there is] the origination of existence [and] one plans for and tends towards the sphere of existence.[61] [Bej 487] The volitions, plans, and tendencies towards this, they, arising due to not fully knowing[62] the ground [and] in order to obtain existence, establish [consciousness] in existence. It is like planting a good seed in moist earth. Herein, there is no knowledge of the cessation of existence. Therefore, "with formations as condition, consciousness".

Due to the not knowing (*apariññā?*) of these [truths], preparation-volitions are produced. Therefore, due to delight in existence, [there is] entering into existence, [and there is] the existence-sign-object. [Der 186A] Due to

60. *Paṭisandhi-samaya/kāla, nying mtshams sbyor ba'i dus kyi sems.*

61. *Srid pa'i skye mched* = *bhava-āyatana*, which is not found in the Chinese nor the Pali works.

62. *Yongs su mi shes pa* = *apariññā*, the opposite of *yongs su shes pa* = *pariññā*.

[kamma] accumulation [there is] adverting to existence and the relinking-consciousness is produced. There is no interruption of this existence mind process. Therefore, "with formations as condition, consciousness".

11 § 45. Simile of the sun and the two bundles of reeds

Without the sun there is no establishing of a ray of light on the ground nor any movement of it, just so, without consciousness there is no descent into the womb (*gabbhāvakkanti*) of name-and-matter, nor is there growth [of it]. It is like bundles of reeds that are leaning against each other. Therefore, "with consciousness as condition, name-and-matter".

The sense base of mind occurs dependent upon the material basis that is born together with name. The other five sense bases arise and occur with name [born] together with the four elements that depend on food and time as condition. Without this condition, there is no [arising of them]. Therefore, "with name-and-matter as condition, the six sense bases".

By the coming together of the sense-faculties, sense objects and consciousness, contact arises. Therefore, "with the six sense bases as condition, contact".

Through contact there is painful, pleasurable, and neither painful nor pleasurable feeling. Without contact, there is no [feeling]. Therefore, "with contact as condition, feeling". [Bej 488]

When foolish worldlings feel pleasure, they become attached to it and they seek it again and again. Even if they feel pain, to subdue the pain they seek pleasure. If they feel neither-pain-nor-pleasure, they are attached to the feeling. Therefore, "with feeling as condition, craving".

When attached to feeling, one grasps the object of craving firmly. Therefore, "with craving as condition, clinging".

The actions done that are associated with clinging are the seed of existence. Therefore, "with clinging as condition, existence".

According to one's particular kamma, one is reborn in the destinations [of rebirth]. Therefore, "with existence as condition, birth".

Through birth, there is ageing and death. Therefore, "with birth as condition, ageing and death".

11 § 46. Simile of the seed and sprout

Another conceptualization: As the husk and the seed, [Der 186B] so are ignorance and the formations. As the seed and the sprout, so are formations and consciousness. As the sprout and the leaf, so are consciousness and name-and-matter. As the leaf and the stalk, so are name-and-matter and the six sense bases. As the stalk and the branches, so are the six sense bases and contact. As the branches and the flower, so are contact and feeling. As the flower and the mass (*piṇḍa*?), so are feeling and craving. As the mass and the fruit, so are craving and clinging. As the fruit and the seed; so are clinging and existence. As the seed and the sprout, so are existence and birth. *"With as condition" is to be read everywhere.*[63] [Bej 489] In such a manner there is the arising of a succession of seeds of which the past end cannot be known and the future end cannot be known. [Chin 450c]

Just so, ignorance and so forth are a succession of dependently arisen [states]. The past end cannot be known and the future end cannot be known. Therefore, if it is asked, "What is the condition of ignorance?", it is to be said, "Only ignorance". With the condition of ignorance, there are the latent tendencies. With the condition of the obsessions, the latent tendencies. With the condition of the latent tendencies, the obsessions. The obsessions are the condition for the latent tendencies. The former are the condition for the former and the latter are the condition for the latter. Alternatively, all the afflictions are the condition. As it is said: "With the origination of the contaminations, there is the origination of ignorance."

11 § 47. In a single mind moment

Furthermore, there is the mode of a single mind state:[64] At the time when foolish people see a form with the eye, greed (*'dod chags*) is born for it, considering the beauty and pleasure [of it], and the mind is deluded—this is ignorance. Ignorance gives rise to excitation[65] of the body and so on—this is ["with ignorance as condition] formations". The mind of greed—this is "with formations as condition consciousness".[66] The mental factors associated with that and the dependent kinds of matter due to that—this is "with consciousness as condition, name-and-matter". With delight born of craving as condition, with matter born of delight as condition, there is no sensitivity[67] of the sense-faculties [Der 187A]—this is "with name-and-matter as condition, the six sense bases". Ignorance-contact is "with the six sense bases as condition, contact". On that occasion, any pleasure (*bde ba* = *sukha, sāta*) is "with contact as condition, feeling". On that occasion, greed is "with feeling as condition, craving". [Bej 490] The grasping of beauty and pleasure due to greed is "with craving as condition, grasping". On that

63. I.e. "with the condition of" (= *paccayā*) is to be added to each of the clauses above.

64. *Sems gcig pa'i tshul* = *eka-citta-vidhi/naya.*

65. *Yongs su g-yo ba* = *pariphandana?*

66. Or "the mind that has attachment", *chags ba'i sems.*

67. *Dbang po rnams kyi rab tu dang ba ma yin pa.* The Tibetan translator misunderstood the meaning of *pasāda* "sensitivity". In § 32 he understood it correctly.

occasion, the intention of greed is "with clinging as condition, existence". The manifestation of those states is "with existence as condition, birth". The alteration of what persists is "ageing". Momentary dissolution is "death". Thus, one should understand it as a succession of twelve factors taking place together in a single moment.

11 § 48. Questions on kamma, defilements, results, etc.

There are ten questions and answers about the twelve factors of dependent arising. Herein, the ten questions are: How many are afflictions? How many are kamma? How many are result? How many are past? How many are future? How many are present? What is dependent arising? What are dependently arisen states? What are the differences between dependent arising and dependently arisen states? What is the profound nature of dependent arising?

The respective answers are: The defilements are three factors, namely, ignorance, craving, and clinging. Two factors are kamma, namely, formations and existence. Seven factors are result, namely, the remaining seven factors. Here, like the preparation of colours in the action of painting, the defilements are the cause for the production of further existence. Like the action of painting [with colours], kamma causes the diversity of inferior and superior. Like the painted form is the result (*vipāka*): action-defilement functions as the condition for the production of existence. [Bej 491] Two factors are past: ignorance and the formations. Two are future: birth and ageing-and-death. Eight [factors] are present, namely, the remaining ones. [Der 187B] Thus, by the apprehending of the three times, the beginningless cycle of saṃsāra is taught.

When the twelve factors are a succession of reciprocal causes, reasons, associated factors, and specific conditions (*'di ni rkyen nyid = idapaccaya?*), it is dependent arising. The twelve factors are the dependently arisen states. With regard to dependent arising: the formations change. Not having fully come into being, they are not to be spoken of; they are not to be spoken of as conditioned; they are not to be spoken of as unconditioned. Dependently arisen states are formations that have fully come into being and are conditioned. This is the difference between these.

[What is the profound nature of dependent arising?] Whatever the modes and characteristics by which ignorance is the condition of the formations, those modes and those characteristics the noble ones, [in]dependent of another, penetrate with the eye of wisdom. Thus, all this is the profound nature of dependent arising.

11 § 49. Seven ways of knowing dependent arising

Another direction. This dependent arising should be understood in seven ways, namely: (1) through the three links, (2) the four summaries, (3) the twenty modes, (4) the wheel, (5) way, (6) analysis, and (7) through inclusion. [Chin 451a]

11 § 50. Three links

Herein, with regard to the three links, [Bej 492] the interval between the formations and consciousness is the first link; the interval between feeling and craving is the second link; the interval between existence and birth is the third link. Herein, past kamma and affliction are the condition of the present result, is the first link. Present action and affliction are the condition of the present result, is the second link. Present action and affliction are the condition of the future result, is the third link. Alternatively, the first and third are the cause-result link. The second is the result link. The existence link does not exist.

11 § 51. Existence link

If it is asked "What is the meaning of "existence link"? It should be said: Immediately upon passing away, there is production of further existence in the non-transmigrating aggregates, sense bases, elements. [Der 188A] This is called the "existence link".

If it is asked "How is there the existence link?" It should be said: The foolish worldling, affected by ignorance and fettered by craving, accumulates merit and demerit. When at that very time he dies he is overcome by a feeling ending in death (*māraṇantika*), he is not close to surpassing death (*'chi ba la lhag par ma nye ba*). At that time, there is origination: he does not see this world; he loses mindfulness and does not regain it; he is oppressed by [painful] feeling; his memory and intelligence decline; bodily strength and power decline; the sense-faculties stop. Like the withering of a palm leaf, the life faculty withers away from either end of the body. At that time it is like he dreams. Four states of kamma appear to him, namely, kamma, kamma-sign, destination, [Bej 493] and destination-sign.

11 § 52. Kamma, kamma-sign, destination, and destination-sign

Herein, with regard to kamma: Whatever merit or demerit has been done, and heavy or light, proximate or action formerly done[68]—that kamma appears. The sign of kamma: that kamma which is done depending upon the

68. *Sngon byas sam las* = "formerly done or action", which is a mistranslation of *kaṭattā vā pana kammaṃ*, "or action done formerly".

basis, in that basis it appears. At that very time it occurs in accordance with the kamma done.

Destination: Due to the condition of meritorious action, a good destination appears, and [when there is] demeritorious action, a bad destination.

Destination-sign: Those born in the womb appear in the mother's belly possessed of season, possessed of blood.[69] With regard to those who are spontaneously born: wherever there is birth, there the opportunity will appear—a celestial mansion, or a sentient being (*sems can*), or a forest, or a tree. According to the destination, the associated sign appears. At that time, whether they are [going, standing] sitting or lying down, they see and grasp it. At that time, the action or action sign, destination or destination sign is made the object, so that there is rebirth. [Der 188B] *And so forth, in detail. [The rest of this section is missing.]*

11 § 53. Four collections

[Chin 451b] The four (summary) collections are the collection of/inclusion in (*bsdus pa = saṅgaha*) past kamma and affliction, collection of present result, collection of present kamma and affliction, and collection of future result. Herein, ignorance and formations are collected in past action and affliction. Consciousness, name-and-matter, six sense bases, contact, and feelings are collected in present result. [Bej 494] Craving, grasping, and existence are collected in present action and affliction. Birth, old age, and death are collected in future result.

11 § 54. Twenty modes

The twenty modes. (1) By grasping ignorance and past craving and clinging, [it is grasped] through the affliction-characteristic. (2) By grasping the formations and past existence, [it is grasped] through the kamma-characteristic. (3) By grasping consciousness, name-and-matter, the six sense bases, contact, and feeling, by grasping present birth and ageing-and-death, [it is grasped] through the result-characteristic. (4) By grasping craving and clinging, and present ignorance, [it is grasped] through the affliction-characteristic. (5) By grasping existence and present formations, [it is grasped] through the kamma-characteristic. (6) By grasping birth and ageing-and-death and future consciousness, name-and-matter, six sense bases, contact, and feeling, [it is grasped] through the result-characteristic. These twenty-four states when completely grasped become twenty.

---

69. *Dus dang ldan zhing khrag dang ldan pa'i ma'i lto bar nye bar gnas par 'gyur ro.* This probably is related to the three objects that come together, as is said in the Chinese parallel.

As is said in the Abhidharma: "In former-action-existence, ignorance, formations, craving, grasping, and existence—these five states are the conditions for relinking here. Here, the consciousness, name-and-matter, six sense bases, contact, and feeling—these five states in former-action-existence are the conditions for rebirth-existence here. Here, due to the maturing of the sense bases, etc., ignorance, formations, [Der 189A] craving, grasping and existence—these five states in action-existence here, [Bej 495] are the conditions for future relinking. Future consciousness, name-and-matter, six sense bases, contact, and feeling—these five states in future rebirth-existence, [their] condition is action done here." Four [times] five are twenty kinds.

11 § 55. Wheel

The Wheel. With ignorance as condition, the formations ... and so forth (*zhes pa nas* = *peyyāla*) ... with birth as condition, ageing, and death. Just so, there is the origination of this entire mass of suffering.

Just so again, with ignorance as condition, the formations and so on. Again, in this manner, there is an endless turning of the wheel of dependent arising.

11 § 56. Way

Way (*tshul lugs* = *naya, vidhi*). [There are] two ways, that is, the way starting with ignorance, and the way starting with old age and death. Therein, the way starting with ignorance is: With ignorance as condition, formations ... and so on until ... old age and death, sorrow, lamentation, pain, distress, grief. Thus is there the origination and so on. The way starting with old age and death is: With the cessation of birth, the cessation of old age and death, the cessation of existence, ... and so on until ... with the cessation of ignorance, the cessation of formations. Furthermore, the way starting with ignorance is the threshold (*sgo* = *mukha*) to the posterior end, [Chin 451c] i.e., the future-part [of] knowledge of the path. The way starting with old age and death is the threshold to the anterior end, i.e., the past-part [of] knowledge of the path.

11 § 57. Analysis

Analysis. There are two kinds of dependent arising: mundane and supra-mundane.

Herein, mundane [Bej 496] is from "with ignorance as condition formations" until "just so, there is the origination of this entire mass of suffering".

Supramundane is again [starting with] suffering; with suffering as proximate cause, faith; with faith as proximate cause, gladness; with gladness as proximate cause, rapture; with rapture as proximate cause, tranquillity; with tranquillity as proximate cause, pleasure; with pleasure as proximate cause, concentration; with concentration as proximate cause, [Der 189B] knowledge and vision according to reality; with knowledge and vision according to reality as proximate cause, disenchantment; with disenchantment as proximate cause, dispassion; with dispassion as proximate cause, freedom; and with freedom as proximate cause, knowledge of destruction.

It is also said in other [texts or traditions]: There are four kinds of dependent arising, namely: caused by kamma and affliction; caused by seed; caused by preparation; and caused by shared kamma.

Herein, caused by kamma and affliction is "with ignorance as condition, formations" until "just so, there is the origination of this entire mass of suffering". Caused by seed is the succession of seed and sprout and so on. Caused by preparation is [magical] creation of forms and so on. Caused by shared kamma is the earth, Himalaya, sea, moon and sun and so on.

11 § 58. Inclusion

Inclusion. There are four kinds of inclusion, namely, inclusion in the aggregates, inclusion in the sense bases, inclusion in the elements, [Bej 497] and inclusion in the truths.

With regard to inclusion in the aggregates: Six factors are included in the aggregate of formations, namely, ignorance, formations, contact, craving, grasping, and existence. Consciousness is included in the aggregate of consciousness. Name-and-matter is included in the five aggregates. The six sense bases are included in the aggregates of matter and consciousness. The factor of feeling is included in the aggregate of feeling. Birth and ageing and death are included in the aggregate of matter and the aggregate of formations.

Inclusion in the sense bases: Nine factors are included in the sense base of mental states, namely, ignorance, formations, contact, feeling, craving, grasping, existence, birth, and ageing and death. The factor of consciousness is included in the sense base of mind.[70] Name-and-matter is included in the sense base of mind and the sense base of mental states [Der 190A] and the five external sense bases. The six sense bases are included in the six internal sense bases.

Inclusion in the elements: Nine factors are included in the element of mental states, namely, ignorance, formations, contact, feeling, craving,

70. *Rnam par shes pa'i khams* is equivalent to *mano-viññāṇadhātu* here, not *viññāṇadhātu*. Cf. § 18 where *rnam par shes pa'i khams 'dus te reg pa* = *manoviññāṇadhātusamphassa*.

grasping, existence, birth, and ageing and death. The factor of consciousness is included in the element of mind-consciousness. Name-and-matter is included in seven elements, namely, the element of forms, the element of sounds, the element of odours, [Bej 498] the element of tastes, the element of touches, the element of mind, and the element of mental-states. The six sense bases are included in twelve elements, namely, the elements of eye, ear, nose, tongue, body and mind, the element of eye-consciousness, eye-consciousness, ear-consciousness, nose-consciousness, tongue-consciousness, body-consciousness, and mind-consciousness.

Inclusion in the truths: Three factors are included in the truth of origination, namely, ignorance, craving, and clinging. The remaining nine factors are included in the truth of suffering, namely, formations, consciousness, name-and-matter, the six sense bases, contact, feeling, existence, birth, and ageing and death. With regard to supramundane dependent arising: suffering is included in the truth of suffering. Ten factors are included in the truth of the path, namely, faith, gladness, rapture, tranquillity, pleasure, concentration, knowledge and vision as they are, disenchantment, dispassion, and freedom. Knowledge of destruction is included in the truth of cessation. [Der 190B]

Through such ways, knowledge of the skill in dependent arising is produced. [Bej 499]

[This is] the skill in dependent arising.

The analysis of dependent arising according to the system of the Sthavira School. The Analysis of the Conditioned and Unconditioned (= Saṃskṛtāsaṃskṛtaviniścaya) compiled by the Great Pandita, the Auspicious Friend of the One with Ten Powers (= Daśabalaśrīmitra), Chapter 14.

11 § 59. Skill in the noble truths

[Chin 452a] What is skill in the noble truths? There are four noble truths: the noble truth of suffering, the noble truth of the origination [of suffering], the noble truth of the cessation of suffering, and the noble truth of the path leading to the cessation of suffering.

11 § 60. Truth of suffering

Herein, if it is asked "What is the truth of suffering?", it should be said: Birth is suffering too; ageing is suffering too; death is suffering too; sorrow and lamentation are suffering too; pain, distress and grief are suffering too; association with those who are not dear is suffering too; separation from those who are dear is suffering too; not getting what is wished for is suffering too; in brief, the five aggregates subject to clinging are suffering too.

Herein, "birth" is the unprecedented arising of the aggregates[71] in various orders of beings. Furthermore, it is the origin (*nye bar sogs par byed pa*) of all suffering. "Ageing" is the maturing of the elements of one who is born. It is suffering in the sense of decline in object *(dmigs pa = ārammaṇa)*, (physical) appearance, activity (*bya ba*), sense-faculties, memory, and intelligence. "Death" is suffering in the sense of creating great fear about the exhaustion of life.

"Sorrow" is the consuming of the mind upon reaching suffering. [Bej 500] It is suffering in the sense of burning (*bsreg pa*) inside and outside. "Lamentation" is the expression by speech when there is suffering. It is suffering in the sense of burning (*sreg pa*) inside and outside. "Pain" is physical [suffering]. It is suffering in the sense of physical torment (*yongs su mnar ba*). "Distress" is mental suffering. [Der 191A] It is suffering in the sense of mental harassment (*yongs su gzir ba*). "Grief" is pervasive fear (*'jigs pa rgyas pa*) when there is suffering. It is suffering in the sense of being deluded.

"Association with those who are not dear is suffering" is being united with disagreeable beings. It is suffering in the sense of creating suffering.

"Separation from those who are dear is suffering" is being separated from agreeable beings. It is suffering in the sense of creating sorrow and lamentation.

"Not getting what is wished for" is when one is desiring separation from those who are disagreeable and desiring association with those who are agreeable, one is not getting it. It is suffering in the sense of the losing of what is wished for.

"In brief, the five aggregates subject to clinging are suffering": There is no separation from the suffering in these five aggregates subject to clinging. Therefore, in brief, the five aggregates subject to clinging are suffering. *[The definition of the five aggregates is missing.]*

11 § 61. Kinds of suffering

Herein, suffering is of two kinds, namely suffering as basis and suffering as intrinsic nature. Herein, [suffering as] basis is "birth is suffering too", and so on until "in brief, the five aggregates subject to clinging are suffering". Suffering as intrinsic nature is sorrow, lamentation, pain, distress, and grief are suffering. [Bej 501]

Furthermore, suffering is of three kinds: the suffering of suffering, the suffering of change, and the suffering of formations. Herein, the suffering of body and speech (*ngag*) is the suffering of suffering. The change of the basis of

71. *Phung po sngar med pa byung ba*. A mistranslation of *abhinibbatti khandhānaṃ pātubhāvo?*

the feeling/experiencing of pleasure that is subject to contaminations is the suffering of change. The five aggregates subject to clinging is the suffering of formations.

This is called the noble truth of suffering.

11 § 62. Truth of the origination of suffering

What is the noble truth of the origination of suffering? This craving that causes further existence, is accompanied by delight and greed, [and] is delighting everywhere. [Chin 452b] *[The first part of the explanation is missing.]*

"Delighting everywhere": [Der 191B] wherever self-hood is produced, there it delights. Furthermore, wherever there is a likeable object or pleasant object, there it delights. Herein, there are three kinds, namely, the craving for sense-pleasure, the craving for existence, and the craving for annihilation. Except for craving for existence and the craving for annihilation, all craving is craving for sense-pleasure. The craving accompanied by the view of eternalism is craving for existence and the craving accompanied by the view of annihilationism is craving for annihilation.

This is called the "noble truth of the origination of suffering".

11 § 63. Truth of the cessation of suffering

What is the noble truth of the cessation of suffering? The remainderless fading away, cessation, relinquishing, renouncing, being delivered from, and dislodging of that very craving". [Bej 502] This is called "the noble truth of the cessation of suffering". *[Question and answer are missing.]*

11 § 64. Truth of the path leading to the cessation of suffering

What is the noble truth of the path leading to the cessation of suffering? It is the noble eightfold path, namely, right view, right intention, right speech, right action, right livelihood, right effort, right mindfulness, and right concentration. Herein, right view is the knowledge of the four truths. Right intention is wholesome intention. Right speech is the abstaining from the four verbal wrong conducts. Right action is abstaining from the three bodily wrong conducts. Right livelihood is abstaining from wrong livelihood. Right effort is the four right efforts. Right mindfulness is the four establishments of mindfulness. Right concentration is the four jhānas.

Furthermore, knowledge and vision of nibbāna due to the development of the noble path—this is right view. The thinking [directed] towards just that nibbāna is right intention. [Der 192A] The abandoning of wrong speech due to just that [nibbāna] is right speech. The abandoning of wrong action due to just that [nibbāna] is right action. The abandoning of wrong livelihood due to just that [nibbāna] is right livelihood. The energy due to just that [nibbāna] is right effort. The recollection of just that nibbāna is right mindfulness. The one-pointedness of mind towards just that nibbāna is right concentration.

Furthermore, the faculty of wisdom, [Bej 503] the power of wisdom, the basis of supernormal power of examination and the enlightenment factor of the investigation of the Dhamma are included in internal right view.

The faculty of energy, the power of energy, the basis of super normal power of energy, the basis of supernormal power of motivation, the enlightenment factor of energy, the enlightenment factor of tranquillity,[72] and the fourfold right effort are included in internal right effort. The faculty of mindfulness, the power of mindfulness, the enlightenment factor of mindfulness, and the four establishments of mindfulness are included in internal right mindfulness. The faculty of concentration, the power of concentration, the basis of supernormal power of mind, the faculty of faith, the power of faith, the enlightenment factor of concentration, the enlightenment factor of rapture, and the enlightenment factor of equanimity are included in internal right concentration.

Thus, the thirty-seven states that are aids to enlightenment are included in the noble eightfold path.

This is called "the noble truth of the path leading to the cessation of suffering".

These are the four noble truths.

11 § 65. Why four noble truths are taught

Now, if it is said: Why are there four noble truths and not three or five? Then it should be said: The mundane and supramundane results and causes are four: [Chin 452c] Suffering is mundane result; origination is mundane cause; cessation is supramundane result; [Bej 504, Der 192B] and the path is supramundane cause. Therefore there are four.

Furthermore, because "to be understood", "to be abandoned", "to be realized", and "to be practised", are four, the truths are four.

11 § 66. Eleven ways of knowing the four noble truths

Furthermore, the distinctions of these four noble truths should be known in eleven ways, namely, through word meaning, through characteristics, through sequence, through (summary) collection, through simile, through

72. As in the Chinese, the enlightenment factor of tranquility should be included in right concentration, where it is missing in the Tibetan.

analysis, through enumeration, through oneness, through diversity, through successive explanation, and through inclusion.

11 § 67. Word meaning

Herein, word meaning is: [they are] numbered "four"; [they are] delimited as "Noble Truths" (or "Truths of the Noble One", *'phags pa'i bden pa*). They are truths taught by the Noble One or they are realized (*sacchikata*) by the Noble One. "Noble Truths" has the meaning of realness, and also of non-deceptiveness due to the realness of the specific characteristic.[73] "Suffering" has the meaning of torment (*mnar ba*). "Origination" has the meaning of arising. "Cessation" has the meaning of ceasing. "Path" has the meaning of practising (*goms par byed pa = bhāvanā?*) the ultimate.

11 § 68. Characteristic

Characteristic. Suffering has the characteristic of disadvantage.[74] Origination has the characteristic of cause. Cessation has the characteristic of non-arising. The path has the characteristic of means.

Furthermore, suffering has the characteristic of harassment (*gzir ba, pīḷana*), the characteristic of burning (*kun du gdung ba, santāpa*), the characteristic of the conditioned, and the characteristic of change. Origination has the characteristic of accumulation, the characteristic of source (*gzhi, nidāna*), [Bej 505] the characteristic of bondage (*kun du tshogs*), and the characteristic of obstruction. Cessation has the characteristic of escape, the characteristic of seclusion, the characteristic of the unconditioned and the characteristic of the deathless. The path has the characteristic of leading out, the characteristic of causing to reach, the characteristic of seeing, and the characteristic of authority.

11 § 69. Sequence

Sequence. Because it has the sense of grossness and the sense of condition, suffering is taught first. Because suffering is born due to this, [Der 193A] therefore origination is taught second. The cessation of origination is the cessation of suffering, therefore the truth of cessation is taught third. It is the means for the cessation of origination, therefore the truth of the way is taught fourth. Just as a skilful physician first diagnoses the disease, then investigates (*yongs su tshol ba*) the cause (*rgyu*) of the disease, then cleanses (*byang ba*) the disease, and [then] prescribes (*ston pa*) appropriate medicine;

---

73. *de bzhin nyid kyi la yang de bzhin nyid rang gi mtshan nyid kyi mi slu ba'i don gyis na ...*
74. A translation of this passage is also given in Skilling 1997b: 143–44.

just so suffering is like the disease, origination is like the source (*gzhi*) of the disease, cessation is like the cleansing of the disease, and the path is to be regarded as the medicine.

11 § 70. Collection

(Summary) collection. Occurrence (*'jug pa = pavatti*) is suffering; causing occurrence is origination; non-occurrence (*ldog pa*) is cessation; and causing non-occurrence is the path. The grounds for afflictions are suffering; afflictions are origination; the abandoning of afflictions is cessation; and the means for abandoning is the path. The defining of suffering destroys the entrance/door of identity view; [Bej 506] the defining of origination destroys the door of the view of annihilationism; the defining of cessation destroys the door of all suffering;[75] and the defining of the path destroys the door of non-action-view.

11 § 71. Simile

Simile. Suffering should be regarded as being similar to a poisonous tree; origination should be regarded as being similar to the seed [of the poisonous tree]; cessation should be regarded as being similar to the burning of the seed; and the path should be regarded as being similar to the fire [burning the seed].

Suffering should be regarded as being similar to the near shore, which is dreadful and fearful; origination should be regarded as being similar to the torrent; cessation should be regarded as being similar to the further shore that is free from fear; and the path should be regarded as being similar to the boat that enables one to cross over [to the further shore]. [Chin 453a]

One should regard suffering as being similar to the carrying of a burden; origination as being similar to the taking up of the burden; cessation as being similar to the laying down of the burden; and the path as being similar to the means for laying down the burden. [Der 193B]

11 § 72. Analysis

Analysis. There are four kinds of truth: truth of speech (*vācā-sacca*), individual truth (*so sor bden pa = pacceka-sacca*), ultimate truth, and noble truth. Herein, the speaking of truth only and not of untruth—this is truth of speech. Wrong views—this is manifold individual truth. "Bhikkhu, that which is false and

---

75. *Sdug bsngal thams cad = sabba-dukkha*. This does not fit in the context of wrong views and must be due to a misunderstanding of *sassatadiṭṭhi*, "eternalist view" (= *rtag par lta ba* in Sav).

which has a delusive nature, is untrue. That which does not have a delusive nature, is nibbāna, absolute truth." The truth to be practised by the noble ones is noble truth (or "truth of the noble ones", *'phags pa'i bden pa*). [Bej 507] Herein, noble truth is intended.

11 § 73. Enumeration

Enumeration. Except for craving, the truth of suffering is the wholesome, unwholesome and indeterminate states of the three planes of the sensual, material and immaterial. The truth of origination is craving. The truth of cessation is the abandoning of craving. The truth of the path is the noble eightfold path.

Another way: Except for craving and the other afflictions, the truth of suffering is the wholesome, unwholesome, and indeterminate states of the three planes of the sensual, etc. The truth of origination is craving and the other afflictions. [The truth of] cessation is the abandoning of craving and the other afflictions. The truth of the path is the noble eightfold path.

Another way: Except for craving, the other afflictions, and all unwholesomeness, the truth of suffering is the wholesome and indeterminate states of the three planes. [The truth of] origination is craving, the other afflictions and all unwholesome states. The truth of cessation is the abandoning of craving, etc. Just so is the truth of the path.

Another way: Except for craving, the other afflictions, all unwholesomeness and wholesomeness of the three planes, the truth of suffering is the indeterminate states of the three planes. [The truth of] origination is craving, the other afflictions, all unwholesomeness and wholesomeness of the three planes. The truth of cessation is the abandoning of craving, etc. Just so is the truth of the path. [Der 194A]

[Bej 508] Herein, craving, in the principal sense (*gtso bor gyur pa'i don gyis = padhānaṭṭhena*) of desiring satisfaction in existence, is origination. The other defilements, in the principal sense of fetter of existence, are origination. All unwholesomeness, in the sense of having to be abandoned, and in the sense of fetter of existence, is origination. The wholesome states of the three planes, in the sense of generating existence, are origination. Therefore craving, the other afflictions, all unwholesomeness, and the wholesome states of the three planes, are the truth of suffering, because of having characteristic of torment (*mnar ba*), burning (*kun du gdung ba*), the conditioned, the limited, and change. Craving and so on, are the truth of origination, because of having the characteristic of accumulation, clinging, obstruction (*kun du spags pa = palibodha*?), and fetter.

11 § 74. Oneness

Oneness. The four truths are one in four ways, namely, in the sense of truth; in the sense of realness; in the sense of doctrine; and in the sense of method (*rigs pa = naya*).

11 § 75. Diversity

Diversity. There are two truths: Mundane and subject to contaminations, subject to fetters, ties, [Chin 453b] torrents, yokes, hindrances, to holding, clinging, and affliction. It is the truth of suffering and the truth of origination.

The second truth is supramundane, not subject to contaminations, fetters, ties, torrents, yokes, hindrances, holding, [Bej 509] clinging, and affliction. It is the truth of cessation and the truth of the path. Three [truths] are conditioned; cessation is unconditioned. Three truths are immaterial. The truth of suffering is material and immaterial. The truth of origination is unwholesome. The truth of the path is wholesome. The truth of cessation is indeterminate. [Der 194B] The truth of suffering is wholesome, unwholesome, and indeterminate.

Suffering is to be understood. Origination is to be abandoned. Cessation is to be realized. The path is to be practised.

11 § 76. Successive explanation

Successive explanation. Through one kind, the body endowed with consciousness is suffering; the conceit "I am" is origination; its abandoning is cessation; and mindfulness of the body is the path.

Through two kinds, name-and-matter are suffering; ignorance and craving are origination; the abandoning of these is cessation; and calm and insight are the path.

Through three kinds, the three kinds of suffering are the truth of suffering; the three roots of unwholesomeness are the truth of origination; the abandoning of these is cessation; and virtue, concentration, and wisdom are the path.

Through four kinds, the four grounds of selfhood are suffering, namely, the suffering of birth, suffering of ageing, suffering of death, and suffering of sickness. The four distortions are origination. The abandoning of them is cessation. [Bej 510] The four establishments of mindfulness are the path.

Through five kinds, the five destinations are suffering. The five hindrances are origination. The abandoning of them is cessation. The five faculties are the path.

Through six kinds, the six bases of contact are suffering, namely, eye contact, ear contact, nose contact, tongue contact, body contact, and mind contact; the [six] groups of craving are origination, namely, craving for forms, craving for sounds, craving for odours, craving for tastes, craving for touch, craving for mental objects; the abandoning of them is cessation.

The six dhammas to be delighted in are the path. Herein, the six dhammas to be delighted in are: (1) He dwells contemplating an internal dhamma as a dhamma,[76] this is the first dhamma to be delighted in. (2) Likewise, an external dhamma. (3) Likewise, external and internal [dhamma]. [Der 195A] (4) Or he dwells contemplating arising [of a dhamma] or contemplating [arising of] a dhamma according to dhamma.[77] (5) Likewise he [dwells] contemplating the ceasing of a dhamma. (6) Or he dwells contemplating arising and ceasing [of a dhamma], [this is] the sixth dhamma to be delighted in.[78]

Through seven kinds: The seven stations of consciousness are suffering. There are beings with different bodies and different perceptions—this is the first station of consciousness. There are beings with different bodies and the same perceptions—this is the second. There are [beings] with the same bodies and different perceptions—this is the third. There are [beings] with the same bodies and same perceptions—this is the fourth. [Bej 511] [There are beings] perceiving space in the immaterial—this is the fifth. [There are beings] perceiving consciousness—this is the sixth. [There are beings] perceiving nothingness—this is the seventh.[79]

---

76. *Nang gi chos la chos kyi rjes su lta zhing gnas pa.* Unlike in the Pali parallels, *chos* or *dhamma* is singular.

77. *Kun du skye ba la rjes su lta ba'am chos la chos dang mthun par lta zhing gnas pa'o.*

78. Cf. D II 301: (1) *Iti ajjhattaṃ vā dhammesu dhammānupassī viharati,* (2) *bahiddhā* ..., (3) *ajjhattabahiddhā* ..., (4) *samudayadhammānupassī vā dhammesu viharati,* (5) *vayadhammānupassī* ..., (6) *samudayavayadhammānupassī vā dhammesu viharati.*

Kun du chags par bya ba'i chos = *ṣaṣ saṃrañjanīyā dharmāḥ*; see Introduction § 4.4. The explanation appears to say, in accordance with the *dhammānupassanā* contemplation: (1) contemplation of *dhamma*-s as *dhamma*-s internally, (2) externally, and (3) both, and (4) the contemplation of the arising of *dhamma*-s, (5) their cessation and (6) their arising and cessation. Cf. Nidd II 161: ... *ajjhattaṃ vedanāsu vedanānupassī viharanto vedanaṃ nābhinandati ... bahiddhā ... ajjhattabahiddhā vedanāsu ... Ajjhattaṃ samudayadhammānupassī vedanāsu vedanānupassī ... ajjhattaṃ vayadhammānupassī ... bahiddhā samudayadhammānupassī ... bahiddhā vayadhammānupassī ... ajjhattabahiddhā samudayadhammānupassī ... ajjhattabahiddhā vayadhammānupassī ... ajjhattabahiddhā samudayavayadhammānupassī vedanāsu ...*

79. D III 253: *Satta viññāṇaṭṭhitiyo. Santāvuso, sattā nānattakāyā nānattasaññino, seyyathā pi manussā ekacce ca devā ekacce ca vinipātikā. ... Santāvuso, sattā sabbaso viññāṇañcāyatanaṃ samatikkamma natthi kiñcī ti ākiñcaññāyatanūpagā. Ayaṃ sattamī viññāṇaṭṭhiti.* Cf. Daśottarasūtra: *sapta vijñānasthitayaḥ, katamāḥ, rūpiṇaḥ santi sattvā nānātvakāyā nānātvasaṃjñinas tadyathā manuṣyā ekatyāś ca devāḥ, iyaṃ prathamā vijñānasthitiḥ, ...*

The seven latent tendencies are origination, namely, the latent tendency of sensual desire, the latent tendency of anger, the latent tendency of conceit, the latent tendency of (wrong) view, the latent tendency of uncertainty, the latent tendency of desire for existence, and the latent tendency of ignorance. The abandoning of these is cessation. The seven factors of enlightenment are the path.

Through eight kinds, the eight worldly states are suffering. The eight kinds of wrongness are origination, namely, wrong view, wrong intention, wrong speech, wrong action, wrong livelihood, wrong effort, wrong mindfulness, and wrong concentration. The abandoning of these is cessation. The eight kinds of rightness are the path, namely, right view, right intention, right speech, right action, right livelihood, right effort, right mindfulness, and right concentration.

Through nine kinds, the nine abodes of beings are suffering: [There are beings with] different bodies and different perceptions, namely, humans and some gods—this is the first abode of beings. [Der 195B] [There are beings with] the same bodies and different perceptions, namely, the deities in the company of Brahmā who are reborn first—this is the second. [There are beings] with different bodies and the same perceptions, namely, the radiant deities—this is the third.[80] [There are beings] with the same bodies and same perceptions, namely, the lustrous deities—this is the fourth. [Bej 512] The base of boundless space, the base of boundless consciousness, the base of nothingness, and the base of neither-perception-nor-non-perception, and beings without perception. [These are] the nine abodes of beings. The nine states rooted in craving are origination. The abandoning of these is cessation. The nine states rooted in reasoned attention are the path.[81]

Through ten kinds, the formations of the ten directions are suffering. The ten fetters are origination, namely, the fetter of greed for sense-pleasures, the fetter of ill will, the fetter of conceit, the fetter of (wrong) view, the fetter of doubt, the fetter of holding on to precepts and observances, the

80. Items two and three should be the other way around, i.e. "There are beings with different bodies and the same perceptions, ...—this is the second. There are beings with the same bodies and different perceptions, ...—this is the third." as in the Pali and as in the seven stations of consciousness given above. D III 263: ... *Santi, bhikkhave, sattā nānattakāyā ekattasaññino, seyyathā pi devā brahmakāyikā paṭhamābhinibbattā. Ayaṃ dutiyo sattāvāso. Santi, bhikkhave, sattā ekattakāyā nānattasaññino, seyyathā pi devā ābhassarā. Ayaṃ tatiyo sattāvāso.* Cf. Daśottarasūtra: ... *rūpiṇaḥ santi satvā nānātvakāyā ekatvasaṃjñinas tadyathā devā brahmakāyikā ye etat prathamābhinirvṛttāḥ, ayaṃ dvitīyaḥ satvāvāsaḥ. rūpiṇaḥ santi satvā ekatvakāyā nānātvasaṃjñinas tadyathā devā ābhāsvarāḥ, ayaṃ tṛtīyaḥ satvāvāsaḥ.*

81. *'Di ltar* indicates that an explanation of these nine states is supposed to follow, as above, but for some unknown reason the explanation is not given.

fetter of greed for existence, the fetter of envy, the fetter of selfishness, and the fetter of ignorance. The abandoning of these is cessation. The ten perceptions are the path, namely, perception of impermanence, perception of worthlessness,[82] perception of the foul, perception of disadvantage, perception of living beings, perception of dispassion, perception of cessation, perception of non-delight towards the whole world, perception of dislike towards all formations, and perception of breathing.

11 § 77. Inclusion

How through inclusion? There are three kinds of inclusion: inclusion in the aggregates, inclusion in the sense bases, and inclusion in the elements. Herein, the truth of suffering is included in the five aggregates. [Bej 513] The truths of origination and the path are included in the aggregate of formations. The truth of cessation is not included in the aggregates. [Der 196A] The truth of suffering is included in the twelve sense bases. Three truths are included in the sense base of mental states. The truth of suffering is included in the eighteen elements. Three truths are included in the element of mental states.

In these [ways] knowledge of the skill in the noble truths arises.

This is called "skill in the noble truths". *[The first sections of Chapter 12 are missing.]*

12 § 23. Knowledge of change of lineage

The attainment of fruition should be discussed.

[Chin 457a] Having transcended the sign of all formations [and] having made nibbāna the object, the knowledge of the partaking of the lineage (*rigs spyod = gotrabhu*) arises.

Herein, if it is asked "What is the meaning of partaking of the lineage?", it should be said: The overcoming of the states of the worldling is partaking of the lineage. Nibbāna is the "lineage". The partaking of this is the partaking of the lineage. As is said in the Abhidharma: "The overcoming of birth, this is called 'partaking of the lineage'. The partaking of non-arising (*anuppādā*), this is 'partaking of the lineage'. The overcoming of the sign [and] turning away, this is called 'partaking of the lineage'. The non-existence of the sign [and] turning away, this is 'partaking of the lineage'. The first focussing on nibbāna and the wisdom with regard to emergence and turning away is knowledge of the partaking of the lineage."

82. Or "perception of meaninglessness", *don med pa'i 'du shes.*

12 § 24. Knowledge of the path

Due to the knowledge of the partaking of the lineage, due to fully knowing suffering, due to abandoning its origination, due to realizing its cessation, and due to practising the path, all the states that are aids to enlightenment together with their retinue, together with the path-knowledge of stream-entry, arise. At this time, due to that, the end of existence, the unconditioned, and the deathless element are seen.

12 § 25. Comprehension of the truths in a single moment

[Bej 514] In a single moment of seeing, due to this knowledge with regard to that, there is simultaneous comprehension of the four truths, namely, the comprehension of the full understanding of suffering, the comprehension of the abandoning of origination, the comprehension of the realization of cessation, and the comprehension of the practice of the path. Here the simile of the boat is taught. [*The verse is missing.*] [Chin 457b] Like a boat moving on water, in a moment, simultaneously, performs four functions thus: It leaves this shore, [Der 196B] cuts the stream, reaches the further shore, and carries goods. Like that respectively are the comprehension of the full understanding of suffering, the comprehension of the abandoning of origination, the comprehension of the realization of cessation, and the comprehension of the practice of the path.

Furthermore, it is said to be like a lamp, which with its appearance performs four functions together simultaneously in one moment, namely, it burns the wick; dispels darkness; consumes oil; and manifests light. Likewise, respectively, the four comprehensions of full knowledge and so forth of the truths of suffering and so forth.

Furthermore, it is said to be like the sun, which performs four functions together simultaneously in one moment, namely, it makes forms cognizable, dispels darkness, eliminates cold, and manifests light. Likewise, respectively, the four comprehensions of full knowledge and so forth of the truths of suffering and so forth. [*Similes and discussions are missing.*]

[Chin 457c] Herein, if it is asked what is the meaning of comprehension of the truths?, it should be said: [Bej 515] The four noble truths are comprehended all together (*mnyam du*) in a single moment, this is called "comprehension of the truths".

At this time, connected with the path, the faculties combine in the sense of authority; the powers in the sense of unshakability; the factors of enlightenment in the sense of leading out; the path factors in the sense of cause; the establishments of mindfulness in the sense of establishing; right effort in the sense of principal;[83] the bases of supernormal power in

83. *Gtso bos don gyis/gtso bo'i don gyis.* This is a misunderstanding due to taking

the sense of succeeding; truth in the sense of suchness; calm in the sense of undistractedness; insight in the sense of contemplation; coupling in the sense of inseparability of those; purity of virtue in the sense of restraint; purity of mind in the sense of undistractedness; purity of view in the sense of vision; [Der 197A] liberation in the sense of release; direct knowledge in the sense of penetration; freedom in the sense of giving up; knowledge of destruction in the sense of cutting off; root in the sense of motivation; attention in the sense of origination; contact in the sense of combining; feeling in the sense of coming together; concentration in the sense of being directed towards;[84] mindfulness in the sense of authority; wisdom in the sense of constancy (*bar med pa*); and the entering into the deathless, cessation, nibbāna, combines in the sense of conclusion.

12 § 26. Three fetters

[Bej 516] Thus knowing, thus seeing, three fetters are abandoned, namely, personal-identity-view, doubt, holding on to precepts and observances, and the afflictions conjoined with them.

Personal-identity-view. Herein, the uninstructed worldling regards matter as self; the self as possessing matter; matter as within self; self as within matter. Likewise, feeling, perception, formations, and consciousness as self; the self as possessing consciousness; consciousness as within self; self as within consciousness. This is called personal-identity-view. This is abandoned by this [seeing and perceiving], and due to this abandoning, the sixty-two included views beginning with personal-identity-view are abandoned.

The doubt and uncertainty regarding suffering, origination, cessation, or the path, or regarding the Buddha, the Dhamma and the Saṅgha, or regarding the past, the future, or the past and future, or regarding dependently arisen states—this is called "doubt". This is also abandoned.

Holding on to precepts and observances is twofold, namely, associated with craving and associated with delusion. [Der 197B] Herein, "Through this precept, through this observance, through this austerity, and through this practice of the holy life, [I] will become a deity, [or] otherwise [I will be born] among [the deities]"—this is holding on to precepts and observances associated with craving. "[There is] purity by precepts, purity by observances, purity by precepts and observances", the holding on to views in any such manner by ascetics or brahmins outside of this [Dhamma] [Bej 517]—this is holding on to precepts and observances associated with delusion. This is abandoned by this. The greed, hatred, and delusion that lead to the bad

---

padhāna as "principal" instead of "exertion".

84. *Mngon du phyogs pa* = *abhimukha* rather than the Pali *pamukha*.

destinations—these are called "the afflictions conjoined with them". These are abandoned by this. [Chin 458a]

12 § 27. Stream-enterer

For as long as he is practising for the fruit of stream-entry, for so long he is not a stream-enterer.

The plane of practice for [stream-entry], the eighth plane, the plane of vision, gone to certainty (*nges par gyur pa* = *niyata-gata*), the wisdom with regard to emergence and turning away from both, knowledge of the path of stream-entry—these are synonyms.[85]

Immediately after the path of stream-entry, [and] the states associated the path, the disassociated unconditioned is made the object, and the knowledge of the fruit of stream-entry arises. Due to the immediate occurrence of two or three fruition minds, due to the abandoning of the three fetters, [the mind] then immediately enters into the bhavaṅga. Having emerged from the bhavaṅga, he reviews the path, reviews the fruit, reviews nibbāna, reviews the abandoned defilements, and reviews the remaining defilements.

He is called "a stream-enterer; one who is not subject to regress; one of fixed destiny; one with enlightenment as his destination; one endowed with comprehension, who has come to the fruit; [Bej 518] born of the breast and the mouth of the Fortunate One, born of the Dhamma, created by the Dhamma; an heir to the Dhamma, [Der 198A] not an heir to material things". Herein, he is one endowed with [right] view, one endowed with vision; one who realized this Dhamma, one who sees the Dhamma, one who is possessed of learner's knowledge, one who is possessed of learner's higher knowledge, one who is rightly practising the method of the Dhamma; a noble one with penetrative wisdom; and one who dwells having entered the door of the deathless. Therefore, it is said thus:

> To being the sole king of earth;
> To going to heaven oneself;
> To being the ruler of the whole universe—
> The fruit of stream-entry is superior.

12 § 28. Once-returner

Established in this plane, he endeavours further for the realization of the fruit of once-returning, beginning with contemplating rise and fall. Look

85. The Tibetan translator misunderstood this passage since only the last two items—i.e. the wisdom with regard to emergence and turning away from both, knowledge of the path of stream-entry—are actually synonyms, as the Chinese translator rightly understood.

at what is properly taught (about this above).[86] Through what has been seen, the faculties, the powers and factors of enlightenment, and also the comprehension of the truths, he cultivates the paths. Thus he practises towards the abandoning of coarse sensual greed, hatred, and the afflictions conjoined with them. Immediately after this path, the fruit of once-returning is realized.

12 § 29. Non-returner

Established in this plane, he endeavours further for the realization of the fruit of non-returning, beginning with contemplating rise and fall. Look at what is properly taught (about this above). [Der 198B, Bej 519] Through what has been seen, the faculties, the powers and factors of enlightenment, and also the comprehension of the truths, he cultivates the paths. Thus he practises towards the abandoning of subtle sensual greed, hatred, and the afflictions conjoined with them. Immediately after this path, the fruit of non-returning is realized.

12 § 30. Arahant

Established in this plane, he endeavours further for the realization of the fruit of arahantship, beginning with contemplating rise and fall. Look at what is properly taught (about this above). Through what has been seen, the faculties, the powers and factors of enlightenment, and also the comprehension of the truths, he cultivates the paths. Thus he practises towards the abandoning of desire for the material and the immaterial [existences]; and he abandons conceit, agitation, ignorance, and the other afflictions without remainder. [Chin 458b] Then immediately after this path he realizes arahantship. He reviews the path and he reviews the fruit, nibbāna, and the abandoned afflictions.

That bhikkhu is an arahant,[87] one who has eradicated the contaminations, has lived the holy life, has done what had to be done, has laid down the burden, has reached the true goal, has destroyed the fetters, and whose mind is well liberated by right knowledge. He has abandoned five factors and is endowed with six factors, has a single guard, is not fettered to death, has dispelled individual truths, has completely given up searching, has unsullied intentions, has tranquillized the bodily formation, [Bej 520] has a well-

86. This refers to the section on the knowledge of rise and fall at 12 § 11 in the Chinese, which Daśabalaśrīmitra does not quote.

87. The Tibetan term *dgra bcom pa* literally means "enemy slayer" or "foe killer", which is one of the etymologies of the word *arahant*; see 8 § 75. Cf. Vism VII.4/p.198: *te ca anena kilesārayo maggena hatā ti arīnaṃ hatattā pi arahaṃ*.

liberated mind, has a well-liberated wisdom, has wholly[88] lived the Holy Life, is the greatest person, supreme person, one who has attained the supreme attainment, who has abandoned all trouble (*pari-igha*?), has crossed the expanse of waves [and] troubles, has left behind seeking due to fear, has no bolt, has raised the victory banner of the noble one, has the burden of a leaf,[89] and is detached; the Brahmin, one who has bathed, [knower of the] highest knowledge, is pure, an arahant, one who has crossed over, one who is tamed, one who is released, one who is appeased.

12 § 31. Three kinds of stream-enterer and the non-returner

Herein, even when the stream-enterer does not strive further in this birth: just as there are the three kinds of reaching certainty (*mtha' rjes su thob*), so there are three [kinds of] stream enterers: one of dull faculties is one who is reborn seven times in the meantime (*de ltar thogs na*), one of middling faculties is one who is reborn from family to family, and one of sharp faculties is one who is reborn once in the meantime (*bar chad*). [*The explanation of these names is missing.*]

[Der 199A] Even when the once-returner does not endeavour further in this birth, having passed away from here and having returned to here once as a human (*mi'i nang 'dir lan cig*), he makes an end of suffering. Even when a non-returner does not endeavour further in this birth, having passed away from here, he is born in a Pure Abode plane.

12 § 32. Five kinds of non-returner

Through a distinction of faculties there are five kinds of reaching certainty. The five [kinds of] non-returners are: One who attains nibbāna in the intermediate state (*bar do = antarābhava*), one who attains nibbāna as soon as he has been born (*skyes nas*), one who attains nibbāna without impetus, one who attains nibbāna with impetus, [Bej 521] and one who goes upstream, to Akaniṭṭha. [*The explanation of these names is missing.*]

---

88. *Tshangs par spyod pa gcig tu gnas pa = kevala-brahmacariya-vusitavā*: "has wholly lived the whole holy life". This probably is an interpretation of *kevalī vusitavā* "one who is complete, who has lived [the Holy Life]"as in Nidd I 21: *... pañcaṅgavippahīno ... suvimuttapañño kevalī vusitavā uttamapuriso paramapuriso paramapattippatto* and S III 61, A V 16: *... kevalī vusitavā uttamapuriso ti vuccati.* Mp V 3: *Kevalīti kevalehi sakalehi guṇehi samannāgato. Vusitavā ti vutthabrahmacariyavāso.* M II 144, A I 162: *Pahīnajātimaraṇo, brahmacariyassa kevalī.* Ps III 396: *Brahmacariyassa kevalī ti yaṃ brahmacariyassa kevalī sakalabhāvo, tena samannāgato, sakalacatumaggabrahmacariyavāsoti attho.*

89. *lo 'dab kyi khur* is a mistranslation of *pannabhāra* (the same in Skt) "put down the burden" misunderstanding it as *paṇṇabhāra* = Skt *parṇabhāra.*

[Chin 458c] With regard to the five non-returners: there are five in [each of] the four[90] planes of Aviha and so on, [making] twenty. In Akaniṭṭha, which is without the one who goes upstream, there are four persons. In this way, there are twenty-four persons.

12 § 33. No further existence for the arahant

Because the arahant has completely cut off all defilements without remainder, there is no further existence since there is no cause for it. The arahant has exhausted the life force upon which existence depends—just this is the cessation of suffering. He is not born elsewhere—just this is the end of suffering. Therefore it is said:

Just as the destination is not known
Of the blazing due to the feeling born,[91]
Of the [blazing] lump of iron that is struck,
And has gradually quenched,
So there certainly is no declaration of the destination
Of the person rightly liberated
By crossing the swamp torrent of sensuality,
By the attainment of the unshakeable state.

[*Section missing.*]

12 § 47. Noble planes

[Chin 459b] Therefore there are two noble planes (*ariyabhūmi*). Herein, the plane of seeing (*mthong ba'i sa* = *dassanabhūmi*) is the path for the fruit of stream-entry. The remaining three paths and the four fruits of recluseship are the path of practice.[92] Herein, the three paths are the path for the fruit of once-returning, the path for the fruit of non-returning, and the path for the fruit of arahantship. The four fruits of recluseship are the fruit of stream-entry, the fruit of once-returning, the fruit of non-returning, and the fruit of arahantship. Herein, the seeing of truth not seen before is the plane of seeing; the practice of what has been seen thus is the plane of practice (*bsgom pa'i sa*). [Der 199B]

Furthermore, there are two planes, namely, the plane of the trainee and the plane of the non-trainee. [Bej 522] Herein, the four paths and the three

---

90. Reading *bzhi*, "four" instead of *gzhi* "basis".

91. *Rigs kyi tshor bas 'bar ba* = *jātiyā vedanāya jalā*. This is due to a misunderstanding of *jalato jātavedasso*.

92. *Bsgom pa'i lam* = *bhāvanāmagga*. This is an error. Below *bsgom pa'i sa* = *bhāvanābhūmi* is used instead.

fruits of recluseship are the plane of the trainee. Herein, the four paths are the path for the fruit of stream-entry, the path for the fruit of once-returning, the path for the fruit of non-returning and the path for the fruit of arahantship. The three fruits of recluseship are the fruit of stream-entry, the fruit of once-returning, the fruit of non-returning. The fruit of arahantship is the plane of the non-trainee.

12 § 48. Three supramundane faculties

The three supramundane faculties: the "I-shall-perfectly-know-what-is-not-yet-known" faculty, the perfect-knowledge faculty, and the one-who-has-perfectly-known faculty. Herein, the knowledge of the path of the fruit of stream-entry, formerly not known with Dhamma knowledge, is the "'I shall-know-what-is-not-yet-known' faculty". The knowledge of the three paths and the knowledge of the three fruits of recluseship is the "perfect-knowledge faculty", knowing again the states one has known. The knowledge of the fruit of arahantship, having known states completely, is the "one-who-has-perfectly-known faculty".

12 § 49. Three liberations

Liberations: There are three, namely, the signless gate to liberation, the desireless gate to liberation, and the emptiness gate to liberation. Herein, according to the path and the knowledge of conformity, the not creating of a sign is the signless gate to liberation; the not creating of a desire is the desireless gate to liberation; and the not creating of attachment is the emptiness gate to liberation. *[Questions and answers are missing.]*

[Chin 459c] If it is asked "What is the difference between liberation and gate to liberation?", it should be said: Only the knowledge of the path. The freedom from the afflictions is liberation. [Bej 523] Only the knowledge in the sense of entry into the door of the deathless is the gate to liberation. [Chin 460a] *[Sentence missing.]*

12 § 50. Hundred thirty-four defilements

Through the three paths twenty afflictions are abandoned, namely, the roots of unwholesomeness, the desirous searches, the contaminations, the ties, the torrents, the yokes, [Der 200A] the clingings, the kinds of going the wrong way, the kinds of selfishness, the hindrances, the roots of dispute, the latent tendencies, the worldly states, the conceits, the grounds for afflictions, the unwholesome [actions], the fetters, the [kinds of] wrongness, the distortions, and the arisings of the unwholesome mind.

12 § 51. Three roots of unwholesomeness

There are three roots of unwholesomeness, namely, greed, hatred, and delusion. Of these, hatred is reduced by [the first] two paths. It is abandoned without remainder by the path of non-returning. Greed and delusion are reduced by three paths. They are abandoned without remainder by the path of arahantship.

12 § 52. Three searches

There are three desirous searches, namely, the search for sense-pleasures, the search for existence, and the search for the holy life. Herein, the desirous search for the holy life is abandoned without remainder by the path of the fruit of stream-entry. The search for sense-pleasures is abandoned by the path of non-returning. The search for existence is abandoned by the path of arahantship. [Bej 524]

12 § 53. Four contaminations

There are four contaminations, namely, the contamination of sense-pleasures, contamination of existence, contamination of views, and the contamination of ignorance. Herein, the contamination of views is abandoned by the path of the fruit of stream-entry; the contamination of sense-pleasures is abandoned by the path of non-returning; the contamination of existence and the contamination of ignorance are abandoned by the path of arahantship.

12 § 54. Four ties

There are four ties, namely, the tie of the body of covetousness, the tie of the body of ill will, the tie of the body of holding on to precepts and observances, and the tie of the body of attachment to "this is the truth". Of these, the tie of the body of holding on to precepts and observances and the tie of the body of attachment to "this is the truth" are abandoned by the path of the fruit of stream-entry. The tie of the body of ill will is abandoned by the path of non-returning. The tie of the body of covetousness is abandoned by the path of arahantship.

12 § 55. Four torrents

There are four torrents, namely, [Der 200B] the torrent of sense-pleasures, the torrent of existence, the torrent of views, and the torrent of ignorance. There are four yokes, namely, the yoke of sense-pleasures, the yoke of existence, the yoke of views, and the yoke of ignorance. These are abandoned in the same way as the four contaminations.

12 § 56. Four clingings

There are four clingings, namely, the clinging to sense-pleasures, clinging to views, clinging to precepts and observances, and clinging to a doctrine of a self. Of these, two clingings are abandoned by the path of the fruit of stream-entry. Clinging to sense-pleasures by the path of non-returning. Clinging to the doctrine of a self by the path of arahantship.

12 § 57. Four kinds of going the wrong way

There are four kinds of going the wrong way, namely, going the wrong way of desire, going the wrong way of anger, going the wrong way of fear, and going the wrong way of delusion. [Bej 525] The four are abandoned by the path of the fruit of stream-entry.

12 § 58. Five kinds of selfishness

There are five kinds of selfishness, namely, selfishness as to dwelling, selfishness as to family, selfishness as to gain, selfishness as to appearance, and selfishness as to doctrine. All are abandoned by the path of non-returning.

12 § 59. Five hindrances

There are five hindrances, namely, sensual desire, ill will, sloth and torpor, agitation and worry, and doubt. Of these, doubt is abandoned by the path of stream-entry. Sensual desire, ill will, and worry are abandoned by the path of non-returning. Sloth, torpor, and agitation are abandoned by the path of arahantship.

12 § 60. Six roots of dispute

There are six roots of dispute, namely, wrath, depreciation, jealousy, craftiness, evil desires, and holding on to one's own views. Of these, craftiness, evil desires, and holding on to one's own views are abandoned by the path of the fruit of stream-entry. Wrath, depreciation, and jealousy are abandoned by the path of non-returning.

12 § 61. Seven latent tendencies

There are seven latent tendencies, namely, the latent tendency of greed for sense-pleasures, [Chin 460b] the latent tendency of aversion, [Der 201A] the latent tendency of conceit, the latent tendency of views, the latent tendency of doubt, the latent tendency of the greed for existence, and the latent tendency of ignorance. Of these, the latent tendency of views and the latent tendency of doubt are abandoned by the path of the fruit of stream-entry. The latent tendency of greed for sense-pleasures and the latent tendency of aversion are abandoned by the path of non-returning. [Bej 526] The latent tendency of conceit, the latent tendency of greed for existence and the latent tendency of ignorance are abandoned by the path of arahantship.

12 § 62. Eight worldly states

There are eight worldly states, namely, gain and non-gain, fame and non-fame, blame and praise, and pleasure and pain. Of these, the aversion towards the four disagreeable things beginning with [non] gain[93] is abandoned by the path of non-returning. The affection towards the four agreeable things beginning with gain is abandoned by the path of arahantship.

12 § 63. Nine conceits

There are nine conceits, namely, the conceit "I am superior" by one who is superior; or the conceit "I am equal" by one who is superior; or the conceit "I am inferior" by one who is superior; or the conceit "I am superior" by one who is equal; or the conceit "I am equal" by one who is equal; or the conceit "I am inferior" by one who is equal; or the conceit "I am superior" by one who is inferior; or the conceit "I am equal" by one who is inferior; or the conceit "I am inferior" by one who is inferior. All the nine conceits are abandoned by the path of arahantship.

12 § 64. Ten grounds for afflictions

There are ten grounds for afflictions, namely, greed, hatred, delusion, conceit, views, doubt, sloth, agitation, consciencelessness, and shamelessness. Of these, views and doubt are abandoned by the path of stream-entry. Hatred is abandoned by the path of non-returning. The remaining seven are abandoned by the path of arahantship.

12 § 65. Ten grounds for anger

There are ten grounds for anger, namely, [thinking:] "He acted for my non-benefit", one gives rise to anger; [Bej 527, Der 201B] "He acts, ..." one gives rise

---

93. *'Dod pa'i dngos po rnyed pa la sogs pa la zhe sdang ba*. The word *rnyed pa* supposedly refers to the first state of gain, however this is not a disagreeable state, of which the first is non-gain, *ma thob pa*. Read *mi rnyed pa*? The parallel clause for the agreeable things also has *rnyed pa*, where it fits. These two clauses are not found in the Chinese version.

to anger; "He will act for the non-benefit ..." one gives rise to anger. Likewise, "He acted, ... acts, ... will act for the non-benefit of those who are dear to me", ... "He acted, ... acts, ... will act for the benefit of those who are not dear and not beloved by me", one gives rise to anger; and one even gives rise to anger for [no]thing.[94] All ten grounds for anger are abandoned by the path of non-returning.

12 § 66. Ten unwholesome actions

There are ten unwholesome actions, namely, taking of life, taking what is not given, sexual misconduct, false speech, harsh speech, malignant speech, frivolous speech, covetousness, ill will, and wrong view. Of these, the taking of life, taking of what is not given, sexual misconduct, lying, and wrong view are abandoned by the path of the fruit of stream-entry. Harsh speech, malignant speech, and ill will are abandoned by the path of non-returning. Frivolous speech and covetousness are abandoned by the path of arahantship.

12 § 67. Ten fetters

There are ten fetters, namely, the fetters of greed for sense-pleasures, ill will, conceit, (wrong) view, doubt, holding on to precepts and observances, greed for existence, envy, selfishness, and ignorance. Of these, the fetters of (wrong) view, doubt, and holding on to precepts and observances are abandoned by the path of stream-entry. The fetters of greed for sense-pleasures, ill will, envy, and selfishness are abandoned by the path of non-returning. The fetters of conceit, greed for existence, and ignorance are abandoned by the path of arahantship. [Bej 528]

12 § 68. Ten kinds of wrongness

There are ten kinds of wrongness, namely, wrong view, wrong intention, wrong speech, wrong action, wrong livelihood, [Der 202A] wrong effort, wrong mindfulness, wrong concentration, wrong knowledge, and wrong freedom. Of these, wrong view, wrong speech characterized by lying, wrong action, wrong livelihood, wrong knowledge, and wrong freedom are abandoned by the path of stream-entry. Wrong intention and wrong speech characterized by harshness and malignance are abandoned by the path of non-returning. Wrong speech characterized by frivolousness, wrong effort, wrong mindfulness, and wrong concentration are abandoned by the path of arahantship.

---

94. *Gnas mal (v.l. sam) la yang mnar sems skye ba.* This likely is a corruption or a misunderstanding. In accordance the required meaning as in the Pali and Chinese, "for no reason" or "for nothing", *aṭṭhāne*, the reading should have been *mi gnas sa.*

12 § 69. Twelve distortions

[Chin 460c] There are twelve distortions, namely, the distortion of perception, distortion of mind, and distortion of view [due to perceiving] "permanence" in the impermanent; just so the distortion of perception, distortion of mind, and distortion of view [due to perceiving] "happiness" in suffering; distortion of perception, distortion of mind, and distortion of view [due to perceiving] "beauty" in the foul; and distortion of perception, distortion of mind, and distortion of view [due to perceiving] "self" in what is without self.

Of these, the three distortions [of perception, mind, and view, due to perceiving] "permanence" in the impermanent; the distortion of view [due to perceiving] "beauty" in the foul; the distortion of view [due to perceiving] "happiness" in suffering; and the distortion of view "self" in what is without self are abandoned by the path of stream-entry. [Bej 529] The distortion of perception and the distortion of mind [due to perceiving] "beauty" in the foul are abandoned by the path of non-returning. The distortion of perception and the distortion of mind [due to perceiving] "happiness" in suffering, and the distortion of perception and the distortion of mind [due to perceiving] "self" in what is without self are exhausted by the path of arahantship.

12 § 70. Twelve arisings of the unwholesome mind

There are twelve arisings of the unwholesome mind, namely: (1) arising of mind accompanied by joy, accompanied by (wrong) view, and without force; [Der 202B] (2) arising of mind (...) with force; (3) arising of mind accompanied by joy, not accompanied by (wrong) view, without force; (4) arising of mind (...) with force; (5) arising of mind accompanied by equanimity, accompanied by (wrong) view [and] understanding[95] (*rtogs pa*), without force; (6) arising of mind (...) with force; (7) arising of mind accompanied by equanimity, not accompanied by (wrong) view, without force; (8) arising of mind (...) with force; (9) arising of mind accompanied by distress, accompanied by aversion, without force; (10) arising of mind (...) with force; (11) arising of mind accompanied by agitation; and (12) arising of mind accompanied by doubt.

Of these, the four arisings of mind accompanied with (wrong) view and the arisings of mind accompanied by doubt are abandoned by the path of stream-entry. The two arisings of mind accompanied by distress are reduced in two paths and abandoned without remainder by the path of non-returning. [Bej 530] The four arisings of mind disassociated from views and the arising of mind accompanied by agitation are reduced in three paths and are abandoned without remainder by the path of arahantship.

---

95. *Lta bar rtogs pa dang ldan pa*. This is not found in the Chinese parallel. The term *rtogs pa* means "realization", "wisdom", "insight", *avabodha*, etc.

12 § 71. Attainments not shared with the worldling

There are two attainments that are not shared with the worldling, namely, fruition attainment and the attainment of cessation of feeling and perception.

12 § 72. Attainment of fruition

With regard to the first [attainment] there are ten questions: What is the attainment of fruition? Why is it called attainment of fruition? Who enters upon it? Why does one enter upon it? How does one enter upon it? How does one attend when one enters? What are the conditions for entering upon this attainment? [What are] the conditions for its persistence? [What are] the conditions for emerging? Is this attainment mundane or supramundane?

Herein, if it is asked, "What is the attainment of fruition?" [It should be said:] The mind of the fruit of recluseship, not including nibbāna[96]—this is called 'attainment of fruition'".

Why is it called "attainment of fruition"? It is neither wholesome nor unwholesome nor functional (*bya ba*), nor born of the result of the supramundane path, therefore it is the attainment of fruition.

With regard to [the question] "Who enters upon it?" [Der 203A] The arahant and the non-returner, since these two are perfect in concentration. *[Two paragraphs are missing.]*

[Chin 461a] Why does one enter upon it? One enters upon it for the sake of a pleasant dwelling in this life. As the Fortunate One taught to Ānanda: "At the time which, Ānanda, the Tathāgata, due to not attending to all signs, due to the cessation of certain feelings, [Bej 531] dwells having entered upon the signless concentration of mind, at that time, Ānanda, the body of the Tathāgata is much more at ease".

How does one enter upon it? Going to a solitary place for the purpose of the attainment of fruition, he, having gone to a solitary dwelling, having sat down or lain down, having composed the mind, sees with insight the formations beginning with contemplation of rise and fall, then [continues up to] change of lineage knowledge. Immediately after change of lineage knowledge, [the mind] becomes fixed in the attainment of fruition, nibbāna. Dependent upon however the path is developed, having concentrated[97] [the mind] on that there will be just that attainment of fruition.

How does one attend? The unconditioned, deathless element is attended to as peaceful.

---

96. Apparently the Tibetan translator understood (or read) *appanā* in *nibbāne appanā* as *apariyāpanna* and therefore translated it as *ma gtogs pa;* see Introduction § 4.4.

97. *Mnyam par bzhag = samāhita, samādahitvā.*

What are the conditions for entering upon that attainment? There are two conditions for entering upon the attainment, namely, the non-attending to all signs and the attending to the signless element.

What are the conditions of [its] persistence? There are three conditions of [its] persistence, namely, non-attending to all signs, attending to the signless element, and previous preparation.

What are the conditions of emergence [from it]? There are two conditions of emergence, namely, attending to all signs and non-attending to the signless element.

Is this attainment mundane or supramundane? This attainment is supramundane, not mundane.

[The rest of the section on the attainment of fruition is missing.]

12 § 73. Attainment of the cessation of perception and feeling

There are fifteen questions about the attainment of the cessation of perception and feeling, namely: [Bej 532, Der 203B] What is the attainment of the cessation of perception and feeling? Who enters upon it? Who does not enter upon it? Endowed with how many kinds of power does one enter upon it? Through the stilling of how many formations is it entered upon? How many preliminary duties are there? Why does one enter upon it? How does one emerge from it? By what does the mind emerge from it? If the mind has emerged, towards what is it inclined? How many [kinds of] contact touch [the mind upon emerging]? Which formations arise first? What is the difference between a corpse and a person who enters upon the cessation of perception and feeling? Is this attainment conditioned or unconditioned?

What is the attainment of the cessation of perception and feeling? The abiding in the non-occurrence of the mind and mental properties—this is the attainment of the cessation of perception and feeling.

Who enters upon it? The arahant and the non-returner, since these are perfect in concentration.

Who does not enter upon it? The worldling, the stream-enterer, the once-returner, and one who is born in the immaterial sphere. [Chin 461b] Herein, the worldling cannot enter upon it since it is not within his range. The stream-enterer and the once-returner cannot enter upon it since they have not yet fully removed the obstacles and afflictions to concentration. One who is born in the immaterial sphere cannot enter upon it since afterwards there is no [material] basis for emerging from it.

Endowed with how many kinds of power is it entered upon? It is entered upon through two kinds of power: through the power of calm [Bej 533] and through the power of insight. Herein, through the power of calm there is mastery of the four jhānas and the four immaterial attainments. Through the power of insight there is mastery of the seven contemplations, namely, the contemplation of impermanence, contemplation of suffering, contemplation of without self, contemplation of disenchantment, contemplation of fading away, [Der 204A] contemplation of cessation, and contemplation of relinquishment. Herein, the power of calm is for the purpose of cessation of the jhāna factors and for the purpose of resolve towards unshakability. The power of insight is for the purpose of seeing danger in occurrence, and for the purpose of resolve towards non-occurrence.

Through the stilling of how many formations is it entered upon? Through the stilling of three it is entered upon, namely, verbal formations, bodily formations and mental formations. Herein, of those who have entered upon the second jhāna, the verbal formations of thinking and exploring are stilled. Of those who have entered upon the fourth jhāna, the bodily formation and inhalations and exhalations are stilled. Of those who have entered upon the attainment of the cessation of perception and feeling, the mental formations of perception and feeling are stilled.

How many are its preliminary duties? There are four preliminary duties, namely, personal belongings, non-damage, delimiting the duration, and observing legal acts and non-legal acts. Herein, "personal belongings" [Bej 534] are the resolve regarding the robes and bowl, body, and whatever is belonging to one [person]. "Non-damage": one resolves "Let there be no arising of any damage to this body through any means (*sbyor ba*)". "Delimiting the duration": by estimating the strength of the body, one sets a limit to the dwelling [in the attainment]. One resolves: "At the time when this period has passed, [I] will emerge from it". "Observing legal acts and non-legal acts": One resolves: "When the time-limit has not yet been reached, and [the Saṅgha] assembles for some reason for legal acts or non-legal acts of the Saṅgha, [I] will emerge at the sound of the ringing of the gong (*gaṇḍi*)". *[Sentence missing.]*

For what purpose is it entered upon? For the purpose of a pleasant dwelling in this life. A pleasant dwelling in this life is due to the ultimate immovable concentration attainments (*tshogs pa rnams*) of the noble ones, [Der 204B] or it is concentration for the purpose of manifesting supernormal power. *[The examples are missing.]*

How is it entered upon? For the purpose of cessation, aspiring for cessation, having gone to a secluded dwelling, one sits down or lies down. Having composed the mind, he enters upon the first jhāna. Having emerged from it, he immediately contemplates that jhāna as impermanent, suffering and without self, until [he reaches] the knowledge of equanimity towards the formations. Likewise for the second jhāna, the third jhāna, the fourth jhāna, the base of boundless space, and the base of boundless consciousness. Having entered and emerged from the base of nothingness, he immediately contemplates that attainment as impermanent, suffering and without self, [Bej 535] until [he reaches] the knowledge of equanimity towards the formations, and then immediately after enters upon the base of neither-perception-nor-non-perception. [Chin 461c] Then having adverted (*bzhag ste*) the mind two or three times to the base of neither-perception-nor-non-perception, there is non-occurrence and cessation of the mind. At the non-occurrence and cessation of mind, he enters upon the [attainment of] cessation of feeling and perception.

How does one emerge from it? Herein, one does [not] attend, "I shall emerge". On the contrary, one only emerges when the previously delimited time has been reached.

Through what does the mind emerge? The non-returner emerges by the fruition mind of non-returning. The arahant emerges by the fruition mind of arahantship.

If the mind has emerged, towards what is it inclined? It is inclined towards seclusion.

How many contacts touch [the mind upon emerging]? Three contacts, namely, emptiness, and signless and desireless [contact].

Which formations arise first? Mental formations and then bodily formations.

What is the difference between a corpse and one who has entered upon the cessation of perception and feeling? [Der 205A] In the case of the dead person, the three formations have ceased and stilled, the life span is exhausted, [bodily] heat has subsided, and the sense-faculties have broken up. In the case of one who has entered upon the cessation of perception and feeling, the three formations have not ceased and are not stilled,[98] the life span is not exhausted, heat has not subsided, and the sense-faculties are clear. This is the difference.

Is the attainment of the cessation of perception and feeling conditioned or unconditioned? [Bej 536] This attainment is not to be spoken of as conditioned or unconditioned.

Why is this attainment not to be spoken of as conditioned or unconditioned? Because conditioned states do not occur in that attainment, and entering upon and emerging from the unconditioned is not known. Therefore this attainment is not to be spoken of as conditioned or unconditioned.

This is the end of the attainment of cessation.

The analysis of the skill in the noble truths ('phags pa'i bden pa la mkhas pa) according to the system of the Noble Sthavira School. The Analysis of the Conditioned and Unconditioned (= Saṃskṛtāsaṃskṛtaviniścaya) compiled by the Great Pandita, the Auspicious Friend of the One with Ten Powers (= Daśabalaśrīmitra), Chapter 15.

---

98. *'Du byed gsum ma 'gags shing rgyun ma chad pa.* According to the Chinese and Pali, the three formations have ceased, and this is also said in the Tibetan earlier in this section in answer to the question, "Through the stilling of how many formations is it entered upon?"

Appendix III

The Pāli Commentaries and their Sources

1. The origins of the Pāli commentaries (*aṭṭhakathā*)

An investigation of the sources of the *Visuddhimagga* and the Pali commentaries, the *aṭṭhakathā*, sheds light on the sources and language of the *Vimuttimagga* as well. Both Upatissa and Buddhaghosa quote the former teachers, the *pubbācariyā* (see Introduction § 4.8), and both draw from the same or similar sources, i.e. the old commentaries that the former teachers had composed.
It has been suggested that Buddhaghosa was an innovator who introduced new ideas into the Theravāda tradition, but this is not so. According to Kalupahana (1970: 167–171), Buddhaghosa introduced some ideas and theories from the Sarvāstivāda school, i.e. the idea of atoms (*paramāṇu*), momentariness (*khaṇika*), intrinsic nature (*sabhāva*), and the distinction between *hetu* as primary cause and *paccaya* as secondary contributory condition.[99] Kalupahana also suggests Buddhaghosa could have accepted some of the ideas of schools other than the Sarvāstivāda, and that the idea of *bhavaṅgaviññāṇa* as found in Buddhaghosa's works could have been related to the *ālāyavijñāna* of the Yogācāra. Skilling (1993: 173) is even more emphatic in lauding Buddhaghosa as an innovator: "The *hadaya-vatthu* ... and the developed *bhavaṅga* theory (along with the Theravādin *khaṇikavāda*) appear only with Buddhaghosa. The great *ācariya* was an Indian monk who almost certainly selectively introduced new material from the tenets of the Indian Sthavira schools: he was not only a codifier but also an innovator ...". All these ideas and theories that are said to be introduced by Buddhaghosa, however, are already found in the *Vimuttimagga*.[100] It could therefore be suggested that Upatissa was the

99. Kalupahana (ib. 171f.) also says that Buddhaghosa "without any provocation ... introduces a type of causal relation which was not contemplated in the Theravāda tradition", i.e. the causal relationship of ignorance (*avijjā*) as an obstruction (*palibodha*) for formations as found in Sv I 101, and that it can only be found in Yogācāra literature. However, in fact, Buddhaghosa quotes from the Paṭisambhidāmagga, so the idea already existed in the canonical Theravāda tradition; see Paṭis I 50: ... *Avijjā saṅkhārānaṃ ... saññogaṭṭhiti ca palibodhaṭṭhiti ca ....*

100. For the idea of momentariness in Vim, see Introduction § 5 idea 21. *Sabhāva* is used at Ch. 8 § 164, Ch. 11 § 4, 18, 61, etc. The distinction between *hetu* and *paccaya* is found in Ch. 12 § 11/p.455a06ff. and also Ch. 11 § 48/p.450c16f. For *kalāpa* or atomic clusters see Ch. 8 § 166, 11 § 11, etc. For *bhavaṅga*, see Ch. 11 § 25, 36–38, Ch. 12 § 27. The *hadayavatthu* as *vatthurūpa* is at Ch. 11 § 5, 7, 10, 15–16, 52, Ch. 12 § 19.

real innovator rather than Buddhaghosa, but this is to be avoided since the ideas could as well have been introduced by Upatissa's predecessors. Just as the *Visuddhimagga* and Buddhaghosa's other commentaries are not original works in the modern sense, but rather are restatements of earlier materials available to Buddhaghosa (see Jayawickrama 1962: xv), so the *Vimuttimagga* could also be a restatement and/or compilation of earlier materials that were available to Upatissa; see Intro. § 4.8.

Buddhaghosa's project of compiling, translating, editing and organising the old Sīhaḷa commentaries into new commentaries was probably not an entirely new idea, but was possibly done in imitation of and reaction to the work of Upatissa and other authors, compilers, and editors of the Abhayagirivihāra and other schools, which also had commentaries; see below § 4. The sophisticated scholastic Pali language of Buddhaghosa's *Visuddhimagga* and other works was probably also influenced by the language used by Upatissa—who refers to grammar, likely Paninian Sanskrit grammar—and others; see below § 6.

What follows is an overview of what is known about the sources of the *aṭṭhakathā* as well as some tentative observations. Since the information about the sources is rather scanty in Pali commentaries and their subcommentaries, not much can be said with certainty and mostly only inferences can be made. Even with regard to the Pali commentaries and subcommentaries themselves, there are uncertainties with regard to the authors, date of composition, etc., and relatively little research has been done on these works; see Horner 1981: 93–94, von Hinüber 1996: 101, § 205, and Endo 2013: 8.

For the sake of convenience, I shall refer to Buddhaghosa as the author of all the commentaries traditionally attributed to him according to the

---

The idea of equating *paṭicca-samuppāda* and *suññatā,* as Nāgārjuna did and as is also found in Buddhaghosa's works (Vism XVI.90, XIX.19), is found in a less developed form in *Vimuttimagga* at Ch. 8 § 144/p.436b11f., along with the idea of the emptiness of the experiencer, *vedaka,* and the doer, *kāraka*: "Emptiness: one should reflect: 'In the absolute sense it cannot be obtained: "This person creates suffering" or "This person experiences suffering." This body is produced by conditions. It is without a being, without a self. It is [merely] a bunch of elements, just like a bunch of straw.'" And in Ch. 12 § 13/455b-c: "Why are all formations unconcerned and indifferent? They persist without having been originated by another [being]. They persist as intrinsic natures and conditions that come together and aggregate as dependently arisen [states]. When, through such-naturedness, they are originated, they [in turn] originate [formations]. Herein, in the sense of soullessness and in the sense of indifference, unconcern should be understood. In the sense of intrinsic nature and in the sense of condition, such-naturedness should be understood. The manifestation of emptiness is unconcern. The manifestation of the kamma that has been done is such-naturedness. The manifestation of unconcern is called 'states'. The manifestation of such-naturedness is called 'formations'".

colophons. Although there is agreement that the *Visuddhimagga* and the Nikāya commentaries are the work of Buddhaghosa, modern scholars have expressed doubts as to whether he was actually the author of the other works traditionally attributed to him, i.e. the *Samantapāsādikā, Kaṅkhāvitaraṇī* and Abhidhamma commentaries (see von Hinüber 1996: 104, 109, 110, 151). The absence of a mention of Buddhaghosa in the Chinese translation of the *Samantapāsādikā*, the 一切善見律毘婆沙 or "Entirely Pleasing to Behold Vinaya Commentary", however, cannot be taken as significant since this work is only a partial translation or digest wherein the translator only selected the materials that he considered most relevant, left out others such as the second part of the colophon and the whole epilogue, and added materials taken from other Theravāda works or earlier Chinese translations of these; see Introduction § 8 and Ñāṇatusita 2014–2015: Part III. In any case, given the date of composition given in its colophon, the texts used, and the references to the *Visuddhimagga*, the *Samantapāsādikā* belongs to the same period as the one Buddhaghosa worked in. If he was not the author then it would have been instigated by him or have been made in consultation with him. Possibly there was at the Mahāvihāra a workshop or collective of commentary compilers that later was called "Buddhaghosa" since it either was directed by him or closely followed his example.

According to the traditional account of the origination of the *aṭṭhakathā* as given in the prefaces to Ācariya Buddhaghosa's commentaries to the four Nikāyas, the *aṭṭhakathā* were communally chanted at the first council, were communally chanted again at the other councils, were brought to Sri Lanka by Mahinda Thera, were then translated into Sīhaḷa and were then retranslated into Pali by Ācariya Buddhaghosa. This is a prose translation of the verses:

> [I will explain the meaning] of the Collection (*āgama*) [of Long Discourses, etc.] [using] the commentary which was first communally chanted [at the First Council] by the five hundred sages for explaining the meaning [of it], and later also communally re-recited [at the Second and Third Councils], but then, when brought to the Island of the Sīhaḷas by the sage Mahinda the Great, was put into the language of the Sīhaḷas for the benefit of those who inhabited the Island. From that [commentary] I have removed the language of the Sīhaḷas replacing it by the pleasing language that conforms with the style of the canonical texts (*tantinayānucchavikaṃ*) and is free from flaws, not disagreeing with the doctrine (*samaya*)101 of the

101. Cf. the preface of Nidd-a: "Established in the study/recitation (of the texts) of the Mahāvihāra ... not making it deviate from the own doctrine and not grasping the doctrine of another"; *mahāvihāravāsīnaṃ, sajjhāyamhi patiṭṭhito; ... Avokkamento samayaṃ sakañ-ca, anāmasanto samayaṃ parañ-ca.* Cf. Paṭis-a 1: *avokkamanto samayā sakā ca, anāmasanto samayaṃ parañ-ca.*

> elders residing in the Great Monastery, who are lights in the Lineage of the Elders, and whose authoritative decisions [on the meaning] are very skilful, leaving out [explanations of the] meaning that occur repeatedly. I will elucidate the meaning [of the Collection of Long Discourses] for pleasing the good people and for the long lasting of the Dhamma.102

A slightly different version is found in the preface to the *Atthasālinī*:

> [I will explain the meaning] of the Abhidhamma recited first at the time of the communal chanting (i.e. council) ..., [using] the commentary that was at first recited by the sage Mahākassapa and other [sages], and afterwards also re-recited by those who were seers, but when Mahinda Thera brought it to the best island, it was prepared in the language of the island dwellers. Having removed the language of the *tambapaṇṇi* dwellers from that [commentary], replacing it by flawless language that conforms with the style of the canonical texts, elucidating the authoritative decision of the Mahāvihāra inhabitants, not mixed with the wrong ideas of different schools (*nikāyantaraladdhīhi*), not confused [by opinions due to different readings, etc.], I will explain the meaning [of the Abhidhamma], taking what is to be taken in the commentaries on the collections (*āgama*), pleasing the wise.[103]

The preface of the *Samantapāsādikā* says:

> ... I will explain unmixedly the Vinaya, relying on the majestic power of the former teachers, ... By the former-teacher-bulls, ... who were skilled in explaining the True Dhamma, ... who were like the banners of the Mahāvihāra, this Vinaya has been gladly commented upon in variegated

---

102. See also Ñāṇamoli 2010: xxxv; Crosby 2004: 74– 78; von Hinüber 1996: 101, § 206. Sv I 1: *Dīghassa dīghasuttaṅkitassa, nipuṇassa āgamavarassa, ..., atthappakāsanatthaṃ, aṭṭhakathā ādito vasisatehi; pañcahi yā saṅgītā, anusaṅgītā ca pacchāpi, sīhaḷadīpaṃ pana ābhatātha, vasinā mahāmahindena, ṭhapitā sīhaḷabhāsāya, dīpavāsīnamatthāya, apanetvāna tatohaṃ, sīhaḷabhāsaṃ manoramaṃ bhāsaṃ, tantinayānucchavikaṃ āropento vigatadosaṃ, samayaṃ avilomento, therānaṃ theravaṃsapadīpānaṃ, sunipuṇavinicchayānaṃ, mahāvihāre nivāsīnaṃ, hitvā punappunāgatamatthaṃ, atthaṃ pakāsayissāmi, sujanassa ca tuṭṭhatthaṃ, ciraṭṭhitatthañ-ca dhammassa.* Cf. D-ṭ I 19–20: ... *Manoramaṃ bhāsan-ti māgadhabhāsaṃ. Sā hi sabhāvaniruttibhūtā paṇḍitānaṃ manaṃ ramayatī ti. Tenevāha tantinayānucchavikanti, pāḷigatiyā anulomikaṃ pāḷibhāsāyānuvidhāyinin-ti attho. Vigatadosan-ti asabhāvaniruttibhāsantararahitaṃ. ...*

103. As 1: *Saṅgītikāle saṅgīto ... abhidhammassa ādito. Yā mahākassapādīhi, vasīhiṭṭhakathā purā; saṅgītā anusaṅgītā, pacchāpi ca isīhi yā. Ābhatā pana therena, mahindenetamuttamaṃ; Yā dīpaṃ dīpavāsīnaṃ, bhāsāya abhisaṅkhatā. Apanetvā tato bhāsaṃ, tambapaṇṇinivāsinaṃ; Āropayitvā niddosaṃ, bhāsaṃ tantinayānugaṃ. Nikāyantaraladdhīhi, asammissaṃ anākulaṃ; Mahāvihāravāsīnaṃ, dīpayanto vinicchayaṃ. Atthaṃ pakāsayissāmi, āgamaṭṭhakathāsupi; Gahetabbaṃ gahetvāna, tosayanto vicakkhaṇe.* Cf. As-mṭ 10.

manners, in accordance with [the intentions of] the Enlightened One.[104] But since this commentary, due to being composed in the language of the Sīhaḷa Island, provides no benefit for any bhikkhus outside of the Island, therefore I will begin on the commentary that conforms with the style [of the language] of the Canonical Texts, ... Beginning on the commentary on that, making the Great Commentary its body, as well as the *Mahāpaccarī*, not abandoning the authoritative decision and the proper meaning stated in the commentaries, in the renowned *Kurundī* and so on, and thence also contained in the Doctrine of the Theras, I shall rightly begin on the commentary. .... The Dhamma and Vinaya spoken by the Buddha, was known by his sons exactly like that, since those who made the commentaries formerly, were not abandoning the opinions (*mati*) of those [sons on the Dhamma and Vinaya], therefore [from] that which is said in the commentaries, having avoided the corrupt readings all, since [this commentary will be] the standard of the wise ones here, of those who respect the training rules, and having removed just the other language[105] from it, and having abridged the extensive way [of wording], not having left out any authoritative decision, not having deviated from the course of the canonical texts,[106] explaining the meaning of statements connected to the suttantas in accordance with the suttas,[107] since this will also be the commentary [on that], it is to be studied carefully.[108]

---

104. Or: "By [the teachers] who came after the excellent Fully Enlightened One". Sp-ṭ I 19: *Sambuddhavaranvayehīti sabbaññubuddhavaraṃ anugatehi, bhagavato adhippāyānugatehi nayehī ti vuttaṃ hoti. Atha vā buddhavaraṃ anugatehi pubbācariyāsabhehīti sambandho kātabbo.*

105. *Bhāsāntara* means "other language/dialect". In Sanskrit it can also mean "translation"; see MW: *bhāṣāntara.*

106. *Tantikkama.* Adikaram translates *kama* as "idiom" and Jayawickrama as "method of exposition". Probably it refers to the arrangement of the text. Vjb-ṭ explains it as *pāḷikkamaṃ*: "order/course/succession of the Canonical Text". Compare Vjb-ṭ 66: "According to the course [of events] of the Canonical Text it appears as if [the Buddha] is dwelling eight rains retreats only in Vesālī", *aṭṭha vassāni vesāliyaṃ yeva viharanto viya pāḷikkamena dissati.*

107. *Suttantikānaṃ vacanānamatthaṃ suttānurūpaṃ paridīpayantī.* The Verañjakaṇḍa, the first part of the Suttavibhaṅga of the Vinaya, starts with the Verañjasutta (also found at A IV 172) which contains passages on the jhānas, etc., and therefore as material connected to the suttas needs explanation in accordance with the suttas. Likewise, the origin story on the third *pārājika* (Vin III 70) contains a section on developing *ānāpānasati*, which also is connected with the the suttas. *Suttantika* usually means "those who are versed in the suttantas", but in Abhidhamma works it is found in compounds such as *suttantikavatthūni*, *suttantikaduka* and *suttantikapariyāya* in the sense of "belonging to/connected to the suttanta(s)".

108. The translation of this difficult passage is in accordance with the explanations

The preface to Dhammapāla's Udāna commentary, which is similar to the prefaces in his other commentaries, says:

> "Whatsoever inspired utterances of the Great Sage, ..., they were [collected] all together into one [text] by the Dhamma compilers who were depositing [texts] into the canon, [and then it] was communally chanted [by them] as the 'Udāna'. (cf. Ud-a 31) ... Since together with a commentary the Teacher's Doctrine continues,[109] and [since] the authoritative decision of the former-teacher-lions still remains, therefore, depending on that [judgment], having plunged into the five Nikāyas, supported by the method of the ancient commentaries (or: commentaries of the ancients), the very pure, unmixed, skilful judgement, not disagreeing with the doctrine of the Mahāvihāravāsins, having properly avoided [explanations of] meaning that occur repeatedly, I shall, according to my capability, make an explanation of the meaning of the Udāna".[110]

---

in the Vjb-ṭ and Sp-ṭ. Sp 1–2: ... *Taṃ vaṇṇayissaṃ vinayaṃ amissaṃ; Nissāya pubbācariyānubhāvaṃ. ... Kāmañ-ca pubbācariyāsabhehi; ... Mahāvihārassa dhajūpamehi; Saṃvaṇṇitoyaṃ vinayo nayehi; Cittehi sambuddhavaranvayehi; Saṃvaṇṇanā sīhaḷadīpakena; Vākyena esā pana saṅkhatattā; Na kiñci atthaṃ abhisambhuṇāti; Dīpantare bhikkhujanassa yasmā. ... Tasmā imaṃ pāḷinayānurūpaṃ; Saṃvaṇṇanaṃ dāni samārabhissaṃ; ... Saṃvaṇṇanaṃ tañ-ca samārabhanto; Tassā mahāaṭṭhakathaṃ sarīraṃ; Katvā mahāpaccariyaṃ tatheva; Kurundināmādisu vissutāsu; Vinicchayo aṭṭhakathāsu vutto; Yo yuttamatthaṃ apariccajanto; Tato pi antogadhatheravādaṃ; Saṃvaṇṇanaṃ samma samārabhissaṃ. ... Buddhena dhammo vinayo ca vutto; Yo tassa puttehi tatheva ñāto; So yehi tesaṃ matimaccajantā; Yasmā pure aṭṭhakathā akaṃsu; Tasmā hi yaṃ aṭṭhakathāsu vuttaṃ; Taṃ vajjayitvāna pamādalekhaṃ; Sabbam-pi sikkhāsu sagāravānaṃ; Yasmā pamāṇaṃ idha paṇḍitānaṃ; Tato ca bhāsantaram-eva hitvā; Vitthāramaggañ-ca samāsayitvā; Vinicchayaṃ sabbamasesayitvā; Tantikkamaṃ kiñci avokkamitvā; Suttantikānaṃ vacanānamatthaṃ; Suttānurūpaṃ paridīpayantī; Yasmā ayaṃ hessati vaṇṇanāpi; Sakkacca tasmā anusikkhitabbāti.*

109. The *satthusāsana* is here the nine-factored one, *navaṅga satthusāsana*, which includes *udāna, itivuttuttaka, gāthā*, etc. Cf. the preface in Nett-a: *Tena yā bhāsitā netti, satthārā anumoditā; Sāsanassa sadāyattā, navaṅgassatthavaṇṇanā.* What Dhammapāla means is that with a commentary a text, and consequently the Teaching, lasts longer because it is understood properly and does not get corrupted. Examples of corrupted texts without commentaries are the *Dīpavaṃsa* and *Peṭakopadesa*.

110. Ud-a 1: ... *Yāni ... udānāni mahesinā, tāni sabbāni ekajjhaṃ, āropentehi saṅgahaṃ, udānaṃ nāma saṅgītaṃ, dhammasaṅgāhakehi yaṃ. ... Sahasaṃvaṇṇanaṃ yasmā dharate satthusāsanaṃ; pubbācariyasīhānaṃ tiṭṭhateva vinicchayo. Tasmā taṃ avalambitvā, ogāhetvāna pañcapi nikāye, upanissāya porāṇaṭṭhakathānayaṃ, suvisuddhaṃ asaṃkiṇṇaṃ, nipuṇatthavinicchayaṃ, mahāvihāravāsīnaṃ samayaṃ avilomayaṃ. Punappunāgataṃ atthaṃ vajjayitvāna sādhukaṃ, yathābalaṃ karissāmi, udānassatthavaṇṇanaṃ.* Cf. It-a, Th-a 1, Vv-a 1, Pv-a 1, Cp-a, Nett-a 1, Vism-mhṭ 1.

Malalasekera (1928: 90–91) says that the appropiate meanings of terms, especially of those borrowed from other Indian philosophies, were discussed and fixed at the first council, and then at the next two councils, when schismatic schools with different ideas had formed, the right interpretations of rules and points of Dhamma were fixed even more precisely: "When, at the Second and the Third Councils, the custodians of the orthodox tradition met together to condemn such heresies, we may be sure that they determined with even greater preciseness and clearness than before the connotations and the implications of the Buddha's teachings. By the time of the Third Council such commentarial literature (using the word in the wider sense) had been more or less fully developed; and when, after the conclusion of that Synod, Mahinda came to Ceylon, he brought over with him the expositions of the teaching which had been sanctioned by the Elders at that meeting".

Malalasekera might have based this on the following *ṭīkā* commentary on the preface of the nikāya commentaries: "Chanted communally: said, having compiled [what was said] to explain the meaning at the appropriate place: 'this is the meaning of this; this is the meaning of this. And communally re-chanted by Yasa Thera, etc., afterwards at the second and third councils'".[111]

---

111. Sv-ṭ I 19: *Saṅgītā ti atthaṃ pakāsetuṃ yuttaṭṭhāne ayaṃ etassa attho, ayaṃ etassa attho ti saṅgahetvā vuttā. vuttā. Anusaṅgītā ca yasattherādīhi pacchāpi dutiyatatiyasaṅgītīsu.* Cf. Sv III 897: *Tisso saṅgītiyo mahākassapattherassa saṅgīti, yasattherassa saṅgīti, moggaliputtatissattherassa saṅgītī ti. Imā tisso saṅgītiyo āruḷhe tepiṭake buddhavacane.*

The Cullavagga's account of the first council does not mention a communal chanting of the Dhamma and Vinaya. Mahākassapa only questions Upāli and Ānanda about the main points of the vinaya rules and suttantas such as the locations where they were given and the persons involved, as are given at the start of the Vinaya origin stories and in suttantas. The terms *saṅgīti* and *saṅgāyana* in Pali and Sanskrit, however, imply a communal chanting or rehearsal (as in the Saṃgītisutta: "Therein, it is to be recited communally by all, not to be disputed about", *tattha sabbeheva saṅgāyitabbaṃ, na vivaditabbaṃ,* D III 210; and as in the Pāsādikasutta: "... the noble eightfold path. These, Cunda, are the dhammas taught by me, having understood them with direct knowledge, wherein you all, meeting together and assembling together, are to communally chant the meaning in accordance with the meaning and the letter in accordance with the letter, and are not to dispute"; ... *ariyo aṭṭhaṅgiko maggo. Ime kho te, cunda, dhammā mayā abhiññā desitā, yattha sabbeheva saṅgamma samāgamma atthena atthaṃ byañjanena byañjanaṃ saṅgāyitabbaṃ na vivaditabbaṃ,* D III 127) although it could mean that one monk recited in front of the assembly as is done at the Pātimokkha recital. In the Cullavagga's account of the second council, which it calls *vinayasaṅgīti,* there is no mention of a compiling or a recital at all. The account of the Sāṃmitīya school does mention a compilation of the Dhamma at the second council; see Skilling 2009: 56. Thus it appears that the Cullavagga's account of the two councils does not give the full picture. Although there are accounts of the first council in Vinayas of various schools translated into Chinese, they give different

The account of the first council in the Cullavagga of the Vinaya Piṭaka (Vin II 285ff.), however, does not indicate that the *aṭṭhakathā* were compiled at that council; it says that the Vinaya (the Suttavibhaṅga) and Dhamma (the Nikāyas) were compiled; see Norman 1983: 119. Nevertheless, since there are commentaries by disciples contained in suttantas, the practice of disciples explaining the meaning of the Buddha's words dates back to the lifetime of the Buddha himself. In the Madhupiṇḍikasutta, the Vedallasuttas, Mahākaccānabhaddekarattasuttas, etc., monks and nuns such as Sāriputta, Mahākaccāna, Ānanda, and Dhammadinnā give their own interpretations of the Buddha's sayings.[112] These interpretations were mostly condoned by the Buddha himself.

Although there are indications that recitation of suttantas and vinaya rules already took place during the lifetime of the Buddha,[113] according to

---

details; for example, in the account in the Mahāsaṃghika Vinaya there is no mention of questioning by Mahākassapa. It says that Ānanda was requested by the assembly to compile the Dhammapiṭaka, which he did by reciting the suttas, and then Upāli was asked to do the same for the Vinaya; see Suzuki 1904.

112. E.g. Madhupiṇḍikasutta, M I 110ff; Mahāvedallasutta, M I 291ff (not condoned by the Buddha); Cūḷavedallasutta, M I 298ff; Sevitabbāsevitabbasutta, M III 45ff; Mahākaccānabhaddekarattasutta, M III 193ff; Uddesavibhaṅgasutta, M III 223ff; Hāliddikānisutta I & II, S III 8–13 (not condoned by the Buddha); S III 35–36, 74–79; Mālukyaputtasutta, S IV 73ff.; Lokantagamanasutta, S IV 93ff; Kāmaguṇasutta, S IV 97ff; the suttas in the Cittasaṃyutta, S IV 281–304 (not condoned by the Buddha).

113. There are indications in canonical Pali works that monks and nuns were already reciting together and teaching recitation during the Buddha's lifetime; see Allon 1997: 39–40. For example in Vin I 169, it is said: "those versed in the suttantas recite together a suttanta" *suttantikehi suttantaṃ saṅgāyantehi*; cf. Vin II 75, III 159. The *suttantika* appears to the predecessor of the *bhāṇaka*; see Adikaram 1953: 25. Another corresponding term appears to be the *dhammadhara* "one who memorises the Dhamma" as in "bhikkhus who are greatly learned, to whom the tradition has been handed down, memorisers of the Dhamma, memorisers of the Vinaya, memorisers of the matrices" D II 125, M I 221: *bhikkhū ... bahussutā āgatāgamā dhammadharā vinayadharā mātikādharā*. The *bhāṇaka* in the role of teacher/preacher might also have taken on tasks of the *dhammakathika* "speaker of the Dhamma" as mentioned with the *suttantika* and *vinayadhara* at Vin I 169. The *mātikādharā* might be the equivalent of the *ābhidhammika* mentioned instead in a similar list at Nidd I 237.

A rule in the Pātimokkha (Bhikkhu Pācittiya 4, Vin IV 13–14, Bhikkhunī Pācittiya 100) that prohibits monks and nuns from making ones who have not received the full admission (*upasampadā*) recite the Dhamma line by line (*anupasampannaṃ padaso dhammaṃ vāceyya*, cf. Skt *padaśas* "step by step" or "word by word") implies that they were teaching the recitation of suttantas only to fully ordained members of the Saṅgha. The Suttavibhaṅga's commentary on *padaso* describes four methods of teaching by reciting, which likely were influenced by Brahmanical recitation teaching methods (on these Brahmanical methods see Wilke & Moebus 2011: 494). This rule is the *Samantapāsādikā* the official reciter groups started at the first council. The preservation of the Vinayapiṭaka was assigned to Upāli and his pupils and the Dīghanikāya to Ānanda and his pupils. Likewise, the other three Nikāyas were respectively assigned to Sāriputta, Mahākassapa, Anuruddha, and their pupils; see Sv 13–14, Adikaram 24, Norman 1983: 8, 1997: 44. There is no mention here that the commentaries were assigned to reciter groups.

At the first council itself, when the five hundred arahants came together after the Buddha's passing away to compile the Dhamma and Vinaya, it is likely that the primary focus was on selecting and arranging the discourses (Dhamma) and legal rulings (Vinaya) of the Buddha into collections and preserving them by assigning the recitation of the collections to arahant monks and their pupils. The Dīgha and Vinaya commentaries say that in a period of seven months the *Buddhavacana* was systematically arranged into the divisions of Dhamma and Vinaya, the first, middle, and last words of the Buddha, the three *piṭakas*, the five Nikāyas, the nine factors of the Teaching, the 84.000 sections of the Dhamma, and communally chanted by the congregation headed by Mahākassapa. Also the manifold divisions

---

reflected in another passage in the Aṅguttara Nikāya (A III 361) where it is said that a monk "makes others recite the Dhamma in detail as he has (or: they have) heard it and learnt by heart" *yathāsutaṃ yathāpariyattaṃ dhammaṃ vitthārena paresaṃ vāceti.* This is commented upon in Mp III 382 as: *Paraṃ* vācetī ti paraṃ uggaṇhāpeti*: "He makes another learn/acquire it". (* The Burmese and European editions of Mp read *paraṃ.*) The non-offence clause to Pacittiya 4 says: "No offence: when making (him) recite it together (with one who has not received the full admission), in studying it together": *Anāpatti ekato uddisāpento, ekato sajjhāyaṃ karonto.* The proposal by two bhikkhus of brahmin birth "with lovely voices", to put the Teaching of the Buddha in metre (*chanda*), i.e. metrical verse, which the Buddha rejected (see Vin II 139) also suggests that disciples tried to preserve the Buddha's teachings in ways that they were used to before they became monks and nuns.

In the Vinaya there is even an allowance for a monk to travel during the rains retreat to learn a discourse from a lay person: "Here, monks, an *upāsaka* recites a known suttanta. If he would send a messenger to the monks [who says]: 'Let the venerable sirs come to learn this suttanta before it is lost.'": *... abhiññātaṃ vā suttantaṃ bhaṇati. ... imaṃ suttantaṃ pariyāpuṇissanti, purāyaṃ suttanto na palujjatī ti*; Vin I 140–41.

As to recitation of the Vinaya: The counterpart of the *suttantika, dhammadhara* and *bhāṇaka* was the *vinayadhara*, "memoriser of the Vinaya". The Pātimokkha or Sutta was already compiled and recited during the Buddha's lifetime. Pupils would have learned to recite it in the same way as the suttantas. The explanation of Pācittiya 72, the rule prohibiting criticism of the minor rules when the Pātimokkha is being recited (unofficially, not on the Uposatha day) has: "When the Pātimokkha is being recited: when reciting it or when making (another) recite it or when studying/reciting it by himself": *Pātimokkhe uddissamāneti uddisante vā uddisāpente vā sajjhāyaṃ vā karonte*; Vin IV 143. The Sp (IV 876) explains that it means that a teacher is reciting it to a pupil or makes the pupil recite it.

of compilation seen in the Tipiṭaka such as mnemonic verses (*uddāna*), chapters, abridged repetitions (*peyyāla*), and the sections of the Nikāyas were arranged.[114] There is no mention of a compilation of the commentaries here.

There would have been no need for composing separate commentaries at the first council since the right way of interpreting the Dhamma was obvious to the arahants. Moreover, explanations of difficult passages by the Buddha's disciples were included in the compilation of texts. After the council however, the arahants would have defined and explained the meanings of difficult words and passages when teaching the texts to their pupils. They would also have told stories related to the suttas and rules. Their pupils would have passed on these definitions, explanations, and stories to their own pupils, adding some additional explanations wherever required. At later councils, when the Saṅgha had become more geographically spread out, and doctrinally divided, and there was therefore a greater need for fixing and condoning the right definitions and interpretations of the texts that the reciter teachers taught, some of these explanations were made part of the Tipiṭaka.

In the preface of the Sp, the former teachers, *pubbācariyā,* who preserved the opinions of "the sons of the Buddha" are equated to those who formerly made the commentaries. Elsewhere (Sv II 567) it is said: "The theory/ statement of the teachers is commentary", *ācariyavādo nāma aṭṭhakathā.* As will be discussed below, the teachers who explained the texts were also reciters of them. The written *aṭṭhakathā* texts therefore began as collections of the definitions, opinions, interpretations, decisions, and stories of reciter teachers. This could have happened in two ways. The first way is as recited collections of brief definitions of the meaning of words and passages made by reciter teachers; the second is as longer explanations and stories that were not recited but taught in vernacular.

With regard to the first way: Simple recitable compilations of word definitions were compiled by teachers to clarify the meaning of obscure words and phrases in verses, Pātimokkha rules, etc. Due to the limitations

---

114. Sv I 24, Sp I 29: ... *dhammavinayādivasena duvidhādibhedaṃ buddhavacanaṃ saṅgāyantena mahākassapappamukhena vasīgaṇena ayaṃ dhammo, ayaṃ vinayo, idaṃ paṭhamabuddhavacanaṃ, ... tīsu piṭakesu sandissamānaṃ saṅgahappabhedaṃ vavatthapetvā eva sattahi māsehi saṅgītaṃ.* See translation by Jayawickrama 1962: 26–27.

It is impossible that what was compiled was the definite form of the canon as we have it today, since, for example, new suttantas were added after the council, i.e. those by Ānanda after the Buddha's passing away (MN 52, 108, DN 10) and the Nāradasuttanta (A III 57ff.) at Pāṭaliputta, in which Ven. Nārada teaches King Muṇḍa, who is said to be a great grandson of King Ajātasattu; see DPPN s.v. "Muṇḍa". The allowance that a monk can travel during the rains retreat and learn a suttanta from a lay person to preserve it, see previous fn. also suggest that materials were added.

of memorisation, these commentaries were simple. The concise definitions of words and phrases (*padabhājana*) contained in the Suttavibhaṅga, and the rudimentary definitions or formulations, often incorporating lists of synonymous concepts and made in answer to brief questions about the meaning of words and phrases, as found in the Niddesa, Dhammasaṅgaṇī,[115] and the Vibhaṅga are examples of these commentaries.

Some compilations of definitions were transmitted as separate texts (i.e. Niddesa); others were incorporated into or attached to the rules and *mātikā*s that they explained (i.e. Suttavibhaṅga, Dhammasaṅgaṇī, etc.). Some of these commentaries might have originated at or were prepared at the councils themselves, as the *Ṭīkā*-s suggest, or were condoned at them. Others might not have been prepared, discussed and condoned at the councils but were transmitted by some reciter teachers. Perhaps an example of this is the old *aṭṭhakathā* that explained the meaning of words of the Jātaka verses and is mentioned in relation to variant readings in the word commentaries explaining the meaning of the words of the verses quoted in the *Jātakaṭṭhakathā*. Probably it differed little from the brief word explanations now found in the *Jātakaṭṭhakathā*. There likely were similar commentaries for the Dhammapada, etc. The same style of word commentary was also used by other early Buddhist traditions, as can be seen in the Bhikṣuṇivinaya of the Mahāsaṃghikas and Prajñāvarman's commentary on the Udānavarga. Among the birchbark manuscripts from Gandhara there is a word commentary called *nideśa* on verses that have parallels in the Theragāthā; see Salomon, 1999: 26–30.

The Suttavibhaṅga of the Vinaya Piṭaka is a commentary that contextualizes and analyses the rules of the Pātimokkha, which is called *sutta* and *mātikā* in the commentaries. It contains word commentaries (*padabhājana*) that explain and fix the meaning of words and phrases in Pātimokkha rules. Possibly, it originally formed an independent text that was recited by Pātimokkha reciters to clarify the proper meaning of the words in the rules; see Ñāṇatusita 2014: civ.

The Niddesa is the best example of an orally transmitted commentary. Thomas (1926: 298) says that "the first distinct evidence of material

115. In Dhs 233–34 the last 10 dhammas of the *suttantamātikā* are not analysed by way of the usual question and answer structure but in the manner of *padabhājana*. (... § 1373. *Tattha katamā diṭṭhivisuddhi? Kammassakatañāṇaṃ saccānulomikañāṇaṃ maggasamaṅgissa ñāṇaṃ phalasamaṅgissa ñāṇaṃ.* § 1374. *Diṭṭhivisuddhi kho panā ti yā paññā pajānanā ... pe ... amoho dhammavicayo sammādiṭṭhi. ...*) Perhaps this abrupt change is due to the author not being able to fit the particles *kho pana* in question format. In any case, it shows that the two ways of analysis are closely related. The following *Atthuddhāra* "Synopsis of the Meaning" section is called *Aṭṭhakathākaṇḍa* in the heading (which might not be original), and in the *Atthasālinī*. It is said to be a commentary made by Sāriputta that got appended to the Dhammasaṅgaṇī (As 409).

intended for definite instruction is found in the Niddesa" and divides its materials into three types: 1. commentaries similar to the ones found in the suttas and consisting of matter drawn from the suttas and often in the language of the suttas; 2. concise definitions of individual words sometimes corresponding to the definitions in the padabhājana in the Vinaya; and, 3. most characteristically, lists of synonyms of the word commented on which, in the case of important words, consist of long lists of synonyms drawn from canonical texts and are unintelligible without knowing the context they are taken from.

The Dhammasaṅgaṇi and Vibhaṅga are commentaries on the *mātikā* or "matrices" given at the start of these texts; see Anālayo 2014: 83. Likewise, the Saṃgītiparyāya—one of the treatises of the Abhidharma of the Sarvāstivādins—is a commentary on the Saṃgītisūtra, the parallel to the Saṅgītisutta.

The Paṭisambhidāmagga contains word commentaries on suttas and verses, which possibly are based on the old word commentaries on the Nikāyas.[116] At Paṭis I 172–76 there is a commentary on Theragāthā verse 548 and a part of the Ānāpānasati-sutta; and at Paṭis II 19–20 there is a commentary (called *niddesa* in the headings and conclusion) on a passage that is partly found in the Saṃyutta Nikāya. There is also a word commentary on a part of the Yuganaddha Sutta of the Aṅguttara Nikāya, which is first quoted in full, at Paṭis II 91-102, and a few other commentaries on sutta passages. Since the explanations are using the unique Paṭisambhidāmagga style of analysis of giving the different senses (*-aṭṭhena, -aṭṭho*) that a term is to be taken as (e.g. *paripuṇṇā ti pariggahaṭṭhena paripuṇṇā, parivāraṭṭhena paripuṇṇā, paripūraṭṭhena paripuṇṇā* at Paṭis I 172), they are probably not exactly the same as early word commentaries.

The *Peṭakopadesa* is also a kind of commentary, i.e. one which shows teachers and reciter-preachers how to interpret and explain texts, but in method and content it is a much more complex text than the Niddesa. Unlike the *Nettipakaraṇa*, it contains *uddāna* (see Ñāṇamoli 1962: xxvi), suggesting that it was transmitted orally at first. Perhaps, like the Parivāra (see fn. 2494), it was an early written text based on older recited materials intended to be memorised by advanced students and teachers.

With regard to the second way that the commentaries originated: Naturally, reciter teachers would also need to give longer explanations that gave extra meaning to what was recited and stories that gave context and life to it. For example, the brief, cryptic discussions in the Kathāvatthu that show the right standpoints to be taken by the Theravādins in response to wrong ideas by members of other Buddhist groups are often hard or impossible to understand without the help of the explanations found in the commentary

116. See also Ñāṇatusita 2014: xcviii.

(see von Hinüber 1996: 72, § 146, and the prefaces by Mrs. Rhys-Davids and B.C. Law to their translations of Kv and Kv-a). Therefore, the discussions would have required extensive explanations by reciter teachers to their pupils in a spoken, vernacular, non-fixed format. These vernacular explanations were passed on by reciters until they were compiled and written down in a Sīhaḷa commentary that formed the basis for the Pali commentary.

Von Hinüber observes (1996: 72, § 146) that the necessary accompaniment of the Kathāvatthu by an oral commentary is similar to how the Jātaka stories were transmitted. Since only the Jātaka verses are canonical, but must have been accompanied by the stories, it is likely that the stories were transmitted not in a fixed format but were narrated in the words of the reciter (see von Hinüber 56–57/§ 113), i.e. in vernacular. The same applies to the introductory stories accompanying the Pātimokkha rules in the Suttavibhaṅga, some of which differ in details or are completely different in the corresponding works of other schools (e.g. in the Mahāsāṃghika Bhikṣuṇivinaya) while the rules themselves are mostly the same or are very similar.[117] Cousins (1983/2005: 103) argues that the "improvisatory element" of oral performance of suttas, similar to the Homeric and Yugoslavian oral epic traditions, caused the differences in the Nikāyas of different schools. This theory has been countered by Allon (1997) who shows that canonical sutta texts were composed as fixed texts employing standardized formulas that were intended to be chanted communally, leaving no space for differences.[118] However, when it comes to the stories and narratives in the commentaries, then Cousin's theory suits better than Allon's.

---

117. On differences in the versions of the origin stories to Pārājika rule 1, see Anālayo 2012b. On the authenticity of the Pali origin stories; see Horner 1949: xxxiv: "Rhys Davids and Oldenberg [in *Vinaya Texts* I, Oxford 1881: xx–xxi] think that when the rules had been formulated and each word interpreted, some explanation was wanted as to how the rules originated. Thus they hold, stories were invented to introduce each rule. Personally, I do not think it necessary to take quite such a hard-and-fast view. For it seems to me possible that in some cases the story may be true, or may have had some historical foundation, so that the rule came to be made on account of the self-same events which, later, were recorded. In other cases, the story may quite possibly be an invention, the original reason for framing the rule and the name of the first wrong-doer involved having long been forgotten. It would now be very difficult to judge which stories may be more or less true and which may be purely fictitious."

118. To give an idea of the precision of recitation of Sri Lankan reciters: When after the Brāhmaṇatissa famine in the 1st century BCE, the sixty reciter bhikkhus who had preserved the Tipiṭaka in Sri Lanka met with the reciter bhikkhus who had returned from India, and were purifying (*sodhentā*) the Tipiṭaka with them (presumably through reciting it together) they did not see a single different letter and word; Mp I 92: *therehi saddhiṃ tepiṭakaṃ sodhentā ekakkharam-pi ekabyañjanam-pi asamentaṃ nāma na passiṃsu*; see Adikaram 1953: 77.

That stories were to be told in the teacher's or preacher's own words is shown in the *Visuddhimagga*, wherein there are brief references to stories that Buddhaghosa assumed his readers would be familiar with since only the names of the stories are given and it is not said where they can be found. Buddhaghosa says that the stories are "to be told" (*kathetabbaṃ*), presumably by a teacher to his pupils; see Rāhula 1966: xxvi. For example, at Vism I 122/p. 42 it is said that the story of the Elder Mahātissa the Mango-eater who lived at Cīragumba (*ciragumbavāsika-ambakhādaka-mahātissatthera-vatthu*) is to be told. If Dhammapāla had not given the story in his *ṭīkā* on the Vism (translated in Ñāṇamoli 2010: 40 fn. 32), we would not know what the story was. The "story of the bhikkhu who went round giving away the alms he had got at first to children of families here and there and in the end got milk and gruel", as referred to at Vism I 82/p. 30 and As 485, however, is a case of a story that cannot be traced anywhere, although it would not be difficult to make up a story based on just these details. Buddhaghosa says that the story of the boy Bhūtapāla, which he summarises, is to be told in detail (*vitthāretabbaṃ*), but it is not found anywhere else in his commentaries. It is mentioned in Mahānāma's commentary on the Paṣtisambhidāmagga(Paṭis-a III 669) where the first part is the same as the one found in the Vism but then has a few more sentences wherein further details are given, such as the reason for his name. In this section of the Vism (XII. 26–35), there are other references to stories that the reader, i.e. teacher, is supposed to be familiar with.

The non-fixed format of stories can also be seen by examining stories in the texts of other early Buddhist schools. The Sanskrit and Tibetan versions of the verse collection called Udānavarga of the (Mūla-) Sarvāstivāda school, which contains verses found also in the Dhammapada and Udāna, contain no stories or word commentaries. The stories are given in the commentary, the *Udānavargavivaraṇa* by Prajñāvarman, who sometimes briefly cites alternate origin stories of "others", some of which correspond to the ones in the *Dhammapada-aṭṭhakathā*; see Skilling 1993: 143–53. The Chinese translation of the Udānavarga (T 212), however, sometimes gives stories in addition to the word commentaries. Stories to verses that are also found in the Udāna can be quite different, or the stories are found with different verses or even in different works; see Anālayo 2009c: 40–41. Likewise, in the Chinese translation of a parallel of the Aṭṭhakavagga of the Suttanipāta (T 198) there are stories with the verses. Bapat (1951: 10) observes "... the Pali text, as it is available, has no such introduction for each chapter incorporated in the text, although it was understood that such a prose narrative was always supposed to be connected with it. It appears that different traditions connected different stories with these chapters. Hence, we find that the stories given in the Pali tradition, incorporated in the SnCm., often differ from those in the Chinese version. These stories were for a long time not written down at all, but formed only a floating mass of tradition, from which the preachers selected stories befitting a text selected by them for a particular occasion". Seven of the sixteen Chinese stories are quite different from those in the *Suttanipāta-aṭṭhakathā*, and even in the ones which are similar there are considerable variations, such as the first sūtra having the structure of the *Jātaka-aṭṭhakathā*, with a present life and past life story and a final identification of the characters by the Buddha; see Bapat 1951: 10–12, Anālayo 2014: 80–81.

With regard to the *Dhammapada-aṭṭhakathā*, von Hinüber (§ 264, p. 133) says: "In contrast to the Ja the joint between prose story and verse is often very awkward, because the contents of both do not really fit together". About 60 of the stories in the *Dhammapada-aṭṭhakathā* were probably copied from the *Jātaka-aṭṭhakathā*. However, whereas the verses and prose stories are identical, the word explanations of the verses are different than in J-a, (e.g., Dhp 125 is explained differrently at Dhp-a III 33, Spk I 49, and J-a II 203). This suggests that there was an old commentary accompanying the Dhammapada verses that contained word definitions, and possibly some short stories, since in the Sp (IV 789) it is said that the *Mahāpaccarī* says that Jātaka reciters should also learn the Dhammapada with its stories.

The *aṭṭhakathā* that Mahinda and his companion reciters are said to have brought to Sri Lanka thus could have consisted of fixed, concise definitions and explanations of words and phrases in the canonical texts, but also, or perhaps mainly, of non-fixed explanations and stories and narratives taught in vernacular spoken language by reciter teachers to their pupils who were learning the meaning of the texts that they recited. The stories gave life and context to otherwise bare rules and verses that, if taught by themselves, would bore and perplex the young monk students and, in the case of the Jātaka and Dhammapada verses, lay audiences. The explanations and narratives would have accorded with texts and doctrines that were condoned at the councils but, due to their non-fixed, vernacular nature, they were more liable to vary from teacher to teacher in details.

Before written texts were commonly used, monk teachers recited by heart the texts that they taught and commented upon; see Adikaram 1953: 25–26. From the first council onwards reciters became the authorities with regard to transmission of the Buddha's teachings and the interpretation and explanation of them. The monks who participated at later councils and the writing down of the Tipiṭaka were mostly, if not all, reciters. Several of the Sīhaḷa theras listed by Adikaram (1953: 65–87) are said to be memorizers of the whole Tipiṭaka and are also found in the lineage of teachers who handed down the Vinayapiṭaka at Vin V 3 and Sp I 62. In the *ṭīkā*-s on the Nikāyas, reciters of the collections of canonical texts (*nikāya*) are identified as former teachers (*pubbācariyā*), teachers of commentaries (*aṭṭhakathācariyā*) and ancients, *porāṇā*; see § 3 below. The reciter teachers belonged to different groups who specialized in recitation of particular collections of texts, e.g. the *majjhimabhāṇakā* or "Majjhima reciters" recited the Majjhimanikāya.[119] As mentioned above, the *Samantapāsādikā*'s account of the first council says that these different groups first appeared at this council when the preservation of Dhamma and Vinaya through recitation was assigned to Upāli, Ānanda, and other monks.

The groups were semi-independent from each other since they did not entirely harmonize the canonical texts that they had in common. For example, there are differences in the verses attributed to Vaṅgisa Thera in the Saṃyutta Nikāya and Theragātha; see Norman 1983: 9, 1997: 45. In the Mahāparinibbānasutta (D II 162), Mahākassapa's consolation to the bhikkhus comes after Subhadda's consolation, while in the Cullavagga (Vin II 284) it comes before it. Another difference is in the two versions of the Satipaṭṭhāna Sutta in the Dīgha and Majjhima Nikāya, which are identical except for the incorporation of a detailed explanation of the four noble truths in the DN. Perhaps the Dīgha reciters, wishing to make their collection more comprehensive (see von Hinüber 1996: 25/§ 49), included it since it is not found elsewhere in the DN while it is found in the Saccavibhaṅgasutta in MN. Variation in standardized formulations or stock phrases in the Nikāyas may also be due to their transmission by different reciter groups; see Allon 1997: 46–47. Differences in the Hirisutta and Hirijātaka will be discussed below.

The Pali commentaries show that the groups of reciters also had their own interpretations of the words and passages in the texts they recited. For example, the *dīghabhāṇakas* and *majjhimabhāṇakās* held different opinions on what a teacher should say to a pupil when the counterpart sign has appeared in meditation. It is likely that longer explanations and stories were passed on from reciter teachers to pupils in a non-fixed, vernacular format and therefore changed more during transmission in different groups. Each group of reciters built up its own body of interpretations and repertoire of stories, which differed somewhat from those in other groups, especially in details. Different explanations and narrations of reciter groups as found in Buddhaghosa's commentaries are discussed by Adikaram 1953: 27–29, 40–41, Norman 1983: 9 and Endo 2013: 52–54, 58–77; see also § 7 below. The differences are only attributed to groups reciting particular texts, such as the *Dīgha* reciters; no names of particular reciters are given. This suggests that the explanations predate the writing down of the *Porāṇaṭṭhakathā* and possibly came from India. Another reason for the differences in the old commentaries may be that each group of reciters had possibly written down and compiled its own commentary on the nikāya it recited so that no commentaries of other Nikāyas had to be consulted; see § 7.

---

119. On the different groups of reciters and their views; see Adikaram 1953: 26–32; Norman 1997: 41–57; Cousins 2013: 13–14; Endo 2013: 47–89.

Sāriputta, the compiler of the *ṭīkā* on the *Aṅguttaranikāya*,[120] points out several apparent contradictions or discrepancies (*virodha*) in explanations and narratives that appear in Buddhaghosa's commentaries, which are listed below in § 8. He accounts for them as being due to the different opinions or understandings (*mata*) of different (groups of) reciters, and emphasises that they should not be ascribed to the Ācariya, i.e. Buddhaghosa. Sāriputta thus equates the passages in Buddhaghosa's commentaries with the materials that the reciters transmitted. If Sāriputta is correct, the differences indicate that Buddhaghosa did not compare and harmonise all the explanations and stories in different commentaries but sometimes just translated or copied materials as they were given in his sources. Adikaram (1953: 40–41) shows some other differences in Pali commentaries.

A comparison of the Hirisutta of the Suttanipāta (Ch. 2.3, p. 45) and its parallel, the Hirijātaka (J 363) and their commentaries displays all the kinds of differences discussed above. Both the canonical Suttanipāta and Jātaka versions only give the verses without any introduction and conclusion. The Suttanipāta commentary (Sn-a I 294–99) gives a story that relates that the verses are the Buddha's reply to the question in verse of a Brahmin ascetic. In the Jātaka commentary (J-a III 195-97), the present and past stories that introduce the verses are not given. After the initial setting, the reader is referred on to the Akatuññujātaka Jātaka (J 90, J-a III 377–79)—which instead has a story about an ungrateful trader who gets his retribution—and it is said that the verse there is to be replaced by the verses given here.[121] The word explanations in the two commentaries are different too. Moreover, in the canonical verses themselves there is a different word in pada c of verse 1: Sn

120. This tentatively assumes that these observations are by Sāriputta himself, however, they might have been copied by Sāriputta from Dhammapāla's *Aṅguttaranikāya-purāṇaṭīka* of which only the first part as edited by Pecenko has been published. According to Kieffer-Pülz (2017) a comparison of the old *ṭīka* by Dhammapāla with the new one by Sāriputta shows there are additions in the latter work, but that most of these have been taken from other of Dhammapāla's commentaries so that what is ascribed to Sāriputta actually comes from Dhammapāla.

121. In several places in the Jātaka commentary* it is said that the two stories (*dvepi vatthūni*, i.e. the stories of the present and the past, *paccuppanna-* and *atīta-vatthu*) are given in full in other Jātakas, indicating that the Jātaka reciters told the same story along with different verses. In the Dhammapada commentary this happens frequently. Von Hinüber (1996: 132, § 262): "As some stories introducing Dhp verses are used repeatedly, their total number is only 299 against 423 verses." (* J-a on J 88 Sārambhajātaka, refers on to J-a on J 28, Nandivisālajātaka; J 127, Kalaṇḍukajātaka to J 125, Kaṭāhakajātaka; J 275 Rucirajātaka to J 274 Lolajātaka; and J 330, Sīlavīmaṃsajātaka I, to J 362, Sīlavīmaṃsajātaka II. J 371, Dīghītikosalajātaka refers on to the Saṅghabhedakkhandhaka, i.e. to the Dīghāvuvatthu in the Mahāvagga, Vin I 342.)

reads *sayhāni* and J *seyyāni* and the commentaries explain accordingly. Padas a & b in verse 2 are completely different; Sn has *ananvayaṃ piyaṃ vācaṃ, yo mittesu pakubbati* and J has *yañhi kayirā tañhi vade, yaṃ na kayirā na taṃ vade.*[122] Finally, the last verse, on "drinking the joy of seclusion", is also found as Dhp verse 205, and has its own story and a different word commentary in Dhp-a.

With regard to different explanations, Norman (1983: 119) observes: "The fact that the *Dīpavaṃsa* sometimes gives two or three different versions of the same event suggests that the tradition of the Mahāvihāra was based upon a mass of disjointed chronicle material, and there is no reason to doubt that the situation with regard to exegetical material was exactly the same, with comments gathered together from a number of sources. This would explain why we sometimes find commentators giving two or more, sometimes contradictory explanations of the same word or phrase." See also von Hinüber 1996: 116–117, § 232.

Opinions and discussions of named Sri Lankan theras on points of Dhamma and Vinaya are also recorded in the Pali commentaries. As far as can be gathered from Adikaram's list (1953: 80–87), these elders worked in the 1st century BCE and 1st century CE, i.e. after the Tipiṭaka and *aṭṭhakathā* had been written down during the reign of King Vaṭṭagāmini Abhaya (circa 89–76 BCE) and after there had been a fallout with the Abhayagirivihāra; see below. Several learned elders lived during the time of King Duṭṭhagāminī (circa 161–137 BCE), when the Sāsana flourished, but no opinions of them or discussions between them are mentioned; there are only anecdotes about them; see Adikaram 1953: 65–70. This absence of a mention of discussions between elders before the writing down of the Tipiṭaka and their appearance shortly afterwards along with the names of the elders involved, is significant since it suggests that during this period there was an actual shift to writing that enabled the transmission of the more complex commentarial materials that are found in Buddhaghosa's commentaries.

The typical Sri Lankan Theravāda abhidhamma ideas (see above and Intro. § 4.1) of the bhavaṅga mind, etc. as found in both the Vim and Vism as well as other Mahāvihāra commentaries, possibly arose out of or in reaction to discussions between Sri Lankan theras, and possibly also out of discussions of Sri Lankan Theravāda theras with Indian theras as well as members of other early Buddhist schools, although this likely took place before the commentaries were written down.

According to Ñāṇamoli (2010: xxxvii), the stories about India in Buddhaghosa's commentaries "in every case where a date can be assigned are not later than Asoka (3rd cent. BCE)". This suggests that no new materials

122. The verse in J is also found at J-a III 369 (J 320), J-a III 253 (J 380, wherein line b of Sn is found in the preceding verse), S I 24, and Th v. 226.

from India had been taken on and transmitted by the Sri Lankan reciter groups apart from what Mahinda and his fellow reciters had brought during the initial period of establisment of Buddhism in Sri Lanka, and that Sri Lankan reciters had become isolated from those in the mainland. As discussed in the Introduction (§ 4.5), the old commentaries that Buddhaghosa consulted appear to have been closed during or soon after the reign of King Vasabha (circa 66–110 CE) since in Buddhaghosa's works there is no mention of learned theras and their opinions after the reign of this king.

2. *Sīhaḷaṭṭhakathā*

The *ṭīkā*-s say that the commentary brought to Sri Lanka by Mahinda Thera was later put into the language of the Sīhaḷas by the great elders of Tambapaṇṇidīpa for the reason of avoiding mixing with the wrong ideas of different schools (*nikāyantaraladdhisaṅkarapariharaṇatthaṃ*).[123] Elsewhere the *ṭīkā*-s say that "at a later time the commentary was put in the Sīhaḷa language for not intermixing with the wrong ideas of different schools" and that therefore the *Mūlaṭṭhakathā* is not shared by all (people) but is exclusively for the islanders.[124] Supposedly, the "different schools" referred to are other early Buddhist schools such as the Mahāsāṃghikas. The introduction of the *Atthasālinī* translated above also refers to "the wrong ideas of different schools" (*nikāyantaraladdhi*) when the commentaries were translated back to Pali. In this case, it could refer to the Abhayagirivihāra since there had been a split with this monastery. A later part of the *Mahāvaṃsa* chronicle—the part now usually called *Cullavaṃsa*, which was composed in the 13th century—says that no commentary was available in India, but that a pure Sīhaḷa language commentary still existed among the Sinhalese; see fn. 2497.

The preface of the *Samantapāsādikā*, Buddhaghosa also says that he started on the commentary for the reason that no foreign monks could understand

---

123. Sv-ṭ II 217: *atthasaṃvaṇṇanābhūto kathāmaggo mahindattherena tambapaṇṇidīpaṃ ābhato pacchā tambapaṇṇiyehi mahātherehi sīhaḷabhāsāya ṭhapito nikāyantaraladdhisaṅkarapariharaṇatthaṃ.* Similarly Sp-ṭ I 19. Cf. Dhs-mṭ 10: *Nikāyantaraladdhīhīti antarantarā anuppavesitāhi. Asammissan-ti avokiṇṇaṃ. Anākulan-ti sanikāyepi anāvilaṃ paricchinnaṃ. Asammisso anākulo ca yo mahāvihāravāsīnaṃ atthavinicchayo, taṃ dīpayanto atthaṃ pakāsayissāmīti.* Nett-ṭ 16: ... *nikāyantaraladdhidosehi antarantarā anuppavesitehi asammissan-ti adhippāyo. Asaṃkiṇṇan-ti sanikāyepi padatthantaraparikappanādinā asaṃkiṇṇaṃ tādisasaṅkararahitaṃ anākulaṃ suparicchinnaṃ.* Abhidh-av-pṭ 137: § 1406. *Nikāyantaraladdhīhīti aññasmiṃ nikāye laddhīhi.*

124. Sv-ṭ I 20, Ps-ṭ I 16, Spk-ṭ I 16, Mp-ṭ I 19: *Aparabhāge hi nikāyantaraladdhīhi (not in Sv-ṭ & Mp-ṭ) asaṅkaratthaṃ sīhaḷabhāsāya aṭṭhakathā ṭhapitāti. Tena (Sv-ṭ: ten'assa, Mp-ṭ: tena sā) mūlaṭṭhakathā sabbasādhāraṇā na hotī ti idaṃ atthappakāsanaṃ ekantena karaṇīyan-ti dasseti. Tenevāha dīpavāsīnamatthāyā ti.*

the meaning of the Sīhaḷa language; see § 6 below. Since the commentaries brought to Sri Lanka by Mahinda and his companion monks (who were all reciters, see Vin V 3) were orally recited commentaries, they supposedly were translated to orally recited commentaries in the Sīhaḷa language, or perhaps they were translated in written form. Then, when they had been translated and written down, they gradually became complemented by more complex interpretations and authoritative decisions (*vinicchaya*) regarding the meaning of terms and points of Dhamma and Vinaya that had been passed on from reciter teachers to pupils in vernacular, but were not recited, as well as new interpretations, opinions and authoritative decisions (*vinicchaya*) that arose in reaction to new sectarian developments. Another possibility is that the explanations and stories passed on in vernacular by reciter teachers to their pupils were considered the *aṭṭhakathā* that are said to have been brought by Mahinda and later written down. Naturally, these explanations and stories were taught in Sīhaḷa vernacular to the islanders and, unlike a recited Pali text, were in no need of formal translation. Since the word commentaries discussed above contain concise and simple definitions useful for students learning Pali texts, and for teachers explaining the meaning to pupils, it seems unlikely that they were in need of recitable Sīhaḷa translations.[125]

---

125. According to von Hinüber (1996: 116/§ 231) the explanations of commonplace words by way of synonyms in the Pali commentaries—such as "minute and large" and "born", i.e. *aṇuṃ thūlan-ti khuddakaṃ vā mahantaṃ vā and uppannaṃ hotī ti jātaṃ hoti* in Sv—are "perhaps retranslations from the Sīhalaṭṭhakathā. Although these indeed are fairly common words, the aim of the commentaries is to be comprehensive and make certain that there is no room for misinterpretations of anyting that could possibly be misinterpreted. The word definitions in the Suttavibhaṅga, Dhammasaṅgaṇī, Niddesa, etc. manifest this same concern when they explain words, including commonplace ones; e.g. Vin IV 80: *Ākaṅkhamānenā ti icchamānena* and Nidd I 7: *sappo vuccati ahi*, I 131: *āsanaṃ vuccati yattha nisīdanti*, II 433: *Pacchā vuccati anāgataṃ* (see also Thomas 1926: 498). The definition of the opposites *aṇu* & *thūla* in Sv shows that in this particular context aṇu is to be interpreted as *khuddaka* "small" and not as *sukhuma* "fine, subtle" and *thūla* as *mahanta* "big" and not as "coarse", *oḷārika*, as in e.g. Paṭis-a I 351: *oḷārikānan-ti thūlānaṃ; sukhumānan-ti aṇūnaṃ*. The same explanation of the pair *aṇu* & *thūla* as *mahanta* & *khuddaka* is not unique to Sv 393: It is also found at Ps III 438, Mp III 373, Dhp-a I 282, Th-a III 11, and J-a IV 192. The explanation of *uppanna* could be an abridged version of longer ones found at Ps I 160: *Uppannanti jātaṃ nibbattaṃ* and A-a I 31: *Uppannoti jāto sañjāto nibbatto abhinibbatto pātubhūto*. These in turn are could be based on the definition in the Dhammasaṅgaṇī (p. 186), whose author found it important enough to give eight synonyms: *Ye dhammā jātā bhūtā sañjātā nibbattā abhinibbattā pātubhūtā uppannā samuppannā uṭṭhitā samuṭṭhitā uppannā*. Thus there is no compelling reason to assume that short definitions of commonplace words are from a Sīhaḷa glossary rather than a Pali one.

The commentaries that Upatissa and Buddhaghosa consulted were books written on *ola* leaves, *potthaka*. Adikaram (1953: 23), with reference to the *porāṇā*, says: "the fact that prose passages of identical form are found quoted more than once suggests strongly that the commentators drew those prose passages from a written compilation"; see also Endo 2013: 110–111, von Hinüber 1996: 101–102/§ 206, Cousins 2012: 115. The *Dīpavaṃsa* and *Mahāvaṃsa* say that the Tipiṭaka and the *aṭṭhakathā* on it were written down during the reign of King Vaṭṭagāmini Abhaya (circa 89–76 BCE),[126] but it is not said which *aṭṭhakathā* were written down, i.e. the Pali *aṭṭhakathā* said to be brought by Mahinda to Sri Lanka or the *Sīhaḷaṭṭhakathā*. Endo (2013: 13) argues that the Sinhalese commentaries were written down, since, if Pali commentaries were available to the Mahāvihāra commentators, they would have given preference to them when quoting them as support. However, since the *aṭṭhakathā* brought by Mahinda may have been simple word commentaries in Pali as well as more lengthy interpretations and stories in vernacular, it is possible that both were written down and merged in what came to be called the *Sīhaḷaṭṭhakathā*.

After the orally transmitted *aṭṭhakathā* had been written down in palm leaf books, they likely grew considerably in size, complexity, and scope because teachers and copyists could now much more easily add new, additional and lengthier explanations, opinions and decisions of theras as well as stories. Since the *aṭṭhakathā* were not regarded as the authentic *buddhavacana* or "Word of the Buddha" there were no reservations about adding new materials, reorganising, or rewriting them. Details in narratives might have been elaborated or amplified; see Adikaram 1953: 35. New works, such as the lost *Mahāpaccarī* and *Kurundī* vinaya commentaries referred to in the Sp as *Sīhaḷa-aṭṭhakathā*, were also considered part of the commentary collection. The observation made by the Greek scholar West (1973: 16) with regard to adaptations in Greek and Latin commentaries can also be applied to Indic commentaries: "Commentaries ... were rightly regarded as collections of material to be pruned, adapted or added to, rather than sacrosanct literal entities."

Cousins (2012: 114) suggests that commentaries probably were produced in many locations in India by the early Buddhist schools and adds: "Eventually, one or more large compilations of this material were made and became authoritative. For the Mahāvihāra this was the *Mahā-aṭṭhakathā*". He draws a pertinent parallel to the *Mahāvibhāṣā* compendia of the Sarvāstivādins. The *vibhāṣā* commentaries on Sarvāstivāda Abhidharma texts are described

126. Dīp xx.20, Mhv xxxiii.103: *Piṭakattayapāḷiñca, tassa aṭṭhakatham-pi ca; Mukhapāṭhena ānesuṃ, pubbe bhikkhū mahāmati. 103. Hāniṃ disvāna sattānaṃ, tadā bhikkhū samāgatā; Ciraṭṭhitatthaṃ dhammassa, potthakesu likhāpayuṃ.*

by Cox (1998: 229–31) as repositories for a "wide range of views, often with explicit attribution to specific figures or schools, on any given doctrinal point, ... possible interpretative positions, arguments and scriptural citations" of various Sarvāstivāda groups and "were compiled in a period of sectarian self-consciousness and intense inter-sectarian debate, as well tremendous growth in both doctrinal interpretation and techniques of argument"; see also Potter 1996: 110ff. These observations can also be applied to the Theravāda *aṭṭhakathā*, and that is why, after the introduction of writing, each Theravāda monastic group in Sri Lanka and South India likely had its own open-ended written *aṭṭhakathā* compilation, to which it could add new materials and works to and could adapt in reaction to new ideological and interpretative developments. Thus, the original core of the *Sīhaḷaṭṭhakathā* compilation would have been the simple oral style Pali *aṭṭhakathā* and vernacular explanations and stories that Indian reciters brought to Sri Lanka. After the compilation and writing down of these various new materials were gradually incorporated, such as the opinions of important Sri Lankan teachers and materials adapted from commentarial texts of other monastic groups and schools. The reason why the South Indian commentator Ācariya Dhammapāla does not refer to the *Sīhaḷaṭṭhakathā* could be because compilations were particular to each monastic group; on the absence the word *sīhaḷa* in the works of Dhammapāla; see Kieffer-Pülz 2013b: 10–11.

The chronicles place the writing down of the Tipiṭaka and commentaries after the founding (Mhv) and enlargement (Dīp) of the Abhayagirivihāra during the reign of King Vaṭṭagāmini Abhaya (circa 89–76 BCE), when, according to the Mhv, there had been a fallout with the Abhayagirivihāra (see Adikaram 1953: 79, Cousins 2013: 18–19). Perhaps the *Sīhaḷaṭṭhakathā,* i.e. its main part called *Mahā-aṭṭhakathā*, was regarded as a work unique to the Mahāvihāra, especially after new explanations and opinions of Mahāvihāra elders were incorporated. The Abhayagirivihāra would have had the same or very similar commentarial texts until the split, but then likewise could have added the opinions of its own teachers, etc.

Sīhaḷaṭṭhakathā can mean both "commentary of the Sinhalese"—in the same way as *Andhakaṭṭhakathā* means "commentary of the Andhakas"—as well as "Sīhaḷa [language] commentary".[127] Therefore, the term *Sīhaḷaṭṭhakathā* does not necessarily mean that it was exclusively in the *Sīhaḷabhāsā*, the language of the Sīhaḷa people. It could also have encompassed works or

127. The *Andhakaṭṭhakathā* were quoted in Vinaya *ṭīkā*-s until the 10th or 11th century; see Kieffer-Pülz 2013a: 30. The *Sīhaḷaṭṭhakathā*, or more commonly specific texts considered as *Sīhaḷaṭṭhakathā*, were quoted to perhaps up to the 10–12th century; see von Hinüber 1996: 104, § 110 & 133 fn. 464; Kieffer-Pülz 2013b: 192; Hettiaratchi 1950: 70–71

sections that were partly or completely in Pali. The prefaces and colophons of Buddhaghosa's commentaries indicate that the most important and central work of the *Sīhaḷaṭṭhakathā* was called *Mahā-aṭṭhakathā*,[128] and perhaps the *Sīhaḷaṭṭhakathā* was sometimes taken as being synonymous with it (see Cousins 2012: 115), but other works apparently were included too, since the colophon of the *Samantapāsādikā* (see § 4) also includes the *Mahāpaccarī* and *Kurundī* in the *Sīhaḷaṭṭhakathā*.

The word *Sīhaḷaṭṭhakathā* is rare. Apart from the above occurrence in Sp, the only time that it is used elsewhere in the Pali commentaries is in the colophon of the *Kaṅkhāvitaraṇī*, where it is equated to the *Porāṇaṭṭhakathā*,

128. Endo (2013: 32 fn. 35, 33–45) suggests that the *aṭṭhakathā* referred to in the commentaries were written down along with the Tipiṭaka in the 1st century B.C., while the *mahā-aṭṭhakathā* were a newer genre of works containing later additions. However, the grounds for this suggestion are untenable, since the only passage that he refers to (Sp 299–300 at Endo 2013: 36) as proof for the distinction between the *Mahā-aṭṭhakathā* and the *aṭṭhakathā* does not actually distinguish them. The passage is on the proper definition of the village boundary (*gāmasīma*). After quoting the interpretation of the *Kurundī* and *Mahāpaccariya*, and the one of the *Mahā-aṭṭhakathā*, Buddhaghosa points out an apparent difference in interpretation between the Vinaya text (*Pāḷi*) and the *Mahā-aṭṭhakathā*, but then endorses the interpretation of the *Mahā-aṭṭhakathā*: "... (Objection:) But that which is said in the *Mahā-aṭṭhakathā* seems to be at odds with the Canonical Text (*pāḷi*). For in the Canonical Text just this much is said: 'the throwing of a clod by an average man standing in the surrounding of the house'. In the *Aṭṭhakathā* (= *Mahā-aṭṭhakathā*), however, the throwing of the clod is reckoned as the village, and a further [throwing of a clod] from there is taught as the surrounding of the village. (Reply:) [To this] it is said [by us]: True indeed, [this] is what is said in the Canonical Text, but the intent is to be understood herein. And this [intent] was understood by the commentary teachers. Therefore, even though the characteristic of the surrounding of the house has not been stated in the Canonical Text herein [i.e. in connection with the phrase] 'of one who is standing in the surrounding of the house', it has been accepted [by us] on account of [what] has been said in the Aṭṭhakathā (= *Mahā-aṭṭhakathā*). Just so the rest [of the explanation] is to be accepted too." Sp 300: *Yañcetaṃ mahāaṭṭhakathāyaṃ vuttaṃ, taṃ pāḷiyā viruddhamiva dissati. Pāḷiyañ-hi gharūpacāre ṭhitassa majjhimassa purisassa leḍḍupāto ti ettakam-eva vuttaṃ. Aṭṭhakathāyaṃ pana taṃ leḍḍupātaṃ gāmasaṅkhepaṃ katvā tato paraṃ gāmūpacāro vutto ti? Vuccate: saccam-eva pāḷiyaṃ vuttaṃ, adhippāyo panettha veditabbo. So ca aṭṭhakathācariyānam-eva vidito. Tasmā yathā gharūpacāre ṭhitassā ti ettha gharūpacāralakkhaṇaṃ pāḷiyaṃ avuttam-pi aṭṭhakathāyaṃ vuttavasena gahitaṃ. Evaṃ sesam-pi gahetabbaṃ.* For a German translation of this passage, see von Hinüber (2009: 239–40; see also Kieffer-Pülz 2013b: 452). Also, the "*Sīhaḷa-Vinaya-aṭṭhakathā*" that Endo (2013: 35) describes as the same *aṭṭhakathā* that is older than the *Mahā-aṭṭhakathā*, as the primary source material for Sp, and as not mentioned in the Sp introduction, is not found in the references given. Only the *Vinayaṭṭhakathā* is mentioned and the passages quoted from it are all found in the Sp.

and in the commentary on the Abhidhammapiṭaka.[129] Buddhaghosa does not refer to the *Sīhaḷaṭṭhakathā* at all in his *Visuddhimagga* and in the Nikāya commentaries. It is found about two dozen times in the *ṭīkā*-s, mostly in the ones on the Vinaya, once in the *Mahāvaṃsa*, and a number of the times in the *Mahāvaṃsaṭīkā*. References to the *Mahā-aṭṭhakathā* are much more common in the commentaries and *ṭīkās*. In the *Visuddhimagga* and the Nikāya commentaries Buddhaghosa refers to and quotes from specific older commentaries such as the *Dīghanikāyaṭṭhakathā, Majjhimanikāyaṭṭhakathā, Saṃyuttanikāyaṭṭhakathā, Aṅguttaranikāyaṭṭhakathā, Dukanipātaṭṭhakathā* (the commentary on the second book of the *Aṅguttaranikāyaaṭṭhakathā*), as well the collections *Vinayaṭṭhakathā, Suttantaṭṭhakathā*, and *Abhidhammaṭṭhakathā*. He also refers to unspecified commentaries as in *aṭṭhakathāyaṃ* "in the commentary" and the commentaries as a whole as in *aṭṭhakathāsu* "in the commentaries".

The chronicle that was the predecessor of the *Mahāvaṃsa* is called *Sīhaḷaṭṭhakathā-mahāvaṃsa* in the *Mahāvaṃsaṭīkā*. It is said to have been a Sīhaḷa language text; see Malalasekera 1935: lvi–lvii. Malalasekera (1935: lvi–lxi) observes that the old *Mahāvaṃsa* probably served as the introduction to the *Mahā-aṭṭhakathā*, but, due to the regular incorporation of new extraneous materials, developed into an independent Mahāvihāra chronicle, which in its final form must have been very large and comprehensive. This incorporation of materials also happened in the *Dīpavaṃsa*, which sometimes contains two different accounts of the same event. Mahānāma, in the preface to the *Mahāvaṃsa* (v. 2, see below § 5 end), says that the old *Mahāvaṃsa* as was overly long in some places, too concise in others, and contained many repetitions, and that he instead made a work free from those blemishes, which was therefore easier to learn and remember.

The same issues probably applied to the *Sīhaḷaṭṭhakathā* as a whole. As with the Sarvāstivāda *Mahāvibhāṣā*, it had become a large, unwieldy repository of different opinions, discussions, stories, etc. that sometimes were conflicting with each other, or were hard to understand. The *Sīhaḷaṭṭhakathā* therefore was in need of revision. An example of this is found in the *Samantapāsādikā*, where Buddhaghosa says about the various commentaries on the five modes of stealing that: "With regard to this point, all commentaries are confused, wavering and having authoritative decisions that are hard to understand": *Imasmiñca ṭhāne sabbaaṭṭhakathā ākulā luḷitā duviññeyyavinicchayā* (Sp II 303), and then gives a clear explanation instead.

129. Kkh 208: *sīhaḷaṭṭhakathānayaṃ; mahāvihāravāsīnaṃ, vācanāmagganissitaṃ* .... Yam-a 83: *Yaṃ pana vibhaṅgappakaraṇassa sīhaḷaṭṭhakathāyaṃ cittasamuṭṭhānaṃ rūpaṃ sattarasamassa cittassa uppādakkhaṇe nirujjhatī ti vuttaṃ, taṃ imāya pāḷiyā virujjhati.*

3. *Porāṇā*

The terms *pubbācariyā* "former teachers", *porāṇācariyā* "ancient teachers" and *porāṇā* "ancients" can refer to the same source, and be identical with the *aṭṭhakathācariyā* "teachers of the commentaries", and *porāṇaṭṭhakathākārā* "makers of the commentaries", i.e. the teachers who composed the *Porāṇaṭṭhakathā*, the "commentaries of the ancients" or "ancient commentary", which Buddhaghosa and other commentators refer to; see Adikaram (1953: 16–22) and Kieffer-Pülz (2014: 68–69; cf. 2013b 159–160). Oldenberg (1879: 2–3) says that in the *Mahāvaṃsa-ṭīkā*, the *porāṇā*, *porāṇaṭṭhakathā*, *aṭṭhakathā*, and *sīhaḷaṭṭhakathā* are identical; so Geiger (1908: 45–47 § 13). Jayawickrama (1962: 95 fn. 1), with reference to the preface of the *Samantapāsādikā*, says that the *porāṇā*, *sīhaḷaṭṭhakathā*, and the *theravāda*, "are evidently to be included among the *pubbācariyā*". In the *Abhidharmakośabhāṣya*, the term *pūrvācāryā* or "former teachers" is used to refer to ideas of former teachers, several of whom can be traced in earlier texts; see Yamabe 2013: 602–606.

The following passages suggest that post-Buddhaghosa authors equated the *porāṇā*, *pubbācariyā*, *aṭṭhakathācariyā*, *aṭṭhakathākārā*, and *bhāṇakā*: "Indeed, today the authoritative decision of the former teachers is still not interrupted;[130] ... therefore I wish to make a commentary on the meaning; depending on just the Teaching and on the authoritative decision of the ancients": *Ajjā pi tu abbocchinno, pubbācariyanicchayo; .... Tasmāhaṃ kātumicchāmi, atthasaṃvaṇṇanaṃ imaṃ; Sāsanañ-ceva nissāya, porāṇañ-ca vinicchayaṃ*; Khp-a 1. "Having taken what is to be taken, the authoritative decision in the [commentaries of] the ancients, ... compiling [it] in accordance with the style of the commentary with the instructions of the former [teachers]"; *gahetabbaṃ gahetvāna, porāṇesu vinicchayaṃ. ... Pubbopadesaṭṭhakathānayañ-ca, yathānurūpaṃ upasaṃharanto;* Nidd-a 1. "The ancients are the commentary teachers; and, [some] say, the ancients are the Majjhima reciters'"; *Porāṇānan-ti aṭṭhakathācariyānaṃ; purātanānaṃ majjhimabhāṇakānan-ti ca vadanti*; Ps-ṭ I 164. "Some [say that] 'these theras', are the Majjhima reciters; but others say that they are 'the commentary teachers', 'the Dīgha reciters'"; *Ime pana therā ti majjhimabhāṇakāti keci; apare pana aṭṭhakathācariyā ti, dīghabhāṇakā ti vadanti*; Sv-ṭ II 104. "The ancient theras are the commentary teachers"; *Porāṇakattherāti aṭṭhakathācariyā*; Sv-ṭ III 134. "The former teachers are the great elders in Tambapaṇṇi who were the makers of the ancient commentaries"; *Pubbācariyā porāṇaṭṭhakathākārā tambapaṇṇiyā mahātherā*; Kkh-pṭ 121. "The ancients are the makers of the Sīhaḷa commentaries in the Island of the Sīhaḷas"; *Porāṇā ti sīhaḷadīpe sīhaḷaṭṭhakathākārakā*; Vmv I 32. "The teachers using the Aṅguttaramahānikāya: the teachers who preserve the Aṅguttaranikāya; i.e. the Aṅguttara reciters"; *Aṅguttaramahānikāyavaḷañjanakaācariyā ti aṅguttaranikāyaṃ pariharantā ācariyā*

130. Cf. Vism XVII.25/p.523, As 130.

aṅguttarabhāṇakā ti vuttaṃ hoti; Mp-ṭ II 186. "The majestic power of the former teachers is the commentary since they formerly made the commentary ...": *Pubbācariyānubhāvan-ti aṭṭhakathā, yasmā pure aṭṭhakathā akaṃsū ti* ...; Vjb-ṭ 16. "The majestic power of the former teachers is the commentary from the perspective of meaning explained by the former teachers, ... Mahākassapa Thera etc. are the very former teachers"; *Pubbācariyānubhāvo nāma atthato pubbācariyehi saṃvaṇṇitā aṭṭhakathā, ... Mahākassapattherādayo pubbācariyā eva* ...; Sp-ṭ 16. "Here the Teaching is the Dhamma of the canonical texts, ... And what is considered the commentary on that is the way of the former teachers"; *Idha sāsanan-ti pāḷidhammamāha, ... Tadaṭṭhakathāsaṅkhāto ca pubbācariyamaggo*; Vism-mhṭ II 242.

A verse attributed to the *porāṇā* at As 84 is attributed to *aṭṭhakathācariyā* at Sv-ṭ III 239. A verse in the *Milindapañhā* (p. 369) that is attributed to the *dhammasaṅgahaka*, the "Dhamma compilers", i.e. the theras who compiled the Suttas at the councils (see Ud-a I 1, 435, It-a II 193, Sv I 7), is instead attributed to the *porāṇā* in the *Visuddhimagga* (I 270) and other commentaries of Buddhaghosa; see Adikaram 1953: 21. Vajirabuddhi (Vjb-ṭ 126) says that the *porāṇā* to which a verse is attributed in Sp are the "council teachers", *porāṇāti saṅgītiācariyā*. Sāriputta (Pāḷim-pṭ I 387, similarly Sp-ṭ III 11) says with reference to the commentaries on the Dhammapada and Jātaka, that these are the *Porāṇaṭṭhakathā* that were fixed at the three councils: ... *Aṭṭhakathanti iminā saṅgītittayāruḷhaṃ porāṇaṭṭhakathaṃ gahetabbaṃ.*

However, the term *porāṇā* can also be used in a more general way. Malalasekera (1928: 92 fn. 1): "... *Porāṇās* merely refer to teachers whose expositions were not necessarily embodied in the Commentaries, but handed down in various schools by oral tradition, sometimes with mnemonic verses to help the memory and that Buddhaghosa, refers to such traditional explanations as the anonymous *Porāṇā*. ...".. See also Malalasekera 1935: lxiv–lxv. Kieffer-Pülz (2013b: 160–161) says that in the *Vajirabuddhi-ṭīkā* the term *porāṇā* can simply refer to older sources, in particular to the old *gaṇṭhipada,* since word definitions are mostly attributed to them in this *ṭīkā*. In two instances,[131] the *porāṇā* refers to the authors of the *porāṇagaṇṭhipada*.

131. At Vjb 125 it is said that the definition of the *porāṇā* fits with the *padabhājana* definition (as found in the Vinaya): ... *Theyyan-ti saṅkhātan-ti theyyasaṅkhātan-ti porāṇagaṇṭhipade vuttaṃ. Taṃ theyyaṃ yassa thenassa kammaṃ, so yasmā theyyacitto avaharaṇacitto hoti, tasmā theyyasaṅkhātan-ti padaṃ uddharitvā theyyacitto avaharaṇacitto ti padabhājanam-pi* (= Vin III 46) *tesaṃ porāṇānaṃ yujjateva, tathā pi aṭṭhakathāyaṃ vuttanayeneva gahetabbaṃ.* Vjb 386: ... *hatthapāsassa avijahitattā ti porāṇagaṇṭhipade vuttaṃ. Tesaṃ porāṇānaṃ matena chandapārivāsiyamevekaṃ na vaṭṭatī ti āpannaṅgañ-ca dassitaṃ.*

4. *Aṭṭhakathā* in other Theravāda traditions

Aṭṭhakathā were not confined to the Mahāvihāra tradition. Buddhaghosa and other Mahāvihāra commentators refer to *aṭṭhakathā* of other Theravāda traditions in Sri Lanka (the Uttaravihāra or Abhayagirivihāra and the Dakkhiṇagirivihāra) and Southeast India (Andhakaraṭṭha).

The Abhayagirivihāravāsins or Uttaravihāra Abhayagirivihāravāsins (i.e. Abhayagirivihāravāsins living in the main Uttaravihāra or Abhayagirivihāra monastery, referred to as Abhayuttara in the *Mahāvaṃsa*) and Dakkhiṇagirivihāravāsins (a sub-sect of the Abhayagirivihāravāsins) each had a commentary on the four main Nikāyas. The commentary of the former was called *Uttaravihāra-aṭṭhakathā* and the one of the latter *Sārasamāsa*; see Sodō Mori 1988: 43–44. Variant readings quoted in Mahāvihāra commentaries suggest that the canonical texts of these other schools were in Pali.[132] Likewise, quotations from their commentarial works[133] suggest that these were in Pali, too. There is no mention in Mahāvihāra works that the commentaries of other schools were in the *Sīhaḷabhāsā*.

It is not exactly known to which degree the commentaries of other Sinhalese schools shared the same materials as the commentaries transmitted by the Mahāvihāra. Likely, they contained mostly the same or similar materials. According to Geiger (1908: 50 § 14), the quotations in the *Mahāvaṃsa-ṭīkā* indicate that the contents of the *Uttaravihāra-aṭṭhakathā* "may have differed from the tradition of the Mahāvihāra monks more in detail than general construction" and (1908: 51 § 14) that "We can rightly suppose that the tradition of the Uttaravihāra transmitted the same material as the Mahāvihāra with approximately the same grouping"; see also Malalasekera 1935: lxvi–lxvii.

The Abhayagirivihāra was probably founded during the reign of King Abhaya Duṭṭhagāminī (circa 161–137 BCE), at least a century after the

---

132. E.g. Sp IV 880: *Sammattan-ti keci paṭhanti, taṃ na gahetabbaṃ.* Ps I 118: *Elamukhātipi pāṭho. Elamugā ti keci paṭhanti, apare elamukātipi, sabbattha elamukhā ti attho.* Sn-a II 416: *Ito paraṃ ye kāme hitvā agahā caranti, susaññatattā tasaraṃva ujjun-ti imam-pi gāthaṃ keci paṭhanti.*

133. E.g. A-a III 272: *Apare pana gaddohanamattan-ti pāḷiṁ vatvā gāviyā ekavāraṁ thana-añchanamattan-ti atthaṁ vadanti.* Ud-a 162: *yaṃ so pubbe agāriyabhūto samāno ti pāḷiṃ vatvā, anubhavī ti vacanasesena keci atthaṃ vaṇṇenti.* Thī-a 226: *Keci kāliṅginin-ti pāṭhaṃ vatvā tassa kumbhaṇḍalatāsadisan-ti atthaṃ vadanti. Aññe pana ...* Th-a I 137: *Apare āsandikuṭikan-ti pāṭhaṃ vatvā āsandippamāṇaṃ kuṭikaṃ katvā ti atthaṃ vadanti.* Vv-a 161: *Keci anojakā pi santī ti pāṭhaṃ vatvā anojakā pī ti vuttaṃ hotī ti atthaṃ vadanti.* Pv-a 14: *Keci pana vihāyasaṃ tiṭṭhasi antalikkhe ti pāṭhaṃ vatvā vihāyasaṃ obhāsento antalikkhe tiṭṭhasī ti vacanasesena atthaṃ vadanti.* Spk-ṭ I 147: *Keci kammante susamāhitā ti pāṭhaṃ vatvā maggasamāhitā ti atthaṃ vadanti.* Spk-ṭ II 424: *Pubbabhāgāvā ti ettha keci pubbabhāgā cā ti pāṭhaṃ katvā pubbeva lokuttarā pubbabhāgā cā ti atthaṃ vadanti.*

Mahāvihāra was founded (see Cousins 2012: 72–76), as a branch monastery of the Mahāvihāra, and for hundreds of years the two monasteries co-existed in close proximity. If the account in the *Mahāvaṃsa* (33: 95–98)—which is not found in the earlier *Dīpavaṃsa*—is correct, there was already very early on a falling out between the two monasteries. Nevertheless, it is likely that they originally shared the same general pre-sectarian Sinhala Theravāda textual tradition that was transmitted by the reciters, including the old commentaries that Mahinda is said to have brought to Sri Lanka.

Buddhaghosa also consulted commentaries from South India: The "Commentary of the Andhakas", *Andhakaṭṭhakathā,* a non-Mahāvihāra commentary on the Vinaya, is quoted and criticized in the *Samantapāsādikā. Andhaka* refers to the people/monks of the Andhaka Country, *Andhakaraṭṭha,* now called Andhra Pradesh in South India. Presumably, the commentary originated there in a Theravāda tradition different from the Mahāvihāra tradition; see Kieffer-Pülz 2010: 147, 2013a: 30.[134] Moreover, the terminology used in the quotations from the *Andhakaṭṭhakathā* is different from the one used in the *Samantapāsādikā*, suggesting that the *Andhakaṭṭhakathā* was composed in Pali; see Kieffer-Pülz 2010: 147; cf. 2013a: 30.

5. The sources of the *Visuddhimagga* and other commentaries of Buddhaghosa

Buddhaghosa had access to the commentaries of other Sinhalese and South Indian schools, so he very likely also had access to the *Vimuttimagga* and used it for his *Visuddhimagga*. In the preface and colophon of the *Visuddhimagga,* he unfortunately gives no information on the exact sources that were used and whether they were in Pali and/or Sīhaḷa; see Pind 1992: 40–41. Since he does give his sources in the preface and colophon of the *Samantapāsādikā*, perhaps this omission was done deliberately, to make the *Visuddhimagga* appear to be an original work that was unique to the Mahāvihāra.

The *Visuddhimagga*'s colophon says that it was made by "collating (*samāharitvā*) almost all of the authoritative decisions [of the Mahāvihāra elders] on the meaning of terms such as virtue in the five Nikāyas in the style of the commentaries, and proclaimed as free from all blemishes due to intermixing".[135] In other words, the colophon says that the *Visuddhimagga* is a

134. The non-Mahāvihāra origin of the *Andhakaṭṭhakathā* is also suggested by there being no quotations from it in the commentary on the Parivāra; see von Hinüber 1996: 105, § 211. Although parts of the Parivāra might be of Indian origins, in its final form it likely was exclusive to the Mahāvihāra tradition; see Norman 1983: 26–29, von Hinüber 1996: 21–23, § 40–45.

135. *Tesaṃ sīlādibhedānaṃ atthānaṃ yo vinicchayo pañcannam-pi nikāyānaṃ vutto aṭṭhakathānaye samāharitvā taṃ sabbaṃ yebhuyyena sanicchayo; sabbasaṅkaradosehi*

compilation of authoritative decisions according to the style or method (*naya*) of commentaries. Given the structure and content of the *Visuddhimagga*, this likely means that the *Visuddhimagga* is a selection of materials from the *Vimuttimagga*—which is clearly its main inspiration and source (see Introduction § 1)—as well as other older exegetical works such as the *Sīhaḷaṭṭhakathā*.[136] The selected materials were often restructured, rewritten, and adapted to fit the opinions and ideas of the Mahāvihāra elders. The 13th century *Cullavaṃsa* reports that Buddhaghosa, after arriving in Sri Lanka, first made the *Visuddhimagga* by compiling the Tipiṭaka and *aṭṭhakathā* in an abridged manner (*saṅgahetvā samāsato*) and that, when it was approved by the Mahāvihāra elders, he translated all the *Sīhaḷaṭṭhakathā* into Pali.[137] On the meaning of doctrinal "intermixing" (*saṅkara*), see below.

---

mutto yasmā pakāsito. Cf. Vism-mhṭ II 534: *Tatthā ti ādīsu ayaṃ padasambandhena saddhiṃ saṅkhepattho tesaṃ sīle patiṭṭhāyā ti gāthāyaṃ vuttānaṃ sīlādippabhedānaṃ atthānaṃ pañcannam-pi mahānikāyānaṃ aṭṭhakathānaye aṭṭhakathātantiyaṃ tattha tattha vutto yo vinicchayo, yebhuyyena taṃ sabbaṃ samāharitvā samānetvā nikāyantarassa nikāyagatavādadosasaṅkarehi mutto so nicchayo yasmā pakāsito, ...*

136. For the reuse of text from other sources by Buddhaghosa and other commentators; see Introduction § 4.8.

137. "Here only the text has been preserved; there is no commentary here, and likewise no Teachers' Doctrine; for that has been allowed to go to pieces and is no longer known. However, a pure Sinhalese commentary still exists among the Sinhalese. It alone was rendered into the Sinhalese tongue by the learned Mahinda with proper regard for the way of commenting that was handed down by the three Councils as taught by the Enlightened One and inculcated by Sāriputta and others. ... ... Having gone to the Mahāpadhānaghara, from Saṅghapāla [he learnt about] the pure Sinhalese Commentary and the whole of the Elders' Doctrine (Theravāda) and decided, 'This alone is the intention of the Master of the Dhamma'. So he assembled the Community there and said, 'Give me all the books to make commentaries'. Then in order to test him the Community gave him two stanzas, saying 'Show your ability with these; when we have seen that you have it, we will give you all the books'. Just with these [two verses] he made [the compendium] named 'Path to Purification' (*Visuddhimagga*) by compiling in an abridged manner the Three Piṭakas together with the commentary. ... Then, he translated all the Sinhalese Commentaries into the words of Magadha, the root-language of all [beings]". (Adapted from Ñāṇamoli, PoP p. xxxix). Mhv xxxvii.227: *Pāḷimattaidhānitaṃ, natthi aṭṭhakathā idha; Tathācariyavādā ca, bhinnarūpā na vijjare.* 228. *Sīhaḷāṭṭhakathā suddhā, mahindena matīmatā; Saṃgītittayamāruḷaṃ, sammāsambuddhadesitaṃ.* 229. *Sāriputtādigītañ-ca, kathāmaggaṃ samekkhiya; Ekā sīhaḷabhāsāya, sīhaḷesu pavattati. ...* 232: *Mahāvihāraṃ sampatto, vihāraṃ sabbasādhūnaṃ; Mahāpadhānagharaṃ gantvā, saṅghapālassa santikā.* 233. *Sīhaḷaṭṭhakathā suddhā, theravādañ-ca sabbaso; Dhammasāmissa esova, adhippāyo ti nicchiya.* 234. *Tattha saṅghaṃ samānetvā, kātumaṭṭhakathāmama; Potthake detha sabbe ti āha, vīmaṃsituṃ sataṃ.* 235. *Saṅgho gāthādvayaṃ tassādāsi sāmatthiyaṃ tava; Ettha dassehi taṃ disvā, sabbe demā ti potthake.* 236. *Piṭakattayamettheva, saddhimaṭṭhakathāya so; Visuddhimagga-*

Only in the preface and colophon of the *Samantapāsādikā* the names of the texts used for this commentary are given: the *Mahā-aṭṭhakathā*, the *Mahāpaccarī*, and *Kurundī*, which in the colophon are said to be *Sīhalaṭṭhakathā*;[138] see von Hinüber 1996: 104, § 210. The preface adds "and so on", *ādi*, after *Kurundī*, which the Sp-ṭ and Vmv-ṭ explain as the *Andhakaṭṭhakathā* and *Saṅkhepaṭṭhakathā* that are also quoted in the Sp; see Kieffer-Pülz 1993: 171.

The prefaces of Buddhaghosa's Nikāya commentaries say that they are founded on the *Visuddhimagga*, i.e. in the sense that the *Visuddhimagga* is to be used as a companion volume, and that they frequently refer back to it for further explanations;[139] see von Hinüber 1996: 112, § 226. The prefaces also state that these commentaries are translations from the *sīhaḷa* language *aṭṭhakathā* but no specific names of texts are given. The colophons, however, do specify them as *Mahā-aṭṭhakathā* and *Mūlaṭṭhakathā*. It is said in the colophons that the essence or gist of the *Mahā-aṭṭhakathā* was taken to compose the commentaries and then another verse states that the gist of the *Mūlaṭṭhakathā* was taken.[140] Although these probably refer to the same text, Pind (1992: 139) observes that Dhammapāla, the author of the *Dīgha-nikāya-ṭīkā*, gives two explanations of *Mūlaṭṭhakathā*. First (and finally too) Dhammapāla identifies it with the *Mahā-aṭṭhakathā*, but then gives the alternative explanation *porāṇaṭṭhakathā*.[141] Pind suggests that this implies that Dhammapāla was uncertain about the identity of the *Mūlaṭṭhakathā* and took the *Porāṇaṭṭhakathā* to be different texts than the *Mahā-aṭṭhakathā*, which is a *Sīhaḷaṭṭhakathā* according to the colophon of Sp. However, the colophon

---

nāmākā, saṅgahetvā samāsato. ... 244. Parivattesi sabbāpi, sīhaḷaṭṭhakathā tadā; Sabbesaṃ mūlabhāsāya, māgadhāya niruttiyā.

138. Sp I 2: ... *Mahāvihārassa dhajūpamehi; Saṃvaṇṇitoyaṃ vinayo nayehi; ... Tassā mahāaṭṭhakathaṃ sarīraṃ; Katvā mahāpaccariyaṃ tatheva; Kurundināmādisu vissutāsu.* Sp VII 1414: *Mahāaṭṭhakathañ-ceva, mahāpaccarim-eva ca; Kurundiñ-cā ti tisso pi, sīhaḷaṭṭhakathā imā.*

139. Sv I 1: *Majjhe visuddhimaggo, esa catunnam-pi āgamānañ-hi; Ṭhatvā pakāsayissati, tattha yathā bhāsitaṃ atthaṃ.* For a translation, see Adikaram 1953: 2. Sv-ṭ I 22: *Tattha majjhe ṭhatvā ti etena majjhebhāvadīpanena visesato catunnaṃ āgamānaṃ sādhāraṇaṭṭhakathā visuddhimaggo, na sumaṅgalavilāsinīādayo viya asādhāraṇaṭṭhakathā ti dasseti. Visesato ti idaṃ vinayābhidhammānam-pi visuddhimaggo yathārahaṃ atthavaṇṇanā hoti yevā ti katvā vuttaṃ.*

140. Sv VII 1414: ... *Sā hi mahāṭṭhakathāya, sāramādāya niṭṭhitā; ... Mūlaṭṭhakathāsāra, mādāya mayā imaṃ karontena; ...*

141. Sv-ṭ III 371: *Mūlakaṭṭhakathāsāran-ti pubbe vuttaṃ dīghanikāyamahāaṭṭhakathāsāram-eva puna nigamanavasena vadati. Atha vā mūlakaṭṭhakathāsāran-ti porāṇaṭṭhakathāsu atthasāraṃ.* Parallels to this explanation are found in the *ṭīkā*-s on the Aṅguttara Nikāya and Saṃyutta Nikāya.

of the *Kaṅkhāvitaraṇī* equates the *Sīhaḷaṭṭhakathā* and *Porāṇaṭṭhakathā* so they were probably the same works.[142]

Pind (1992: 141) also observes that "there is no post Buddhaghosa aṭṭhakathā in which it is expressly stated that it is a translation into Pali from a Sinhalese source. The colophons of Paṭis-a and Nidd-a, for instance, state that they are based upon the method of exposition of the former aṭṭhakathās (*pubbaṭṭhakathānaya*). There is not a single indication that these works are based upon sources written in Sinhalese". In all of the post-Buddhaghosa commentaries, mostly made by Dhammapāla (i.e. Ud-a, Th-a, It-a, Cp-a, Pet-a, Vv-a, Nett-a), the *Mahā-aṭṭhakathā* is only referred to once (at Ud-a 399). In the *ṭīkā*-s on the Vinaya the *Mahā-aṭṭhakathā* is referred to many times, in the *ṭīkā*-s on the Abhidhamma eighteen times and in the ones on the Nikāyas only nine times. The *Mahā-aṭṭhakathā* quotations in the *ṭīkās*, however, can be from quotations in the commentaries and other works rather than from the original *Mahā-aṭṭhakathā* itself; see Kieffer-Pülz 2013b 191–92.

Does the commentator Ācariya Dhammapāla, when he refers to the *Porāṇaṭṭhakathā* of the *pubbācariyā* in his prefaces to his commentaries, refer to different texts than the *Sīhaḷaṭṭhakathā* Buddhaghosa refers to? Perhaps partly. A possible reason for the distinction might be that Dhammapāla only used Pali materials from the old Sīhaḷa commentaries, that is, although he might have had access to the Sīhaḷa commentaries he did not use them completely because he could not read the Sīhaḷa parts. Dhammapāla lived about two hundred years after Buddhaghosa—i.e. about seven centuries after the *Sīhaḷaṭṭhakathā* were first written down—was from South India, did not use the word *sīhaḷa* in his commentaries and possibly did not know the Sīhaḷa language, especially the old form of the Sīhaḷa language that the *Sīhaḷaṭṭhakathā* were composed in; see Cousins 2013: 4 fn. 23; Kieffer-Pülz 2013b: 10–11. Only in the It-a (II 154) there is a reference to *laṅkādipa* with reference to those going forth there doing so by following Mahinda. In Dhammapāla's commentaries no reciters (*bhāṇaka*) are referred to (their views are referred to a few times in his Nikāya commentaries though, i.e. the *majjhimabhāṇakas* in M-ṭ and S-ṭ), and—at least in his Ud, It, Cp and Nett commentaries—there is no mention of Sinhalese theras who have discussions or opinions about points. On Dhammapāla's works, see Masefield 2002.

142. Kkh 208: ... *sīhaḷaṭṭhakathānayaṃ; mahāvihāravāsīnaṃ vācanāmagganissitaṃ ... ādāya sabbaso; Sabbaṃ aṭṭhakathāsāraṃ, pāḷiyatthañ-ca kevalaṃ. Na hettha taṃ padaṃ atthi, yaṃ virujjheyya pāḷiyā; Mahāvihāravāsīnaṃ porāṇaṭṭhakathāhi vā.* Kkh-ṭ 486: ... *Pāḷiyatthañ-ca kevalan-ti sakalaṃ pāḷi-atthañ-ca, ubhatovibhaṅgañcā ti vuttaṃ hoti. ... Sīhaḷaṭṭhakathānayan-ti sīhaḷamātikaṭṭhakathānayaṃ. Aṭṭhakathāsāran-ti sīhaḷamātikaṭṭhakathāyaṃ atthasāraṃ, atha vā vinayaṭṭhakathāsu atthasāraṃ. ...*

6. Translation of the *Sīhaḷaṭṭhakathā*

In the prefaces to the Nikāya commentaries (see § 1), Buddhaghosa says: "... removing (*apanetvā*) the Sīhaḷa language from that [commentary], replacing it by the delightful language that conforms with the style [of the language] of the Canonical Texts ...". Although this might be a liberal way of saying that he translated the commentary, perhaps it can also be taken to mean that he removed the parts in the Sīhaḷa language and left the parts that were already in Pali. In the preface of the *Samantapāsādikā* (Sp I 2), traditionally also attributed to Buddhaghosa, the author says that he will start on "the commentary that conforms with the style of [language of] the Canonical Texts (*pāḷinayānurūpa*)" and that he "is taking out just the different language" from what is said in the commentaries (*... tato ca bhāsantarameva hitvā*), which is explained in the *ṭīkā* as removing the Sīhaḷa language.

The author of the *Mahāvaṃsa* said that he compiled it from the ancient *Sīhaḷaṭṭhakathāmahāvaṃsa* by "leaving out just the different language" (*bhāsantarameva vajjiya,* p. 687). The preface of the *Vaṃsatthapakāsinī* or *Mahāvaṃsa-ṭīkā* says that the *Mahāvaṃsa* is a translation of the old Sīhaḷa commentary called *Mahāvaṃsa*: "In this way, having taken out the Sīhaḷa language [from it], I tell here in the language of Māgadha the traditional old commentary of the residents of the Mahāvihāra which has gotten the name *Mahāvaṃsa*,".: *Evaṃ mahāvaṃsan-ti laddhanāmaṃ mahāvihāravāsīnaṃ vācanamaggaṃ porāṇaṭṭhakatham-ettha sīhalabhāsaṃ hitvā māgadhikabhāsāya pavakkhāmī ti. ...*; see Oldenberg 1879: 2. This would account for the usage of *Sīhaḷaṭṭhakathā-mahāvaṃsa* "Sīhaḷa-commentary-*Mahāvaṃsa*" or "Great Historical Chronicle of the Sīhaḷa-commentary" later in the *ṭīkā*. For more on the *Mahāvaṃsa*, see § 8 below.

The usage of verbs denoting removal (*apaneti* and *jahati*) is remarkable since the verb *parivattati* "to translate" is used in the Vibhaṅga commentary to denote translations.[143] Although large parts of the *Sīhaḷaṭṭhakathā* were likely in Sīhaḷa, and Buddhaghosa would have translated these, other parts were apparently in Pali, as will be discussed below. Possibly Buddhaghosa partly "translated" the *Sīhaḷaṭṭhakathā* by comparing with and/or extracting Pali text from the definitions and explanations in these commentaries as well as from non-Mahavihāra works such as the *Vimuttimagga*. By copying and adapting existing Pali passages and explanations from various texts that were available to him, as well as translating passages from Sīhaḷa, Buddhaghosa could have compiled his commentaries.

---

143. Vibh-a 387, Paṭis-a 6: *Tattha sesā oṭṭakirāta-andhakayonakadamiḷabhāsādikā aṭṭhārasa bhāsā parivattanti. Ayamevekā yathābhuccabrahmavohāra-ariyavohārasaṅkhātā māgadhabhāsā na parivattati.*

There are several untraced quotations from the *aṭṭhakathā* in Buddhaghosa's Nikāya commentaries that may have been copied from Pali passages in the old commentaries and not translated from *Sīhaḷa*. Pind (1992: 141) writes: "... there are at least a couple of instances where the nature of the quotations forces one to conclude that they stem from a Pali source". For example, in the *Manorathapūraṇī*, a phrase is quoted from the *aṭṭhakathā* which contains the Eastern nominative singular forms ending in *-e* as found in the Kathāvatthu.[144] There are also other indications in Pali commentarial works that suggest this. The *Vajirabuddhiṭīkā* (9th or 10th CE) gives variant readings of Pali words and passages from the *Mahā-aṭṭhakathā* (see Kieffer-Pülz 2013b: 192) suggesting that the *Mahā-aṭṭhakathā* could partially have been in Pali. It is also difficult to account for a statement in the *Samantapāsādikā* that the quotation from the *Kurundī* is "just like that" or "just the same" (*tādisameva*) in the *Mahāpaccarī*, if both were not quoting the same Pali passage. The *Mahā-aṭṭhakathā* is also quoted as if it is from a Pali text.[145]

Compelling evidence for the Vinaya commentaries being partly in Pali is found in the preface of *Samantapāsādikā*, wherein Buddhaghosa said that he cleared the corrupt readings (*pamādalekhaṃ*) from the commentaries" (Sp I 2: ... *tasmā hi yaṃ aṭṭhakathāsu vuttaṃ; taṃ vajjayitvāna pamādalekhaṃ* ...). The term *pamādalekha* literally means "careless writing" and refers to a "copyist mistake" or "corruption"; see Endo 2013: 113. This only makes sense if what he was referring to was in Pali, and indeed, in their discussions of this passage the *ṭīkā*-s give as example a *pamādalekha* in Pali from the *Mahā-aṭṭhakathā* as quoted in the *Samantapāsādikā*.[146]

As mentioned in § 1, the simple word commentaries brought from India by Mahinda were possibly not translated into Sīhaḷa but could have been incorporated in Pali into the *Sīhaḷaṭṭhakathā*. Therefore the *Sīhaḷaṭṭhakathā*

---

144. See Pind 1992: 148–149. Mp II 273: *Tena vuttaṃ aṭṭhakathāyaṃ samanuyuñjatī ti vā samanuggāhatī ti vā samanubhāsatī ti vā esese ekaṭṭhe same samabhāge tajjāte taññevā ti.*

145. Sp II 299: *Tasmiṃ gharūpacāre ṭhitassa leḍḍupāto gāmūpacāroti kurundaṭṭhakathāyaṃ vuttaṃ. Mahāpaccariyam-pi tādisam-eva. Mahāaṭṭhakathāyaṃ pana gharaṃ nāma, gharūpacāro nāma, gāmo nāma, gāmūpacāro nāmā ti ....*

146. Sp-ṭ I 21: *Tattha pamādalekhan-ti aparabhāge potthakāruḷhakāle pamajjitvā likhanavasena pavattaṃ pamādapāṭhaṃ. Idaṃ vuttaṃ hoti pamādena satiṃ apaccupaṭṭhapetvā adinnādānassa pubbapayoge saccepi alikepi dukkaṭan-ti vuttavacanasadisaṃ yaṃ likhitaṃ, taṃ vajjayitvā apanetvā sabbaṃ pamāṇanti. Vakkhati hi tattha Mahāaṭṭhakathāyaṃ pana saccepi alikepi dukkaṭam-eva vuttaṃ, taṃ pamādalikhitan-ti veditabbaṃ. Na hi adinnādānassa pubbapayoge pācittiyaṭṭhāne dukkaṭaṃ nāma atthīti* (Sp II 310). Vjb-ṭ 19: *Yaṃ atthajātaṃ aṭṭhakathāsu vuttaṃ, taṃ sabbam-pi pamādalekhakānaṃ pamādalekhamattaṃ vajjayitvā. Kiṃ sabbesam-pi pamāṇaṃ? Na, kintu sikkhāsu sagāravānaṃ idha vinayamhi paṇḍitānaṃ, mahāaṭṭhakathāyaṃ pana saccepi alikepi dukkaṭam-eva vuttaṃ, taṃ pamādalekhan-ti veditabbaṃ. Pamādalekhaṃ vajjayitvā pamāṇaṃ hessatī ti sambandho.*

might have been texts in both Pali and Sinhala, with words, phrases, verses from Canonical texts, and the old word commentaries on these quoted in Pali and with the additional explanatory prose on these in Sīhaḷa; see also Geiger 1908: 45–46 § 13, Pind 1992: 150. In Sri Lanka there are many exegetical works in mixed Pali-Sinhala called *sannaya/sannē, gaṇṭhipada/gäṭapadaya, padārtha,* and *piṭapota*; see Hettiaracchi 1950: 70–97, Blackburn 1997: 76–78. Most of these are from the 18th century and beyond, but some are older. The oldest one, the *Dhampiyā-aṭuvā-gäṭapadaya*, might be from the 10th century. It comments in Sīhaḷa on difficult Pali words and passages in the *Dhammapadaṭṭhakathā* and is said to contain four (corrupt) quotations from the *Sīhaḷaṭṭhakathā* (called *Heḷaṭuvā*); see Hettiaratchi 1950: 70–71. A *gaetapadaya* explains in Sinhala the difficult, knotty passages of a Pali text, while a *sannaya* or *padārtha* or *piṭapota* is a word by word Pali-Sinhala translation of a whole Pali text. The distinctions between *gaetapadaya* and *sannaya*, etc. are sometimes unclear; see Hettiaratchi 1950: 76. There are also other mixed Pali-Sinhala texts, for example, the *Heraṇasikha* (11th–12th century, with Pali verses and Sinhala prose), the *Vimukti-saṃgrahaya* (14c, with Pāli verses, a sannaya on these, and Sinhala prose), meditation instruction books such as the *Vidarśanā bhāvanā pota* (with formulae in Pali and instructions in Sinhala), and works such as the *Kaṅkhāvitaraṇīpiṭapota* (13c) and *Moggallāna-pañcikā-pradīpaya* (15c, in Sinhala with many quotations in Pali); see Ñāṇatusita 2011. *Gaṇṭhipada*s on the *Samantapāsādika* soon appeared after its composition and are quoted in *ṭīkā*s; see Kieffer-Pülz 2015: 431.

The ancient *Sīhaḷaṭṭhakathā*, or parts of them, could have been similar to these later exegetical mixed Pali-Sinhala texts, with the words, phrases, and verses that were commented upon in Pali. In one explanation, the Dīgha-nikāya commentary says that the variant reading in the canonical Pali text is not found in the commentary and elsewhere remarks that the reading in the commentary is different on all occasions from the one in the Pali text.[147] The former remark is with reference to a word in a prose text, while the latter is with reference to a word found in verses. In the *Jātakaṭṭhakathā* there are references to variant readings in the (old) commentary, indicating that the verses commented upon were quoted in Pali.[148] In two cases, the readings in the commentary are preferred over the one in the canonical Jātaka text.

147. Sv I 113: *khiḍḍāya padussanti vinassantī ti khiḍḍāpadosikā, padūsikātipi pāḷiṃ likhanti, sā aṭṭhakathāyaṃ natthi.* Sv II 686: *Pāḷiyaṃ pana mahabbalā ti likhanti. Aṭṭhakathāyaṃ sabbavāresu mahābalā ti pāṭho.*

148. J-a II 175: *Haṃsā koñcā mayūrā cā ti ... aṭṭhakathāyaṃ pana haṃsakoñcamayūrānan-ti pāṭho. So sundaratarā*; I 488: *kaliṃ pāpeti attānaṃ, ... Pāḷiyaṃ pana phalaṃ pāpeyyā ti likhanti. Taṃ byañjanaṃ aṭṭhakathāyaṃ natthi, attho pissa na yujjati. Tasmā yathāvuttam-eva gahetabbaṃ*; II 241: *Kasmā nu tvan-ti ... aṭṭhakathāyaṃ pana kasmā tuvan-ti pāṭho*; II 294: *Evaṃ vaṇṇitā agiddhitāpi sādhu. Pāḷiyaṃ pana agiddhimā ti likhitaṃ, tato*

Some of the glosses in Buddhaghosa's commentaries seem to be quoted from a dictionary similar to the *Abhidhānappadīpikā* and there are also explanations that appear to come from the Niddesa; see Von Hinüber 1996: 116, § 231, & 117, § 234. Passages quoted from *aṭṭhakathās* in which *nāma* is used as quotation marker instead of *iti*, and others in which unusual, colloquial Pali terms are used, also suggest that the quoted passages were originally in Pali; see von Hinüber 1996: 125–126, § 249.

Possibly, there were even some texts completely in Pali that were referred to as *Sīhaḷaṭṭhakathā,* such as word commentaries or glossaries, *gaṇṭhipada*, and perhaps commentaries such as the *Kurundī.*

Just as Buddhaghosa was not an innovator in the sense of introducing new ideas into the Theravāda tradition from other traditions, it is unlikely that the advanced commentarial terminology and the commentarial, scholastic Pali language as found in Buddhaghosa's works were entirely developed by himself. Rather, it was the product of an already advanced commentarial Pali tradition. The development of commentarial Pali terminology and language is unlikely to have stopped with the composition of the *Peṭakopadesa* and *Netti*—which do not contain the Sri Lankan abhidhamma concepts and ideas (see Intro. § 4.1) and which might have originated in another school (see Intro. § 6)—only to be resumed centuries later by Buddhaghosa. Since the Sri Lankan abhidhamma ideas are found in the *Vimuttimagga,* Buddhaghosa might have gotten them from there and from other commentarial works in Pali.

The *Vimuttimagga*'s style of language might also have influenced Buddhaghosa. In the explanation of the word *bhāva*, Upatissa (at 418b25/Ch. 8 § 30) refers to a definition from "grammar" (聲論 "exposition of words" = *saddasattha*), which might be a commentary on Pāṇini's grammar; see fn 871. Although there are no other grammatical discussions in the Vim, this passage nevertheless suggests that Upatissa was familiar with Pāṇinian Sanskrit grammar (*śabdaśāsana/śabdaśāstra*), just as Buddhaghosa was. Possibly Upatissa, as well as other Abhayagirivihāra and South Indian authors, had composed more works in Pali that could have influenced Buddhaghosa.

7. Structural changes

Buddhaghosa's "translations" from the *Sīhaḷaṭṭhakathā* are not translations in the modern sense of the word, that is, translations that literally represent the texts translated. As pointed out above, they are rather a "best of" selection that

---

ayaṃ aṭṭhakathāpāṭhova sundarataro; II 334: *Haritāmayoti ... aṭṭhakathāyaṃ pana samāluharitāmayo ti pāṭho*; II 354: ... *mahesīsīti ... aṭṭhakathāyaṃ pana mahesī cā tipi pāṭho*; IV 223: *Goṭṭhaṃ majjaṃ kirāṭan-ti ayaṃ potthakesu pāṭho, aṭṭhakathāyaṃ pana goṭṭhaṃ majjaṃ kirāsañcāti*; etc. See Adikaram 1953: 33.

matches the original to a certain degree but not completely since materials were left out, abridged, rearranged, and adapted, and materials from other commentarial sources were incorporated. Moreover, a substantial amount of the used materials would have been in Pali already. Parts of the original commentaries were left out in Buddhaghosa's commentaries or were given in abridged form. In the prefaces and colophons to his commentaries on the four Nikāyas, Buddhaghosa writes that his commentaries were made "taking the essence" (*sāraṃ ādāya*) of the old commentaries, suggesting that his works were a kind of digest and reinterpretation of the older commentaries. As Jayawickrama (1962: xv) says about the Sp: "As is usually the case with all his commentaries, it is by no means an original exegesis, but a restatement of the material available to him in the Sīhaḷa Aṭṭhakathā".

An example of an omission is the account of the foundation of the Bhikkhunī-saṅgha, which is given in full in Buddhaghosa's *Manorathapuraṇī*, while it is given in brief in the *Samantapāsādikā*. Von Hinüber (1996: 121, § 241) writes: "Thus a piece of the old Vinaya-Aṭṭhakathā might survive in this particular case in the commentary on the Aṅguttaranikāya". Further on (1996: 122, § 242) he says: "As demonstrated for Sp (§ 215), the structure of the old Aṭṭhakathā was changed to a large extent, if not almost completely, but perhaps also in those on the Nikāyas, which are called Aṭṭhakathāsāra 'essence of the (old) Aṭṭhakathā' (Ps I 109, 15* etc.), which seems to point at an abbreviation". In the *Visuddhimagga* (VI.42/p. 184), Buddhaghosa quoted a passage from the old *Majjhimaṭṭhakathā* on the potential attractiveness of a woman's corpse that is not found in the *Papañcasūdanī*; see Pind 1992: 141. The same applies to a quotation from the *Saṃyuttaṭṭhakathā* in Vism (XIII.117/p. 442) that is not found in Buddhaghosa's *Sāratthappakāsiṇī*; see von Hinüber (1996: 113, § 227), who observes: "it is not unlikely that Vism occasionally quotes and thus preserves material from the 'old' Aṭṭhakathā otherwise lost, because it was not included elsewhere into the 'new' Aṭṭhakathā".

Another quotation from the old commentary, not mentioned by Pind and von Hinüber, is a passage likening *vitakka* and *vicāra* to a bird rising up and flying in the air. In the Vism and other commentaries, it is said to be from *Dukanipātaṭṭhakathā*,[149] however, it cannot be found in the *Dukanipātaṭṭhakathā*, nor in any other commentary. Buddhaghosa apparently quoted it from the old *Dukanipātaṭṭhakathā* but did not use it in his new *Dukanipātaṭṭhakathā* itself. Finally, in *Mahāvaṃsaṭīkā* there is a story about the Ājīvaka Janasāna

149. Vism IV.89/p.142, Paṭis-a I 182, Nidd-a I 128: *Dukanipātaṭṭhakathāyaṃ pana ākāse gacchato mahāsakuṇassa ubhohi pakkhehi vātaṃ gahetvā pakkhe sannisīdāpetvā viya ārammaṇe cetaso abhiniropanabhāvena pavatto vitakko; so hi ekaggo hutvā appeti; vātagahaṇatthaṃ pakkhe phandāpayamānassa gamanaṃ viya anumajjanasabhāvena pavatto vicāro ti vuttaṃ*. Cf. As 115: *Aṭṭhakathāyaṃ pana ākāse gacchato ... vuttaṃ*.

and the strange longings of King Asoka's pregnant mother that is said to be from the *Majjhimasaṅgītī Cūḷasīhanādasuttavaṇṇanā Sīhalaṭṭhakathā*, but is not found in the *Papañcasūdanī*; see Malalasekera 1935: lxxxiv, 193.

With regard to changes to the arrangement of the texts: In the Sp the arrangement of the subject matter of the old commentaries was changed. It is said in the commentary on the first *pārājika* rule: "But all commentaries discuss the going forth and the full admission here.[150] However, we will discuss it in the Khandhaka, as it is situated in the (canonical) Pali text. And not only this: Whatever else is discussed in the [commentary on the] (Sutta) Vibhaṅga by the *aṭṭhakathā* teachers but [instead] is to be discussed in [the commentary on] the Khandhaka or Parivāra, that we will all discuss just there, for only when it is discussed in such a manner, the explanation is done in the order of the (canonical) Pali text".[151] Von Hinüber (1996: 106, § 215) gives more examples and concludes: "it shows that a very considerable amount of text has been shifted from the Pārājikakaṇḍa to later parts of Sp, changing the structure of the commentary completely". According to Frauwallner (1994: 16–17), besides abridging the *Vinayaṭṭhakathā* in the Sp, "Buddhaghosa goes beyond his source" and also "enlarged and embellished it" in two places in narrations by adding details and descriptions from the *Vinayaṭṭhakathā,* since otherwise it "would not be understandable that the *Vaṃsatthappakāsinī* quotes the *Samantapāsādikā* here, when the same could be found in the original source, namely the *Vinayaṭṭhakathā*".

Buddhaghosa probably did the same with the *Vimuttimagga,* the main inspiration and template for his *Visuddhimagga*, albeit in a much more drastic manner: He changed the structure of the text, left out some materials, inserted other materials such as explanations, stories, etc., from various commentaries and texts in use by the Mahāvihāra, rewrote parts, adapted passages to fit the Mahāvihāra tenets, and gave it a slightly different name.

This omission of materials from the old *aṭṭhakathā* in Buddhaghosa's commentaries could account for the divergent opinions of reciters therein,

---

150. This suggests that all the commentaries used for the Sp were exclusively commentaries on the Pātimokkha and Suttavibhaṅga, which would discuss *upasampadā* and in extension *pabbajjā* as part of the meaning of *bhikkhu* in the first Pārājika rule. Similarly, the *Kaṅkhāvitaraṇī*, the commentary on the Pātimokkha, lists the eight different types of *upasampadā* here, although it does not further comment on them, presumably since they were already discussed in the Sp.

151. Sp 206: *Ettha pana ṭhatvā sabba-aṭṭhakathāsu pabbajjā ca upasampadā ca kathitā. Mayaṃ pana yathāṭhitapāḷivaseneva khandhake kathayissāma. Na kevalañcetaṃ, aññampi yaṃ khandhake vā parivāre vā kathetabbaṃ aṭṭhakathācariyehi vibhaṅge kathitaṃ, taṃ sabbaṃ tattha tattheva kathayissāma. Evañ-hi kathiyamāne pāḷikkameneva vaṇṇanā katā hoti. Tato tena tena vinicchayena atthikānaṃ pāḷikkameneva imaṃ vinayasaṃvaṇṇanaṃ oloketvā so so vinicchayo suviññeyyo bhavissatī ti.*

even in the commentaries of those Nikāyas that the reciters recited themselves. For example, in the Dīgha commentary (Sv I 15) it is said that the Dīgha reciters included the texts of the Khuddakagantha (= Khuddakanikāya) in the Abhidhammapiṭaka, while the Majjhima reciters included it in the Suttapiṭaka and included two more texts (Bv and Cp). By attributing it to the Dīgha reciters, and referring to the longer and preferred list as given by the Majjhima reciters, i.e. in the old Majjhimanikāya commentary, Buddhaghosa showed what accorded with the opinion of the Mahāvihāra elders.

Other examples of Buddhaghosa apparently indirectly referring to the old commentary on a text when instead referring to the reciters of this text are in passages on different opinions of reciters listed by Endo (2013: 65–77): The Majjhima and Aṅguttara commentaries (Ps IV 178 & and Mp III 127–28) say that the shortness of the duration of the light that pervaded the universe when the Bodhisatta descended into his mother's womb is said differently by the Dīgha reciters. This different wording is found in the parallel in the Dīgha commentary without attribution (Sv II 434, also Sp-ṭ I 276). In the Dīgha commentary (Sv III 1036), it is said that signless liberation of mind (*animittācetovimutti*) is the fruition attainment of the arahant. However, in the Aṅguttara commentary (Mp III 347) it is said that this liberation is powerful insight (*balavavipassanā*) and that the Dīgha reciters say that it is fruition attainment. The *Atthasālinī* (As 159) says that the Dīgha reciters give a different definition of rectitude of view, which is found in the Dīgha commentary (Sv III 1000; cf. It-a II 26) without attribution. In the Suttanipāta and Cariyapiṭaka (Sn-a I 186, Cp-a 154) commentaries it is said that Diṭṭhamaṅgalikā took Mātaṅga by his hand, and add that the *Jātakaṭṭhakathā* reciters say that she carried him on her back, just as is said in the Jātaka commentary (J-a IV 376). Finally, the Saṃyutta commentary (Spk I 302) says that Sūciloma went forth (i.e. became a bhikkhu) during the teaching of Buddha Kassapa. The Suttanipāta commentary (Sn-a I 302), however, says that he was a lay-follower of this Buddha, and that the Saṃyutta reciters said that he was a bhikkhu.

Perhaps Buddhaghosa did not wish to refer to the old commentaries directly so as not to lower their worth, or he did so to avoid confusion with his own commentaries with the same names. The subcommentator Sāriputta similarly referred to the opinions of different reciters when he found contradictory explanations or narratives in the different commentaries of Buddhaghosa; see § 1 and 8.

In one case, the version of the reciters is not found in the Nikāya they recited, but in another one. In the Vinaya Commentary's account of the first council (Sp I 12, also Khp-a 96) it is said that the arahant Ānanda went to the assembly by diving into the earth and manifesting himself on his seat. This way of going is attributed to the Majjhima reciters in the account of the first council in the Dīgha commentary (Sv I 10) but is not found in the Majjhima commentary, wherein there is no account of the first council. Possibly, there was such an account in the old Majjhima commentary but since Buddhaghosa had already used the old Dīgha commentary's version, he decided that there was no need for the account again. Therefore passages and opinions that Buddhaghosa attributes to reciters of other Nikāyas, but cannot be found in the relevant places in Buddhaghosa's commentaries on those Nikāyas, could simply have been left out by him because he had already used them in another commentary and therefore he gave a commentary instead that, as stated in the preface of the Nikāya commentaries, is "leaving out [explanations of the] meaning that occur repeatedly".

A good reason for repetitions in the old commentaries is given by Adikaram (1953: 25–26): "Provision also seems to have been made to enable a Bhāṇaka of one Nikāya to have as comprehensive a knowledge as possible without resorting to the study of other Nikāyas and their Commentaries. The preliminary detailed explanations often given in the same style, and practically in the same words at the beginning of the Commentaries of each Nikāya, would warrant this inference".[152] The canonical texts and old commentaries were compiled and written down with the intention that they would just serve as a backup and reference guide for reciters. Each group of nikāya reciters likely desired a commentary to a nikāya as comprehensive as possible so that they would not have to consult other Nikāyas and commentaries. Possibly the different groups even compiled and wrote down their own commentaries independent of the ones of other groups.

The differences in the explanations and narratives attributed to the different groups of reciters could therefore have reflected differences in the old nikāya commentaries. The editor and compiler Buddhaghosa, wishing to standardize materials and not to repeat explanations and narratives, especially when they conflicted with others, might have chosen what he considered the best explanation or narrative and left out others, except for referring sometimes to them as being the words or opinions of reciters. However, he was not entirely consistent in standardization since there are still different explanations of words and phrases in his commentaries, even

152. See also Sp 790 on what a monk has to learn to qualify as "very learned", *bahussuta* and be an advisor to the bhikkhunīs, i.e. he "has to learn the three piṭakas with their commentaries. If he is not able to do so, he has to be familiar with one commentary [of the four commentaries] on the four Nikāyas, for [when familiar with the commentary] with one nikāya he will also be able to answer a question about [the contents of] the other Nikāyas": *Bhikkhunovādakena pana sāṭṭhakathāni tīṇi piṭakāni uggahetabbāni, asakkontena catūsu nikāyesu ekassa aṭṭhakathā paguṇā kātabbā, ekanikāyena hi sesanikāyesupi pañhaṃ kathetuṃ sakkhissati.* ... See also von Hinüber 1996: 25, § 49.

within one commentary. These can be accounted for as possibly being due to each section of the Nikāyas (e.g. the three sections of the Majjhimanikāya) being accompanied by its own written Sīhaḷa commentary; see von Hinüber 1996: 116–117, § 232 & fn. 412, see also 25/§ 49.

8. Differences in commentaries as pointed out in the *Sāratthamañjūsā*

In the *Sāratthamañjūsā* or *Aṅguttaranikāya-ṭīkā* of Sāriputta (Mp-ṭ),[153] it is pointed out a number of times that different commentaries attributed to Ācariya Buddhaghosa disagree on points or differ in details. The *ṭīkā* emphasises that the differences are not due to contradictions in the expositions of Ācariya Buddhaghosa, but are due to differences in the expositions of different groups of reciters, in other words, in these cases Buddhaghosa just reproduces the expositions of the reciters.

At Mp-ṭ II 342, it is said the accounts in the Mp, Vism, As, with respect to the modes of progress of the arahants Mahāmoggallāna (= M) and Sāriputta (= S), disagree with each other. In two suttas in the Aṅguttaranikāya (A II 154–155), it is said that M attained arahantship with unpleasant practice and quick realization while S did so with pleasant practice and quick realization. The commentary on these suttas (Mp III 142) adds that M attained the three lower paths with pleasant practice and slow realization, while S did so with pleasant practice and slow realization. Vism (XXI.118/p. 668), however, says that M attained the first path with pleasant practice and quick realization and the other three with unpleasant practice and slow realization, and that S attained all the four paths with pleasant practice and quick realization, just as the Buddha did. *Atthasālinī* (p. 236) says the same for S but says that M attained the first path with pleasant practice and quick realization and the three higher ones with unpleasant practice and slow realization. The *ṭīkā* concludes: "All that does not conform to each other. There is no agreement with regard to this in the Canonical text and the Commentary. Therefore it is to be investigated or it is to be taken [as] it has been said here and there [in the commentaries] in such and such a manner according to the opinion of this and that [group of] reciters": ... *taṃ sabbaṃ aññamaññaṃ nānulometi.*

153. Since Sāriputta took over most of the materials in this *ṭīkā* from Dhammapāla's *Aṅguttara purāṇaṭīkā* (see Kieffer-Pülz 2017: 423), of which only the first part has been published by the PTS, it is uncertain whether all statements discussed in this section are by Sāriputta or by Dhammapāla. The statement at Mp-ṭ I 198 (Ee Mp-nṭ Ee III 277 in Mp-pṭ 434 note 4) is by Sāriputta since it is only found in Sāriputta's *ṭīkā* but not in the older *ṭīkā* or in in any other *aṭṭhakathā* or *ṭīkā*. However, other statements have been taken by Sāriputta from the older commentary, i.e. Mp-ṭ I 164 = Mp-pṭ 166; Mp-ṭ I 188 = Mp-pṭ 195–96; Mp-ṭ I 179 = Mp-pṭ 185.

Imāya pāḷiyā imāya ca aṭṭhakathāya na sameti, tasmā vīmaṃsitabbam-etaṃ. Taṃ taṃ bhāṇakānaṃ vā matena tattha tattha tathā tathā vuttan-ti gahetabbaṃ.

Mp-ṭ II 63, gives the different definitions of purification of view (*diṭṭhivisuddhi*) and the effort in accordance with that view (*yathādiṭṭhissa ca padhānaṃ*) as found in Mp, Sv, an untraced source, and As. The *ṭīkā* concludes: "But here the different kinds of explanation are because of different kinds of opinion of this and that [group of] reciters. It is not to be assumed that the statements of the commentaries are in contradiction with each other": *Ettha ca taṃ taṃ bhāṇakānaṃ matabhedenāyaṃ vaṇṇanābhedo ti na aṭṭhakathāvacanānaṃ aññamaññavirodho saṅkitabbo.*

At Mp-ṭ III 243 (and also in Sp-ṭ III 349) the list of causes for the disappearance of the Dhamma as given in Mp IV 136 is said to be of the reciters of the *khandhakas* since it is given in this very manner in the Sp. After giving different lists as in Sv and Spk, the Mp-ṭ concludes: "Therefore it is to be accepted that it is the mere opinion of this and that [group of] reciters that is shown here and there by the *ācariya* (= Buddhaghosa). For otherwise there would indeed be an implication of contradiction of the former and latter [explanations] of the *ācariya*": *tasmā tesaṃ tesaṃ bhāṇakānaṃ matam-eva ācariyena tattha tattha dassitan-ti gahetabbaṃ. Aññathā hi ācariyasseva pubbāparavirodhappasaṅgo siyā ti.* Coḷaraṭṭhakassapa, the author of *Vimativinodanī*, also gives the different reasons for decline at Vmv II 263, and concludes in a similar way: "... that all, even though they are contradicting each other, has been written down by the ācariya, having taken only the meaning (*naya*) handed down in the written commentaries of the Sīhaḷas in accordance with the opinion of this and that [group of] reciters, because in such contradictions in expositions there is no decline of the Teaching and because there is no means to clean away [such contradictions]. For only a contradiction of the ultimate truth is to be cleaned away by the method of the suttas, etc., not a contradiction of an exposition.": ... *taṃ sabbaṃ aññamaññaviruddham-pi taṃ taṃ bhāṇakānaṃ matena likhitasīhaḷaṭṭhakathāsu āgatanayam-eva gahetvā ācariyena likhitaṃ īdise kathāvirodhe sāsanaparihāniyā abhāvato, sodhanupāyābhāvā ca paramatthavirodho eva hi suttādinayena sodhanīyo, na kathāmaggavirodho ti.*

At Mp-ṭ I 198 (Ee Mp-nṭ Ee III 277; in Mp-pṭ 434 note 4) the *ṭīkā* points out that a verse (Dhp 102) is worded differently in the story on Kuṇḍalakesittheriyā as found in the Therigāthā and Dhammapada commentaries and concludes: "It has been said here and there in such and such a manner according to the expositions of this and that [group of] reciters. It is not to be assumed that there is a contradiction between the former and latter [expositions] of the teacher (= Buddhaghosa)": *Taṃ taṃ bhāṇakānaṃ kathāmaggānusārena tattha tattha tathā [tathā] vuttan-ti na idha ācariyassa pubbāparavirodho saṅkitabbo.*

At Mp-ṭ III 193, the *ṭīkā* notices a different order of two items between the canonical text (A IV 117) and the way it is quoted in the Dīgha commentary (Mp IV 58) and explained in its *ṭīkā*. The *ṭīkā* concludes: "But this order is shown through the usage order of the Dīgha reciters. It is not to be assumed that there is a contradiction/discrepancy of the teacher": *Ayañca anukkamo dīghabhāṇakānaṃ vaḷañjanānukkamena dassito, na ettha ācariyassa virodho āsaṅkitabbo.*

There are also several other indirect references to differences, as follows.

At Mp-ṭ I 164 (= Ee Mp-pṭ 166) the *ṭīkā* says that due to the opinion of the Aṅguttara reciters (= Mp I 238), it is said in the commentary that the yakkha Sātāgira, after he had become stream-enterer upon hearing a discourse of the Buddha, wonders where his friend Hemavata is, wishing him to hear the Dhamma too. Sāriputta says that in the *Suttanipātaṭṭhakathā* (Sn-a I 198), however, Sātāgira does not attain any distinction because when he thinks whether Hemavata has come or not and not seeing him, he feels deceived.[154]

At Mp-ṭ I 188 (= Ee Mp-pṭ 195–96), the *ṭīkā* notices a difference in the story of Mahākappina thera as found in the Aṅguttara and Dhammapada commentaries (Mp I 323 and Dhp-a II 215). In Mp the Buddha, after having established Queen Anojā and her retinue in the fruit of stream-entry, and having made King Mahākappina (now a bhikkhu and arahant along with his retinue) and queen and their respective retinues visible to each other, thinks "let Uppalavaṇṇā come". When the Therī came, she made all the ladies go forth and then took them to the Bhikkhunī residence. According to Mp-ṭ: "this is said by showing the exposition of the Aṅguttara reciters. With respect to just that it is said in the Dhp-a, 'They, having paid respect to the Teacher, standing on one side, asked for the going forth'. Reportedly, when this was said so, some say that the teacher thought about the coming of Uppalavaṇṇā. However, the teacher said to those upāsikās: 'Having gone to Sāvatthī, you will go forth in the Bhikkhunī residence'."[155]

At Mp-ṭ I 179 (= Ee Mp-pṭ 185), the *ṭīkā* refers to different accounts of the going forth of Pilindavacccha, i.e. at Mp I 276 and Th-a I 53/Ap-a 321. In Mp, Pilindavacccha, after hearing a discourse by Buddha Padumuttara, aspires to become a deity. Eventually, he is reborn in a Brahmin family and goes forth after hearing the Buddha Gotama giving a talk. In Th-a, Pilindavacccha first

---

154. *Dasabalassa dhammakathaṃ sutvā sotāpattiphale patiṭṭhāya cintesīti idaṃ aṅguttara-bhāṇakānaṃ matena vuttaṃ. Suttanipātaṭṭhakathāyaṃ pana "sapariso bhagavantaṃ upasaṅkamma dhammadesanaṃ assosi, na ca kañci visesaṃ adhigañchi. ...*

155. *Satthā uppalavaṇṇā āgacchatūti cintesi. Therī āgantvā sabbā pabbājetvā bhikkhunīupassayaṃ gatā ti idaṃ aṅguttarabhāṇakānaṃ kathāmaggaṃ dassentena vuttaṃ. Teneva dhammapadaṭṭhakathāyaṃ vuttaṃ: Tā satthāraṃ vanditvā ekamantaṃ ṭhitā pabbajjaṃ yāciṃsu. Evaṃ kira vutte satthā uppalavaṇṇāya āgamanaṃ cintesīti ekacce vadanti. Satthā pana tā upāsikāyo āha sāvatthiṃ gantvā bhikkhunīupassaye pabbājethā ti.*

goes forth as a non-Buddhist wanderer who masters "lesser Gandhara" magic power and then goes forth again under the Buddha, wishing to learn the "greater Gandhara" magic power from him. The *ṭīkā* concludes that the former is "the exposition of the Aṅguttara reciters" but that "others" tell the latter.[156]

In a discussion of the factors that aid right view, as given in Mp on a passage that is also found in the Majjhima-nikāya, and therefore commented upon in M-a (II 346), the *ṭīkā* (Mp-ṭ III 7) says: "This explanation of the meaning has been undertaken in accordance with the opinion of the Aṅguttara reciters. However, the Majjhima reciters say the meaning in another way. For it is said in the Majjhima Commentary: ...": ... *aṅguttarabhāṇakānaṃ matena ayaṃ atthavaṇṇanā āraddhā, majjhimabhāṇakā panettha aññathā atthaṃ vadanti. Vuttañ-hetaṃ majjhimaṭṭhakathāyaṃ* ... The simile comparing the factors that aid right view to the factors that aid the growth of a mango tree is worded and explained differently in both commentaries, with M-a not fully explaining all the five factors in relation to the simile.

At Mp-ṭ III 175, a difference is pointed out in the story of Anāthapiṇḍika's slave-girl Puṇṇā persuading the Buddha to return to the Jetavana and not to set out on a tour. Mp-ṭ points out that in accordance with the opinion of the Aṅguttara reciters it is said (at Mp IV 34) that the Buddha left after the Rains retreat and Invitation and took along his two main disciples (i.e. Sāriputta and Moggallāna), but the Majjhima reciters say (at Ps II 136) that he went "with the rains retreat coming close" (i.e. before the rains retreat) and was followed by the bhikkhu community, and that therefore the King and others were trying to stop him leaving at the wrong time. The reason, according to M-a, is that they wished the Buddha to spend the rains at Jetavana so that they could listen to the Dhamma and make merit for three months.[157]

At Mp-ṭ II 210, the *ṭīkā* points out that the story of the circumstances leading up to the Gotamakacetiyasuttanta as found in Mp II 373 is the version of the Aṅguttara reciters and then gives the version of the Majjhima reciters from the commentary on the Mūlapariyāyasutta at Ps I 56–58.

9. *Dīpavaṃsa* and *Mahāvaṃsa*

The *Mahāvaṃsa* is probably a revised and enlarged version of the earlier chronicle *Dīpavaṃsa*, containing additions from the *Sīhalaṭṭhakathā-mahāvaṃsa* and other sources, leaving out repetitive materials, and containing less faults

---

156. *Satthu dhammadesanaṃ sutvā paṭiladdhasaddho pabbajitvā ti idaṃ aṅguttara-bhāṇakānaṃ kathāmaggena vuttaṃ. Apare pana bhaṇanti ...*

157. *... vutthavasso pavāretvā ... pe ... nikkhamīti aṅguttarabhāṇakānaṃ matenetaṃ vuttaṃ. Majjhimabhāṇakā pana vadanti bhagavā upakaṭṭhāya vassūpanāyikāya jetavanato bhikkhusaṅghaparivuto cārikaṃ nikkhami. Teneva ca akāle nikkhantattā kosalarājādayo vāretuṃ ārabhiṃsu. Pavāretvā hi caraṇaṃ buddhāciṇṇanti.*

in terms of grammar and metre; see Frauwallner 1994: 17–19; Norman 1983: 116–118.

The author of the *Mahāvaṃsa* says that he compiled it from the ancient *Sīhaḷaṭṭhakathā-mahāvaṃsa* by taking just the "essence/heartwood of the [explanation of the] meaning" (*atthasāram-eva gahetvā,* p. 687, cp. *aṭṭhakathāsāra*), removing just the different language (*bhāsantaram eva vajjiya,* p. 687), and "abandoning the blemish of being overly lengthy/detailed and repetitious" (*ativitthāra-punar-utta-dosabhāvam pahāya,* p. 42) from the *Sīhaḷaṭṭhakathā Mahāvaṃsa*; see Malalasekera 1935: lvii fn. 2). In the preface of the Mhv itself, it is said, "This what has been made also by the ancients is overly lengthy in some places, in some overly brief, having many repetitions; but when voided of those blemishes, it is easy to learn and remember."[158] Malalasekera (1935: lvii) writes: "[The *Mahāvaṃsa*] should be considered rather as an adaptation, a work of an eclectic character, the author having obtained his materials from diverse sources, sifted them with great care ... according to his own lights. It is nevertheless true that the *Aṭṭhakathā* (as the older Mhv. was called) formed the foundation of Mahānāma's *Mahāvaṃsa* and supplied most of the material contained therein, which the author of the Pali poem put into more artistic form, making it more readable and easier to grasp." Oldenberg (1879: 3–4) suggests that both the *Mahāvaṃsa* and *Dīpavaṃsa* are "based on the historical Introduction to the great Commentary of the Mahāvihāra", which he describes as the historical narrative which forms the foundation to the Sinhalese commentaries, and which is similar but more extensive than Buddhaghosa's account of the origin of the Tipiṭaka prefixed to the *Samantapāsādikā.* Frauwallner (1994: 10–17), however, points out that the Sinhalese *aṭṭhakathā* were not a single work, that the introduction of the Sp is based on the old *Vinayaṭṭhakathā,* and that, therefore, the Mhv and Dīp draw from a different, older text called Mhv. Whether the sources of Mhv and Dīp only belonged to the Mahāvihāra is also uncertain since they, like the Vim and other old commentaries, could have been part of the general pre-sectarian Sinhala Theravāda textual tradition. Geiger (1908: 51–52 § 14) says that since the *Mahāvaṃsaṭīkā* does not refer to the *Uttaravihāra-aṭṭhakathā* (i.e. the historical introduction of it) and *Uttaravihāra-mahāvaṃsa* beyond its first part, this could indicate that these Abhayagirivihāra texts stopped with the story of Mahinda, just as the *Samantapāsādikā* does.

After the sectarian split with the Abhayagirivihāra, the Mahāvihāra tradition emphasised its school identity through its revised version of the Mhv, just as it did through the Vism and the Pali commentaries. The older *Dīpavaṃsa* sometimes gives two accounts of the same event, while

158. Mhv 2–3: *Porāṇehi kato'peso, ativitthārito kvaci; Atīva kvaci saṃkhitto, anekapunaruttako, Vajjitaṃ tehi dosehi, sukhaggahaṇadhāraṇaṃ.*

the *Mahāvaṃsa* only gives one; see Geiger 1908: 66–68 § 23; Malalasekera 1935: lx; Norman 1983: 116; Frauwallner 1994: 19–21; Gunawardana 1988: 6.[159] According to Frauwallner (1994: 20–21), the accounts from the old *Mahāvaṃsa* chronicles of both the Mahāvihāra and Abhayagirivihāra are likely given in these cases. The Abhayagirivāsins had their own *Mahāvaṃsa* from which the *Mahāvaṃsaṭīkā* quotes; see Geiger 1908: 50–52 § 14, Frauwallner 1994: 20–21. Some passages in the *Dīpavaṃsa* that are ascribed to the Uttaravihāra (= Abhayagirivihāra) are left out of the later *Mahāvaṃsa* and therefore Von Hinüber (1996: 90–91, § 184 & 186) says: "Mhv is much more a true Mahāvihāra text than Dīp". While the old part of the Mhv ends with the desertion of the Mahāvihāra under King Mahāsena (circa 277–304 CE) and its re-establishment, the Dīp ends with King Mahāsena coming under the influence of evil bhikkhus without there being any mention of the Mahāvihāra or Abhayagirivihāra.

The *Dīpavaṃsa* possibly consists of the Pali verses extracted from the old *Mahāvaṃsa Sīhaḷaṭṭhakathā*—called *Porāṇaṭṭhakathā* in the preface to the *Mahāvaṃsa-ṭīkā* and later on referred to as *Sīhaḷaṭṭhakathā-mahāvaṃsa*—which also would have contained a Sinhala prose explanation on the Pali verses; see Oldenberg 1879: 4 and Geiger 1908: 52–53 § 14. With regard to the language of the verses in the old *Sīhaḷaṭṭhakathā*, Oldenberg says: "The Pali verses ... taken apparently from the introduction to the whole work, render it highly probable that all these stanzas were composed in Pali". He also thinks that the *Dīpavaṃsa* is a compilation of verses, possibly from different sources: "..., a great part of the *Dīpavaṃsa* has the appearance not of an independent, continual work, but of a composition of such single stanzas extracted from a work or works like that Aṭṭhakathā ..." (1879: 6). Likewise, Geiger (1908: 5 § 1) writes: "It gives the impression, not of an evenly worked out whole, but of a stringing together of fragments ...". According to Frauwallner (1994: 19–31) there are two separate sources for the *Dīpavaṃsa*: one a history of the Buddhist community and the other a chronicle of the kings of Sri Lanka (*rājavaṃsa*), each in turn consisting of an older and newer part, composed in India and Sri Lanka respectively. Gunawardana (1988: 14–17)—in his discussion of the tendency of the *Dīpavaṃsa* to give the history of the Bhikkhunī Saṅgha and it therefore probably being a work composed by bhikkhunīs—suggests that the author of the *Samantapāsādikā* selected the list with the succession of bhikkhu teachers from the *Porāṇā*, excluding the list of bhikkhunī teachers, while the author(s) of the *Dīpavaṃsa* only selected the list of bhikkhunī teachers from the same source.

---

159. Gunawardana points out that the *Dīpavaṃsa* contains three different lists with names of bhikkhunīs who accompanied Saṅghamittā; ch. 15 v.77, ch. 18 vv. 11–12 & 24–5.

10. Different attributions of ideas

In at least two cases, there is a divergent attribution of ideas in Pali commentaries, showing a change of understanding of the Mahāvihāravāsins with regard to certain ideas that were originally in common with the Abhayagirivihāra, probably due to sharing the same commentaries.

In the *Visuddhimagga* (XIV.71) the inclusion of birth of matter (*jātirūpa*) and three other kinds of dependent matter, "matter as strength", "matter as origination", and "matter as disease" (*balarūpaṃ sambhavarūpaṃ, rogarūpaṃ*) in the list of kinds of dependent matter is attributed to the *aṭṭhakathā*. In the *Atthasālinī* (p. 339) and *Abhidhammāvatāra* (p. 72), however, it is attributed to "others" (*apare*), and in the *Mohavicchedanī* (p. 79) to "some" (*keci*).[160] *Jātirūpa* is part of the *Vimuttimagga*'s list, but the other three are not. Apparently, the old commentary included these four kinds of matter in its list. The *Visuddhimagga* adds that "in the opinion of certain ones (*ekacca*)", also "matter as torpor" (*middharūpa*) is included. This might refer to the inclusion of matter as torpor in the list of the recension of the same commentary transmitted in the Abhayagirivihāra or perhaps in the *Vimuttimagga*; see Introduction § 5 idea 1. By the time Buddhaghosa wrote the *Visuddhimagga*, the Mahāvihāra elders had changed their opinion about these four kinds of dependent matter and considered them non-existent due to being included in other types of matter. Nevertheless, due to being given in the old commentary, the four were still not regarded questionable enough to be attributed as the ideas of "others" as later commentators did. It is odd that the *Visuddhimagga* and the *Atthasālinī*, both ascribed traditionally to Buddhaghosa, attribute these four kinds of matter to different sources.[161]

The second case is an idea that Dhammapāla attributes to "some" (*keci*) in the *Visuddhimagga-mahāṭīka* and then rejects it—i.e. that there is no seeing of rise and fall of the immaterial aggregates by way of the moment (*khaṇato*). However, in the *Paṭisambhidāmagga-aṭṭhakathā*, Mahānāma presents this idea as if it is an accepted Mahāvihāra idea. Perhaps Mahānāma incorporated it from

160. Vism XIV.71/p.450: *Aṭṭhakathāyaṃ pana balarūpaṃ sambhavarūpaṃ jātirūpaṃ rogarūpaṃ, ekaccānaṃ matena middharūpanti, evaṃ aññānipi rūpāni āharitvā* ... As 340: *Keci pana middharūpaṃ nāma atthī ti vadanti. ... Apare balarūpena saddhiṃ sattavīsati, sambhavarūpena saddhiṃ aṭṭhavīsati, jātirūpena saddhiṃ ekūnatiṃsati, rogarūpena saddhiṃ samatiṃsati rūpānīti vadanti.* ... Abhidh-av 72: *Keci pana middhavādino middharūpaṃ nāma atthīti vadanti. ... Apare balarūpena saddhiṃ ekūnatiṃsa, sambhavarūpena saddhiṃ tiṃsa, jātirūpena saddhiṃ ekatiṃsa, rogarūpena saddhiṃ dvattiṃsa rūpānīti vadanti.* Moh 79: *Keci pana middharūpaṃ balarūpaṃ sambhavarūpaṃ jātirūpaṃ rogarūpan-ti imānipi pañca gahetvā tettiṃsa rūpāni hontī ti vadanti.* See fn. 75 for more complete passages.

161. Modern scholars have expressed doubts about Buddhaghosa being the author of the *Atthasālinī*. On the *Atthasālinī* and *Sammohavinodanī* not being works of Buddhaghosa, see Pind 1992: 136–137 and von Hinüber 1996: 151, §312.

the old commentary or from an Abhayagirivihāra work, not knowing that it was to be disapproved of, or he presented an understanding that was still held among some in the Mahāvihāra tradition but not by Dhammapāla. A similar idea as given by Mahānāma is found in Vim, see Introduction, § 5 idea 21.

The colophon to the *Visuddhimagga* says that this exposition of the authoritative decision or judgement (*vinicchaya*) [as found in the *aṭṭhakathā* of the Mahāvihāra] is "free from all blemishes due to intermixing": *sabbasaṅkaradosehi mutto*. "Blemishes due to intermixing",[162] according to the *Visuddhimaggamahāṭīkā* (II 534) means "free from intermixing with doctrine blemishes (*vādadosa*) of members of different schools": *nikāyantarassa nikāyagatavādadosasaṅkarehi mutto so nicchayo*. The preface to the *Atthasālinī* (p. 2) clarifies the meaning of this: "elucidating the judgement of the Mahāvihāra inhabitants, not mixed with the wrong ideas (*laddhi*) of different schools (*nikāyantaraladdhīhi*), not confused [by opinions due to different readings, etc.]".[163] Buddhaghosa thus says that the *Visuddhimagga* is free from the wrong ideas of other schools. This suggests that the older commentaries, or some of them, were taken to contain ideas that contradicted those of the Mahāvihāra and therefore needed revision.

Once such wrong idea might be found in Buddhaghosa's commentary on the Yamaka. It says that a statement in the *Sīhaḷaṭṭhakathā* on the Vibhaṅga, i.e. that matter ceases at the moment of arising of the seventeenth mind, contradicts the Canonical text, which is more authoritative.[164] This idea is also rejected in the commentary on the Vibhaṅga, where it is attributed to the *aṭṭhakathā*.[165]

---

162. Cf. MW: "*saṃkara*: m. mixing together, commingling, intermixture confusion (esp. of castes or races...) ... the confusion or blending together of metaphors which ought to be kept distinct. ..."

163. As 2: *Āropayitvā niddosaṃ, bhāsaṃ tantinayānugaṃ. Nikāyantaraladdhīhi, asammissaṃ anākulaṃ; Mahāvihāravāsīnaṃ, dīpayanto vinicchayaṃ, atthaṃ pakāsayissāmi, āgamaṭṭhakathāsupi, gahetabbaṃ gahetvāna, ...* Cf. Dhs-mṭ 10: *Nikāyantaraladdhīhīti antarantarā anuppavesitāhi. Asammissan-ti avokiṇṇaṃ. Anākulan-ti sanikāyepi anāvilaṃ paricchinnaṃ. Asammisso anākulo ca yo mahāvihāravāsīnaṃ atthavinicchayo, taṃ dīpayanto atthaṃpakāsayissāmīti.* Sp-ṭ I 19: *...mahātherehi nikāyantaraladdhīhisaṅkarapariharaṇatthaṃ sīhaḷabhāsāya ṭhapito.* Nett-ṭ 16: ... *nikāyantaraladdhidosehi antarantarā anuppavesitehi asammissan-ti adhippāyo. Asaṃkiṇṇan-ti sanikāyepi padatthantaraparikappanādinā asaṃkiṇṇaṃ tādisasaṅkararahitaṃ anākulaṃ suparicchinnaṃ.* Abhidh-av-pṭ 137: § 1406. *Nikāyantaraladdhīhīti aññasmiṃ nikāye laddhīhi.*

164. Yam-a 82: *Esā cittasamuṭṭhānarūpassa dhammatā ti niyamato cittasaṅkhārena saddhiṃ ekakkhaṇe nirujjhanato āmantā ti vuttaṃ. Yaṃ pana vibhaṅgappakaraṇassa sīhaḷaṭṭhakathāyaṃ: cittasamuṭṭhānaṃ rūpaṃ sattarasamassa cittassa uppādakkhaṇe nirujjhatī ti vuttaṃ, taṃ imāya pāḷiyā virūjjhati. Aṭṭhakathāto ca pāḷiyeva balavatarā ti pāḷiyaṃ vuttam-eva pamāṇaṃ.*

165. Vibh-a 27: *Ettha pana yadetaṃ sattarasamassa bhavaṅgacittassa uppādakkhaṇe*

An idea from the *Mahā-aṭṭhakathā* that is disagreed with in the *ṭīkā*-s is the idea that there are noseless beings in the sensuous sphere: "For one who is spontaneously born blind, deaf, noseless, and genderless, thirty kinds of matter are produced by way of the tongue-, body-, and [material] basis-decads." This is quoted and rejected as a "corrupt reading" (*pamādapāṭha*) in Dhammapāla's *Visuddhimagga-mahāṭīkā* and Ānanda's *Vibhaṅga-mūlaṭīkā*.[166] The idea of spontaneously born noseless beings is also found in a verse in Buddhadatta's *Abhidhammāvatāra* (5th c.) and troubled Sumaṅgala, the author of its *navaṭīkā*, who says that Buddhadatta took the "theory of the *Aṭṭhakathā*" (*aṭṭhakathāvāda*).[167] As part of their refutation of this idea, the *ṭīkā*-s refer to Buddhaghosa's commentary on the Abhidhammapiṭaka, which denies the existence of spontaneously born noseless beings in the sensuous sphere. Buddhadatta might not have been aware of this rejection or did not agree with it.

11. Reasons for Buddhaghosa's commentary project

What could be the reason for Buddhaghosa's commentary project for the Mahāvihāra? Ñāṇamoli (2011: xxx–xxxi) suggests that Buddhaghosa helped the Mahāvihāra to regain status for its Theravāda tradition and the Pali language in the face of the growing popularity of Sanskrit and the Buddhist traditions that used it: "unless it could successfully compete with Sanskrit, it had small hope of holding its position. With that the only course open was to launch a drive for the rehabilitation of Pali—a drive to bring the study of that language up to a standard fit to compete with the 'modern' Sanskrit in the field of international Buddhist culture." Similarly, Pind (1992: 150) says that it

---

yeva nirujjhatī'ti ādinā nayena ekassa cittassa uppādakkhaṇe uppannaṃ rūpaṃ aññassa uppādakkhaṇe nirujjhat 'ti aṭṭhakathāyaṃ āgatattā vuttaṃ, taṃ yassa kāyasaṅkhāro nirujjhati, tassa cittasaṅkhāro nirujjhatī ti? Āmantā ti imāya pāḷiyā virujjhati. ...

166. Vism-mhṭ II 308, Vibh-mṭ 123: *Ye pana opapātikassa jaccandhabadhira-aghānakanapuṃsakassa jivhākāyavatthudasakānaṃ vasena tiṃsa rūpāni uppajjantī ti mahāaṭṭhakathāyaṃ vuttan-ti vadanti, taṃ na gahetabbaṃ, so hi pamādapāṭho. Evañ-ca katvā āyatanayamakavaṇṇanāyaṃ (Yam-a 75): kāmadhātuyaṃ pana aghānako opapātiko natthi. Yadi bhaveyya, kassaci aṭṭhāyatanāni pātubhavantī ti vadeyyā ti vuttaṃ. ...*

167. Abhidh-av-nṭ II 179 (on Abhidh-av v. 756, see below): *Jaccandhabadhirā ti chandānurakkhaṇatthaṃ dīghakaraṇaṃ. Na hi jaccandhabadhira-aghānarahite napuṃsake vatthukāyajivhādasakavasena idha tiṃsā ti yujjati, idañ-ca opapātikassa jaccandhabadhiraghānarahite napuṃsake jivhākāyavatthudasakānaṃ vasena tiṃsa rūpāni uppajjantī ti aṭṭhakathāvādaṃ gahetvā vuttaṃ. Ānandācariyo pana taṃ pāḷiyā na sametī ti vatvā paṭikkhipati (see Vibh-mṭ 123)*.... *Dhammahadayavibhaṅge (Vibh § 1009) hi: kāmadhātuyā upapattikkhaṇe ... kassaci navāyatanāni, kassaci sattāyatanāni pātubhavantī ti vuttaṃ. Na vuttaṃ: aṭṭhāyatanāni pātubhavantī ti.* Abhidh-av 756: ... *Jaccandhabadhirāghāna-rahite tu napuṃsake.* 757. *Vatthuno kāyajivhānaṃ, vasā tiṃsāvakaṃsato ...*

is "probably first of all an attempt at consolidating the religious and political prerogatives of the tradition of the Mahāvihāra, which he clearly considered to be the true representative of the Buddhist dhamma."

Ñāṇamoli's theory implies that the Abhayagirivihāra was also using the Sanskrit language, but this is not indicated anywhere, rather, there are indications that it was using Pali; see Cousins 2012: 85–90. However, a modernisation and rehabilitation of the Pali language was likely one of the reasons for Buddhaghosa's project. According to Norman (1983: 119), the *Sīhaḷabhāsā* had developed so much in the five centuries between the 1st century BCE and the 5th century CE—that is, between the supposed writing down of the *aṭṭhakathā* and the time of Buddhaghosa—that even Sri Lankan bhikkhus would have had difficulty understanding the old *aṭṭhakathā*. The archaic nature of the *Sīhaḷabhāsā* used in the *aṭṭhakathā* was therefore an important reason to translate the *Sīhaḷabhāsā* parts into Pali. The old commentaries likely also contained Pali materials from different periods and provenances that were using different non-standardized spellings, sanskritizations, dialect forms, etc.; see Cousins 2013: 35–37. Instead, Buddhaghosa used one standardized form of the Pali language in his commentaries. Works in standardized, modern Pali made the commentaries accessible to both Sinhalese and foreign monks.

Making the Sīhaḷa commentaries accessible to the South Indian Theravāda communities was likely also a reason for Buddhaghosa's project. The preface to the Vinaya commentary translated in § 1 says, "But since this commentary, due to being composed in the language of the Sīhaḷa Island, provides no benefit for any bhikkhus outside of the Island, I will start on the commentary that conforms with the style [of the language] of the Canonical Texts." According to the *Dakkhiṇaindiyaraṭṭhikabhāvayutti* chapter of the *Visuddhimagganidānakathā* (composed for the Sixth Council in the 1950s), Buddhaghosa was South Indian, and two of the monks who requested the composition of the Nikāya commentaries, i.e. Jotipāla from Kañcipura, who requested the composition of the Spk and Mp, and Buddhamitta, who requested the Ps, and who had stayed with Buddhaghosa at Mayūradūtapaṭṭana; see also von Hinüber 2015: 356. The Jātaka commentary was also made upon the request of Buddhamitta and of Buddhadeva, a member of the Mahiṃsāsaka School, which was a prominent school in South India. Buddhadatta, a contemporary of Buddhaghosa and the composer of the *Buddhavaṃsa-aṭṭhakathā* and other works, was from Uraga in South India.

The translation of the old commentaries into the sophisticated and "pleasing language" (*manoramaṃ bhāsaṃ;* Sv I 1) that Buddhaghosa used would have increased the status of the Mahāvihāra in Theravāda Buddhist communities in Sri Lanka and South India, and perhaps also with ones further afield, such as in Southeast Asia, and strengthened ties with them.

A parallel can be drawn to the modern (digital) editions of the Tipiṭaka made by modern Buddhist groups such as Dhammakāya. The groups claim that their editions are authoritative or authentic and use them to boost their prestige and legitimacy. Buddhaghosa's works were possibly a similar prestige and legitimacy project. Since the concept of an official edition of the Tipiṭaka was unknown in Buddhaghosa's time, and since the content of the Tipiṭaka was fixed, changing, and adapting, it was not an option. However, the commentaries could be adapted and modernised due to not being the word of the Buddha.

Apart from school prestige and a need to modernise the language, there were also other and perhaps even more important reasons for Buddhaghosa's project for the Mahāvihāra. One major reason could have been the existence of the *Vimuttimagga*, an important work of the Abhayagirivihāra that would have given it prestige in Sri Lanka and abroad, to the dismay of the Mahāvihāra. The *Visuddhimagga*, Buddhaghosa's first official work for the Mahāvihāra, could have been the Mahāvihāra's response to the *Vimuttimagga*. Possibly Buddhaghosa's other commentaries were also a reaction to similar commentaries composed by Abhayagirivihāra authors. In order to keep up with its Abhayagirivihāra neighbours and competitors, the Mahāvihāra could have felt compelled to come up with a treatise on the path to nibbāna and modernise its commentaries.

As discussed above, the older commentaries also contained different and sometimes conflicting ideas that did not always agree with the Mahāvihāra elders. Some differences in explanations and narratives, mostly in details and not in doctrinal ideas, are still found in parallel passages in different commentaries of Buddhaghosa, and in *ṭīkās* these are said to be due to different opinions of different groups of reciters, see § 1 and 8. However, explanations of important words and phrases are identical in the commentaries of Buddhaghosa, e.g. the explanations of *evaṃ me sutaṃ* and *bhagavā* are identical in the beginning of the four Nikāya commentaries. The discussion of *ānāpānasati* is mostly the same in the *Visuddhimagga* and *Samantapāsādikā*, and the latter refers back to the discussion in the former for the full explanations of points, as is done also in other commentaries.

The prefaces to Buddhaghosa's commentaries also indicate that the old commentaries were repetitive (*punappunāgatamattha*) and contained corrupt readings (*pamādalekha*). As discussed in § 7, Buddhaghosa abridged the materials from the old commentaries. It is also likely that old commentaries were probably not well structured, not always following the order of materials of the canonical texts; see § 7. For the corrupt readings rejected by Buddhaghosa, see § 6.

Instead of these unwieldy works, Buddhaghosa made commentaries that were more concise, orderly, accessible, consistent, and accorded with the latest doctrinal ideas and exegetical methods of the Mahāvihāra. After Buddhaghosa's Vinaya Commentary was finished, a Mahāvihāra monk studying or teaching the Vinaya would only have to consult one authoritative and accessible Pali Vinaya commentary in a modern standardized form of Pali instead of the several older Vinaya commentaries that were in archaic Sīhaḷa and non-standardized forms of Pali.

Due to the rise of the Abhayagirivihāra, other schools, and the Mahāyāna, the Mahāvihāra elders likely also felt that the survival of their tradition, and therefore the true Dhamma, was threatened. By calling in the help of Ācariya Buddhaghosa to compose the modern and authorative *Visuddhimagga* and the commentaries they ensured the "endurance of the True Dhamma" as said in the colophon of the *Visuddhimagga*, and the "longevity of the Dhamma", as said in the preface of the Nikāya commentaries.

To sum up, the main reasons for Buddhaghosa's project were authority, school-identity, prestige, competition, modernisation, doctrinal, linguistic and exegetical consistency and standardization, accessibility in terms of language and structure, making the commentaries available abroad, and survival of the true Dhamma.

Appendix IV

The Reasons for the Split between the Mahāvihāra and Abhayagirivihāra

According to the Pali chronicles, a dispute about the interpretation of Vinaya rules caused the official split between the Mahāvihāra and Abhayagirivihāra during the reign of King Mahāsena (circa 277–304 CE); see Cousins 2012: 96–98. Why did this happen?

In the final part of the *Dīpavaṃsa* (Ch. 22 vv. 66–76), the "evil" bhikkhus Mitta, Soṇa, and other "shameless persons" are condemned for misleading the king by teaching that some Vinaya regulations of the Mahāvihāra were unallowable and unlawful. Two Mahāvihāra regulations that were rejected are specified: (1) giving the full admission (*upasampadā*) to one who is twenty rainy seasons old by counting the time from conception (rather than birth), and (2) the use of ivory [for handles of hand fans].[168]

The school affiliation of the "evil" bhikkhus is not mentioned in the *Dīpavaṃsa*, however, according to the *Mahāvaṃsa* and *Mahāvaṃsaṭīkā* they were connected to the Abhayagirivihāra. The *Mahāvaṃsaṭīkā* also says that they created the schism by reason of differences as to the meaning (*atthantara*) and differences in readings (*pāṭhantara*) of the Khandhakas and Parivāra of the Vinaya Piṭaka and that they left the Theravāda (i.e. Mahāvihāra) to form the Dhammarucikavāda, which was the official name of the school or monastic sect (*nikāya*) of the Abhayagirivihāravāsins; see Cousins 2012: 68, 94.[169]

Their rejection of the use of ivory (*danta*) for monks' paraphernalia[170] is a relatively minor Vinaya point. However, teaching that the full admission

---

168. *Ubhatosamaggabhāvissaṃ (=upasampadaṃ gabbhavisaṃ?) anuññātaṃ kumārakassape, akappiyan-ti dīpesuṃ dussīlā mohapārutā / Chabbaggiyānaṃ vatthusmiṃ ananuññātaṃ dantavattakaṃ, anuññātaṃ ti dīpesuṃ alajjī dantagaṇikā* ... The *Dīpavaṃsa* text is quite corrupt here and, as Oldenberg (1879: 112, 220–221) does, is to be interpreted according to the account in the *Mahāvaṃsaṭīkā* (II 676–77): *Chabbaggiyabhikkhūnaṇi vatthumhi anuññātaṃ dantamayavījanim pi, aḍḍhakāsikagaṇikāya vatthumhi anuññātaṃ dūteyya-upasampadam pi, kumārakassapavatthumhi anuññātaṃ gabbhavāsena paripuṇṇa-vīsativassūpasampadam pi na vaṭṭatī ti* ... *Sīmantarikanimittavasen'eva anajjhottharitaṃ khaṇḍasīmaṃ ajjhottharitan ti ca, tattha dantakaṭṭhakiccapariyosāne cāletvā khelaṃ bhūmiyaṃ na khipitabban ti ca keci vadantā.*

169. Mhv-ṭ II 676: *Abhayagirivāsino hi pubbe yeva bhagavato āhaccabhāsitavinayapiṭakato khandhakaparivāraṃ atthantarapāṭhantarakaraṇavasena bhedaṃ katvā theravādato nikkhamitvā dhammarucikavādā nāma jātā.*

170. The *Dīpavaṃsa* text, as in Oldenberg's edition, says that the shameless bhikkhus, who are said to be "of the ivory-faction"* taught that the use of ivory was allowed

into the bhikkhu-saṅgha is not allowable when it is carried out within twenty rainy seasons from conception certainly is important. The stricter interpretation of counting the years from birth and rejecting the months spent in the womb, i.e. counting the actual twentieth year[171] as the earliest limit, entails that all those who had received the admission by counting twenty years from conception—of whom there likely were many—had actually not been ordained (as regulated in Pācittiya rule 65 at Vin IV 130). This certainly would have led to bitter dispute and schism and would have given a good reason to King Mahāsena to penalize the Mahāvihāra bhikkhus (as related in the *Mahāvaṃsa*). Perhaps the Abhayagirivāsins took the stance that Mahāvihāra bhikkhus who had been ordained by including the time from conception were not properly ordained and had to be re-ordained, and when

---

(*anuññāta*) although it was *not* allowed (*ananuññāta*) in the story of the group of six monks in the Khandhakas. However, the *Mahāvaṃsaṭīkā* says that they rejected the use of ivory fans: *Chabbaggiyabhikkhūnaṃ vatthumhi anuññātaṃ dantamayavījanim pi na vaṭṭatī ti*: "The ivory fan [handle] allowed in the origin story of the group of six monks is also not fitting". (* *dantagaṇikā*, "of the ivory-faction", not "ivory harlots"; cf. *Sāsanavaṃsa*: *ekaṃsikagaṇikā bhikkhū*: "one-shoulder-faction monks".) Ivory is not in the list of three allowable materials for [the handles of] fans (*vījanī*) at Vin II 130, but it is not explicitly forbidden either. As Cousins points out (2012: 96), the commentary to the Cullavagga (Sp VI 1209f., commenting on Vin II 130) allows ivory (handles) for fans: *Vidhūpanan-ti vījanī vuccati. Tālavaṇṭaṃ pana tālapaṇṇehi vā kataṃ hotu veḷudantavilīvehi vā morapiñchehi vā cammavikatīhi vā sabbaṃ vaṭṭati.* The Khandhakas do allow ivory collyrium boxes (*añjanī*, Vin I 203), penknife handles (*satthakadaṇḍā*, Vin II 115), earwax removers (*kaṇṇamalaharaṇī*, Vin II 135), and robe tiers (*gaṇṭhika*, Vin II 136). The non-offence clause to the Pātimokkha rule on needle cases in the Suttavibhaṅga (Pācittiya rule 86 at Vin IV 167) allows ivory for several paraphernalia, including the ones mentioned in the Khandhakas: robe tier, a [handle] of a stick for making fire (*araṇika*), a buckle, collyrium box, collyrium stick, axe-handle, and some kind of water wiper: Vin IV 167: *Anāpatti gaṇṭhikāya, araṇike, vidhe (v.l.l. vīṭhe, vithe. Cf. Skt vīṭhaka), añjaniyā, añjanisalākāya, vāsijaṭe, udakapuñchaniyā ....* Given these various allowances, it would be odd that fan handles made of ivory were not allowed. In the origin stories (*vatthu*) to all of these Khandhaka allowances the group of six monks are mentioned as the culprits who gave rise to the regulations, however the group of six is not mentioned in the origin story to the allowed materials for hand fans as well as to the origin story to the Pātimokkha rule on needle cases. According to Pācittiya rule 86 (Vin IV 167), ivory is not allowable as a material for needle cases. Therefore, the Abhayagirivāsin bhikkhus perhaps took the Pātimokkha rule on ivory not being an allowable material for needle cases to apply to all monks' paraphernalia, and rejected the laxer allowance for the use of ivory in the Khandhakas and in the non-offence clause in the Suttavibhaṅga.

171. *Vassa* means "rainy season" and "year". However, here "rainy season" seems to be implied, i.e. even if the applicant for full admission is born just after the rainy season, then he has to wait until the 20th rainy season is finished.

this was rejected, the king took sides and dispelled the Mahāvihāravāsins from their monastery.

According to the Mhv-ṭ (p. 676), the Abhayagirivāsins held three other views regarding Vinaya regulations: (1) they rejected the allowance of full admission [of bhikkhunīs] by way of a messenger (as at Vin II 277, see Cousins 2012: 97–98); they held (2) that just the markers of the interspace between monastery boundaries (*sīmantarikā*, see Vin I 111) were not sufficient to separate a subsidiary boundary [from the great boundary (*mahāsīmā*)],[172] and (3) that one should not spit on the ground after cleaning the teeth (see Cousins 2012: 97).

The second view appears to reject the Mahāvihāra commentarial concept of *khaṇḍasīmā* or subsidiary boundary which is not found in the canonical Vinaya and is based on the Khandhaka regulation for marking the interspace of boundaries (Vin I 111). This rejection entails that bhikkhus who are received the full admission in a village area covered by a *mahāsīmā* are ordained properly and this is in line with the *sīmā* regulations as found in the canonical Vinaya. This also could have been a cause of dispute about the validity of the full admissions since the Mahāvihāra could have rejected these outside of a *khaṇḍasīmā* and could have considered invalid any of the full admissions that had been carried out in this manner. In the 19th century, a dispute about the validity of a *sīmā* led to a split in the Amarapura Nikāya in Sri Lanka. Some monks held that all the full admissions were invalid that had been held in a particular monastic boundary (*sīmā*) that they considered invalid and others disagreed with this; see Kieffer-Pülz 1998: 214–217.

What can be gathered from the accounts in the *Dīpavaṃsa* and *Mahāvaṃsaṭīkā* is that the Abhayagirivāsin bhikkhus who influenced King

172. "A subsidiary boundary (*khaṇḍasīmā*) not overlapped [by the great boundary (*mahāsīmā*)] merely by means of the marks of the boundary-interspace [between the subsidiary and great boundary] is overlapped [by the great boundary]": *sīmantarika-nimittavasen'eva anajjhottharitaṃ khaṇḍasīmaṃ ajjhottharitan ti ca.* This could mean that the Abhayagirivāsins held that just placing the boundary-interspace marks does not prevent the overlapping of the subsidiary boundary by the great boundary and that extra markers for the subsidiary boundary are needed. However, the Mahāvihāra tradition says that markers for the subsidiary boundary as well as the boundary space are needed and that the *khaṇḍasīmā* has to be determined first. Sp V 1054: *Sace pana khaṇḍasīmāya nimittāni kittetvā tato sīmantarikāya nimittāni kittetvā mahāsīmāya nimittāni kittenti, evaṃ tīsu ṭhānesu nimittāni kittetvā yaṃ sīmaṃ icchanti, taṃ paṭhamaṃ bandhituṃ vaṭṭati.* Therefore, it seems to be a rejection of the *khaṇḍasīmā* concept as expounded in Mahāvihāra commentaries and that only the *mahāsīmā* as taught in the canonical Vinaya was acccepted. In contrast to the first three views, these two statements are not Mahāvihāra allowances that are rejected (*na vaṭṭati*) by the Abhayagirivāsins, but they rather express the Abhayagirivāsin views (*keci vadantā*).

Mahāsena were not lax monks but zealous reformists who had a stricter and more conservative interpretation of some Vinaya rules and regulations than the Mahāvihāravāsins; see also Cousins 2012: 82–85. The Pali commentaries and subcommentaries support this since they mention that the Abhayagirivāsins had more strict or severe interpretations of some Vinaya rules than the Mahāvihāra had.[173]

Significant in the passage in the Mhv-ṭ is its specification of the falling out as being due to differences as to the meaning and readings of the Khandhakas and Parivāra (*khandhakaparivāraṃ atthantarapāṭhantarakaraṇa*). With "different meaning" (*atthantara*) is probably meant that the reformists did not accept the way the regulations were interpreted in the Mahāvihāra commentaries (see Cousins 2012: 96) and that the Abhayagirivihāra commentaries had different interpretations of regulations. On different interpretations of Vinaya rules by *keci*, i.e. Abhayagirivāsins, as mentioned in Mahāvihāra commentaries, see fn. 2533. "Different reading" or "different text," *pāṭhantara* means that the text of the Khandhaka and Parivāra texts transmitted by the Abhayagirivihāra had different readings than the text of the Mahāvihāra.[174] It usually applies to words and parts of sentences in a text. This matches with the different readings of words and parts of sentences attributed to "some", etc. (*keci/ye ... paṭhanti*) that are found in

173. They had a stricter interpretation of the fourth Pārājika in respect of making false claims of attainments in past lives. The Mahāvihāra held that this is not a pārājika but *keci* or "some" held that it is (Sp II 496). Vajirabuddhi says that *keci* are residents of the Uttaravihāra, i.e. Abhayagirivihāra (Vjb-ṭ 172). At Sp 1025 it is said that in the case of giving *upasampadā* without an preceptor (*upajjhāya*) the legal act is valid, but that "some" hold that it is invalid. Vajirabuddhi says that some are the Abhayagirivāsins (Vjb-ṭ 433–34). On this and other stricter interpretations of Vinaya rules by Abhayagiri monks, see Kieffer-Pülz 2013b: 244–47. Other stricter interpretations attributed to *keci* are mentioned at Sp 265 and Sp 377 (stealing).

174. See also von Hinüber 1996: 22 § 43. A verse quoted from the *Khuddasikkhā* of the Abhayagirivāsins in the *Khuddasikkhā-purāṇaṭīkā*, which says that animal fats are among the excellent foods that can be kept for seven days (see Cousins 2012: 89),* suggests that their version of the Khandhakas did not include the regulation found in the Bhesajjakkhandhaka (Vin I 200) or that it was worded differently. In the regulation, as transmitted by the Mahāvihāravāsins, the Buddha allows the oil extracted from animal fats to be kept for seven days at most (since oil is a seven day medicine allowed in Pācittiya rule 39 [of which the word commentary includes oil made from animal fat, *vasātela*, into oil] see Vin IV 88) when these fats are accepted, cooked and mixed in time, i.e. in one morning before noon, but there is no allowance for keeping the animal fats themselves beyond the noon of the day they are accepted.
* Khuddas-pṭ 114: ... *uttaravihāravāsīnaṃ khuddasikkhāya āgatanayena vuttaṃ. Tesaṃ pana: Sappi-navanītaṃ telaṃ, madhu-phāṇitapañcamaṃ; Acchamacchavasādi ca, honti sattāhakālikā ti.*

the Pali commentaries. On passages containing both different readings and explanations that are attributed to *keci*, suggesting that at least some of the different explanations are due to different readings in the canonical texts; see fn. 2493.

The rejection of the allowance by which the Buddha settled the doubt of Kumārakassapa whether his full admission (*upasampadā*) had been valid or not—i.e. that the time he in spent in the womb from the moment of the arising of the first mentality (i.e. conception) can be included in counting the twentieth year (as found in the Mahākhandhaka of the Mahāvagga at Vin I 93)—indicates that the Abhayagirivāsins accepted the rule as it is literally stated in the Pātimokkha and the Suttavibhaṅga and that the Abhayagirivihāra version of the Khandhakas did not contain the allowance. Possibly the Vibhaṅga's origin story with Kumārakassapa is unique to the Mahāvihāra Theravādins. The explanation of the rule on giving full admission to a person younger than twenty years in the Vinayavibhaṅga of the Mahāsāṃghikas as translated into Chinese (T 1425: 383b18–c23) contains a detailed analysis of what constitutes twenty rains and how it is to be ascertained, but there is no mention that the time starting from conception can be included in the counting, or that the age can be reduced in another manner.[175] The Vinayavibhaṅgas of other schools, in the definitions of "non-offence" in the same rule, do briefly mention that the twenty years can be counted by including the time spent in the mother's womb. None of the Vinayavibhaṅgas, however, contains an origin story or a mention of Kumārakassapa.[176]

The rejection of the full admission of a bhikkhunī by way of a messenger, found in the Khandhakas, could indicate a different reading in the Khandhakas of the Abhayagirivāsins, or a stricter interpretation in their commentaries (see Cousins 2012: 97–98). The rejection of the *khaṇḍasīmā* suggests that it was rejected or not found in their commentaries. The regulation on spitting on the ground cannot be traced in the Vinaya Piṭaka or in Pali commentarial works, nor in the Prātimokṣasūtras of other early schools. Perhaps the Vinaya commentary of the Abhayagirivihāra took the Pātimokkha rule on not spitting on vegetation (Sekhiya 74, Vin IV 205) to apply also to spitting on the ground after cleaning the teeth. Alternatively, perhaps the reformist Abhayagirivihāra bhikkhus had made their own stricter interpretations that

175. The analysis is found more briefly in § 210 of the Bhikṣuṇīvinaya of the Mahāsāṃghika Lokottaravādins.

176. The Dharmaguptaka Vinayavibhaṅga has: "Non offence: ... If ordained already [and he] has doubt, the Buddha said: it is allowed to count the time-period [he spent] inside the womb, to count the leap months of the years, or count all fourteen day uposathas ...." T 1428: 680c24–26. Similarly in the Mahīśāsaka VinVibh at T 1421: 061b15–17; Sarvāstivāda VinVibh at T 1441: 578c06-07 and *Vinayamātṛka* at T 1463: 841b08-13 (cf. T 1463: 803a17-20).

were not found in commentaries and perhaps they were only a small but influential group of bhikkhus within the wider Abhayagirivihāra tradition.

The *Mahāvaṃsa* (Ch. 37) records that the Mahāvihāravāsins were evicted by King Mahāsena because he was made to believe by the evil bhikkhus that they did not teach the true Vinaya.[177] It is unlikely that Mahāsena—overall an able Bodhisattva king[178] who did many good deeds such as building reservoirs, as well as building and repairing monasteries—would have evicted them without any kind of prior investigation and demand for improvement. It is therefore possible that if the Mahāvihāravāsins had complied with the stricter interpretations as endorsed by the king, they could have stayed on. Since it was to be expected that the Mahāvihāravāsins would adhere to the allowances as given in their version of the Khandhakas, and therefore would not want to get re-ordained, it indeed would have been a clever pretext to get rid of them.

What could possibly have taken place is that the Mahāvihāra's allegations of corruption in doctrine, i.e., the practice of vetullavāda or Mahāyāna at the Abhayagirivihāra, or more likely by a faction residing at this monastery complex, led to counter allegations of corruption in monastic discipline at the Mahāvihāra. Since the new king Mahāsena sided with the Mahāyāna faction at the Abhayagirivihāra, who he might have regarded as more virtuous and progressive, he warned and then punished the "quarrelsome" Mahāvihāra monks.

There is significant inscriptional evidence for the split between the Mahāvihāra and Abhayagirivihāra in a fragmentary edict inscription found at the Jetavana Stupa that King Mahāsena built. The first parts of all thirteen lines are missing and it is therefore hard to interpret the edict. The translations and interpretations of Paranavitana (1943: 273–285) and Dias (2001: 83–84) differ. What can be gleaned from it is that it was made in the first year of the reign of its royal author (line 1)—presumably King Mahāsena—who blames those of the Five Great Monasteries or Mahāvihāra (*paca maha-avasa*) and the whole

177. Mhv xxxvii.3: ... *Mahāvihāra-viddhaṃsaṃ, kātukāmo asaññato. 4. Avinayavādino ete, mahāvihāravāsino; Vinayavādī mayaṃ rāja, iti gāhiya bhūpabhiṃ. 5. Mahāvihāravāsissa, āhāraṃ deti bhikkhuno; Yo so sataṃ daṇḍiyo'ti, raññā daṇḍaṃ ṭhapāpayi. ...*

178. The *Mahāvaṃsa* says that Saṅghamitta—a monk from the Coḷa country who became a disciple of one of the Abhayagiri monks and who was banished to southern India by King Gothābhaya (circa 254–267 CE) on account of following Vetullavāda, i.e. Mahāyāna, and who was skilled in sorcery (*bhūtavijjā*)—performed the *abhiseka* annointing of Mahāsena at his coronation. Since Buddhist monks traditionally do not perform rituals at coronations, Saṅghamitta could have carried out a Mahāyānist initiation to make Mahāsena a bodhisattva king. Mahāsena was not the first and only Sri Lankan king who was a bodhisattva. King Saṅghabodhi (circa 252–254 CE) preceded him and many followed him.

Saṅgha (*sava-saga*) [of ...] for transgressing (*pave*) in various ways, despite being rebuked for it (line 3 & 4). He says that Vaitulya books (*vayatudala pota*) create a path of [welfare?] and that he has faith [in this path?] (line 5 & 6). Then the Mahāvihāra is mentioned again (line 7), followed by "those who cause disturbance to one another and ... are quarrelsome" (line 8). Towards the end of the inscription (line 11) there is reference to the Abhayagirivihāra (*Abagiri-mahavihara*), wherein a copy of the edict was to be placed, as well as in the square hall on the highway (line 13). The unintelligible line (no. 12) in between these two lines suggests that another copy was to be placed elsewhere, possibly the Mahāvihāra.

In another inscription found at the Rājagala or Rāssahela—a large monastery complex located on a remote mountain in the traditionalistic Rohaṇa province, far away from the capital—Mahāsena says that he made a donation for the benefit of the monks at the two local monasteries and "whole great Bhikkhu Saṅgha of all monasteries" (*sakala-veherahi sakala-maha-biku-saga*), so that those who constantly abide in the "mansion of True Dhamma" (*sadhama-pate*) gain distinction in virtue, concentration, and wisdom, [instead of] division (*bidini*); see Dias 2001: 86.

The inscriptions show that Mahāsena was troubled by the quarrels in the Saṅgha and desired peace. Since the edict was also to be placed at the Abhayagirivihāra there apparently were also Abhayagiri monks who Mahāsena considered "quarrelsome". These could have been orthodox Abhayagiri monks opposed to the Mahāyāna faction at their monastery. Since the edict was also to be placed at an important public place and since "the whole Saṅgha" is mentioned, other monasteries could also have been involved in the dispute.

Mahāsena's declaration of his faith in the Mahāyāna suggests that there was a dispute about this new doctrine and that Mahāsena considered this dispute as wrong. However, the emphasis in the Rājagala inscription on practice by way of virtue, concentration and wisdom (i.e. the three divisions of the eightfold path, as described in the *Vimuttimagga* and *Visuddhimagga*) suggests that Mahāsena was not opposed to the Theravāda. The *Mahāvaṃsa* (Ch. 37 v, 45) relates that besides repairing many derelict monastery residences on the island, Mahāsena gave robes to all monks each year. The absence of archeological evidence of Mahāyāna practices at Rājagala also indicates that Mahāsena supported orthodox Theravāda monks there.

Appendix V

Attabhāvavatthu and *Ātmavastu*

1. *Attabhāvavatthu*

The term *attabhāvavatthu* "ground of selfhood" is used in three passages in the *Peṭakopadesa*, and once in the *Nettipakaraṇa*. It is also found three times in the Chinese translation of the *Vimuttimagga*, in passages that parallel ones in the *Peṭakopadesa*.

There is no specific explanation of the term *attabhāvavatthu* in the *Peṭaka*, *Netti*, or *Vimuttimagga*, but from the usage and context in these works, as well as the explanation in the *Netti* commentary and subcommentary, the meaning can be gathered. Its rarity and its usage in the *Peṭakopadesa* and *Nettipakaraṇa* works, which are said to have been imported into the Mahāvihāra tradition from other schools, suggests that *attabhāvavatthu* was not a term that originated in the Theravāda tradition. Since Upatissa does not explain the term, he assumes that readers of the *Vimuttimagga* are familiar with it.

In the first usage in the *Peṭakopadesa* (Peṭ 15), it is given as *attabhāvato ... vatthu* "ground of/for selfhood" in "... and the fourfold ground of selfhood–this is suffering".[179] This is found in the analysis of the herdsman simile in the Gopālasutta (A V 347–352) wherein "four establishments of mindfulness" is given instead. This usage suggests that the compound *attabhāvavatthu* is to be interpreted as a genitive/dative *tatpuruṣa* compound and that the *Peṭaka* takes it as the objects of mindfulness.[180]

The second passage in the *Peṭaka* wherein the four grounds of selfhood are found (Peṭ 121; see below) indicates that they are the five aggregates contemplated in terms of the four *satipaṭṭhānas*—with the *saññā* and *vedanā* aggregates combined into the ground/object of *dhammas*—as foul, suffering, without self, and impermanent respectively, with the aim of opposing the four distortions through which the four grounds of selfhood are regarded as beautiful, etc. The four grounds of selfhood are thus equal to the four grounds of distortion (*vipallāsavatthu*) earlier in the same passage. However, later the *Peṭaka* (Peṭ 224; see below) says that the fourfold ground of selfhood is called 'self' due to ignorance being the place for the four distortions' range

---

179. Peṭ 15: *... catubbidhaṃ ca attabhāvato ca vatthu, idaṃ dukkhaṃ.*

180. *-bhāvato* usually is ablative/instrumental, but "from/due to selfhood" does not fit here and therefore it rather is to be understood as a masculine noun ending in *-ant*. The text might be corrupt.

of predominance (*vipallāsagocarādhipateyyabhūmi*). The fourfold ground of selfhood can therefore be said to be the identity-view, *sakkāyadiṭṭhi* or grasping of a doctrine of self, *attavādūpādāna*[181] that is caused by the four distortions in the four grounds. Each and all of the four distortions cause the wrong perception, mind, and view of a "self".

The *Netti* (85; see below) says that the distortions occur in the four grounds of selfhood, that is, the four modes of regarding a self with regard to the five aggregates. In the Saṃyutta Nikāya (S III 102, etc.), these four modes are said to be the causes for identity-view, *sakkāyadiṭṭhi*. Then the *Netti* says that matter, feelings, perceptions and formations, and consciousness (i.e. the objects of the four establishments of mindfulness) are the grounds of distortion, and finally that the four grounds of distortion are the five aggregates contemplated in terms of the objects of the four *satipaṭṭhānas*. Therefore, as Ñāṇamoli notes (1964: 166 fn. 485/1, 1977: 119 fn. 493/1), unlike the *Peṭaka* at first, the *Netti* does not take the four grounds of selfhood as the five aggregates contemplated in terms of the four *satipaṭṭhānas*, but rather as the four modes through which the five aggregates are regarded as "self", i.e. as the causes for identity-view, as in the last passage in the *Peṭaka*.

In his commentary on the *Netti* (Nett-a 142; see below), Dhammapāla explains the term *attabhāvavatthu*. In brief, he says that it is the awareness and designation that there is a "self" in the four grounds due to the I-conceit established by the distortions therein. The old subcommentary summarises: "The selfhood caused by the occurrence of that awareness and designation in the ground of happiness, etc. is called 'ground of selfhood'".

There are three different translations of the term *attabhāva-vatthu* in the Chinese translation of the *Vimuttimagga*: 義性處, *attha-bhāva-vatthu* at 447c02, 自性處, *sabhāva/attabhāva-vatthu* at 450a14 and 身性處, *attabhāva-vatthu* at 453b12. The Tibetan translation (Sav 182b) first has *bdag gi rang bzhin yongs = attā + sabhāva* but in the next paragraph it instead has *bdag gi dngos po = attā + vatthu/bhāva = attabhāva*. Later (Sav 194b), it has *bdag gi ngo bo'i dngos po* corresponding to *attabhāva*.

The term is not explained in Vim. These are the three occurrences:

1. The Buddha taught the [five] aggregates by way of the grounds of selfhood (Vim 450a14).
2. The not knowing of the grounds of selfhood is the cause for the four distortions of perception, i.e. perceiving beauty in the foul, etc. and

181. See Vibh-a 182: *Vīsativatthukā sakkāyadiṭṭhi attavādupādānaṃ. Yathāha (Vibh 375): Tattha katamaṃ attavādupādānaṃ? Idha assutavā puthujjano ... rūpaṃ attato samanupassati ... vipariyesaggāho. ...* Nett-a 195: *Ucchedasassataṃ samāsato vīsativatthukā sakkāyadiṭṭhīti attā ucchijjati attā nicco ti ca ādippavattanato ucchedasassatadassanaṃ saṅkhepato vīsativatthukā sakkāyadiṭṭhi eva hoti. Sabbo pi hi attavādo sakkāyadiṭṭhi-antogadho evā ti.*

the knowing of them is cause for the four [true] perceptions, i.e. of the foul, suffering, impermanence, and without self (Vim 447b29ff).

3. The four grounds of selfhood are [the truth of] suffering, the four distortions are [the truth of] the origination of suffering, and the four establishments of mindfulness are the path (Vim 453b12).

The first two occurrences parallel the passage at Peṭ 121 which says that the five aggregates are the four grounds of selfhood, that the perception of beauty in the body, etc., are distortions, and that the four establishments of mindfulness eradicate these distortions (see also Nett 83, 85). The third one parallels the passage at Peṭ 15, which says that the fourfold ground of selfhood is suffering.

2. Translations of Pāli passages

Peṭ 121: "What are the four grounds of distortion? The body, feelings, mind, and dhammas. ... What are the three distortions? Perception, mind, and view. ... Herein, the grasping of the sign [of beauty, etc.] in an agreeable ground ..., this is the distortion of perception. Herein, when there is intimation by one whose mind is distorted with regard to the [agreeable] ground, this is the distortion of mind. Herein, when one whose mind is distorted with regard to that [agreeable] form [by perceiving] beauty in the foul, that which is liking, preference, regarding, judgement, view... this is the distortion of view. Therein, when analysing by way of the grounds, the three become twelve distortions: three with regard to the body, three with regard to feelings, three with regard to the mind, and three with regard to dhammas. ... Herein, the five aggregates are the four grounds of selfhood. The aggregate of matter is the body as ground of selfhood; the aggregate of feelings is the feelings as ground of selfhood; the aggregate of perception and the aggregate of formations are dhammas as ground of selfhood; and the aggregate of consciousness is the mind as ground of selfhood. Thus, the five aggregates are the four grounds of selfhood. Herein, [the perception of] beauty in what is foul with regard to the body is a distortion; [happiness in what is suffering with regard to feelings is a distortion; permanence in what is impermanent with regard to the mind is a distortion;] self in what is without self with regard to dhammas is a distortion. Herein, for the purpose of eradication of the four distortions, the Fortunate One taught and declared the four establishments of mindfulness. For one who dwells contemplating the body in the body, the distortion of beauty in what is foul is eradicated; and so for feelings, mind and dhammas".[182]

---

182. Peṭ 121: *Katamāni cattāri vipallāsavatthūni? Kāyo vedanā cittaṃ dhammā ca. ... Katamāni tīṇi vipallāsāni? Saññā cittaṃ diṭṭhi ca. ... Tattha manāpike vatthumhi indriyavatthe vaṇṇāyatane*

Peṭ 224: "... Therein, the resort [and] plane of predominance of the distortions is ignorance. For, as it perceives, as it cognizes, as it perceives and cognizes, [and] as it likes, it designs/intends these four distortions whereby beings call 'self' the fourfold ground of selfhood, which is a disease, a boil."[183]

Netti 85: "What is it that it distorts? Three things: perception, mind, and view. Wherein does it distort? In the four grounds of selfhood [i.e.] 'He regards matter as self, or as self as possessing matter, matter as in self, or self as in matter.' So for feelings, perceptions, formations, and consciousness. Herein matter is the first ground of distortion [by regarding] beauty in what is foul;

---

vā yo nimittassa uggāho, ayaṃ saññāvipallāso. Tattha viparītacittassa vatthumhi sati viññatti, ayaṃ cittavipallāso. Tattha viparītacittassa tamhi rūpe asubhe subhan-ti yā khanti ruci upekkhanā nicchayo diṭṭhi nidassanaṃ santīraṇā, ayaṃ diṭṭhivipallāso. Tattha vatthubhedena tayo sā dvādasa vipallāsā bhavanti. Tayo kāye tayo vedanāya tayo citte tayo dhamme, cattāro saññāvipallāsā cattāro cittavipallāsā cattāro diṭṭhivipallāsā, ... Tattha pañcakkhandhā cattāri attabhāvavatthūni bhavanti. Yo rūpakkhandho, so kāyo attabhāvavatthu. Yo vedanākkhandho, so vedanā attabhāvavatthu. Yo saññākkhandho ca saṅkhārakkhandho ca, te dhammā attabhāvavatthu. Yo viññāṇakkhandho, so cittaṃ attabhāvavatthu. Iti pañcakkhandhā cattāri attabhāvavatthūni. Tattha kāye asubhe subhan-ti vipallāso bhavati. Evaṃ vedanāsu ... pe ... citte ... pe ... dhammesu ca attā ti vipallāso bhavati. Tattha catunnaṃ vipallāsānaṃ samugghātanatthaṃ bhagavā cattāro satipaṭṭhāne deseti paññapeti kāye kāyānupassī viharato asubhe subhan-ti vipallāsaṃ samugghāteti, evaṃ vedanāsu, citte, dhammesu ca kātabbaṃ. Cf. Nett 83: *Kāye kāyānupassī viharanto asubhe, subhan-ti vipallāsaṃ pajahati, ... Vedanāsu vedanānupassī viharanto dukkhe sukhan-ti vipallāsaṃ pajahati ... Vedanāsu vedanānupassī viharanto dukkhe sukhan-ti vipallāsaṃ pajahati ... Dhammesu dhammānupassī viharanto anattani attā ti vipallāsaṃ pajahati.* Nett 124: *cattāro vipallāsā tesaṃ paṭipakkho cattāro satipaṭṭhānā.* Cf. *Śrāvakabhūmi* Ms.87a2L, Sh.303-4: *tatra caturṇāṃ viparyāsānāṃ pratipakṣeṇa bhagavatā catvāri smṛtyupasthānāni vyavasthāpitāni /tatrāśucau śucīti viparyāsapratipakṣeṇa kāyasmṛtyupasthānaṃ vyavasthāpitam / tathā hi bhagavatā kāyasmṛtyupasthānabhāvanāyām aśubhāpratisamyuktāś catasraḥ śivapathikā deśitāḥ, yā asya bahulaṃkurvanmanasikurvataḥ, aśucau śucīti viparyāsaḥ prahīyate /tatra duḥkhe sukham iti viparyāsapratipakṣeṇa vedanāsmṛtyupasthānaṃ vyavasthāpitam / vedanāsu vedanānudarśī viharan yat kiṃcid veditam idam atra duḥkhasye ti yathābhūtaṃ prajānāti, evam asya yo duḥkhe sukham iti viparyāsaḥ sa prahāyate /tatra anitye nityam iti viparyāsapratipakṣeṇa cittasmṛtyupasthānaṃ vyavasthāpitam / tasya sarāgādicittaprabhedena teṣāṃ teṣāṃ rātriṃdivasānām atyayāt kṣaṇalavamuhūrtānām anekavidhānāṃ bahunānāprakāratāṃ (Śbh II 196) cittasyopalabhya yo 'nitye nityam iti viparyāsaḥ sa prahīyate /tatrānātmany ātme ti viparyāsapratipakṣeṇa dharmasmṛtyupasthānaṃ vyavasthāpitam / tasya yeṣām ātmadṛṣṭyādikānāṃ saṃkleśānāṃ sadbhāvād yeṣām anātmadṛṣṭyādikānāṃ kuśalānāṃ dharmāṇām asadbhāvāt skandheṣv ātmadarśanaṃ bhavati, nānyasya, svalakṣaṇataḥ sāmānyalakṣaṇataś ca dharmān dharmānudarśino yathābhūtaṃ paśyataḥ, yo 'nātmany ātme ti viparyāsaḥ sa prahīyate.* Cf. Wayman 1961: 98.

183. Peṭ 224: *Tattha avijjā vipallāsagocarādhipateyyabhūmi, yathā hi taṃ sañjānāti yathā vijānāti yathā sañjānāti ca vijānāti ca. Yathā khanti ceteti ime cattāro vipallāsā sattā yehi catubbidhaṃ attabhāvavatthuṃ rogabhūtaṃ gaṇḍabhūtaṃ attā ti vadanti.*

feeling is the second ground of distortion [by regarding] happiness in what is suffering; perceptions and formations are the third ground of distortion [by regarding] self in what is without self; consciousness is the fourth ground of distortion [by regarding] permanence in what is impermanent."[184]

The only clear explanation of the term *attabhāvavatthu* is given by Dhammapāla in his explanation of this passage:

Nett-a 142: "Now, to show the object-range and place of occurrence of the distortions, it is said 'Wherein does it distort? In the four grounds of selfhood.' The self is the I-conceit that is established by them herein (i.e. by the distortions in the four grounds). Selfhood (*attabhāva*) is the awareness/ discernment (*buddhi*) and designation (*vohāra*) that there is a 'self' (*attā ti bhavati*) herein. And just that is called 'ground of selfhood' [since] it is a ground due to being the basis (*adhiṭṭhāna*) for the distortion of beauty [in the foul,] etc. 'He regards matter as self' etc.: having shown the ground of selfhood by the occurrence of the identity view which is the root of all distortions of those [aggregates], to show again the reason for the occurrence of the distortions, having analysed it together with the object-range (*visaya*) [i.e. the establishments of mindfulness] it is said 'matter is the first ground of distortion [by regarding] beauty in what is foul'".[185]

The old *ṭīkā* on the *Netti*, also attributed to Dhammapāla, comments on this. Nett-pṭ 86: "It is said 'by them', etc.: due to Indra's Net etc., and in the manner of the gem etc., [the distortions] appear in the five aggregates subject to clinging through the action of [regarding these as] I and mine etc., [and] through the way of language (*nirutti-naya*) it is called 'self'. The selfhood

---

184. Nett 85: *So kiṃ vipallāsayati? Tayo dhamme: saññaṃ cittaṃ diṭṭhimiti. So kuhiṃ vipallāsayati? Catūsu attabhāvavatthūsu: Rūpaṃ attato samanupassati, rūpavantaṃ vā attānaṃ, attani vā rūpaṃ, rūpasmiṃ vā attānaṃ. Evaṃ vedanaṃ...pe... saññaṃ... pe... saṅkhāre...pe... viññāṇaṃ attato samanupassati, viññāṇavantaṃ vā attānaṃ, attani vā viññāṇaṃ, viññāṇasmiṃ vā attānaṃ. Tattha rūpaṃ paṭhamaṃ vipallāsavatthu asubhe subhanti. Vedanā dutiyaṃ vipallāsavatthu dukkhe sukhanti. Saññā saṅkhārā ca tatiyaṃ vipallāsavatthu anattani attāti. Viññāṇaṃ catutthaṃ vipallāsavatthu anicce niccan-ti.* Paṭis-a 339: *Lokassa attā ti ca attaniyan-ti ca ubhayathā gāhasambhavato tadubhayagāhapaṭisedhanatthaṃ attābhāvo ca attaniyābhāvo ca vutto.*

185. Netti-a 142: *Idāni vipallāsānaṃ pavattiṭṭhānaṃ visayaṃ dassetuṃ so kuhiṃ vipallāsayati, catūsu attabhāvavatthūsū ti āha. Tattha attabhāvavatthūsū ti pañcasu upādānakkhandhesu. Tehi āhito ahaṃ-māno etthā ti attā. Attā ti bhavati ettha buddhi-vohāro cā ti attabhāvo. So eva subhādīnaṃ vipallāsassa ca adhiṭṭhānabhāvato vatthu cā ti attabhāvavatthū ti vuccati. Rūpaṃ attato samanupassatī ti ādinā tesaṃ sabbavipallāsamūlabhūtāya sakkāyadiṭṭhiyā pavattiṭṭhānabhāvena attabhāvavatthutaṃ dassetvā puna vipallāsānaṃ pavatti ākārena saddhiṃ visayaṃ vibhajitvā dassetuṃ rūpaṃ paṭhamaṃ vipallāsavatthu asubhe subhan-ti vuttaṃ.*

caused by the occurrence of that awareness and designation in the ground of happiness, etc. is called 'ground of selfhood'".[186]

Similar to Netti-a, Sv-ṭ explains *attabhāva* as: "Selfhood is the thought (*citta*) that there is a self herein, [i.e. in] the aggregate-mass". Spk-ṭ and Vism-mhṭ likewise: "Selfhood is the conceit that there is a self herein, [i.e. in] the five aggregates subject to clinging. Some say the body," and Vism-mhṭ "Selfhood is the designation (*abhidhāna*) and the thought that there is a self herein, [i.e. in] the body or [in] just the fivefold aggregates".[187] In Pali commentarial works, *attabhāva* is often explained as the five aggregates and is sometimes equated with *attā*.[188]

3. *Ātmavastu*

An exact Sanskrit equivalent of *attabhāvavatthu*—i.e. **ātmabhāvavastu*—cannot be traced. However, in texts attributed to Asaṅga and other texts connected the Yogācāra school the term *ātmavastu* "ground of self" is used in a similar way as *attabhāvavatthu* is in Theravāda texts, i.e. it is a mode in which the delusion of a self manifests in relation to the five aggregates.

Asaṅga incorporated doctrinal opinions of the Mahīśāṣaka school in his works and is said to have originally been a member of this school.[189] His

186. Nett-pṭ 86: *Indajālādivasena maṇi ādi ākārena upaṭṭhahante upādānakkhandhapañcake ahaṃmamādikāraṇatāya niruttinayena attā ti vuccamāno taṃbuddhivohārappavattinimittatāya attabhāvo sukhādīnaṃ vatthutāya attabhāvavatthū ti pavuccatī ti āha tehī ti ādi. Tesan-ti upādānakkhandhānaṃ. Vipallāsānaṃ pavatti-ākāro asubhe subhanti ādi. Visayo kāyavedanācittadhammā.* Cf. Nett-ṭ 221: ... *imāni attabhāvavatthūni vipallāsapavattiṭṭhānavisayānīti dassetuṃ so kuhiṃ vipallāsayati catūsu attabhāvavatthūsū ti vuttaṃ. Catūsu rūpakāyavedanācittadhammasaṅkhātesu attabhāvavatthūsu so sabbo vipallāso saññācittadiṭṭhiyo vipallāsayati. ...*

187. Sv-ṭ II 427: *attā ti bhavati ettha cittan ti attabhāvo, khandhasamūho.* Spk-ṭ I 92; Vism-mhṭ I 6: *attā ti bhavati ettha abhimāno ti attabhāvo, upādānakkhandhapañcakaṃ; sarīran-ti keci.* Vism-mhṭ I 367: *attā ti bhavati ettha abhidhānaṃ, cittañ cā ti attabhāvo, sarīraṃ khandhapañcakam-eva vā* (= Vism IX.54/p.310). Cf. Th-a 8: *Atha vā bhāvitattānan-ti bhāvitattābhāvānaṃ, attabhāvo hi āhito ahaṃ-māno etthā ti attā ti vuccati, ...*

188. Nett-a 237: ... *attabhāvato samuṭṭhāyā ti attho vutto, taṃ sādhento āha snehajā attasambhūtāti. ... Tathā jāyantā ca pañcupādānakkhandhabhede attabhāvasaṅkhāte attani sambhūtā.* Th-a III 32: *Attasamuṭṭhānan-ti ahan-ti mānaṭṭhānatāya attā ti ca laddhanāme attabhāve sambhūtaṃ.* Nett-a 241: ... *saka-attabhāvasaṅkhātesu upādānakkhandhesu.* As 308: *Ayaṃ me attā ti bālajanena pariggahitattā attabhāvo vuccati sarīram-pi khandhapañcakampi.* Vibh-a 77: ... *pañcakkhandhasaṅkhātassa attabhāvassa ....* Th-a II 47: ... *tuccho kāyo adissatha niccasārādivirahito tuccho khandhapañcakasaṅkhāto attabhāvakāyo. ....* Mp II 209: ... *puggalassa attabhāvo nibbattati, khandhā pātubhavanti.* It-a I 180: ... *upādānakkhandhasaṅkhātassa attabhāvassa ....* Ud-a 174: *Pahitattoti ... pesitatto vissaṭṭha-attabhāvo.*

189. See e.g. Bareau 1993: 5: "It is ... sufficiently obvious that Asaṅga had been a

usage of *ātmavastu* in a manner similar to its usage of *attabhāvavatthu* in the *Peṭakopadesa* therefore might lend further support to the *Paṭisambhidāmagga-gaṇṭhipada*'s statement that the *Peṭaka*—i.e. the source of the anomalous quotation in Vism, etc. (see Introduction § 6)—is a work of the Mahiṃsāsakas. This school was present in South India and Sri Lanka in the first half of the first millennium; see Warder 2000: 280, Cousins 2012: 121. In Sri Lanka, Faxian obtained a copy of the Mahīśāṣaka Vinaya and Buddhamitta of the Mahiṃsāsaka tradition was one of the initiators of the Jātaka Commentary (see J-a I 1). However, to ascertain whether the term *ātmavastu* originated in the Mahīśāṣaka school more research would need to be done to see whether it is found in other Sanskrit works and in Tibetan and Chinese translations.

Chapter 1 § 2a-c of the *Abhidharmasamuccaya* has: "Because of what [reason] are there only five aggregates? Because of the manifestation of the five modes of the ground of self: Because of the ground of self that is the body with its possessions (*saparigraha*), the ground of self that is experience (*upabhoga*), the ground of self that is verbalization/designation (*abhilāpa*), the ground of self that is the formation/construction of all dharmas and non-dharmas, and the ground of self that is based upon those."[190]

And Chapter II § 90: "What is the object for the establishments of mindfulness? The body, feelings, mind, and dharmas. Moreover, it is the ground based on self (*ātmāśrayavastu*), the ground of experience of self, the ground of self, and the ground of the defiling and purifying of self."[191]

On the first passage, Jinaputra's *Abhidharmasamuccayabhāṣya* comments: "Because of the manifestation of the five modes of the ground of self: herein the four modes that are the ground of self (*ātmano*) are "ground of self", the

---

Mahīśāsaka when he was a young monk, and that he incorporated a large part of the doctrinal opinions proper to this school within his own work after he became a great master of the Mahāyāna ...."

190. Ch. 1 § 2a-c: *kimupādāya skandhāḥ pañcaiva / paṃcākārātmavastūdbhāvanatāmupādāya / saparigrahadehātmavastu upabhogātmavastu abhilāpātmavastu sarvadharmādharmābhisaṃskārātmavastu tadāśrayātmasvastu* copādāya.* (* The last *vastu* in the Chinese translation 我自體事 corresponds to *atmā-svabhāva-vastu/atmābhāva-vastu*, instead of 我事 = *ātma-vastu*. So does the *vyākhyā*. The Tibetan translation has *bdag gi gzhi* = *ātma-vastu*. See Hayashima 2003: 16, 17, 19.) This passage is also found in the Chinese translation of the Yogācāra text *Vijñaptimātratāsiddhi-śāstra* at T 1831: 619c08–10 and in the earliest Chinese commentary on the Heart Sūtra at T 1710: 537c23–24.

191. *smṛtyupasthānānāmālambanaṃ katamat | kāyo vedanā cittaṃ dharmāḥ|| api khalvātmāśrayavastu ātmopabhogavastu ātmavastu* ātmasaṃkleśavyavadānavastu ca*; see Hayashima 2003: 550. As above, the Chinese translation of the *vyākhyā* uses 我自體事 for this item instead of 我事, while the Tibetan translation of the *Bhāṣya* has *bdag gi dngos po* = *ātma-vastu* or *ātma-bhāva*.

fifth is the ground that is just the characteristic of self, thus "ground of self" is to be understood. By grasping the body together with its possessions, the grasping of the external and internal aggregate of matter is to be understood. The state of experiencing etc. of feelings etc. is made known in the exposition on their characteristics [i.e. in Ch. 1 § 4A (1)]. Consciousness is the ground, which is the characteristic of self that is based on the body together with its possessions etc. This is the meaning. For in that manner in the world there mostly is grasping of self in consciousness, and there is grasping of what belongs to a self in the other [aggregates]."[192]

On the second passage the *Bhāṣya* comments: "Herein, the object for the establishments of mindfulness, respectively, are the body, feelings, mind, and dharmas. What is the purpose of positing the object thus again? Because fools with distorted awareness mostly are imagining (*vikalpayanta*) a self based on the body with its sense-faculties, [a self that is] experiencing happiness etc., [a self that is] apprehending/perceiving (*upaladbhi*) the characteristic [of the sense-object], [a self] that is defiled by lust etc. and purified by faith etc. Therefore, one first has to rightly examine the characteristics of the grounds. Thus, the positing of the four kinds of object is to be understood."[193]

The Chinese translation of the *Viniścaya* section of the *Yogācārabhūmiśāstra* has a related explanation: "Again, because depending on the ground[s] that are requisites for self (我眾具事 = *ātmūpakaraṇavastu?*) and the ground of self, you should know the aggregates taught respectively, namely the self that is based on the body, that experiences suffering and happiness with regard to sense-objects, that gives rise to verbalization (言說 = *abhilāpa*) in oneself and in others (i.e.): 'such name', 'such category', 'such clan', etc. Based on these two kinds [of aggregates, i.e. feeling and perception], dharmas and non-dharmas accumulate [in the formations aggregate]. Thus, you should know the ground[s] that are requisites for self. And you should know the last aggregate [i.e. consciousness], which is the ground of self [based on] those [first four]."[194]

---

192. For the Sanskrit, see Hayashima 2003: 17.

193. For the Sanskrit, Hayashima 2003: 551.

194. T 1579: 596b10–15. The commentary on this at T 1828: 627c29–628a04 says: "Dependent on the ground[s] that are the requisites for self, the first four aggregates are established. Dependent on [these first four aggregates], the ground of self, the last [aggregate, i.e.] the consciousness aggregate is established. Namely, the self dependent on the body is [the aggregate of] matter; [the self] that experiences suffering and happiness with regard to sense-objects is [the aggregate of] feeling; [the self] that gives rise to verbalization in oneself and in others is [the aggregate of] perception; [the self] that is the accumulation of dharmas and non-dharmas based on these two kinds, [i.e. the aggregates of] feeling and perception, is the aggregate of formations. ..."

The second chapter of the *Śrāvakabhūmi* section of the *Yogācārabhūmiśāstra* places *ātmavastu* in the context of removing delusion with regard to the four grounds of self by means of the four establishments of mindfulness: "... contemplating dharmas as dharmas, seeing them as they really are, the distortion of [regarding a] self in what is without self is abandoned. In another way, the world mostly proceeds thus: Not knowing as it really is with regard to the aggregates that they are merely aggregates and merely dharmas, namely, [the regarding of a self] that is based upon the body, and based upon [the body] is experiencing happiness and suffering, and is defiled and purified by dharmas and non-dharmas. Therein, the establishment of mindfulness of the body is to be established for the purpose of removing delusion with regard to the ground based upon that self; the establishment of mindfulness of feelings is to be established for the purpose of removing delusion with regard to the ground which is the experiencing of just that self; the establishment of mindfulness of the mind is to be established for the purpose of removing delusion with regard to the ground of self wherein they are deluded by grasping a self in mind (*citta*), mentality (*manas*), and consciousness; and the establishment of mindfulness of dharmas is to be established for the purpose of removing delusion with regard to the ground of the defiling and purifying of the mind."[195]

Finally, Chengguan (澄觀, CE 738–839) says in his commentary on the *Buddhāvataṃsaka-mahāvaipulya-sūtra,* the 大方廣佛華嚴經疏 (T 1735: 791a17–19): "And [the aggregates of] perception and formations are combined for the contemplation of dharmas: because for knowledge/wisdom [the four grounds, i.e.] the ground that is based on the self, the ground that is the experience of self, the ground that is selfhood, and the ground that is affliction and purification of the self, are necessary. [There are] these four [contemplations]: because they oppose the distortions, namely, contemplation of the body opposes the distortion of beauty in what is foul, contemplation of feelings [opposes the distortion of happiness in what is]

195. Śbh II 196: ... *dharmān dharmānudarśino yathābhūtaṃ paśyataḥ, yo 'nātmany ātmeti viparyāsaḥ sa prahīyate // aparaḥ paryāyaḥ / prāyeṇa hi loka evaṃ pravṛttaḥ / skandheṣu skandhamātraṃ dharmamātraṃ yathābhūtam aprajānan yathā kāya (Shukla/DSBC: kāye) āśritaḥ, yadāśritaś ca sukhaduḥkham upabhuñje, dharmādharmābhyām saṃkliśyate vyavadāyate ca / tatrātmana āśrayavastusaṃmohāpanayanārthaṃ kāyasmṛtyupasthānaṃ vyavasthāpitam / tasyaivātmano 'nubhavanavastusaṃmohāpanayanārthaṃ vedanāsmṛtyupasthānaṃ vyavasthāpitam / yatraiva ca te citte manasi vijñāna (Shukla/DSBC: vijñāne) ātmagrāheṇa saṃmūḍhā ātmavastusaṃmohāpanayanārthena cittasmṛtyupasthānaṃ vyavasthāpitam / tasyaiva ca cittasaṃkleśavyavadānavastusaṃmohāpanayanārthaṃ dharmasmṛtyupasthānaṃ vyavasthāpitam.* From the GRETIL edition by Klaus Wille based on: *Śrāvakabhūmi: The Second Chapter*, Tokyo 2007. Chinese translation at T 1579: 441c22 and T 1828: 456c17–c21.

suffering, contemplation of mind [opposes the distortion of permanence in what is] impermanent, contemplation of dharmas [opposes the distortion of self in what is] without self."

Bibliography

Vimuttimagga Bibliography

Chinese Translation of the *Vimuttimagga*

The critically edited and punctuated Taishō edition of the 解脫道論 or *Jiě-tuō-dào-lùn* or "Exposition of the Path to Freedom" by 僧伽婆羅 or Saṅghapāla, is part of the 論集部, Śāstra or "Exposition", section of the Chinese Tripiṭaka at T 32, as text no. 1648, pp. 399c–461c.[1] This edition is available in digital format in the CBETA Chinese Electronic Tripitaka Collection of the Chinese Buddhist Electronic Text Association (CBETA), Taipei, Taiwan, and in the SAT Daizōkyō Text Database of the University of Tokyo, Tokyo, Japan.

Tibetan Translations of the *Vimuttimagga*

Partially abridged sections of chapters 10, 11 and 12 of the *Vimuttimagga*, and a few smaller parts, (see § 3) are quoted in the *'Dus byas dang 'dus ma byas rnam par nges pa = *Saṃskṛtāsaṃskṛtaviniścaya* or "Ascertaining of the Conditioned and Unconditioned" by Stobs bcu dpal bshes gnyen = *Daśabalaśrīmitra. The text, etc. is described in Skilling 1987; see § 3 above. This text is found in the *Bstan 'gyur dbu ma* section of the Tanjur, Dergé edition, vol. Ha, f. 109a1–317a7. A digital romanized text edition of the Asian Classics Input Project (ACIP, Release 6), Catalogue Number TD3897, is available at http://aciprelease.org/r6web/flat/td3897m_t.txt (Retrieved 9.4.2012). PDF files of several Tibetan script xylograph editions of this text are available at the website of the Tibetan Buddhist Resource Centre (TBRC). There is also a collated, critical edition of the text, generally called Peking edition, i.e., *bstan 'gyur/ (dpe bsdur ma), krung go'i bod rig pa zhib 'jug ste gnas kyi bka' bstan dpe sdur khang* (Comparative Edition of the Tengyur by the Bureau for the Collation of Tripitaka of the China Tibetology Research Center). 120 volumes. Beijing: *krung go'i bod rig pa dpe skrun khang* (China Tibetology Publishing House), 1994-2008, Vol. 63, pp. 293-864. Digital pictures of this text are available at Tibetan Buddhist Research Centre (TBRC) at http://tbrc.org/link?RID=O2MS16391|O2MS163912MS19324$W1PD95844. This collated text takes the Dergé edition as the main text and the Peking and Narthang editions as subordinate texts from which variant readings are given in endnotes.[2]

1. See Mizuno 1982: 51 and Bapat 1970: xiii.
2. See Huimin 2005.

A complete translation of Chapter 3, the "Exposition of the Ascetic Qualities" or *Dhutaguṇaniddesa*, as an independent text is called *Rnam par grol ba'i lam las sbyangs pa'i yon tan bstan pa zhes bya ba* or *Vimuktimārga-dhutaguṇa-nirdeśa-nāma* (i.e., the Tibetan transliteration given in the colophon of this text) or *Rnam par grol ba'i lam la sbyangs pa'i yon tan bstan pa'i mdo* or *Vimuktimārga-dhutaguṇa-nirdeśa-sūtra*. A critical edition and translation of this text was made by P.V. Bapat: *Vimuktimārga Dhutaguṇanirdeśa*, Delhi 1964. The text, and the editions of it, etc. are described in Skilling 1993: 135–140. A digital file with the Dergé edition (D 4143, 'dul ba, su 161b2-172b7) of this text is available on the websites of the Tibetan and Himalayan Library at www.thlib.org and the Buddhist Canons Research Database at www.aibs.columbia.edu. The digital text of the Lhasa edition (H 309, mdo sde, la 202b3-214a2, vol. 72) is available at the same sites. PDF files of several Tibetan script xylograph editions of this text are available at the Tibetan Buddhist Resource Centre (TBRC). Various Kanjur editions of this text are also listed on the website of the Resources of Kanjur & Tanjur Studies (RKTS) of the Universität Wien, where the text is numbered rKTs-K306. Several variant titles, etc. are also listed. See www.istb.univie.ac.at/kanjur/xml3/xml/verif2.php?id=306 (retrieved 10.10.2012).

Digital text files with the Tibetan quotations from the *Vimuttimagga* in the Beijing collated edition and Dergé (ACIP) edition *Saṃskṛtāsaṃskṛtaviniścaya* as well as a text file with Bapat's edition of the Tibetan text of the *Dhutaguṇanirdeśa*, with some notes with regard to the right readings, etc., made while preparing the translations in this book, are available online at Nyanatusita at www.academia.edu.

English Translation of the Chinese Translation

Ehara, N.R.M. Soma Thera, and Kheminda Thera, *The Path of Freedom*, Colombo, 1961. Reprinted Kandy 1977.[3]

Japanese Translations of the Chinese Translation

These Japanese translations have not been consulted and are only listed for reference.

Hikata, Ryūshō (tr.) *Gedatsudōron*, in *Kokuyaku issaikyō Ronshū* vol. 7, Tokyo, 1933. (干潟　龍祥　解脱道論, 國譯一切經　論集部　七, 東京：大東出版社, 昭和八年.) (The translation into Japanese that was consulted by Ehara et al.)

3. See "Old Buddhist Manuscripts in Japanese Collections" at http://koshakyo-database.icabs.ac.jp/index_en.html (accessed on 21.10.2013) and, for more detail, Toshinori Ochiai, 2008.

Naniwa, Senmyō. *Gedatsudōron*, Tokyo 2001. (浪花宣明, 解脱道論, 大蔵出版. (Edition and exegetical, annotated translation with a word-by-word correspondence of Chinese and Japanese words arranged according to the Japanese syntax.)

General Bibliography

Adikaram, E.W. *Early History of Buddhism in Ceylon*, Colombo, 1953.

Allon, Mark. "The Oral Composition and Transmission of Early Buddhist Texts", in Connelly, P. & Hamilton, S. eds. *Indian Insights: Buddhism, Brahmanism and Bhakti*, London, 1997: 39–62.

Anālayo Bhikkhu. "Vimuttimagga", in W.G. Weeraratne ed. *Encyclopaedia of Buddhism*, Vol. 8 no. 3, Colombo, 2009a: 622–632.

— "The Treatise on the Path to Liberation (解道論) and the *Visuddhimagga*", *Fuyan Buddhist Studies*, Vol. 4, 2009b: 1–15.

— "The Development of the Pāli Udāna Collection", *Bukkyō Kenkyū*, Vol. 37, 2009c, pp. 39-72.

— *Excursions Into the Thought-World of the Pali Discourses*, Onalaska, 2012a.

— "The Case of Sudinna: On the Function of Vinaya Narrative, Based on a Comparative Study of the Background Narration to the First Pārājika Rule"; *Journal of Buddhist Ethics*, Vol. 19, 2012b, pp. 396–438.

Andreeva, Anna & Steavu, Dominic. "Introduction: Backdrops and Parallels to Embryological Discourse and Reproductive Imagery in East Asian Religions", in Andreeva, A. & Steavu, D., eds. *Transforming the Void: Embryological Discourse and Reproductive Imagery in East Asian Religions*, Leiden, 2015: 1–52.

Bagchi, Prabodh Chandra. *Le canon bouddhique en Chine: les traducteurs et les traductions, Tome 1*, Paris, 1927.

Bapat, P.V. "Unidentified Sources of the Vimuttimagga", *Annals of the Bhandarkar Oriental Institute* 15.3–4, Poona, 1935.

— "Vimuttimagga and the school of Abhayagirivihāra in Ceylon", *Journal of the Asiatic Society of Bengal* (Calcutta) I.2, 1936.

— *Vimuttimagga and Visuddhimagga, a Comparative Study*. Poona, 1937. Reprinted Kandy, 2010.

— "Vimuttimagga and Peṭakopadesa", *Indian Culture* (Calcutta) III, 1937: 743–746.

— "Nā-lo-tho of the Vimuttimagga", *New Indian Antiquary* I, 1938–39: 599–600.

— "Interpolations in the fragmentary Tibetan version of the Vimuktimārga", *New Indian Antiquary*. Vol. VII, 1944: 58–60.

— *Arthapada-sūtra*, Santinekan, 1951.

— *Vimuktimārga Dhutaguṇanirdeśa*, Delhi, 1964.

— with A. Hirakawa. *Shan-chien-p'i-p'o-sha: A Chinese version by Saṅghabhadra of Samantapāsādikā commentary on Pali Vinaya*. Poona, 1970.

— "Review of Ratnajoti and Ratnapāla 1963", *Journal of the Vidyalankāra University of Ceylon* 1(1), 1972: 172–190.

Bareau, André. "The List of the *Asaṃskṛta-dharma* according to Asaṅga", in Sharma R. K. ed. *Researches in Indian and Buddhist Philosophy: Essays in Honour of Professor Alex Wayman*, Delhi, 1993: 1–6.

Bechert, Heinz. "*Vimuttimagga* and *Amaṭakaravaṇṇanā*", in N. H. Samtani and H. S. Prasad eds. *Amalā Prajñā: Aspects of Buddhist Studies, Professor P.V. Bapat Felicitation Volume. Bibliotheca Indo-Buddhica* No. 63, Delhi, 1989: 11–14.

— *Singhalesische Handschriften Teil II*, Stuttgart, 1997.

Bingenheimer, Marcus. "Problems and Prospects of Collaborative Edition and Translation Projects in the Era of Digital Text", in Meisig, Konrad, ed. *Translating Buddhist Chinese: Problems and Prospects*, Wiesbaden, 2010: 21–43.

Blackburn, Anne M. "Sūtra Sannayas and Saraṇaṃkara: Changes in Eighteenth-Century Buddhist Education", *The Sri Lanka Journal of the Humanities*, Vol. 23, Nos. 1-2, 1997: 76-99.

Bodhi, Bhikkhu. *The Connected Discourses of the Buddha*, Somerville, 2000.

— *A Comprehensive Manual of Abhidhamma: The Abhidhammattha Saṅgaha of Ācariya Anuruddha*, Kandy, 2007a.

— *The All-Embracing Net of Views: The Brahmajāla Sutta and its Commentaries*, Kandy, 2007b.

— *The Discourse on the Fruits of Recluseship: The Sāmaññaphala Sutta and its Commentaries*, Kandy, 2008.

Bodiford, William M. *East Asian Buddhist Studies: A Reference Guide*, Los Angeles, 2005.

Boucher, Daniel. "Gāndhāri and the Early Chinese Buddhist Translations Reconsidered: The Case of the Saddharmapuṇḍarīkasūtra", *Journal of the American Oriental Society* 11–8.4, 1998: 471–506.

Bretfeld, Sven. "Purifying the Pure: The *Visuddhimagga*, Forest-Dwellers and the Dynamics of Individual and Collective Prestige in Theravada Buddhism", in *Discourses of Purity in Transcultural Perspective (300-1600)*, Leiden, 2015: 320–347.

Bucknell, Roderick S. "Taking account of the Indic source-text", in Meisig, Konrad, ed. *Translating Buddhist Chinese: Problems and Prospects*, Wiesbaden, 2010: 45–52.

Buswell, Robert E. Jr. and Jaini, Padmanabh S. "The Development of Abhidharma Philosophy", in Potter, Karl H., ed. *Encyclopedia of Indian Philosophies Volume VII: Abhidharma Buddhism to 150 A.D.* Delhi, 1996: 73–120.

Chan, Yiu-wing. *An English Translation of the Dharmatrāta-Dhyāna-Sūtra*（*達摩多羅禅經 T15, no.618*）*—With Annotation and a Critical Introduction*, unpublished PhD thesis, University of Hongkong, 2013.

Chattopadhyaya, A. and Chimpa, Lama, transl. Chattopadhyaya, A. ed. *Tāranātha's History of Buddhism in India*, Delhi, 1990: 279.

Ch'en, Kenneth. *Buddhism in China: A Historical Survey*, Princeton, 1964.

Chen, Shu-fen & Montoneri, Bernard. "A Study of the Punctuation Errors Found in the Taisho Diamond Sutra—Based on Sanskrit-Chinese Comparative Studies" in NACCL Proceedings Online - NACCL-23 (2011), Zhuo Jing-Schmidt, ed. Columbus,,2011: 279–295.

Chimpa, Lama. "The Methodology of Translations from Classical Tibetan", in Doboom Tulku ed. *Buddhist Translations: Problems and Perspectives*, New Delhi, 2001: 14–19.

Chödrön, Gelongma Karma Migme. *The Treatise on the Great Virtue of Wisdom by Nāgārjuna (Mahāprajñāpāramitāśāstra), Étienne Lamotte*, unpublished manuscript with English translation of Lamotte's *Le Traité de la Grande Vertu de Sagesse de Nāgārjuna*, 2001.

Coedès, George. *The Indianized States of Southeast Asia*, Hawaii, 1968: 57–58.

Collins, Steven. "Remarks on the *Visuddhimagga* and on its treatment of the Memory of Former Dwelling(s) (*pubbenivāsānussatiñāṇa*)", *Journal of Indian Philosophy*, 37, 2009: 499–532.

Cousins, L.S. "The Paṭṭhāna and the Development of the Theravādin Abhidhamma", *Journal of the Pali Text Society* IX, 1981: 22–46.

– "Pali Oral Literature", in Williams, P. ed. *Buddhism: Critical Concepts in Religious Studies*, Vol. I, 2005: 96–104.

– "The Teachings of the Abhayagiri School", in Skilling, P., Carbine J. A., Cicuzza C., Pakdeekham S., eds. *How Theravāda is Theravāda? Exploring Buddhist Identities*, Chiang Mai, 2012: 67–127.

– "Tambapanniya and Tāmraśātiya", *Journal of Buddhist Studies* XI, 2013: 21–46.

– "The Early Development of Buddhist Literature and Language in India", *Journal of the Oxford Centre for Buddhist Studies* 5, 2013: 89–135.

– "The Sutta on Mindfulness with In and Out Breathing", in Dhammajoti, KL, ed. *Buddhist Meditative Praxis: Traditional Teachings & Modern Applications*, Hong Kong, 2015: 1–24.

Crosby, Kate. "History versus modern myth: the Abhayagirivihāra, the *Vimuttimagga* and *Yogāvacara* meditation", *Journal of Indian Philosophy*, 27, 1999: 503–550.

– "Tantric Theravāda: A Bibliographic Essay on the Writings of François Bizot and others on the Yogāvacara Tradition", *Contemporary Buddhism*, Vol. 1, No. 2, 2000: 141–198.

– "The Origin of Pali as a Language Name in Medieval Theravada Literature", *Journal of the Centre for Buddhist Studies, Sri Lanka* 2, 2004: 70–116.

– "Differences between the *Amatākaravaṇṇanā* and the *Vimuttimagga-uddāna*", *Journal of the Centre of Buddhist Studies, Sri Lanka* 3, 2005: 139–149.

Deeg, Max. *Das Gaoseng-Faxian-Zhuan als religionsgeschichtliche Quelle*, Wiesbaden, 2005.

– "Abhayagirivihara—Geschichte und »Geschichte« eines ceylonesischen Klosters", in Hase, Thomas, ed. *Mauss, Buddhismus, Devianz: Festschrift für Heinz Mürmel zum 65. Geburtstag*, Marburg, 2009: 135–151.

Deleanu, Florin. "Mindfulness of Breathing in the Dhyāna Sūtras", *Transactions of the International Conference of Orientalists in Japan*, No. 37, 1992: 42–57.

– "A Preliminary Study of An Shigao's Translation of the Yogācārabhūmi", *The Journal of the Department of Liberal Arts of Kansai Medical University*, Vol. 17, 1997: 33–52.

– "A preliminary study on meditation and the beginnings of Mahāyāna Buddhism", in Williams, P. ed. *The Origins and Nature of Mahāyāna Buddhism*, Volume III of *Buddhism: Critical Concepts in Religious Studies*, London & New York, 2005.

— *The Chapter on the Mundane Path (Laukikamārga) in the Śrāvakabhūmi: A Trilingual Edition (Sanskrit, Tibetan, Chinese), Annotated Translation, and Introductory Study* (2 vols.), Tokyo, 2006.

— "Far From the Madding Strife for Hollow Pleasures: Meditation and Liberation in the *Śrāvakabhūmi*", *Journal of the International College for Postgraduate Buddhist Studies*, Vol. 16, 2012: 1-38.

Delhey, Martin. *Sanskrit text of the Samāhitā Bhūmiḥ*, electronic text of the critical edition in Delhey, M.: *Samāhitā Bhūmiḥ: Das Kapitel über die meditative Versenkung im Grundteil der Yogācārabhūmi*, Vienna 2009. Retrieved from www.academia.edu on 9.10.2016.

Demiéville, Paul. "La *Yogācārabhūmi* de Saṅgharakṣa." *Bulletin de l' École Française d' Extrême-Orient*, Tome 44 N°2, 1951: 339–436.

Dhammadharo, Ajahn Lee. *Keeping the Breath in Mind*, Bangkok, 1993.

Dhammajoti, K.L. "The Sixteen-mode Mindfulness of Breathing", *Journal of the Centre for Buddhist Studies, Sri Lanka* 6, 2008: 251-288.

— "The Doctrine of the Six-stage Mindfulness of Breathing", in Dhammajoti, K.L. and Karunadasa, Y., eds. *Buddhist and Pali studies: in Honour of Venerable Professor Kakkapalliye Anuruddha*, Hong Kong, 2009a: 639–650.

— *Sarvāstivāda Abhidharma*, Hong Kong, 2009b.

— "The Contribution of Saṃghabhadra", in Dessein, Bart and Teng, Weijen, *Text, history, and philosophy : Abhidharma across Buddhist scholastic traditions*, Leiden, 2016.

Dias, Malini. *The Growth of Buddhist Monastic Institutions in Sri Lanka from Brahmi Inscriptions, Epigraphia Zeylanica, Vol. VIII*. Colombo, 2001.

Ehara, N.R.M., Soma Thera, Kheminda Thera. *The Path of Freedom*, Colombo 1961. Reprinted Kandy, 1977.

Endo, Toshiichi. "The Asgiriya Manuscript of the Pali Vimuttimagga: An Inquiry into Its Authenticity", *Kalyāṇi, Journal of Humanities and Social Sciences of the University of Kelaniya* 1, 1983: 100–108.

— *Buddha in Theravāda Buddhism—A Study of the Concept of Buddha in the Pali Commentaries*, Dehiwela, 2002a.

— "Potthaka (Book or Manuscript) in the Pali Commentaries", in *Buddhist and Indian Studies in Honour of Prof. Sodo Mori*, Hamamatsu, 2002b: 79–90.

— *Studies in Pali Commentarial Literature: Sources, Controversies and Insights*, Hong Kong, 2013.

– "The Sevenfold Purification (*sattavisuddhi*) as the Structural Framework of the *Visuddhimagga*: Some Observations", in Dhammajoti, KL, ed. *Buddhist Meditative Praxis: Traditional Teachings & Modern Applications*, Hong Kong, 2015: 51–80.

Frasch, Tilman. "Notes on Dipavamsa: An Early Publication by U Pe Maung Tin", *The Journal of Burma Studies*, Vol. 9, 2004: 70–81.

Frauwallner, Erich. "On the Historical value of the Ancient Ceylonese Chronicles", in *Erich Frauwallner's Posthumous Essays, Volume 1*; New Delhi, 1994: 9–33.

– *Studies in the Abhidharma Literature and the Origins of Buddhist Philosophical Systems*, Albany 1995.

Freschi, Elisa. "The Reuse of Texts in Indian Philosophy: Introduction", *Journal of Indian Philosophy*, 43(2), 2015: 85–108.

Gaffney, S. "Do the Tibetan Translations of Indian Buddhist Texts Provide Guidelines for Contemporary Translators?", *SOAS Literary Review* 2 (July) 2000: 1–15.

Geiger, Wilhelm. *The Dīpavaṃsa and Mahāvaṃsa and their historical development in Ceylon*, Colombo, 1908.

Glass, Andrew. "Guṇabhadra, Bǎoyún, and the Saṃyuktāgama", *Journal of the International Association of Buddhist Studies*, Vol. 31 No. 1–2, Vienna, 2008: 184–203.

Goonatilake, Hema. "Sri Lanka-Cambodia Relations with Special Reference to the Period 14th–20th Centuries" *Journal of the Royal Asiatic Society of Sri Lanka*, New Series, Vol. XLVIII, 2003: 191–211.

Gornall, A.M. "Some Remarks on Buddhaghosa's use of Sanskrit Grammar: Possible Hints of an Unknown Commentary in Buddhaghosa's Grammatical Arguments", *Journal of the Oxford Centre for Buddhist Studies*, Vol. 1, 2011: 89–107.

Greene, Eric Matthew. *Meditation, Repentance, and Visionary Experience in Early Medieval Chinese Buddhism*, unpublished PhD thesis, University of California, Berkeley, 2012.

Gunasinghe, P.A.T. *The Political History of the Kingdoms of Yāpahuva, Kurunägala and Gampala (1270–1400)*, Colombo, 1987

Gunawardana, R.A.L.H. *Robe and Plough: Monasticism and Economic Interest in Early Medieval Sri Lanka*, Tucson, 1979.

— & Sakurai, Yumio. "Sri Lankan Ships in China", *The Sri Lanka Journal of the Humanities*, Vol. VII, no. 1 & 2, 1981: 147–152.

— "Changing Patterns of Navigation in the Indian Ocean and their Impact on Pre-colonial Sri Lanka", in Chandra, Satish ed. *The Indian Ocean: Explorations in History, Commerce and Politics*, New Delhi, 1987.

— "Subtle Silks of Ferrous Firmness: Buddhist Nuns in Ancient and Early Medieval Sri Lanka and Their Role in the Propagation of Buddhism", *The Sri Lanka Journal of the Humanities*, Vol. XIV, no. 1 & 2, 1988: 1–59.

Guruge, Ananda. "Shan-Jian-Lu-Piposha as an authentic source on the early history of Buddhism and Aśoka", in *Dhamma-Vinaya: Essays in Honour of Venerable Professor Dhammavihari (Jotiya Dhirasekera)*, Colombo, 2005: 91–110.

Har Dayal, Lala. *The Bodhisattva Doctrine in Buddhist Sanskrit Literature*, London 1932.

Hayashi, Takatsugu. "On the Peṭakopadesa and the Vimuttimagga", *Journal of Indian and Buddhist Studies,* Vol. 51, No. 2, 2003: 852–848. (In Japanese.)

— "The Vimuttimagga and Early Post-Canonical Literature (I)", *Buddhist Studies*, Vol. 31, 2004: 90–121.

— "The Vimuttimagga and Early Post-Canonical Literature (II)", *Buddhist Studies,* Vol. 32, 2004: 59–82.

— "The Vimuttimagga and Early Post-Canonical Literature (III)", *Buddhist Studies*, Vol. 34, 2005: 5–33.

— "アバヤギリ派の五蘊。十二処。十八界—『有為無為決択』第13章—", 佛教研究, Vol. 36, 2008: 167–208. (= "The Aggregates, Bases, and Elements According to the Abhayagiravāsins: A Japanese Translation of the *Saṃskṛtāsaṃskṛtaviniścaya,* Chapter 13".)

— "Metaphors for Simultaneous Comprehension (*abhisamaya*) of the Truths in Theravada Buddhism", *The Journal of Korean Association for Buddhist Studies*, 2008: 76–86.

— "アバヤギリ派の十二縁起—『有為無為決択』第14章—", 佛教研究, Vol. 38, 2010: 191–222. (= "Dependent origination according to the Abhayagiravāsins: A Japanese Translation of the *Saṃskṛtāsaṃskṛtaviniścaya,* Chapter 14".)

Hahn, Michael. "Striving for Perfection: On the Various Ways of Translating Sanskrit into Tibetan", *Pacific World Journal*, 3rd series, no. 9, 2007: 123–149.

Heirman, Ann. "The Chinese Samantapasadika and its school affiliation", *Zeitschrift der Deutschen Morgenländischen Gesellschaft* 154.2, 2004: 371–396.

– "Vinaya: from India to China", in Heirman, Ann & Bumbacher S. P. eds. *The Spread of Buddhism*, Leiden, 2007.

Hettiaratchi, D.E. *Vesaturu-dā-sannē*; Colombo, 1950.

Hikata, Ryūshō. *Gedatsudōron*, in *Kokuyaku issaikyō Ronshu*, Vol. 7, Tokyo 1933 (干潟 龍祥 解脱道論, 國譯一切經 論集部 七, 東京：大東出版社, 昭和八年).

von Hinüber, Oskar. "The Oldest Pali Manuscript: Four Folios of the Vinaya-Piṭaka from the National Archives, Kathmandu", *Abhandlungen der Akademie der Wissenschaften und der Literatur*, Nr. 6, Stuttgart, 1991.

– *Handbook of Pali Literature*, Berlin, 1996.

– *Kleine Schriften Teil I*, Wiesbaden, 2009.

Hirakawa, Akira. *A History of Indian Buddhism: From Śākyamuni to Early Mahāyāna*, New Delhi 1993.

Horner, I.B. *The Book of the Discipline (Vinaya-Piṭaka) Volume I (Suttavibhaṅga)*, London, 1949.

– The Book of the Discipline (Vinaya-Piṭaka) Volume VI (Parivāra), London, 1966.

– *Milinda's Questions I & II*, London, 1969.

– "*Keci* 'some' in the Pali commentaries", *Journal of the Pali Text Society* IX, 1981: 87–95.

Huimin, Bhikkhu. "Techniques for Collating Multiple Text Versions in the Digitization of Classical Texts: The CBETA Taishō Buddhist Canon as an Example", *Chung-Hwa Buddhist Journal*, No. 18, Taipei, 2005: 299–324.

Hureau, Sylvie. "Translations, Apocrypha, and the Emergence of the Buddhist Canon", in Lagerwey, J. Lü Pengzhi, eds. *Early Chinese Religion Part II. The Period of Division (220-589 AD)*, Leiden, 2010: 741–774.

Jha, Lalan Kumar. *The Vimuttimagga: A Critical Study*, Delhi, 2008.

Janakābhivaṃsa Mahāthera. "Nidāna to *Visuddhimagga-Mahāṭīkā Nissaya* of Mahāsi Sayādaw", Rangoon 1966. Unpublished translation by W. Pruitt.

Jayawickrama, N. A. *The Inception of Discipline and the Vinaya Nidāna*; London, 1962.

Karashima, Seishi. "Underlying languages of early Chinese translations of Buddhist scriptures", in Anderl C. and Eifring, H. eds. *Studies in Chinese Language and Culture: Festschrift in Honour of Christoph Harbsmeier on the Occasion of His Sixtieth Birthday*. Oslo 2006: 355–366.

Kalupahana, D. J. "Schools of Buddhism in Early Ceylon", *The Ceylon Journal of the Humanities*, Vol. 1, no. 2, 1970: 159-190.

Karunadasa, Y. *Buddhist Analysis of Matter*, Hong Kong, 2015a.

— *The Theravāda Abhidhamma: Its Inquiry into the Nature of Conditioned Reality*, Kandy, 2015b.

Katre, S. M. *Introduction to Indian Textual Criticism*. Bombay, 1941.

Kieffer-Pülz, Petra. "Zitate aus der Andhaka-Aṭṭhakathā in der Samanta-pāsādikā", in *Studien zur Indologie und Buddhismuskunde. Festgabe des Seminars für Indologie und Buddhismuskunde für Prof. Dr. Heinz Bechert*, Bonn, 1993: 171–212.

— "A Legal Judgement regarding a Sīmā Controversy: Ñeyyadhamma's Sīmāvivādavinicchayakathā", in Sinha ed. Reinhold Grünendahl and others, *Facets of Indian Culture: Gustav Roth Felicitation Volume*, Patna, 1998: 210–218.

— "Zitate aus der Andhakaṭṭhakathā in den Subkommentaren", in *Studien zur Indologie und Iranistik*, Heft 27, 2010: 147–235.

— "Buddhist Nuns in South India as Reflected in the Andhakaṭṭhakathā and in Vajirabuddhi's Anugaṇṭhipada", *Annual Report of The International Research Institute for Advanced Buddhology at Soka University* [= ARIRIAB], Vol. XVI, Tokyo, 2013a: 29–46.

— *Verlorene Gaṇṭhipadas zum buddhistischen Ordensrecht. Untersuchungen zu den in der Vajirabuddhiṭīkā zitierten Kommentaren Dhammasiris und Vajirabuddhis. Teil 1: Disziplinarrecht: Pārājika bis Saṅghādisesa (Z 1-132)*, Wiesbaden, 2013b.

— "Quotatives Indicating Quotations in Pāli Commentarial Literature, II: Quotatives with *āha*", *Annual Report of The International Research Institute for Advanced Buddhology at Soka University* [= ARIRIAB], Vol. XVII, Tokyo, 2014: 61–76.

— "Vinaya Commentarial Literature in Pali", in Silk, J.A. ed. *Brill's Encyclopaedia of Buddhism*, Vol. 1. Leiden, 2015: 430–441.

— "Reuse of Text in Pāli Legal Commentaries", *Buddhist Studies Review* 33.1-2, 2016a: 9–45.

– "[Review on] Pecenko, Primo (Hg.) posts. compl. by Ditrich, Tamara: *Aṅguttaranikāya-Purāṇaṭīkā Catutthā Līnatthapakāsinī*, Bristol 2012", *Orientalistische Literaturzeitung*, Vol. 112, Issue 4–5, 2017: 422–26.

Kieschnick, John. *Primer in Chinese Buddhist Writings, Vol 1: Foundations*, Stanford, 2014.

Kim, Kyungrae. "Observations on Some Technical Terms in the **Vimuttimagga* and their English Translations: An Examination of *Jiā* (夾) and *Visayappavatti*", *Buddhist Studies Review* 32.2, 2015: 231–243

van Kooij, K. R. "A Meaningful Tree: The Bo Tree", in Zijlmans, K. ed. *Site-seeing*, Leiden, 2006.

Kritzer, Robert. "Life in the Womb: Conception and Gestation in Buddhist Scripture and Classical Indian Medical Literature", in Sasson, V.R. & Law, J. M. eds. *Imagining the Fetus: the Unborn in Myth, Religion, and Culture*, Oxford, 2008: 73–90.

– *Garbhāvakrāntisūtra: the Sūtra on Entry into the Womb*, Tokyo, 2014.

Kulatunge, T. G. *Abhayagiri Vihāra at Anuradhapura*, Central Cultural Fund, Colombo, 1999.

Legge, James. *A Record of Buddhistic Kingdoms*, Oxford, 1886.

Malalasekera, G.P. *The Pāli Literature of Ceylon*, London, 1928. (Reprinted Kandy, 1994.)

– *Vaṃsatthappakāsinī: Commentary on the Mahāvaṃsa*, London, 1935.

– *Dictionary of Pāli Proper Names*, London, 1937.

Masefield, Peter. "The Composition of the Itivuttakaṭṭhakathā", in *Buddhist and Indian studies in honour of professor Dr. Sodo Mori*, Hamamatsu 2002: 103–115.

Mirando, A. H. *Buddhism in Sri Lanka in the 17th and 18th Centuries*, Dehiwala, 1985.

Mizuno, Kōgen. *Buddhist Sutras: Origin, Development, Transmission*, Tokyo, 1982.

Monier-Williams, Monier. *A Sanskrit English Dictionary*, Oxford 1899.

Mori, Sodō. "Shin shiryō *Vimuttimagga*", *Indogaku bukkyōgaku kenkyū*, Vol. 17, no. 1, 1968: 132–133.

– "*Uttaravihāraṭṭhakathā* and *Sārasamāsa*", *Journal of the Pali Text Society* XII, 1988: 1–48.

Muller, Charles, editor. *Digital Dictionary of Buddhism*, at http://buddhism-dict.net/ddb.

— *CJKV-English Dictionary: A Dictionary of Sinitic Characters and Compounds Related to East Asian Cultural, Political, and Intellectual History*, at www.buddhism-dict.net/dealt/.

Nagai, Makoto. "The Vimutti-magga: The 'Way to Deliverance': The Chinese Counterpart of the Pāli Visuddhi-magga", *Journal of the Pali Text Society* VII, 1917–1919: 69–80.

Ñāṇamoli, Bhikkhu. *Minor Readings and Illustrator*, London, 1960.

— *The Piṭaka-disclosure (Peṭakopadesa) according to Kaccāna Thera*, London, 1964.

— *The Guide (Netti-ppakaraṇaṃ) according to Kaccāna Thera*, London, 1977.

— *Path of Discrimination*, London, 1982.

— & Bodhi, Bhikkhu. *The Middle length Discourses of the Buddha*, Boston, 1995.

— *The Dispeller of Delusion (Sammohavinodanī) Part I & II*, Oxford, 1996.

— *The Path of Purification: Visuddhimagga*, Kandy, 2010 (4th edition).

Ñāṇatusita, Bhikkhu. "A Reference Table of Pali Literature", in Webb, Russell and Ñāṇatusita, Bhikkhu: *An Analysis of the Pali Canon and A Reference Table of Pali Literature*, Kandy, 2011.

— *Analysis of the Bhikkhu Pātimokkha*, Kandy, 2014.

— "Translations or Adaptations? Chinese Hybrid Translations of Vinaya Texts", *Journal of Buddhist Studies, Centre for Buddhist Studies, Sri Lanka and The Buddha-Dharma Centre of Hong Kong*, Volume XII, 2014–2015: 123–186.

Nanjio, Bunjiu. *A catalogue of the Chinese translation of the Buddhist Tripitaka, the sacred Canon of the Buddhists in China and Japan*, Oxford, 1883.

Norman, K.R. *Pāli Literature*, Wiesbaden, 1983.

— "The Literary Works of the Abhayagirivihārins", in *Collected Papers IV*, Oxford, 1993: 207–17.

— *A Philological Approach to Buddhism: The Bukkyō Dendō Kyōkai Lectures 1994*, London, 1997.

Ochiai, Toshinori. "The Digital Archives of Old Japanese Buddhist Manuscripts: Currrent Plans and Their Implementation", presentation given at Dharma Drum Buddhist College (DDBC), Taipei, in 2008. Accessed on www.ddbc.edu.tw/downloads/download_document.html?gid=425 on 21.10.2013.

Oldenberg, Hermann. *The Dîpavaṃsa: An Ancient Buddhist Historical Record*. Berlin, 1879.

Ooi, Keat Gin. *Southeast Asia: a Historical Encyclopaedia*, Vol. 1, Santa Barbara, 2004.

Paranavitana, S. "A Fragmentary Inscription from Jētavanārāma now in the Colombo Museum", *Epigraphia Zeylanica*, Vol. IV, Colombo, 1943: 273-285.

Pelliot, Paul. "Le Fou-nan". *Bulletin de l'Ecole Française d'Extrême-Orient* III, 1903: 248-303.

Pind, Ole Holten. "Buddhaghosa: His Works and Scholarly Background", *Bukkyō Kenkyū*, Vol. XXXI, March 1992: 135–156.

Pinte, Gudrun. *Lost in Translation: A Case Study of Saṅghabhadra's Shanjian lü piposha (T.1462)*, Gent, 2011. (Unpublished thesis.)

Pradhan, Pralhad. *Abhidharma Samuccaya of Asaṅga*, Santinekan, 1950.

Pruden, Leo M. *Karmasiddhiprakarana: the Treatise on Action by Vasubandhu, by Étienne Lamotte, English Translation by Leo M. Pruden*, Berkeley, 1987.

— *Abhidharmakośabhāṣyam by Louis de La Vallée Poussin, Vol III, English Translation by Leo M. Pruden*, Berkeley, 1988.

Rāhula, Walpola. *History of Buddhism in Ceylon*, Colombo, 1966.

Raine, Roberta. "Translating the Tibetan Buddhist Canon: Past Strategies, Future Prospects", *Forum* 9 (2), 2011: 157–186.

Ratanajoti, Galkätiyagama & Ratanapāla, Karalliyaddē: *Vimuttimaggo, Bhadantārahanta-Mahāriṭṭha-Upatissa-tthera-vara-ppaṇīto*, Colombo, 1963.

Rhys-Davids, T.W. and Stede, W.: *The Pali Text Society's Pali-English Dictionary*, London, 1921–25.

Ronkin, Noa. *Early Buddhist Metaphysics: The making of a philosophical tradition.* Oxon, 2005.

Ruegg, Seyfort D. "On Translating Tibetan Philosophical Texts", in Doboom Tulku ed. *Buddhist Translations: Problems and Perspectives*, New Delhi, 2001: 75–86.

Salomon, Richard. *Ancient Buddhist Scrolls from Gandhāra*, London, 1999.

Samtani, N.H. *The Arthaviniścaya-sūtra & its Commentary (Nibandhana)*, Patna, 1971.

Silk, J. A. "Further Remarks on the *yogācāra bhikṣu*", in Bhikkhu Pāsādika and Bhikkhu Tampalawela Dhammaratana, eds. *Dharmadūta: Mélanges offers au Vénérable Thích Huyēn-Vi á l'occasion de son soixante-dixiéme anniversaire*, Paris, 1997: 233–250.

— "The Yogācāra Bhiksu", in Silk J. A. ed. *Wisdom, Compassion and the Search for Understanding: The Buddhist Studies Legacy of Gadjin M. Nagao*, Honolulu, 2000: 265–314.

Skilling, Peter. "The *Saṃskṛtāsaṃskṛtaviniṣcaya* of Daśabalaśrīmitra", *Buddhist Studies Review*, Vol. 4, No. 1, 1987: 3–23.

— "Theravādin literature in Tibetan translation", *Journal of the Pali Text Society* XX, 1993: 67–191.

— "*Vimuttimagga* and Abhayagiri: The Form-Aggregate according to the *Saṃskṛtāsaṃskṛtaviniścaya*", *Journal of the Pali Text Society* XX, 1994: 171–210.

— "The Advent of Theravāda Buddhism to Mainland Southeast Asia", *Journal of the International Association of Buddhist Studies* 20(1), 1997a: 93–107.

— "New Pali Inscriptions from South-east Asia", *Journal of the Pali Text Society* XXXIII, 1997b: 123–157.

— "A Note on King Milinda in the *Abhidharmakośabhāṣya*"; *Journal of the Pali Text Society*, Vol. XXIV, 1998: 81–101.

— "Redaction, recitation, and writing: Transmission of the Buddha's teaching in India in the early period", in Berkwitz, S.C. *Buddhist Manuscript Cultures,* Oxon, 2009: 53–75.

Somadasa, K.D. *Catalogue of the Hugh Nevill Collection of Sinhalese manuscripts in the British Library*, Vol I, London, 1987.

Stache-Rosen, Valentina. "Gunavarman (367–431): A Comparative Analysis of the Biographies found in the Chinese Tripitaka", *Bulletin of Tibetology*, X, No. 1, 1973.

Strong, John, S. *The Legend and Cult of Upagupta: Sanskrit Buddhism in North India and Southeast Asia*, Princeton, 1992.

Sundberg, J. "The wilderness monks of the Abhayagirivihara and the origins of Sino-Javanese esoteric Buddhism", *Bijdragen tot de Taal-, Land- en Volkenkunde* 160, no: 1, 2004: 95–123.

— "The Abhayagirivihāra's *Pāṃśukūlika* Monks in Second Lambakaṇṇa Śrī Laṅkā and Śailendra Java: The Flowering and Fall of a Cardinal Center of Influence in Early Esoteric Buddhism", *Pacific World* 3S,16, 2014: 49-185.

Suzuki, Teitaro. "The First Buddhist Council", *The Monist*, 14 (2), 1904: 253-282.

Szántó, Péter-Dániel. "A Sanskrit Fragment of Daśabalaśrīmitra's *Saṃskṛtā-saṃskṛtaviniścaya*", unpublished handout for Kyoto University presentation, 2015.

Tarling, Nicholas. *Cambridge history of South East Asia*, Cambridge, 1999.

Ṭhānissaro, Bhikkhu. *Buddhist Monastic Code I*, Valley Center, 2007.

Thomas, E. J. "Buddhist Education in Pāli and Sanskrit Schools", *The Indian Historical Quarterly*, Vol. II, 1926: 495-508.

Toru, Funayama. "Masquerading as Translation: Examples of Chinese Lectures by Indian Scholar-Monks in the Six Dynasties Period", *Asia Major*, Volume 19, No 1/2, 2006: 39–55.

— "The work of Paramārtha: An example of Sino-Indian cross-cultural exchange", *Journal of the International Association of Buddhist Studies*, Vol. 31 No. 1–2, 2008 (2010): 141–184.

Vachissara, Koṭagama. *Vaelivița Saraṇaṅkara and the Revival of Buddhism in Ceylon*, London 1961. (Unpublished Ph.D. thesis, University of London.)

Vickery, Michael. "Funan Reviewed: Deconstructing the Ancients", *Bulletin de l'Ecole Française d'Extrême-Orient*, Vol. 90, 2003: 101–143.

Warder, A. K. *Indian Buddhism*; New Delhi, 2000.

Wayman, Alex. "The Lamp and the Wind in Tibetan Buddhism", *Philosophy East and West*, Vol. 5, No. 2, 1955: 149-154.

— *Analysis of the Śrāvakabhūmi Manuscript*, Berkeley & Los Angeles, 1961.

West, Martin L. *Textual Criticism and Editorial Technique Applicable to Greek and Latin Texts*, Stuttgart, 1973.

Wilke, A. & Moebus, O. *Sound and Communication: An Aesthetic Cultural History of Sanskrit Hinduism*, Berlin, 2011.

Williams, Paul. *Mahāyāna Buddhism: The Doctrinal Foundations, Second Edition*, Oxon 2009.

Woodward, F.L. *Manual of a Mystic*, Oxford, 1916.

Wujastyk, Dominik. "Jambudvīpa: Apples or Plums", in *Studies in the History of the Exact Sciences in Honour of David Pingree*, Leiden, 2004: 287–301.

Yamabe, Nobuyoshi. "New Fragments of the "Yogalehrbuch"", *Kyushu Ryukoku Tanki Daigaku kiyo*, 43, 1997: 11-39.

— *The Sūtra on the Ocean-Like Samādhi of the Visualization of the Buddha: The Interfusion of the Chinese and Indian Cultures in Central Asia as Reflected in a Fifth Century Apocryphal Sūtra*, unpublished PhD thesis, Yale University, 1999.

— "Parallel Passages between the Manobhūmi and the *Yogācārabhūmi of Saṃgharakṣa", in Kragh, Ulrich Timme, eds. *The Foundation for Yoga Practitioners: The Buddhist Yogācārabhūmi Treatise and Its Adaptation in India, East Asia, and Tibet.* Harvard Oriental Series 75. Cambridge, 2013: 596–737.

Yuanci. "A Study of the Meditation Methods in the DESM and Other Early Chinese Texts", presentation given at 2nd International Association of Buddhist Universities Conference: Buddhist Philosophy & Praxis, at the International Buddhist Conference on the United Nations Day of Vesak 2012, Bangkok, 2012. Available at www.undv.org/vesak2012/iabudoc/31YuanciFINAL.pdf. Accessed 18.8.2012.

Yokoyama, Kōitsu & Hirosawa, Takayuki. *Chinese-Sanskrit-Tibetan Table of Buddhist Terminology based on the Yogacarabhumi*, Tokyo, 1996.

Zacchetti, Stefano. "Some Remarks on the *Peṭaka* Passages in the *Da zhidu lun* and their Relation to the Pāli *Peṭakopadesa*", *Annual Report of The International Research Institute for Advanced Buddhology at Soka University*, Vol. V, Tokyo, 2001: 67–85.

— "An early Chinese translation corresponding to Chapter 6 of the *Peṭakopadesa*—An Shigao's *Yin chi rujing* T 603 and its Indian original: a preliminary survey", *Bulletin of the School of Oriental and African Studies*, Vol. 65, No. 1, London, 2002: 74–98.

— "Mind the Hermeneutical Gap: A Terminological Issue in Kumārajīva's Version of the Diamond Sutra", in Xie, D. ed. *Hanchuan fojiao yanjiu de guoqu xianzai weilai - Chinese Buddhism: Past, Present and Future*, 2015: 157-194.

Zürcher, E. *The Buddhist Conquest of China: The Spread and Adaptation of Buddhism in Early Medieval China*, Leiden, 2007.

Index

A

abandon 30, 50, 75, 99, 149, 150, 168, 202, 206, 266, 351, 352, 360, 427, 437, 556, 603. *See also* jahati
abandoning 16–20, 26, 27, 30, 49, 54, 59, 66, 69, 109, 110, 136, 145, 148, 149, 159, 162, 164–166, 193, 194, 197, 200, 210–213, 221, 222, 232, 236, 238, 240, 241, 243–248, 252, 258, 264, 313, 370, 399, 402, 403, 427, 530, 536, 539, 540, 542–544, 557, 568, 584–586, 590, 593, 595, 596, 599, 600, 602
Abhayagiri Vihāra cxxiii
Abhidhamma 3, 16, 74, 82, 83, 90, 95, 100, 104, 265, 325, 327, 383, 425, 438, 445, 456, 477, 481, 493, 519, 570, 583, 624, 628
Abhidhamma method xxxiv, lxiii
Abhidhammamūlaṭīkā, cvii
abhidharma 91, 281, 380, 465, 473, 474
Abhidharmakośabhāṣya xliii, lvii, xcii, xciv, 9, 306, 307, 336, 445, 506, 509, 512, 609
Abhidharmasamuccaya 618
abhisamācārika xlix, cxxxii
abodes of beings 543, 555, 578, 579
abridged 16, 30, 195, 213, 299, 398, 519, 543, 586
abridgement 309
absorption 89, 152–156, 159–161, 165, 172, 182, 193, 200, 209, 218, 224, 228, 231, 258, 284, 357, 367, 371–373, 437, 626
ācāra 21, 35, 38
ācāragocara 38
Ācariya Ānanda cvii
accumulation 7, 8, 18, 95, 340, 430, 433, 447, 476, 502, 519, 520, 534, 540, 549
acquisition 356. *See also* upadhi
adaptation 393, 406, 523, 524
adhicitta 8, 9. *See also* higher miad
adhipaññā 8. *See also* higher wisdom
adhisīla 8, 9. *See also* higher virtue
ādikammika-yogāvacara 139
aggadhamma 50, 278. *See also* supreme Dhamma
aggregate of concentration 7, 8, 49, 477
aggregate of matter 215, 391, 437, 458, 475, 477, 493, 495, 523, 549, 560, 561, 606
aggregate of virtue 7, 49, 477
aggregate of wisdom 7, 8, 49, 477
Aggregates 7, 437
ahiri 19, 25, 468
ājīvapārisuddhi 42, 48
akālika 30, 287
akappiya 72. *See also* unallowable
ākāsa 121, 224, 373, 440
alms-food 45–47, 54, 56, 59, 60, 66, 72, 73, 74, 104
āḷolayamāno 116, 117
alteration 455, 509
alternative interpretation lxxx, 582
amanasikārā cxv, 194, 218–220, 265, 629. *See also* non-attending
Amatākaravaṇṇanā cxvi, cxvii, 303
āmisa cxliv. *See also* worldliuess
Amoghavajra cxxiv
Ānandaśrī li, lvi, lxvi
ānāpānasati 122, 123, 131, 297, 303, 320. *See also* mindfulness of breathing
ānāpānasmṛti lxxxiv, lxxxv
anāsava 4, 458. *See also* without contaminations
anattā 426, 460, 554, 567, 611, 615
anattasaññā 321, 544

anavajja 20, 23, 79, 129
anavajja-sukha 20
ancients lxxiv, lxxxi, cxi
aniccasaññā 321, 544
anicchā lxii, lxiii
anindriyabaddharūpa 453, 478
ānisaṃsa 15, 20, 141, 176
Aññe 16, 21, 478, 522, 584
anomalies 544
anottappa 19, 25
An Shigao lxxxviii, lxxxix, cxi, cxxxiv
antidotes for the defilements lxxxv
anupādiṇṇa-rūpa 454
anupasampanna 35, 49
anupubbābhisamaya xcv
Anuruddha 177
anuttara 4, 291, 324. *See also* unexcelled
apara lxxix
aparaṃ 8
apare 78, 522, 635
api ca 8, 214, 426, 486, 501
apocryphal suttantas lxxvii
appanā 89, 152, 154, 155, 165, 167, 174, 182, 206, 305, 626, 627, 630
appreciative joy 371
arahant 11, 31, 33, 79, 100, 177, 322, 344, 347, 407, 424, 596, 597, 600, 620, 627, 628, 630, 631, 634–636
arahantship 14, 19, 36, 290, 344, 399, 402, 596, 610, 616–626, 634, 636
araññavāsin xciii
arati 149, 314, 329, 365. *See also* dissatisfaction
arising and falling away 559, 561, 568, 587
ariya-dhamma 4, 86. *See also* noble States
Ariya-sthavira-nikāya xlvi
arpaṇā lix
arūpāvacara 10. *See also* concentration of the inmaterial
Āryasthavira xli, xlii, lxv
Asaṅga xliii, lvii, lxxxii, lxxxiv, lxxxvi–lxxxix
asaṅkhārena 492, 600
asantuṭṭhi 25, 34
asceticism 22, 54, 74, 75, 77–79, 81, 104, 485, 547
ascetic practices 34, 75
ascetic qualities 53, 104
Asgiriya cxiv, cxv, cxvi, cxvii, cxxi, cxxii, cxxiii
Asgiriyē Talpata cxv, cxxii
ashamed 33, 348, 468
asmi-māna lv
aśoka-rāja-sūtra cxxiv, cxxx
aśubha lxxxiv, lxxxv
asubhasaññā 122, 544. *See also* ten perceptions of the foul
Aśvaghoṣa lxxxviii
ātmavastu lxvi, xciv
atoms lxxxii. *See also* paramāṇu
attabhāvavatthu 460, 497, 542. *See also* ground of selfhood
attainment 5, 18, 28, 37, 81, 84, 94, 95, 99, 129, 139, 159, 167, 173, 175, 180, 190–192, 199, 200, 205, 208, 209, 215–224, 226–235, 239, 247–251, 268, 275, 279, 290, 305, 361, 399, 408, 409, 472, 485, 583, 596, 611, 612, 614, 615, 626–637
attainment of cessation 84, 94, 173, 234, 485, 626, 630, 634, 637
attainment of freedom 5
attainment of fruition 612, 626, 627, 629, 630, 634. *See also* phalasamāpatti
attains freedom 34, 82
attakilamathānuyoga 13, 47, 165
attavāda 565
attavādupādāna 619
authors 435
avaṭṭhiti 82, 313, 403
avikkhepa 4, 196, 557. *See also* undistractedness

avippaṭisāra 12, 165, 293
avītikkama 15, 17, 30
avoidance 25, 26, 45, 58, 64, 66, 156, 428

B

bad destinations xcii, 14, 26, 51, 158, 235, 401, 421, 547, 553, 591. *See also* duggati
Bagchi cxxx, cxxxii-cxxxiv
Bǎo-chàng cxxiv, cxxv, cxxvii, cxxviii, cxxx, cxxxi, cxxxiv, cxxxv
Bapat xxviii, xxxii-xxxiv, xli, xlvii, xlviii, li, lii, liv, lxx, lxxv, lxxvii, lxxxi, xcvi, xcix, cii, cviii, cx, cxiv, cxv, cxviii, cxxiv, cxxxvi, cxlvii, cxlviii, 6, 48, 66, 70, 76, 121, 182, 183, 321, 337, 601, 605, 635
bare insight cii, ciii, 606-609
base of boundless consciousness cxli, 18, 124, 223-228, 232, 248, 344, 371, 373, 635
base of boundless space 18, 124, 217-219, 222-225, 247, 251, 344, 371, 372, 635
base of neither-perception-nor-non-perception xxxix, cxli, 18, 122, 124-232, 235, 238, 250, 251, 344, 395, 399, 633, 635
basic discipline xlix, cxxxii, 39
beautification 45, 46
beauty 40, 44, 65, 130, 242, 264, 460, 461, 497, 507, 509, 624, 625
beginner meditator xxxvii, lxxxvii, xciv, 99, 130, 139, 237, 240, 241, 243-248, 253, 257, 263, 268, 286, 289, 292, 294, 296, 298, 306, 308, 321, 329, 330, 343, 347, 363, 365, 375, 391, 406, 413-415, 417, 418, 420, 422, 437, 438
being produced xcvii, 333, 454, 455
benefits xxx, xxxviii, xxxix, xcii, xciv, cxxxv, cxxxviii, cxli, cxlviii, 15, 20, 21, 51, 57-64, 66-71, 81, 85, 87, 100, 135, 136, 143, 145, 158, 159, 175, 176, 184, 198, 208, 214, 216, 223, 226, 229, 232, 236-248, 252, 259-263, 267, 268, 285, 286, 288, 292-295, 297, 298, 318, 320, 321, 328, 329, 342, 343, 346, 350, 362-366, 371, 374, 375, 390, 391, 395, 408, 425, 426
bhāṇaka lxxxi, cxvi
bhaṅga cvii, 510, 568
bhāva li, lxxxii, 55, 86, 196, 230, 374, 375, 381, 389, 442, 454
bhāvanābhūmi xcvi, cxii, 592, 609
bhavaṅga xliii, lxxiii, lxxxii, 472, 473, 484, 487-492, 495, 516, 593
bhavaṅga-citta xliii, lxxiii
bhavaṅga mind xliii, lxxiii, 484, 488-492
bhaya 33, 466, 554
bhikkhu xxxix, lxxvii, cxlvii, cxlviii, 8, 21-25, 28, 29, 35, 37, 38, 39, 40-44, 49, 50, 55, 58, 59, 60, 62, 68, 71, 73, 75, 76, 86, 87, 95, 96, 99, 100, 104, 148, 155, 156, 161, 184, 185, 189, 190, 191, 195, 198, 201, 207, 208, 210, 211, 214, 219, 225, 228, 231, 252, 266, 292, 299, 313, 315, 318, 319, 326, 343, 344, 346-349, 357, 369, 370, 371, 374, 384, 385, 398, 400, 401, 403, 404, 411, 412, 416, 421, 425, 432, 435, 466, 468, 505, 527, 538-540, 551, 570, 577, 581, 582, 585, 596, 597, 607, 610, 620, 627, 631, 634, 637
bhikkhunī 35, 40
bhikkhunīs xxxvii, cxix, cxx, 40, 51
bhojane amattaññutā 25, 151
bhūmi xcv, 129, 143, 217, 317, 319, 362, 606, 608
birth of matter xcvi, 439, 442, 444, 456. *See also* jātirūpa
blamelessness xxxviii, 13, 20, 23, 45, 46, 166, 292, 293
bodhi cxliv, 145, 267, 275, 278, 392

Bodhisatta xlv, xlviii, 36, 221, 276, 277, 359
Bodhisatta ideal xlv
bodhisattva lxxxii
Bodhisattvabhūmi xlv, lxxxii
body xlvii, li, lix, lxv, lxx, lxxiii, lxxvii, lxxxi, lxxxiv, lxxxviii, xcii, xciv, xcviii, c, civ, cxiii, cxxvii, cxxviii, cxxix, cxxxviii, cxxxix, cxl, 12, 15, 19, 20, 22, 25, 26, 28, 30, 32, 38, 39, 45, 46, 58, 63, 68, 70, 75, 85, 103, 116, 117, 122, 123, 126–129, 131, 137, 145, 148, 153, 156, 160, 161, 163, 165, 172, 176, 185, 186, 192, 194, 195, 198, 199, 200, 203, 206, 207, 208, 211, 214, 215, 236, 239, 241, 242, 248, 252, 255, 256, 259, 260, 262–266, 268, 298, 299–303, 306–311, 317, 318, 321, 322–325, 328–344, 348, 355, 375–377, 379, 382, 384, 386, 389–394, 398, 405, 406, 407, 409–412, 414, 415, 417, 419, 428, 438, 441–445, 447–452, 454, 455, 459, 461, 463, 469, 470, 479, 480, 481, 483, 484, 494, 502, 515, 516, 526, 527, 542, 549, 558, 573, 600, 612–614, 618, 620, 628, 629, 633, 634
body endowed with consciousness lix, 542
breath should not be extended c
Buddhabhadra lxxxv, lxxxvi, cxxxiv
Buddha-fields xxviii. *See also* buddhakkhetta
Buddhaghosa xxviii, xxxii–xxxiv, xxxviii, xlii, xlvi, lxx, lxxii–lxxiv, lxxvi, lxxix–lxxxii, lxxxvii, xcv, cii, ciii, cvi, cx, cxii, cxiii, cxv, cxviii, cxix, cxlvii, 196, 305, 330, 422, 615
buddhakkhetta xxviii. *See also* Buddha-fields
buddhānusmṛti lxxxv
burning head 44, 547

C

cāga cxliv, 557. *See also* giving up
cakras cxvi
caṇḍāla cxlvii, cxlviii, 51, 72, 468. *See also* outcasts
catubhūmi lx
cause l, lxviii, cvi, cxiv, cxlvi, 101, 119, 139, 142, 147, 150, 171, 173, 188, 197, 234–236, 258, 275, 278, 279, 287, 318, 321, 323, 348, 349, 354, 371, 382, 425, 434, 437, 456, 463, 474, 505, 509, 511, 512, 514, 521, 522, 523, 529, 532–534, 559–562, 566, 567, 572, 573, 578, 579, 580, 587, 589, 600. *See also* hetuto
causes of temperament xxxii
causes of virtue 15, 24, 25
cessation xl, lix, lxii, lxxxvii, cii, ciii, civ, cvi, 18, 36, 37, 84, 94, 95, 101, 173, 193, 194, 200, 203, 209, 210, 212, 213, 215, 221, 233, 234, 277, 279, 285, 287, 288, 299, 315, 316, 342, 344, 352, 355, 390, 435, 436, 469, 485, 498, 501, 524, 525, 529, 531, 535, 536, 537, 538, 539, 540–545, 552, 561–563, 568, 571, 581, 584–587, 591, 604, 614, 626, 628–637
cessation of perception and feeling xl, lix, civ, 344, 626, 631, 633, 634, 636, 637
cetanā lvi, lxii, lxiii, ci, 15–17, 30, 163, 179, 309, 462, 463, 502, 507, 520, 523. *See also* volition
cetovimutti lxi, 82, 126, 155, 349, 363, 369, 370, 592, 609, 616, 632
change l, lix, cii, cvi, cvii, cxxvi, 18, 89, 154, 235, 242, 246, 383, 392, 407, 487, 512, 527, 534, 540, 559, 571, 582, 583, 584, 587, 588, 608, 628, 629, 630
characteristic xxx, xlii, xlviii, xlix, liii, xciv, ciii, cxii, cxliv, 15, 19, 20, 31, 49, 50, 79, 82, 109, 110, 132, 135,

136-138, 144, 146, 167, 168, 170, 172, 177, 179, 186, 194-197, 203-205, 212, 213, 233, 236, 238, 240, 241, 243-248, 252, 259-263, 267, 285, 286, 288, 292, 294, 295, 297, 320, 325, 328, 329, 331, 342, 346, 350, 360, 362-366, 374, 380-382, 387, 388, 391, 425, 426, 438, 445, 455, 456, 458, 460, 463, 475, 476, 481, 496, 497, 518, 519, 532-535, 548, 554, 559, 562, 565, 567, 581, 587
Chinese pilgrims xlv
Chinese team lxix, cxlv
Chinese translation of the Vimutti-magga xxix, xlii, liv, lxx, cxxxvi, cxlii, cxliii
Chinese translations xlix, lxix, lxx, lxxxiv, xciv, cxxxiii, cxxxv, cxxxvi, cxli, cxliv, cxlvi, cxlvii, 277, 336
Chinese Tripiṭaka xxxi, cxxxvi, cxlii
chronicles lxxiii
citta xliii, l, lxxiii, ci, cvii, 3, 9, 11, 88, 94, 109, 135, 136, 155, 193, 265, 281, 314, 327, 346, 355, 385, 386, 388, 389, 405, 410, 415, 444, 448, 464, 465, 469, 484, 487, 488, 489, 495, 499, 502, 506, 508, 516, 517, 523, 558, 571, 593, 631
citta-khaṇa cvii, 327, 355, 506, 571. *See also* Mind-moments
clean use 48
clear knowing 20, 204-206, 208, 217, 252, 259-263, 320, 426, 557
clinging lv, lvii, 88, 428, 429, 457, 474, 476-478, 498, 500, 504-506, 509, 511, 518-520, 523-527, 541, 550, 552, 554, 556, 564, 565, 619
coarse afflictions 19, 344
colophons xxxi, xlii, lxxiii
comfortable abiding 45, 46
commentarial texts xlii, lxxii, 122, 227
conceit lv, lxi, xcix, 24, 28, 31, 107, 108, 328, 421, 462, 467, 542, 596, 621-624. *See also* mana
conceit 'I-am lv
concentration xxvii, xxix, xxxi, xxxv, xxxvi, xxxviii-lxxx, lxxxvii, xc, cii, ciii, civ, cix, cxiv, cxxxvii, cxxxviii, cxl, cxliv, 3-5, 7-14, 35, 45, 49-51, 54, 81-99, 106, 122, 138, 145, 147, 149, 153-162, 165, 171, 173, 180-185, 189, 192-195, 197-199, 203, 205, 216, 217, 219, 221, 226, 235, 239, 271, 274, 280, 291-293, 303-305, 309, 310, 317, 318, 343, 350, 369, 397, 398, 399, 403-405, 419, 420, 422-424, 429, 462, 467, 468, 477, 478, 522, 529-531, 542, 556, 557, 576, 577, 587, 588, 589, 593, 607, 612, 613, 624, 627-629, 631, 634. *See also* samādhi
concentration and insight xxxvi
concentration attainments cii, ciii, 84, 94, 271
concentration of the immaterial 10, 91. *See also* arūpāvacara
concentration of the material 91, 219. *See also* rūpāvacara
concentration of the path 10
concentration partaking of distinction 10
concentration partaking of penetration 5, 162
concept xxviii, xliii-lv, xcvii, xcix, ciii, 126, 146, 179, 322, 485, 620
condition lvi, lxiii, lxv, lxviii, cv, cvi, cvii, 122, 125, 152, 163, 234, 275, 293, 327, 332-334, 385-388, 417, 443, 444, 456, 469-471, 482-484, 487, 489, 490, 492, 493, 498, 500-509, 511, 513-516, 518, 520, 521, 535, 551, 552, 559-562, 566, 567. *See also* paccayato
conduct lxi, xc, cxxxvii, 19, 21, 23, 25, 26, 37, 38, 39, 40, 41, 73, 101, 103, 159, 188, 189, 271-273, 280, 281, 324, 362, 623
confession 29, 50, 73

consciencelessness 25, 462, 622
contact between Sri Lanka and China cxix
contentment xxxviii, 19, 25, 34, 53, 58, 62, 76, 87
copyists lii, lxv, lxviii, cxliv
corruptions cxii, cxliv, cxlvi
cotton wool c, 142, 302, 406
Councils lxxvii

D

Daśabalaśrīmitra xxxii, xli, xlii, xlvi, xlvii, lii, lxv, lxvii, lxviii, lxix, 16
dassanabhūmi xcv, cxii, 592, 609
Dasuttarasutta lxiii, lxiv, 542, 544
date of composition lxx, lxxxiv
death lxi, xc, xci, xcviii, cvii, cxiii, cxiv, cxx, cxxxviii, 3, 22, 30, 51, 68, 122, 127, 128, 131, 132, 158, 162, 187, 199, 209, 215, 223, 226, 229, 232, 252, 275, 320–328, 342, 347, 364, 437, 498, 500, 504, 506, 510, 511, 515, 516, 518–521, 523–526, 551–553, 571, 596
debt 47, 352, 353, 466
deceiving 42, 43, 392
delusion l, lxxx, lxxxv, xc, xcix, cxxxix, 19, 76–78, 106–119, 131, 133, 163, 165, 205, 215, 230, 257, 308, 309, 312, 313, 357, 415, 426, 456, 462, 506, 509, 519, 520, 568, 591, 616, 619, 622
dependences li, cxlviii, 66. *See also* nissaya
dependent arising in a single moment cvii
dependent matter lii, liii, liv, lv, xcvi, xcvii, 383, 442, 443, 445, 449, 465, 620
dependent origination xxxv, xxxvii, lvi, lix, lxxxvii, xc, 506, 507
detachment 4, 163, 164, 390. *See also* visaṃyoga, Visesikā
Dhammapāla xxx, xxxi, xxxii, xliv–xlvi, liv, lvii, lxxi, lxxvi, lxxx, lxxxii, xcix, cii, ciii, civ, cv, cxi, cxii, cxiii, cxvii, cxlvii, 9, 485
dhammatā 35, 407, 564
dhāraṇa xlviii, 380, 381, 525
Dharmarakṣa lxxxviii
Dharmatrāta-dhyāna-sūtra lxxxvi, lxxxix, 331
dhātuprabheda lxxxvi, lxxxvii
dhuta liii, ciii, 54, 75, 78, 104, 485
Dhutaguṇaniddesa xxix, xlii, lxv, cxxxv
dhutaṅga xliv, lxxii, xcix, ciii, 22, 65, 75, 76, 485
Dhyāna Sūtras lxxxiv–lxxxvi, xciv, cxxxiv
different interpretations lxxxi
Dīpavaṃsa xxxvii, xlvi, lxxi, lxxviii, lxxix, cxii, cxix, 635
disaccumulation lx, 54, 95, 430, 433
disciple cxxvii, cxxix, 29, 45, 216, 345, 348, 349
discontentment 34
diseases xciv, 47, 341, 394
disenchantment xlix, 7, 12, 18, 48, 49, 77, 190, 256, 322, 328, 392–394, 433, 434, 522, 579, 614, 632
dispassion lxii, 12, 18, 70, 82, 119, 190, 215, 221, 265, 315, 522, 544
disqualification 49. *See also* pārājika
dissatisfaction cxlv, 45, 365, 368, 370, 375. *See also* arati
dissolution cvi, cvii, cviii, cxlii, 30, 322, 327, 506, 510, 568, 569, 570, 571, 575–578, 636
distinction lvii, lxxxvi, cxliv, 3, 9, 10, 34, 35, 70, 76, 90, 128, 149, 153, 158, 170, 188, 190, 193, 200, 209, 218, 224, 227, 230, 342, 352, 368, 370, 403, 438, 599
distortion lv, 273, 286, 304, 624, 625

divine abiding civ, 184–186, 198, 199, 208, 214, 215, 634
division of monastic vocations into practice xciii. *See also* paṭipatti
Dpal Brtsegs xli
drowsiness cxxxix, 63
dubious 32, 33
dubious virtue 32, 33
duggati 14, 26, 51, 158, 235, 401. *See also* bad destinations
dukkha lxx, 210, 354, 374, 525, 526, 527, 529, 533, 545, 611
duration and continuity civ, cv, cvi, cviii
dussīlamala 11
Dvādaśāṅga-pratītyasamutpādaḥ cxxiii
dweller xciii, 55, 56, 64, 65, 66, 67, 68, 69, 73, 74, 75, 78

E

ease 33, 51, 86, 102, 315, 331, 365, 366, 629
effortless l, 492
Ehara xxxi, xxxii, li, lxxv
ekābhisamaya xcv, 605, 606
ekacce, eke xxxii, lxxix, lxxx, xcvi, xcix, 112, 302, 440, 602
elements xxxix, xli, xliv, liii, lvi, lviii, lix, lxi, lxxxiv, lxxxvi, lxxxvii, lxxxix, xc, xci, xcvii, xcviii, xcix, c, cxvi, cxxviii, cxlvi, 86, 104, 112, 113, 122, 123, 126–132, 137, 138, 240, 264, 274, 279, 306, 330–332, 355, 374–380, 382–390, 400, 401, 403, 437, 438, 440, 442, 444, 445, 448, 453, 461, 477, 479, 481, 489, 491, 493–497, 503, 514, 523, 524, 525, 545, 547, 548, 549, 554, 606
elements in excess c
eleven different kinds of concept *(paññatti)* liv
embryo xciv, 335, 336
Emperor Wen cxx
Emperor Wu of Liáng cxvii, cxxxiii, cxxxiv
emptiness lxxxix, xci, cxliv, 18, 68, 129, 264, 325, 331, 332, 352, 374, 540, 555, 567, 611, 612, 614, 615, 636. *See also* suññata
energy xcvii, cxxxvii, cxxxviii, 22, 23, 37, 48, 52, 54, 55, 83, 94, 148, 149, 157, 158, 177, 179, 184, 189, 276, 280, 284, 313, 318, 360, 361, 383, 403, 404, 406, 427, 462, 464, 466, 468, 515, 531, 547
enlightenment xlviii, lxi, cxxxviii, cxliv, 13, 14, 145, 171, 201, 202, 267, 270, 275, 276, 278, 282, 286, 298, 318, 319, 390, 392, 531, 543, 576, 582, 584, 587, 588, 589, 594, 595, 596, 608
enters upon the path to freedom cxl, 8, 12, 13, 14
equanimity xcix, ciii, civ, cxliv, 90, 96, 122, 130, 160, 166, 173, 182, 183, 200–203, 206, 208–210, 212–217, 235, 276, 280, 281, 305, 306, 315, 319, 360, 361, 366, 367, 369–371, 373, 374, 393, 404, 415, 458, 459, 462, 473, 504, 531, 557, 576, 580, 609, 625, 634, 635. *See also* upekkha
escaping lx, lxi, 4, 5, 162, 216, 543
eternalist view lxvii
etymologies xxxiv, lxxii
evil signs 44
exegetical system xxxiv, xlii
exhausting oneself 13, 47, 77, 165
existences 14, 86, 270, 279, 418, 514
expediencies xxxvii, lxxix, cxxxv, cxlvi, 70, 72, 73, 74
expositions xxix, xxxv, cxxix, 131, 435. *See also* niddesa

F

factors of asceticism xxviii, xliv, liv, lxxii, xcix, ciii, 22, 75
faith xlix, lxi, cxxxviii, 19, 25, 26, 40, 48, 51, 52, 83, 103, 107–111, 118, 119, 131, 132, 145, 153, 157, 171, 172, 184, 194, 235, 267, 268, 283, 284, 291, 295, 296, 345, 349, 350, 352, 415, 462, 464, 521, 531, 599, 603, 612
fame 4, 28, 350, 621
fascicles lxxxviii, cxix, cxxiii, cxxiv, cxxv, cxxvi, cxxx, cxxxi, cxliii
Fawning 43
Faxian cxvii, cxx, cxxiii
five aggregates xxxix, xl, lvi, lviii, lix, lxi, lxv, lxviii, lxxxix, xc, xcii, cvii, 306, 437, 475–478, 500, 523, 525–527, 545, 552, 553, 556, 581, 606
foolishness 33, 34
forest asceticism xxxvi, lxxxii
forest dweller xciii
formation of the embryo xciv, 336
formations l, lviii, lix, lxii, lxiii, lxviii, ciii, cvii, 110, 163, 174, 207, 220, 221, 230, 231, 235, 273, 274, 285, 299, 311–313, 315–319, 322, 384, 390, 410, 437, 462, 468, 476, 492, 498, 500–502, 504, 506–508, 511–513, 518–521, 523, 524, 526, 527, 544, 545, 548, 550–562, 564–571, 576, 577, 580–582, 587, 588, 590, 593, 607, 612–614, 629, 631, 633, 635–637
former causes 36, 573
former teachers lxxiii, lxxiv, lxxviii, lxxix, lxxxi, 47, 50, 140, 275, 305, 323, 377, 384, 414, 586
four assemblies 40, 51
four establishments of mindfulness cxxxviii, 41, 282, 286, 298, 318, 319, 464, 530, 531, 542, 582
four kinds of use 47
four noble truths xxxiii, xl, lxix, lxxxviii, xcii, 13, 100, 178, 290, 390, 426, 428, 464, 500, 525, 531, 532, 544, 547, 548, 584, 588, 591
four paths lv, lx, 91, 430–434, 602, 603, 610
four planes lx, 430, 433
four resolves xxviii, 360, 361
four right efforts 37, 282, 286, 530, 582
freedom xxvii, xxix, xxxi–xxxiv, xxxviii, xl, l, cxl, 3–8, 11–14, 21, 27, 28, 29, 32, 34, 54, 76, 82, 85, 160, 163, 164, 184, 273, 275, 276, 278, 280, 283, 287, 291, 298, 317, 318, 319, 342, 343, 427, 477, 478, 492, 522, 544, 589, 615, 624. *See also* vimutti
Freedom, Path of xix freedom through eradication xxvii, xxxi, xl, cxxxvii, cxl, cxli, cxlii, cxliii, 4, 5, 395, 424, 436, 545, 637, 638. *See also* nissarana; *See also* samuccheda freedom through escaping
freedom through 4, 5. *See also* vikkha-mbhana- vimutti
suspension 4
freedom through the [opposite] factor. *See also* patippassaddha fruit of recluseship; *See also* tadanga freedom through tranquillizing
Funan cxxi, cxxv–cxxvii, cxxix, cxxxii, cxxxiii, cxxxv, cxlii
functional-causeless mind l
functional-indeterminate l, lx, 430, 433
fundamentals of the holy life 28, 29

G

gāmavāsin xciii
Gaṇṭhipada cx
general characteristic xciv, 179, 548
generosity 40, 122, 127, 128, 159, 294, 295, 296, 345, 350, 361

Girimānandasutta lxii, lxiii, lxvi, 544
giving up xc, cxliv, 44, 101, 110, 294, 360, 393, 466, 589. *See also* caga gladness; *See also* pamojja good destination
good friend xxxvii, xxxix, 40, 99, 100, 102, 103, 350
Gotama xxxviii, 3, 4
gotta 20, 583
gradual physical formation 332, 335, 336
gradual realization xxviii, xcii, xcv, 601, 602
grammar xxxiv, lxxii, lxxxii, cxvii, 196
Great Emperor of Liáng cxxvii, cxxix
ground of selfhood xxxvii, li. *See also* attabhavavatthu
growth and continuity xcvii. *See also* upacaya-santati Guangzhou
guards one's mind 49
guard the sense-faculties 45
guṇa cxliv, 8, 54, 104, 109, 176, 179, 278, 291, 292, 294, 295, 303, 353, 491
Guṇabhadra cxvii, cxxvii, cxxix, cxxx, cxxxii, cxxxiii, cxxxv
Guṇavarman cxvii, cxxiii
Guṇavṛddhi cxvii, cxxii–cxxiv, cxxx

H

hadayavatthu lxxxii, xcvii, 439, 442, 445, 453, 471, 503, 508, 517. *See also* heart basis hanabhagiya
happiness of purity 33
heart basis xcvii. *See also* hadayavatthu heaviness
hetuto cvi, 527, 537, 559. *See also* adhicitta higher training; *See also* cause higher mind
higher virtue cxiv, 8, 9, 10, 11, 310. *See also* adhicitta higher training; *See also* adhipañña; *See also* adhisila higher wisdom
hita xlix, 9, 110, 346
holy life 28, 29, 45, 46, 100, 106, 591, 617
Hsüan-tsang xlv

I

Ichi-shan-jian-lu-piposha lxx, lxxvii, cxviii, cxxxvi
idamatthitā l, 53, 76
idioms xxxvii, cxlvi
idleness 25, 69, 70, 158, 177
immaterial aggregates lviii, lix, lxiv, lxv, civ, cv, cvi, cvii, cviii, 482, 497, 606
immeasurables xxxix, lxxx, lxxxvi, c, ciii, 122, 125–131, 133, 202, 238, 303, 367, 368, 369, 370, 466
immediate xl, 30, 167, 235, 286, 287, 488
immoderation 64
immorality 39, 51
impure virtue 32, 33
inclusion liv, lvi, xcv, xcix, 475, 477, 482, 493, 513, 523, 524, 532, 545, 565. *See also* saṅgaha
inconsistency cxlv
indeterminate *(abyākata)* virtue l, lx, 23, 24, 75, 424, 430, 432, 433, 456, 457, 539, 541
indeterminate mind 24
indriyasaṃvara 44, 159
inferior virtue 34
inheritance 47, 48
insight for the attainment of fruition cii, 630
insight is without strength cii
insight knowledges xxxiii, xl, xliii, cxlii
interpolations lxiv, lxix, lxx, 340

intoxication 45, 46, 252, 253, 264
intrinsic nature lxxxii, xcvii, xcviii, ciii, cvii, 179, 254, 256, 309, 325, 381, 382, 438, 455, 456, 458, 496, 526, 527, 560, 564, 566, 567, 571, 618. *See also* sabhāva
intrusions lxix
iṭṭha xlix, 109, 110

J

jahati. *See also* abandon
jalati xlix, 381
Jātaka xxviii, cxviii, 276
Jātaka-aṭṭhakathā cxviii
jātirūpa xcvii, 439, 456. *See also* birtli of matter
Jingxiu cxx, cxxi, cxxiv
joy xlix, cxliv, 106, 166, 170, 210, 295, 365–369, 371, 373, 415, 458, 459, 473, 608, 609, 614, 625. *See also* muditā

K

kalāpa xliii, xcvii, ciii, cviii, 382, 383, 444, 447, 448, 475, 569
kalyāṇa cxliv, 12, 37, 100. *See also* three kinds of goodness
kāmacchanda lv, lvii, 164, 176
kāmāvacara ci, 9, 14, 95, 175, 465, 490. *See also* sensuous sphere
kāmupādāna lv, lvii
Karmavibhāgaya li, lvi
kasiṇa xxxvi, 93, 125, 136, 137, 139, 331, 485
Kassapa 36, 171
Kathāvatthu xxviii, lxxi, xcv, cii, 233, 601, 606
keci, ekacce and apare lxxix, lxxx, xcvi, xcvii, xcix, cii, ciii, civ, cv, cviii, cix, 139, 280, 293, 329, 432, 465, 597, 635, 637
khaṇato civ, cvi, cviii, cix, 327, 447, 560, 571
khaṇika lxxxii, 322, 355. *See also* momentariness
Kheminda li, cxliii, cxlvii
kikī 52
kilesa lxxxii, cxliv, 162, 178, 389, 405, 423, 536, 556, 600, 613
kinds of worms xlvii, li, lxix, xciv, xcv, 325, 332, 336, 337, 339, 340
King Mahānāma xlv, lxxv, cxx, cxxiv, cxxvi
King Mahāsena lxxi, lxxiii, lxxv
King Parākramabāhu lxxvi
King Saṅghabodhi lxxxiii
kiriyāhetuka l, 489
kiriyāvyākate l, 430, 489
knowledge and vision according to reality 12, 19, 522, 550
knowledge in conformity with the truths 429, 431
knowledge of rise and fall civ, 568
knowledge of the ownership of kamma lxi, 422, 423, 429, 431
knowledge of the path xl, 10, 279, 521, 582, 587, 588, 589, 593, 610, 615
kodha 24, 114. *See also* wrath
kuhanā 42
Kulumbasutta lxxvii
Kumārajīva lxxxv, lxxxvi, lxxxix, cxxxiv–cxxxvi, cxlv, 7
kusala xcix, ci, cxliv, 54, 143, 289, 432, 437, 456, 460, 465, 627
kusalattikavinimutta xliv, 75
Kusalāvyākate l

L

lakkhaṇa ciii, cxliv, 15, 101, 176, 360, 387, 391, 455, 513, 534
latent tendencies cxxxvi, 11, 279, 505, 506, 543, 616, 621

lay-follower 35
learning lxxiv, cxxvii, cxxix, 40, 51, 106, 112, 149, 264, 290, 295, 296, 345, 350, 429, 597
Ledi Sayādaw cviii
Liáng Dynasty cxxiv, cxxvii, cxxxiii
limitation 27, 28
living being lv, 322, 358, 378, 506
lodgings 47, 55, 57, 67, 69
lokiya lxi, 27, 532
loss of mindfulness 25
loving-kindness xxxvi, xxxvii, lxxxvii, lxxxix, xc, cxxxviii, 122, 131, 147, 202, 276, 284, 346, 347, 349–352, 354, 356–372, 400, 401

M

macchariya 24, 114. *See also* selfislmess
magga-ñāṇa 10, 589
Mahā-aśoka-rāja-sūtra cxxiv, cxxx
Mahānāma xlv, lxxii, lxxv, cv, cxviii, cxx, cxxiv, cxxvi
Mahāsāṃghika xliii, xlix, lxxxiii, cxxxii, 65
mahāsatta lxxxiii, 359
Mahāvaṃsa xlv, xlvi, lxxii, lxxvi, lxxxii, lxxxiii, cxii, cxix, 635
Mahāvihāra xxviii, xxxiii, xxxiv, xlii, xliv–xlvii, li, liii, liv, lxv, lxx, lxxii–lxxiv, lxxvii, lxxviii, lxxx, xcv, xcvi–xcix, ci, cii, cv, cxi–cxiii, cxlvi, 125, 442, 465, 620
Mahāyāna xxviii, xxxvi, xlii, xliv, xlv, lxxiv, lxxv, lxxxii–lxxxv, lxxxix, cxviii, cxx, cxxii, cxxix–cxxxii, cxxxv, cxxxviii
Mahāyāna forest asceticism xxxvi
Mahiṃsāsaka xlvi. *See also* Mahīsāsaka
Mahīsāsaka. *See also* Mahiṃsāsaka
maitri lxxxv
majjhimā paṭipadā 13, 286
Malwatta cxv, cxxiii
māna lv, 24, 28, 108, 421, 467. *See also* conceit
Mandra cxvii, cxxi, cxxv, cxxvii, cxxix–cxxxi, cxxxiii, cxxxvi, cxlii
mantras cxvi
manual xxvii, xxix, xxx, xxxiv–xxxvi, xxxviii, xliv, lxxi, lxxxiii, lxxxiv, lxxxvi–lxxxviii, xcii, cxi, cxxxv
manuscript xlv, l, li, lii, lvi, lxiv, lxvi, lxviii, cxiv, cxvii, cxix, cxxi, cxxx, cxxxi, cxxxv, cxlii, cxliii, cxlvii, 142, 230, 419, 457, 508
mārga lxxxvi, xcii, xcv, cxxiv, cxxx, 9
material basis xliii, xcvii, 439, 442, 443, 449, 454, 455, 471, 503, 516, 573. *See also* vatthurūpa
material cluster xcvii, ciii, 382
material sphere lxxviii, xcvii, 98, 166, 170, 197, 217, 219, 221, 222, 372, 403, 413, 417, 424, 431, 432, 433, 450
mātikā summaries xxx
matter as intrinsic nature xcvii, 455, 456
matter not bound up with faculties cii, 453, 478
matter that are not-clung-to xcvii
medicines 47, 62, 103
meditation xxvii, xxix, xxx, xxxiv, xxxvi–xxxix, lxx, lxxv, lxxxii–lxxxviii, xc, xciii, xciv, xcv, xcviii, cxv, cxvi, cxvii, cxxxi, cxxxiv, cxxxv, cxli, 25, 43, 49, 51, 65, 98, 101–105, 107, 121–133, 139, 140, 148, 149, 151, 177, 191, 192, 205, 257, 258, 263, 266, 278, 284, 303, 320, 392, 395, 428, 557
meditation manual xxix, xxxiv, xxxvi, xxxviii, lxxxiii, lxxxvi, lxxxvii, lxxxviii, cxxxv
meditation subjects xxxvi, xxxvii,

xxxix, lxxxiv, lxxxv, lxxxvii, 98, 101, 121–130, 132, 133, 191, 303, 320, 395, 557
memorisation lxxiii
merchants cxx, cxxiv, cxxvii
middha xliv, liv, xciv, xcvii, xcviii, xcix, civ, cv, 176, 442, 449, 450, 542, 620. *See also* physical torpor
middharūpa xliv, xcvi, xcvii, xcviii, cxii, 439, 449, 620. *See also* torpor of matter
middle way 13, 14, 46, 47, 290
Milindapañhā xxviii, lxxi, lxxii, lxxvii, lxxxii, xciii, xciv, xcviii, ci, cxii, cxxii, 54
mind xxxiv, xxxv, xliii, l, lv, lviii, lix, lxi, lxv, lxxiii, lxxviii, lxxxvii, lxxxix, xci, xcvii, xcviii, xcix, c, cvii, cix, cxiv, cxxvii, cxxix, cxlii, 3, 8–12, 17, 20, 23, 24, 29, 30, 36, 40, 41, 45, 49, 51, 52, 57, 64, 74, 81–83, 85, 86, 89, 94, 96, 97, 106, 109, 116, 131, 135–137, 139, 143–163, 165–168, 170, 172, 174, 176–186, 192, 193, 195–200, 203, 206, 208, 209, 211, 212, 214–218, 220, 222, 224–226, 228, 229, 231, 233, 236, 238, 240, 241, 243–249, 252, 253, 256–263, 265, 267, 268, 278, 281, 283, 284, 286, 288, 289, 291–310, 313–318, 320–322, 327, 328, 329, 331, 340, 342, 343, 345–352, 355–357, 359, 362, 363, 365–368, 371–376, 385–394, 398, 403–405, 409–412, 414–418, 420, 421, 425, 428, 442, 444, 448, 449, 457–474, 477–479, 481–484, 486–497, 499, 502, 503, 506–508, 516, 517, 523–527, 530, 531, 547, 549, 554–559, 562, 568–571, 574, 575, 576, 577, 580, 587, 588, 589, 593, 596, 612–616, 618, 624–626, 629, 631, 635, 636
mindfulness xxxvi, xlvii, lxiii, lxxvii, lxxxvii, lxxxix, xc, xci, c, cxxxviii, cxliv, 8, 20, 25, 26, 40, 41, 48, 49, 83, 101, 122–124, 126–131, 133, 142, 145, 148, 149, 157, 165, 179, 184, 189, 195, 202, 204–208, 210, 213, 214, 217, 252, 253, 256, 267, 268, 280, 282, 284–286, 288, 291–299, 302, 303, 305–313, 317–321, 323–329, 342, 345, 351, 391, 403, 462, 464, 514, 515, 529, 530, 531, 542, 557, 576, 582, 589, 624
mindfulness of breathing xxxvi, xlvii, lxiii, lxxvii, lxxxvii, lxxxix, xc, xci, c, cxliv, 122–124, 126–131, 133, 148, 285, 297, 298, 302, 303, 305, 308–312, 317–320. *See also* ānāpānasati
mind-moments xliii, 327. *See also* citta-khana
mind will be guarded 52
minor rules xlix, 39
misconduct xc, 38, 39, 623
mistakes xlviii, xlix, l, lxv, lxvi, lxvii, cxxxv, cxxxvi, cxlvi
mnemonic verses xxx, lxxii, cxix
moderation 25, 46, 48, 62, 63, 87, 118, 151
moha 33, 107, 109
moment xxxv, xxxvii, lxiii, lxv, ci, civ, cv, cvi, cvii, cviii, cx, 130, 210, 319, 327, 355, 386, 447–452, 470, 499, 506, 509, 510, 517, 560, 561, 571, 574–576, 584–586, 588, 605, 611, 614–616
momentariness lxxxii, xcv, xcvi, cvii, cviii, 323, 327, 509, 571. *See also* khaṇika
momentary arising, presence cvii
momentary death 322
mosquitoes 47, 237
muditā cxliv, 122, 365, 369, 370, 373, 543. *See also* appreciative joy
mundane lxi, lxxxvii, 27, 88, 307, 424, 428, 431, 456, 474, 521, 532, 541, 577, 626, 627, 629, 630
Mundane knowledge 10

mundane virtue 27
muṭṭhasati 25

N

Nagai xxxi, xxxiv
nāmarūpa lvi, lviii, lix, lxv, 523, 524
name-and-matter lvi, lxiii, lxv, 199, 390, 427, 470, 497, 498, 502–504, 506, 508, 518–520, 542, 548–551, 561, 572
ñāṇa 10, 12, 131, 133, 150, 197, 270, 274, 278, 322, 361, 374, 398, 422, 508, 551, 581, 589
Nanda xciv, 45, 75, 100
negligence 25, 301
neither-trainee-nor-non-trainee 33
netripada-sūtra cix, cxiii
Netti lxxvii, lxxviii, ci, cxi–cxiv, cxviii, cxix, 6, 17, 460, 497, 506, 542
Nettipada-sutta lxxvii, cxiii
nibbāna xxvii, xxix, xxxiv–xxxvi, xxxviii, xl, lix, lxxxii, 3, 5, 35, 162, 215, 273, 275, 277, 285–287, 290, 314–316, 344, 482, 484, 493, 495, 530, 539, 577, 578, 581–583, 587, 588, 590, 593, 596, 599, 607, 613–616, 626, 628, 629, 635
nibbatti cvi, cix, 442, 500, 507, 509, 512, 559
nibbedhabhāgiya 9, 34. *See also* virtue partaking of penetration
nibbidā xlix, 7, 12, 215, 252, 256, 328, 433, 521, 579, 614
niddesa xxix, xxxi, 15, 174. *See also* expositions
nimitta cxliv, 101, 130, 136, 149, 167, 224, 274, 300, 301, 302, 354, 373, 391, 406, 485, 502, 515. *See also* sign
nipphanna xcvii, 450, 455
nissarana. *See also* freedom through escaping
nissaraṇa lxi, 4, 164, 287, 535
nissaraṇīya lxi, lxii
nissaya li, cxlviii, 66, 184, 325, 341, 386, 387. *See also* dependences
nivāraṇa c, 465
noble states 4
noble States. *See also* ariya-dhamma
non-attachment 79, 373
non-attending 44, 354, 629. *See also* amanasikāra
non-humans 68, 140, 325, 346
non-moderation with regard to food 25
non-remorse xxxviii, xlviii, 12, 165, 171, 293, 348
non-trainee xxxiii, lxxxix, xc, xcii, xcvi, xcviii, cxiii, 11, 33, 37, 86, 90, 94, 609, 610
non-transgression lxvii, 15–17, 22, 24, 30, 37
not fully ordained 27, 35, 49
nothingness cxli, 18, 122, 124, 126, 128, 221, 226–232, 251, 344, 371, 373, 374, 395, 399, 485, 633, 635
not to be spoken of liii, liv, xcix, 75, 126, 127, 128, 413, 419, 512, 637

O

ojā lii, 383, 442, 444, 445, 451, 453, 480
old commentaries lxxiii, lxxiv, lxxviii, lxxxi
omissions cxlv, cxlvi, 299
opposing 44, 152, 193, 200, 209, 218, 224, 227, 230, 312, 366, 368, 369, 370, 371. *See also* paṭipakkha
opposite of sensual desire cix, 164, 181
opposites of the five hindrances 181
opposites *(paṭipakkha)* of the five hindrances cxii, 25, 180, 181, 368, 456
originality lii, lxxvi

outcaste 51, 468
outcastes 72
outcasts cxlvii. *See also* caṇḍālas
overcoming evil 45
overturning the bowl cxlviii. *See also* pattanikkujjana

P

paccaya 46, 163, 180, 275, 355, 385, 386, 388, 417, 483, 487, 489, 535, 536, 554, 566
paccayato cvi, cviii, cix, 125, 333, 559. *See also* condition
Paccekabuddhas 29, 324, 345, 368, 414, 416, 419, 423
padaṭṭhāna xxxvii, 15, 341
pahāna lxii, lxx, 26, 213, 427, 557
painful feelings 45, 46, 47
pakati lxxxii, 21, 25, 35, 108, 196, 305, 350
Pāli lvi, 39, 144, 465
Pali commentaries xxxiii, xxxvi, xxxviii, xliii, xlix, lv, lxi, lxvi, lxxii, lxxiii, lxxiv, lxxvi, lxxix-lxxxii, xcvi, xcviii, cviii, cix, cxiii, cxvi, 6, 18, 139, 156, 179, 270, 336, 359, 361, 362, 428, 456, 459, 481, 614
pāmojja cxliv, 171, 373. *See also* gladness
pāṇa lxii
Pañcaśata-jātaka-sūtra cxviii, cxix
paṇihita 32
Pāṇini lxxii, 196
paññā xxix, xxx, xxxiii, xxxv, xxxviii, xci, cxl, 3–7, 10, 49, 82, 86, 93, 97, 110, 132, 171, 177, 204, 252, 276, 296, 310, 315, 359, 362, 419, 425–436, 464, 478, 508, 531, 548, 553, 554, 569, 578, 579, 580, 584, 593, 632. *See also* wisdom
paññatti xliv, liv, lv, xcix, ciii, 75, 76, 126, 127, 179, 322, 436, 478, 484, 485, 486, 576. *See also* prajñapti
pārājika 49. *See also* disqualification
parallels xlvii, lv, lvi, lix, lxvii, lxviii, lxxix, cviii, cxiii, cxliv, cxlv, cxlvii, 24, 49, 55, 61, 77, 94, 150, 166, 174, 180, 197, 208, 214, 222, 223, 238, 249, 268, 364, 397, 419, 479, 481, 520, 536, 564, 572, 585, 607, 634
paramāṇu lxxxii, 384. *See also* atoms
paramaṭṭha 34
pāramitā lxxxiii, 269
paribhoga 47
paritāpana l
paritta l, li, lvi, lxvi, 92, 125, 136, 142, 150, 416, 419, 422, 474
Parivāra lxxi, lxxii, lxxiv, lxxvii-lxxix, xciv, cxxii, 54, 461
pariyanta 27, 30, 534, 562, 584
pariyatti xciii. *See also* división of monastic vocations into practice *(patipatti)* and study
pariyuṭṭhāna 11, 189, 506
pasāda lxvi, c, 439, 445, 464, 479, 508, 520
Passasukha xlix
Path of xxxi, xxxv, xl, cx, cxliii, 210, 335
path of arahantship liv, lv, lvii, xcvii, 19, 290, 399, 402, 616–626
Path of Freedom xxxi, xl, cxliii. *See also* PoF
path of non-returning lv, 19, 290, 616–626
path of once-returning 19, 290
path of practice xxvii, xxxi, 5
path of stream-entry lv, xcv, 19, 290, 593, 603, 609, 617–626, 628
path to freedom xxxi, xxxii, xxxiv, xxxviii, cxl, 3–5, 7, 8, 11–14, 275
Pātimokkha xxxvii, cxli, 19, 22, 35, 37, 38, 39, 41, 42, 48, 49, 71, 283

Pātimokkha restraint xxxvii, 22, 35, 37, 38, 48, 49
pātimokkha-saṃvara 35, 465
paṭipakkha 44, 84, 180, 212, 312, 358. *See also* opposing
paṭipatti xciii, 75. *See also* division of monastic vocations into practice *(patipatti)* and study
Paṭisambhidāmagga xxix–xxxii, xxxv–xxxvii, xliii, xlvii, lxiv, lxxi, lxxii, lxxvii, lxxix, lxxxii, xc, xciii, xcv, xcix, ci, ciii, cxxvi, cxlvi, cxlvii, 165, 191, 293, 399, 402, 544, 612
paṭisaṅkhā 46, 47, 62, 72, 569, 579, 580
pattanikkujjana cxlviii, 73. *See also* overturning the bowl
perception xxxvi, xxxix, xl, l, lv, lviii, lix, lxii, lxiii, xci, civ, cxxxvii, cxli, cxliv, cxlvi, 17, 18, 48, 62, 68, 87, 95, 122–131, 136, 137, 139, 145, 146, 150, 151, 164, 167, 169, 189, 190, 207, 215, 216, 218–220, 224, 227–233, 235, 236, 238, 240, 241, 243–248, 250–252, 259–266, 268, 297, 300, 302, 304, 308, 312, 313, 328, 329, 331, 344, 350, 354, 374, 384, 390–395, 399, 400, 401, 405, 409, 410, 419–421, 437, 450, 452, 460, 461, 462, 476, 497, 526, 550, 553–556, 557–559, 569–571, 577, 578, 590, 624, 625, 626, 631, 633–637
perception of breathing lxii
perception of cessation lxii
perception of creatures lxii
perception of disadvantage lxii, 329
perception of dislike lxii, lxiii
perception of dispassion lxii
perception of happiness 18, 460, 554
perception of impermanence lxii, 151, 252, 328, 329, 460
perception of non-delight lxii
perception of the foul lxii, xci, cxlvi, 238, 329, 331, 460
perception of worthlessness lxii
personal knowledge 12, 98
Peṭaka xlvi, li, lxi, lxxvi–lxxviii, xcvi, xcviii, ci, cviii, cix, cx, cxi, cxii, cxiii, cxiv, cxv, cxviii, cxix, 6, 132, 165, 168, 181, 184, 435, 460, 542
Peṭakopadesa xxx, xlii, xlvi, li, lxxi, lxxii, lxxvi, lxxvii, lxxxii, xciii, xciv, xcv, xcvi, xcviii, cviii, cx, cxi, cxii, cxxii, cxlvii, 6, 94, 165, 168, 169, 542, 566
phalasamāpatti lix, lxxx, 95, 626, 627, 630, 632, 637. *See also* attainment of fruition
phassa xlix, lxiii
phāsu 33, 86, 102, 315, 350, 366
phoṭṭhabba lii, liv, 383, 445, 448
physical basis 156, 157, 428, 516
physical torpor xxviii, 620. *See also* middha
pīti cxii, cxliv, 85, 89, 95, 96, 144, 160, 161, 170–174, 176, 179–181, 185, 187, 192, 198, 207, 212, 248, 285, 304, 305, 312, 368, 462, 521, 544, 576, 577, 608. *See also* rapture
plagiarism lxxvi
plane of development cxii, 609
plane of practice xcvi, 592, 609
plane of the non-trainee xcvi, 609, 610
plane of the trainee xcvi, 609, 610
plane of vision xcv, cxii, 592
pleasant dwelling in this life 57, 85, 86, 629, 634
pleasant practice cii, 91, 92, 608, 609, 630
pleasure xxxviii, xlix, cii, cix, 5, 12–14, 18, 20, 21, 65, 70, 85, 90, 96, 97, 108, 139, 143, 144, 149, 153, 158, 160, 161, 165, 166, 170, 172–175, 179– 181, 184–186, 193, 197–200, 203, 206–215, 217, 218, 240, 241,

243–248, 258, 287, 292, 293, 298, 299, 303, 304, 308, 309, 312, 317, 318, 327, 344, 356, 367, 370, 373, 405, 409, 410, 457, 458, 473, 504, 507, 509, 522, 528, 556, 576, 621, 630
pleasure of seclusion 65, 143, 173
PoF cxli, cxliii, cxlvii. *See also* Path of Freedom
porāṇā lxxiv, lxxix, lxxxi, cx, 510, 569, 572, 579, 580, 634
porāṇācariyā lxxiii, lxxxi
Porāṇaṭṭhakathā lxxiii, lxxiv, lxxxi
prajñapti lv, lvi. *See also* paññatti
pratītyasamutpāda lxxxiv, lxxxv, 505, 512
prayoga-mārga lxxxvi, xcii. *See also* path of effort
prefaces xxxi, xlii, lxxiii
process of mind xliii, 482, 487, 493, 497, 502
production cvi, 36, 413, 511, 514, 559, 562
protect one's virtue 52
proto-Mahāyāna xxviii, lxxxiv
pubbācariyā lxxiii, lxxiv, lxxix, lxxxi, 47, 484
puna caparaṃ lxxviii
punctuation l, cxlvii, 98
pure virtue 29, 32, 33, 53, 81
purity of livelihood lxix, 37, 42, 48, 49
purity of mind 11, 149, 414, 589
purity of practice xcix, 182, 183
purity of view 11, 550, 589
purity of virtue 11, 49, 50, 171, 589
pursuing gain lxix, 42, 43

Q

Qizil Yoga Manual lxxxiv, 384
question and answer xxx, lxviii, lxix, 97, 220, 320, 385, 400, 526, 529
quotations xxvii, xxxii, xxxv, xli, xlii, xlvi, xlvii, lii, liii, lvi, lix, lxiv, lxv, lxviii, lxx, lxxv, lxxvii, lxxx, cviii, cx, cxiii, cxxvi, cxxxvi–cxxxviii, cxl, cxlii, 196, 527, 628

R

rapture xl, xciii, cix, cxliv, 12, 13, 17, 85, 89, 90, 96, 97, 137, 149, 153, 161, 170–172, 174, 175, 179, 180, 181, 184–186, 193, 197–200, 202, 203, 205–209, 211–213, 217, 258, 299, 303–305, 308, 309, 312, 317, 318, 344, 367, 368, 370, 373, 421, 462, 463, 522, 531, 576, 606, 608. *See also* pīti
Ratnamegha-sūtra cxxv, cxxix, cxxxi, cxliii
real nature cvi
reborn as a deity 34, 187, 215, 216, 232, 591
reborn as a human 34
recitation cxix, cxxii, 25, 102, 392
reciters lxxiv, lxxviii, lxxxi, cxvi
recluseship lix, xc, xcvi, 283, 287, 478, 609, 610, 626
recollection of stillness xxxvii, 122, 128, 131, 342–345
reflect lxxxv, 45, 47–50, 326, 340, 347, 348, 350–355
reflection on avoiding 46
reflection on using 46
reflection on what is to be developed 46
reflections 46, 47, 237
refraining lxvii, lxxxix, c, ci, 15, 16, 17, 19, 30
rejoicing 20, 24, 79, 183, 313, 373
releases of mind lxi
remorse xxxviii, xlviii, 12, 20, 32, 50, 51, 79, 165, 171, 293, 348
renunciation lxxxvii, xc, ci, 16–18, 87, 141, 143–145, 155, 164, 276, 286, 359,

361, 402, 459, 460, 576
requisite 28, 31, 173
requisites lxxxvii, 19, 37, 42, 45, 47-50, 81, 87, 88, 188, 321, 511, 633
resort 37, 38, 40, 41, 112, 117, 118, 205
restraining lxvii, c, cxiv, 16, 17, 157, 462
restraint xxxvii, lxvii, lxxxvii, lxxxix, xci, ci, 4, 15–20, 22, 25, 35, 37, 38, 41, 42, 44, 45, 48, 49, 50, 159, 465, 589. *See also* saṃvara
restraint of sense-faculties 48, 49
revivalist movement lxxxiii
right mindfulness cxxxviii, 8, 49, 142, 204, 213, 267, 286, 288, 292, 294, 295, 297, 329, 342, 529, 530, 531
right view xxx, lxi, lxvi, 6, 204, 270, 426, 431, 529, 530, 531, 594
right view endowed with ten grounds lxi, 431
robes xxxvii, lxvii, lxviii, lxxii, lxxiv, cxx, cxxxv, cxxxvii, cxxxviii, cxxxix, cxlvi, 42, 47, 54–59, 66, 69-72, 76, 102, 103, 105, 112, 115, 117, 118, 393, 633
rūpakkhandha cvi, 475
rūpāvacara xcvii, ci, 9, 10, 217, 465. *See also* Concentration of the material

S

sabhāva li, lxxxii, ciii, 25, 146, 163, 179, 196, 222, 308, 325, 354, 381, 455, 458, 466, 496, 513, 526, 527, 554, 564, 566, 571. *See also* intrinsic nature
sacca 359, 532, 538, 556
saccānulomika-ñāṇa 10
sakkāyadiṭṭhi lv, 537, 590, 619
salakkhaṇa xciv, 137, 138, 179, 274, 374, 380, 388, 548, 557
samādhi xxix, xxx, xxxiii, xxxviii, cxii, cxiv, cxl, cxliv, 3, 4, 7-10, 81-85, 89–95, 98, 99, 122, 135, 153, 156, 160, 165, 174, 180-182, 187-189, 195, 196, 217, 218, 233, 234, 274, 284, 293, 298, 303, 305, 310, 313, 368, 370, 398, 403-405, 422, 425, 464, 521, 543, 577, 607, 630, 634. *See also* concentration
sāmaññalakkhaṇa xciv, 179, 548
Samantapāsādikā lxx, lxxiii, lxxv, lxxvii, cxviii, cxix, cxx, cxxiv, cxxxvi, cxliii, 183
sāmānyalakṣaṇa xciv, 548
samāpatti cxliv, 89–91, 94, 95, 99, 175, 180, 192, 200, 205, 217, 234, 271, 305, 626, 634. *See also* attainment
samatha-vipassanā xxxvi, 361, 428
sambhāra 28, 31, 173, 511
Saṃghabhadra lxx, cxvii, cxviii, cxx, cxxi, cxxiv, cxxxiii
sammādiṭṭhi lxi, 8, 93, 204, 270, 278, 426–428, 431, 432, 436, 462, 513, 529, 530, 531, 540, 592
saṃsāra xliii, l, xci, 98, 270, 277, 287, 354, 427, 437, 512, 547, 585
Saṃskṛtāsaṃskṛtaviniścaya xl, xli, xlii, xlvi, xlvii, lii–liv, lvii, lx, lxiv-lxvi, lxviii, lxxv
samuccheda 4, 322. *See also* freedom through eradication samvara; *See also* restraint
saṃyama 17
saṅgaha lvi, 274, 381, 476, 477, 496, 545, 565. *See also* inclusion
saṅghādisesa 50
Saṅghapāla xlviii, xlix, l, li, lii, liii, lxix, cix, cxiii, cxvii-cxix, cxxi, cxxii, cxxiv-cxxvi, cxxviii-cxxxvi, cxliii-cxlvi, cxlviii, 12, 16, 24, 39, 43, 52, 54, 55, 66, 68, 69, 70, 76, 77, 93, 98, 110, 116, 118, 129, 142, 144, 146, 157, 161, 167, 169, 183, 202, 205, 216,

222, 230, 244, 251, 265, 268, 356, 365, 376, 379, 382–386, 397, 419, 430, 432, 445, 456, 458, 489, 508, 520, 534, 535, 575, 593, 596, 601, 614
Saṅghapāla's mistakes xlviii
Saṅgharakṣa xliii, lxxxii, lxxxv, lxxxviii, lxxxix, xc, xci, xcii, xciv, xcv
Saṅghasena cxxii, cxxiii
saññā lxi, lxii, lxiii, lxx, cxliv, 131, 136, 145, 150, 151, 158, 167, 179, 218, 219, 220, 221, 228, 230, 231, 302, 304, 308, 309, 325, 344, 354, 391, 406, 429, 437, 460, 462, 463, 475, 476, 496, 499, 523, 560, 624, 633
Sanskrit xxxi, xxxvii, xli, xlvii, xlviii, xlix, l, li, lvii, lx, lxi, lxii, lxix, lxxii, lxxvi, lxxxii, lxxxiv, xciii, xciv, cxx, cxxii, cxxv, cxxxi, cxxxii, cxxxiv, cxxxv, cxxxvi, cxl, cxliv, cxlv, 5, 52, 54, 70, 93, 110, 144, 161, 281, 293, 307, 365, 384, 440, 454, 485, 499, 574, 576, 611, 614, 623
santati cvii, 354, 439, 442, 445, 446, 447, 453, 454, 455, 505, 512, 553
sāraṇīyā lxi, lxii, lxvi
Sāriputta xxxi, civ, 324, 399, 440, 634
Sarvāstivāda xxviii, xxxvi, xliii, liii, lv, lxiii, lxxv, lxxxii-lxxxvi, lxxxix, xcii, xciii, xciv, xcv, xcvi, ci, cxiii, cxxi, cxxxi, cxxxii, 242, 380, 445, 544, 548, 609
Sarvāstivāda Abhidharma lxiii, lxxxii, xciv, cxxxii, 548
Sarvāstivāda practice scheme of paths lxxxvi, xcii
sassatadiṭṭhi lxvii
sati-sampajañña 20, 557
satta xxxiii, lv, cxxxvi, 41, 85, 87, 126, 156, 282, 298, 318, 322, 354, 428, 435, 439, 485, 486, 564, 582, 591, 594, 598, 608, 609, 621, 632
sattakkhattuparama xcvi, 598
satta visuddhi xxxiii
sāvaka 29, 94, 216, 289, 348, 349
saviññāṇaka kāya lix
scheme of the five paths lxxxix, xcv
scholastic Sanskrit xxxvii
scorching l, 142
season xcvii, xcix, 71, 75, 78, 177, 385, 386, 387, 388, 389, 444, 449, 450, 503, 516, 517, 523
seclusion lxxviii, lxxxviii, cxxvii, cxxix, 3, 43, 65, 69, 85, 96, 143, 144, 153, 154, 160–166, 170, 171, 173, 175, 176, 181, 184–186, 197, 203, 216, 256, 258, 292, 294, 343, 390, 535, 584, 587, 629, 636
sectarian split lxxiii
sekha 33, 37, 627
self-control lxvii, ci, 16, 17, 19, 22, 37
selfishness 24, 60, 66, 70, 114, 294, 295, 321, 616, 619, 623, 624. *See also* macchariya
semhika xlviii
Sendha-pa lxxiv
senior monks lxxiii, lxxxi, 38, 39
sense bases xxxix, liv, lvi, lviii, lix, lxiii, lxv, 86, 104, 194, 221, 274, 437, 442–445, 450–453, 477, 479, 480, 482, 484, 485, 493–499, 503, 504, 506, 508, 514, 518–520, 523, 524, 545, 547–549, 551, 553, 554, 574
sense-faculties lxvi, lxvii, 19–21, 25, 37, 39, 44, 45, 48, 49, 50, 87, 101, 151, 328, 344, 352, 354, 450–453, 488, 503, 506, 508, 515, 525, 637
sense-pleasures lv, lvii, 13, 47, 49, 64, 75, 77, 91, 140, 141, 143, 144, 161–166, 171, 175, 176, 180, 190, 191, 211, 237, 252, 265, 266, 368, 391, 433, 434, 617, 618, 619, 621, 623, 624. *See also* kāmāvacara

sensitivity lix, lxvi, c, 439, 440, 445, 479, 480, 494, 508, 519, 520
sensuous sphere 14, 91, 95, 98, 175, 222, 235, 431–433, 450, 451, 457
seven groups *(of offences)* 41, 49
shamelessness 19, 25, 462, 622
sign lxxxi, c, cxliv, 18, 45, 68, 73, 93, 97, 101, 104, 125, 128, 130, 135–140, 145–152, 154–158, 160, 165, 167, 168, 181, 183, 185, 189, 193, 200, 201, 209, 214, 218, 227, 233, 236–241, 243–249, 252–266, 284, 297, 301–304, 308, 309, 311, 327, 330–332, 345, 354, 364, 373, 390, 391, 404, 413, 414, 417, 485, 490, 491, 497, 502, 515, 516, 527, 554, 556–559, 562, 578, 582, 583, 587, 588, 593, 611, 612, 614, 615. *See also* nimitta
Sīhaḷaṭṭhakathā cxix
sikkhā 8, 11, 29, 39, 151. *See also* three trainings
sīla xxix, xxx, xxxiii, xxxviii, xli, cxl, 4, 9, 15, 17, 22, 23, 25–27, 31, 33–36, 42, 44, 49, 50, 54, 75, 76, 279, 350, 359. *See also* virtue
similes lxxi, lxxxviii, xci, xcii, cx, cxi, 141, 170, 311, 462, 576, 586
simultaneous comprehension xcv
sira 21, 338
sītala ciii, 21, 381
sitter lxxix, cxxxvii, cxxxix, 55, 57, 69, 70, 74
soka 33, 158, 322, 364, 368
solid food lii, 49, 391, 439, 442, 444, 454, 455
somanassa cxliv, 210, 366–369, 608, 609
sorrow 20, 33, 34, 322, 368, 389, 498, 525, 526, 551–553
space l, xciv, cxliv, 18, 121, 124–129, 133, 146, 150, 217, 218, 219, 222–227, 247, 248, 251, 260, 303, 344, 371–373, 384, 389, 402, 403, 405–409, 438, 440, 442, 444, 447, 448, 454, 456, 635
sparśa xlix
specific characteristic xciv, 137, 138, 179, 360, 380, 548
speech ci, 7, 15, 20, 25, 26, 29, 39, 40, 100, 101, 149, 163, 281, 343, 350, 417, 421, 422, 434–436, 442, 448, 449, 454, 455, 463, 465, 527, 529, 530, 538, 623, 624
Śrāvakabhūmi lxxxiv, lxxxvi, lxxxvii, lxxxviii, xciii, xciv, 107, 131, 144, 147, 192, 224, 307, 310, 320, 388, 548, 611
Śrāvakayāna xlv, lxxv, lxxxix
stain of ignorance 11
stain of poor virtue 11
stain of the obsessions 11
stations of consciousness lx, 543, 555, 578, 579
steadfastness l, 82
Sthavira xxxii, xli, xlii, xliii, xlvi, lxv, lxvii, cxviii, cxix, cxxi, cxxxii, 16
Sthavira Nikāya xlii
Sthavira-vinaya cxviii
stillness xxxvii, 13, 122, 128, 131, 158, 196, 305, 342–345, 361, 468
stories, opinions of elders xxx, xxxiv, lxxii, 275, 276, 277, 435
stream-enterer lv, xci, xcii, xcvi, 235, 347, 594, 597, 598, 603, 610, 631
structural difference lxviii
structure of the Vimuttimagga xxix
subcommentaries xliii, lxxvi, xcvi, c, 6, 125
subsistence 46
subtle afflictions 19, 344
subtle matter liii, 445, 453, 493
successive explanation lx, 532, 542, 544
suffering lv, lix, lxi, lxvii, lxviii, lxxxix, xci, xcii, cvi, 6, 9, 18, 49, 78, 100, 141, 143, 158, 165, 202, 210, 215,

274, 276, 278, 279, 318, 321, 327, 328, 348, 349, 352, 354, 355, 359, 362–364, 371–373, 388, 390, 427, 431, 435, 436, 460, 478, 493, 496, 497, 498, 514, 520, 521, 524–529, 531, 532, 534–537, 539–545, 548, 550–555, 560–562, 567, 570–572, 574, 578, 580, 581, 584–587, 591, 598, 599, 600, 602–606, 612–614, 618, 624, 625, 632, 635
suffering of suffering lix, 527, 542
sugati 21, 27, 253, 268
sukha cii, 13, 20, 173, 304, 367, 374, 507, 509, 630
sukhapaṭipadā cii, 608, 630
sukhumarūpa liii, 445, 481
sukkhavipassaka cii, 630
suññata. *See also* emptiness
suññatā cxliv, 129, 227, 332, 355, 541, 616
supersession cxii
supramundane virtue 27, 88
supramundane wisdom xliii, 88, 428
supreme Dhamma 50, 268. *See also* aggadhamma
suspension 4, 50, 152, 162, 163, 174. *See also* saṅghā-disesa
sustaining the body 45, 46, 58
Sūtra of Hundred Parables cxxiii
Suttanettipada cxiii, cxiv, 268
Suttavibhaṅga cxviii
svalakṣaṇa xciv, 205, 380, 548

T

tadaṅga 4. *See also* freedom through the [opposite] factor
Tāmraparṇīya xliii, lxxii
Tāmraśāṭīyas lxv, lxxxii
tangibles lii, liii, liv, lv, 163, 219, 439, 441, 445, 446, 453, 461, 469, 479, 480, 481, 484, 558
Tāranātha lxvi, lxxiv, lxxvii
team translation cxlv
tebhūmi lx
temperament xxix, xxxii, lxxx, lxxxv, xc, 77, 78, 107–119, 121, 130–133, 188, 265, 332
ten packages of texts cxx
ten perceptions of the foul xxxix, cxliv, 121, 123, 126–131. *See also* asubhasaññā
ten perfections xxviii, 359, 360, 361
ten topics of discussion 64
terminology xxxvii, lxvi, lxvii, cxxxv, cxxxviii
thera lxxiii, lxxxi, 38, 104, 635
Theravāda xxvii, xxviii, xxxii, xxxiv, xxxvii, xlii, xliii, xlv, xlvii, xlviii, xlix, l, li, lii, liii, lvi, lx, lxiii, lxiv, lxv, lxvi, lxx, lxxii, lxxiii, lxxxii, lxxxiii, lxxxiv, lxxxviii, xc, xciii, xciv, xcv, xcvi, cix, cxii, cxviii–cxxi, cxxvi, cxxxi, cxlii, 381, 383, 456, 477, 481
Theravāda abhidhamma xliii, xlviii, lii, lx, lxxiii, 381
thirteen factors of asceticism lxxii
thirty-eight meditation xxvii, xxix, xxxix, 121, 122, 132, 557
thirty-eight meditation topics xxvii, xxix
this-is-sufficient'-ness l, 76
ṭhiti l, lxiii, cvii, 4, 81, 82, 195, 305, 313, 403, 510, 524, 563
ṭhitibhāga 27
ṭhitibhāgiya 9, 34, 99, 284
three aggregates lvi, lxiii, 7, 8, 560, 561
threefold division of the noble eightfold path xxxiii
three kinds of goodness xcix, cxl, 12, 13, 176, 182, 198, 208, 214, 223, 226, 229, 232, 286. *See also* kalyāṇa
three kinds of pleasure 13
three planes lx, xci, 430, 433, 539, 540

three trainings xlvii, 8, 11, 310. *See also* sikkhā
Tibetan translators xli, liv, lxiv, lxvii, lxviii, cxxxv, cxlvi, 456, 525, 590, 601
tiny faults 33, 37, 41, 292
Tipiṭaka xxviii, xxxii, xxxiv, xlii, li, lxxiii, lxxvi, lxxvii, lxxix, lxxxi, lxxxii, xcix, cviii, cix, cxviii, cxxii, 168
torpor xxviii, xliv, xlvi, liv, xciv, xcvii, xcviii, xcix, cix, cxl, 17, 67, 69, 87, 148, 151, 165, 176, 177, 179, 181, 246, 302, 383, 421, 439, 442, 444, 448–450, 454, 455, 620
torpor of matter xliv, xcvii, 439, 442, 444, 449, 455. *See also* middharūpa
torpor of the elements xcvii, 442
totalities xxxvi, xxxix, cxlv, 121, 123–131, 133, 135, 136, 138, 139, 145, 146, 216, 237, 238, 239, 242, 243, 246, 248, 249, 251, 264, 303, 331, 332, 402, 403, 413, 417, 420
touch xlix, c, cxi, 68, 241, 298–303, 308, 320, 383, 479, 494, 573, 631, 636
training in higher wisdom cxiv, 10
training in virtue 8, 9
training in wisdom 8, 10
training rule 11, 41
tranquillity lxxvii, 5, 12, 85, 168, 172, 186, 287, 303, 308, 318, 462, 522, 531, 576, 613
transgression lxvii, 15, 16, 17, 22, 24, 30, 33, 37, 485
translation team lxix
translator's notes lxix
truths xxviii, xxxiii, xxxiv, xl, xli, lvi, lxviii, lxix, lxxxviii, xcii, xcv, cii, cvi, cx, cxlvi, 9, 10, 13, 100, 178, 267, 290, 390, 426–429, 431–434, 437, 464, 477, 478, 493, 496, 499, 500, 523, 524, 525, 529, 531, 532, 540, 541, 544, 545, 547, 548, 552, 554, 555, 584, 586, 587, 588, 589, 591, 595, 596, 601, 603, 605, 606
two extremes 13, 14, 46, 289, 290

U

udayabbayañāṇa civ, 568
uddāna lxxii, lxxix, cxii, cxvi, cxvii, cxxii
unallowable cxlviii, 72. *See also* akappiya
unbroken ciii, 292
understanding xxviii, xxxvii, xli, liv, lxxxii, ci, civ, cv, cvii, cviii, cxliv, cxlviii, 4, 103, 149, 169, 204, 235, 239, 286, 287, 386, 391, 425, 427, 502, 520, 560, 561, 565, 567, 584
undistractedness 4, 17, 82, 87, 165, 351, 403, 557, 589. *See also* avikkhepa
unexcelled xxxiii, xxxviii, 3, 14, 270, 273, 274, 289, 291, 324. *See also* anuttara
unexcelled freedom xxxviii, 3, 14
unincluded plane lx
unwholesome mind 24, 36, 41, 506, 616, 625
unwholesome virtue 23, 24, 36
upacayasantati xcvii
upādāna lv, 381, 382
upadhi cxliv. *See also* acquisition
Upagupta lxxxv, cxiv, cxxxi, 321
upāsaka 35
upasampanna 50
Upatissa xxvii, xxviii, xxx–xxxviii, xlii, xliv, xlvi, li, lxiii, lxx–lxxxiv, xcii, xcv, xcvi, xcvii, xcix, cii, cvii, cviii, cxii, cxiii, cxiv, cxv, cxxii, cxxiv, cxlii, cxlvii, 3, 76, 123, 132, 133, 227, 303, 398, 402, 408, 461, 605
upekkha. *See also* equanimity
upekkhā cxliv, 96, 122, 124, 166, 179,

200–202, 208, 213, 214, 217, 281, 305, 315, 359, 366, 369, 370, 374, 459, 557, 576
uppāda cvii, 95, 456, 474, 510, 533, 578, 612
Uttarakuru 36

V

Vaibhāṣikas liii, 445, 604
Vaipulya cxxvii, cxxix, cxxx, cxxxii
vāritta 25, 26
vāsana lxxxii, ci
Vasubandhu xliii, lxxxii, lxxxiv
vata lvi, 15, 22, 23, 42, 75, 76, 144, 165, 195, 221, 233, 295, 326, 406, 564, 582, 591
vatthu li, 33, 49, 75, 77, 118, 136, 142, 144, 156, 162, 176, 181, 203, 205, 207, 271, 272, 297, 316, 325, 341, 349, 392, 428, 429, 445, 449–451, 458, 469, 470, 471, 482, 489, 497, 501, 503, 515, 516, 526, 527, 536, 621, 630
vatthurūpa xliii, xcvii, 439, 442, 443, 449, 450, 489, 516, 573. *See also* material basis
Vedabahulo xlix
vematika 33, 461
veramaṇī ci, 16, 17, 466, 530
vetullavāda xlv, lxxv, lxxxii
vicāra cx, 258, 312, 370, 473, 608
Vidarśanā Pota cxvi, cxvii
Vidyākaraprabha xli
vikkhambhana- vimutti. *See also* freedom through suspension
vikkhambhana-vimutti 4
village dweller xciii
Vimokṣa-mārga-śāstra cxxiv, cxxx
Vimuktimārga xxxi, xli, cxxvi, cxxviii
vimutti xxxiii, l, cxl, 3, 4, 162, 273, 287, 319, 362, 521, 543, 613, 632. *See also* freedom
Vimuttimagga xxvii–xlvii, xlix, li–liv, lvi, lxii, lxiii, lxv, lxvi, lxviii–lxxiii, lxxv–lxxvii, lxxix, lxxx, lxxxii–lxxxiv, lxxxvi–lxxxix, xcii, xciii, xciv, xcv, xcvi, xcviii, xcix, ci, cvii, cviii, cx, cxi, cxii, cxiii, cxiv, cxv, cxvi, cxvii, cxxi, cxxii, cxxiv, cxxv, cxxviii, cxxxi, cxxxii, cxxxiv, cxxxv, cxxxvi, cxl, cxli, cxlii, cxliii, cxliv, cxlv, cxlvi, cxlvii, 6, 121, 169, 174, 191, 265, 302, 303, 306, 321, 352, 369, 415, 478, 481, 611
Vimuttimagga, doctrinal alterations lii
Vinaya-piṭaka cxxix
Vinaya regulations xxxvii, lxxxiii
Vinaya terminology lxvii, cxxxv
vipallāsa 233, 273, 304, 467, 542, 587
vipariṇāma l, cvi, 455, 512, 534, 559
vipassanāñāṇa xxxiii, xliii, 88
virāga lxx, 12, 119, 190, 215, 315, 529, 538
virati ci, 15–17, 30, 31, 42, 465, 530, 589
viriya 22, 37, 93, 94, 158, 359
virtue xxvii, xxix, xxxi, xxxiii, xxxv, xxxvii, xxxviii, lxvii, xcix, ci, cxiv, cxxxiv, cxxxvii, cxxxviii, cxxxix, cxl, 4, 5, 7–17, 19–37, 40, 42, 44, 45, 48–54, 75, 81, 87, 88, 122, 127, 128, 159, 171, 173, 271, 275, 276, 291–296, 310, 343, 345, 348, 350, 359, 361, 426, 466, 477, 478, 542, 547, 589. *See also* sīla
virtue and observance 15, 22
virtue due to fear 33
virtue of non-transgression 15, 17
virtue of restraint 15
virtue of the noble ones 9
virtue of the trainee 33
virtue of volition lxvii, 15
virtue partaking of distinction 9, 34, 35. *See also* visesabhāgiya virtue]

partaking of falling back
virtue partaking of penetration 9, 35. *See also* nibbedhabhāgiya
virtue that is not transgressed 29
virtue with a time limit 30
visaṃyoga 4, 163. *See also* detachment
visesabhāgiya 3, 9, 34. *See also* virtue partaking of distinction visualisations
visuddha 33
visuddhi xxxiii, 11, 184, 551
Visuddhimagga xxvii-xxxviii, xlii, xlvi, xlvii, lvi, lxx, lxxii, lxxiii, lxxvi, lxxvii, lxxx, lxxxi, lxxxiii, lxxxvi, lxxxvii, lxxxix, xc, xciv, xcv, xcvi, c, ci, cx, cxii, cxiv, cxv, cxvi, cxxvi, cxli, cxlv, cxlvi, cxlvii, 3, 33, 48, 53, 62, 109, 121, 157, 218, 227, 254, 265, 358, 368, 382, 415, 440
Visuddhimagga-nidānakathā xxxii, xlvi
vitakka cx, cxliv, 107, 109, 133, 165, 168, 298, 299, 320, 473, 485, 530, 607
vital essence lii, liii, 383, 442, 445, 448, 480
vīthi-citta xliii
vitthambhana xlviii, 381
Vivaṭṭati xlix
viveka lxxviii, lxxxvii, 5, 69, 82, 161, 173, 184, 196, 256, 315, 390
volition lv, lvi, lxvii, ci, 15–17, 19, 462, 485, 500, 502, 507, 509, 519, 520, 553, 558

W

walking up and down l, 118, 119
way of its real nature cvi
way of the moment civ, cv, cvi, cvii, cviii, 560, 561
wholesome indeterminate l
wholesome mind 24, 36
wholesome virtue 13, 23, 36, 54
wilderness-dweller 55, 64, 66, 73, 74, 75
wind xlviii, liii, lxxx, ciii, 47, 67, 81, 106, 112, 113, 121, 128, 130, 142, 146, 185, 215, 237, 240, 241, 302, 303, 306–308, 310, 320, 325, 335, 336, 375–385, 387, 388, 392, 405, 406, 409, 438, 439, 441, 445, 453, 480, 481, 484, 558
wisdom xxvii, xxix, xxxi, xxxv, xxxviii, xxxix, xliii, lvi, lx, lxvii, lxxv, lxxviii, cxiv, cxxxiv, cxxxvii, cxxxviii, cxl, 4, 5, 7, 8, 10–14, 19, 25, 39, 40, 48, 49, 51, 83, 88, 104, 110, 129, 131, 133, 144, 157, 158, 165, 171, 183, 184, 204, 235, 268, 276, 280, 284, 291, 295, 296, 310, 324, 331, 342, 343, 345, 348, 349, 350, 360, 361, 375, 390, 419, 425–437, 462, 477, 478, 513, 515, 525, 531, 542, 557, 559–561, 583, 589, 590, 593, 594, 596, 609, 614, 628. *See also* paññā
without contaminations 4, 416. *See also* anāsava
without interval l, 488
worldliness cxliv, 166. *See also* āmisa
worldly gain 28
worms xlvii, xlviii, li, lxix, xciv, xcv, 325, 332, 336–340, 393, 394
wrath 24, 106, 620. *See also* kodha writing down of commentarial texts
wrong livelihood lxix, 23, 38, 42, 44, 47, 50, 530, 624

Y

yakkha civ, 379, 411, 634
yathābhūta-ñāṇadassana 12
yāthāvasarasato cvi, 423, 560. *See also* way of its real nature

yogācāra lxxxvii, lxxxviii, xc, xci, xciii, xciv, xcviii
Yogācārabhūmi xxxvi, xliii, lxxxii, lxxxvi-lxxxix, xc, xcii, xciii, xcv, xcviii, 215
Yogācārabhūmiśāstra xxxv, lxvi
Yogalehrbuch lxxxiv, 336, 384
yogāvacara xxix, xxxvii, lxxxvii, xciii, xciv, xcviii, cxvi, cxvii, 53, 139
yogi xciii, 81, 237
Yuān-yùn cxxiv, cxxvii, cxxx, cxxxi, cxxxv

ABOUT PARIYATTI

Pariyatti is dedicated to providing affordable access to authentic teachings of the Buddha about the Dhamma theory (*pariyatti*) and practice (*paṭipatti*) of Vipassana meditation. A 501(c)(3) nonprofit charitable organization since 2002, Pariyatti is sustained by contributions from individuals who appreciate and want to share the incalculable value of the Dhamma teachings. We invite you to visit www.pariyatti.org to learn about our programs, services, and ways to support publishing and other undertakings.

Pariyatti Publishing Imprints

Vipassana Research Publications (focus on Vipassana as taught by S.N. Goenka in the tradition of Sayagyi U Ba Khin)

BPS Pariyatti Editions (selected titles from the Buddhist Publication Society, copublished by Pariyatti)

MPA Pariyatti Editions (selected titles from the Myanmar Pitaka Association, copublished by Pariyatti)

Pariyatti Digital Editions (audio and video titles, including discourses)

Pariyatti Press (classic titles returned to print and inspirational writing by contemporary authors)

Pariyatti enriches the world by

- disseminating the words of the Buddha,
- providing sustenance for the seeker's journey,
- illuminating the meditator's path.

www.ingramcontent.com/pod-product-compliance
Lightning Source LLC
Chambersburg PA
CBHW020345170426
43200CB00005B/52
* 9 7 8 1 6 8 1 7 2 7 1 8 9 *